Handbook of Social Support and the Family

The Plenum Series on Stress and Coping

Series Editor:
Donald Meichenbaum, *University of Waterloo, Waterloo, Ontario, Canada*

Editorial Board: Bruce P. Dohrenwend, *Columbia University* • Marianne Frankenhauser, *University of Stockholm* • Norman Garmezy, *University of Minnesota* • Mardi J. Horowitz, *University of California Medical School, San Francisco* • Richard S. Lazarus, *University of California, Berkeley* • Michael Rutter, *University of London* • Dennis C. Turk, *University of Pittsburgh* • John P. Wilson, *Cleveland State University* • Camille Wortman, *University of Michigan*

Current Volumes in the Series:

BEYOND TRAUMA
Cultural and Societal Dynamics
Edited by Rolf J. Kleber, Charles R. Figley, and Berthold P. R. Gersons

COMBAT STRESS REACTION
The Enduring Toll of War
Zahava Solomon

COMMUTING STRESS
Causes, Effects, and Methods of Coping
Meni Koslowsky, Avraham N. Kluger, and Mordechai Reich

COPING WITH WAR-INDUCED STRESS
The Gulf War and the Israeli Response
Zahava Solomon

HANDBOOK OF SOCIAL SUPPORT AND THE FAMILY
Edited by Gregory R. Pierce, Barbara R. Sarason, and Irwin G. Sarason

INTERNATIONAL HANDBOOK OF TRAUMATIC STRESS SYNDROMES
Edited by John P. Wilson and Beverley Raphael

PSYCHOTRAUMATOLOGY
Key Papers and Core Concepts in Post-Traumatic Stress
Edited by George S. Everly, Jr. and Jeffrey M. Lating

STRESS AND MENTAL HEALTH
Contemporary Issues and Prospects for the Future
Edited by William R. Avison and Ian H. Gotlib

TRAUMATIC STRESS
From Theory to Practice
Edited by John R. Freedy and Stevan E. Hobfoll

THE UNNOTICED MAJORITY IN PSYCHIATRIC INPATIENT CARE
Charles A. Kiesler and Celeste G. Simpkins

Handbook of Social Support and the Family

Edited by

Gregory R. Pierce

Hamilton College
Clinton, New York

Barbara R. Sarason

University of Washington
Seattle, Washington

and

Irwin G. Sarason

University of Washington
Seattle, Washington

PLENUM PRESS • NEW YORK AND LONDON

Library of Congress Cataloging-in-Publication Data

Handbook of social support and the family / edited by Gregory R.
  Pierce, Barbara R. Sarason, and Irwin G. Sarason.
        p.   cm. -- (Plenum series on stress and coping)
    Includes bibliographical references and index.
    ISBN 0-306-45232-4
    1. Family. 2. Child rearing. 3. Social interaction in children.
  4. Social psychology.   I. Pierce, Gregory R. II. Sarason, Barbara
  R. III. Sarason, Irwin G. IV. Series.
  HQ515.H335 1996
  649'.1--dc20   96-17181
                                                                 CIP

ISBN 0-306-45232-4

© 1996 Plenum Press, New York
A Division of Plenum Publishing Corporation
233 Spring Street, New York, N. Y. 10013

Printed in the United States of America

Contributors

Linda K. Acitelli, Department of Psychology, University of Houston, Houston, Texas 77204-5341

Manuel Barrera, Jr., Department of Psychology, Arizona State University, Tempe, Arizona 85287-1104

Steven R. H. Beach, Department of Psychology, University of Georgia, Athens, Georgia 30602

Thomas N. Bradbury, Department of Psychology, University of California at Los Angeles, Los Angeles, California 90024-1563

Inge Bretherton, Department of Child and Family Studies, University of Wisconsin–Madison, Madison, Wisconsin 53706

Brant R. Burleson, Department of Communication, Purdue University, West Lafayette, Indiana 47907-1366

Rebecca P. Cameron, Applied Psychology Center, Kent State University, Kent, Ohio 44242

Heather A. Chapman, Applied Psychology Center, Kent State University, Kent, Ohio 44242

Helen M. Coble, Counseling Psychology Program, College of Education, University of Oregon, Eugene, Oregon 97503-5251

Carolyn E. Cutrona, Department of Psychology, Iowa State University, Ames, Iowa 50014

Peggye Dilworth-Anderson, Department of Human Development and Family Studies, University of North Carolina at Greensboro, Greensboro, North Carolina 27412

Christine Dunkel-Schetter, Department of Psychology, University of California at Los Angeles, Los Angeles, California 90024-1563

Pamela Feldman, Department of Psychology, University of California at Los Angeles, Los Angeles, California 90024-1563

Marnie Filer, Ferkauf Graduate School of Psychology and Department of Epidemiology and Social Medicine, Albert Einstein College of Medicine, Bronx, New York 10461-1924

Frank D. Fincham, Department of Psychology, University of Illinois at Urbana–Champaign, Champaign, Illinois 61820

Robert W. Gallagher, Applied Psychology Center, Kent State University, Kent, Ohio 44242

Diana L. Gantt, Day Treatment Program, Providence Medical Center, Portland, Oregon 97213

Gemma L. Gladstone, Psychiatry Unit, Prince of Wales Hospital, Randwick 2031, Australia

Ciarda A. Henderson, Department of Psychology, Hamilton College, Clinton, New York 13323

Stevan E. Hobfoll, Applied Psychology Center, Kent State University, Kent, Ohio 44242

Christine Johnson, Department of Sociology and the Center for Family Research in Rural Mental Health, Iowa State University, Ames, Iowa 50011

Helene J. Joseph, Department of Psychology, Hamilton College, Clinton, New York 13323

Jennifer Katz, Department of Psychology, University of Georgia, Athens, Georgia 30602

Christine Killingsworth, Department of Psychology, University of California at Los Angeles, Los Angeles, California 90024-1563

Adrianne W. Kunkel, Department of Communication, Purdue University, West Lafayette, Indiana 47907-1366

Brian Lakey, Department of Psychology, Wayne State University, Detroit, Michigan 48202

Molly Lependorf, Department of Child and Family Studies, University of Wisconsin–Madison, Madison, Wisconsin 53706

Susan A. Li, Department of Psychology, Arizona State University, Tempe, Arizona 85287-1104

Catherine J. Lutz, Department of Psychology, Wayne State University, Detroit, Michigan 48202

Brent Mallinckrodt, Counseling Psychology Program, College of Education, University of Oregon, Eugene, Oregon 97503-5251

John Mariani, Ferkauf Graduate School of Psychology and Department of Epidemiology and Social Medicine, Albert Einstein College of Medicine, Bronx, New York 10461-1924

Sheree Marshall, Department of Human Development and Family Studies, University of North Carolina at Greensboro, Greensboro, North Carolina 27412

Rudolf H. Moos, Center for Health Care Evaluation, Department of Veterans Affairs Health Care System, and Stanford University Medical Center, Palo Alto, California 94304

Gordon Parker, Psychiatry Unit, Prince of Wales Hospital, Randwick 2031, Australia

Jennifer S. Paul, Department of Psychology, Hamilton College, Clinton, New York 13323

Gregory R. Pierce, Department of Psychology, Hamilton College, Clinton, New York 13323

Karl Pillemer, Department of Human Development and Family Studies, Cornell University, Ithaca, New York 14583

J. T. Ptacek, Department of Psychology, Bucknell University, Lewisburg, Pennsylvania 17837

Karen S. Rook, School of Social Ecology, University of California at Irvine, Irvine, California 92717

Lisa B. Rosenbaum, Department of Psychology, Hamilton College, Clinton, New York 13323

Richard M. Ryan, Department of Psychology, University of Rochester, Rochester, New York 14627

Lynda M. Sagrestano, Department of Psychology, University of California at Los Angeles, Los Angeles, California 90024-1563

Kristine E. Santoro, Department of Psychology, Hamilton College, Clinton, New York 13323

Barbara R. Sarason, Department of Psychology, University of Washington, Seattle, Washington 98195

Irwin G. Sarason, Department of Psychology, University of Washington, Seattle, Washington 98195

Tonya L. Schuster, School of Social Ecology, University of California at Irvine, Irvine, California 92717

Ronald L. Simons, Department of Sociology and the Center for Family Research in Rural Mental Health, Iowa State University, Ames, Iowa 50011

Jessica A. Solky, Department of Psychology, University of Rochester, Rochester, New York 14627

Jill Suitor, Department of Sociology, Louisiana State University, Baton Rouge, Louisiana 70803

Christine Timko, Center for Health Care Evaluation, Department of Veterans Affairs Health Care System, and Stanford University Medical Center, Palo Alto, California 94304

Reghan Walsh, Department of Child and Family Studies, University of Wisconsin–Madison, Madison, Wisconsin 53706

Thomas A. Wills, Ferkauf Graduate School of Psychology and Department of Epidemiology and Social Medicine, Albert Einstein College of Medicine, Bronx, New York 10461-1924

Penny L. Yee, Department of Psychology, Hamilton College, Clinton, New York 13323

Preface

While insights sometimes are slow in coming, they often seem obvious when they finally arrive. This handbook is an outcome of the insight that the topics of social support and the family are very closely linked. Obvious as this might seem, the fact remains that the literatures dealing with social support and the family have been deceptively separate and distinct. For example, work on social support began in the 1970s with the accumulation of evidence that social ties and social integration play important roles in health and personal adjustment. Even though family members are often the key social supporters of individuals, relatively little research of social support was targeted on family interactions as a path to specifying supporter processes. It is now recognized that one of the most important features of the family is its role in providing the individual with a source of support and acceptance.

Fortunately, in recent years, the distinctness and separateness of the fields of social support and the family have blurred. This handbook provides the first collation and integration of social support and family research. This integration calls for specifying processes (such as the cognitions associated with poor support availability and unrewarding family constellations) and factors (such as cultural differences in family life and support provision) that are pertinent to integration. The handbook has two primary goals: (1) to provide an overview of important topics currently being addressed by investigators at the intersection of social support and the family, and (2) to call attention to the challenges for and promises of future research at this intersection. Researchers and theorists in the fields of social support and the family are now focusing attention on issues that lie at the intersection of the two fields. We believe the time is ripe to recognize and build on these integrative efforts.

The handbook is organized in three parts. The first part addresses conceptual and methodological issues in research on social support and the family. How are family relationships cognitively processed? While families provide support, they also provide opportunities for friction and psychological pain. How can close relationships within the family be dealt with in a holistic way that attends to both the positive and the negative sides of social relationships?

The second part explores the ways in which social support plays its role in family relationships. These relationships include established families (parents, children, siblings, extended family) and the critical spousal relationship that plays such a crucial role in overall family functioning and the present and future lives of children. This part of the book recognizes the family as a developing social organization with members who play changing roles over time.

The third part deals with a number of real-world issues, including the role social support plays during pregnancy and the earliest stages of family formation; how families confront crises (such as the need to provide care for a victim of Alzheimer's disease); and family support—and its absence—when psychological distress is high and behavior problems are evident.

The handbook, by design, is integrative—not only in its content, but also in the fields that are influencing work at the intersection of social support and the family. The authors include experts in the areas of psychology, sociology, family studies, and communication. While these are not the only fields participating in the ferment at this intersection, they are among the leaders. We find it interesting and intriguing that so many scholars with these diverse backgrounds and interests are addressing themselves to similar issues. They are all interested in investigating the social support processes of marital, parent–child, and sibling relationships and the development or unfolding of these relationships.

For us, the handbook has been an adventure in widening our horizons and provoking new ways of thinking about interpersonal relationships. We hope readers will also feel this sense of adventure. The adventure could not have taken place without the contributing authors, who have presented thoughtful and stimulating analyses of research in the domain of social support and the family. Of course, there are many mysteries yet to be solved. As with all scientific explorations, what seem to be final answers are usually mirages. We hope that this handbook contributes to a higher level of integration and extensions of the frontiers of theory and research.

Acknowledgments

We wish to thank several individuals and institutions for making this handbook a reality. Hamilton College generously provided sabbatical leave to Gregory Pierce, which greatly facilitated the development of this book. In addition, three former Hamilton students, two of whom are currently in graduate school, collaborated in writing chapters for this handbook: Ciarda Henderson, Helene Joseph, and Jessica Solky. Their contributions to this handbook serve to illustrate the active role of young scholars—as well as established scholars—in the fields of social support and the family. Tracy Hildebrand, a current Hamilton student, invested considerable energy and time in helping to complete the index for the handbook.

We also wish to thank Eliot Werner, Executive Editor at Plenum, for encouraging the pursuit of this handbook; his support and assistance aided greatly in the production of this volume.

Contents

PART III. STRESS, CLINICAL PROBLEMS, AND SUPPORT NEEDS FOR FAMILIES

I

Conceptual and Methodological Issues in Research on Social Support and the Family

1

Conceptualizing and Assessing Social Support in the Context of the Family

GREGORY R. PIERCE, BARBARA R. SARASON,
IRWIN G. SARASON, HELENE J. JOSEPH,
and CIARDA A. HENDERSON

Social support and family researchers have made enormous strides in document-ing the many links between the supportive elements within family relationships, on one hand, and important personal outcomes, such as psychological adjust-ment, on the other. These efforts have contributed to a better understanding of the multidimensional nature of the social support construct and to recognition that the impact that supportive relationships have on personal outcomes is com-plex and requires attention to a broad range of pertinent variables. Despite these impressive developments, several topics—topics that lie at the heart of research on social support and the family—still need to be addressed. This chapter exam-ines some of these topics and seeks to offer a new perspective from which to examine them.

The chapter has two themes. First, despite recognition of the multifaceted nature of the social support construct, too little attention has been paid to the interconnections among these elements. Second, most research on social support has focused on the short-term consequences that support has for coping with life events; the long-term consequences of support for personality development and healthy functioning have remained largely unexplored. We begin the chapter with

GREGORY R. PIERCE, HELENE J. JOSEPH, and CIARDA A. HENDERSON • Department of Psychology, Hamilton College, Clinton, New York 13323.   BARBARA R. SARASON and IRWIN G. SARASON • Department of Psychology, University of Washington, Seattle, Washington 98195.

Handbook of Social Support and the Family, edited by Gregory R. Pierce, Barbara R. Sarason, and Irwin G. Sarason. Plenum Press, New York, 1996.

an overview of the social support construct. We then describe the components of the support construct and highlight both the interconnections among these features and their impact on situation-specific coping and developmental outcomes. The chapter concludes with a discussion of the implications of these observations for further study of the support construct.

Before discussing specific components of social support, we wish to comment on the topic of social support and the family more generally. Researchers in the social support tradition have typically credited investigators such as Cobb, Cassell, and Caplan as the early pioneers in the field. And it is certainly the case that their work in the mid-1970s marks the emergence of a field of study that clearly identifies itself as focusing on social support. If you ask researchers in the field of family studies about the beginnings of interest in the topic of social support, however, a quite different answer emerges. Scholars concerned with the contributions of the family environment to children's social development have a long tradition of acknowledging the important role played by a supportive, caring environment. For example, Rollins and Thomas (1979) cite Symonds (1939) as an early pioneer in the study of parental support. Thus, family scholars are likely to tell you that interest in social support began at least half a century before "social support" researchers became interested in the topic. Our goal here is not to determine who is to be credited as the torchbearer of research on social support and the family. Instead, we wish to point out that, to date, these two fields have been pursued largely independently of each other.

One of the many important contributions made by both social support and family researchers has been the acknowledgment that the construct of social support is broad and encompasses many different components. This recognition has brought with it increased attention to matters of construct validity with regard to the instruments employed in a growing number of studies. One consequence of this attention has been that we know more about increasingly small parts of the social support construct. And, unfortunately, researchers may have lost interest too soon in elements of the social support construct that may, in the end, prove to be highly important; for example, social researchers have argued that one's perceptions of support are more critical for healthy adjustment than are the actual supportive behaviors provided by network members. As we will argue in this chapter, one's perceptions of support are not independent of the supportive transactions that give rise to them, and so such an emphasis on one piece of the support equation may direct attention away from other important elements involved in social support processes. In some ways, social support research has been characterized by increasing specificity, at the cost of breadth of coverage.

CONCEPTUALIZING SOCIAL SUPPORT

In general, two broad views of social support are discernible: (1) a situation-specific view in which social support is tied to coping with a particular stressful event (Cohen & Wills, 1985) and (2) a developmental approach in which social support is seen as a contributor to personality and social development (Rollins &

Thomas, 1979). The former orientation is more typical of researchers identified with the social support tradition, while the latter approach is more characteristic of researchers in the field of family relationships. Our analysis of the social support construct acknowledges and builds on these two different orientations. The point we wish to underscore is that social support, broadly speaking, has both short- and long-term implications for psychological functioning. Programs of research on social support need to investigate both types of consequences.

Components of Social Support

Social support is a complex construct and encompasses at least the following three components: support schemata, supportive relationships, and supportive transactions. These elements of the social support construct are not mutually exclusive; they overlap and mutually influence each other in important ways. For example, support schemata derive from a history of supportive (or unsupportive) transactions; potentially supportive transactions occurring in the context of supportive relationships are especially likely to have beneficial effects; individuals who expect others to be supportive (i.e., those with positive support schemata) are more likely than others to develop supportive relationships in new social contexts. For this reason, while we discuss each aspect of the support construct separately, we focus throughout the following sections on the many interconnections among these distinct elements.

Support Schemata. Of the various ways in which social support has been assessed, it has come to be generally agreed that measures that tap individuals' perceptions of the availability of others upon whom they can rely for support—referred to as "perceived social support"—have proved to be the most consistent and strongest predictors of personal adjustment. Evidence indicating that perceived social support is stable across time and situations has led researchers to speculate about the possible role of personality factors in these perceptions (Pierce, I. G. Sarason, B. R. Sarason, Solky, & Nagle, 1996; I. G. Sarason, B. R. Sarason, & Shearin, 1986). For example, B. R. Sarason, Pierce, and I. G. Sarason (1990) have hypothesized that these general appraisals of the supportiveness of the social environment reflect support schemata—knowledge structures whose content include information about the likelihood that others, in general, will be able or willing to meet one's needs for support.

Support schemata encompass one's expectations about the forthcomingness of the social environment in providing aid should one need it. They are analogous to Bowlby's concept of working models (Bowlby, 1980) that influence information processing related to social interaction. This approach is consistent with research on person perception and social schemata showing that people develop rich and elaborate schemata about others that include expectations for their future behavior and assumptions about their motivations and intentions (Fiske & Taylor, 1984; Markus & Zajonc, 1985). This cognitive orientation to social support has been facilitated, in part, by the application of methodological paradigms developed by experimental psychologists (Baldwin, 1992) (see also Chapter 2).

Children whose interactions with their parents are supportive, sensitive, and well-matched to their needs develop positive expectations about the willingness of others in general to provide support; children whose needs for support are not met develop a generalized view of others as unwilling or unable to meet their needs for support. The latter outcome is particularly unfortunate, because evidence indicates that perceived social support is positively related to self-appraisals; those who believe others, in general, to be supportive ascribe to themselves more positive and fewer negative attributes (Lakey & Cassady, 1990; B. R. Sarason, Pierce, Bannerman, & I. G. Sarason, 1993). These findings therefore suggest that parental support impacts schemata concerning the nature of supportive relationships (e.g., that others desire to be of assistance) and the self (e.g., I am a worthwhile person and am loved and valued by others).

Lakey and his colleagues, using a variety of methodologies, have demonstrated that support schemata influence appraisals of supportive stimuli. For example, individuals high in perceived social support interpret novel supportive stimuli as significantly more helpful than do those low in perceived social support (Lakey & Cassady, 1990; Lakey, Moineau, & Drew, 1992). Of course, support schemata are not independent of supportive transactions (B. R. Sarason et al., 1990; I. G. Sarason et al., 1986). Evidence suggests that individuals high in perceived social support, compared with persons low in perceived social support, are more effective in developing supportive relationships in new social environments (Lakey & Dickinson, 1994). Reciprocal processes appear to operate such that persons high in perceived social support—that is, those who expect others to be supportive—create supportive relationships in new social settings, thereby further confirming their expectations that others are likely to be supportive (cf. Heller & Swindle, 1983; Heller, Swindle, & Dusenbury, 1986).

Support schemata also influence the responses of potential support providers. Studies have shown that those high in perceived social support are more interpersonally sensitive and are more strongly desired as potential sources of social support (B. R. Sarason, I. G. Sarason, Hacker, & Basham, 1985). These findings mesh with the analysis by Sroufe and Fleeson (1986) of the consequences of attachment experiences. They suggest that individuals learn the roles of both participants in a relationship; for example, by receiving support that is sensitive to their needs, children learn not only how to receive but also how to provide support. The vast majority of research on social support has focused on perceived social support and its impact on the recipient's role in potentially supportive transactions; there is great need for further research that examines the influence of support schemata on potential support providers' contributions to supportive transactions.

Our analysis of support schemata has emphasized the long-term impact of parental support; that is, over time, parental support leads children to make inferences about the nature of supportive relationships that serve to guide their social behavior later in life. These early parental experiences also have short-term implications. Supportive interactions with parents provide children with an opportunity to acquire coping skills that enable them to meet the challenges posed by stressful situations. Parental support also reduces children's distress by increasing their coping resources, thereby reducing the threat posed by stressful situations.

These observations illustrate the two major themes of this chapter. First, the various components of social support are interconnected: Supportive transactions with parents lead children to develop positive support schemata that, in turn, influence the development of supportive relationships later in childhood and into the adult years—in terms of both receiving *and* providing supportive behavior. Second, social support has both short- and long-term implications. For example, supportive parental behavior enables children to acquire interpersonal skills that facilitate peer interaction (i.e., a short-term consequence) as well as a positive view of self and others that guides their interactions with the social environment, increasing both their own personal effectiveness and their ability to acquire and make use of support from others (i.e., a long-term consequence).

Supportive Relationships. While individuals have support schemata that incorporate their expectations about how others, in general, will respond to them, they also have expectations about how specific supportive others are likely to respond should assistance be needed. These relationship-specific schemata are distinct from general support schemata, although they are likely to mutually influence each other (Pierce, I. G. Sarason, & B. R. Sarason, 1991). As is the case with general support schemata, relationship-specific support schemata impact appraisals of support-relevant behavior. Pierce, B. R. Sarason, and I. G. Sarason (1992) had 54 undergraduates complete a packet of questionnaires, including measures of students' global perceptions of support (i.e., the availability of support from others in general) and perceptions of the supportiveness (and conflictualness) of their relationship with their mothers. Each student–mother pair then participated in a laboratory task that involved having the student prepare and give a speech arguing for the value of a college education. Before the student began preparing the speech, the mother was taken to another laboratory room, where she copied in her own handwriting two standardized notes that were supportive in content. The experimenter subsequently asked the student to stop and read one of the notes at each of two points in time during presentation of the speech and then to rate the degree to which each note was supportive; all the students believed that their mothers had written the notes.

Substantial variation was observed in students' ratings of how supportive their mothers' notes were. In addition, the measures of general and relationship-specific support schemata were positively related; general and relationship-specific support schemata were also positively correlated with students' support ratings. Regression analyses indicated that students' perceptions of the amount of support and conflict in their maternal relationship each predicted their appraisals of the supportiveness of their mothers' notes; the measure of general support schemata did not uniquely predict students' support ratings. These findings suggest that while both general and relationship-specific schemata each influence the interpretation of potentially supportive behavior, relationship-specific support schemata may play a larger role in the interpretation of supportive transactions occurring in the context of that relationship than do general support schemata. General support schemata may have a particularly great impact on the appraisal of potentially supportive behavior involving those whom we do not know well; relationship-specific schemata—which develop as a consequence of a history of support-relevant experiences with a particular other—may be more important when interpreting supportive transactions occurring in the context of close relationships (i.e., those for which we have relationship-specific support schemata).

Research on social support has typically involved studying supportive relationships in such a way that one participant is identified as the support provider and the other as the support recipient. This approach is particularly likely to have been taken in investigation of parental relationships; the approach has some merit in that parents have been found to be a major source of support for their children, especially in childhood, although recent research in the area of adult aging indicates that children become important sources of social support for their elderly parents. However, this orientation has two fundamental flaws. First, it neglects the fact that an individual is, in any relationship, both a source and a recipient of social support. Thus, while we may study relationships in such a way that one participant in a relationship dyad enacts (or fails to enact) supportive behavior toward the other, in everyday life, no such distinction in participants' roles can be drawn. This problem arises, at least in part, from the fact that we have attempted to isolate relationship participants' responses to a life event that is presumed to impact only one person in the dyad. In a sense, we have separated specific supportive transactions from the everyday fabric of relationships in which people mutually support each other as they cope with challenges that indirectly and directly impact themselves and each other. Support providers do not simply forgo their own needs for support in order to provide others with assistance; instead, they continue to deal with their own concerns, presumably by receiving support from others, some or all of whom may be those to whom they are also currently giving support.

A second flaw concerns an implicit bias in the social support literature that sees providing social support as a "cost" and receiving social support as a "benefit." In truth, the opportunity to provide others with support is itself an important social resource that contributes to self-esteem and healthy functioning. Weiss (1974) identified this feature of relationships, which he referred to as the *opportunity for nurturance*, as one of six supportive functions served by social bonds. People need to give as well as receive social support in their close relationships. Results from several studies make clear that individuals experience higher levels of satisfaction in relationships in which they provide as well as receive social support, particularly when support exchanges are distributed equally between the two participants (Cutrona & Suhr, 1994). Even very young children evidence a need to be helpful to others in the family (Bowlby, 1980), suggesting that reciprocity is an important feature of supportive relationships across the life span.

Conceptualizing supportive relationships in terms of the efforts both participants make in mutually supporting each other emphasizes the interconnectedness of what have typically been investigated as two distinct roles: support provider and support recipient. Our analysis suggests that a more realistic view of supportive relationships requires attending to supportive transactions initiated by both participants as they seek to cope with a range of life events that require personal and social resources. The pattern of supportive or unsupportive transactions exchanged between the participants serves to shape the relationship-specific schemata each participant forms across time regarding the nature of their relationship. The latter observation underscores the point that supportive relationships influence coping with respect to specific life events as well as the development of relational schemata that may influence individuals' behavior in those as well as other relationships.

Supportive Transactions. By asserting that participants in a supportive relationship are likely, across time, to be both providers and recipients of aid, we do not mean to imply that specific supportive transactions cannot profitably be conceptualized or studied in terms of each participant's primary role as a support provider or recipient with respect to a particular life event. Supportive transactions involve behavioral exchanges between at least two individuals. Although not all supportive interactions involve each of the following elements, many transactions include efforts on the part of the potential support recipient to elicit support from another person, the enactment of supportive behaviors on the part of the provider, and, consequently, the receipt of supportive behaviors by the individual who attempted to elicit support. We begin our analysis of supportive transactions by discussing supportive behavior per se.

Supportive Behavior. Efforts to develop definitions of supportive behavior have served to highlight the complexity of delineating the social support construct. Considerable attention has been given to developing typologies that classify various behaviors into categories of support. In the social support literature, this approach to defining supportive behaviors has been referred to as the *functional approach* because it seeks to categorize behaviors on the basis of functions that they might serve (Cutrona & Russell, 1987). Instruments developed to assess specific functions of socially supportive behavior have yielded different results in terms of the number and content of supportive functions. For example, factor analysis of the Inventory of Socially Supportive Behaviors (Barrera, 1981) by Stokes and Wilson (1984) revealed four components: emotional support, tangible assistance, cognitive information, and directive guidance. A principal components analysis of a revised version of the Social Support Behaviors scale (Vaux, Riedel, & Stewart, 1987) to assess supportive behaviors provided by caregivers to the parents of young children indicated five functions: emotional support, socializing, practical assistance, financial assistance, and advice/guidance (Caruso, 1992). A quite different approach was taken by Dakof and Taylor (1990), who coded interview data from 55 cancer patients and identified specific supportive actions enacted by members of their support networks: physical presence; expressions of concern; calm acceptance of patient's cancer; expression of optimism about prognosis or cancer patient's ability to live successfully with cancer; provision of useful information or advice; expression of special understanding because of similar experience; provision of technically competent medical care; and being pleasant and kind.

Although the categorical schemes proposed by various researchers differ substantially, most distinguish between two general forms of support: *emotional support* (i.e., behaviors that communicate that an individual is cared for and loved) and *instrumental support* (i.e., behaviors that provide assistance in task-directed coping efforts). However, even this simple dichotomy is not without its pitfalls in that it is possible for behaviors that serve to bolster task-focused coping (e.g., a loan of money when one has just lost a job) to lead the recipient to conclude that he or she is valued and loved by the provider of such assistance. Thus, a particular behavior may serve several functions. This situation creates problems for investigators who try to develop instruments to assess discrete categories of supportive behaviors. A measure of instrumental support may correlate positively with effective personal functioning and reflect the fact that such behaviors are communicating to the recipient that he or she is loved and cared for, thereby bolstering his or her confidence, rather than assisting directly in his or her efforts to cope with a specific stressful event. This overlap in the functions served by specific behaviors may account for the substantial correlations observed across subscales intended to assess discrete functions of support (Pierce, B. R. Sarason, & I. G. Sarason, 1990). Difficulties can also arise in experimental studies in which the type of supportive behavior received by subjects is experimentally manipulated. For example, in a recent study by Pierce, Ptacek, Contey, and Pollack (1996), subjects were randomly assigned to receive either instrumental or emotional support from a confederate of the experimenter. The subjects' ratings of the confederate's behavior indicated that instrumental support was perceived as being both instrumentally and emotionally supportive. Emotional support, on the other hand, was perceived as serving only to reduce subjects' distress in the stressful situation; it was not perceived as directly aiding their efforts to cope.

While social support researchers have spent considerable time drawing distinctions among a wide range of potentially supportive behaviors, surprisingly little attention has been paid to the need to define the boundaries of the social support construct in general—that is, to state where the construct of social support ends and other constructs begin. It is possible to define an enormously wide range of behaviors as potentially supportive. Imagine a situation in which John, an 11-year-old, observes his mother while she helps his younger sister, Julie, complete a mathematics assignment for her class the following day. The mother shows Julie how to structure the problem in such a way that the solution is easier to obtain. The next day, John adopts the approach his mother showed Julie as he works on his own homework for his mathematics course. The mother's behavior facilitated John's efforts to cope with the challenges posed by his mathematics homework. But should we categorize the mother's behavior as supportive of John?

Because the behavior of John's mother had an impact on her son's coping efforts, the mother's behavior was—in a sense—supportive. However, such an approach to defining supportive behavior runs the risk of developing circular arguments: Supportive behavior is behavior that is found to be supportive. This orientation is similar to that adopted by many behaviorists in defining reinforcers as outcomes that serve to increase the likelihood that a particular behavior will occur in the future. Our own view is that since John did not perceive that his mother was trying to be supportive and his mother did not intend her behavior in that situation to be helpful to John (although she probably would not be disappointed to find that her actions had been helpful to him as well as to his sister), it is probably best not to label the mother's behavior as supportive with respect to John (although we would undoubtedly define the mother's behavior as supportive with respect to Julie).

Consider another example involving an interaction between Sally, a high-school senior who wants to purchase a car, and her parents. Sally has recently found a car that costs $3000; unfortunately, she has managed to save only $1500 from her weekend job. Sally asked her parents to help her pay for the car by providing the remaining $1500 on the grounds that having her own car would enable her to be more independent (i.e., she would not have to rely on the availability of her parents' car to go to work and visit friends). Although acknowledging the merits of Sally's arguments, her parents told her that she must earn the rest of the money to pay for her car on the grounds that part of learning to be self-reliant means working hard to achieve her personal goals. Sally's parents clearly intended their behavior to be supportive; they too wanted to foster her independence. Perhaps not surprisingly, Sally interpreted their behavior quite differently. She perceived her parents' behavior as unsupportive; in Sally's view, her parents were actively thwarting her efforts to achieve independence. Clearly, the discrepancy between Sally's view and her parents' perception of their interaction does not simply reflect a difference in the category of support to which they each assign the interaction (e.g., emotional support vs. instrumental support). Instead, they disagree about whether or not the interaction was supportive. Is Sally's parents' behavior supportive or not?

The second example is more complicated than the first in that the family members perceive the interaction in different ways. Particularly in family relationships, individuals may share different goals or have different views about the best way to achieve (or aid another family member to achieve) a specific goal. This is likely to be the case, for example, in relationships between parents and their children. Parents may frequently have long-term developmental goals that are not of central concern to their children; for example, while children may wish to have their parents purchase a toy they have recently seen advertised on television, the parents may wish to help their children learn to delay gratification of such impulses (and may therefore elect not to purchase the toy for the child).

A resolution to this problem of categorization can be achieved by defining supportive behavior in such a way that it attends to the appraisals of both potential support providers and potential support recipients. Definitions of supportive behavior should consider limiting the scope of behaviors to be considered to those interactions that are either intended by the provider to be supportive or are perceived by the recipient as supportive. Social interaction that has the potential to facilitate either (1) coping with respect to a particular life event (short-term view) or (2) adaptive personal functioning (long-term view) might be considered. We believe that definitions of supportive behavior need to take into account the goals and intentions of those who are providing (or not providing) potentially supportive behavior as well as the appraisals made by those who are receiving (or not receiving) potentially supportive behavior.

This approach to conceptualizing supportive behavior has clear methodological implications. Investigators need to study the behavior and perceptions of both the potential support provider *and* the potential recipient of supportive behavior (see Chapter 5). This approach has several advantages, two of which we address here. First, by studying both participants' behavior and perceptions, we make it possible to investigate similarities and discrepancies in the way in which each person is construing and responding to the interaction. Deal, Wampler, and Halverson (1992) have suggested that the degree of mutuality in marital partners' perceptions of important facets of their relationship is itself a crucial feature of the relationship, with greater similarity in partners' views being a positive element in the relationship. The point we wish to emphasize here is that researchers need to avoid the temptation to assign one view as a criterion by which to judge the veridicality of another person's appraisals of an interaction. Indeed, it is more profitable to investigate the factors that serve to increase or decrease the degree to which individuals share common perceptions of their interactions.

Second, by studying the behaviors and perceptions of both relationship participants, we acknowledge that supportive interactions reflect behavioral transactions between two individuals. While we wish to avoid the "chicken or egg" issue, it seems reasonable to assume that support providers elect to give support in response to their perception that another person needs their support; these perceptions, in turn, are likely to be based, at least in part, on the providers' observations of the potential recipients' behavior. Of course, a potential recipient's choice of whom to seek support from is itself likely to be a function of previous supportive (or unsupportive) experiences with particular network members. We now turn our discussion to the specific elements involved in the seeking, provision, and receipt of social support.

Support Seeking.   There is little doubt that individuals who are able to seek out and elicit support fare better in life than those who are unable to garner assistance when they need it. Milgram and Palti (1993) studied 52 culturally disadvantaged Israeli youth to identify characteristics that discriminated between resilient and less successful children. They found that resilient children, compared to others, possessed personal characteristics that facilitated seeking and attracting social support from peers and adults. This finding is especially important in light of other evidence indicating that low levels of support seeking are associated with lower levels of support receipt (Searcy & Eisenberg, 1992). Burleson and his colleagues (see Chapter 6) argue that a contributing factor to the social support process may be social skills that enable a person to negotiate supportive transactions. The acquisition of these skills begins in the family with early interactions between children and their parents and siblings. These skills are then generalized to interactions with peers and other non-family members. Another determinant of support seeking may be the ability to trust. Grace and Schill (1986) found that individuals high in interpersonal trust were more likely than others to seek social support following stressful experiences.

While family relationships carry with them strong social obligations and prescriptions concerning the provision of social support, individuals are by no means assured of obtaining support from family members should they need it. Thus, the ability to elicit support, even from family members, is crucial. The degree of fit between children's temperamental styles and the personal charac- teristics of potential family support providers (e.g., parents) is crucial in ensuring optimal support provision to facilitate children's coping efforts (Compas, 1987; Lerner, Baker, & Lerner, 1985; Lerner & Lerner, 1983). These findings make clear that even young children play a role in determining whether their needs for support are met by others.

It is ironic that many individuals who need social support apparently either lack the skills to seek, or experience anxiety about seeking, social support. In a study of 107 Israeli mothers of young children being seen for possible health problems, Hobfoll and Lerman (1988) found that mothers who reported discom- fort in seeking support received less support in response to their children's potential illness. Interestingly, the mothers' reports of their discomfort in seeking support across a 1-year period were quite stable ($r = 0.69$), suggesting the possible role of personality characteristics in seeking social support. Discomfort in seeking support may be especially problematic because the act of contemplating seeking support is distressing and because the person may be less likely to seek support, thereby possibly reducing the effectiveness of his or her efforts to cope with stressful events (Hobfoll & Lerman, 1988).

Given these findings, it is puzzling that the majority of research on supportive transactions has focused on the process at the point at which assistance is ren- dered by a provider; the topic of support seeking has been largely ignored. The implicit model for supportive transactions is that providers perceive a need for support on the part of a potential recipient and then decide whether to give support to that person. This orientation is understandable, yet unfortunate, because a considerable amount of activity relevant to supportive transactions may occur before the provider renders assistance (Milgram, 1989). This approach has had a strong impact on assessment procedures. For example, researchers may assume that assessments of support receipt are an indication of recipients' prefer- ences. Or they may assume that the person from whom one actively seeks support is the person from whom one most desires to obtain support. However, neither of these assumptions may be warranted. An individual may consider seeking support from several potential providers before electing to seek support from one of them—or he or she may decide not to seek support from any network member. The latter point makes it clear that an individual's failure to actively seek support from others does not mean that he or she did not wish to obtain support from others or did not consider seeking support from members of his or her network. This view of support seeking suggests that researchers need to attend to the cognitive and behavioral aspects of support seeking and that such attention needs to be directed at activities occurring prior to behavioral indicators that a person is seeking support from a particular network member.

Support-seeking attempts can be either direct or indirect. *Direct attempts* to elicit support from others involve making explicit requests for assistance; *indirect attempts* focus on communicating one's need for support without actually asking for assistance (e.g., by displaying distress with the goal of drawing a potential support provider's attention to one's need for aid). Unfortunately, we know relatively little about the content or efficacy of particular support-seeking strategies. Direct support-seeking efforts may be especially likely to communicate one's need for support and thus increase the likelihood that potential providers will be cognizant of one's desire to obtain help. This advantage also has costs in that it may be more difficult for potential providers to decide not to render assistance because of the direct request for aid that has been made, thereby possibly engendering feelings of ambivalence and obligation and, ultimately, undermining one's efforts to enlist aid. Indirect support-seeking attempts involve a higher level of risk in terms of clarity of communication (i.e., the provider may not perceive that the potential recipient is asking for help); on the other hand, assuming that the provider does get the message, he or she may more easily decline to provide assistance without directly rebuffing the support seeker. Whether one uses either direct or indirect methods to seek support, and which of the two methods is more likely to yield supportive behavior, may depend strongly on the type of situation being confronted by the person seeking support. For example, when a person perceives a stressor as significantly exceeding her or his personal resources, she or he may engage in direct support-seeking efforts because the consequences of failure are relatively high; in contrast, the person may use an indirect support-seeking strategy when faced with a less challenging life event, in which case not obtaining support would be less costly. Further research is needed to investigate the situational determinants and efficacy of each approach to support seeking.

The decision to seek support from a family member or peer begins, in part, with the recognition that assistance in some form may be needed. This process may begin, in some instances, during secondary appraisal when the individual assesses his or her available resources with which to confront a specific stressful event that has already occurred (Lazarus & Folkman, 1984). However, an individual may begin thinking about seeking support before a stressful event has even occurred. This may be the case in instances in which the individual has some control over whether the event is likely to occur. For example, prior to undertaking a challenging task, an individual may assess the availability of social support from particular family members. In this sense, family members (e.g., parents) may serve as a secure base from which individuals explore their environment (Bowlby, 1980). The point here is that support seeking may begin prior to, rather than simply subsequent to, the occurrence of a stressful life event, and that these early support-seeking efforts may strongly influence whether such life events even occur (Pierce, I. G. Sarason, & B. R. Sarason, 1996).

Other factors may also influence support-seeking efforts. For example, evidence indicates that the elderly look to family members, particularly their adult daughters, for instrumental support, but prefer to seek companionship from peers. Since family members are expected to provide support, feelings of obligation or the need to reciprocate immediately may be minimized (Clark, 1983). As new family structures become more common in society, these expectations may become less useful as guides to seeking support. As Jacobson (1990) has noted, family relationships involving step-family members have less clear-cut culturally defined norms for the giving and getting of social support. Substantial differences in expectations across cultural groups have also been found (see Chapters 4 and 16).

As with definitions of supportive behavior, we believe that conceptualizations of support-seeking behavior need to have boundaries. For example, it is possible to define a support-seeking behavior as any social interaction that has the consequence of eliciting supportive behavior from others. This definition, however, again has associated with it the problem of circularity—that is, of defining the antecedent behavior by its consequence—a situation we believe needs to be avoided. Thus, we advocate delimiting the construct of support-seeking behaviors to those acts intended by the potential recipient to elicit support. Of course, behaviors that lead to the receipt of support, but are not intended to do so, are also worthy of empirical attention and might be incorporated into models of social support processes.

Support Provision (Level 4). As one typically learns from one's own experience, giving support is not as easy as intuition might lead one to believe. Several important steps are involved in this part of the social support process. As a first step, the potential provider of support must perceive that another person either desires or needs assistance. This part of the equation, in itself, is likely to be complex. For example, the potential recipient may or may not have actively sought support from the potential provider. Whether or not the potential recipient has actively sought support (using either direct or indirect methods), the potential provider must evaluate the nature of the challenge to which the potential recipient's coping efforts are (or will be) directed. The provider must also assess the potential recipient's personal resources for dealing with the challenge. From this perspective, it is easy to see why individuals frequently report not receiving the support they desire (Dakof & Taylor, 1990). A provider may fail to give aid—even when it is desired by the potential recipient—if the provider evaluates the challenge as nonthreatening or if the provider overestimates the potential recipient's personal resources with which to face the challenge. The provider's estimation of the potential recipient's resources includes an assessment of that individual's personal coping repertoire as well as of the likelihood that others in the person's network will provide assistance. Thus, the potential provider might fail to enact support that is desired, not because she or he fails to perceive the potential recipient's need for support, but rather because she or he believes that others will be lending assistance and that her or his support is therefore not needed.

Of course, the process does not end when the potential provider has determined that his or her assistance is needed. The provider must then decide what type of support to provide. This assessment is undoubtedly based, in part, on the potential recipient's expressed desire for a particular type of support (if the potential recipient has communicated this information). As in the previously described example of Sally and her parents, however, it is possible for the provider to recognize that the potential recipient desires a particular type of support without being willing (or able) to provide that specific assistance. As we have already mentioned, discrepancies in the type of support that is desired by the recipient and provided by a network member are especially likely to occur when the recipient and provider have different goals regarding the short- or long-term outcome of the support that is rendered. Discrepancies may also occur when providers and recipients fail to communicate about and coordinate their supportive transactions. This point is worth underscoring because, while some supportive interactions may be mutually orchestrated by relationship participants, other interactions are likely to be initiated by the provider without explicit communication with the recipient regarding the nature and amount of support the provider is willing or intends to provide.

Part of the decision concerning the type of support to be provided undoubtedly involves the provider's assessment of her or his willingness to provide particular kinds of aid. For example, the provider may discern that an individual desires and needs a loan of money, but may be unwilling to risk giving a loan to that person. Or the provider may currently be dealing with significant personal difficulties that make it difficult or impossible to give assistance to the other person, despite the desire to be of help. In other words, support may fail to materialize not because the provider fails to perceive the other person's need, but because the provider is unwilling to help, or because the provider is unable to provide assistance.

Other factors probably also play a role in the provision of support. For example, network members may attempt to be supportive but may inadvertently engage in behaviors that are actually unsupportive (Dakof & Taylor, 1990). Such unsupportive transactions appear to be especially likely when providers attempt to aid those who are coping with victimizing events (Dunkel-Schetter & Wortman, 1982; Wortman & Dunkel-Schetter, 1987). For example, Peters-Golden (1982) found that a substantial number of breast cancer patients were the recipients of inappropriate or unhelpful support attempts. Results from these and other studies make clear that unsupportive behavior is not simply the absence of supportive behavior; instead, unsupportive behavior is distinct from supportive behavior and may have significant and negative consequences for a person's efforts to cope with stressful life events (Hirsch, 1979; Pierce et al., 1991).

Having determined on a course of action, the provider is still faced with the task of providing aid. Even the apparently simple act of lending money may be difficult. For example, for the loan of money to be optimally beneficial, the provider must give the assistance without undermining the recipient's self-esteem or confidence in his or her personal resources; either of these outcomes may lead the recipient to respond defensively to the aid (Nadler & Fisher, 1986; Tessler & Schwartz, 1972). Timing may also be an important feature of the supportive transaction. Supportive behavior that is enacted too early in the coping process may prevent the individual from developing personal coping skills that might reduce the person's need for assistance in the future; conversely, support enacted late in the coping process may come too late to prevent the individual from experiencing personal failure. As is the case with support seeking, social skills may play an important role in the provision of supportive behavior.

As we discussed earlier in the chapter, the act of giving assistance provides an individual with an opportunity to enhance self-esteem and to increase a sense of reciprocity in a relationship. Viewed in this way, supportive transactions may yield positive effects for the provider *and* the recipient of support; this perspective differs markedly from the current focus on the costs associated with providing assistance. By acknowledging the important role of reciprocity in relationships, we also emphasize the potential long-term impact of support provision—that is, enhanced satisfaction in supportive relationships. This does not mean that there may not be short- or long-term costs associated with providing support. By focusing on the other person's needs for assistance, the provider may overlook or ignore her or his own current needs for support; this inattention may lead to ambivalence or resentment on the provider's part, a situation that may undermine her or his efforts to provide support.

Support Receipt. The receipt of supportive behavior involves several steps. This stage of the support transaction begins for the recipient when he or she recognizes that another person has enacted supportive behavior that may facilitate his or her coping efforts. In other words, receiving support is a conscious act that requires that the individual perceive that potentially supportive behavior has been provided by a network member. A recipient may be especially likely to recognize supportive efforts on the part of a provider when the recipient has requested assistance from that person or when he or she has received aid from that person in the past; the latter point makes clear that the fact that the recipient has not explicitly requested help does not mean that he or she will not be anticipating receiving support from others. Other aspects of the interaction may also influence support appraisals. For example, a father may try to help his daughter fix her toy truck by reattaching a broken wheel to the truck's axle. The impact of this potentially supportive act may differ, depending on whether the assistance is preceded by a comment such as, "Here, let me do that, you'll probably just break it more," rather than one such as, "I think you just need to push the tire onto the axle with a little more pressure ... there you go, you did it!" Our point it that supportive behavior occurs in an interpersonal context (Pierce et al., 1992) and that this context strongly influences recipients' appraisals of potentially supportive behavior.

As we mentioned earlier in the chapter, it is tempting to frame the issue of whether support providers and recipients appraise their potentially supportive transactions similarly in terms of veridicality. This approach is likely to be unproductive because providers and recipient may appraise a social interaction in very different ways and still each be correct (i.e., the provider may have enacted behavior that she or he intended to be supportive, and the potential recipient of the behavior may evaluate the behavior as unsupportive or may not take notice of the other person's support attempts). The issue needs to be recast such that the central issue concerns the mechanisms by which providers and recipients come to hold similar (or dissimilar) perceptions of their potentially supportive transactions (cf. Chapter 5).

Assuming that the potential recipient perceives that the provider is willing to enact or has enacted supportive behavior, the recipient must still decide whether he or she will make use of the proffered support. Support may be provided but not received in the sense that the potential recipient may decide not to make use of the assistance available from a family member. This decision may be made for at least two reasons. First, although family relationships carry with them strong societal prescriptions about providing support, a family member may still elect not to receive assistance from other family members because of concerns about obligation, because of the desire to develop or maintain independence from other members of the family, or because the potential recipient may be worried about stigmatization associated with being perceived as taking advantage of the support provider (Martin & Martin, 1978). Second, potentially supportive behavior that is offered by the provider may not match the recipient's perceived need for a specific type of support; the recipient may therefore need to make significant revisions in his or her coping strategy if he or she is to make use of the offered support. Provision of mismatched support (i.e., support that differs from the type of support desired by the recipient) may be especially problematic when the recipient feels ambivalent about the obligations he or she might incur if he or she were to make use of the support.

Our discussion of supportive transactions has understandably emphasized their impact on coping with a specific life event. Our analysis of support schemata and supportive relationships suggests that these transactions also have important implications for personality development. Supportive transactions over time, particularly with one's parents early in life, contribute to support schemata that incorporate expectations about the supportiveness of the social environment. These transactions with others also lead to the development of relationship-specific schemata about the supportiveness of particular others. As Pierce et al. (1992) recently demonstrated, the appraisal of supportive transactions depends strongly on recipients' support schemata and on the quality of the relationship between recipient and provider.

Implications for Future Research

The conceptualization of social support presented herein has several implications—both theoretical and methodological—for an agenda for further research on social support. In particular, we see a need for efforts in two directs: (1) studies of supportive relationships, with an emphasis on the dyad, as opposed to a single participant, and (2) developmental studies that examine social support processes over time.

Studies of Supportive Relationships.   Throughout this chapter, we have made the point that social support involves transactional processes between two relationship participants. Studies need to employ methodologies that incorporate assessments of cognition and behavior engaged in by each of the participants (Chapter 5). These efforts would make it possible to examine questions pertaining to the conditions under which participants are most likely to appraise their own and each other's behavior in a similar manner, the strategies that individuals use to seek social support and their impact on potential providers' thoughts and actions, and the consequences that enacted support has for both the recipient and the provider.

Although studies have appeared in the literature that obtain measures of both participants, there has been no development of statistical techniques that would enable researchers to make optimal use of the data that are being collected. For example, structural equation modeling can be employed to isolate unique and shared variance in each participant's perceptions of their potentially supportive transactions; yet such analyses ignore the fact that while orthogonal partitioning of the variance in perceptions is possible, these two portions of each participant's perceptions (i.e., unique and shared) do not operate independently of each other and instead probably exert mutual influences. For example, a recipient's support schema probably impacts her or his "unique" as well as "shared" appraisal of support provided by a network member. In other words, available statistical techniques fail to clarify—and may even obscure—important interconnections among the different elements in the social support equation. An important challenge for further research concerns the development of analytical approaches to explicate the complex processes linking cognition and social behavior in family (and other) relationships.

By focusing on the dyad, we hope that future research will avoid the unidirectional bias present in much of past and current social support research—the tendency to view one relationship participant as the support provider and the other participant as the support recipient. As we have argued in this chapter, each relationship participant is both a provider and a recipient of social support. In some cases, an individual may play a primary role as a support provider while the other relationship participant struggles with a challenging life event. Coyne's work (Coyne, Ellard, & Smith, 1990) demonstrates, however, that even a life event that has traditionally been conceptualized as occurring to an individual, such as myocardial infarction, requires that both members of a dyad cope with the ramifications of the event. Adopting a dyadic approach will serve as an impetus for theoretical formulations that seek to account for the mutual influences that relationships exert on each other as well for methodological techniques that will enable researchers to evaluate hypotheses stemming from such an orientation.

Developmental Studies. Growing recognition of the role played by individual differences in social-support processes raises several important questions requiring empirical attention. Studies demonstrating the role of support schemata in appraisals of potentially supportive behavior lead to speculation about the developmental sequelae of support schemata. One plausible hypothesis is that support schemata emerge as a consequence of a history of experiences with important support providers (B. R. Sarason et al., 1990). Which features of these experiences, however, are most pertinent to the formation of support schemata? To what extent can supportive experiences with a particular caregiver buffer conflictual experiences with other family members? Can support schemata change over time and, if they can, which experiences in later life are most likely to lead to change in support schemata derived from previous experience?

Developmental studies are also needed to examine change in the nature of supportive relationships over time. Parental relationships evolve over time, with a shift in emphasis from parents serving as primary support providers to their young children to parents relying increasingly on their adult children for support, particularly assistance in dealing with activities that challenge the elderly in later life (Brubaker, 1990). Changes in the roles played by family members in each other's lives may require adaptation that, in turn, may be facilitated by supportive relationships in the family members' larger social networks.

By attending to the long-term implications of supportive family relationships, we do not wish to draw attention away from the short-term consequences of specific supportive interactions. For example, in addition to leading, across time, to the acquisition of support schemata, supportive interactions enhance coping efforts directed toward specific life events. These experiences provide children with opportunities to acquire coping skills, thereby increasing their personal effectiveness. Supportive interactions also reduce recipients' distress and arousal. Longitudinal studies are therefore needed that incorporate assessments of situation-specific and long-term impacts of social support.

CONCLUSION

The social-support construct is complex and includes the following elements: support schemata, supportive relationships, and supportive transactions. This conceptualization of social support emphasizes two important features of social support. First, although the concept of social support can be disaggregated into components, these components do not operate in isolation from each other; instead, they are interconnected aspects of a superordinate construct. Research methodologies are needed to explore each of these features of the support construct, particularly in terms of the reciprocal influences they exert on one another. Second, social support has both short- and long-term implications with respect to coping and personal development. Investigations of social support need to examine its consequences across time to delineate the situation-specific and developmental impact of social support.

REFERENCES

Baldwin, M. W. (1992). Relational schemas and the processing of social information. *Psychological Bulletin, 112,* 461–484.
Barrera, M., Jr. (1981). Social support in the adjustment of pregnant adolescents: Assessment issues. In B. H. Gottlieb (Ed.), *Social networks and social support* (pp. 69–96). Beverly Hills: Sage Publications.

Bowlby, J. (1980). *Attachment and loss*, Vol. 3, *Loss: Sadness and depression*. New York: Basic Books.

Brubaker, T. H. (Ed.) (1990). *Family relationships in later life*. Newbury Park, CA: Sage Publications.

Caruso, G.-A. L. (1992). The development of three scales to measure the supportiveness of relationships between parents and child care providers. *Educational and Psychological Measurement, 52*, 146–160.

Clark, M. S. (1983). Some implications of close social bonds for help-seeking. In B. M. DePaulo, A. Nadler, & J. D. Fisher (Eds.), *New directions in helping*, Vol. 2, *Help-seeking* (pp. 205–233). San Diego: Academic Press.

Cohen, S., & Wills, T. A. (1985). Stress, social support, and the buffering hypothesis. *Psychological Bulletin, 98*, 310–357.

Compas, B. E. (1987). Coping with stress during childhood and adolescence. *Psychological Bulletin, 101*, 393–403.

Coyne, J. C., Ellard, J. H., & Smith, D. A. F. (1990). Social support, interdependence, and the dilemmas of helping. In B. R. Sarason, I. G. Sarason, & G. R. Pierce (Eds.), *Social support: An interactional view* (pp. 129–149). New York: Wiley.

Cutrona, C. E., & Russell, D. (1987). The provisions of social relationships and adaptation to stress. In W. H. Jones & D. Perlman (Eds.), *Advances in personal relationships*, Vol. 1 (pp. 37–67). Greenwich, CT: JAI.

Cutrona, C. E., & Suhr, J. A. (1994). Social support communication in the context of marriage: An analysis of couples' supportive interactions. In B. R. Burleson, T. L. Albrecht, & I. G. Sarason (Eds.), *Communication of social support: Messages, interactions, relationships, and community* (pp. 113–135). Thousand Oaks, CA: Sage Publications.

Dakof, G. A., &Taylor, S. E. (1990). Victims' perceptions of social support: What is helpful from whom? *Journal of Personality and Social Psychology, 58*, 80–89.

Deal, J. E., Wampler, K. S., & Halverson, C. F. (1992). The importance of similarity in the marital relationship. *Family Processes, 31*, 369–382.

Dunkel-Schetter, C., & Wortman, C. B. (1982). The interactional dynamics of cancer: Problems in social relationships and their impact on the patient. In H. S. Friedman & M. R. DiMatteo (Eds.), *Interpersonal issues in health care* (pp. 69–100). New York: Academic Press.

Fiske, S. T., & Taylor, S. E. (1984). *Social cognition*. Reading, MA: Addison-Wesley.

Grace, G. D., & Schill, T. (1986). Social support and coping style differences in subjects high and low in interpersonal trust. *Psychological Reports, 59*, 584–586.

Heller, K., & Swindle, R. W. (1983). Social networks, perceived social support, and coping with stress. In R. D. Felner, L. A. Jason, J. M. Moritsugu, & S. S. Farber (Eds.), *Preventive psychology: Theory, research and practice* (pp. 87–103). Elmsford, NY: Pergamon.

Heller, K., Swindle, R. W., & Dusenbury, L. (1986). Component social support processes: Comments and integration. *Journal of Consulting and Clinical Psychology, 54*, 466–470.

Hirsch, B. (1979). Psychological dimensions of social networks: A multimethod analysis. *American Journal of Community Psychology, 7*, 263–277.

Hobfoll, S. E., & Lerman, M. (1988). Personal relationships, personal attributes, and stress resistance: Mothers' reactions to their child's illness. *American Journal of Community Psychology, 16*, 565–589.

Jacobson, D. (1990). Stress and support in stepfamily formation: The cultural context of social support. In B. R. Sarason, I. G. Sarason, & G. R. Pierce (Eds.), *Social support: An interactional view* (pp. 199–218). New York: Wiley.

Lakey, B., & Cassady, P. B. (1990). Cognitive processes in perceived social support. *Journal of Personality and Social Psychology, 59*, 337–348.

Lakey, B., & Dickinson, L. G. (1994). Antecedents of perceived support: Is perceived family environment generalized to new social relationships? *Cognitive Therapy and Research, 18*, 39–53.

Lakey, B., Moineau, S., & Drew, J. B. (1992). Perceived social support and individual differences in the interpretation and recall of supportive behavior. *Journal of Social and Clinical Psychology, 11*, 336–348.

Lazarus, R. S., & Folkman, S. (1984). *Stress, appraisal, and coping*. New York: Springer.

Lerner, J. V., Baker, N., & Lerner, R. M. (1985). A person-centered goodness of fit model of adjustment. In P. C. Kendall (Ed.), *Advances in cognitive–behavioral research and therapy*, Vol. 4 (pp. 111–136). New York: Academic Press.

Lerner, J. V., & Lerner, R. M. (1983). Temperament and adaptation across life: Theoretical and empirical issues. In P. B. Baltes & O. G. Brim, Jr. (Eds.), *Life-span development and behavior*, Vol. 5 (pp. 197–231). New York: Academic Press.

Markus, H., & Zajonc, R. B. (1985). The cognitive perspective in social psychology. In G. Lindzey & E. Aronson (Eds.), *Handbook of social psychology*, Vol. 1 (pp. 137–230). New York: Random House.

Martin, E. P., & Martin, J. M. (1978). *The black extended family.* Chicago: University of Chicago Press.

Milgram, N. A. (1989). Social support versus self-efficiency in traumatic and post-traumatic stress reactions. In B. Lehrer & S. Gershon (Eds.), *New directions in affective disorders* (pp. 455–458). New York: Springer-Verlag.

Milgram, N. A., & Palti, G. (1993). Psychosocial characteristics of resilient children. *Journal of Research in Personality, 27,* 207–221.

Nadler, A., & Fisher, J. D. (1986). The role of threat to self-esteem and perceived control in recipient reaction to aid: Theory development and empirical validation. *Advances in experimental social psychology*, Vol. 19 (pp. 81–123). San Diego: Academic Press.

Peters-Golden, H. (1982). Breast cancer: Varied perceptions of social support in the illness experience. *Social Science and Medicine, 16,* 483–491.

Pierce, G. R., Ptacek, J. T., Contey, C., & Pollack, K. (1996). Supportive behavior and support appraisals: An experimental study (submitted).

Pierce, G. R., Sarason, B. R., & Sarason, I. G. (1990). Integrating social support perspectives: Working models, personal relationships and situational factors. In S. Duck & R. C. Silver (Eds.), *Personal relationships and social support* (pp. 173–189). London: Sage Publications.

Pierce, G. R., Sarason, B. R., & Sarason, I. G. (1992). General and specific support expectations and stress as predictors of perceived supportiveness: An experimental study. *Journal of Personality and Social Psychology, 63,* 297–307.

Pierce, G. R., Sarason, I. G., & Sarason, B. R. (1991). General and relationship-based perceptions of social support: Are two constructs better than one? *Journal of Personality and Social Psychology, 61,* 1028–1039.

Pierce, G. R., Sarason, I. G., & Sarason, B. R. (1996). The role of social support in coping. In M. Zeidner & N. Endler (Eds.), *Handbook of coping: Theory, research, and applications* (pp. 434–451). New York: Wiley.

Pierce, G. R., Sarason, I. G., Sarason, B. R., Solky, J. A., & Nagle, L. C. (1996). Assessing the quality of personal relationships: The Quality of Relationships Inventory (submitted).

Rollins, B. C., & Thomas, D. L. (1979). Parental support, power, and control techniques in the socialization of children. In W. R. Burr, R. Hill, F. I. Nye, & I. L. Reiss (Eds.), *Contemporary theories about the family*, Vol. 1 (pp. 317–364). New York: Free Press.

Sarason, B. R., Pierce, G. R., Bannerman, A., & Sarason, I. G. (1993). Investigating the antecedents of perceived social support: Parents' views of and behavior toward their children. *Journal of Personality and Social Psychology, 65,* 1071–1085.

Sarason, B. R., Pierce, G. R., & Sarason, I. G. (1990). Social support: The sense of acceptance and the role of relationships. In B. R. Sarason, I. G. Sarason, & G. R. Pierce (Eds.), *Social support: An interactional view* (pp. 97–128). New York: Wiley.

Sarason, B. R., Sarason, I. G., Hacker, T. A., & Basham, B. R. (1985). Concomitants of social support: Social skills, physical attractiveness, and gender. *Journal of Personality and Social Psychology, 49,* 469–480.

Sarason, I. G., Sarason, B. R., & Shearin, E. N. (1986). Social support as an individual difference variable: Its instability, origins, and relational aspects. *Journal of Personality and Social Psychology, 50,* 845–855.

Searcy, E., & Eisenberg, N. (1992). Defensiveness in response to aid from a sibling. *Journal of Personality and Social Psychology, 62,* 422–433.

Sroufe, L. A., & Fleeson, J. (1986). Attachment and the construction of relationships. In W. W. Hartup & Z. Rubin (Eds.), *Relationships and development* (pp. 51–71). Hillsdale, NJ: Erlbaum.

Stokes, J. P., & Wilson, D. G. (1984). The Inventory of Socially Supportive Behaviors: Dimensionality, prediction, and gender differences. *American Journal of Community Psychology, 12,* 53–69.

Symonds, P. (1939). *The psychology of parent–child relationships.* New York: Appleton-Century-Crofts.

Tessler, R. C., & Schwartz, S. H. (1972). Help seeking, self-esteem, and achievement motivation: An attributional analysis. *Journal of Personality and Social Psychology, 21,* 318–326.

Vaux, A., Riedel, S., & Stewart, D. (1987). Modes of social support: The Social Support Behaviors (SS-B) scale. *American Journal of Community Psychology, 15,* 209–237.

Weiss, R. S. (1974). The provisions of social relationships. In Z. Rubin (ed.), *Doing unto others* (pp. 17–26). Englewood Cliffs, NJ: Prentice-Hall.

Wortman, C. B., & Dunkel-Schetter, C. (1987). Conceptual and methodological issues in the study of social support. In A. Baum & J. Singer (Eds.), *Handbook of psychology and health* (pp. 63–108). Hillsdale, NJ: Erlbaum.

2

Information Processing Approaches to the Study of Relationship and Social Support Schemata

PENNY L. YEE, KRISTINE E. SANTORO, JENNIFER S. PAUL, and LISA B. ROSENBAUM

In 15 minutes, Sam would be leaving to begin his first year in college. As he buckled the last straps on his bags, his father popped his head into the room and said, "Hey, give us a call when you arrive." Sam recognized the tone of his dad's voice. He was still uncertain about Sam's ability to cope with the challenges of college life. Sam had already decided not to call home for several weeks—not until he was completely settled into his classes and could prove his ability to handle the demands of college.

Sam's thoughts drifted back to his last visit with his high school physics teacher. She was like the grandmother he had never known; she had always been there to listen to his troubles. When she asked him to call when he arrived at college, he knew it reflected her genuine interest in how he would be getting along—and she assumed he'd do just fine.

Sam patted his shirt pocket as he passed through the door to check that he had the phone number his new roommate had given to him. His roommate would be working when he showed up, so he had written to ask Sam to call when he arrived. Sam hadn't met his roommate and was a bit nervous about calling up someone he didn't know, but he was eager to call and meet his new roommate.

In this hypothetical episode, three similar requests—to telephone someone when he arrives on campus—have been made of Sam, and yet each request has elicited a different reaction within him. Intriguing questions for researchers in the areas of social support and relationships are how and why ostensibly similar behavioral acts evoke such different responses within an individual. Questions like these can be and have been examined from a cognitive perspective adopting

PENNY L. YEE, KRISTINE E. SANTORO, JENNIFER S. PAUL, and LISA B. ROSENBAUM • Department of Psychology, Hamilton College, Clinton, New York 13323.

Handbook of Social Support and the Family, edited by Gregory R. Pierce, Barbara R. Sarason, and Irwin G. Sarason. Plenum Press, New York, 1996.

information processing models. Our reactions in social interactions are guided by implicit rules that assign meaning to events and function as road maps for navigating our social world. Information processing theory provides a novel approach for investigating the thoughts, feelings, and expectations that are represented in these rule structures. Understanding the origins of our differential responses to situations will provide another link between social support and relationships research.

SOCIAL SUPPORT RESEARCH AND INFORMATION PROCESSING: A BRIEF OVERVIEW

The links among social support, psychological adjustment, and physical health outcomes have been of interest since the first epidemiological studies linked psychological variables to a variety of outcomes (Berkman & Syme, 1979; Blazer, 1982; Brown & Harris, 1978; Cassel, 1976; House, Robbins, & Metzner, 1982). These findings triggered efforts to discover the nature of these relationships and the mechanisms by which social ties influence an individual's overall well-being. Initial research on the topic of social support implicitly assumed that the key ingredient in social support processes was the exchange of supportive behaviors that might bolster an individual's coping efforts (Pierce, B. R. Sarason, & I. G. Sarason, 1990). This early focus has shifted to an emphasis on the cognitive appraisals that individuals make regarding their interactions with members of their support networks (Coyne & DeLongis, 1986; B. R. Sarason, Shearin, Pierce, & I. G. Sarason, 1987). There is growing evidence to suggest that the attributions a person makes regarding a support provider's behaviors significantly influence the effectiveness of supportive behaviors in buffering the effects of negative life events (Wethington & Kessler, 1986). In essence, a person may not benefit from "supportive" behaviors if that person does not view the actions or the intent of the actions as helpful. The perceptions or interpretations of the "supportive" behavior seem to be a crucial factor.

If these observations reflect genuine connections between perceptions and the facilitatory effects of social support, then it is important to examine where these perceptions come from. Why do people differ in their perceptions and interpretations of the same objective events? Differences may emerge across individuals as well as within individuals. Two individuals may differ in their response to the same behavior enacted by the same provider. For instance, one person may welcome a phone call from a friend following major surgery, while another person may view the same behavior as intrusive. On the other hand, differences may be observed within an individual also. A phone call from a close friend may be welcome, while a call from a sibling who has been out of touch for several years may be viewed as disingenuous. These examples emphasize the importance of considering the specific relationships between support providers and recipients in understanding differences in perceptions of social support.

What is it that individuals bring to the situation to produce such different impressions of what appears to be the same objective behavior? The answer to this question lies, in part, in the personal experiences that individuals have had within the context of specific relationships. The memories from personal social experiences create a mental structure that not only maintains a history of experiences in different situations, but also influences the way an individual is likely to interpret or perceive another's behavior.

Mental structures that serve to facilitate the comprehension and organization of incoming information have been described using a number of different terms such as "scripts" (Bower, Black, & Turner, 1979; Schank & Abelson, 1977), "schemas" (Bartlett, 1932; Markus, 1977), "mental models" (Johnson-Laird, 1980, 1983), and "working models" (Bowlby, 1969). Because Bowlby framed his discussion of working models specifically around the development of significant social relationships, we will rely on his term "working models." When we refer to more general cognitive structures, we will use the term "schema." Working models comprise a set of expectations of how typical interactions between oneself and specific others are likely to progress based on past experience. Consequently, observed behaviors will be interpreted with these sets of expectations in mind. The examination and ultimate understanding of these behaviors and responses are optimally suited for investigation using social–cognitive paradigms.

The purpose of this chapter is to discuss the information processing approach to studying the nature and influences of these mental structures on our perception of supportive behaviors exchanged within significant social relationships. If we are to understand why individuals differ in their perceptions of social support, it is important first to discuss the general role of working models in guiding our social behavior. The emphasis will be on *how* these structures impact the manner in which people process social information, and not simply on *what* components of an interaction are processed. By using what we know about how social information is dealt with, we may gain useful insights into the question of why there are individual differences in the effectiveness of supportive interactions. We discuss how one can investigate the mental processes that are engaged when individuals are in significant relationships to examine questions such as the following: How is attention drawn to specific behavioral acts in an interaction? How are relevant cues identified in a social situation? How do we perceive events as supportive in a social interaction? And how does past experience affect our perceptions? This chapter explores how adopting an information processing framework can address questions such as these. First, a general model of information processing is presented, and then applications of this model are discussed in the context of social interactions.

The proposed techniques are considered *implicit* as opposed to *explicit* measures of thought processes. Implicit processing reflects spontaneous processing that is guided by stimulus cues rather than subject-initiated activities (Schachter, 1987). Implicit tests measure the effects of previous experience on tasks in which the explicit conscious retrieval of experiences is not necessary. In short, implicit measures are indices of unconscious knowledge. Prior experience is reflected in current behavior and thought, but is not consciously recollected. One implicit technique frequently used is based on the notion of priming effects. Priming measures the extent to which previous learning or exposure to a stimulus facilitates performance of a task or skill (Gardiner, 1989; Schachter, 1987). Priming effects can be observed in processing time and in accuracy. For instance, priming is evident if a person processes or makes judgments about previously studied information faster and more efficiently than about nonstudied information.

Another characteristic of the proposed techniques is their emphasis on thoughts that are spontaneously triggered when working models are activated, and not just the resulting memory of the interaction. This marks a distinction between *on-line* processes and the memorial consequence of processing. On-line processing refers to processes that occur *while engaged* in an activity—for instance, telling a story, counseling a friend, or driving a car. They are most commonly examined with time–course analyses, by which measures of active thought processes can be assessed on a moment-to-moment basis. Applications of these techniques to the investigation of social support within the context of close relationships are also presented.

The focus on implicit, on-line thought processes is advantageous because it allows researchers to investigate the unintentional, automatic cognitions that are activated when individuals are engaged in social behavior. These thoughts are not easily identified through self-report and are subsequently not easily censured by defensive mechanisms that serve to cast a person in a more positive light. These techniques provide promising directions for investigations of people's working models of support within specific relationships.

TRADITIONAL COGNITIVE INFORMATION PROCESSING APPROACHES AND SOCIAL SUPPORT: A REVIEW OF THEORY AND RESEARCH

Information processing theory provides a convenient means of conceptualizing the systematic behaviors that individuals produce in response to informational stimuli. The model distinguishes between the types of information being processed and the nature of that processing at particular stages, and assumes that behavior results from information passing through a series of cognitive processes. The general model that guides our discussion is summarized in Figure 1. Conventional information processing models consist of the following three functionally distinct structures: a sensory memory, a working memory (similar to short-term memory proposed in early models of memory), and a long-term memory. Operating in this system are processes that monitor the flow of information within these structures. These monitoring processes are often overlooked, yet they are fundamental in guiding our attention to, and our perception and comprehension of, real world events. Below, we briefly describe the functions of the basic information processing system, highlighting those components most relevant for dealing with social support processes in the context of relationships.

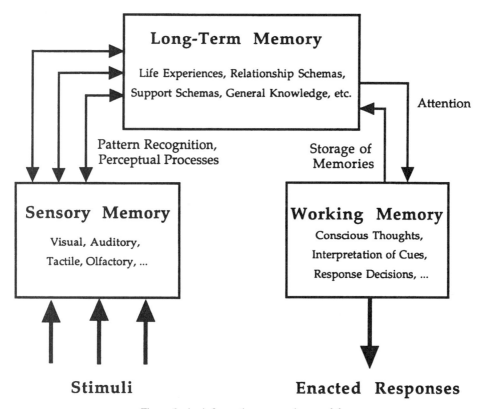

Figure 1. An information processing model.

General Information Processing Theory

Basic Structures. The basic structures in the classic information processing system are *sensory memory, working memory,* and *long-term memory.* These structures provide the basic framework within which cognitive psychologists try to understand mental processes and behavior. We describe sensory memory here primarily for completeness in presentation of the model. However, we will devote little attention in this chapter to it, primarily because representations at this level are relevant mainly for basic perceptual processes such as object or feature recognition. Environmental events enter the system through sensory memory. In sensory memory, transient and primitive mental representations of stimuli are retained just long enough for information to be identified and channeled into working memory. Information in sensory memory is not processed beyond the development of extremely rudimentary representations of the physical features that are ultimately used for stimulus identification. For example, in sensory memory, we would be able to distinguish between different colors or different voices, but the stimulus would not carry any meaning beyond that.

The role of working memory is more central to our discussion of the role of relationships in social support interactions. Thought processes of which we are consciously aware are said to reside in working memory. Conscious thoughts, interpretation of social cues, and decisions about intentional acts of behavior are dealt with here. (See Baddeley [1986] for a more detailed description of functions and activities of working memory.) When the patterns in sensory memory have been linked with meaningful representations in long-term memory and attended to by control mechanisms, they become part of working memory. This process is represented in Figure 1 by the arrow labeled "Attention" that connects long-term memory to working memory. Thus, once a voice is identified, we can begin to think about the content of the message. The meanings of the words contribute to one's understanding of the explicit verbal message, while one's relationship with the speaker provides one with information for interpreting the speaker's emotional state through nonverbal behavior. The nonverbal behavior gives us implicit information. All these cues make important contributions to the overall impact of the communication, and it is in working memory that integration and interpretation of these cues takes place. Returning to our initial example, Sam did not interpret his father's utterance as a simple request to phone home. Intonation and knowledge about their father–son relationship also influenced Sam's interpretation of their interaction.

Long-term memory is considered a permanent storage area in which we retain memories about personal life experiences and general knowledge (e.g., vocabulary, facts, motor skills). For instance, memories of successful support-seeking experiences, past conflicts, and an understanding of social and cultural norms are stored here. Thus, it follows that Sam's working models for interacting with family and friends would be stored here. Information in long-term memory is organized into a highly interconnected structure in which associated concepts are tightly linked. The interconnected links facilitate the activation of facts when processing related information.

Although the components of the general information processing model are typically explained in a manner that emphasizes a sequential flow through the system (i.e., entering sensory memory and ultimately being stored in long-term memory), it should be noted that the transmission of information occurs in both directions in a parallel fashion. That is, working and long-term memory are not sitting idle waiting for the completion of processing in sensory memory. For example, Sam will process the visual and auditory cues of his father at the same time that expectations and memories of past interactions become salient in working memory. Thus, stimulus events are continually entering our information processing systems and competing for available mental resources. The processing capacity of working memory is limited, so we must make decisions to prioritize our processing efforts.

Basic Processes.   Control processes represent a set of operations in working memory that demand mental resources and may be thought of as strategies or goal-oriented processes that allow our thoughts and behaviors to be purposeful and planful. Although we have conscious control over the general goals to be accomplished, we have little direct access to how they are achieved. For instance, control processes are involved when Sam integrates the verbal and nonverbal cues in the interaction with his father. He knows what cues he is attending to, but he would not always be able to explain how they contributed to his insight into the interaction. Control processes require attention and assist in prioritizing the information dealt with by working memory.

Our behavior is also influenced by another set of processes over which we exert even less control. These are more reflexive or *automatic* processes. They are reflected in the expectations and spontaneous emotional responses that are triggered when we find ourselves in support-seeking or support-providing situations. Simply interacting with a familiar individual will activate memories and emotional responses of past interactions. These past memories form a working model of one's understanding of the relationship—in other words, one's expectations for acceptance by this individual, expectations of how much support one is likely to receive, and the other's personal attributes.

Information Processing and Social Support

Although all components in the general information processing model are important for efficient cognitive functioning, some (e.g., sensory memory) are less relevant when examining perceptions of social support in relationships. Social information processing theory emphasizes the cognitive processes involved in an individual's response to supportive behaviors. Thus, the theory's contribution to understanding supportive behaviors lies in understanding the assumptions and processes that are evoked in individuals. Although attempts have been made to provide objective definitions of supportive behavior, mounting evidence suggests that adequate definitions of supportive behavior need to incorporate reference to the appraisals of support providers and recipients (see Chapter 1). It is important to understand how individuals perceive social cues, how they make attributions and inferences about these cues, and how they arrive at decisions about appropriate responses. Consequently, more central to social psychologists is the interplay among long-term memory structures, automatic and control processes, and the behavioral responses formulated and enacted in working memory. That is, how do early attachment experiences influence one's attention to and perception of support interactions? What sort of impact do beliefs about oneself and others have on how one elicits support from others? For instance, Sam's personal history with his father led him to focus on the tone of his father's voice. This in combination with Sam's past experiences with his father gave the interaction a very different meaning than would seem to have been embodied in the explicit verbal request. The request was not viewed as a sincere gesture of affection or concern. Instead,

Sam perceived his father as lacking confidence in him. This perception—accurate or not—influenced Sam's behavior.

Previous researchers have identified key processes that are crucial in understanding social behavior: encoding of cues, interpretation of cues, response decision, and response enactment (Dodge & Crick, 1990; McFall, 1982; McFall & Dodge, 1982; Wyer & Srull, 1989). The role of attention is important in focusing and encoding cues that are relevant to the interaction. The individual's past experiences in similar situations are key in directing attention to significant aspects of the interaction and in providing meaning to ambiguous social cues. These past experiences also provide a means for inferring another's intentions and for making attributions regarding the causes and motivations for behavior. Thus, they play a significant role in social-cue reading (Lipton, McDonel, & McFall, 1986) and intention-cue detection (Dodge, Murphy, & Buchsbaum, 1984). Working memory is an important component in this process because it is where integration of social and cognitive processing occurs.

Historically, psychologists have been interested in the knowledge structures that arise from our experiential histories. These structures or storage bins of information reside in long-term memory and guide our understanding of and our behavior in social situations (Schank & Abelson, 1977). They represent "organizations of conceptually related representations of objects, situations, events and of sequences of events and actions" (Markus & Zajonc, 1985, p. 143). Researchers have identified a number of different structures that facilitate our understanding and behavior in situations in the world around us. For instance, several researchers have examined the role of schemas/schemata (Bartlett, 1932; Cantor & Kihlstrom, 1982; Markus, 1977; Rumelhart, 1976), scripts (Gerrig, 1988; Schank & Abelson, 1977), mental models (Johnson-Laird, 1980, 1983), and working models (Bowlby, 1969, 1988). Each emphasizes a slightly different application of the memory structure, but they all serve to facilitate processing and enactment of appropriate behavioral responses and memories.

Bartlett (1932) was one of the first to systematically assess the function of these cognitive structures. He argued that schemata are derived from past experience and guide the individual in construing new experiences—properties of schemata that are still accepted today. Schemata develop through experience and over time. Because they affect the construction of new experiences, it follows that they impact the formation of new relationships. Bowlby's model of attachment emphasized the importance of healthy attachment relationships between parent and child early in life. The ability to develop and maintain healthy adult relationships within which support is easily offered and requested may very well lie in our experiences of support early in life (Lakey & Dickinson, 1994; I. G. Sarason, Sarason, & Shearin, 1986). These experiences provide the foundation upon which supportive acts in other (current) relationships are interpreted. For instance, how parents treat a child elicits a response from the child. How the child reacts reinforces the parents' treatment of him or her. As the child grows older, this pattern continues and becomes a property of the parent–child relationship (Main, Kaplan, & Cassidy, 1985). More important, the pattern also becomes a property of the child, who imposes it on new relationships. In other words, the child internalizes the types of interactions that exist within the relationship with his or her parents. The child then applies this knowledge when dealing with others. In this way, the pattern established in the child's first relationships carries over to later relationships (Hazan & Shaver, 1987; Sroufe & Fleeson, 1986). Because our working models are products of the personal experiences we have had with people, events, and situations, it follows that our understanding of individual differences in perceptions of social behavior ought to focus on these structures.

Impact of Schemata on Behavior and Cognitive Processing. Schemata have a powerful influence on how we perceive a social interaction and what we remember about it. They provide the mechanism through which past experience influences current behavior. We rely on schemata to direct our attention, guide behavior, and organize the memory of events. Schemata are dynamic structures. Past and present experiences influence them as they serve to guide current behavior. They tell us what to expect in certain situations as well as what are appropriate and effective responses. As we grow in experience, we abstract rules about how the world works. It is through these rules that we are able to direct attention to key features of an interaction. There are many subtle nuances involved in interpersonal behaviors; to consciously evaluate each and every head tilt, every voice tremor, and every shift of one's gaze would be an overwhelming feat and would place extraordinary demands on our cognitive systems. The use of schemata allows us to take shortcuts. Schemata allow us to prioritize the elements of an interaction; they provide us with expectations. Expectations direct our attention to defining elements of the interaction. We don't look and evaluate each aspect of the interaction, just the aspects necessary for confirming understanding of what is going on. For instance, when requesting a favor, we look at past experiences to assess the likelihood that assistance will be offered—for example, how often has support been available in the past? But we also read other behavioral and situational cues to determine the best time to make the request. Seeing a parent's furrowed brow or stacks of unpaid bills on the kitchen table may persuade us to request help at another time. In some instances, we make conscious and deliberate use of the available cues—for example, the stack of unpaid bills. But it is very likely that we also process cues of which we are unaware. We appear to be sensitive at a preconscious level to subtle behavioral cues that influence our behavior. The cue may be a slight twitch of an eyebrow, a quick, sideways glance, or a change in physical distance between members in the interaction, but these subtle cues are detected and influence our behavior.

In addition to influencing what is attended to, schemata influence our perceptions or interpretations of behaviors. This influence occurs in two ways. First, it directs our attention. Our perceptions will be guided by the cues we permit to enter working memory. The second means is through past experience. Our personal histories assist us in assigning meaning to the information brought into working memory. We can quickly and easily distinguish between a serious, committed "No" response from a more flippantly sarcastic "No" response that is intended to mean a resounding "Yes, or course!" We also know from our working models the likelihood that particular individuals will respond seriously or humorously.

Our memories of supportive events will also be influenced by past schemata. This influence occurs in a way that creates an illusion of circularity. First, we are more likely to remember what we attend to, which is typically what we expect on the basis of past experience. However, our expectations are based on information in our schemata. Once a schema is established, we tend to seek out information to reinforce or strengthen its organization. Second, when we fail to retrieve specific aspects of a supportive interaction, we rely on internal schemata to infer the missing information. Since we attend to only a subset of the details present during an interaction, this situation is likely to arise frequently. Schemata assist us in integrating the pieces of an event to create a coherent, meaningful memory based on what is most probable from our experience. This integration is not a conscious process, which makes it difficult to determine when a recollection is a genuine or reconstructed memory. Thus, schemata streamline our understanding and responses in social interactions, but at a cost of not knowing what was constructed and what was the true experience. This streamlining again serves to reinforce the strength of associations within activated schemata. This view is consistent with the claim of Fiske and Taylor (1989) that schemata persist despite evidence that supports contrary or conflicting information. Because events, concepts, and behaviors are subjective, individuals create their own reality consistent with their schemata.

Relationship Schemata. The significance of schemata in understanding supportive behaviors becomes even more apparent when framed in the context of specific relationships. Thus, when entering a support-seeking situation, the question becomes, "How likely am I to receive support from person X?" Individuals with a long shared history will have well-developed frameworks or lists of assumptions regarding the knowledge, intentions, and behaviors that a particular individual will have and manifest (Pierce, I. G. Sarason, & B. R. Sarason, 1991). In these instances, working models will have a very powerful impact on how an individual's behaviors will be interpreted (Pierce, B. R. Sarason, & I. G. Sarason, 1992). Surra and Bohman (1991) have asserted that individuals possess different schemata that correspond with every relationship they form. Surra and Bohman (1991) define relationship schemata as "organized representations of traits, beliefs, behaviors and action sequences relevant to a particular other person and to one's relationship with that person" (p. 288). In addition to these specific relationship schemata, Surra and Bohman propose the existence of general prototypes relevant to general close relationships, that is, beliefs about what a typical relationship is like, what the rules for behavior are, and what makes a relationship good or bad (see also Pierce et al., 1991, 1992).

Relationships with primary caregivers present the most logical target for exploring the significance of relationship schemata on perceptions of social support. Investigations of our earliest relationships have identified the existence of differential attachment bonds and behaviors (Ainsworth, Blehar, Waters, & Wall, 1978). Three attachment styles have been identified: secure, anxious–ambivalent, and anxious–avoidant. These attachment styles persist into adulthood, most likely in the form of schemata. As mentioned earlier, the first relationships that individuals have influence the formation of specific relationship schemata. These attachments, internalized during childhood, influence the formation of new relationships. In order for these patterns to persist, the child must possess an internal model of the self and the parent. Thus, individuals' relationship schemata include such things as their feelings toward themselves and others, reflected appraisals, how others treat them, and how they expect to be treated. Because the model is habitual (activated spontaneously) and unconscious, Bowlby (1988) argues that people continue to interact with others as they had with their parents, despite how others treat them.

APPLICATION OF INFORMATION PROCESSING PARADIGMS TO THE STUDY OF SOCIAL SUPPORT

The social information processing techniques used to study social support and relationships rely on procedures that are *implicit* and *on-line*. As mentioned in the introduction, implicit, on-line procedures measure the effects of previous experience on tasks that do not require conscious retrieval of those experiences. In other words, one can measure responses to stimuli that may evoke memories for a supportive episode or relationship rather than ask for explicit recall of the memory itself. On-line procedures are those that examine mental activity while performing a task rather than one's memory of it. In the discussion that follows, techniques for investigating relationship working models are outlined. Each of the techniques assumes that spontaneous associations and processing are triggered when particular working models are activated.

Priming in Lexical Decision Tasks

The first procedure is a priming procedure in which simple word targets are presented for subjects to identify. The idea is to present two target letter strings either simultaneously or within about 2 seconds of each other. Subjects simply decide if the letter strings are words in the English language—this decision being referred to as a "lexical decision task." If the concepts (words) are strongly associated in memory, identification of them should be easier and faster than if the words are not associated. For instance, imagine four trials in which the following word pairs are presented: MOM–WARM, DAD–WARM, MOM–COLD, DAD–COLD. An individual who is securely attached to parents might respond more quickly to the MOM–WARM and DAD–WARM word pairs because these two ideas would be stored closely together in long-term memory. Consequently, a time-consuming, exhaustive search of one's memory would not be necessary to identify the words. Responses would be faster than those to the MOM–COLD and

DAD–COLD word pairs. To carry the example even further, assume that a person's parents are divorced and the child holds deep affection for the father and blames the mother for splitting up the family. Differential response times to adjectives presented with the MOM and DAD primes would be expected.

Pilot studies similar to this example are being conducted in our laboratory. In one study, three different classes of relationship primes are used: mother, father, and self terms. These prime items are intended to activate working models relevant to specified relationships and are paired with different adjective types that were selected to reflect different attachment styles. For instance, terms such as "warm" and "secure" would be associated with secure attachment, "distant" and "detached" with ambivalent attachment, and "cold" and "critical" with avoidant attachment.

The viability of this approach is demonstrated in its successful application to other domains of social behavior. A similar task was used by Markus (1977) in investigations of self-schemata. Markus used a lexical decision task to demonstrate that schema-consistent information was more easily attended to than schema-inconsistent information. She found that subjects' reaction times to schema-consistent adjectives correlated with their self ratings on the adjectives. Reaction times were faster for adjectives that were rated as more descriptive. These results suggest that information that is consistent with the self-schema is processed more efficiently and is more easily accessed in memory. Baldwin, Fehr, Keedian, Seidel, and Thomson (1993) also adopted a lexical decision task to examine the extent to which individuals differing in attachment styles responded to schema-relevant descriptors. Schemata were activated by priming subjects with sentence fragments intended to activate social expectations within a specific attachment relationship (e.g., "If I try to get closer to my partner then my partner will …"). Presentation of the sentence fragment was followed by a target word that might or might not serve as a suitable conclusion (e.g., "leave") to the fragment. Target words could be compatible or incompatible with a subject's attachment style. Baldwin and colleagues' results showed that targets compatible with one's schematic expectations were responded to more quickly than incompatible completions. Together, these studies attest to the merit of the lexical decision procedure in identifying schema-relevant information.

Stroop Color-Naming Tasks

A second approach is based on the spontaneous activation of schema-related information. This procedure relies on the classic Stroop color-naming task. In the standard Stroop paradigm, color names are presented in different-colored inks—for example, word BLUE printed in red. It is believed that the time taken to name the color in which the work is printed reflects the amount of interference generated by automatic reading of the printed word. Since the task is to name the ink color and ignore the printed word, any interference observed is assumed to be caused by the automatic activation of the word's meaning. This activation is considered automatic because it is outside an individual's direct control and conscious awareness. Despite the intention to name the ink color, it is not possible to block the activation of meanings associated with the presented word. Although one is not always aware that such activation has taken place, its occurrence is inferred from the degree of interference observed in naming the color of the ink.

The basic assumptions of the Stroop task may be extended to examine the spontaneous activation of concepts relevant to relationship schemata. The key is to prime or activate the relevant schema for an individual. Once a schema is primed, associated concepts are closer to threshold levels for detection and recognition. Schemata can be activated by having subjects read sentence fragments, as Baldwin did for the lexical decision task. The fragments should then be followed by a colored target word that is relevant to the activated schema. If the schema is properly activated, schema-consistent concepts should be primed through automatic activation (Collins & Loftus, 1975), and interference in naming the ink color should be observed. For instance, imagine that you are presented with the sentence fragment, "If I were feeling lonely, I would feel better if I called my ..." followed by the target word MOTHER printed in green. Response times for naming the color of the target word should be *slowed* if an individual often relied on one's mother for support. Color naming would be slowed because the target word MOTHER would be primed by the sentence fragment. That the word is a schematically as well as syntactically acceptable completion of the statement allows rapid activation and recognition of the word, thereby introducing a source of interference in naming the color of ink in which the word is printed.

Geller and Shaver (1976) used a similar technique to examine the automatic activation of self-schema-related information. In their study, self-relevant and self-irrelevant words were presented, and subjects named the ink color of each word. When self-relevant words were presented, reaction times for naming the ink colors were significantly slowed. Even though we are not actively searching for schema-consistent information, it attracts our attention, thereby interfering with the current task at hand—naming the ink color in which the words are printed. Thus, in the examination of support in specific relationships, excitation of a particular relationship schema leaves one sensitized to schema-consistent information or cues that are present in the situation. This heightened sensitivity would be reflected in interference observed when naming colors of support-related concepts that are tied to expectations in the relationship.

These results are consistent with Markus's conclusion regarding self-schemata. Schema-consistent information is more available to decision processes, and so presentation of self-relevant words slows color-naming responses in the Stroop task but facilitates response times in lexical decision. Successful application of lexical decision and Stroop color-naming techniques would confirm the automatic activation of schema-related concepts for specific supportive relationships. Carefully selected targets items would allow researchers to examine the specific content of relationship and support schemata and perhaps identify sources for individual differences in perceptions of social-support situations.

Dual-Task Procedures

A third approach for investigating social support in relationships focuses on the limitations of the resources available in working memory. This approach is the classic dual-task approach frequently used in studies of attentional processing. An underlying assumption in dual-task procedures is the belief that there is a fixed and limited amount of cognitive resources available for performing tasks and controlling behavior. Simply put, when the performance of a task or set of tasks exhausts available mental resources, the processing demands of each additional task can be observed in and measured by decrements in performance in another. A classic dual-task procedure is the probe-detection task of Posner and Boies (1971). In this paradigm, a primary task, in this case a letter-matching task, is combined with a secondary task, probe detection. Participants were instructed to devote full attention to the primary task, thereby maximizing performance in this task, and to use any remaining resources to respond to the secondary task. In the letter-matching task, subjects were required to make simple judgments of whether or not two visually presented letters were the same. The secondary task was to press a button whenever they detected the probe signal, a brief burst of white noise. The probe signal was sounded at random points during the presentation of a letter pair. Reaction times to the probe reflected the availability of unused mental resources at the time the probe appeared. Faster response times indicate the availability of more resources; the availability of more mental resources allows efficient responding to the signal. Slower responses indicate a lower level of resource availability—suggesting that subjects were engaged in more demanding mental activities when the probe was presented.

This procedure can be adapted to investigations of relationships and social support working models through simple modification of the primary task. Rather than a simple letter-detection task, the primary task could be made more personally and socially relevant. For instance, a dichotic listening task in which subjects shadowed sentences describing supportive or unsupportive interactions could be effective in activating relationship schemata. Shadowing techniques require subjects to repeat out loud one of several simultaneous auditory messages. Alternatively, subjects could make decisions about whether or not selected adjectives were descriptive of their parental relationships or relationships with significant others. Responding to carefully placed probes would reveal the effort expended in shadowing support-related messages or making judgments about supportive behaviors. As in traditional dual-task procedures, faster reaction times would reflect more efficient probe processing due to the availability of more mental resources. We predict that more resources would be available for probe processing when the processing of the primary task was facilitated by established relationship and support schemata. That is, when a relationship schema is consistent with statements, the processing effort for the primary task is reduced, leaving more resources available to deal with the secondary probe task.

Predictions for this approach are consistent with the investigation of self-schemata by Bargh (1982). He adopted a dual-task procedure to demonstrate automatic processing of self-relevant information—information present in the schemata one possesses about oneself. Bargh combined a dichotic listening task with a probe-detection task. In the dichotic listening task, pairs of words (one noun and one adjective) were presented, one in each ear. The primary task was to shadow the words presented in a predesignated ear. A visual probe was presented at random intervals during the task. When the shadowing task is easier, response times to the probe task should be fast. Bargh observed that schema-relevant information in the attended channel facilitated shadowing and probe-response times. Subjects made fewer shadowing errors and probe reaction times were fast. Thus, when information is consistent with one's schema, fewer overall demands are placed on limited resources in working memory and performance in the secondary task will be high. Interestingly, when schema-relevant information was presented to the unattended ear, shadowing was *more* difficult, because schema-relevant information will attract attention. Consequently, more resources were required to prevent the to-be-ignored words from interfering with task-relevant words. Bargh's study illustrates the underlying principle guiding the interpretation of dual-task applications in this context. When information in a dual-task procedure is relevant both to one's schema and to performance in a task, the demands on resources will be low and probe response times will be fast. When information is schema-relevant but task-irrelevant, demands are higher due to the need to suppress the spontaneously activated cues. The consequence will be slower probe response times.

Memory Tasks

A fourth approach to investigating support relationships relies on a priming technique that differs from those we have been discussing. This technique is an implicit memory task that examines the unconscious memorial consequences of schematic processing. See Roediger (1990) for a review of implicit memory tasks. For instance, in the lexical decision task we described earlier in this chapter, subjects were presented with attachment-related target adjectives paired with primes intended to activate mother, father, and self-schemata. Adjectives were associated with secure, ambivalent, and avoidant attachment styles.

At the end of the testing session, we could have presented subjects with a word fragment completion task. The word fragments would have provided about half the letters for each target adjective presented in the lexical decision portion of the study. The word fragment task, however, would have been presented to the subjects as an exercise to be considered completely independent of the lexical decision task they just completed. Subjects would have been instructed to complete the fragments with the first word that came to mind. We predict that recently activated schematic information would be more available, causing subjects to provide more correct solutions for schema-consistent items than for schema-inconsistent items.

The advantage of this approach is that subjects are not explicitly asked for the content of their relationship schemata. Thus, performance is less likely to be contaminated by self-monitoring behaviors. The implicit nature of the task is also believed to access aspects of memory that we typically have difficulty accessing at an explicit, conscious level. This disparity in the availability of memories was first demonstrated by the famous amnesic patient H.M. (Milner, 1966). After experiencing a serious accident, H.M. was unable to recall events that occurred after his injuries. In short, he seemed unable to transfer information from working memory to long-term memory. He did, however, show effects of learning in his behavior. He showed improvement in tasks of motor skill even though he could not remember ever performing the tasks before. The case of H.M. clearly illustrates that there is a dichotomy between implicit and explicit memory processes and that past experience can unknowingly and unintentionally influence present performance and behavior.

Baldwin, Keelan, Fehr, Enns, and Koh-Rangarajoo (1995) were successful in using an implicit-memory procedure to investigate the memorial consequences of schematic processing of relationship information. They observed that subjects were more likely to recall information that was consistent with their attachment schemata. Because a period of time elapses between explicit study of material and implicit memory testing, this study is important for demonstrating that schemata can unconsciously impact thoughts and behavior for extended periods of time.

SUMMARY

The purpose of this chapter was to illustrate how the application of information processing techniques can be useful in the study of relationships and social support. A difficulty faced by researchers is explaining the differential impact across individuals of the same supportive acts. Individuals ascribe their own interpretations to behavioral acts that are dependent upon the relationship in which they occur. This ascription is very likely due to the operation of relationship-specific schemata. Schemata exert powerful influences over our experiences and our memory of those experiences. We have described standard cognitive procedures that can be adapted to investigate social support and relationship working models. They provide a means of understanding the mechanisms and processes through which schemata exert their influence. Priming techniques such as lexical decision and Stroop color-naming tasks are useful procedures that can reveal the content of specific schemata. Demonstrating differences in working model content represents one step in understanding the cause of different perceptions. Implicit memory procedures are also useful in identifying what sort of cues are likely to influence memory and behavior after an interaction has ended. Together, the techniques described provide insight into how schemata direct attention to support relevant cues, why we differ in our perceptions for social interactions, and why we have selective memory for events.

REFERENCES

Ainsworth, M. D. S., Blehar, M. C., Waters, E., & Wall, S. (1978). *Patterns of attachment: A psychological study of the Strange Situation.* Hillsdale, NJ: Lawrence Erlbaum.

Baddeley, A. (1986). *Working memory.* Oxford: Oxford University Press.

Baldwin, M. W., Fehr, B., Keedian, E., Seidel, M., & Thomson, D. W. (1993). An exploration of the relational schemas underlying attachment styles: Self-report and lexical decision approaches. *Personality and Social Psychology Bulletin, 19,* 746–754.

Baldwin, M. W., Keelan, J. P. R., Fehr, B., Enns, V., & Koh-Rangarajoo, E. (1995). Social cognitive conceptualization of working models: Availability and accessibility effects (submitted).

Bargh, J. A. (1982). Attention and automaticity in the processing of self-relevant information. *Journal of Personality and Social Psychology, 43,* 425–436.

Bartlett, F. C. (1932). *Remembering: A study in experiment and social psychology.* New York and London: Cambridge University Press.

Berkman, L. F., & Syme, S. L. (1979). Social networks, host resistance, and mortality: A nine-year follow up study of Alameda County residents. *American Journal of Epidemiology, 109,* 186–204.

Blazer, D. (1982). Social support and mortality in an elderly community population. *American Journal of Epidemiology, 115,* 684–694.

Bower, G. H., Black, J. B., & Turner, T. J. (1979). Scripts in memory for text. *Cognitive Psychology, 11,* 177–220.

Bowlby, J. (1969). *Attachment and loss,* Vol. 1, *Attachment.* New York: Basic Books.

Bowlby, J. (1988). *A secure base.* New York: Basic Books.

Brown, G. W., & Harris, T. (1978). *Social origins of depression.* New York: Free Press.

Cantor, N., & Kihlstrom, J. F. (1982). Cognitive and social processes in personality. In G. T. Wilson & C. Franks (Eds.), *Contemporary behavior therapy* (pp. 142–201). New York: Guilford Press.

Cassel, J. (1976). The contribution of the social environment to host resistance. *American Journal of Epidemiology, 104,* 107–123.

Collins, A. M., & Loftus, E. F. (1975). A spreading-activation theory of semantic processing. *Psychological Review, 82,* 407–428.

Coyne, J. C., & DeLongis, A. (1986). Going beyond social support: The role of social relationships in adaptation. *Journal of Consulting and Clinical Psychology, 54,* 454–460.

Dodge, K. A., & Crick, N. R. (1990). Social information processing bases of aggressive behavior in children. *Personality and Social Psychology Bulletin, 16,* 8–22.

Dodge, K. A., Murphy, R. R., & Buchsbaum, K. (1984). The assessment of intention-cue detection skills in children: Implications for developmental psychopathology. *Child Development, 55,* 163–173.

Fiske, S. T., & Taylor, S. E. (1989). *Social cognition.* New York: Random House.

Gardiner, J. M. (1989). A generation effect in memory without awareness. *British Journal of Psychology, 80,* 163–168.

Geller, V., & Shaver, P. (1976). Cognitive consequences of self-awareness. *Journal of Experimental and Social Psychology, 12,* 99–108.

Gerrig, R. E. (1988). Text comprehension. In R. J. Sternberg & E. E. Smith (Eds.), *The psychology of human thought* (pp. 242–262). New York: Cambridge University Press.

Hazan, C., & Shaver, P. (1987). Romantic love conceptualized as an attachment process. *Journal of Personality and Social Psychology, 52,* 511–524.

House, J. S., Robbins, C., & Metzner, H. M. (1982). The association of social relationships and activities with mortality: Prospective evidence from the Tecumseh Community Health Study. *American Journal of Epidemiology, 116,* 123–140.

Johnson-Laird, P. N. (1980). Mental models in cognitive science. *Cognitive Science, 4,* 71–115.

Johnson-Larid, P. N. (1983). *Mental models.* Cambridge, MA: Harvard University Press.

Lakey, B., & Dickinson, L. G. (1994). Antecedents of perceived support: Is perceived family environment generalized to new social relationships? *Cognitive Therapy and Research, 18,* 39–53.

Lipton, D. N., McDonel, E. C., & McFall, R. M. (1986). Heterosocial perception in rapists. *Journal of Consulting and Clinical Psychology, 55,* 17–25.

Main, M., Kaplan, N., & Cassidy, J. (1985). Security in infancy, childhood, and adulthood: A move to the level of representation. In I. Bretherton & E. Waters (Eds.), *Growing points of attachment theory and research: Monographs of the Society for Research in Child Development, 50(1–2)*, Serial No. 209 (pp. 66–106).

Markus, H. (1977). Self-schemas and processing information about the self. *Journal of Personality and Social Psychology, 35,* 63–78.

Markus, H., & Zajonc, R. B. (1985). The cognitive perspective in social psychology. In G. Lindzey & E. Aronson (Eds.), *The handbook of social psychology,* 3rd ed. (pp. 137–230). New York: Random House.

McFall, R. M. (1982). A review and reformulation of the concept of social skills. *Behavioral Assessment, 4,* 1–35.

McFall, R. M., & Dodge, K. (1982). Self-management and interpersonal skills learning. In P. Karoly & F. H. Kanfer (Eds.), *Self-management and behavior change: From theory to practice* (pp. 353–392). Elmsford, NY: Pergamon Press.

Milner, B. (1966). Amnesia following operation on the temporal lobes. In C. W. M. Whitty & O. L. Zangwill (Eds.), *Amnesia* (pp. 109–133). London: Butterworths.

Pierce, G. R., Sarason, B. R., & Sarason, I. G. (1990). Integrating social support perspectives: Working models, personal relationships, and situational factors. In S. Duck & R. C. Silver (Eds.), *Personal relationships and social support* (pp. 173–189). London: Sage.

Pierce, G. R., Sarason, B. R., & Sarason, I. G. (1992). General and specific support expectations and stress as predictors of perceived supportiveness: An experimental study. *Journal of Personality and Social Psychology, 63,* 297–307.

Pierce, G. R., Sarason, I. G., & Sarason, B. R. (1991). General and relationship-based perceptions of social support: Are two constructs better than one? *Journal of Personality and Social Psychology, 61,* 1028–1039.

Posner, M. I., & Boies, S. J. (1971). Components of attention. *Psychological Review, 78,* 391–408.

Roediger, H. L. (1990). Implicit memory: Retention without remembering. *American Psychologist, 45,* 1043–1056.

Rumelhart, D. E. (1976). Understanding and summarizing brief stories. In D. LaBarge & S. D. Samuels (Eds.), *Basic process in reading: Perception and comprehension* (pp. 265–302). Hillsdale, NJ: Lawrence Erlbaum.

Sarason, B. R., Shearin, E. N., Pierce, G. R., & Sarason, I. G. (1987). Interrelationships of social support measures: Theoretical and practical implications. *Journal of Personality and Social Psychology, 52* 813–832.

Sarason, I. G., Sarason, B. R., & Shearin, E. N. (1986). Social support as an individual difference variable: Its stability, origins, and relational aspects. *Journal of Personality and Social Psychology, 50,* 845–855.

Schachter, D. L. (1987). Implicit memory: History and current status. *Journal of Experimental Psychology: Learning, Memory and Cognition,13,* 501–518.

Schank, R. C., & Abelson, R. (1977). *Scripts, plans, goals, and understanding.* Hillsdale, NJ: Lawrence Erlbaum.

Sroufe, L. A., & Fleeson, J. (1986). Attachment and the construction of relationships. In W. W. Hartup & Z. Rubin (Eds.), *Relationships and development* (pp. 51–71). Hillsdale, NJ: Lawrence Erlbaum

Surra, C. A., & Bohman, T. (1991). The development of close relationships: A cognitive perspective. In G. J. O. Fletcher & F. D. Fincham (Eds.), *Cognition in close relationships* (pp. 281–305). Hillsdale, NJ: Lawrence Erlbaum.

Wethington, E., & Kessler, R. C. (1986). Perceived support, received support, and adjustment to stressful life events. *Journal of Health and Social Behavior, 27,* 78–89.

Wyer, R. S., & Srull, T. K. (1989). *Memory and cognition in its social context.* Hillsdale, NJ: Lawrence Erlbaum.

3

Social Support in Marriage

A Cognitive Perspective

STEVEN R. H. BEACH, FRANK D. FINCHAM, JENNIFER KATZ, and THOMAS N. BRADBURY

Social support is a widely used construct in the psychological literature. Although multiple conceptions of the construct have been offered, an issue common to many analyses is the extent to which support is perceived or experienced by recipients of "supportive" behaviors. In this chapter, we offer a cognitive framework designed to illuminate the construct of "perceived support." Our analysis focuses on perceived support in marriage, as this relationship provides a relatively homogeneous context within which to examine a number of important issues regarding social support, the resolution of which may have implications for the literature on social support in general. This chapter does not attempt, however, to redefine social support, provide a new theory of social support processes in marriage, or argue that support processes in marriage are fundamentally different from support obtained in other enduring, intimate relationships. Mindful of the need for new perspectives in the social support area that integrate the influences of social context with concern for the match of specific stressors to socially supportive responses and the *cognitive* component of support (e.g., Pierce, Sarason, & Sarason, 1990; I. G. Sarason, B. R. Sarason, & Pierce, 1994), we provide herein a cognitive framework for examining the impact of supportive (and nonsupportive) transactions on "perceived support."

We begin by asking why it is important to examine social support in marriage before turning to examine, in turn, the direct effect of prior beliefs about partner

STEVEN R. H. BEACH and JENNIFER KATZ • Department of Psychology, University of Georgia, Athens, Georgia 30602.   FRANK D. FINCHAM • Department of Psychology, University of Illinois at Urbana–Champaign, Champaign, Illinois 61820.   THOMAS N. BRADBURY • Department of Psychology, University of California at Los Angeles, Los Angeles, California 90024-1563.

Handbook of Social Support and the Family, edited by Gregory R. Pierce, Barbara R. Sarason, and Irwin G. Sarason. Plenum Press, New York, 1996.

supportiveness on perceived support, the potentially limited role of partner behavior in influencing reports of support, and the impact of prior belief on partner behavior. Next, we examine the potentially important moderating influence of accessibility of prior belief on the relationship between prior beliefs and its effects, and the potentially moderating influence of cognitive/motivational factors in social support. Finally, we offer a preliminary synthesis of our analysis using the cognitive perspective developed in the emerging literature on attachment style.

WHY STUDY SOCIAL SUPPORT IN MARRIAGE?

A better understanding of social support provision in marriage is of critical theoretical (cf. Cutrona, 1994) and practical significance. Spouses are often named as the persons most likely to be turned to for support in time of need (Dakof & Taylor, 1990; Berg-Cross, 1974), to play a critical role in the provision of some types of support (Reiss, 1990), and to be the providers of almost all types of supportive behavior among married persons (Beach, Martin, Blum, & Roman, 1993). Likewise, in many circumstances, support provided by an intimate other appears to be uniquely beneficial (Brown & Harris, 1978), and it is the provisions of close relationships, rather than relationships in general, that are related most robustly to various health and mental health outcomes (e.g., Lin, Dean, & Ensel, 1986; Rogers, 1987). Finally, positive and negative self-views are more resistant to change when one is involved in a relationship with a partner who provides a congruent view of the self (Swann, De La Ronde, & Hixon, 1994). Accordingly, marriage is an important context in which to examine social support and its effects.

By the same token, marital distress has been shown to relate to less mobilization of spousal support (Julien & Markman, 1991), and relationships characterized by high levels of conflict are less likely to be perceived as sources of support (Pierce et al., 1990). Likewise, although individuals who find that their social support needs are not met within their marital relationships are likely to seek support from other members of their social network, they do not appear to be mentally healthier as a result (Julien & Markman, 1991). From a number of perspectives, then, transactions within the marital relationship appear to be critical in predicting the quality of social support available to a given individual (Veiel, Crisand, Stroszeck-Somschor, & Herrle, 1991). Accordingly, we believe it is timely to focus specifically on social support processes in marriage and to develop models that clarify important aspects of social support in this context.

How can one advance an understanding of social support in marriage? Unfortunately, social support is a diffuse construct, and there is considerable debate about the best way to increase its theoretical precision (e.g., Gotlieb, 1985; Pierce et al., 1990). Even when attention is confined to intimate dyads, it is difficult to isolate the specific characteristics that make a behavior "supportive." Indeed, it has been particularly difficult to define the topography of supportive behaviors and at the same time capture an essential characteristic of social support: the sense of being supported, or "perceived support" (Cutrona, Suhr, & MacFarlane, 1990). Hence, for example, perceived support is not well explained by frequency of social contact or by specific behaviors of supportive individuals (Cutrona et al., 1990; Vinokur, Schul, & Caplan, 1987).

Yet perceived support appears to be important, as there is considerable evidence of the mental health benefits that come from a "sense of support," or the belief that one is embedded in a network that would provide support if support were needed (e.g., Wethington & Kessler, 1986). The benefits of perceived support for general well-being and physical health have also been documented (e.g., Joseph, Williams, & Yule, 1992; Slack & Vaux, 1988; Vaux, 1988). Because perceived support is stable and covaries with individual difference variables (e.g., Lakey, Tardiff, & Drew, 1994), a focus on intraindividual variables, and particularly cognitive variables, may be necessary if we are to understand more fully the sense of support experienced by spouses.

A COGNITIVE FRAMEWORK FOR UNDERSTANDING PERCEIVED SUPPORT

Any attempt to understand the determinants of "perceived support" without explicit reference to the basic literature on the way in which prior beliefs and knowledge structures may influence, constrain, or change the interpretation of experience seems limited at best and, as we shall argue, most likely to produce misleading conclusions. We therefore introduce such basic research where appropriate.

Knowledge Structures, Partner Behavior, and Perceived Support

An important starting point for cognitive formulations of perceived support is the distinction between controlled and automatic cognitive processes (Shiffrin & Schneider, 1977) (for application to close relationships, see Fincham, Bradbury, & Scott, 1990; Fletcher & Fincham, 1991; Fletcher & Fitness, 1993). Briefly stated, controlled processing is initiated deliberately (such as when one answers questions about perceived support), whereas automatic processing is triggered by stimuli and operates outside awareness. Thus, what one professes to "know" consciously may not be what structures one's perceptions, reactions, and behavior when one is actively engaged in the moment-to-moment process of living (Taylor & Crocker, 1981). Accordingly, self-report of "perceived support" or "availability of support" cannot be assumed to assess directly the knowledge structures that are influencing behavior at times of stress. At the same time, assuming some modicum of self-awareness, we might predict that in many cases self-reported "perceived support" will be substantially related to these important sets of beliefs. This argument implies that self-reported "perceived support" and self-reported "attitudes" or "beliefs about the partner," while they offer a good initial approximation, may best be viewed as providing an indirect measure of the constructs of greatest interest from a cognitive perspective.

Potential Direct Effects of Existing Knowledge Structures on Perceived Support.   Most often, as we interact with others, we process information automatically without awareness and accept the results as the factual representation of what has transpired (Rock, 1983). The knowledge structures we bring to social interaction may cause us to be selective in what we see (Hirt, 1990) or to reinterpret what has occurred and what our response should be (Bodenhausen, 1988). When applied to marital relationships, these considerations lead to the prediction that perceived support from one's spouse often may be relatively stable in the face of apparently disconfirming evidence and may influence a wide range of reactions and behaviors. A spouse with a generalized positive view of the partner's supportiveness (e.g., partner is trustworthy, considerate, loyal, helpful) should be more likely to respond to the occurrence of a specific nonsupportive partner behavior by overlooking it, forgetting it, reinterpreting it, or excusing it. Further, any ambiguity about the behavior should be resolved in such a way that it supports the view that the partner is supportive. Conversely, a spouse with a negative view of the partner's supportiveness should be more likely to respond to nonsupportiveness by noticing it, remembering it, exaggerating it, and filling in ambiguous or missing information such that the partner appears even worse. It follows that a negative partner behavior—for example, spouse fails to pay attention when support seeker needs help—could ultimately be a nonevent in the first case but an instance of a serious pattern of breach of faith in the second.

Thus, a preliminary look at the functioning of knowledge structures suggests that a given partner behavior should be subject to multiple interpretations and capable of producing rather different reactions depending on the knowledge structures that guide its interpretation. While some behaviors may be sufficiently unambiguous to permit little initial distortion, even these behaviors are likely to be subject to differential patterns of use in memory and elaboration during recall and to lead to potentially divergent feelings of support depending on prior sets of beliefs about the partner.

The (Potentially Limited) Role of Partner Behavior in Understanding Perceived Support.   In the social support literature, a common assumption is that perceived support is in some sense an aggregate of transactions that have occurred in the relationship (Cutrona et al., 1990). That is, it is typically hypothesized that particular partner behaviors have occurred over time and in some way form the basis for the partner's judgment of perceived support. This seems to be a reasonable working hypothesis, even if we adopt the position that the relationship between behavior and perceived support is far from linear. From a cognitive perspective, however, it is necessary to add two additional considerations. First, partner behaviors do not come prelabeled, and the label given to the behavior will be important for subsequent processing and recall. Accordingly, the partner behavior that forms the experiential basis of perceived support must first be experienced as either "helpful" and "caring" or, conversely, as "hurtful" and "uncaring." Second, after the behavior is labeled, the likelihood that it will be analyzed further will depend on whether it "fits" (or can be made to fit) with prior beliefs or, alternatively, somehow challenges prior beliefs.

How is a partner behavior noticed and categorized so that it can influence the more stable representation of the partner as supportive or not? Presumably, for a behavior to be noticed, it must be salient and so contain information not readily generated on the basis of already accessed concepts. That is, the behavior must be in some sense surprising. As we have seen above, however, when preconceptions are strong, it may be difficult to make a behavior surprising. The strongly conservative nature of information processing seems likely to require any or some combination of (1) repeated experience that is made salient, (2) an external source that can validate the nature of the experience, or (3) some way of disrupting those processes that would bring the interpretation of the behavior back in line with prior belief.

Behavior that is surprising and salient should have greater effect in changing levels of perceived support. So, for example, kindness from a stranger in a place where everyone was believed to be vicious should be salient and surprising and lay the ground work for changed beliefs about "that place" or "those people." Of course, in keeping with the nature of information processing, it should take relatively little cruelty experienced in the same place to strengthen or to reestablish the original belief. Because prosocial exchanges are normative within marriage, however, supportive interactions with a spouse may provoke little surprise and so provide little stimulus for a change in beliefs about spousal supportiveness. Conversely, evaluating a stimulus as negative is one of the conditions that typically gives rise to further and more controlled processing in marriage (cf. Bradbury & Finchman, 1989, 1990, 1991, 1992). Accordingly, events perceived as "negative" are more likely to be noticed and so are likely to carry disproportionate weight in determining spouses' perceived support (see Coyne & DeLongis, 1986; Pagel, Erdly, & Becker, 1987). As a consequence, negative exchanges rather than positive exchanges may ultimately account for more variance in emotional reactions to social interactions (Beach et al., 1993) and ultimately account for more variance in perceived support. Consistent with this view, negative behaviors observed in marital interaction or reported by spouses on a daily basis account for a greater proportion of the variance in marital satisfaction than do positive behaviors (for reviews, see Weiss & Heyman, 1990; Fincham, Fernandes, & Humphreys, 1993).

For persons who have experienced little need for partner support (or indicated little need to the partner), and so have had little opportunity to be surprised by partner behavior, prior beliefs about partner supportiveness should go unchallenged. Accordingly, perceived support should be influenced more heavily by prior beliefs about partner supportiveness to the extent that there have been few opportunities for the spouse to respond supportively (i.e., few instances of felt need for support). In such circumstances, one might expect perceived support to be almost entirely a product of personality traits and the prior generalized beliefs of the person making the rating. While the partner may, in fact, behave pleasantly during interactions, it would be variability in the support recipient's prior beliefs rather than nuances in the support provider's behavior that would determine variability in level of perceived support. Likewise, if the support-seeking spouse had very negative prior beliefs about partner supportiveness and the partner was relatively neutral, one would anticipate that this circumstance would be interpreted as confirmation of the prior generalized beliefs. Again, nuances in partner behavior would not be predicted to have much effect on variability in perceived support beyond prior beliefs in this case.

On the other hand, if there have been repeated occasions for the partner to respond (i.e., occasions of felt need for support), and if partner responses have been absent or negative or discrepant from what was expected, there should be maximal opportunity for change in "perceived support." In such circumstances, one might expect that the pattern of negative partner behavior could begin to override prior positive beliefs about partner supportiveness. Similarly, for a spouse with initially negative beliefs about partner supportiveness, only if the support-providing spouse were persistently positive and surprisingly supportive would one predict any impact on negative prior evaluation of perceived support. This change might happen, for example, if the support-providing partner were motivated to dramatically and persistently disconfirm the expectation of nonsupportiveness, and so made persistent and dramatic efforts to display support (e.g., Swann & Read, 1981). Under such circumstances, one might expect at some point to see a rather sudden and dramatic change in the supported spouse's evaluation as beliefs and expectations were reorganized to fit with incongruent data.

Thus, when partner behavior is not seen as surprising, which should be most of the time, prior beliefs rather than the topography of support providers' behavior should best predict perceived support. Only when support seekers have been in need of support and have experienced a negative or surprisingly positive response from the partner would one expect any change in belief. However, the situations in which topography of partner behavior accounts for variance in perceived support beyond the prior beliefs of the support seeker may be relatively infrequent. In particular, it may be that persons with negative prior beliefs about partner supportiveness often create the very partner behavior that leaves them feeling unsupported, while those with positive prior beliefs often elicit more supportive behavior from their partners.

Impact of Prior Belief on Partner Behavior. Demonstrations of self-fulfilling prophecies and behavioral confirmation now abound (Snyder, 1992). In addition to the classic laboratory experiment in which the behavioral attractiveness of partners was changed through subtle expectancy manipulations delivered to subjects who were interacting with them (Snyder, Tanke, & Berscheid, 1977), there are now demonstrations in which the behavior of the partner has been changed by providing the subject with expectations about personality (e.g., Snyder & Swann, 1978) or expectations of being liked (e.g., Curtis & Miller, 1986). In each case, it has been shown that a person's expectations have the power to change the behaviors of others. An important implication of this finding is that others often come to behave in the way they are initially expected to behave (Snyder, 1992).

A related concept receiving attention in recent years is self-verification, derived from theories concerned with self-concept and self-consistency (Ritts & Stein, 1994). Self-verification refers to the tendency to seek social information about the self that is consistent with one's self-schema. Accordingly, a given person is likely to interpret, as well as elicit from others, behaviors that will corroborate his or her self-view. Swann, Stein-Seroussi, and Giesler (1992) have suggested that self-verification processes occur in an attempt to increase predictability and control within social situations, rather than for the sake of consistency itself. Other research indicates, however, that even individuals with positive self-views may be uncomfortable with being overvalued (Swann, De La Ronde, & Hixon, 1994). Indeed, recent research has suggested that people with positive self-concepts may be motivated to self-verify for both positivity and self-confirming reasons. For these subjects, positive feedback will be both self-enhancing and self-confirming. For subjects with negative self-concepts, however, self-confirmation may be more important than self-enhancement (Swann, Stein-Seroussi, & Giesler, 1992).

Of considerable importance for understanding social support in marriage, it has been found that marital satisfaction, commitment, and intimacy are enhanced within self-verifying relationships, regardless of whether or not spousal behaviors are positive or negative (Swann, De La Ronde, & Hixon, 1994; Swann, Hixon, & De La Ronde, 1992). That is, individuals with more negative views of their own competence report higher levels of marital satisfaction when their partners also report more negative views of their competence. Potentially, then, spouses may be directly reinforced for adopting a less supportive posture if their partner is insecure and views herself or himself negatively.

In sum, people with negative self-views, although in need of support when dealing with a stressful life event, may nonetheless seek or elicit negative feedback (cf. Joiner, Alfano, & Metalsky, 1993). Further, even when provided with positive evaluations and support, they may tend to discount such feedback as erroneous or invalid. Indeed, especially favorable evaluations by the partner may decrease commitment and intimacy for those with low self-esteem (Swann, De La Ronde, & Hixon, 1994; Swann, Hixon, & De La Ronde, 1992).

From the standpoint of empirical research on social support, this literature has at least two important implications. First, our previous indictment of spouse behavior as having minimal effect on "perceived support" beyond the effect of prior belief may have been based on an overly simple model. In some cases, support-provider variables may fail to account for variance in level of perceived support beyond various intrapersonal characteristics of the support receiver because the provider's behavior has been influenced by those characteristics rather than because the provider's behavior is irrelevant (Swann & Predmore, 1985). That is, rather than being viewed as a competing explanatory variable, the support provider's behavior may be viewed as integral to a more complete account of the process leading to "perceived support."

Second, and relatedly, it may be unrealistic be view the support provider's behaviors as the starting point in a casual chain that leads to perceived support. Rather, provider behavior might more reasonably to viewed as a mediating link in a causal chain that begins with expectations about support and ends with perceived support. This formulation still allows the possibilities that provider behavior could contribute uniquely to perceived support in some cases and that efforts to change partner behavior could result in changes in perceived support. This does not imply, however, that the provider's behavior always or even usually influences level of perceived support independent of the effect of prior beliefs (cf. I. G. Sarason et al., 1994).

Paradoxically, confirmation of the support seeker's a priori beliefs may be particularly likely to occur when the support seeker is motivated to "find out" if the spouse will be supportive rather than simply create a pleasant interaction (Snyder & Haugen, 1990 [cited in Snyder, 1992]). In particular, when perceivers were told to "get to know the other person," they were most likely to produce behavioral confirmation effects, whereas when they were instructed simply to get along with the other person, no behavioral confirmation effects occurred. Accordingly, persons who are the least sure of others and the most cautious about others' motives and dependability should produce the greatest changes in others' behavior toward them, bringing out their worst. However, for those who are already more trusting and positive in their expectations, and who may be more oriented to enjoy rather than to reassure themselves about others, interactions should go more smoothly and positively and be experienced as more supportive when support is required.

Again, because some types of persons may be particularly likely to create nonsupportive responses in others, it seems likely that this pattern will be associated with intrapersonal factors. Specifically, this pattern seems most likely for those who are insecure about the support that others will provide, but who feel in need of support (cf. Joiner et al., 1993). In these cases especially, partner behavior may predict little unique variance in perceived support or in outcomes of support because the partner's supportive behavior is so strongly driven by the a priori assumptions of the support seeker. Because this pattern seems to be one of insecure adult attachment, and because adult attachment may both have important implications for social support research (Pierce et al., 1990) and be interpretable within a cognitive framework, we consider later the issue of adult attachment style.

As can be seen, these initial cognitive considerations entail a change in our view of perceived support. Rather than viewing the effect of partner behavior on perceived support as a fixed product of a set of antecedent partner behaviors, it seems more appropriate to view it as being subject to moderation by a number of different intrapersonal factors as well as being caused by these same factors. Because the idea of moderation is sometimes more easily conveyed by figures, we provide a schematic of hypothesized relationships in Figure 1.

As shown in Figure 1, prior experience of having been "in need" of support, due to personality or circumstance, should be directly related to one's view of the partner's supportiveness. Persons who often find themselves in need of partner support should have a higher probability of being disappointed by the other's

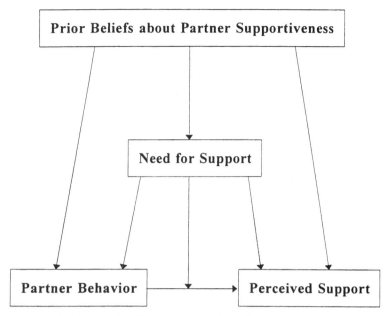

Figure 1. Direct and indirect effects of prior belief on perceived support.

response, and they should, on average, be less positively disposed toward their partners' supportiveness. Having been "in need" more often, however, should also moderate the effect of partner behavior on perceived support because partner behaviors should be more highly related to perceived support as need for support increases. In addition, it is hypothesized that generalized beliefs about partner supportiveness will have direct effects both on perceived support and on experience of being "in need" of support, because persons with some types of beliefs (e.g., that others may abandon them) will show greater levels of need for support regardless of external forces. Finally, it can be inferred from Figure 1 that partner behavior will account for variance in perceived support beyond that due to intraindividual characteristics to the extent that there is greater experience of being "in need" due to external stressors, but will account for relatively less variance beyond intraindividual variables to the extent that the experience of being "in need" is created by the support seeker's own uncertainities and insecurity.

Accordingly, a cognitive perspective does not support a summative model that posits that partner behavior of a certain topography produces "perceived support" additively over time. Rather, it suggests that partner behavior will be more consequential in some circumstances than in others, perhaps for some types of people more than for others, an often may be accounted for in large measure by the support seeker's own prior beliefs. In all, these considerations suggest that it may be difficult and relatively uncommon for partner behavior to account for variance in perceived support beyond the variance associated with the prior beliefs and personality style of the support seeker. Again, this is not to say that the robust behavioral differences associated with marital satisfaction will fail to correlate with "perceived support," only that these behavioral differences may account for little variance beyond the support seeker's prior belief (which will be quite negative among the maritally discordant) and that finding clear evidence of the importance of actual spouse behavior may require considerable sophistication.

Role of Cognitive Accessibility

One of the most robust findings in the cognitive and social cognitive literatures is that knowledge structures in memory that are made available through situational manipulations (e.g., priming) or naturally occurring states (e.g., depression) can influence the encoding of new information, judgments made about the information, and responses to it (e.g., Srull & Wyer, 1989). Concepts easily accessed from memory can therefore have a pervasive impact on spouse's information processing, judgments, and behavior. When information processing occurs, however, not all concepts are equally accessible or brought to mind with equal ease. In fact, the importance of individual differences in concept accessibility is well documented (Markus & Smith, 1981). Thus, even if a concept is chronically accessible to all spouses, individual differences in accessibility may still exist.

Again, such findings from basic research on cognition have important implications for understanding perceived support. For example, those knowledge structures that have been recently primed or that are chronically primed will be most potent in structuring the interpretation of events (Bargh & Pietromonaco, 1982). Moreover, to the extent that the situation is ambiguous, missing information will be supplied by the general knowledge structure that has been activated (Uleman & Bargh, 1989). Likewise, over time, information that was inferred may become indistinguishable from things that actually happened, leading to the fabrication of compelling evidence in support of one's initial biases (O'Sullivan & Durso, 1984). Accordingly, the more chronically activated a particular knowledge structure regarding partner supportiveness, the greater its potential impact on the perception of the partner and the development of the relationship with the partner.

In a similar vein, not all individuals should be expected to have equal access to their assumptions or prior beliefs about partner availability and supportiveness. Ratings of the partner by persons with readily accessible knowledge structures about partner supportiveness should be more stable and more robust across changing circumstances than ratings made by persons with less readily accessible knowledge structures. This distinction is important for at least two reasons. First, for those with more accessible knowledge structures, prior beliefs should exert an ongoing conservative effect with regard to beliefs about the spouse. In the absence of events that produce a change in level of need for support, therefore, we should be able to predict future ratings of spouse supportiveness well for those with highly accessible constructs. The ratings of those with high construct accessibility should also be more predictive of their memories of partner supportiveness and their reactions to future partner behavior. By implication, then, the ratings of spouse supportiveness should be more *valid* for many uses when made by persons with high construct accessibility. Accordingly, consideration of individual differences in construct accessibility has the potential to alleviate some of the problem of measurement error in the area of social support.

Second, even for those who do not display chronically high levels of construct accessibility, it should be possible to increase construct accessibility through priming manipulations and so increase the validity of their reports. Those requiring priming (those who do not have chronically activated constructs) would still be expected to show lower conservation of their initial assumptions leading to less stability in rated support over time and less predictability than for their chronically activated counterparts. By implication, then, predictive validity should always be less for reports from persons with low chronic construct accessibility than for persons with high chronic construct accessibility, even if constructs are situationally primed before subjects are asked to report on them. If constructs are primed before subjects are asked questions about partner support, however, responses from those with low construct accessibility should better correspond to the representation being assessed, and so at least show enhanced concurrent validity.

In sum, constructs that are chronically accessible should be associated with larger correlation coefficients between prior beliefs and ratings of perceived support as well as between prior beliefs and observed partner behavior. In addition, constructs that are situationally primed before being assessed should be more accurate representations of the beliefs one hopes to tap. This elaboration represents a second layer of moderation in the relationship of partner behavior to "perceived support." Figure 2 summarizes the proposed relations among accessibility, prior beliefs, and perceived support.

As shown in Figure 2, the relationship of prior beliefs to both partner behavior and perceived support should be moderated by the accessibility of prior beliefs about partner supportiveness. As level of construct accessibility increases, the amount of variance accounted for in dependent variables should increase. Of course, to the extent that situational priming is used, it should be the match between the target situation and the prime used that determines the degree of predictive validity.

One implication of this line of reasoning is that social support researchers may be able to increase the amount of variance accounted for in outcomes of social support if they use measures of accessibility of perceived support in addition to reports of perceived support. An example of this sort of effect can be seen in research conducted by Fazio and Williams (1986). They found that the accessibility of evaluative judgments of Ronald Reagan moderated the relationship between their subjects' self-reported attitudes toward Reagan and their judgments about the 1984 presidential and vice-presidential debates. For those with highly accessible attitudes, the correlation was 0.738; for those with less accessible attitudes, the correlation was 0.404. Recently, this same logic has been applied

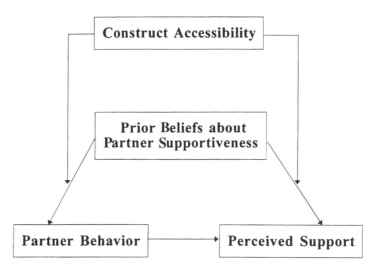

Figure 2. Construct accessibility as a moderator of the effects of prior belief.

successfully to marriage. Fincham, Garnier, Gano-Phillips, and Osborne (1995) found that both husbands and wives with more highly accessible attitudes toward their spouses had greater correspondence between their evaluation of the relationship and their attributions for hypothetical partner behavior. For husbands with highly accessible attitudes toward their wives, the correlation was 0.52; for wives with highly accessible attitudes, the correlation was 0.51. In each case, for those with less accessible attitudes, the correlation was significantly less. Clearly, there appears to be considerable potential for the assessment of construct accessibility to enhance observed relationships in the social support area.

Cognitive/Motivational Considerations in Perceived Social Support

There may also be motivated effects on the interpretation of the partner's supportive behavior. Although motivational factors have not yet been well integrated into the literature on marital relationships or in the area of social support, there is a broad literature on motivated cognitive processes that can be instructive in thinking about social support.

Social support is most likely to be sought in response to an event that is threatening, often an event with troubling implications for self-esteem, and one way that social support may be effective is to help the sufferer regain or protect her or his self-evaluation. A potential obstacle to providing effective social support in marriage is that the partner's supportive behaviors often carry with them the potentially troubling implication that the partner providing the "help" is "stronger," "more able in the area," or "more competent" than the person being "helped." Thus, at the very time the person is in need of support, the partner's support may further undermine the needful partner's self-evaluation. As we discuss below, if the area in which the support seeker is having difficulty is an achievement domain, and if it is important or self-defining to the support seeker to do well in that area, instrumental support from the partner (or anyone else who is close) has the potential to be especially unpleasant. To help elaborate these possibilities, we first briefly review the Self-Evaluation Maintenance (SEM) model (Tesser, 1988) and then discuss its implications for research on social support.

Overview of the SEM Model. The SEM model (Tesser, 1988) identifies two antagonistic processes that are central to the maintenance of a positive self-evaluation: reflection and comparison. The comparison process leads to adjustments to avoid the threat to one's self-evaluation that might result from comparison to the outstanding accomplishments of a close other (cf. Suls & Wills, 1991; Wills, 1981) or serves to bolster self-evaluation through comparison with the poor performance of another (Gibbons, 1986; Taylor, Wood, & Lichtman, 1983; Wood & Taylor, 1991). Examples of negative comparison are quite common, as when one spouse feels threatened because he or she sees the partner as smarter or more verbal or because the partner makes more money. The SEM model predicts that persons will tend to avoid situations that threaten self-evaluation but be attracted to situations that bolster self-evaluation.

The reflection process can be seen as the mirror image of the comparison process. In this process, self-evaluation is bolstered by the outstanding accomplishments of a close other (cf. Cialdini et al., 1976) and threatened by the poor performance of another. Examples of the positive side of this process are frequent, as when one spouse takes pride in the other's accomplishments at work or in the community (e.g., one partner basks in the reflected glory of the other partner's fame, attractiveness, or standing in the community).

What determines when spouses bask in reflected glory rather than wither under negative comparison? According to the SEM model, the relative balance of comparison and reflection processes is determined by the *relevance* of the performance dimension involved. That is, although the self may recognize good performance on a variety of dimensions, the self aspires to be "good at" only a few such dimensions. Those dimensions that a spouse finds "self-defining" or *relevant* prompt comparison. Those dimensions that a spouse finds unimportant or *irrelevant* prompt reflection. Thus, self-evaluation maintenance is facilitated when one outperforms a close other on a dimension high in self-relevance and when one is outperformed by a close other on a dimension low in self-relevance.

In sum, it can be seen that the SEM model has three basic parameters—closeness, relevance (importance), and performance—and these parameters are assumed to interact with each other. The interaction of these parameters is predicted to be important in determining which types of situations spouses will seek out and which they will avoid, as well as which will produce relatively positive affect and which more negative affect. It is assumed that these processes will often operate outside awareness (cf. Pilkington, Tesser, & Stephens, 1991; Pleban & Tesser, 1981; Tesser & Collins, 1988; Tesser, Millar, & Moore, 1988; Tesser & Paulhus, 1983).

SEM and Social Support.   Let us consider a typical case of support provision in which a spouse provides instrumental support or gives advice to another about how best to handle a problem. In terms of the SEM model, the impact of this behavior should be very different depending on the importance of the area to the recipient of the advice. Receiving help from the spouse should produce more negative affective reactions if the help is perceived to be on a highly self-relevant dimension than if it is on a dimension that is not self-relevant. Conversely, if the partner is perceived as providing aid in an area that is not self-relevant, there should be little discomfort (cf. Nadler & Fisher, 1986).

In addition to felt discomfort, the SEM model predicts different reactions toward the partner depending on the importance of the domain. One possible reaction is envy of the partner. Indeed, envy should be most likely to be experienced when comparisons with another person are negative for the self (Salovey & Rodin, 1984) and these comparisons are in a domain especially important or relevant to the person's self-definition (Salovey & Rothman, 1991). Further, as Salovey (1991) points out, one should expect the envious individual to engage in some response to "correct" the threat to self-evaluation implied by the negative comparison. The nature of this response may vary greatly depending on situational constraints; it could range from not taking the advice (i.e., refusing to be outperformed) to denigrating the person giving the advice or creating greater distance in the relationship in order to reduce the intensity of the negative comparison. In each case, the supportive behavior offered by the partner could precipitate relationship discord or discomfort in the other partner and fail to deliver "perceived support." Accordingly, the potential for the supportive behavior to trigger comparison processes seems important in providing a complete picture of the impact of support in marriage.

An immediate implication of the SEM model for research on social support is that topographically similar behavior can have opposite impacts depending on the relevance of the domain to the support receiver's self-evaluation. No matter how caringly delivered, help that engenders a negative comparison process is unlikely to result in perceived support. Because relevance is an intraindividual variable, and because it should moderate the impact of partner behavior, it follows that investigation of partner behavior in the absence of intraindividual variables in the recipient should fail to account for much variance in either perceived support or its hypothesized outcomes.

On the other hand, taking into account the motivational impact of spousal offers of support may help resolve certain ambiguities in the social support area. In particular, the optimal matching model (Cutrona & Russell, 1990) indicates that advice and direct feedback should be most facilitative and best received when the stressor is one that is potentially controllable. The SEM model suggests, however, that advice will be most facilitative when it does not engender comparison processes, but will produce much more complex reactions if comparison processes are provoked. Because events in areas that are self-defining are likely to be the most stressful, such events are potentially important in formulating an optimal matching model.

Giving greater weight to the possibility that satisfaction with support may be more complex than initially proposed, it was found that spouses offered more advice and information when the stressor was controllable, but greater frequency of advice was associated with *lower* rather than higher recipient satisfaction (Cutrona & Suhr, 1992). Perhaps consideration of the extent to which the controllable areas were important for self-definition might help account for such otherwise anomalous reactions to support that "matches" the stressor. Indeed, it may well be that among the most troubling of all interactions in marriages is one in which well-meaning support, offered in good faith, is angrily turned down by the partner. Such interactions may lead to confusion and a variety of maladaptive attributions by both parties. Accordingly, consideration of motivational aspects of support provision potentially has implications for marital therapy as well as for social support research (cf. Beach, 1991).

Another, somewhat paradoxical implication of this perspective is developed by Nadler and Fisher (1986). They note that greater effort toward self-help may be stimulated by a threatening rather than a nonthreatening situation if the person perceives the goal to be potentially controllable. So, for outcomes perceived as potentially controllable, aid from the partner in an area important to the self may produce redoubled efforts to reduce the need for the aid. In this way, while help from the spouse may not make the partner feel good and perhaps not even create high levels of perceived support, it may motivate greater efforts to achieve. To return to the model of optimal matching, this possibility suggests that high levels of spousal advice and information may sometimes lead the partner to feel awful and may not result in "perceived support," but still produce effective coping as a result. The SEM model therefore highlights the possibility that some spouse behaviors that are not topographically similar to other supportive behaviors, and may not be rated by the recipients as very pleasant, may have a positive impact on achievement or coping. Again, the important implication would seem to be that topography of the support-provider's behavior may tell us little in the absence of more fine-grained analysis of the cognitive processes operative for the support seeker. In addition, this analysis suggests that different dependent variables may provide rather different perspectives on the "helpfulness" of partner support.

One additional consideration also follows from this perspective. Consider Jane, someone with a rather negative view of the likely helpfulness of others, who finds herself in a relationship with John, for whom it is self-defining to be seen as friendly and supportive. As John learns that Jane expects him to be rejecting and uncaring at times when she may need his support, he should become especially strongly motivated to disconfirm this expectation (cf. Swann & Read, 1981). Under these circumstances, one might expect John to go to extraordinary lengths to meet unreasonable requests, put up with negative reactions, and endure various tests and provocations. Indeed, under such circumstances, John's response might be exactly what is needed to disconfirm Jane's prior negative beliefs while creating a strong bond between him and Jane.

One might expect, however, that if the support provider wished to reduce his level of support before the support seeker had changed her fundamental beliefs, it could lead to an extremely dysfunctional series of interactions. The support provider might attempt to withdraw, leading the support seeker to counter with greater displays of neediness. The support seeker might then feel increasingly conflicted and trapped. She might begin to suspect that her initial negative beliefs were correct all along and see confirmation in the support provider's behavior. In brief, a dynamic rather like the depressogenic processes outlined by Coyne (1976) might emerge. Thus, while a motivated partner might in some cases be sufficient to provide the new learning needed to challenge and change negative prior beliefs about the behavior of partners, if this support falls short, it may play a part in precipitating depressogenic interactions.

Melding the Cognitive Model with Attachment Theory and Research

Our analysis would be incomplete if we did not discuss possible origins of knowledge structures that are likely to influence processing of support-relevant behavior. Is a sense of the partner's trustworthiness and supportiveness initially determined on the basis of early interactions with the spouse, only later becoming more independent of particular spouse behaviors? Or are some sets of beliefs already present when spouses marry, influencing their subsequent interactions and the development of their relationships? It seems to us that the emerging literature on adult attachment style (e.g., Hazen & Shaver, 1987) has a variety of pertinent insights that can add to our discussion. Accordingly, we review briefly the literature on adult attachments with a focus on implications for the cognitive view of social support in marriage.

Borrowing from developments in infant attachment research, the Bowlby (1969, 1973, 1980) theory of attachment was recently extended to the study of adult intimate relationships (Hazen & Shaver, 1987). Specifically, Ainsworth and colleagues' attachment classifications have been posited as attachment styles evident among adults (e.g., Ainsworth, Blehar, Waters, & Wall, 1978). Hence, "securely" attached adults were described as those for whom closeness and trust were comfortable, while "anxiously/ambivalently" attached adults were described as worrying about abandonment and wanting to get closer. Finally, "avoidantly" attached adults were described as being uncomfortable in relationships because they did not trust or feel they could depend on close others. Bartholomew (Bartholomew, 1990; Bartholomew & Horowitz, 1991) has further divided this group into two types of avoidantly attached persons: (1) a fearful group composed of individuals who desire social contact and intimacy, but experience a pervasive fear of rejection and therefore actively avoid situations and relationships in which they perceive themselves as vulnerable to rejection, and (2) a dismissing group who develop models of the self as fully adequate and capable and view social contact and intimacy as unnecessary.

As with the earlier work on children, the attachment framework appears to be largely compatible with a cognitive perspective (e.g., Baldwin, 1992). Adult attachment styles are hypothesized to reflect mental models that strongly resemble cognitive schemata with affective as well as propositional information represented, and appear to include representations of the self, important others, and the nature of relationships in general (Bowlby, 1973). Internal working models guide expectations about the self and others as well as interpretations of social interactions and, in this respect, appear to function in the same manner outlined earlier for beliefs about supportiveness. Internal working models are presumed to derive from the individual's relationship with a primary caregiver and other social experiences from the past (Main, 1991). Thus, persons enter new relationships with sets of expectations about themselves and others as partners. It is widely hypothesized, however, that despite the obstacles to new learning in this area, current relationships may provide the opportunity for revision of internal working models (e.g., B. R. Sarason et al., 1991). Likewise, Main (1991) suggests that some persons may have multiple models of attachment that may alternate in organizing their perception and behavior. If so, a cognitive framework is likely to be particularly fruitful in accounting for changing reactions to others across situations.

Attachment theory appears to provide straightforward hypotheses about which individuals should feel most supported by partners. Because they expect their needs to be met, securely attached adults report less neuroticism (Shaver & Brennan, 1992), and securely attached women report higher levels of support from their husbands than do their insecure counterparts (Benoit, Zeahan, & Barton, 1989). In contrast, anxious–ambivalent individuals have reported feeling more anxious and more jealous in their relationships than securely attached subjects (Pietromonaco & Carnelley, 1994), but tend to idealize their attachment figures (Feeney & Noller, 1991), at least early in relationships. Persons with both types of avoidant attachment (fearful and dismissive) tend to display low emotional intensity in describing their romantic partners (Feeney & Noller, 1991) and often are characterized by low levels of agreeableness and openness to feelings and high neuroticism (Shaver & Brennan, 1992). Thus, particular attachment styles appear to be associated with characteristic sets of expectations and, as a result, characteristic modes of relating to the social environment.

While the securely attached perceive more available social support as well as high levels of satisfaction with available support (B. R. Sarason et al., 1991), for the insecurely attached, the reverse is true. Securely attached adults are less likely than insecurely attached adults to report expectations that seeking help from others will be risky, costly, and futile. Among the insecure-attachment groups, the avoidantly attached are more likely to focus on needs for autonomy and independence, while the anxious–ambivalently attached report greater mistrust of others (Wallace & Vaux, 1993). To the extent that attachment style continues to emerge as a coherent way of organizing individual differences in orientation toward close relationships, these initial findings suggest that early attachment experiences may be an important influence on later beliefs that shape support seeking and support provision.

In a direct test of the proposition that attachment style influences patterns of support-seeking behavior and support provision, Simpson, Rholes, and Nelligan (1991) found that attachment style influenced support-elicitation behaviors of female subjects in an anxiety-provoking situation and the subsequent responses of their male dating partners. As expected, when left alone with their partners, avoidant women were less likely than securely attached women to mention the stressful event to their dating partners. Conversely, at lower levels of anxiety, avoidant women were more likely to seek support from their partners than were secure women.

The findings of this study have important implications for support behaviors within marriage. As would be expected from the cognitive model developed above, behaviors most characteristic of self-reported attachment styles were most likely during conditions of high stress. Likewise, attachment styles organize sets of support-relevant beliefs and behaviors into coherent clusters (Kobak & Hazen, 1991). Unfortunately, little work has yet been done to examine attachment models using an information processing approach (for an exception, see Baldwin, Fehr, Keedian, Seidel, & Thomson, 1993). Combining the advantages of the cognitive perspective put forward earlier with the conceptual benefits of the attachment approach appears useful for examining continuities and individual differences in support-seeking behavior and in perceived support within a life-span developmental perspective.

IMPLICATIONS FOR FUTURE RESEARCH ON SOCIAL SUPPORT IN MARRIAGE

The foregoing cognitive analysis of social support suggests that in order to achieve stronger and more reliable effects, it will be necessary for social support researchers to consider carefully the effects of basic cognitive processes in seeking to understand perceived support. In particular, the effects of expectation of support on both the support seeker and the support provider, the perseverance of prior beliefs about the probability of support in the face of contradictory evidence, and the cognitive creation of need for support where none would otherwise exist seem to have important implications for social support research. Even cursory attention to these factors warns against an overly optimistic assessment of the likelihood that topography of partner behavior will account for much variance in perceived support beyond that accounted for by intrapersonal variables.

Perhaps more important, the foregoing analysis suggests that it is inappropriate to *control for* intraindividual variables when examining the contribution of partner behavior to perceived support. Rather than conceptualize partner behavior as a competing factor, it seems more appropriate to conceptualize it as partially caused by the support seeker's behavior and as having its effects on perceived support moderated by intraindividual factors associated with the support seeker. Accordingly, it is important to examine the effects of intraindividual variables on partner behavior or their effects in combination with partner behavior in the form of interaction terms.

At a methodological level, the potential effects of differential accessibility of prior beliefs about partner supportiveness suggest that considerably less variance in outcomes is currently being accounted for than could be if accessibility measures were included in social support assessment procedures. In addition, the potential for partner effects on perceived supportiveness of a given interaction seems considerably greater for persons with low accessibility of prior beliefs about partner supportiveness than for persons with high accessibility of these beliefs. The study of accessibility of beliefs therefore appears to offer considerable potential to advance understanding of social support.

Likewise, because motivational factors appear capable of changing the impact of certain types of partner supportive behavior, it may be useful to examine the extent to which spouses provide support that is potentially threatening to self-evaluation (i.e., help that implies an expert status in an area of importance to the partner) vs. nonthreatening (i.e., help that implies no expert status or implies expert status in an area that is not important to the partner). The self-evaluation maintenance model suggests that the relationship between spouse behavior and perceived support should be stronger if it is confined to nonthreatening situations.

Finally, developments in the study of adult attachment have clear implications for the study of social support in marriage, but these implications become more striking when attachment style is viewed from a cognitive perspective. Seen as a set of interlocking prior beliefs, attachment models represent strong examples of the way in which prior beliefs may intrude on perception of current interaction. It seems likely that by melding the insights of attachment research with considerations derived from a cognitive perspective, it may be possible to create more powerful assessments of attachment style and better explicate both the effects of partner supportive behavior and the conditions that give rise to the perception of having a supportive spouse.

REFERENCES

Ainsworth, M. D. S., Blehar, M. C., Waters, E., Wall, S. (1978). *Patterns of attachment: A psychological study of the Strange Situation.* Hillsdale NJ: Lawrence Erlbaum.

Baldwin, M. W. (1992). Relational schemas and the processing of social information. *Psychological Bulletin, 112,* 461–484.

Baldwin, M., Fehr, W., Keedian, B., Seidel, E., & Thomson, M. (1993). An exploration of the relational schemata underlying attachment styles: Self-report and lexical decision making. *Personality and Social Psychology Bulletin, 19,* 746–754.

Bargh, J. A., & Pietromonaco, P. (1982). Automatic information processing and social perceptions: The influence of trait information presented outside of conscious awareness on impression formation. *Journal of Personality and Social Psychology, 43,* 437–449.

Bartholomew, K. (1990). Avoidance of intimacy: An attachment perspective. *Journal of Social and Personal Relationships, 7,* 147–178.

Bartholomew, K., & Horowitz, L. M. (1991). Attachment styles among young adults: A test of a four category model. *Journal of Personality and Social Psychology, 61,* 226–244.

Beach, S. R. H. (1991). Social cognition and the relationship repair process: Toward better outcome in marital therapy. In G. J. O. Fletcher & F. D. Fincham (Eds.), *Cognition in close relationships* (pp. 307–328). Hillsdale, NJ: Lawrence Erlbaum.

Beach, S. R. H., Martin, J. K., Blum, T. C., & Roman, P. M. (1993). Effects of marital and co-worker relationships on negative affect: Testing the central role of marriage. *American Journal of Family Therapy, 21,* 312–322.

Benoit, D., Zeanah, C. H., & Barton, M. L. (1989). Maternal attachment disturbances in failure to thrive. Special issue: Internal representations and parent–infant relationships. *Infant Mental Health Journal, 1,* 185–202.

Berg-Cross, L. (1974). *Basic concepts in family therapy,* New York: Horwath Press.

Bodenhausen, G. V. (1988). Stereotypic biases in social decision making and memory: Testing process models of stereotype use. *Journal of Personality and Social Psychology, 55,* 726–737.

Bowlby, J. (1969). *Attachment and loss,* Vol. 1, *Attachment.* New York: Basic Books.

Bowlby, J. (1973). *Attachment and loss,* Vol. 2, *Separation.* New York: Basic Books.

Bowlby, J. (1977). The making and breaking of affectional bonds. *British Journal of Psychiatry, 130,* 201–210.

Bowlby, J. (1980). *Attachment and loss,* Vol. 3, *Loss, sadness, and depression.* New York: Basic Books.

Bradbury, T. N., & Fincham, F. D. (1989). Behavior and satisfaction in marriage: Prospective mediating processes. *Review of Personality and Social Psychology, 10,* 119–143.

Bradbury, T. N., & Fincham, F. D. (1990). Attributions in marriage: Review and critique. *Psychological Bulletin, 107,* 3–33.

Bradbury, T. N., & Fincham, F. D. (1991). A contextual model for advancing the study of marital interaction. In G. J. Fletcher & F. D. Fincham (Eds.), *Cognition in close relationships* (pp. 127–147). Hillsdale, NJ: Lawrence Erlbaum.

Bradbury, T. N., & Fincham, F. D. (1992). Attributions and behavior in marital interaction. *Journal of Personality and Social Psychology, 51,* 1173–1182.

Brown, G. W., & Harris, T. O. (1978). Social origins of depression: A study of psychiatric disorder in women. New York: Free Press.

Cialdini, R. B., Borden, R. J., Thorne, A., Walker, M. R., Freeman, S., & Sloan, L. R. (1976). Basking in reflected glory: Three (football) field studies. *Journal of Personality and Social Psychology, 34,* 366–375.

Coyne, J. C. (1976). Depression and the response of others. *Journal of Abnormal Psychology, 85,* 186–193.

Coyne, J. C., & DeLongis, A. M. (1986). Going beyond social support: The role of social relationships in adaptation. *Journal of Consulting and Clinical Psychology, 54,* 454–460.

Curtis, R. C., & Miller, K. (1986). Believing another likes or dislikes you: Behaviors making the beliefs come true. *Journal of Personality and Social Psychology, 51,* 284–290.

Cutrona, C. E. (August, 1994). Interplay of social support and conflict in relationship satisfaction. Paper presented at the 102nd Annual Convention of the American Psychological Association. Los Angeles.

Cutrona, C. E., & Russell, D. (1990). Type of social support and specific stress: Toward an optimal theory of matching. In I. G. Sarason, B. R. Sarason, & G. R. Pierce (Eds.), *Social support: An interactional view* (pp. 319–366). New York: Wiley.

Cutrona, C. E., & Suhr, J. A. (1992). Controllability of stressful events and satisfaction with spouse support behaviors. *Communication Research, 19,* 154–172.

Cutrona, C. E., Suhr, J. A., & MacFarlane, R. (1990). Interpersonal transactions and the psychological sense of support. In S. Duck (Ed.), *Personal relationships and social support* (pp. 30–65). London: Sage.

Dakof, G. A., & Taylor, S. E. (1990). Victims' perceptions of social support: What is helpful from whom? *Journal of Personality and Social Psychology, 58(1),* 80–89.

Fazio, R. H., & Williams, C. J. (1986). Attitude accessibility as a moderator of the attitude–perception and attitude–behavior relations: An investigation of the 1984 presidential election. *Journal of Personality and Social Psychology, 51,* 505–514.

Feeney, J. A., & Noller, P. (1991). Attachment style and verbal descriptions of romantic partners. *Journal of Social and Personal Relationships, 8,* 187–215.

Fincham, F. D., Bradbury, T. N., & Scott, C. K. (1990). Cognition in marriage. In F. D. Fincham & T. N. Bradbury (Eds.), *The psychology of marriage: Basic issues and applications* (pp. 118–149). New York: Guilford Press.

Fincham, F. D., Fernandes, L. O., & Humphreys, K. H. (1993). *Communicating in relationships: A guide for couples and professionals.* Champaign, IL: Research Press.

Finchman, F. D., Garnier, P. C., Gano-Phillips, S., & Osborne, L. N. (1995). Pre-interaction expectations, marital satisfaction, and accessibility: A new look at sentiment override. *Journal of Family Psychology, 9,* 3–14.

Fletcher, G. J., & Fincham, F. D. (1991). Attribution processes in close relationships. In G. J. Fletcher & F. D. Fincham (Eds.), *Cognition in close relationships* (pp. 7–35). Hillsdale, NJ: Lawrence Erlbaum.

Fletcher, G. J. O., & Fitness, J. (1993). Knowledge structures and explanations in intimate relationships. In S. Duck (Ed.), *Individuals in relationships* (pp. 121–143). Newbury Park, CA: Sage.

Gibbons, F. X. (1986). Social comparison and depression: Company's effect on misery. *Journal of Personality and Social Psychology, 51,* 140–148.

Gotlieb, B. H. (1985). Social support and the study of personal relationships. *Journal of Social and Personal Relationships, 2,* 351–375.

Hazen, C., & Shaver, P. (1987). Romantic love conceptualized as an attachment process. *Journal of Personality and Social Psychology, 52,* 511–524.

Hirt, E. R. (1990). Do I see only what I expect? Evidence for an expectancy guided retrieval model. *Journal of Personality and Social Psychology, 58,* 937–951.

Joiner, T. E., Alfano, M. S., & Metalsky, G. I. (1993). Caught in the crossfire: Depression, self-consistency, self-enhancement, and the response of others. *Journal of Social and Clinical Psychology, 12,* 113–134.

Joseph, S., Williams, R., & Yule, W. (1992). Crisis support, attributional style, coping style, and post-traumatic symptoms. *Personality and Individual Differences, 13,* 1249–1251.

Julien, D., & Markman, H. J. (1991). Social support and social networks as determinants of individual and marital outcomes. *Journal of Social and Personal Relationships, 8,* 549–568.

Kobak, R., & Hazen, C. (1991). Attachment in marriage: The effects of security and accuracy of working models. *Journal of Personality and Social Psychology, 60,* 861–869.

Lakey, B., Tardiff, T. A., & Drew, J. B. (1994). Negative social interactions: Assessment and relations to social support, cognition, and psychological distress. *Journal of Social and Clinical Psychology, 13,* 42–64.

Lin, N., Dean, A., & Ensel, W. M. (1986). *Social support, life events, and depression.* Orlando, FL: Academic Press.

Main, M. (1991). Metacognitive knowledge, metacognitive monitoring, and singular (coherent) vs. multiple (incoherent) models of attachment: Findings and directions for future research. In C. M. Parkes, P. Marris, & J. Stevenson-Hinde (Eds.), *Attachment across the life cycle* (pp. 127–159). New York: Routledge.

Markus, H., & Smith, J. (1981). The influence of self-schemata on the perception of others. In N. Cantor & J. F. Kihlstrom (Eds.), *Personality, cognition, and social interaction* (pp. 233–262). Hillsdale, NJ: Lawrence Erlbaum.

Nadler, A., & Fisher, J. D. (1986). The role of threat to self-esteem and perceived control in recipient reaction to help: Theory development and empirical validation. In L. Berkowitz (Ed.), *Advances in experimental social psychology,* Vol. 19 (pp. 81–121). Orlando, FL: Academic Press.

O'Sullivan, C. S., & Durso, F. T. (1984). Effects of schema-incongruent information on memory for stereotypical attributes. *Journal of Personality and Social Psychology, 47,* 55–70.

Pagel, M. D., Erdly, W. W., & Becker, J. (1987). Social networks: We get by with (and in spite of) a little help from our friends. *Journal of Personality and Social Psychology, 53,* 793–804.

Pierce, G. R., Sarason, B. R., & Sarason, I. G. (1990). Integrating social support perspectives: Working models, personal relationships, and situational factors. In S. Duck (Ed.), *Personal relationships and social support* (pp. 30–65). London: Sage.

Pietromonaco, P. R., & Carnelley, K. B. (1994). Gender and working models of attachment: Consequences for perceptions of self and romantic relationships. *Personal Relationships, 1,* 63–82.

Pilkington, C. J., Tesser, A., & Stephens, D. (1991). Complementarity in romantic relationships: A self-evaluation maintenance perspective. *Journal of Social and Personal Relationships, 8,* 481–504.

Pleban, R., & Tesser, A. (1981). The effects of relevance and quality of another's performance on interpersonal closeness. *Social Psychology Quarterly, 44,* 278–285.

Reiss, H. T. (1990). The role of intimacy in interpersonal relations. *Journal of Social and Clinical Psychology, 9,* 15–30.

Ritts, V., & Stein, J. R. (1994). Verification and commitment in marital relationships: An exploration of self-verification theory in community college students. Paper presented at the Midwest Psychological Association. Chicago.

Rock, I. (1983). *The logic of perception.* Cambridge: MIT Press.

Rogers, K. R. (1987). Nature of spousal supportive behaviors that influence heart transplant patient compliance. *Journal of Heart Transplant, 6,* 90–95.

Salovey, P. (1991). Social comparison processes in envy and jealousy. In J. Suls & T. A. Wills (Eds.), *Social comparison: Contemporary theory and research* (pp. 261–285). Hillsdale, NJ: Lawrence Erlbaum.

Salovey, P., & Rodin, J. (1984). Some antecedents and consequences of social comparison jealousy. *Journal of Personality and Social Psychology, 47,* 780–792.

Salovey, P., & Rothman, A. (1991). Envy and jealousy: Self and society. In P. Salovey (Ed.), *The psychology of jealousy and envy* (pp. 271–286). New York: Guilford Press.

Sarason, B. R., Pierce, G. R., Shearin, E. N., Sarason, I. G., Waltz, J. A., & Poppe, L. (1991). Perceived social support and working models of self and actual others. *Journal of Personality and Social Psychology, 60,* 273–287.

Sarason, I. G., Sarason, B. R., & Pierce, G. (1994). Social support: Global and relationship-based levels of analysis. *Journal of Social and Personal Relationships, 11,* 295–312.

Shaver, P. R., & Brennan, K. A. (1992). Attachment styles and the "Big Five" personality traits: Their connections with each other and with romantic relationship outcomes. *Personality and Social Psychology Bulletin, 18(5),* 536–545.

Shiffrin, R. M., & Schneider, W. (1977). Controlled and automatic human information processing. II. Perceptual learning, automatic attending, and a general theory. *Psychological Review, 84,* 127–190.

Simpson, J. A., Rholes, W. S., & Nelligan, J. S. (1991). Support seeking and support giving within couples in an anxiety-provoking situation: The role of attachment styles. *Journal of Personality and Social Psychology, 62,* 434–446.

Slack, D., & Vaux, A. (1988). Undesirable life events and depression: The role of event appraisals and social support. *Journal of Social and Clinical Psychology, 7,* 290–296.

Snyder, M. (1992). Motivational foundations of behavioral confirmation. *Advances in Experimental Social Psychology, 25,* 67–114.

Snyder, M., & Haugen, J. A. (August, 1990). Why does behavioral confirmation occur? A functional perspective. Paper presented at the 98th Annual Convention of the American Psychological Association. Boston.

Snyder, M., & Swann, W. B. (1978). Behavioral confirmation in social interaction: From social perception to social reality. *Journal of Experimental Social Psychology, 14,* 148–162.

Snyder, M., Tanke, E. D., & Berscheid, E. (1977). Social perception and interpersonal behavior: On the self-fulfilling nature of social stereotypes. *Journal of Personality and Social Psychology, 35,* 656–666.

Srull, T. K., & Wyer, R. S. (1989). The role of category accessibility in the interpretation of information about persons: Some determinants and implications. *Journal of Personality and Social Psychology, 38,* 841–856.

Suls, J., & Wills, T. A. (1991). *Social comparison: Contemporary theory and research.* Hillsdale, NJ: Lawrence Erlbaum.

Swann, W. B., Jr., De La Ronde, C., & Hixon, J. G. (1994). Authenticity and positivity strivings in marriage and courtship. *Journal of Personality and Social Psychology, 66,* 857–869.

Swann, W. B., Jr., Hixon, J. G., & De La Ronde, C. (1992). Embracing the bitter "truth": Negative self-concepts and marital commitment. *Psychological Science, 3,* 118–121.

Swann, W. B., Jr., & Predmore, S. C. (1985). Intimates as agents of social support: Sources of consolation or despair? *Journal of Personality and Social Psychology, 49,* 1609–1617.

Swann, W. B., Jr., & Read, S. J. (1981). Self-verification processes: How we sustain our self-conceptions. *Journal of Experimental Social Psychology, 17,* 351–372.

Swann, W. B., Jr., Stein-Seroussi, A., & Giesler, R. B. (1992). Why people self-verify. *Journal of Personality and Social Psychology, 62,* 392–401.

Taylor, S. E., & Crocker, J. (1981). Schematic bases of social information processing. In E. T. Higgins, C. P. Herman, & M. P. Zanna (Eds.), *Social cognition: The Ontario Symposium* (pp. 89–134). Hillsdale, NJ: Lawrence Erlbaum.

Taylor, S. E., Wood, J. V., & Lichtman, R. R. (1983). It could be worse: Selective evaluation as a response to victimization. *Journal of Social Issues, 39,* 19–40.

Tesser, A. (1988). Toward a self-evaluation maintenance model of social behavior. In L. Berkowitz (Ed.), *Advances in experimental social psychology,* Vol. 21 (pp. 181–227). San Diego: Academic Press.

Tesser, A., & Collins, J. E. (1988). Emotion in social reflection and comparison situations: Intuitive, systematic, and exploratory approaches. *Journal of Personality and Social Psychology, 55,* 695–709.

Tesser, A., Millar, M., & Moore, J. (1988). Some affective consequences of social comparison and reflection processes: The pain and pleasure of being close. *Journal of Personality and Social Psychology, 54,* 49–61.

Tesser, A., & Paulhus, D. (1983). The definition of self: Private and public self-evaluation maintenance strategies. *Journal of Personality and Social Psychology, 44,* 672–682.

Uleman, J. S., & Bargh, J. A. (1989). *Unintended thought.* New York: Guilford Press.

Vaux, A. (1988). Social and emotional loneliness: The role of social and personal characteristics. *Personality and Social Psychology Bulletin, 14,* 722–734.

Veiel, H. O. F., Crisand, M., Stroszeck-Somschor, H., & Herrle, J. (1991). Social support networks of chronically strained couples: Similarity and overlap. *Journal of Social and Personal Relationship, 8,* 279–292.

Vinokur, A., Schul, Y., & Caplan, R. D. (1987). Determinants of perceived social support: Interpersonal transactions, personal outlook, and transient affect states. *Journal of Personality and Social Psychology, 53,* 1137–1145.

Wallace, J. L., & Vaux, A. (1993). Social support network orientation: The role of adult attachment style. *Journal of Social and Clinical Psychology, 3,* 354–365.

Weiss, R. L., & Heyman, R. (1990). Observation of marital interaction. In F. D. Fincham & T. N. Bradbury (Eds.), *The psychology of marriage: Basic issues and applications* (pp. 87–117). New York: Guilford Press.

Wethington, E., & Kessler, R. C. (1986). Perceiving support, received support, and adjustment to life events. *Journal of Health and Social Behavior, 27,* 78–89.

Wills, T. A. (1981). Downward comparison principles in social psychology. *Psychological Bulletin, 90,* 245–271.

Wood, J. V., & Taylor, K. L. (1991). Serving self-relevant goals through social comparison. In J. Suls & T. A. Wills (Eds.), *Social comparison: Contemporary theory and research* (pp. 23–49). Hillsdale, NJ: Lawrence Erlbaum.

4

Social Support in Its Cultural Context

PEGGYE DILWORTH-ANDERSON and SHEREE MARSHALL

Understanding social support within a cultural context requires knowledge of the culture in which support is given and received. This chapter focuses on cultural factors that shape giving and receiving social support among African-American, Hispanic-American, Asian-American, and Native American families. Although these groups are a part of American society, they also function within distinct cultural boundaries that define and provide them with an identity that is uniquely different from the identity of those who are not a part of their group's culture. Findings suggest that their history, social position, minority group status, and entrance into American society have played major roles in shaping their cultural definition and identity.

This chapter is organized into a discussion on each of these four cultural groups as they give and receive social support within their cultural context. Sociohistorical information provides a conceptual grounding for understanding the cultural context of social support for each group. This sociohistorical information identifies distinct cultural characteristics that shape the giving and receiving of social support.

The concept of culture is critical to this discussion. As is evidenced in almost all social and behavioral science literature in which this concept is used, no one definition is consistently cited. As a result, we have used a definition that fits our conceptual ideas about the groups that are discussed in this chapter. Conceptually, culture is viewed as a core feature of one's identity. It defines, prescribes, directs, and gives meaning to life. Using the definition of Keith (1991), culture is

PEGGYE DILWORTH-ANDERSON and SHEREE MARSHALL • Department of Human Development and Family Studies, University of North Carolina at Greensboro, Greensboro, North Carolina 27412.

Handbook of Social Support and the Family, edited by Gregory R. Pierce, Barbara R. Sarason, and Irwin G. Sarason. Plenum Press, New York, 1996.

"a design for living, the shared understanding underlying a shared way of life. The essential attribute of culture is that it is shared, and that is provides a vocabulary of symbols to express and assign meaning to various aspects of social life" (p. 95). According to Geertz (1973), culture is both objective and subjective, and subsumes racial and ethnic rituals, symbols, language, and general ways of behaving. Culture also places one with others in a society based on characteristics that are distinctly unique to certain people.

Given the terms in which these definitions are cast, culture can influence people's beliefs, attitudes, expectations, and behaviors. The culture of a people therefore provides the contextual grounding for social support to be given and received. This contextual grounding allows for the expression of certain needs that would require providing social support. The shared belief system of the group, along with attitudes, norms, and expectations, also provides direction and guidance to the form in which social support is given and received. Although numerous factors, such as social class, gender, and age, can impact giving and receiving social support in different families, cultural context is also important. The context in which these supportive behaviors occur expands our understanding of how cultural norms, attitudes, beliefs, and behaviors shape support networks in families (Mutran, 1985; Silverstein & Waite, 1993).

CULTURAL IDENTITIES AND THE CONTEXT OF SOCIAL SUPPORT

This section focuses on the influence of cultural identity on shaping the context of social support. The context of social support allows for understanding the structure (informal vs. formal or both) that different groups use to provide social support, the type of support that is given, and the configuration of social support (i.e., who gives it). In Table 1, we have provided a summary of the following discussion on cultural identities and the context of social support.

African-Americans

At present African-Americans represent the largest minority group in this society. They account for approximately 12% of the total population and reside primarily in inner cities (Zinn & Eitzen, 1993). The cultural context in which African-Americans give and receive social support in their families is shaped by the veil of slavery behind which these families developed. For example, the institution of slavery provided few mechanisms for individuals and families to receive support for survival outside the slave community. The availability of social support was therefore internal to the slave community; survival was a group effort. Although this type of survival structure reflected the oppressive outcomes of slavery, it nevertheless was also indicative of the slaves' African heritage. In traditional African communities, social support was embedded within the tribe, community, and village in which families belonged (Escott, 1979).

The expectation that one's survival depended on the effort of the collective slave community for African-Americans is commonly found in historical docu-

Table 1. Cultural Identities and the Context of Social Support

Social support	African-Americans	Asian-Americans	Hispanic-Americans[a]	Native Americans
Structure				
Informal				
Close kin	+	+	+	+
Distant kin	+	−	−	+
Fictive kin	+	−	−	+
Neighbors	+	−	±	+
Friends	+	−	±	+
Formal				
Place of religion	+	−	−	−
Institutions and agencies	−	−	−	−
Type				
Material	+	−	+	+
Financial	−	+	−	−
Instrumental	+	+	+	+
Emotional	+	+	+	+
Configuration				
Parents	+	+	+	+
Siblings	+	+	+	+
In-laws	+	+	+	+
Friends	+	−	±	+
Distant kin	+	−	+	+

[a](±) Indicates that this characteristic exists in some Hispanic groups, but not in others. Cubans are more likely to have friends as a part of their social support system than are Mexicans.

ments that depict life in the slave community (Escott, 1979; Gutman, 1976). Although slavery ended in 1865, Jim Crow laws restricted African-Americans from gaining access to the society that could provide measures of support to the family, such as health care, education, employment, legal rights, and adequate housing, to name a few. Legally, Jim Crow laws were abolished by the middle 1960s in this society; however, the practice of prohibiting African-Americans from using resources to facilitate their individual and family well-being did not stop (Jaynes & Williams, 1989). As a result, the family and church in the African-American community have provided the social support that was often lacking due to discrimination from enacted laws and accepted practices within American society (Lincoln & Mamiya, 1991).

Within African-American families, support is primarily provided through relational networks that consist of consanguine relationships as well as nonkin (Dilworth-Anderson, 1992; Taylor, 1986; Taylor & Chatters, 1991). Boundaries in African-American families tend to be fluid and flexible, allowing for the acceptance of dependent generations into existing households. Family support has traditionally included helping with child care, sharing households, and providing emotional support to close, distant, and even fictive kin (Burton & Dilworth-Anderson, 1991).

Hispanic-Americans

Unlike African-American families, Hispanics came to this country as free immigrants. Although the general descriptor "Hispanic" is used to represent people of Spanish origin in this society, they have very different backgrounds. They are a diverse people, coming from different societies such as Mexico, Puerto Rico, Cuba, and the nations of Central and South America. As a group, they have limited education and health care and generally work in low-paying occupations. Today, Hispanics comprise about 9% of the American population and are the second largest minority group in this society. Hispanics are expected to be the largest minority group by the year 2010 (Zinn & Eitzen, 1993).

Although very diverse as a group, Hispanics are similar in regard to having family-centered cultures that serve as the core of their social support system. These family-centered cultures include a social support system that reflects close and distant kin and the godparents of children in the family. They therefore operate within an extended family system in which emotional, instrumental, and material exchanges are given to provide support to immediate and extended kin relations. Because Hispanics are so strongly rooted in family affiliation and connectiveness, they live in close proximity to one another, share in child-rearing, speak their native language, and preserve their customs through family and community rituals. Families are therefore responsible for primary social and emotional support in which mutual obligation and reciprocity are expected (Vega, 1990).

Among certain Hispanic groups such as Cubans, however, friends in addition to family give and receive social support from one another. By including both family and friends in their social support network, Cuban-Americans have largely duplicated their culture of origin in culturally homogeneous ethnic enclaves in which their sociocultural needs can be easily met. The enclave is a source of effective social support in later life.

Among Mexican-Americans, however, it is the family that is a major source of identity, self-worth, and social support (Keefe, 1984; Salgado de Synder, 1986). Mexican-Americans tend to live near a large number of kin with whom they maintain frequent interaction as a reciprocal aid system (Salgado de Synder, 1986). They are more likely than non-Hispanics to use support from relatives but not friends (Keefe, Padilla, & Carlos, 1979; Vega & Kolody, 1985), and to have more contact with relatives (Antonucci, 1985).

Asian-Americans

The term "Asian-American" incorporates people from several countries, including China, Japan, Korea, Samoa, Guam, the Philippines, Thailand, Laos, Cambodia, and Indonesia. Asians represent the smallest ethnic minority group in the United States, accounting for about 3% of the American population (Zinn & Eitzen, 1993). Even more diverse than Hispanics, Asian-Americans, similar to

Hispanics, share a common thread of family-centered social support systems in which emotional, financial, and instrumental support is given. This support system is maintained through a cultural sense of family loyalty and the predominance of group over individual concerns.

Asian-American families generally adhere to rules regulating respect for older adults and strict gender hierarchies. There is also a great deal of respect and obligation due individual family members, especially one's parents. Two other characteristics define relationships among Asian families: shame and harmony. Shame is used to reinforce certain behaviors that are appropriate in society. Harmony encourages lifestyles that show moderation in behavior, self-discipline, modesty, and patience. The social support system in Asian-American families incorporates both shame and harmony in giving and receiving help. Further, because Asian-Americans have been described as existing in highly organized ethnic enclaves that foster and support individuals and families, they are able to reinforce and maintain cultural values that help shape their support system (Serafica, 1990).

Native Americans

Native American families, representing less than 2% of the American population, still maintain unique customs and traditions. They have a variety of values, religions, and languages depending on the tribe. Native American families tend to live in relational networks that foster strong interrelationships and a mutual assistance network, in which emotional, material, and instrumental support is given. The extended family is a very important and a core feature of this network (Snipp, 1989).

Extended familism of the Native American social support system is evidenced in parenting and child-rearing and in the care of the elderly. Individuals who take part in child-rearing include parents as well as grandparents, uncles, and aunts, all of whom serve as primary role models for children. This kin network of relatives encourages the strong value of autonomy in children, which is also highly valued and respected in Native American families. The children are generally allowed freedom in making decisions within the relational networks in which they reside. Another important aspect of parenting and child-rearing in Native American families is the focus on spirituality. Spirituality, guided by both material and immaterial forces, is important in the rearing of children (Yee, 1990).

Although family structure and values of Native Americans suggest evidence of social support, few studies have attempted to define and measure social support among Native American peoples. Social support in Native American cultures carries considerable colloquial meaning and must therefore be defined within the confines of particular tribal culture. For example, social support is not especially defined in the Navajo language; however, to give individual or group support is clearly defined. When social support is attributed to the Navajo, it includes the culturally determined definitions of family, kinship, and parentship (Kekahbah &

Wood, 1980). Traditional affiliation with their cultural group, rather than their individual affiliation, provides the framework for social support.

PROVIDING SOCIAL SUPPORT
IN DIFFERENT CULTURAL CONTEXTS

The remainder of this chapter is organized around the social support given to the young and old in each cultural group discussed. Before we discuss the provision of social support among the different groups, however, it is important to point out that the context of social support is impacted by gender, age, and social class. For this chapter, however, the focus is on how the cultural context influences the social support among diverse groups. Further, this discussion makes no claim that more or less social support is given or received in one group vs. another. Instead, this discussion describes the cultural context of social support among diverse people as evidenced in the familial support given to the young and the old.

Providing social support to the young and the old among cultural groups was chosen as the focus of this discussion because it provides an exemplary model for understanding how cultural beliefs help shape social support to needy family members. Further, the high demands that the young and the old place on families and their level of dependence will allow for assessing the cultural responses each group uses to address social support to their neediest group members.

African-Americans

Children. Motherhood and parenting among African-Americans have very strong cultural meaning. On the basis of traditional cultural beliefs: (1) mothering occurs in the extended family as opposed to the nuclear family; (2) sex-role segregation in parenting is not salient in families; and (3) motherhood is not tied to economic dependency on a male breadwinner in the home (Wilson, 1989). Due to the perception of what parenting and motherhood entails, African-American mothering is not "privatized" and reserved exclusively for biological mothers (Collins, 1991). Instead, parenting and mothering are roles assumed by others in the family or even outside the family. Parenting and mothering therefore occur within extended family networks, rather than being limited to settings that include only the biological parents.

For instance, "othermothers" have been identified in many African-American families. Othermothers are individuals who assist biological mothers with parenting responsibilities. These "othermothers" are central to adequate monitoring of children. Families in which othermothers share the responsibility for children are viewed as "defended families." In these defended families, the monitoring of the children is largely responsible for identifying positive times that children should leave the home and identifying places they are allowed to go. Additionally, monitoring may prevent the children from being involved in culturally undesirable community relationships. As a result, the assumption of parenting roles by several responsible adults is commonplace in many African-American families (Dilworth-Anderson & Rhoden, in press).

The socialization of children to develop racial and cultural identities in traditional African-American families is also facilitated by their parents and significant others in the community. Children are not socialized or afforded the opportunity to "make it" on their own; thus, individuation is not necessarily viewed as an adaptive developmental task (Watson & Protinsky, 1988). Instead, the goals of socialization are to encourage family enmeshment, which fosters a sense of intergenerational reciprocity, responsibility, and the maintenance of the kin network. For example, the authoritarian parenting style among African-Americans encourages children to fell respectful toward their elders, obedient to parents, and responsible for others. As a result, the cultural norm of enmeshment without emphasis on individual value is maintained (Collins, 1991).

Elderly.   Studies conducted around two decades ago (Cantor, 1979; Hays & Mindel, 1973; Jackson, 1972; Seelbach, 1978) as well as those in more recent years (Chatters, Taylor, & Jackson, 1985, 1986; Mutran, 1985; Taylor, 1986; Taylor & Chatters, 1991) found that elderly blacks receive a great deal of support and caregiving from their children. In a review of the literature of intergenerational family support, Taylor and Chatters (1991) note, however, that there is a gender difference in the receipt of support from adult children. Older women are more likely to receive support from their children than are older men (Chatters et al., 1986).

In addition to receiving direct assistance from their offspring, the elderly have a second advantage if they have adult children. Research indicates that elderly blacks with adult children are more likely to have larger extended kin networks to provide support than are older blacks without children (Chatters et al., 1986).

Hispanic-Americans

Children.   In Hispanic families, the parent–child dyad is often considered more important than the marital dyad, which reflects the value of a child-centered culture. As a result, caretaking of children is more likely to be the responsibility of parents, aunts and uncles, and godparents. These individuals not only care for the basic needs of children, but also are responsible for their cultural socialization. This cultural socialization fosters cohesiveness in the Hispanic culture and helps maintain the future of the extended family as the core of social support for individuals (Vega, 1990). It also teaches Hispanic children biculturalism. This bicultural socialization provides Hispanic children with cultural values and behaviors that are needed for them to function within American society (Gutierrez & Sameroff, 1990). For example, when Hispanic children are encouraged to speak Spanish at home and in their communities and at the same time become proficient in English at school, parents are encouraging their children in the basics of a bicultural life.

Elderly.   Age and gender hierarchies among Hispanic families are strongly respected and have an impact on the social support system of the elderly. As a result, older males are generally held in higher esteem than their younger counterparts. Older women, however, particularly grandmothers, are revered in the culture. The caretaking of these older women is typically based on a system of intergenerational reciprocity. The cultural norm of providing for older generations who once cared for younger generations is generally adhered to among Hispanics, as evidenced by the care of older women.

The care of the elderly includes providing material and emotional support. Although there is an increase of Hispanic elderly living alone in the American culture, they are more likely than their white counterparts to live with adult children in later life (Burr & Mutchler, 1993). Although research shows that both health and economic factors play a significant role in the social support that the Hispanic elderly receive from their extended family, cultural factors have also been found to have an impact on the social support that the Hispanic elderly receive (Golding & Baezconde-Garbanati, 1990).

Asian-Americans

Children.   The diverse population in Asian-American communities, coupled with limited research among them, make it difficult to provide a detailed discussion on social support given to children (Depner & Bray, 1993). Nevertheless, some specific research findings provide insight into how the cultural context in Asian-American communities impacts supporting and caring for children. As noted earlier, Asian-American communities generally operate around strong cultural values such as shame and harmony (Serafica, 1990). For example, the value of harmony is expressed in the care of Asian-American children, which encourages consideration of family over individual needs, self-control, and ancestral worship. Children are given support from their family of origin and their extended family when they adhere to these cultural values. This is not to suggest, however, that when children do not adhere to cultural values they are not cared for or supported, but when children are in balance or harmony with their cultural values, stronger support is often given (Serafica, 1990).

Julian, McKenry, and McKelvey (1994) found several differences in parenting styles of Asian-Americans as compared to those of Caucasians, African-Americans, and Hispanics. Asian-American parents with younger and older children placed more importance on self-control and academic achievement as compared to other groups. Paradoxically, honor in the Asian-American community is perceived as belonging to the group, but individual achievements are highly valued. Thus the individual academic achievements of children bring honor to the group and are therefore not envied. Although the findings of Julian et al. (1994) do not specifically address support given to children, they do provide a view of the cultural context in which social support may be given to children. Thus, social support takes place in the context of discipline, self-control, and extended family networks. These cultural values may be observed, for example, in Asian-American parents' emphasis on using discipline, self-control, and family support for educational attainment and achievement.

Elderly.   Social support provided to the elderly in Asian-American families is based on strong cultural values of parent obligation and honor. The expression of these values, as evidenced through support provided to the elderly, is often impacted by language proficiency as an indication of acculturation, by time of immigration, and by income level. For example, Burr and Mutchler (1993) found that Asian-American women are more likely than their white counterparts to live in complex kin households. They also found that the income of Asian-American women influenced whether they lived alone or lived with relatives. The higher the income, the less likely the elderly were to live with relatives. Time of immigration was also found to impact whether Asian-American women lived alone or lived with relatives. Women who immigrated to the United States after the implementation of the 1965 Immigration Act were more likely to co-reside with relatives than were earlier immigrants or native-born Asian-Americans (Burr & Mutchler, 1993).

Researchers (Osaka & Liu, 1986) have also found that the caregiving and other social support needs of the Asian-American elderly are generally met by the extended family. This extended family is comprised of multiple generations typically living in close proximity to one another who adhere to the traditional cultural values of their group. Care and support to the elderly are therefore provided in the context of adhering to cultural values, as noted earlier, with multiple generations addressing social, economic, and health needs.

Native Americans

Children.   The great diversity among Native Americans and the paucity of data on their cultures limit understanding the cultural influences of social support given to children. As discussed earlier, however, several studies do provide some insight into the cultural context in which Native American families provide support to their children. Care and support of Native American children are provided within the cultural context of tribe and community. Traditional Native American cultures socialize their children within a large extended kin system that provides emotional, economic, protective, educational, cultural, and spiritual support. Needs of children are therefore met not only by their parents, but also by others in the kin system, such as uncles, aunts, and grandparents (John, 1988). Further, because children are highly valued by the kin network in Native American cultures, most social activities in the community include them. Also, adults seldom punish the children, but instead encourage them to develop self-control (Cross, 1986). Although limited information is available that can provide insight into the cultural meaning of this behavior, inferences can be drawn. For example, Native Americans encourage free expressions and interpretations that foster feelings of self-control. It may be assumed, then, that Native American children are supported by their kin networks to feel free, make connections with others on the basis of their own interpretations of relationships with others (relational kin), and understand their individual self-worth.

Elderly.   Care and support given to the Native American elderly are given within the cultural context of honoring the elderly. The cultural values of the importance of the group, a sense of individual autonomy, and lack of competition provide the foundation for supporting the elderly among Native American cultures. As a result, in traditional Native American communities, the elderly are given important tribal roles, are respected by younger generations, and receive and give intergenerational caregiving, and many (66%) live in extended family households (Manson & Callaway, 1990). Manson (1989) reported that although elderly Native Americans are in great need of care alternatives other than in-home care, strong cultural beliefs and distrust of governmental programs contribute to the underutilization of other services. Instead, Native American cultures typically provide support and care to the elderly using community-based and in-home services. This support and care is provided by the extended kin system, which includes spouses, adult children, grandchildren, and even fictive kin.

CONCLUSION

This discussion on social support in a cultural context shows that many similarities exist among ethnic groups regarding the structure, type, and configuration of their family social support. These similarities, however, are not influenced by similar sociohistorical experiences of different cultural groups. Instead, the specific history of a group helped shape the cultural context in which social support is given. For example, family social support in the African-American community is greatly shaped by slavery and discrimination. In the Asian community, time of immigration and who immigrated (male or female) influence social support.

The need to better understand social support among diverse groups is evidenced by the paucity of information available on the subject. Scholars need to question the relevance of information that permeates the literature on white middle class studies that are used as a basis for interpreting other groups. The limited number of studies that include, for example, Native American families fail to take advantage of a vast landscape of knowledge that could enrich most disciplines and areas of study. This limitation has many implications, especially for future empirical studies on diverse cultural groups, and it speaks to researchers acquiring knowledge about diverse populations and using relevant methods to study these groups (Dilworth-Anderson, Burton, & Johnson, 1993). To advance knowledge in the area of social support will therefore require the use of more culturally sensitive conceptual and theoretical views, diverse sampling strategies, and culturally sensitive instruments. Further, both qualitative and quantitative methods need to be developed in order to study the range of issues in understanding social support where diverse cultures are included.

Beyond issues of theory and methods are others that address interpretation and relevance of information. When researchers acquire more relevant and in-depth knowledge about diverse cultural groups, the likelihood of their using inappropriate and irrelevant norms or reference points to distinguish groups from one another will be diminished. Therefore, researchers will have to carefully question when differences occur, how they will be interpreted, and what value judgment will be used to evaluate "normal" behavior across groups.

Because the changing demographic profile of the American population shows a significant increase in the number of diverse groups, the issue of diversity has become an integral part of the American culture (U.S. Bureau of the Census, 1992). Research efforts in the future will therefore need to reflect this reality by providing information and knowledge that will address the different people of American society. As a result, the paucity of information at present available on social support among diverse cultural groups will no longer be an issue for future readers of studies on topics raised in this chapter.

REFERENCES

Antonucci, T. C. (1985). Personal characteristics, social networks and social behavior. In R. H. Binstock & E. Shanas (Eds.), *Handbook of aging and the social sciences*, 2nd ed. (pp. 94–128). New York: Van Nostrand Reinhold.

Burr, J. A., & Mutchler, J. E. (1993). Nativity, acculturation, and economic status: Explanations of Asian American living arrangements in later life. *Journal of Gerontology, 48(2)*, S55–S63.

Burton, L. M., & Dilworth-Anderson, P. (1991). The intergenerational family roles of aged black Americans. *Marriage and Family Review, 16(3/4)*, 311–330.

Cantor, M. H. (1979). The informal support system of New York's inner city elderly: Is ethnicity a factor? In D. Gefland & A. Kutzik (Eds.), *Ethnicity and aging: Theory, research, and policy* (pp. 67–73). New York: Springer.

Chatters, L. M., Taylor, R. J., & Jackson, J. S. (1985). Size and composition of the informal helper networks of elderly blacks. *Journal of Gerontology, 40*, 605–614.

Chatters, L. M., Taylor, R. J., & Jackson, J. S. (1986). Aged blacks' choices for an informal helper network. *Journal of Gerontology, 41*, 94–100.

Collins, P. H. (1991). *Black feminist thought: Knowledge, consciousness, and the politics of empowerment.* New York: Routledge.

Cross, T. L. (1986). Drawing on cultural tradition in Indian child welfare practice. *Social Casework, 67*, 283–289.

Depner, C. E., & Bray, J. H. (1993). *Nonresidential parenting: New vistas in family living.* Newbury Park, CA: Sage Publications.

Dilworth-Anderson, P. (1992). Extended kin networks in black families. *Generations, 17* 29–32.

Dilworth-Anderson, P., Burton, L., & Johnson, L. (1993). Reframing theories for understanding race, ethnicity, and families. In P. Boss, W. Doherty, R. LaRossa, W. Schumm, & S. Steinmetz (Eds.), *Sourcebook of family theories and methods: A contextual approach* (pp. 627–646). New York: Plenum Press.

Dilworth-Anderson, P., & Rhoden, L. (in press). A sociohistorical view of African-American women and their caregiving roles. In N. Burgass & E. Brown (Eds.), *African American women: An ecological perspective.* Hamden, CT: Garland.

Escott, P. D. (1979). *Slavery remembered: A record of twentieth-century slave narratives.* Chapel Hill: University of North Carolina Press.

Geertz, C. (1973). *The interpretation of cultures.* New York: Basic Books.

Golding, J. M., & Baezconde-Garbanati, L. A. (1990). Ethnicity, culture, and social resources. *American Journal of Community Psychology, 18(3)*, 465–486.

Gutierrez, J., & Sameroff, A. (1990). Determinants of complexity in Mexican-American and Anglo-American mothers' conceptions of child development. *Child Development, 61*, 384–394.

Gutman, H. (1976). *The black family in slavery and freedom: 1750–1925*. New York: Pantheon Books.

Hays, W., & Mindel, C. H. (1973). Extended kinship relations in black and white families. *Journal of Marriage and the Family, 35*, 51–56.

Jackson, J. J. (1972). Comparative life styles of family and friends relationships among older black women. *Family Coordinator, 3*, 477–485.

Jaynes, G. D., & Williams, R. M. (1989). *A common destiny*. Washington, DC: National Academy Press.

John, R. (1988). The Native American family. In C. H. Mindel, R. W. Habenstein, & R. Wright (Eds.), *Ethnic families in America: Patterns and variations* (pp. 325–363). New York: Elsevier.

Julian, T. W., McKenry, P. C., & McKelvey, M. W. (1994). Cultural variation in parenting: Perceptions of Caucasian, African-American, Hispanic, and Asian-American parents. *Family Relations, 43*, 30–37.

Keefe, S. (1984). Real and ideal extended familism among Mexican Americans and Anglo Americans: On the meaning of "close" family ties. *Human Organization, 43*, 65–70.

Keefe S. E., Padilla, A. M., & Carlos, M. L. (1979). The Mexican-American extended family as an emotional support system. *Human Organization, 38*, 144–152.

Keith, J. (1990). Age in social and cultural context: Anthropological perspectives. In R. H. Binstock & L. K. George (Eds.), *Handbook of aging and the social sciences*, 3rd ed. (pp. 91–111). San Diego: Academic Press.

Kekahbah, J., & Wood, R. (1980). *Life cycle of the American Indian family*. Norman, OK: American Indian/Alaska Native Nurses Association.

Lincoln, C. E., & Mamiya, L. H. (1991). *The black church in the African American experience*. Durham, NC: Duke University Press.

Manson, S. M. (1989). Long-term care in American Indian communities: Issues for planning and research. *Gerontologist, 29*, 38–44.

Manson, S. M., & Callaway, D. G. (1990). Health and aging among American Indians. In U.S. Department of Health and Human Services, *Minority aging*. Washington, DC: U.S. Public Health Service.

Mutran, E. (1985). Intergenerational family support among blacks and whites: Response to culture or to socioeconomic differences. *Journal of Gerontology, 40*, 382–389.

Osaka, M. M., & Liu, W. T. (1986). Intergenerational relations and the aged among Japanese Americans. *Research on Aging, 8*, 128–155.

Salgado de Snyder, V. M. (1986). Mexican immigrant women: The relationship of ethnic loyalty, self-esteem, social support, and satisfaction to acculturative stress and depressive symptomatology. Unpublished doctoral dissertation. Los Angeles: University of California, School of Social Welfare.

Seelbach, W. (1978). Correlates of aged parents' filial responsibility expectations and realizations. *Family Coordinator, 27(4)*, 341–350.

Serafica, F. C. (1990). Counseling Asian-American parents: A cultural developmental approach. In F. C. Serafica, A. I. Schwebel, R. K. Russell, P. D. Isaacs, & L. James-Myers (Eds.), *Mental health of ethnic minorities* (pp. 222–244). New York: Praeger.

Silverstein, M., & Waite, L. (1993). Are blacks more likely than whites to receive and provide social support in middle and old age? Yes, no, and maybe so. *Journal of Gerontology, 48*, S212–S222.

Snipp, C. M. (1989). *American Indians: The first of this land*. New York: Sage.

Taylor, R. J. (1986). Receipt of support from family among black Americans: Demographic and familial differences. *Journal of Marriage and the Family, 48*, 67–77.

Taylor, R. J., & Chatters, L. M. (1991). Extended family networks of older black adults. *Journal of Gerontology, 46*, S210–S217.

U.S. Bureau of the Census (1992). *Statistical abstract of the United States*, 112th ed. Washington, DC: U.S. Government Printing Office.

Vega, W. A. (1990). Hispanic families in the 1980s: A decade of research. *Journal of Marriage and the Family, 52*, 1015–1024.

Vega, W. A., & Kolody, B. (1985). The meaning of social support and the mediation of stress across cultures. In W. A. Vega & M. R. Miranda (Eds.), *Stress and Hispanic mental health: Relating research to service delivery* (pp. 48–75). Rockville, MD: U.S. Department of Health and Human Services.

Watson, M. F., & Protinsky, H. O. (1988). Black adolescent identity development: Effects of perceived family structure. *Family Relations, 37,* 288–292.

Wilson, M. N. (1989). Child development in the context of the black extended family. *American Psychologist, 44,* 380–385.

Yee, B. W. (1990). Gender and family issues in minority groups. *Generations, 14(3),* 39–42.

Zinn, M. B., & Eitzen, D. S. (1993). *Diversity in families,* 3rd ed. New York: Harper.

II

The Role of Social Support
in Family Relationships

5

The Neglected Links between Marital Support and Marital Satisfaction

LINDA K. ACITELLI

There is an assumption, largely unexamined, that spouses' assessments of marital satisfaction often involve considerations of social support from their partners (Fincham & Bradbury, 1990). If this assumption is true, then spouses' perceptions of social support available from their partners should be related to their marital satisfaction. Surprisingly, there have been very few studies that test this prediction. Thus, as the title of this chapter suggests, the link between marital support and satisfaction has been neglected. Furthermore, marital status is sometimes used as an index of social support without assessing the extent to which the partners in the relationship perceive the marriage to be supportive (for discussions of the pitfalls of this practice see Coyne & De Longis, 1986; Fincham & Bradbury, 1990; Leatham & Duck, 1990). The literature on marriage has "virtually ignored the role of the support that spouses get from and give to each other in determining marital outcomes" (Julien & Markman, 1991, p. 549). The social support literature has also virtually ignored the link between social support and marital outcomes (McGonagle, Kessler, & Schilling, 1992). Thus, two areas of research (marriage and social support) that have become natural topics for the study of close relationships have hardly begun to tap their potential to inform one another (Acitelli & Antonucci, 1994).

In attempting to search for reasons that researchers have not forged stronger links between social support and marital outcomes, three interlocking propositions emerge. First, research on social support needs to be expanded from

LINDA K. ACITELLI • Department of Psychology, University of Houston, Houston, Texas 77204-5341.

Handbook of Social Support and the Family, edited by Gregory R. Pierce, Barbara R. Sarason, and Irwin G. Sarason. Plenum Press, New York, 1996.

assessments of global support to include more studies of relationship-specific support (Pierce, Sarason, & Sarason, 1991; Sarason, Sarason, & Pierce, 1994). Second, both providers and recipients of support should be included in study designs (Kessler, 1991). Third, although there are plenty of studies linking social support to individual outcomes, more studies are needed that link support in relationships to relationship outcomes (Acitelli & Antonucci, 1994; Julien & Markman, 1991; McGonagle et al., 1992). The issues involved in addressing these recommendations are both methodological and theoretical and are not easily categorized as one or the other. Methods embody unstated "theories," and the choice of method is always a theory-based decision (Acitelli & Duck, 1987; Duck, 1977; Duck & Sants, 1983). By addressing these recommendations, this chapter will demonstrate the heuristic value of studying social support within a specific relationship, marriage, collecting data from both providers and recipients of support (husbands and wives), and linking marital support to marital outcomes. Marriage deserves particular attention because it is probably the most common context within which adults find a special relationship that is so vital to psychological and physical well-being. In addition, age, length of relationship, and gender of respondents are additional variables that may moderate the links between support and satisfaction and should not be overlooked in research designs and analyses.

RELATIONSHIP-SPECIFIC SOCIAL SUPPORT

Pierce et al. (1991) conclude that past research demonstrating the connection between global support and personal adjustment has not given sufficient attention to the contribution of relationship-specific support. Their study demonstrated that perceptions of available support from a specific relationship are distinct from perceptions of available support in general. In a review of their studies designed to examine this proposition, Sarason et al. (1994) further demonstrate that relationship-specific support makes a significant independent contribution to the prediction of adjustment, over and above the more global perceptions of support. They recommend that future research on social support take into account possible environmental or situational variables as well as individual difference variables. A fitting way to take these variables into account is to examine the relationship between the provider and the recipient of support. The relationship itself can be construed as providing the context within which support occurs. Whether behavior is seen as supportive depends not only on the characteristics of the person proffering the support (Pierce et al., 1991), but also on the relationship the provider has with the recipient (Sarason et al., 1994). For example, behaviors that are seen to be supportive when provided by teacher to student may not be seen as supportive when provided by husband to wife. Although researchers do need to go beyond the support–outcome correlations as Sarason et al. (1994) suggest, there are still some missing support–outcome links to be forged within the relationship sphere. Studies rarely investigate the link between relationship-based social support and relationship satisfaction as an outcome. This chapter will highlight studies that do so and will point to the need for more refined analyses and designs in this area.

INCLUDING BOTH RECIPIENTS AND PROVIDERS IN STUDIES OF SOCIAL SUPPORT

In addition to considerations of relationship-specific support, researchers need to consider including both partners within the specific relationship when designing studies of social support. Often, researchers study relationships by studying just one partner. Thus, some investigations of reciprocity are really assessing individuals' perceptions of reciprocity. While investigations of social support given to and provided by individuals are valuable, they are, by design, one-sided. This kind of approach is acceptable if it is acknowledged that the topic of investigation is individuals' perceptions of interactions or relationships. But if the focus of study is to compare partners on various dimensions, to see how similar their views are, or how reciprocal their behaviors are, then the research design must include both partners in a relationship. Several scholars have noted the importance of consensus within relationships. Duck (1994) discusses partners developing a shared relational reality (Berger & Kellner, 1964) as the most important process in relationship adjustment and satisfaction. Deal, Wampler, and Halverson (1992) underscore Duck's point by arguing that similarity in perceptions about the relationship between spouses is a crucial dimension of the family system, and it underlies such concepts as "agreement," "consensus," "understanding," and "shared meaning." The studies of Acitelli (1988, 1992, 1993) of relationship awareness also recognize the crucial role that partner's perceptions of their relationship can play in both individual and relationship outcomes. The advantages of including both partners of a relationship in social support research are also emphasized by Kessler (1991) in his recommendation that more studies include both providers and recipients of support. Further-more, Kenny (1988a) emphasizes the need for dyadic designs in the study of interpersonal perception.

Studies of Interpersonal Perception

The focus on social support within marriage can easily fit into the theoretical framework of studies on interpersonal perception in close relationships. Several studies emphasize the importance of viewing the level of support as a subjective perception of the individual (e.g., Depner & Ingersoll-Dayton, 1985; Sarason, Levine, Basham, & Sarason, 1983). Researchers of interpersonal perception are often interested in multiple perspectives on the same phenomena (Kenny, 1988a). Studying interpersonal perception in married couples, investigators typically use data based on spouses' rating of self and partner on various behaviors, attitudes, feelings, or characteristics. The literature on interpersonal perception between intimates can provide bases for hypothesizing about the congruence of perceptions of support between spouses (see Sillars, 1985).

Earlier studies of interpersonal perception in marriage have compared *perceived reciprocity* to *actual reciprocity*. These perceptual congruence variables (Acitelli, Douvan, & Veroff, 1993) have been variously labeled as perceived and actual reciprocity, perceived and actual similarity, or assumed and actual agreement (Kenny, 1988a). As is the case with many concepts, researchers have not settled on a consistent set of terms. However, the choice of term often depends on the perceptual referent. For example, if partners are rating each other's characteristics, researchers may say they are deriving a measure of similarity between partners. But if they are rating each other's attitudes about a particular issue, then researchers may say they are calculating a measure of agreement. (For a more detailed discussion of the meaning of similarity, see Duck [1994].) Because the focus is on giving and receiving social support, the terms "perceived reciprocity" and "actual reciprocity" will be used here.

In this chapter, perceived reciprocity refers to one partner's view that the social supports given to his or her spouse are reciprocated in kind. Actual reciprocity refers to a comparison of both spouses' separate reports. While assessment of perceived reciprocity involves a comparison of self-perceptions and other perceptions, assessment of actual reciprocity involves a comparison of two separate self-perceptions.

Studies of interpersonal perceptions between spouses (both newlywed and diverse couple groups) have consistently shown that estimates of perceived reciprocity based on one spouse's report are greater than those of actual reciprocity based on both partner's separate reports (Acitelli & Antonucci, 1994; Acitelli et al., 1993; Dymond, 1954; Levinger & Breedlove, 1966). These findings are consistent with the literature on assumed similarity in marriage (e.g., Acitelli et al., 1993; Levinger & Breedlove, 1966) and with previous literature on the "false consensus effect" (Ross, Greene, & House, 1977), whereby persons assume that others are more like themselves than the others report themselves to be. One explanation offered for the false consensus effect is that people overestimate commonness because they make judgments about themselves and others by identifying a normative standard (Fenigstein & Abrams, 1993; Marks & Duval, 1991). The spouses in these studies may have been relying on equity norms or the common belief that marriage involves give and take. Therefore, they may have perceived more reciprocity than a comparison of spouses' separate reports would indicate. Results also support the contention of Sillars (1985) that people use themselves as the basis for making judgments about others more than they actually use the others (or "targets" of perception). Similarly, studies of social cognition show that when judging others, people often rely on their own self-schemata (Higgins, King, & Mavin, 1982; Markus, Smith, & Moreland, 1985).

These studies highlight the importance of having both partners in a relationship in the same study. The investigators of interpersonal perception in marriage would not have been able to compare perceived and actual reciprocity had their studies been designed to include individuals without their partners. Furthermore, if studies are based on individuals' perceptions of their relationships, researchers' perspectives on reciprocity within relationships might be quite discrepant from the perspective that could be gained by studying both partners. The question of which perspective is more "accurate" is an issue that goes well beyond the scope of this chapter, but suffice it to say that the more observations one can obtain of the same experience in a relationship, the more knowledge we have of that relationship. For example, a relationship that outsiders agreed is reciprocal may be a different relationship from one that is adjudged reciprocal only by the insiders (or by just one insider). Instead of viewing discrepancies between perspectives as sources of error, Duck and Sants (1983) believe that different perspectives provide useful information about the nature of the relationship. Therefore, the issue is not that there are discrepancies, but how such discrepant data can be used to develop theoretical formulations (Olson, 1977).

Studies of Marital Support with Data from Both Spouses

Three studies (Bolger, Kessler, & Schilling, 1990; Cutrona & Suhr, 1994; Acitelli & Antonucci, 1994) are briefly discussed here to demonstrate the heuristic value of utilizing both partners of the marital pair. In the first, a study of married couples (Bolger et al., 1990) provides an excellent example of how discrepancies between spouses can be used to develop theoretical formulations. In this study, married couples completed a short daily diary questionnaire each day. From these diaries, the investigators discovered that nearly one third of the supports given by one spouse were not reported as being received by the other. They called such supportive actions "invisible support" and noted that husbands reported a smaller percentage of the supportive behaviors described by their spouses than wives did. The researchers offer the example of a wife reporting that she kept the children away from her husband when he had a stressful day at work. Her husband, on the other hand, would report a relaxing evening at home, not how his wife gave him such support. Bolger et al. (1990) found that there was a significant association between these invisible supports and adjustments to stress. If both support providers and recipients were not included in the study design, such a finding and the resultant theoretical formulation would not have been possible.

Similar results were obtained in an observational study of married couples' interactions (Cutrona & Suhr, 1994). The investigators had couples interact with each other twice, each partner taking a turn being the stress discloser and the support provider. Results showed that depression and marital satisfaction predicted men's ratings of their wives' supportiveness, whereas the extent to which wives perceived their husbands as supportive in the earlier interaction was related to the number of support behaviors received from their husbands. This finding is consistent with the idea that wives' supportive behaviors do not have a "visible" effect on men. In this study, the men's perceptions of support depended on how they felt, not on what the wives did. Such a pattern of results would obviously not have been possible without the inclusion of both partners in the study design.

Furthermore, without both partners, Acitelli and Antonucci (1994) would not have discovered why actual reciprocity of support was the only variable (among giving, receiving, actual reciprocity, and perceived reciprocity) in their study relating to husbands' well-being. In their study of older married couples, all the predictor variables were significantly related to wives' well-being. By comparing the husbands' and wives' separate reports, Acitelli and Antonucci (1994) sought explanations for the link between husbands' well-being and actual reciprocity. They discovered that when analyzing both partners' receiving separately, it was wives' receiving (not husbands') that was driving the association. It was then surmised that the link was due to the correlation between husbands' and wives' well-being. When wives' well-being was entered into the regression equation (along with wives' receiving and husbands' receiving) predicting husbands' well-being, both husbands' and wives' receiving were no longer significant. Thus, it was concluded that the relationship between actual reciprocity and husbands' well-being was a methodological artifact. (Or, again, one might make a more theoretical interpretation by surmising that the variable predicting a husband's well-being is not the support the wife provides, but the extent to which she is happy.) None of these analyses would have been possible had the study been designed to assess the perceptions of individual respondents only. Such studies illustrate how researchers can expand their knowledge of relationships by including both partners in the design of the study. Thus, it is recommended not only that studies of social support be relationship-specific, but also that they include both partners within the particular relationship to be studied.

Analytical Considerations

Several complex problems arise when analyzing data from both partners in a dyad. What some researchers may consider error is grist for the theoretical mill to others. Researchers employing structural equation modeling have sometimes used both partners' perceptions as separate measures of the same construct, thereby focusing on shared variance. The assumption in these models is that discrepancies between partners are sources of error. One might argue that, in the strictest of methodological senses, they are right. Many tests of reliability are based on such assumptions. But for the most part, formal reliability checks are conducted with people who are trained to observe the data from within very specific sets of guidelines that practically force them to see the data in similar ways. Consider that husbands and wives are not trained to view their behaviors and attitudes in similar ways. The extent to which they do is an interesting research question in its own right. If similarity and shared reality are crucial dimensions to relationship quality (e.g., Deal et al., 1992; Duck, 1994), then the meaning of discrepancies between partners is a very important psychological and sociological problem and deserves more attention than the residual status it is often accorded (see also Duck & Sants, 1983; Olson, 1977).

Similarly, researchers must also give special consideration to what they consider artifactual. Measuring similarities (or discrepancies) between partners is a more complex procedure than it appears on the surface and often involves controlling for the artifactual inflation of similarity scores. Difficult questions need to be addressed. Many of these questions have been discussed at length by Kenny and Acitelli (1994), so they will be considered only briefly here. For example, are partners similar to one another in their views of their relationship because they are similar to all others in that regard? That is, do people have stereotypical ways of viewing relationships that can inflate the degree of similarity assessed in a research study? Kenny and Acitelli (1994) have developed a method for removing the variance in similarity that is due to cultural consistencies (the *stereotype effect*, or consistent ways of responding within the study sample). With this method, researchers can determine the extent to which partners are uniquely similar.

In addition, another important question is, once a researcher derives the measure of unique similarity, does similarity vary between couples? That is, are some couples more similar than others? Kenny and Acitelli (1994) have also discussed ways of determining whether there is significant variance in the degree of similarity across couples. Interestingly, in their study, they found married couples varied in the extent to which they similarly endorsed the stereotype, but not in the extent to which they were uniquely similar. They also found that partner similarity in the extent to which both spouses responded as typical husbands did was associated with marital satisfaction. Thus, the authors concluded that a stereotype effect may be a psychologically meaningful phenomenon rather than simply a statistical artifact (Kenny & Acitelli, 1994). Issues of what constitutes error and artifact are only two of the several analytical considerations that arise when studying dyads. See Kenny (1988b) for a more complete discussion of the statistical analysis of dyadic data.

So far, it has been recommended that more studies of social support be relationship-specific and that such studies include both partners within the particular relationship to be studied. Let us now turn from how social support in relationships should be studied to more substantive issues of what should be studied. Although the social support–individual outcome link has been researched extensively, there is one link that has been neglected: the social support–relationship outcome connection.

LINKING MARITAL SUPPORT TO MARITAL OUTCOMES

Very few studies focus on the link between marital support and marital satisfaction (Julien & Markman, 1991; McGonagle et al., 1992). Instead of assuming that marriages are supportive, researchers need to find out whether spouses perceive their partners as supportive and whether such perceptions relate to marital satisfaction. Again, both members of a couple are needed for such research. Studies in the social support literature that assess the supports given and received within marriage using both spouses of the marital pair as respondents are few in number, but growing (e.g., Cutrona & Suhr, 1994; Cutrona, Suhr, & MacFarlane, 1990; Julien & Markman, 1991; McGonagle et al., 1992; Vinokur & Vinokur-Kaplan, 1990). Most of the social support literature that does look at the marital relationship as a potential source of support utilizes married individuals as respondents without linking them to their spouses in the same study. Thus, for the most part, the literature provides information on individual respondents' views of the supportiveness of their spouses and individual respondents' perceptions of the reciprocity of supportive behaviors within marriage (e.g., Antonucci & Akiyama, 1987; Billings & Moos, 1982; Depner & Ingersoll-Dayton, 1985; Ingersoll-Dayton & Antonucci, 1988; Pina & Bengtson, 1993; Vanfossen, 1981; Vinokur & van Ryn, 1993). There are very few analyses that incorporate how the spouses of these respondents view the supports given and received within their marriages, nor do we know how congruent the partners' perceptions of support are. Moreover, very few studies assess the link between the degree of congruence of social support perceptions and marital outcomes (Acitelli & Antonucci, 1994).

In addition, age, length of relationship, and gender must also be considered as contextual variables that can affect the meaning of perceptions and behaviors in marriage. Much of the literature on marital relationships involves the study of relatively young couples even though many marriages last for decades (Levenson, Carstensen, & Gottman, 1993). As the population becomes older, the number of older married couples will increase (Weishaus & Field, 1988). Thus, research on older couples has the potential to become increasingly relevant with time. Moreover, as people age, they purposefully narrow their social environments and place an increasing importance on significant relationships (Carstensen, 1992). Because aging is associated with changes in role obligations, financial status, and health status, older couples may need to make adjustments to such transitions within their marriages (Depner & Ingersoll Dayton, 1985). These life changes coupled with narrower social environment make the study of social support within older marriages increasingly important. This section, while it does not focus exclusively on older couples, highlights studies that demonstrate the fruitfulness of examining the ages of the couples as an influential variable. As will be seen, however, it is difficult to determine the separate effects of the individuals' ages and the length of the relationship.

Moreover, researchers must not lose sight of the important insight that men and women may experience marriage differently (Bernard, 1972). As women, more than men, derive a sense of well-being from the emotional qualities of marriage (Gove, Hughes, & Style, 1983; Mills, Grasmick, Morgan, & Wenk, 1992), husbands and wives may have different conceptions of marital satisfaction and the social support exchanged within their marriages. In addition to different conceptualizations, the relations between marital satisfaction, well-being, and social support may also be different for husbands and wives. Thus, studies will be highlighted that indicate that gender also contributes to the different meanings spouses may impart to social support and marital satisfaction.

Gender Differences in the Link between Social Support and Satisfaction

Lakey and Cassady (1990) and Sarason, Sarason, and Shearin (1986) have demonstrated that social support and satisfaction with support are individual difference variables that are relatively stable over time. Other researchers (Acitelli & Antonucci, 1994; Antonucci & Akiyama, 1987; Barbee et al., 1993; Sarason et al., 1986) have also shown that variables associated with support are different for men and women, suggesting the hypothesis that the relationship between social support and marital satisfaction is different for husbands and wives. With regard to reciprocity, Sprecher (1992) found that women expect to be more distressed in inequitable exchanges than men expect to be. Thus, one would expect that wives more than husbands would be affected by the extent to which they experience the availability of social support as reciprocal.

Several studies have shown that women rate supportive behaviors as more satisfying than men rate them to be (Barbee et al., 1993). More specifically, in their study of young and midlife couples, Julien and Markman (1991) have shown that the link between wives reporting support from husbands and wives' marital satisfaction is stronger than the link between husbands reporting support from wives and husbands' satisfaction. This finding relates to several other studies (Acitelli, 1992; Lamke, 1989; Murstein & Williams, 1985; Noller, 1980; White, Speisman, Jackson, Bartis, & Costos, 1986) demonstrating that husbands' interpersonal skills (e.g., relationship awareness, expressiveness, intimacy maturity) are more predictive of relationship and life satisfaction than are the same skills in wives. Similarly, Ferraro and Wan (1986), studying older married couples, have shown that the husband, more than the wife, shapes the trajectory of marital well-being.

A Study of Older Married Couples.   One study by Acitelli and Antonucci (1994) exemplifies the need for considering both age and gender when studying the link between marital support and satisfaction. This study examines data from both spouses in older marital pairs. The data include ratings of self and partner on whether or not social support is available to and from the other. In their study, social support is conceptualized as *perceived* support or *available* support—that is, the cognitions about, respectively, whether or not support is available when one needs it and whether or not one is available to provide support to the spouse when he or she needs it. This study does not focus on support *received* or actual interpersonal exchanges of support (House, 1981; Kahn & Antonucci, 1980; for a review that clarifies the distinction between received and available support, see Dunkel-Schetter & Bennett, 1990). As Kessler (1991) has noted, the relationship between perceived support and adjustment to stress is more powerful and more consistent than the relationship between actual support and adjustment to stress.

Data for this study were taken from a larger study, Social Networks in Adult Life, conducted by the Survey Research Center at the University of Michigan (Kahn & Antonucci, 1984). Respondents were 69 married couples who were drawn from a larger national representative sample of individuals 50 years of age and older. Their average age was 74 and length of marriage was 43 years. (Further details of the larger sample can be found in Antonucci and Akiyama [1987], and see Acitelli and Antonucci [1994] for further details of the subset of this sample used in this study.) During interviews, spouses were asked to indicate to whom in their social network they provided various kinds of social support and from whom in their network they received these same supports. Respondents were asked to list people who were close and important to them on a personal network diagram consisting of a set of three concentric circles with another smaller circle in the center in which the word *you* was written. They were then asked to choose from this list and indicate to whom and from whom they gave and received six different types of social support (i.e., confiding, reassurance, respect, care when ill, talk when upset, and talk about health).

The number of times the respondent identified his or her spouse as the recipient or provider of each of these six types of support was noted. By summing the number of times respondents identified their spouses on these items, aggregate scores of both giving and receiving social support were derived. The researchers also calculated the level of reciprocity reported by one spouse (perceived reciprocity) and a reciprocity score based on both spouses' separate reports (actual reciprocity). The indices of well-being were responses to questions on positive and negative affect, health, and marital and life satisfaction.

Separate analyses were conducted using general well-being and marital satisfaction as dependent variables. Because results were virtually identical, a global measure of well-being was created and used to simplify the final presentation of the results (Acitelli & Antonucci, 1994). In addition, analyses were performed separately for men and women. Results clearly demonstrated that perceptions of giving, receiving, and reciprocity were most consistently related to wives' well-being than to husbands' well-being. These findings hold up when controlling for length of relationship, age, and health of respondent (Acitelli & Antonucci, 1994).

Possible Reasons for the Gender Difference. As noted, the findings from the study of older couples suggest that perceptions of social support within marriage are more important to the marital satisfaction and general well-being of wives than of husbands. Such results were interpreted both methodologically and theoretically (Acitelli & Antonucci, 1994). Perhaps the measures of social support are assessing behaviors that women, but not men, perceive as supportive. Note that most of the social support items are indicative of partners talking intimately to each other, a behavior that is often shown to vary by gender. For example, data from a national survey analyzed by Veroff, Douvan, and Kulka (1981) show that women more than men wished their spouses talked more about their thoughts and feelings. While women may feel supported by such talk from their husbands, perhaps men feel socially supported in other ways not covered by these items.

Other work has revealed findings that are consistent with this interpretation (Vanfossen, 1981). In relating social support to depression in a probability sample of urban adults, Vanfossen (1981) found that affirmation negatively predicted depression for both men and women, while intimacy was a better negative predictor of depression for men than for women. While this finding seems inconsistent with the gender difference found in the study of older couples above (Acitelli & Antonucci, 1994), a closer inspection of both measures of social support used in the Vanfossen (1981) study reveals that the aspects of social support being assessed are different from those assessed in the Acitelli and Antonucci (1994) study. Vanfossen (1981) measures affirmation (being valued and appreciated for being oneself) and intimacy (talk, sex, and affection), while Acitelli and Antonucci (1994) primarily assess emotional support through talk. Although being able to talk to one's spouse is one aspect of intimacy, it is by no means the primary domain of the intimacy measure used in the Vanfossen study. Sexual and affectionate behaviors are quite distinct from talking. Thus, Vanfossen's finding that intimacy was a better negative predictor of depression for men than for women may underscore the idea that men and women respond differently to different types of social support.

Other factors may also contribute to the lack of connection between social support in older couples and men's well-being. Barbee et al. (1993) suggest that sex-role expectations may make males more hesitant to acknowledge the extent to which they value their wives' emotional support. Furthermore, the support received from wives may match husbands' expectations of marriage so well that it has no effect on husbands' marital satisfaction. Other scholars (Hochschild, 1983; Thompson, 1993) suggest that when wives' actions confirm their husbands' sex-role expectations, there may be little recognition of those actions. In other words, it is not that these older husbands do not need support from their wives, but rather than they take such support for granted. Furthermore, Bolger et al. (1990) present concrete evidence that husbands do not recognize the extent to which their wives provide them with support.

Having been socialized to expect socially supportive, nurturant behaviors from their wives, husbands may not appreciate that their wives are performing their expected role. Therefore, having a supportive wife is expected, more the norm than the exception, and may not affect husbands' evaluation of the marriage. Indeed, in the larger data set from which the sample was taken, a higher proportion of men than of women reported giving and receiving more support to and from their spouses, whereas women reported giving and receiving more support to and from their children and friends (Antonucci & Akiyama, 1987; Depner & Ingersoll-Dayton, 1985). These findings lend credence to the idea that perceptions of the availability of social support within marriage are more normative (i.e., typical and expected) for men than for women.

Another possible explanation is that men are supported more by factors outside marriage than by factors within marriage. Billings and Moos (1982) show that the relations between work support and personal functioning are stronger among men than among women. Julien and Markman (1991) showed that socially supportive behaviors of friends rather than of wives were related to fewer symptoms in men. Gilford (1986) states that "men's happiness may be less dependent than women's upon events within marriage" (p. 17). Men may thus require less of marriage to be happy. Similarly, other research indicates that marital status is a more important predictor of men's well-being than the emotional quality of the marriage (Gove et al., 1983; Hess & Soldo, 1985).

At first glance, the conclusion that *being married* is more important to men than to women but that the *perceived quality of the marital relationship* is more important to women than to men may seem contradictory. This conclusion makes sense, however, in light of the robust findings that women are socialized to be more attuned to their social environments than men are (e.g., Antonucci, 1994; Belle, 1987) and that women think more about relationships once they are formed than men do (Acitelli, 1992; Burnett, 1987; Martin, 1991). While men are more likely to think about a relationship in its formative stages, women are more likely to think about the internal dynamics of the relationship after the relationship has been established (Burnett, 1987).

Furthermore, Scott, Fuhrman, and Wyer (1991) have shown that women are more likely than men to store conversations with partners as relationship memories, while men are more likely to store them in terms of the issue discussed. Presumably, then, there are more ongoing interactions for women that have implications for the relationship. Perhaps the more interactions that have implications for the relationship, the higher the probability that perceived interactions with a spouse can influence one's satisfaction with the relationship. For example, when a husband provides comfort to his wife when she is upset about a conflict with a friend, the husband's providing comfort may stimulate different thoughts in each partner. While the husband may think that it is unfortunate that his wife is having trouble with her friend, the wife may think that she is pleased that her husband shows that he cares about her. Thus, Acitelli and Antonucci (1994) speculate that men may not make as strong a connection between perceived support and relationship satisfaction as women do. As social support is more salient to women than to men (Sarason et al., 1986), it is reasonable to suggest that social support in marriage would affect women's more than men's satisfaction with relationships. Likewise, in a study of young married couples, Acitelli (1992) found that the more the husband attends to the marital relationship, the happier a wife is with regard to both her marriage and her life.

Murstein and Williams (1985) interpret such a pattern of results as indicative that men have more power in the relationship. More specifically, this pattern may also indicate that husbands' behaviors are especially salient to wives' well-being especially when husbands take on a more "wifely" role. When a husband exhibits caring and nurturant behaviors, his wife is relieved of some of the relationship work (Fishman, 1978) that is expected of her and is more satisfied with her relationship and her life when she sees that her husband cares about the relationship (Acitelli, 1992). In a related vein, Ward (1993) demonstrates that both husbands' and wives' "perceived unfairness in household labor" reduced marital happiness for wives, but not for husbands. Ward draws a parallel between household labor and social support, adding that both matter more to wives. Perhaps it is because emotionally supportive behaviors matter more to wives that wives' marital and life satisfaction are so linked to them.

A recent article by Levenson et al. (1993) makes a similar point by stating that wives' physical and psychological health are more closely tied to marital satisfaction than are husbands'. They explain that when a marriage is in trouble, wives take on the emotional work of repairing it while husbands are more likely to withdraw. This withdrawal not only buffers husbands from the unhealthy consequences, but also adds to the wives' emotional burden. Thus, when marriages are distressed, wives' health suffers (see also Gove & Hughes, 1979; Kessler & McLeod, 1985).

Comparable Longitudinal Studies.   While the findings of Acitelli and Antonucci (1994) supported their prediction regarding differences between husbands and wives, the data did not permit the identification of a definite causal direction. It is possible that the causal direction is reversed such that more satisfied wives are more likely to perceive that they are giving and receiving more social support to and from their husbands than less satisfied wives are. However, there are data from longitudinal studies (Billings & Moos, 1982; McGonagle et al., 1992) that suggest that social support affects marital outcomes and well-being, and more specifically predict that wives' (and not husbands') perceptions of spouse support affects marital quality and general well-being. These studies will be summarized below.

In a longitudinal study of 778 married couples (mean age = 42), McGonagle et al. (1992) showed that wives' perceptions of husband support predicted wives' marital quality 3 years later. This relationship was not found for husbands' perceptions of wives' support. The investigators assessed marital quality by determining the frequency of marital disagreements. Perceived support from friends, relatives, and spouse was assessed. In the cross-sectional analysis, the researchers found spouse support to be the most powerful type of support predicting marital disagreement frequency for both spouses. Over time, however, the results showed that wives' perceptions of husbands' support predicted fewer disagreements for wives, while husbands' perceptions of wives' support did not predict disagreement frequency for husbands. This finding suggests that it may take some time for gender differences to emerge, indicating, perhaps, that these differences may be more apparent in long-term marriages.

Similar results are found in a longitudinal study of social support and personal functioning (Billings & Moos, 1982). The researchers demonstrated that in a representative community sample of adults, the cross-sectional relationships between family support and functioning were stronger among women than among men, and in the longitudinal analyses, there was significant covariation in family support and personal functioning only among women. In addition, other longitudinal studies (Berkman, Leo-Summers, & Horwitz, 1992; Sherbourne & Hays, 1990) show that individuals' mental and physical health are influenced by perceptions of social support.

Previous research (Lakey & Cassady, 1990) also shows that perceived support is not explained as a "mere reflection of negative affectivity" (p. 341). In a study conceptualizing perceived social support as a cognitive personality variable (Lakey & Cassady, 1990), the results of a factor analysis showed that perceived support did not load highly on the Negative Affectivity factor. Thus, even though causal direction in the Acitelli and Antonucci (1994) study cannot be specified with certainty, there is some literature that suggests that perceived support influences well-being and that it is not driven primarily by negative affect.

Age, Length of Relationship, and Social Support

Another limitation of the Acitelli and Antonucci (1994) study is that there was no younger sample with which to compare the results. There are very few studies on older marriages and few studies linking social support in marriage to marital outcomes. Thus, the investigators cannot say with complete certainty whether their findings are unique to older couples or can be generalized to all couples in the United States.

This section will present results from another study (Acitelli, 1994) as a way to compare an older sample with a younger sample using almost identical variables and analyses. In order to clearly distinguish one study from the other, the Acitelli and Antonucci (1994) study will be referred to as the "older couples' study," and the Acitelli (1994) study as the "younger couples' study."

The younger couples' study (Acitelli, 1994) was designed to examine the links between social support, relationship satisfaction, and well-being. It also highlights some interesting gender differences and may provide some guidance for future analyses. The data were taken from the first wave of a longitudinal study with myself as principal investigator and conducted by the Survey Research Center of the Institute for Social Research. The sample is an area probability sample of 238 unmarried and married couples from the metropolitan Detroit area. In this sample, 90 couples are unmarried, have never been married, and have been together 6 months or longer. The married couples (N=148) are in their first marriage and have been married up to 25 years. Their ages range from 18 to 60, and their average age is 33 years. The questions asked of these couples were very similar to those in the older couples' study (Acitelli & Antonucci, 1994). Instead of concentric circles, however, respondents were provided with a list of people to choose from. Thus, when they were asked, "Who reassures you when you are feeling uncertain about something?," respondents could choose as many as applied from the following list: partner/spouse, children, parents, other relatives, friends/coworkers, professionals, or no one. A measure was constructed that indicates the total number of times the respondents mention their partners as providers of four types of support (i.e., confiding, reassurance, care when ill, and talk when upset).

The sample is a much younger sample than the one used in the older couples' study, in which the respondents' average age was 74 years. Thus, issues of both age and gender can be addressed by comparing the results of the Acitelli (1994) and Acitelli and Antonucci (1994) studies. Preliminary analyses of data from the younger sample indicate that there were no gender differences in the link between support in the relationship and relationship satisfaction, but there were gender differences in the link between support and general well-being. The former finding (no gender difference) will be discussed first. This finding could mean that either length of relationship, age, or cohort might provide a context that modifies the extent to which there are gender differences in associations between support and relationship satisfaction. Perhaps the older couples were raised in a time when more traditional sex roles were an acceptable norm. Maybe the younger couples are not as bound to such traditions, and the partners are more likely to value similar things in their relationship than the older couples are. On the other hand, the younger couples' relationships, being of shorter duration, may be less routine or taken for granted. Therefore, each partner notices when the other gives him or her support. Nevertheless, the reason for the differences in the results of these two studies is not completely clear because it is difficult to separate the effects of age from those of length of relationship. Part of the difficulty is that the variables age and length of relationship are always highly correlated.

Another, more methodological interpretation can also be considered. Perhaps the way in which the studies were presented to respondents could account for the different results causing a "social desirability effect," particularly in the men (Russell & Wells, 1992). Although a study of social desirability in marriage may seem far removed from the study of social support, it is relevant to the interpretations presented here. The younger couples' study was designed to investigate the relationships of married and unmarried couples. It is called the "Couples and Well-Being" study and is presented as such when the potential respondent is approached to participate. The older couples' study was presented to the respondents as the "Social Networks in Adult Life" study, not designed to study premarital and marital relationships specifically. Perhaps partners participating in a study of relationships become more conscious of how their relationship appears to the interviewer and are more concerned with presenting their relationships in a positive light than are those in a study of more general social networks. If so, those who reported their relationships as happy would also be likely to say that their spouse/partner provides them with various social supports. This may be particularly true for the men in the younger couples' study.

Supporting this line of reasoning, Russell and Wells (1992) investigated the relationship between marital quality and social desirability in 94 couples. They were closer in age to those in the younger couples' study (average age = 33 years), ranging from 19 to 73 years (average age = 38 years), than to those in the older couples' study (average age = 74 years). Russell and Wells (1992) found that the two factors, social desirability and marital quality, were unrelated in women, but related in men. Therefore, the men in the younger couples' study might be likely to adopt a response set that puts their relationship in a positive light. Thus, marital satisfaction and marital support might be naturally connected in the minds of some respondents just as Fincham and Bradbury (1990) assumed, especially if respondents want to portray their relationships as happy ones.

There are still, however, gender differences in the support–outcome link in the younger couples' study that are consistent with those in the older couples' study. Recall that results from the older couples' study (Acitelli & Antonucci, 1994) showed gender difference in the links between spousal support and both marital and general well-being. Interestingly, in the younger couples' study, Acitelli (1994) found these same gender differences with regard to anxiety and depression. The fewer social supports provided within the relationship, the more depression and anxiety was reported by women, but not by men. The same explanations could be given for this finding as were offered for the same finding in the older couples' study.

However, if social desirability was a factor for the men in the younger couples' study, why did it not seem to play a role in reports of anxiety and depression? Perhaps, in the respondents' minds, the measures of depression and anxiety are seen to be directed toward the individual, not the relationship. Without the respondents' having made the cognitive connection between individual well-being and relationship satisfaction, the findings may reflect a link less biased by the social desirability response set. While the men may have made the connection in their minds that good relationships mean give and take, the questions about anxiety and depression may not have been as easily influenced by a social desirability response set. For example, one anxiety question is, "How often have you been bothered by nervousness, feeling fidgety and tense?," and one depression question is, "How often do you feel that your life is interesting?" Most likely these items would not be as recognizably connected to how much support one receives from a partner as items about how satisfied one is with one's relationship would be. For women, however, the fact that supports received from their partners were related to their depression and anxiety underscores the point made by Levenson et al. (1993). Their empirical work indicates that women's psychological and physical health are more closely tied to marital satisfaction than are husbands'. If women automatically make the connection between social support from their male partners and relationship satisfaction, then the link between social support in marriage and general well-being should also be strong.

Nevertheless, the questions regarding age and length of relationship as factors contributing to these gender differences are not answered. However, both the older and younger couples' studies (Acitelli & Antonucci, 1994; Acitelli, 1994) do point to a pervasive gender difference with regard to the link between social support in an intimate relationship and general well-being. The link is much stronger for women than for men.

SUMMARY AND CONCLUSIONS

In sum, this chapter addressed three main recommendations. First, emphasis was given to the need for more studies of relationship-specific social support, as opposed to global social support. This recommendation is presented in a more elaborate form in the work of Pierce et al. (1991) and Sarason et al. (1994), which demonstrates the additional contribution that relationship-specific support makes to personal adjustment. Second, the benefits of including both recipients and providers in studies of social support were illustrated. Links between studies of interpersonal perception and social support were uncovered, demonstrating the theoretical and methodological value of including both partners of a relationship in study samples. Third, the merits of studying the social support–relationship outcome connection were noted. More specifically, studies investigating the association between marital support and satisfaction were described. The theoretical and methodological aspects of these three interlocking recommendations were also discussed. In addition, gender, age, and length of relationship were demonstrated to be variables that are likely to modify the relationship support–relationship outcome association.

When investigating the marital support–marital satisfaction link, gender should always be considered as a possible moderating variable. Future work needs to address the different meanings that men and women may attach to socially supportive behaviors (for reviews of gender differences in social support see Antonucci, 1994; Antonucci & Akiyama, 1987; Barbee et al., 1993). Work on social support in marriage reveals that the use of marital status as an indication of adequate social support oversimplifies the complex phenomenon of perceived support within marriage. Several studies clearly indicate that in the same environment, with basically comparable perceptions of social support, social support in marriage has different correlates for husbands and wives. Husbands and wives seem to differ in the implications that perceptions of support have for their well-being. For wives in general, regardless of age, these perceptions seem to have implications for the well-being of themselves and their marital relationships, while for husbands, the implications are not so clear.

The main recommendations outlined in this chapter can be boiled down to a single sentence: We need more investigations of the association between specific relationship support and relationship outcomes with study designs that include both partners in the relationship. The implications that this recommendation has for future research are as numerous as the different types of relationships human beings create with one another. By studying more relationship-based social support, investigators can compare different types of relationships both within and outside the respondents' immediate family. Parent–child, sibling relationships, gay and lesbian relationships, friendships, and even work-related friendships could be grist for the research mill. Several of these types of relationships have been studied from the individual's perspective, but more could be learned from looking at these relationships from both partners' points of view. For example, is reciprocity of social support more important to the quality of a marital relationship than to the quality of a parent–child relationship? How do the ages of both partners modify such effects? Perhaps the effects of reciprocity on the quality of either type of relationship vary with time.

By learning more about social support within specific relationships, researchers may reinforce the idea that the meaning of particular behaviors is greatly influenced by the relationship between the people doing the behaving. Planalp (1987), in her pioneering studies of relationship schemata, explains how seemingly ambiguous actions are interpreted in such a way as to maintain consistency with the prevailing schema of the relationship with the person performing those actions. She shows that relational schemata function like schemata for persons and objects, except that relational schemata are grounded in patterns of interpersonal interaction (see also Baldwin, 1992). Her research has demonstrated that people use their knowledge of a relationship to interpret events. For example, if friends are talking, and one of them directs a sarcastic remark toward another, it may be interpreted as playful. If an enemy makes the exact same remark, it will probably be interpreted as insulting (Planalp, 1987). Thus, researchers of social support may also benefit from incorporating various threads of research on cognition in relationships. How the person thinks about the relationship (Acitelli, 1992; Cate, Koval, Lloyd, & Wilson, 1995; Martin, 1991) may be seen as a vital component of how supportive interactions are interpreted to be. The extent to which partners' views of the relationship are shared may indeed be the most important process in relationship adjustment and satisfaction (Duck, 1994). An essential ingredient of a couple's shared reality is likely to be the shared perception of the support they give to and receive from one another.

ACKNOWLEDGMENTS

The preparation of this chapter was supported, in part, by a grant to the author from the National Institute of Mental Health (R01 MH46567). I am grateful to Toni Antonucci for her insights and contributions to several aspects of this chapter.

REFERENCES

Acitelli, L. K. (1988). When spouses talk to each other about their relationship. *Journal of Social and Personal Relationships, 5,* 185–199.

Acitelli, L. K. (1992). Gender differences in relationship awareness and marital satisfaction among young married couples. *Personality and Social Psychology Bulletin, 18,* 102–110.

Acitelli, L. K. (1993). You, me, and us: Perspectives on relationship awareness. In S. W. Duck (Ed.), *Understanding relationship processes,* Vol. 1, *Individuals in relationships* (pp. 144–174). Newbury Park, CA: Sage Publications.

Acitelli, L. K. (November, 1994). Reciprocity of social support in marriage. Paper presented at the National Council on Family Relations Annual Conference. Minneapolis.

Acitelli, L. K., & Antonucci, T. C. (1994). Gender differences in the link between marital support and satisfaction in older couples. *Journal of Personality and Social Psychology, 67,* 688–698.

Acitelli, L. K., Douvan, E., & Veroff, J. (1993). Perceptions of conflict in the first year of marriage: How important are similarity and understanding? *Journal of Social and Personal Relationships, 10,* 5–19.

Acitelli, L. K., & Duck, S. (1987). Intimacy as the proverbial elephant. In D. Perlman & S. W. Duck (Eds.), *Intimate relationships: Development, dynamics, and deterioration* (pp. 297–308). Beverly Hills: Sage Publications.

Antonucci, T. C. (1994). A life-span view of women's social relations. In B F. Turner & L. E. Troll (Eds.), *Women growing older: Psychological perspectives* (pp. 239–269). Thousand Oaks, CA: Sage Publications.

Antonucci, T. C., & Akiyama, H. (1987). An examination of sex differences in social support among older men and women. *Sex Roles, 17,* 737–749.

Baldwin, M. W. (1992). Relational schemas and the processing of social information. *Psychological Bulletin, 112,* 461–484.

Barbee, A. P., Cunningham, M. R., Winstead, B. A., Derlega, V. J., Gulley, M. R., Yankeelov, P. A., & Druen, P. B. (1993). Effects of gender role expectations on the social support process. *Journal of Social Issues, 49,* 175–190.

Belle, D. (1987). Gender differences in the social moderators of stress. In R. Barnett, L. Biener, & G. K. Baruch (Eds.), *Gender and stress* (pp. 257–277). New York: Free Press.

Berger, P., & Kellner, H. (1964). Marriage and the construction of social reality. *Diogenes, 46,* 1–24.

Berkman, L. F., Leo-Summers, L., & Horwitz, R. I. (1992). Emotional support and survival after myocardial infarction: A prospective, population based study of the elderly. *Annals of Internal Medicine, 117,* 1003–1009.

Bernard, J. (1972). *The future of marriage.* New York: World Publishing.

Billings, A. G., & Moos, R. H. (1982). Social support and functioning among community and clinical groups: A panel model. *Journal of Behavioral Medicine, 5,* 295–311.

Bolger, N., Kessler, R. C., & Schilling, E. A. (1990). Visible support, invisible support, and adjustment to daily stress. Unpublished manuscript.

Burnett, R. (1987). Reflection in personal relationships. In R. Burnett, P. McGhee, & D. D. Clarke (Eds.), *Accounting for relationships: Explanation, representation and knowledge* (pp. 175–191). London: Methuen.

Carstensen, L. L. (1992). Social and emotional patterns in adulthood: Support for socioemotional selectivity theory. *Psychology and Aging, 7,* 331–338.

Cate, R. M., Koval, J. E., Lloyd, S. A., & Wilson, G. (1995). The assessment of relationship thinking in dating relationships. *Personal Relationships, 2,* 77–95.

Coyne, J. C., & DeLongis, A. (1986). Going beyond social support: The role of social relationships in adaptation. *Journal of Consulting and Clinical Psychology, 54,* 454–460.

Cutrona, C. E., & Suhr, J. A. (1994). Social support communication in the context of marriage: An analysis of couples' supportive interactions. In B. R. Burleson, T. Albrecht, & I. G. Sarason (Eds.), *Communication of social support: Messages, interactions, relationships, and community* (pp. 113–135). Thousand Oaks, CA: Sage Publications.

Cutrona, C. E., Suhr, J. A., & MacFarlane, R. (1990). Interpersonal transactions and the psychological sense of support. In S. Duck with R. C. Silver (Eds.), *Personal relationships and social support* (pp. 30–45). London: Sage Publications.

Deal, J. E., Wampler, K. S., & Halverson, C. F. (1992). The importance of similarity in the marital relationship. *Family Process, 31,* 369–382.

Depner, C. E., & Ingersoll-Dayton, B. (1985). Conjugal social support: Patterns in later life. *Journal of Gerontology, 40,* 761–766.

Duck, S. W. (1977). *The study of acquaintance.* Farnborough, UK: Teakfields/Saxon House.

Duck, S. W. (1994). *Meaningful relationships: Talking, sense, and relating.* Thousand Oaks, CA: Sage Publications.

Duck, S. W., & Sants, H. K. A. (1983). On the origin of the specious: Are personal relationships really interpersonal states? *Journal of Social and Clinical Psychology, 1,* 27–41.

Dunkel-Schetter, C., & Bennett, T. L. (1990). Differentiating the cognitive and behavioral aspects of social support. In I. G. Sarason, B. R. Sarason, & G. R. Pierce (Eds.), *Social support: An interactional view* (pp. 267–296). New York: Wiley.

Dymond, R. (1954). Interpersonal perception and marital happiness. *Canadian Journal of Psychology, 8,* 164–171.

Fenigstein, A., & Abrams, D. (1993). Self-attention and the egocentric assumption of shared perspectives. *Journal of Experimental Social Psychology, 29,* 287–303.

Ferraro, K. F., & Wan, T. T. H. (1986). Marital contributions to well-being in later life: An examination of Bernard's thesis. *American Behavioral Scientist, 29,* 423–437.

Fincham, F. D., & Bradbury, T. N. (1990). Social support in marriage: The role of social cognition. *Journal of Social and Clinical Psychology, 9,* 31–42.

Fishman, P. (1978). Interaction: The work women do. *Social Problems, 25,* 397–406.

Gilford, R. (1986). Marriages in later life. *Generations, 10,* 16–20.

Gove, W. R., & Hughes, M. (1979). Possible causes of the apparent sex differences in mental health. *American Sociological Review, 44,* 59–81.

Gove, W. R., Hughes, M., & Style, C. B. (1983). Does marriage have positive effects on the psychological well-being of the individual? *Journal of Health and Social Behavior, 24,* 122–131.

Hess, B., & Soldo, B. (1985). Husband and wife networks. In Anonymous (Ed.), *Social support networks and the care of the elderly: Theory, research and practice* (pp. 67–92). New York: Springer.

Higgins, E. T., King, G. A., & Mavin, G. H. (1982). Individual construct accessibility and subjective impressions and recall. *Journal of Personality and Social Psychology, 73,* 35–47.

Hochschild, A. (1983). *The managed heart.* Berkeley: University of California Press.

House, J. S. (1981). *Work, stress and social support.* Reading, MA: Addison-Wesley.

Ingersoll-Dayton, B., & Antonucci, T. C. (1988). Reciprocal and non-reciprocal social support: Contrasting sides of intimate relationships. *Journal of Gerontology, 43,* S65–S73.

Julien, D., & Markman, H. J. (1991). Social support and social networks as determinants of individual and marital outcomes. *Journal of Social and Personal Relationships, 8,* 549–568.

Kahn, R. L., & Antonucci, T. C. (1980). Convoys over the life course: Attachment, roles, and social support. In P. B. Baltes & O. Brim (Eds.), *Life span development and behavior* (pp. 253–286). San Diego: Academic Press.

Kahn, R. L., & Antonucci, T. C. (1984). *Supports of the elderly: Family/friends/professionals (Final report to the National Institute on Aging).* Washington, DC: U.S. Government Printing Office.

Kenny, D. A. (1988a). Interpersonal perception: A social relations analysis. *Journal of Social and Personal Relationships, 5,* 220–248.

Kenny, D. A. (1988b). The analysis of data from two-person relationships. In S. W. Duck (Ed.), *Handbook of personal relationships: Theory, research, and interventions* (pp. 57–77). New York & Chichester: John Wiley.

Kenny, D. A., & Acitelli, L. K. (1994). Measuring similarity in couples. *Journal of Family Psychology, 8,* 417–431.

Kessler, R. C. (1991). Perceived support and adjustment to stress: Methodological considerations. In H. O. F. Veiel & U. Baumann (Eds.), *The meaning and measurement of social support* (pp. 259–271). New York: Hemisphere.

Kessler, R. C., & McLeod, J. D. (1985). Social support and mental health in community samples. In S. Cohen & S. L. Syme (Eds.), *Social support and health* (pp. 219–240). San Diego: Academic Press.

Lakey, B., & Cassady, P. B. (1990). Cognitive processes in perceived social support. *Journal of Personality and Social Psychology, 59,* 331–343.

Lamke, L. K. (1989). Marital adjustment among rural couples: The role of expressiveness. *Sex Roles, 21,* 579–590.

Leatham, G., & Duck S. (1990). Conversations with friends and the dynamics of social support. In S. Duck with R. C. Silver (Eds.), *Personal relationships and social support* (pp. 1–29). London: Sage Publications.

Levenson, R. W., Carstensen, L. L., & Gottman, J. M. (1993). Long-term marriage: Age, gender, and satisfaction. *Psychology and Aging, 8,* 301–313.

Levinger, G., & Breedlove, J. (1966). Interpersonal attraction and agreement: A study of marriage partners. *Journal of Personality and Social Psychology, 3,* 367–372.

Marks, G., & Duval, S. (1991). Availability of alternative positions and estimates of consensus. *British Journal of Social Psychology, 30,* 179–183.

Markus, H., Smith, J., & Moreland, R. L. (1985). The role of the self concept in the perception of others. *Journal of Personality and Social Psychology, 49,* 1494–1512.

Martin, R. W. (1991). Examining personal relationship thinking: The Relational Cognition Complexity Instrument. *Journal of Social and Personal Relationships, 8,* 467–480.

McGonagle, K. A., Kessler, R. C., & Schilling, E. A. (1992). The frequency and determinants of marital disagreements in a community sample. *Journal of Social and Personal Relationships, 9,* 507–524.

Mills, R. J., Grasmick, H. G., Morgan, C. S., & Wenk, D. (1992). The effects of gender, family satisfaction, and economic strain on psychological well-being. *Family Relations, 41,* 440–445.

Murstein, B. I., & Williams, P. D. (1985). Assortative matching for sex-role and marriage adjustment. *Personality and Individual Differences, 6,* 195–201.

Noller, P. (1980). Misunderstandings in married communication: A study of couples' nonverbal communication. *Journal of Personality and Social Psychology, 39,* 1135–1148.

Olson, D. H. (1977). Insiders' and outsiders' views of relationships: Research studies. In G. Levinger

& H. L. Rausch (Eds.), *Close relationships: Perspectives on the meaning of intimacy* (pp. 115–135). Amherst: University of Massachusetts Press.

Pierce, G. R., Sarason, I. G., & Sarason, B. R. (1991). General and relationship-based perceptions of social support: Are two constructs better than one? *Journal of Personality and Social Psychology, 61,* 1028–1039.

Pina, D. L., & Bengtson, V. L. (1993). The division of household labor and wives' happiness: Ideology, employment, and perceptions of support. *Journal of Marriage and the Family, 55,* 901–912.

Planalp, S. (1987). Interplay between relational knowledge and events. In R. Burnett, P. McGhee, & D. D. Clarke (Eds.), *Accounting for relationships: Explanation, representation, kand knowledge* (pp. 175–191). London: Methuen.

Ross, L., Greene, D., & House, P. (1977). The "false consensus effect": An egocentric bias in social perception and attribution processes. *Journal of Experimental Social Psychology, 13,* 279–301.

Russell, R. J. H., & Wells, P. A. (1992). Social desirability and quality of marriage. *Personality and Individual Differences, 13,* 787–791.

Sarason, I. G., Levine, H. M., Basham, R. B., & Sarason, B. R. (1983). Assessing social support: The social support questionnaire. *Journal of Personality and Social Psychology, 44,* 127–139.

Sarason, I. G., Sarason, B. R., & Pierce, G. R. (1994). Social support: Global and relationship-based levels of analysis. *Journal of Social and Personal Relationships, 11,* 295–312.

Sarason, I. G., Sarason, B. R., & Shearin, E. N. (1986). Social support as an individual difference variable: Its stability, origins, and relational aspects. *Journal of Personality and Social Psychology, 50,* 845–855.

Scott, C. K., Fuhrman, R. W., & Wyer, R. S. (1991). Information processing in close relationships. In G. J. O. Fletcher, & F. D. Fincham (Eds.), *Cognition in close relationships* (pp. 37–67). Hillsdale, NJ: Lawrence Erlbaum.

Sherbourne, C. D., & Hays, R. D. (1990). Marital status, social support, and health transitions in chronic disease patients. *Journal of Health and Social Behavior, 31* 328–343.

Sillars, A. L. (1985). Interpersonal perception in relationships. In W. Ickes (Ed.), *Compatible and incompatible relationships* (pp. 277–305). New York: Springer-Verlag.

Sprecher, S. (1992). How men and women expect to feel and behave in response to inequity in close relationships. *Social Psychology Quarterly, 55,* 57–69.

Thompson, L. (1993). Conceptualizing gender in marriage: The case of marital care. *Journal of Marriage and the Family, 55,* 557–569.

Vanfossen, B. E. (1981). Sex differences in the mental health effects of spouse support and equity. *Journal of Health and Social Behavior, 22,* 130–143.

Veroff, J., Douvan, E., & Kulka, K. (1981). *The inner American.* New York: Basic Books.

Vinokur, A. D., & van Ryn, M. (1993). Social support and undermining in close relationships: Their independent effects on the mental health of unemployed persons. *Journal of Personality and Social Psychology, 65,* 350–359.

Vinokur, A. D., & Vinokur-Kaplan, D. (1990). "In sickness and in health": Patterns of social support and undermining in older married couples. *Journal of Aging and Health, 2,* 215–241.

Ward, R. (1993). Marital happiness and household equity in later life. *Journal of Marriage and the Family, 55,* 427–438.

Weishaus, S., & Field, D. (1988). A half century of marriage: Continuity or change? *Journal of Marriage and the Family, 50,* 763–774.

White, K. M., Speisman, J. C., Jackson, D., Bartis, S., & Costos, D. (1986). Intimacy maturity and its correlates in young married couples. *Journal of Personality and Social Psychology, 50,* 152–162.

6

The Socialization of Emotional Support Skills in Childhood

BRANT R. BURLESON and ADRIANNE W. KUNKEL

INTRODUCTION

Of all the varied forms of social support people seek and provide—appraisal, esteem, informational, instrumental, network, tangible (see Cutrona, Suhr, & MacFarlane, 1990; House, 1981)—none is more ubiquitous than *emotional support*. Everybody needs emotional support, and most of us are providers of it at one time or another. Emotional support is sought on diverse occasions from a variety of potential providers, including friends, family members, coworkers, and professionals such as counselors and clergy. Most people report that the emotional support they receive from these sources helps them feel better about things, relieves hurts and stresses, and improves their quality of life. Not surprisingly, people view the emotional support skills of others as quite important. Studies (Burleson & Samter, 1990; Samter, Burleson, Kunkel, & Werking, July 1994) indicate that people value highly the emotional support skills of friends, lovers, and family members, and may even choose relationship partners on the basis of their competence at providing emotional support (Samter & Burleson, June 1990a).

Although seeking and dispensing emotional support are activities that pervade most people's lives, the provision of sensitive, effective emotional support is no easy task. People often report that they don't know what to say to help a distressed friend or family member feel better about some unhappy circumstance (e.g., Lehman, Ellard, & Wortman, 1986). And there is abundant evidence (Dakof & Taylor, 1990; Lehman & Hemphill, 1990; Wortman & Lehman, 1985) that people are routinely exposed to well-meaning but insensitive and ineffective support

BRANT R. BURLESON and ADRIANNE W. KUNKEL • Department of Communication, Purdue University, West Lafayette, Indiana 47907-1366.

Handbook of Social Support and the Family, edited by Gregory R. Pierce, Barbara R. Sarason, and Irwin G. Sarason. Plenum Press, New York, 1996.

efforts. On the other hand, some people are remarkably skillful at providing highly sensitive and sophisticated emotional support. Such "peer counselors" (Burleson & Waltman, 1987; Samter & Burleson, June 1990a) may be regularly sought out by those in their social network for their special competence at providing warmth, compassion, and comfort.

Although the capacity for empathy and the impulse to provide support are widespread and may be a part of the genetic legacy of our species (see Hoffman, 1975; Rheingold & Emery, 1986), the skillful provision of verbal comfort and other forms of emotional support are clearly *acquired* abilities. How do people learn to provide emotional support? What skills must they master over the course of development? And what types of learning experiences are associated with competence at providing more sensitive, timely, and effective forms of comfort and emotional support?

Few persons outside the clinical context receive explicit, formal instruction in how to provide emotional support. Rather, most people learn to provide support in the same context they learn so many other of life's truly important lessons: in the home, from primary socializing agents, especially parents. The informal "lessons" that children receive from parents about how to provide emotional support constitute a powerful influence on how the children come to respond to the emotional needs of others over the life course.

In the last decade, social scientists have begun to examine how children acquire various emotional support skills and the types of parental behavior that contribute to children's ability to be sensitive providers of emotional support. Unfortunately, the findings of these studies are scattered across multiple literatures in a broad range of disciplines, including psychology, communication, family studies, and sociology. As a result, a comprehensive understanding of the development and socialization of emotional support skills has been slow to emerge. This chapter aims to synthesize and integrate the growing but fragmented literature concerned with the socialization of emotional support skills during childhood. The chapter also offers a fresh theoretical perspective on the socialization of support skills—a perspective that, we believe, will prove useful in organizing the findings of existing research and directing future research efforts.

We begin by briefly reviewing the significance and functions of emotional support, especially in the world of the child. Next, we develop a component model of emotional support, identifying several specific competencies children must acquire if they are to provide sensitive and appropriate forms of support. Our intention here is to specify the skills and proclivities of the child that may be affected by various socialization influences. We then review literature concerning developmental and individual differences in children's emotional support skills and describe some of the major parental practices that facilitate or inhibit development of these skills. Particular attention is given to several theoretical mechanisms through which parental behaviors may affect child competencies. The concluding section touches upon some unresolved problems in our analysis and indicates some directions for future theory development and empirical study.

SIGNIFICANCE AND FUNCTIONS OF EMOTIONAL SUPPORT

A Brief Look at Some Effects of Emotional Support across the Life Span

Emotional support *matters*. It is one of the more important forms of behavior in which intimates engage, and it has powerful consequences affecting life quality for both its recipients and its providers. People who receive more emotional support or perceive that emotional support is readily available are happier, healthier, and better able to cope with life's travails (see Cutrona & Russell, 1990; Pierce, Sarason, & Sarason, 1990). In particular, the receipt of support or the perception of its availability helps people cope with hassles, upsets, disappointments, and hurts that, if left unattended, can have serious negative effects on physical, psychological, and emotional health (Burleson, 1990).

Emotional support serves several important functions and results in numerous positive outcomes across the life span.[1] During childhood, the consistent availability and regular provision of sensitive emotional support by parents fosters secure attachment (e.g., Kestenbaum, Farber, & Sroufe, 1989). Parental nurturance and support enhances the child's social adjustment (East, 1991) and promotes psychological and emotional health both during childhood and later in life (Mallinckrodt, 1992). Sensitive emotional support also facilitates the child's development of numerous social competencies (e.g., Roberts & Strayer, 1987) and contributes to the child's success in school and with peers (see the review by Cauce, Reid, Landesman, & Gonzales, 1990).

A continuing belief throughout adolescence and the young adult years that emotional support is readily available from friends and family members has been found to be associated with several indices of personal happiness, social adjustment, and academic success (see Cutrona & Russell, 1990; Pierce et al., 1990). During midlife, spouses look to each other for emotional support, and the availability and quality of spousal support have been found to be major predictors of marital satisfaction (see the review by Cutrona & Suhr, 1994). Late in life, the emotional support that adults provide to their aging parents helps preserve both physical and psychological health (e.g., Russell & Cutrona, 1991; Silverstein & Bengston, 1994). Thus, at each stage of the life cycle, emotional support serves several powerful and beneficial functions.

Given the valuable functions emotional support serves, it is not surprising that people think emotional support is an important provision of social relationships, value the support skills of others, and choose relationship partners on the

---

[1]Note, however, that several researchers have drawn attention in recent years to the dilemmas and potentially negative effects of emotional support (see Albrecht, Burleson, & Goldsmith, 1994, pp. 431–435). Even well-intended support efforts may occasionally do more harm than good. Moreover, support giving may create undesirable dependencies, undermine skill development by the target, and prove costly to the provider. Although these dangers and costs must be acknowledged, emotional support still remains necessary for the healthy development and functioning of the individual and is an indicator of a healthy and moral social system. The problem for most people is not an excess of emotional support, but a shortage.

basis of their willingness and ability to provide sensitive emotional support. People of all ages routinely look to family members, romantic partners, and especially friends for emotional support (see Burleson, 1990; Cutrona & Russell, 1990). Across the life span, friends are expected to "be there" for one another, especially during times of emotional turmoil and upset. Buhrmester, Furman, Wittenberg, and Reis (1988) found that the degree of satisfaction young adults reported with their friends was more strongly predicted by perceived competence at providing emotional support than by any other form of interpersonal competence. Other studies indicate that people view the ability to provide emotional support as among the most important of friends' and lovers' communication skills (Burleson & Samter, 1990; Samter et al., July 1994). Moreover, some research indicates that people choose friends, in part, for their skill in providing sensitive emotional support (Samter & Burleson, June 1990a) and the extent to which they value support skills (Samter & Burleson, 1990b). Thus, skill at providing emotional support has significant consequences for providers as well as recipients.

Functions of Children's Emotional Support Skills

The ability to provide emotional support to peers seems to be especially important in shaping the quality of children's social relationships. Contemporary theorists (e.g., Eisenberg & Mussen, 1989; Zahn-Waxler & Radke-Yarrow, 1990) view the capacity to provide emotional support as a central component of the child's social competence. Children, too, report that they value the emotional support skills of their peers (Clark, 1994). Consistent with the views of both theorists and children, an expanding body of research has found children's acceptance within the peer group to be associated with several aspects of the ability to provide emotional support.

One line of research has examined the relationship between peer acceptance and children's abilities to recognize and understand the emotional states of others. Several studies (e.g., Edwards, Manstead, & MacDonald, 1984) indicate that children better able to recognize the emotional states of others are more popular among peers. Similarly, research indicates that peer popularity among children is predicted by the ability to engage in affective perspective taking—the capacity to appreciate what another is feeling and understand the causes for that emotional state (Burleson, Delia, & Applegate, 1992; Cassidy, Parke, Butkovksy, & Braungart, 1992; Garner, Jones, & Miner, 1994).

A second line of research, undertaken by Farver and her colleagues (Farver & Branstetter, 1994; Howes & Farver, 1987; Phinney, Feshbach, & Farver, 1986), has examined preschoolers' responses to distressed (crying) peers. In each of these studies, it was found that children who were more likely to engage in comforting and other prosocial responses were better liked by peers than children who showed little concern for the crying peer.

A third line of research has examined qualitative features of the messages with which grade-school children to seek comfort their peers. This research indicates that children capable of producing sophisticated comforting messages may be better liked by peers (Burleson et al., 1992). Although not all studies have found a positive association between comforting skill and peer popularity (see Burleson & Waltman, 1987), some research (Burleson et al., 1986) indicates that children who use *insensitive* messages when seeking to provide comfort may be actively *rejected* by peers.

Children's emotional support skills thus appear to play a key role in the development and maintenance of relationships with peers. These skills take on added significance in light of the central role peer relationships have been found to play in the child's social and emotional development. Numerous studies indicate that children who lack friends, especially those actively rejected by peers, are at risk for a host of social, emotional, and behavioral problems both during childhood and later in life, including poor performance in and dropout from school, delinquency, substance abuse, and emotional disturbances (see the reviews by Burleson, 1986; Kupersmidt, Coie, & Dodge, 1990). Because emotional support skills play a prominent role in the child's social relationships, as well as reflect the child's ability to manage challenging social and emotional situations, some theorists (e.g., Bryant, 1987; Hay, 1993) have suggested that these skills may be useful as an indicator of more general social and emotional development.

Research Trends in the Study of Children's Emotional Support Skills

Although we now know they are quite important, children's emotional support skills did not receive much research attention until fairly recently. Several factors may have contributed to the delay in undertaking systematic examinations of these skills and their antecedents. Social concerns with violence, delinquency, and aggression have, quite legitimately, caused much research to focus on antecedents of and remedies for these forms of antisocial behavior (see the review by Parke & Slaby, 1983). Understanding and promoting positive behaviors like emotional support may have seemed less urgent, and perhaps less important, than understanding and inhibiting aggression. In the last few years, however, both theorists and agents of social change have come to appreciate that not all social problems arise from an excess of negative behaviors; at least some stem directly from an absence of appropriate positive behaviors (see Radke-Yarrow & Zahn-Waxler, 1986).

Once research on altruism and positive social behaviors was under way, a belief in the generality of prosocial conduct led researchers to focus on easily studied tangible forms of support such as sharing resources, cooperating on tasks, and providing physical assistance. Unfortunately, subsequent research showed that there is only a low level of generality among varied forms of prosocial behavior (see Payne, 1980; Underwood & Moore, 1982a), so knowledge about the factors that influence sharing, for example, may provide only minimal information about emotional support skills. Indeed, some studies (e.g., Richman, Berry, Bittle, & Himan, 1988) indicate that there is little association between the tendencies to provide instrumental help and emotional support, suggesting that each form of behavior must be examined.

As might be anticipated, emotional support is a difficult phenomenon to study. Some early observational studies of children found naturally occurring instances of peer-directed emotional support to be so rare as to preclude meaningful analysis (e.g., Iannotti, 1985; F. F. Strayer, 1981). Past middle childhood, social pressures to maintain a positive public "face" (Goffman, 1967) make it unlikely that scientific observers would be privy to many naturally occurring instances of emotional support. Further, much emotional support is conveyed through verbal communication, and thus requires sophisticated methods for the analysis of interactions and messages (see Burleson, 1994).

Despite the difficulties associated with the study of children's emotional support skills, the research reviewed previously suggests several good reasons for exploring how children acquire and develop these skills. With advancing age, children increasingly turn to peers for emotional support. Older children and adolescents expect their friends to provide them with emotional support when it is needed. Further, the emotional support children provide to distressed peers has important effects: Sensitive, appropriate support helps distressed peers work through difficult situations and strengthens the bond between the provider and the recipient. In contrast, inappropriate forms of support, even if well intended, may exacerbate the recipient's distress and undermine the provider's relationships with peers.

Because differences in children's tendencies and abilities to provide emotional support may have significant, long-term consequences for both providers and recipients, it is important to understand the genesis of these differences. Moreover, research investigating the antecedents of individual differences in children's emotional support skills may help us understand more about the general character of the socialization process, increase our comprehension of how children learn complex forms of social behavior, and improve our capacity to design effective interventions aimed at enhancing children's support skills. Before the ways in which varied forms of parental behavior impact on the child's developing emotional support skills can be examined, a more fine-grained portrait of these skills is needed. The next section presents a detailed model of the emotional support process and identifies several constituent skills involved in the provision of emotional support.

COMPONENTS OF EMOTIONAL SUPPORT

Definitional Issues

"Emotional support" is a broad term that can encompass a wide range of behaviors (see Cutrona et al., 1990; House, 1981). For example, East (1991) suggests that emotional support involves aspects such as affection (caring actions), intimacy (availability as a confidant), enhancement of worth (validating the other's value and competence), companionship (sharing experiences), reliable alliance (manifesting a lasting and dependable bond), and help (providing comfort, guidance, and advice). Theoretically, then, emotionally supportive actions include those directed at enhancing positive emotional states, as well as those aimed at helping others overcome negative emotional states.

Some theorists define emotional support more narrowly, limiting focus to the comforting function. For example, Cutrona and Russell (1990) suggest that emotional support "appears to represent the ability to turn to others for comfort and security during times of stress, leading the person to feel that he or she is cared for by others" (p. 322). Although theorists may differ in their conceptual definitions of emotional support, practically there is little difference in the phenomena actually being studied. That is, virtually all research has focused on support efforts directed at overcoming sadness, anxiety, fear, anger, and other negative emotions. Indeed, in most research, "comforting" is an adequate synonym for "emotional support." Comforting has been defined as behavior "having the intended function of alleviating, moderating, or salving the distressed emotional states of others" (Burleson, 1984a, p. 64).

In what follows, we emphasize that comforting and related forms of emotional support are appropriately viewed as *skills*. Some studies indicate that valuable health outcomes can result simply from people's perception that support is available to them (see Pierce et al., 1990). This finding has led to empirical work focused on the intrapsychic determinants of perceived support availability. Recent research emphasizes, however, that the *quality* of the emotional support that people receive, and not just its perceived availability, is an important predictor of psychological and emotional well-being. It has been found that sophisticated forms of emotional support—especially "person-centered" messages that acknowledge, elaborate on, legitimize, and contextualize the feelings and perspective of a distressed other—are preferred by recipients, are relatively effective at moderating emotional distress, and bring about desirable relationship outcomes (see Burleson, 1994). There are broad individual differences in the ability to produce such sophisticated forms of verbal support (Burleson, 1985). Thus, it is useful to view at least certain forms of emotional support as a skill—a skill that develops over the life course and that individuals possess in differing degree.

Constituents of Emotional Support

Comforting and related forms of emotional support have been conceptualized in numerous ways by scholars in a variety of academic disciplines and research traditions. In particular, emotional support has been viewed as a form of *social competence* (e.g., Dodge, 1986), an approach that emphasizes social–cognitive processes and abilities; as a class of *social support* (e.g., Barbee & Cunningham, 1995), a conception that emphasizes the personality and situational determinants of behavior; as a type of *functional communication skill* (e.g., Burleson, 1984a), a view that emphasizes message-production abilities; as a kind of *altruistic or prosocial behavior* (e.g., Zahn-Waxler & Radke-Yarrow, 1990), an orientation that emphasizes developmental and motivational factors; and even as a form of *therapeutic practice* (e.g., Elliott, 1985), an approach that stresses the outcomes of different behaviors for distressed individuals. Each of these perspectives sheds some light on the nature and development of emotional support skills. However, these literatures tend to be quite segregated and inform each other only minimally. In developing our analysis of emotional support skills, we draw from all these diverse literatures in an effort to articulate a rich portrait of the constituents underlying the delivery of sensitive emotional support (also see Burleson, 1994). Secondarily, we hope that our analysis contributes to the integration of overly balkanized literatures and research specialities.

What skills must children develop to be competent providers of sensitive emotional support? In elaborating a developmental perspective on social competence, Waters and Sroufe (1983) argue that analyses of the constituents of social competence must make provision for at least the following elements: (1) recognition of the opportunity or demand for response, (2) prior acquisition of response alternatives, (3) selection from among response alternatives, (4) motivation to respond, (5) persisting or changing the response as required, and (6) modulation (fine-tuning) of the response. Waters and Sroufe's analysis thus emphasizes that the provision of emotional support is not an event, but a *process*—a process that taps several distinct competencies of the individual.

Two recent discussions of the components involved in providing emotional support appear to be generally consistent with the criteria articulated by Waters and Sroufe. In evaluating the emotional support skills of preschoolers, Zahn-Waxler and Radke-Yarrow (1990) note that the competence to provide emotional support depends on the development of three sets of skills: "(a) the cognitive capacity to interpret the physical and psychological states of others, (b) the emotional capacity to experience affectively the states of others, and (c) the behavioral repertoire that permits the possibility of trying to alleviate discomfort in others" (pp. 113–114). Zahn-Waxler and Radke-Yarrow thus suggest that the competence to provide support is dependent on the acquisition and development of certain cognitive, affective, and behavioral skills.

Burleson (1984a) proposed a model of the factors underlying comforting behavior that appears to fit the Waters–Sroufe standard even more closely. Burleson's model begins by distinguishing between factors that underlie the *competence*, or abstract ability, to provide sensitive comfort and factors that motivate the *performance* of comforting acts in concrete social contexts. According to this model, support givers must possess at least three analytically distinct types of knowledge if they are to be competent providers of comfort (and other forms of emotional support).

First, a provider must be capable of acquiring knowledge about the feelings and psychological states of the recipient; as suggested by Zahn-Waxler and Radke-Yarrow (1990), sensitive support presupposes an awareness of the recipient's affective state. Social perception skills, including the abilities to recognize and interpret emotional cues, integrate social information, and take the other's perspective, are the chief means through which people acquire knowledge about the affective states of others.

Second, a support giver must possess general knowledge about human emotional dynamics—for example, what circumstances typically lead to particular emotions, how the confluence of characteristic motivational and situational factors can invoke specific patterns of psychological coping and defense, how subjective appraisals of events can result in certain feeling states (see Lazarus, 1991). It appears that many assessments of social perception skills, which typically are intended to measure the individual's capacity to acquire knowledge about a specific other's affective state, also tap an individual's general knowledge about human emotional and motivational dynamics.

Third, the competent comfort giver must possess knowledge of the nonverbal, linguistic, and rhetorical resources through which supportive intentions can be realized in specific message strategies. As Waters and Sroufe (1983) stress, it is not enough merely to understand the other's psychological state (listener knowledge) and the general character of human emotional dynamics (topic knowledge). Rather, support givers must also possess a repertoire of interaction strategies and tactics through which knowledge of the listener and topic can be integrated and effectively applied. In sum, Burleson's model maintains that the competence to provide emotional support depends on *rhetorical knowledge* (knowledge of appropriate interaction strategies), as well as listener and topic knowledge.

Having the competence to provide support does not ensure, of course, that this competence will be exercised (see Chapman, Zahn-Waxler, Cooperman, & Iannotti, 1987). As Dunn and Munn (1986, p. 266) emphasize: "To behave in a prosocial manner depends not only on the capability of recognising the needs and feelings of another person, but on the motivation to act practically upon that recognition." The model of Burleson (1984a) distinguishes between two facets of the motivation to provide emotional support, *desire* and *willingness*. "Desire" refers to wanting to improve another's affective state or alleviate suffering. Dispositional factors associated with the desire to provide comfort should include traits such as commitment to prosocial values orientation (Feinberg, 1977) and emotional empathy (Mehrabian & Epstein, 1972). "Willingness" pertains to acceptance of, commitment to, and involvement with the task of working through the other's feelings and providing support. The willingness to undertake comforting acts should be affected by beliefs regarding the ability of the self to exert control over external events, the efficacy of the self in social situations, and the viability of verbal communication as a resource for managing interpersonal encounters.[1]

The model of Burleson (1984a) suggests that factors such as social perception ability and a flexible repertoire of communication strategies should be associated with comforting competence or the capacity to produce sensitive comforting

---

[1]Burleson's model recognizes that situational factors substantially influence the occurrence and sensitivity of emotional support. Variables such as the perceived need of the recipient, the perceived deservingness of the recipient, the type of social relationship between provider and recipient, presence of others, temporary states of the provider (e.g., fear, exhaustion), and numerous other factors have all been found to influence the occurrence, amount, and quality of comfort provided in various situations (see Burleson, 1984a, 1985). However, these situational factors are not dealt with here since this chapter focuses on individual differences in emotional support skills and the socialization factors associated with the genesis of these individual differences.

messages. Motivational factors, on the other hard, should primarily be associated with aspects of the situated performance of comforting, such as the likelihood of engaging in comforting acts, the frequency of providing support, and the persistence with which comfort is given (perhaps in the face of resistance or limited success). Unfortunately, most research on comforting has not distinguished clearly between, or included separate assessments of, comforting competence and comforting performance. The available findings thus do not permit a rigorous evaluation of the fine details of Burleson's model. Extant research indicates quite clearly, however, that variables such as social perception skill, message production abilities, and certain motivational factors are predictive of the occurrence and/or quality of comforting efforts and related forms of emotional support.

Research on the Cognitive and Motivational Correlates of Emotional Support

Social Perception Skills. Numerous studies have found linkages between measures of social perception skills and indices of comforting behavior. One line of research has examined the association between measures of affective perspective taking or social perspective taking and varied indices of comforting behavior. Most of these studies have found significant, positive associations between the perspective-taking measures and assessments of comforting behavior (e.g., Applegate, Burleson, & Delia, 1992; Burleson, 1984b; Garner et al., 1994; J. Strayer & Roberts, 1989). However, several studies have not found significant relationships between perspective taking and comforting (e.g., Howe & Ross, 1990; J. Strayer, 1980; Zahn-Waxler, Iannotti, & Chapman, 1982; Zahn-Waxler, Radke-Yarrow, & Brady-Smith, 1977).

Most of the studies that failed to find a relationship between perspective-taking skills and comforting were conducted with preschoolers, while most of the studies that found a significant relationship between these variables were conducted with samples of grade-school children. This pattern suggests that the relationship between perspective taking and comforting is developmental. That is, the capacity to use information provided by perspective-taking skills may become integrated with message formulation processes only gradually. Another possibility is that the measures of perspective-taking ability used with younger children suffered from poor reliability and validity; numerous critics have identified problems in many of the common measures employed with younger children (see Underwood & Moore, 1982b). In any event, it appears that by the time children reach grade school, perspective-taking skills are a reliable predictor of comforting behavior.

A second line of research has found consistent associations between individual differences in interpersonal cognitive complexity and the ability to produce sensitive, person-centered comforting messages. The *constructivist* theoretical perspective (Burleson, 1989; Delia, O'Keefe, & O'Keefe, 1982) views all social perception processes (e.g., attribution, information integration, impression formation, perspective taking) as occurring through the elements that Kelly (1955) termed "interpersonal constructs." These are the cognitive schemes or structures through which persons represent, anticipate, and evaluate the thoughts and behaviors of themselves and others. Persons with more differentiated, abstract, and organized systems of interpersonal constructs are regarded as more cognitively complex and as having more advanced social perception skills (see Delia et al., 1982). Numerous studies have found interpersonal cognitive complexity positively associated with comforting skill in samples of both children (e.g., Applegate et al., 1992; Burleson, 1984b) and adults (e.g., Applegate, 1980; Burleson, 1983) (these studies are reviewed extensively by Applegate, 1990).

Message Production Skills.   Only a few studies have examined the association between the availability of response alternatives and the sensitivity or quality of the comforting messages people use. Availability of response alternatives has been assessed by presenting hypothetical comforting situations to participants and repeatedly asking them what they would say in response to those situations until they could express no new strategies (e.g., Burleson, 1982a). In general, these studies have found positive associations between the quantity of strategies that participants produce and the tendency to use sensitive, person-centered comforting messages (Applegate, 1980; Burleson, 1982a; Burleson, Waltman, & Samter, 1987). These findings support the notion that the competence to engage in sensitive, appropriate forms of emotional support is partially attributable to the development of a repertoire of response alternatives.

Motivational Factors.   Researchers have examined several motivational factors that influence the provision of emotional support. Emotional empathy is the variable that has received the greatest research attention with respect to comforting and related forms of support.

Research on emotional empathy and its effects has been complicated by numerous, often incompatible conceptual and operational definitions of "empathy" (see Eisenberg & Mussen, 1989; Goldstein & Michaels, 1985). In recent years, however, a consensus has begun to emerge among researchers that "empathy" is most appropriatcly used to refer to "vicarious affective arousal" (Eisenberg & Fabes, 1990). Eisenberg and Fabes suggest that the vicarious emotional arousal associated with an empathic response to a distressed other can take one of two forms: a state of personal distress or a state of sympathetic concern. Empathically induced personal distress is not usually associated with prosocial responses such as emotional support; those experiencing personal distress often provide aid to a distressed victim only if escape from the situation is blocked (see Batson, Dyck, & Brandt, 1988). In contrast, empathically induced sympathetic concern represents an important force motivating expressions of care, comfort, and emotional support.

Most studies examining the association between comforting and emotional empathy have employed measures of affect contagion and sympathetic concern derived from the self-report assessments of dispositional empathy of Mehrabian and Epstein (1972) or Davis (1983). The results of these studies are generally consistent, with most finding a positive relationship between empathy and assessments of comforting behavior (e.g., Burleson, 1983; Burleson & Waltman, 1987;

Tamborini, Salomonson, & Bahk, 1993). However, a few studies (Samter & Burleson, 1984; J. Strayer & Roberts, 1989) have not found significant associations between self-report measures of empathy and assessments of emotional support. Similarly, Eisenberg-Berg and Lennon (1980) found no relationship between a situational measure of preschoolers' empathy and their frequency of comforting behavior in natural settings.

Importantly, Eisenberg et al. (1993) found that behavioral measures of children's personal distress reactions to a sad film or crying infant were *negatively* correlated with the amount of verbal comfort expressed to the crying infant. Interestingly, these researchers also found that a behavioral index of the sympathetic concern children manifested in reaction to the sad film was *positively* associated with the amount of comfort children offered the crying infant. The findings of Eisenberg and colleagues underscore that not all types of vicarious emotional arousal facilitate the provision of emotional support: Arousal leading to sympathetic concern motivates prosocial acts of comforting, whereas arousal manifest as personal distress inhibits attention to the other's state and may even lead to a denigration of the other.

Another motivational factor potentially associated with the desire to provide emotional support is a prosocial values orientation. People who place a high value on interpersonal relationships and the qualities that foster these relationships (such as intimacy, trust, and commitment) should be more motivated to provide emotional support in times of need than those who endorse more instrumental and self-focused values. Consistent with this reasoning, endorsement of values that reflect concern for the quality of interpersonal relationships has been found positively associated with the likelihood of providing emotional support to a distressed other (Feinberg, 1977; Grodman, 1979).

Factors potentially associated with the willingness to provide emotional support include communication apprehension (Burgoon, 1976), locus of control orientation (Rotter, 1966), and social self-efficacy (Bandura, 1977). People who feel comfortable communicating with others should be more willing to engage in acts of emotional support than the socially anxious. Similarly, people who believe they can affect external states of affairs and see themselves as efficacious agents in social contexts should be more willing to provide emotional support than those who see themselves as lacking control over external events or efficacy in social contexts. Unfortunately, few studies examining the effects of these factors have been reported, and the results of the available studies are less than conclusive. For example, Samter and Burleson (1984) found, as predicted, that communication apprehension was inversely associated with the proclivity to provide comfort to an emotionally distressed other. However, these researchers also found, contrary to expectations, that having an internal locus of control orientation was not associated with an increased likelihood of providing comfort. Clearly, more research is needed on factors that underlie the motivation to provide support, especially those associated with the willingness to provide support.

Summary. Theoretical analysis of the support-giving process suggests that the capacity to provide sensitive emotional support is dependent on both social perception and message production skills, while the likelihood of actually engaging in supportive actions is a function of factors associated with the desire and willingness to provide support. Consistent with this theoretical analysis, the available research indicates that the capacity to provide comfort (and probably other forms of emotional support) is dependent upon the ability to recognize and understand the emotional states of others, the ability to construct sensitive and appropriate responses to these states, and the motivation to alleviate distress in others. The next section examines how individual differences in these constituent skills emerge and develop over the course of childhood.

DEVELOPMENTAL AND INDIVIDUAL DIFFERENCES IN CHILDREN'S EMOTIONAL SUPPORT SKILLS

To understand how individual differences in emotional support skills unfold, and how socialization factors such as parenting practices impact on the emergence and growth of these differences, it is necessary to have some appreciation of the general developmental course of skills related to the provision of emotional support. Thus, we begin this section with a brief sketch of the development of emotional support skills during childhood. We then summarize evidence indicating that there are important individual differences in these skills.

Development of Emotional Support Skills in Childhood

Children are sensitive to the emotional cues of others from the beginning of life. Newborns can distinguish the cries of infants from other noises and (to the exasperation of their caregivers!) often cry in tandem with one another (Sagi & Hoffman, 1976; Simner, 1971). By 6 months of age, infants frequently notice when another child is crying or expressing distress, attend to those distress cues, and often begin manifesting distress themselves (Hay, Nash, & Pedersen, 1981). By the end of their first year, some children exhibit primitive efforts to comfort distressed others; young toddlers have been observed to respond to others' distresses with behaviors such as pats and hugs (Zahn-Waxler, Radke-Yarrow, & King, 1979).

During the second year, the child's ability to provide emotional support grows substantially. The tendency to respond to distress by becoming upset declines, and the child begins to exhibit more active interventions on behalf of distressed others. By 18 months, children display a diversity of nurturant, comforting, and caregiving acts (Rheingold & Emery, 1986). By 2 years of age, children make practical attempts to comfort distressed others, expressing sympathy both verbally and nonverbally, bringing objects (such as teddy bears) to the other, and recruiting others (such as parents or other adults) to help provide aid (e.g., Dunn & Munn, 1986; Zahn-Waxler et al., 1982). By the end of their second year, children have developed several aspects of the competence to provide emotional support, exhibiting "(a) the cognitive capacity to interpret, in simple ways, the physical and psychological states of others, (b) the emotional capacity to experience, affectively, the state of others, and (c) the behavioral repertoire that permits the possibility of attempts to alleviate discomfort in others" (Zahn-Waxler & Radke-Yarrow, 1990, p. 107).

Comforting and other acts of emotional support are a standard part of the behavioral repertoire of most preschoolers (2- to 5-year-olds). Although children do not always exhibit emotional support when confronted with a distressed other, they are capable of providing various forms of comfort and do so with some frequency in both home and preschool environments. Preschoolers have been observed to intervene actively on behalf of crying peers (e.g., Farver & Branstetter, 1994; Howes & Farver, 1987), will attempt to console a sad or upset peer on the playground (e.g., Eisenberg-Berg & Lennon, 1980; J. Strayer, 1980), and may even try to comfort an adult displaying distress cues (Chapman et al., 1987; Yarrow & Waxler, 1976).[1]

Children are able to discriminate among most basic emotional states by the third year of life (Borke, 1971; Thompson, 1987). There is also evidence that the capacity to empathize, or experience vicarious affective arousal, grows throughout childhood (see Barnett, 1987). By age 5, children are capable of recognizing and distinguishing among varied emotional states, some quite subtle. The individual's understanding of emotional dynamics continues to develop throughout childhood and adolescence (Whiteman, 1967), as does the ability to understand the causes of others' emotional states (Burleson, 1982b).

During the middle- and late-childhood periods and throughout adolescence, youngsters progressively develop broader and more sophisticated verbal repertoires for addressing the distressed emotional states of others. Several studies (e.g., Burleson, 1982a; Clinton & Hancock, 1991; Ritter, 1979) have found that from middle childhood through late adolescence, children develop more differentiated and diverse repertoires of comforting strategies. They also gradually become more able to produce sensitive comforting messages that acknowledge, elaborate on, legitimize, and contextualize the feelings and perspectives of distressed others. During this period, children also become more adept at adapting their comforting messages to fit the characteristics of a particular target and the requirements of the specific situation (see Burleson, 1980, 1982b).

An important aspect of the child's developing competence for emotional

---

[1]Some observational studies have reported very low base rates of peer-directed comforting by preschoolers (e.g., Eisenberg, Cameron, Tyron, & Dodez, 1981; F. F. Strayer, 1981), which contrasts with the results of research conducted in home and laboratory settings (e.g., Hay et al., 1981; Zahn-Waxler et al., 1979) suggesting that young children rather frequently orient to the distressed affective states of others (especially peers) and regularly seek to provide aid and comfort. This contradiction was addressed in a study by Caplan and Hay (1989), who carefully observed the responses of preschoolers to the distress cues of peers in the classroom context. Children often paid attention to the distress cues of peers, but only occasionally undertook prosocial actions directed at relieving the peer's distress. Interviews with the children indicated that many were capable of engaging in appropriate forms of emotional support, but did not undertake such actions because they believed they were not supposed to provide help when competent adult caregivers were present. These findings suggest that children's prosocial tendencies may sometimes be attenuated by the acquisition of social norms defining appropriate conduct (see Hay, 1993). Thus, with respect to peer-directed emotional support, children may often be more competent than their performances imply.

support is learning whom *not* to support and when *not* to engage in supportive activities (see Caplan, 1993). That is, children must learn to be discriminating with respect to support recipients and occasions. For example, over the course of development, children learn that some relationship partners (e.g., friends, siblings) are more "deserving" of support than others (e.g., strangers). Although preschoolers appear to be somewhat indiscriminate in their selection of support recipients, by the time they are ready for school, most children are much more likely to provide emotional support to a friend than an acquaintance (e.g., Costin & Jones, 1992)—a tendency that persists through adolescence and the adult years (e.g., see Ritter, 1979). Children must also learn to distinguish among distress cues that should be responded to and those that should be ignored, circumstances that merit supportive actions and those that do not, and social settings in which it is appropriate to provide support and those in which it is not. Thus far, little research has addressed these important aspects of emotional support competence.

In sum, skills associated with both the capacity and the motivation to provide sensitive emotional support develop throughout childhood and adolescence. Rudimentary acts of comforting and support appear either during or shortly after the first year of life. Toddlers display differentiated acts of comforting, some of which include verbal expressions of sympathy. Throughout the preschool years, children become more likely to perform spontaneous acts of comforting, especially when it is normatively appropriate for them to do so. By the time children enter grade school, they are quite capable of recognizing emotional distress in others, empathizing with those distressed others, and formulating more or less supportive responses. These capacities continue to grow in sophistication through adolescence, and perhaps into adulthood.

Individual Differences in Children's Emotional Support Skills and Behaviors

Although there is a clear developmental course for children's emotional support skills, noticeable individual differences in the ability and proclivity to provide support are apparent from early childhood and onward. Individual differences have been observed among quite young children in their responsiveness to distress cues of peers, parents, and siblings. For example, substantial individual differences have been observed in preschoolers' responsiveness to crying by peers (e.g., Farver & Branstetter, 1994). Important differences have been observed among toddlers in the likelihood of intervening on behalf of a distressed sibling (Dunn & Munn, 1986), other children (Zahn-Waxler et al., 1979), and adults (Zahn-Waxler & Radke-Yarrow, 1990). Later in childhood, individual differences have been documented in children's empathy (Eisenberg et al., 1993), affective perspective-taking skills (e.g., Barnett, 1984), and verbal strategies for comforting distressed peers (Applegate et al., 1992; Burleson, 1984b). Thus, individual differences are manifest initially in children's responsiveness to distressed others and later in the quality of the verbal strategies they use to comfort distressed others.

The individual differences observed in children's emotional support skills appear to be stable, even quite early in life. Cummings, Hollenbeck, Iannotti, Radke-Yarrow, and Zahn-Waxler (1986) examined the stability of individual differences in emotional support (responsiveness to another's distress) during the second year of life, finding a high degree of stability over a 9-month period in the levels of supportiveness displayed by children. Dunn and Munn (1986) found a moderate degree of stability in the tendency of toddlers to behave supportively toward siblings over a 6-month period. Similarly, Zahn-Waxler, Radke-Yarrow, Wagner, and Chapman (1992) found that individual differences in supportive behavior children displayed in response to witnessed distress were moderately stable from 18 to 24 months of age. Other research has shown that later in childhood, individual differences in skills associated with the provision of sensitive verbal comfort exhibit considerable stability over a 1-year period (Applegate et al., 1992).

The early appearance and stability of individual differences in emotional support suggest that there may be a biological basis for these differences. Zahn-Waxler, Robinson, and Emde (1992) assessed the heritability of emotional support orientations by examining the reactions of 94 monozygotic (MZ) twins and 90 same-sex dizygotic (DZ) twins to staged instances of distress when the children were both 14 and 20 months of age. MZ twins were more similar than DZ twins at both 14 and 20 months in their expressions of empathic concern, and were also more similar than DZ twins at 14 months in degree of overt support displayed to the distressed other. These results are consistent with studies of adult twins that have found MZ twins more similar than DZ twins in self-reports of empathic concern (Matthews, Batson, Horn, & Rosenman, 1981) and altruism (Rushton, Fulker, Neale, Nias, & Eysenck, 1986). It appears, then, that some aspects of the orientation to provide emotional support may be heritable.

But while biology can predispose, it cannot compose. That is, a genetically inherited predisposition may lead some individuals to be comparatively responsive to the distress of another. But composing, delivering, and revising sensitive, sophisticated comforting messages involves much more than the predisposition to act on behalf of others. As argued above, comforting and other forms of emotional support—especially beyond the early childhood years—are complex, skilled forms of behavior. These skills are not genetically programmed; rather, they must be learned. Moreover, as detailed below, substantial social influences on a broad array of emotional support skills have been found. Hence, individual differences in emotional support skills need to be explained, at least in part, in terms of socialization factors.

SOME PARENTAL PRACTICES AND THEIR EFFECTS ON CHILDREN'S EMOTIONAL SUPPORT COMPETENCIES

Several general reviews addressing the socialization of prosocial behavior have appeared in the last dozen years (e.g., Barnett, 1987; Brody & Shaffer, 1982; Eisenberg & Mussen, 1989; Goldstein & Michaels, 1985; Grusec, 1982; Radke-

Yarrow & Zahn-Waxler, 1986; Radke-Yarrow, Zahn-Waxler, & Chapman, 1983). For the most part, these reviews have focused on behaviors such as sharing, cooperation, and the provision of instrumental help, with none having focused on emotional support skills. In this review, we focus exclusively on research pertaining to emotional support skills, for both practical and theoretical reasons. Practically, there is a need to delimit the literature covered to render it manageable. More important, many studies have found only weak associations among various forms of prosocial behavior (e.g., Payne, 1980; Richman et al., 1988; see the review by Underwood & Moore, 1982a). The lack of generality among different forms of prosocial behavior means that factors that predict one type of behavior (e.g., sharing) will not necessarily be associated with other forms of prosocial conduct (e.g., comforting). Consequently, each form of behavior requires distinct examination.

Some forms of prosocial behavior are relatively straightforward and can be taught by caregivers through simple, if frequent, imperatives ("Share," "Take turns," "Don't hit"). But the process of providing emotional support typically involves much more complicated cognitive abilities and behaviors. The skills and orientations associated with the provision of sensitive emotional support must be acquired by the child over a period of years within social environments that implicitly "instruct" the child in relevant skills and afford opportunities for practice. Hence, understanding the development of and individual differences in children's emotional support skills requires attention to contexts and processes of socialization, especially primary socialization processes involving parents. There is little evidence that parents intentionally and explicitly teach their children emotional support skills, which is a touch ironic since parents clearly do intentionally teach their children simpler and less demanding forms of prosocial behavior such as sharing.

Adequate explanations of the socialization of emotional support skills must specify three factors: (1) the emotional support skills and proclivities of the child that are of interest, (2) the behavioral practices of parents (or other socialization agents) that are believed to act on the child's competencies, and (3) the theoretical mechanisms that link parental practices to the child's competencies. Skills and proclivities of the child pertinent to this discussion were detailed in the model of emotional support developed in the section entitled "Components of Emotional Support." This section describes several behavioral practices by parents that potentially influence the child's emotional support skills, discusses the nature of some theoretical mechanisms through which these practices may affect children, and summarizes the results of empirical studies assessing ties between parental practices and child skills. A list of relevant parental practices, socialization mechanisms, and child competencies is presented in Figure 1.

There is a wide variety of parental practices that may facilitate the acquisition of emotional support skills by children, among which are expressing care, affection, and warmth to the child; modeling appropriate forms of comfort and emotional support; telling the child how to display sympathy and support; reinforcing the child for observed supportive acts; inculating prosocial and humanis-

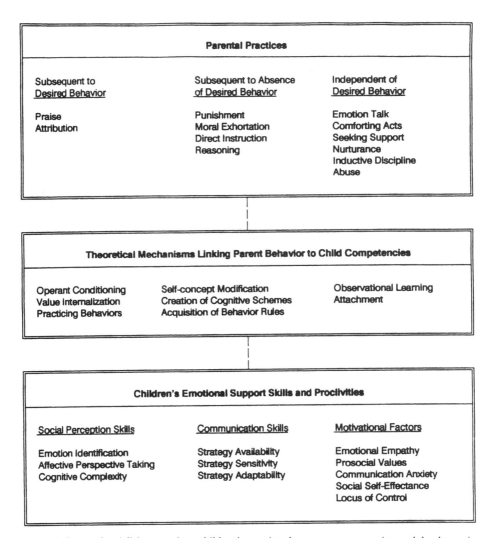

Figure 1. Parental socializing practices, children's emotional support competencies, and the theoretical mechanisms that link them.

tic values; disciplining the child in a compassionate and sensitive manner; discussing feelings, intentions, and other internal states with the child; and labeling the child as caring and compassionate. Grusec (1982) has suggested that behavioral practices potentially influencing the socialization of some prosocial proclivity or skill can be divided into three groups: (1) those administered after the occurrence of the desired prosocial behavior, (2) those that follow an absence of a desired prosocial behavior, and (3) those that occur independently of the child's prosocial behavior, but that later facilitate concern for others. This simple typology provides a convenient framework for assessing the effects of different parental practices on the socialization of the child's emotional support skills. For purposes of analytical clarity, the subsequent discussion separately considers practices falling into each of Grusec's categories. Clearly, though, parents may engage in multiple behaviors within a single episode, so many practices relevant to the socialization of emotional support skills may occur more or less simultaneously.

Parental Practices Following Desired Child Behaviors

Some of the things that parents do after observing a desired prosocial behavior by their child may have the effect of stabilizing that behavior or increasing the likelihood of its occurrence. Among the more important parental behaviors falling in this category are praise (and other positive reinforcements) and attributing the child's behavior to internal dispositions such as caring and compassion.

Praise.   Praise and related forms of positive reinforcement may be used by parents if they observe their child displaying appropriate forms of emotional support. Principles of operant conditioning maintain that positively reinforced behaviors increase in frequency. Thus, parental praise of their children's emotionally supportive acts should enhance the child's motivation to engage in such acts, thereby increasing the likelihood, frequency, and persistence of these acts. There is some evidence that praise can increase the amount or frequency of prosocial behaviors such as sharing in laboratory contexts (e.g., Rushton & Teachman, 1978). However, little research has examined the effects of praise and other reinforcers in naturalistic contexts, and virtually no research has examined how praise influences comforting and other forms of emotional support in either laboratory or naturalistic contexts. An observational study in the home environment conducted by Grusec (1991) found that praise and other symbolic rewards were rarely used by parents to positively reinforce the prosocial behaviors of their children (and parents almost never used material rewards as reinforcers). Hence, although praise may have the potential to enhance the child's motivation to undertake emotionally supportive acts, there is little evidence that this practice is actually used by parents or that it functions to increase displayed levels of children's emotional support.

Attributing Supportive Acts to Prosocial Dispositions.   A second practice that might occur subsequent to the observation of an emotionally supportive act is verbally attributing that act to prosocial dispositions within the child (e.g., "You were so kind to comfort Pat. You are a very caring and sympathetic person"). Such attributions make use of what Goffman (1967) termed "alter-casting," the imposition of a particular social identity on another through the use of labeling. This practice is held to influence the child's subsequent behavior through the mechanism of self-concept modification (Grusec, 1982). Presumably, the individual's self-concept or self-schema is a basis for action; persons seek to act in ways consistent with their self-concepts. Labeling the child's actions with prosocial terms and attributing those actions to prosocial dispositions may lead the child to think of himself *as* a kind and caring person who engages in compassionate acts.

Attributing observed actions to particular dispositional states is a potentially powerful socializing practice that has been shown—in laboratory studies—to enhance prosocial behaviors such as cooperation, sharing, and helping (see the review by Radke-Yarrow et al., 1983, pp. 511–512). The impact of this practice on emotional support skills and proclivities has not been examined, however. Moreover, there is little evidence that parents systematically use this practice with their children in the home environment (Grusec, 1991). Thus, it is currently unknown whether this practice fosters the development of emotional support skills and proclivities in children.

Parental Practices Following the Absence of Desired Child Behaviors

At times, parents may expect to desire their child to behave in a prosocial way, but the child fails to act in the anticipated manner. Indeed, some observational research (e.g., Iannotti, 1985; F. F. Strayer, 1981) indicates that young children have many opportunities to provide emotional support to distressed peers, siblings, and adults, but often fail to do so. Further, children occasionally act in ways directly contrary to parental desires (e.g., with aggression rather than compassion). When confronted with the child's failure to exhibit a desired behavior, parents may engage in several practices intended to make the occurrence of that behavior more likely, including punishment, moral exhortation, behavioral instruction, and reasoning.

Punishment. Clearly, parents punish their children for all kinds of misdeeds. But there is little indication that parents, at least in this culture, punish children for failing to engage in acts of emotional support. And this makes sense given how the practice of punishment works: Punishment is the application of negative reinforcement, which, through the mechanism of operant conditioning, seeks to extinguish an undesirable behavior (Walters & Grusec, 1977). Punishment may be effective in extinguishing an undesirable behavior, but there is no indication that it is effective in promoting desired behaviors. Hence, it is unlikely that punishing children for failing to behave in an emotionally supportive manner increases their support competencies.

Although punishing children for failing to act supportively may not increase the likelihood of subsequent supportive behaviors, punishment other misdeeds may enhance aspects of children's support orientations. For example, Eisenberg, Fabes, Schaller, Carlo, and Miller (1991) found that parents who reported being restrictive about their children's display of emotions that might hurt others (e.g., aggressive anger) had children with higher levels of dispositional sympathy and empathy. Though important, this finding pertains to punishment for inappropriate actions, not to punishment for the failure to engage in desirable actions. If parents are frustrated by an absence of emotionally supportive acts, it is more likely that, rather than punishing their children, they would exhort them to undertake such acts, instruct them about how and when to engage in such actions, or reason with them about the situation.

Moral Exhortation, Direct Instruction, and Reasoning. Moral exhortation refers to the practice of telling a child what is good, worthy, and right, while direct instruction involves telling a child when and how to behave in a desired manner. Reasoning, in the current context, pertains to systematically reflecting on elements of a situation with the child. If children fail to behave supportively when parents think they should, some parents may respond by telling their children that they *should* have acted supportively in that situation and that they should be more supportive (or caring and helpful) in future situations. Parents may also use such occasions to assert the value of virtues such as care, compassion, and sympathy. These exhortations may lead to the internalization of the desired values. In addition, if parents believe that the child's failure to act supportively stems from ignorance about appropriate actions, they may provide some direct instruction in suitable forms of conduct (e.g., "Say you're sorry that he's feeling sad," or "Put your arm around her and give her a little hug"). Clear instructions may help the child acquire appropriate behavioral rules and tactics. Parents may also engage in reasoning with their child about the absence of supportive actions (e.g., inquiring if the child was aware that another was distressed, asking the child why he or she didn't act, getting the child to think about the consequences of his or her inaction, and encouraging the child to think about why it is important to be supportive and how he or she might be able to act more supportively in the future). Such reasoning may facilitate both the internalization of norms and the acquisition of behavioral rules, as well as promote more general cognitive capacities (e.g., consequential thinking, means–ends reasoning).

Although there is plentiful anecdotal evidence that parents engage in these practices, they have not been the object of systematic research in contexts in which children have failed to provide emotional support. Nor has their effect on children's emotional support skills and dispositions been determined. There is, however, evidence from laboratory investigations (e.g., Grusec, Kuczynski, Rushton, & Simutis, 1978; see the review by Eisenberg & Mussen, 1989) indicating that moral exhortations and direct instruction can increase the amount of prosocial behavior children display. Further, the use of reasoning by parents in the context of disciplining children for misdeeds appears to facilitate the development of several skills involved in the provision of sensitive emotional support (research on the effects of parental discipline is reviewed below). There is good reason, then, for thinking that when children fail to act supportively, parental use of practices such as moral exhortation, instruction, and reasoning may increase both children's tendency to undertake supportive actions and their skill in addressing others' feelings.

Parental Practices Independent of the Child's Emotional Support Behaviors

As indicated previously, it appears that only rarely do parents directly attempt to teach their children how and when to engage in acts of emotional support. Rather, children appear to acquire the competencies needed to act supportively from a variety of everyday practices in which parents (and other socialization agents) routinely engage. Such practices include discussing emotions and other internal states with the child, comforting the child when he or she is upset, seeking support from the child, nurturing the child warmly, using inductive modes of disciplining the child, and avoiding abusive treatment. Substantial research has been done on many of these practices, and they appear to be important anteced-ents of the child's emotional support skills and proclivities.

Emotion Talk. One practice that appears to contribute substantially to the child's ability to recognize and understand another's emotions is talking with the child about feelings, intentions, and related internal states.[1] Parents may talk to their children about the emotions of others in a wide variety of contexts, includ-ing, for example, while playing, observing others, reading stories, regulating the child's behavior, or watching television. Such talk creates an awareness of the nature and range of human emotions, leads to an appreciation of the circum-stances that motivate various emotional states, and implicitly teaches the child that emotions are significant and need to be taken into account (see Goldstein & Michaels, 1985). This learning is important, since young children spontaneously think about others in concrete, physical, and behavioral terms.

More specifically, talk by parents about feelings and related internal states semiotically mediates the world to the child, drawing attention to "invisible" features of others, making them a more salient part of the child's world (see Dunn, Bretherton, & Munn, 1987). Further, talk about emotions helps create the inter-personal constructs or cognitive schemes that children come to use in interpret-ing and acting upon their world. Children with more cognitive schemata pertain-ing to emotions should be more likely to orient to and focus on the emotions of others, contemplate others' feelings, and take emotions into account when gener-ating goals for social situations and developing lines of action.

Consistent with this hypothesis, an observational study by Dunn et al. (1987) found that the number of references to feeling states occurring in the talk of mothers and older siblings when a target child was 18 months old predicted the child's speech about feeling states 6 months later. Moreover, in two other studies, Dunn and her colleagues have found that the number of references to feeling states occurring in conversations between children and their mothers or siblings

---

[1]The amount of talk about emotions in which the members of a family engage should not be confused with the level of emotional expressiveness in that family. The latter construct pertains to the degree to which emotions are overtly expressed, not the extent to which emotions are discussed. Recalled levels of family emotional expressiveness have been found unassociated with self-reported dispositional empathy (sympathetic concern) and perspective-taking skill among college students (Eisenberg et al., 1991).

predicted children's performances on measures of affective perspective taking both 7 months later (Dunn, Brown, Slomowski, Tesla, & Youngblade, 1991) and 36 months later (Dunn, Brown, & Beardsall, 1991). However, Howe and Ross (1990) found no relationship between the frequency of references to feeling states in conversations between mothers and first-borns and the tendency of first-borns to comfort second-borns when they were distressed. This latter finding suggests that there is more to emotional support than perspective-taking skill: Children must also acquire effective comforting strategies, as well as good perspective-taking skills, if they are to be sources of sensitive emotional support.

Comforting Acts. The comforting acts that children observe parents performing are surely one of the most important influences on the children's developing emotional support skills. Obviously, most children are the recipients of numerous comforting acts by parents. They also may witness such actions being directed toward others (e.g., siblings, other family members). Depending on their particular character, the comforting actions of caretakers may influence the child's support skills and proclivities through a variety of mechanisms. Clearly, observational learning is an important mechanism: Children learn how and when to dispense emotional support by observing and imitating parental models. It is no accident that most comforting behaviors displayed by toddlers include warm hugs, gentle pats, verbal reassurances, and expressions of affection; these are the very behaviors parents routinely direct at their upset children. Consistent with this anecdotal evidence, a multimethod study by Zahn-Waxler et al. (1979) found that toddlers whose mothers engaged in empathic caregiving were more likely to produce comforting acts in experimentally structured situations and more frequently engaged in spontaneous comforting acts in natural situations than children whose parents typically employed a less empathic style of providing support.

Substantial laboratory research indicates that children frequently imitate the altruistic actions of models they observe (see Eisenberg & Mussen, 1989; Radke-Yarrow et al., 1983). Moreover, several studies by Eisenberg and her colleagues (Eisenberg et al., 1992; Eisenberg, Fabes, et al., 1991; Fabes, Eisenberg, & Miller, 1990) have found that children whose parents exhibit a high level of empathy or sympathetic concern report and/or display greater sympathy and affective perspective-taking skills than children whose parents exhibit lower levels of empathy and sympathetic concern. Some research, however, has found the association between parent–child sympathy and empathy to be moderated by the sex of the child (e.g., Barnett, King, Howard, & Dino, 1980) or to be absent altogether (e.g., J. Strayer & Roberts, 1989).

The comforting efforts of parents may also involve a good deal of emotion talk, which, as discussed previously, can foster the development of cognitive schemata for feeling states. Consistent with this view, Applegate et al. (1992) found that maternal use of comforting messages encouraging the child to think about emotional states was associated with several aspects of children' social–cognitive skills. Similarly, Bryant (1987) found that children of mothers who responded to their children's stressful experiences with "expressive" behaviors exhibited higher levels of empathy, while Eisenberg et al. (1993) found that a child-oriented discussion of feelings by mothers while providing comfort was associated with children's manifesting a low level of personal distress when watching a sad film.

Parental talk about feelings while providing comfort may also model appropriate verbal strategies for conveying emotional support. Eisenberg et al. (1993) found that an emphasis by mothers on problem solving and the exploration of feelings while comforting their children was associated with the amount of verbal comfort their children directed at a crying infant. Further, Applegate et al. (1992) found that the sophistication of mothers' comforting messages was associated with the person-centered quality of the comforting messages their children produced in a laboratory peer-comforting situation. In sum, the manner in which parents convey comfort and other forms of emotional support to their children represents a powerful influence on children's ability to recognize others' emotional states, their tendency to empathize or sympathize with others' distress, and their capacity to produce appropriate behavioral and verbal responses to those distressed states.

Seeking Support.   Interestingly, one parental practice that may enhance children's abilities to provide support is occasionally seeking support from those children. This notion is suggested by the finding of Rehberg and Richman (1989) that single-parent mothers who reported being emotionally dependent on their children had offspring more likely to provide functional comfort to distressed peers. Providing support to a distressed parent gives children the opportunity to practice and refine their support skills. Responding to others' needs may also lead children to become accustomed to, and even comfortable in, the role of support provider. Clearly, though, the emotional problems and needs of adults can easily overwhelm the capacity of child support givers. For example, Zahn-Waxler, Kochanska, Krupnick, and McKnew (1990) found that young children of chronically depressed mothers exhibited greater responsiveness to the distress of others than did the children of nondepressed mothers. By middle childhood, however, this trend had reversed, with the offspring of chronically depressed mothers exhibiting less responsiveness to the distress of others than the children of nondepressed mothers.

Parental Nurturance.   "Nurturance" has been defined as "warmth and involvement in caregiving, sensitivity and responsiveness to the child's needs, and expression of affection" (Eisenberg & Mussen, 1989, p. 79). Parental nurturance may facilitate the development of emotional support skills in several ways. For example, "parental nurturance presumably contributes to prosocial development because responding to a child's signals of need reduces a child's self concern, creates a positive affective orientation toward people, and increases identification with and imitation of these prosocial parents" (Bryant & Crockenberg, 1980, p. 529). Radke-Yarrow et al. (1983) suggest that parental nurturance may promote the development of a sensitive, supportive child by modeling care, concern, and compassion. Nurturant behavior may also foster the child's emotional support skills and proclivities by promoting a secure attachment relationship between caretaker and child.

Consistent nurturance and warmth by parents has been found to be one of the most powerful predictors of a secure attachment style in children (see Bretherton & Waters, 1985). Secure attachment may enhance the emotional support competencies of children in several ways (see Elicker, Englund, & Sroufe, 1992). For example, securely attached individuals have had their past emotional needs met, and thus may be better attuned to the emotional needs of others (Kestenbaum et al., 1989). Congruent with this view, studies have found parental warmth affection, and nurturance to be associated with children's social–cognitive abilities (e.g., Garner et al., 1994), empathic tendencies (Barnett, Howard, King, & Dino, 1980; Eisenberg-Berg & Mussen, 1978; Feshbach, 1975), and inclination to provide comfort (Bryant & Crockenberg, 1980; Garner et al., 1994).

Securely attached children may acquire positive social orientations and prosocial values, which serve to motivate emotionally supportive acts. Waters, Wippman, and Sroufe (1979) found that children who had a secure attachment style at 15 months of age were rated 2 years later as being more sympathetic to distressed preschool playmates. And an impressive longitudinal study by Koestner, Franz, and Weinberger (1990) found that nurturant behavior by parents toward their 5-year-old children was associated 25 years later with the degree of concern for others expressed by those now-grown children.

The working models of interpersonal relationships developed by securely attached children tend to portray these relationships as stable, consistent sources of support, and this picture may translate into principles that guide behavior in these relationships (e.g., provide comfort and support when it is needed). Children exhibiting anxious–avoidant and anxious–resistant attachment styles have not had their emotional needs consistently met and thus are less likely to have elaborated a framework for adequately responding to the distresses of others. In line with this reasoning, Kestenbaum et al. (1989) reported that children classified as securely attached at 12 and 18 months engaged in more spontaneous comforting of distressed playmates at 48 months of age than did children initially classified as anxious–avoidant. Insecurely attached children may become aroused by another's distress, but that arousal can take the form of fear, anger, or other unpleasant emotions. Sadly, there is growing evidence that children with insecure attachment histories may act aggressively toward emotionally distressed peers (e.g., Main & George, 1985).

Inductive Discipline.   Discipline is an omnipresent feature of the parental role, and the effects of different disciplinary styles are one of the most intensively researched topics in the social sciences. One group of disciplinary techniques capturing considerable attention are those termed *induction* (Hoffman, 1977), *authoritative parenting* (Baumrind, 1989), or *reflection-enhancing regulation* (Applegate et al., 1992). In general, induction refers to disciplining children through reasoning, encouraging reflection about the consequences of problematic behaviors, and emphasizing principles that ought to govern actions. Induction is typically contrasted with *power assertion* or *authoritarian parenting*, which involves the use of physical punishment and the exercise of material power in an effort to control the child.

Several theorists (Eisenberg & Mussen, 1989; Goldstein & Michaels, 1985; Radke-Yarrow & Zahn-Waxler, 1986) have suggested that the use of induction and related disciplinary techniques may facilitate the development of children's emotional support skills. This is an interesting theoretical suggestion, since if inductive discipline affects children's emotional support capacities, it must do so through mechanisms other than modeling or observational learning. Induction appears most likely to affect children's support proclivities and skills by promulgating prosocial values that motivate supportive acts. Consistent with this reasoning, some studies have found parental power assertion negatively associated with children's other-oriented values (Dlugokinski & Firestone, 1974) and empathic dispositions (Feshbach, 1975). However, other studies (e.g., Barnett, King et al., 1980) have failed to find an association between parental induction and children's empathic dispositions.

The emotion talk that is a part of many inductive efforts may enhance children's social perception skills by helping the child elaborate cognitive schemes focused on others' feelings and perspectives. Indeed, Applegate et al. (1992) found the use of inductive discipline by mothers to be positively associated with several of their children's social–cognitive abilities, as well as with the children's ability to produce sensitive comforting messages. Similarly, Miller, Eisenberg, Fabes, Shell, and Gular (1989) found maternal induction to be positively associated with children's emotional responsiveness to a sad film stimulus, while maternal power assertion was negatively associated with children's responsiveness to this stimulus.

Abuse and Emotional Support Pathologies.   Although inductive discipline may promote support-giving abilities, harsh and abusive treatment by parents seriously undermines children's supportive orientations. For example, in several studies, Camras and her colleagues (e.g., Camras et al., 1990; Camras, Grow, & Ribordy, 1983) have shown that children abused or maltreated by their mothers are less able than nonmaltreated children to recognize facially expressed emotions. More seriously, abuse does not merely result in children's lacking support skills, but additionally leads to emotional support pathologies in which maltreated children act hostilely toward peers exhibiting emotional distress. Main and George (1985) compared the responses of 10 abused and 10 nonabused toddlers to distress exhibited by playmates at a daycare center. None of the abused children showed concern in response to playmates' distress; moreover, several of the abused toddlers reacted to peer distress with anger and even physical attack. None of the nonabused children exhibited such dysfunctional behaviors. Three other studies (Howes & Eldrige, 1985; Howes & Espinosa, 1984; Klimes-Dougan & Kistner, 1990) comparing abused and nonabused children have also found that abused children exhibit some likelihood of responding to peer distress with anger, teasing, and aggression (both verbal and physical). The inappropriate responses of abused children to peer distress may reflect the operation of modeling processes; these children probably have seen the expression of distress provoke hostile and aggressive actions by maltreating parents. Abused children also have poor attachment to their caregivers and develop dysfunctional working models of interpersonal relationships. No doubt all these factors, along with others, contribute to the emotional support pathologies displayed by abused children.

CONCLUSION

The research reviewed in this chapter provides convincing evidence that features of parents' behaviors influence their children's emotional support skills and proclivities. In particular, the available literature suggests that parental practices such as talking to children about emotions, engaging in comforting, providing nurturance, creating opportunities to practice giving support, and using inductive forms of discipline foster support-relevant aspects of the child's social–cognitive abilities, message production skills, and motivational orientations. These parental practices appear to promote child competencies primarily through the mechanisms of observational learning, attachment processes, schema development, and value internalization.

The results of the research reviewed here, although intriguing and suggestive, are far from definitive. The current findings give us some reasonably good ideas about the parental practices that affect children's emotional support competencies; we are also in a position to formulate some reasonable speculations about the mechanisms through which these practices may influence children's skills. Clearly, though, the current state of the research permits only tentative conclusions. Future research should aim to enhance both the precision and the scope of our understanding about how children develop emotional support skills.

One source of impression stems from most studies having been designed to examine how one (or at most a few) parental practices influence one (or a very few) of the child's competencies. This approach to research is problematic, since many parental practices are probably correlated with one another (e.g., parents who comfort their children regularly also may provide lots of nurturance as well as use inductive discipline). If our understanding of how parent behaviors affect children's skills is to be improved, we need to identify more precisely the "effective ingredients" of various parental practices, how these ingredients might combine and work together, and how they separately and collectively impact on the child's skills. This can be done only through studies that simultaneously assess and compare the effects of multiple parental practices.

More precise understandings of how socialization practices influence children's skills can also be obtained through experimental research, especially studies comparing different methods of teaching children emotional support skills. Very few experimental training efforts have been reported (for one example, see Yarrow, Scott, & Waxler, 1973). Yet such research may afford the best context for developing a precise appreciation of which practices most affect children's skills. The results of such experimental research not only promise to enhance our theoretical understanding of the socialization process, but also should provide a sound basis for developing interventions and educational programs designed to improve children's support skills.

The research reviewed in this chapter suggests that the parental practices most commonly associated with children's emotional support competencies are those that occur apart from the contexts in which children provide, or might be expected to provide, support (e.g., parental comforting of the child, nurturing the child, talking about emotions, using inductive discipline). This finding is reasonable since there are many more opportunities for parents to nurture, discipline, and comfort their children than there are for them to offer feedback on children's successes and failures at providing support. However, the major reason there is more evidence supporting the role of practices such as parental comforting and nurturance with respect to children's support skills is that much more research has been carried out on these practices than on practices that follow either the display of emotional support (praise, attribution of prosocial dispositions) or the failure to observe desired acts of support (exhortation, instruction, reasoning). Thus, it would be inappropriate to conclude that practices such as emotion talk and nurturance are more powerful or more important socializing influences with respect to the child's support skills. Clearly, additional research is needed, especially on how parents (and other caretakers) respond to children's supportive actions, as well as to children's lack of action in contexts in which they could provide support to a distressed other. Important questions to be pursued in the latter case include whether parents notice and talk with the nonintervening child in these situations, what practices they use if and when they confront their children, and how different parental practices subsequently affect children's emotional support skills and proclivities.

Another way of improving precision in the analysis of socialization processes is to take better account of factors that may moderate the influence of parental practices on children's emotional support competencies. For example, both the emotional expressivity of parents and the intensity of emotions expressed have been found to moderate the effects of parental discipline and comforting on children's support competencies (see Eisenberg, Fabes, Schaller, Carlo, et al., 1991; Miller et al., 1989). Other research indicates that parental depression (see Hay, 1993; Zahn-Waxler et al., 1990) and marital discord (see Zahn-Waxler & Radke-Yarrow, 1990) may influence the impact of various socialization practices on children's support skills.

One moderating factor that merits special attention is gender. Emotional support is a heavily gendered activity in our culture (Wood, 1994), and there is abundant evidence of reliable gender differences in empathy (see the reviews by Eisenberg & Lennon, 1983; Lennon & Eisenberg, 1987) and various forms of helping (see Eagly, 1987). How does the socialization process contribute to the origin and development of these gender differences? In what ways do mothers and fathers model comfort and support differently to their offspring? Do sons and daughters respond differently to the parental practices to which they are exposed?

Research addressing these questions will enhance our understanding of how emotional support skills are acquired and developed, as well as deepen our appreciation of the social construction of gender.

There are several ways in which the scope of research on the socialization of emotional support skills needs to be expanded. For example, most research has focused on the emotional support behaviors of young children and the parental practices that affect these behaviors. Far fewer studies have examined factors that underlie the support competencies of older children and adolescents. Undertaking research with older populations will require developing more sophisticated conceptions of supportive behaviors as well as more sophisticated methods for examining the presumably advanced skills of older children and adolescents. In particular, the simple frequency counts of supportive behaviors so common in research with young children are unlikely to capture meaningful differences in the skills and proclivities of older persons. Frequency counts assume that all supportive actions are equal in quality or effectiveness and therefore that "more is better." Clearly, though, some support efforts are more sensitive and effective than others (e.g., Dakof & Taylor, 1990; Lehman et al., 1986), so more is not always better. Methods useful in the analysis of the complex verbal strategies used by older persons to provide support have recently been developed and validated (see Applegate et al., 1992; Burleson, 1994).

A second way in which research on the socialization of emotional support needs to expand its scope is in the range of behaviors examined. As noted previously, many theoretical characterizations of emotional support encompass a broad range of behaviors (e.g., celebrating with others, enhancing others' esteem, building confidence) (see East, 1991). Yet existing research has focused almost exclusively on comforting behaviors. Future research should examine emotional support skills other than comforting, consider the roles these other skills play in children's lives and relationships, identify the cognitive and motivational constituents of these skills, and specify the socialization experiences that help develop them.

Research also needs to consider socialization agents other than parents. There is only a smattering of research on how agents other than parents affect the child's support skills, but there are indications that these skills are influenced by siblings (e.g., Dunn & Munn, 1986), peers (Brody & Shaffer, 1982; Burleson & Kunkel, May, 1995), and teachers (e.g., Eisenberg et al., 1981). Other agents that potentially influence the child's emotional support abilities include grandparents, daycare programs, churches and religious organizations, the media, and community groups such as Scouts. As children grow older and spend more time outside the home, it is likely that the influence of nonparental agents will increase.

Finally, insufficient attention has been given to the processes through which children come to see themselves as providers of support. At what point in development do children come to see themselves as sources of emotional support? Are children aware of and do they value their own emotional support skills? Do those who value the activity of providing support come to develop more sophisticated support-giving skills? Addressing these issues may help us better understand when and how the role of support provider becomes salient to the child, how this role may enter the child's self-concept, and why children come to care about caring.

ACKNOWLEDGMENT

We are grateful to Greg Pierce for suggesting the research questions in the final paragraph of this chapter.

REFERENCES

Albrecht, T. L., Burleson, B. R., & Goldsmith, D. (1994). Supportive communication. In M. L. Knapp & G. R. Miller (Eds.), *Handbook of interpersonal communication*, 2nd ed. (pp. 419–449). Thousand Oaks, CA: Sage Publications.

Applegate, J. L. (1980). Adaptive communication in educational contexts: A study of teachers' communicative strategies. *Communication Education, 29*, 158–170.

Applegate, J. L. (1990). Constructs and communication: A pragmatic integration. In G. Neimeyer (Ed.), *Advances in personal construct psychology*, Vol. 1 (pp. 203–230). Greenwich, CT: JAI Press.

Applegate, J. L., Burleson, B. R., & Delia, J. G. (1992). Reflection-enhancing parenting as antecedent to children's social–cognitive and communicative development. In I. E. Sigel, A. V. McGillicuddy-Delisi, & J. J. Goodnow (Eds.), *Parental belief systems: The psychological consequences for children*, 2nd ed. (pp. 3–39). Hillsdale, NJ: Lawrence Erlbaum.

Bandura, A. (1977). Self-efficacy: Toward a unifying theory of behavioral change. *Psychological Review, 84*, 191–215.

Barbee, A. P., & Cunningham, M. R. (1995). An experimental approach to social support communications: Interactive coping in close relationships. In B. R. Burleson (Ed.), *Communication yearbook 18* (pp. 381–413). Thousand Oaks, CA: Sage Publications.

Barnett, M. A. (1984). Perspective taking and empathy in the child's prosocial behavior. In H. E. Sypher & J. L. Applegate (Eds.), *Communication by children and adults: Social cognitive and strategic processes* (pp. 43–62). Beverly Hills: Sage Publications.

Barnett, M. A. (1987). Empathy and related responses in children. In N. Eisenberg & J. Strayer (Eds.), *Empathy and its development* (pp. 146–162). New York: Cambridge University Press.

Barnett, M. A., Howard, J. A., King, L. M., & Dino, G. A. (1980). Antecedents of empathy: Retrospective accounts of early socialization. *Personality and Social Psychology Bulletin, 6*, 361–365.

Barnett, M. A., King, L. M., Howard, J. A., & Dino, G. A. (1980). Empathy in young children: Relation to parents' empathy, affection, and emphasis on the feelings of others. *Developmental Psychology, 16*, 243–244.

Batson, C. D., Dyck, J. L., & Brandt, R. J. (1988). Five studies testing two new egoistic alternatives to the empathy–altruism hypothesis. *Journal of Personality and Social Psychology, 55*, 52–77.

Baumrind, D. (1989). Rearing competent children. In W. Damon (Ed.), *Child development today and tomorrow* (pp. 349–378). San Francisco: Jossey-Bass.

Borke, H. (1971). Interpersonal perception of young children: Egocentrism or empathy? *Developmental Psychology, 5*, 263–269.

Bretherton, I., & Waters, E. (Eds.) (1985). Growing points of attachment theory and research. *Monographs of the Society for Research in Child Development, 50(1-2)*, Serial No. 209.

Brody, G. H., & Shaffer, D. R. (1982). Contributions of parents and peers to children's moral socialization. *Developmental Review, 2*, 31–75.

Bryant, B. K. (1987). Mental health, temperament, family, and friends: Perspectives on children's empathy and social perspective taking. In N. Eisenberg & J. Strayer (Eds.), *Empathy and its development* (pp. 245–270). New York: Cambridge University Press.

Bryant, B. K., & Crockenberg, S. B. (1980). Correlates and dimensions of prosocial behavior: A study of female siblings with their mothers. *Child Development, 51*, 529–544.

Buhrmester, D., Furman, W., Wittenberg, M. T., & Reis, H. T. (1988). Five domains of interpersonal competence in peer relationships. *Journal of Personality and Social Psychology, 55,* 991–1008.

Burgoon, J. K. (1976). The unwillingness to communicate scale: Development and validation. *Communication Monographs, 43,* 60–69.

Burleson, B. R. (1980). The development of interpersonal reasoning: An analysis of message strategy justifications. *Journal of the American Forensic Association, 17,* 102–110.

Burleson, B. R. (1982a). The development of comforting communication skills in childhood and adolescence. *Child Development, 53,* 1578–1588.

Burleson, B. R. (1982b). The affective perspective-taking process: A test of Turiel's role-taking model. In M. Burgoon (Ed.), *Communication yearbook 6* (pp. 473–488). Beverly Hills: Sage Publications.

Burleson, B. R. (1983). Social cognition, empathic motivation, and adults' comforting strategies. *Human Communication Research, 10,* 295–304.

Burleson, B. R. (1984a). Comforting communication. In H. E. Sypher & J. L. Applegate (Eds.), *Communication by children and adults: Social cognitive and strategic processes* (pp. 63–104). Beverly Hills: Sage.

Burleson, B. R. (1984b). Age, social–cognitive development, and the use of comforting strategies. *Communication Monographs, 51,* 140–153.

Burleson, B. R. (1985). The production of comforting messages: Social–cognitive foundations. *Journal of Language and Social Psychology, 4,* 253–273.

Burleson, B. R. (1986). Communication skills and childhood peer relationships: An overview. In M. L. McLaughlin (Ed.), *Communication yearbook 9* (pp. 143–180). Beverly Hills: Sage Publications.

Burleson, B. R. (1989). The constructivist approach to person-centered communication: Analysis of a research exemplar. In B. A. Dervin, L. Grossberg, B. J. O'Keefe, & E. Wartella (Eds.), *Rethinking communication,* Vol. 2, *Paradigm exemplars* (pp. 29–46). Newbury Park, CA: Sage Publications.

Burleson, B. R. (1990). Comforting as everyday social support: Relational consequences of supportive behaviors. In S. Duck with R. Silver (Eds.), *Personal relationships and social support* (pp. 66–82). London: Sage Publications.

Burleson, B. R. (1994). Comforting communication: Significance, approaches, and effects. In B. R. Burleson, T. L. Albrecht, & I. G. Sarason (Eds.), *The communication of social support: Messages, interactions, relationships, and community* (pp. 3–28). Thousand Oaks, CA: Sage Publications.

Burleson, B. R., Applegate, J. L., Burke, J. A., Clark, R. A., Delia, J. G., & Kline, S. L. (1986). Communicative correlates of peer acceptance in childhood. *Communication Education, 35,* 349–361.

Burleson, B. R., Delia, J. G., & Applegate, J. L. (1992). Effects of maternal communication and children's social–cognitive and communication skills on children's acceptance by the peer group. *Family Relations, 41,* 264–272.

Burleson, B. R., & Kunkel, A. W. (May, 1995). Parental and peer contributions to the emotional support skills of the child: From whom do children learn how to express support? Paper presented at the International Communication Association convention. Albuquerque.

Burleson, B. R., & Samter, W. (1990). Effects of cognitive complexity on the perceived importance of communication skills in friends. *Communication Research, 17,* 165–182.

Burleson, B. R., Waltman, M. S., & Samter, W. (1987). More evidence that cognitive complexity is *not* loquacity: A reply to Beatty and Payne. *Communication Quarterly, 35,* 317–328.

Burleson, B. R., & Waltman, P. A. (1987). Popular, rejected, and supportive preadolescents: Social–cognitive and communicative characteristics. In M. L. McLaughlin (Ed.), *Communication yearbook 10* (pp. 533–552). Newbury Park, CA: Sage Publications.

Camras, L. A., Grow, J. G., & Ribordy, S. C. (1983). Recognition of emotional expression by abused children. *Journal of Clinical Child Psychology, 12,* 325–328.

Camras, L. A., Ribordy, S., Hill, J., Martino, S., Sachs, V., Spaccarelli, S., & Stefani, R. (1990). Maternal facial behavior and the recognition and production of emotional expression by maltreated and nonmaltreated children. *Developmental Psychology, 26,* 304–312.

Caplan, M. A. (1993). Inhibitory influences in development: The case of prosocial behavior. In D. F. Hay & A. Angold (Eds.), *Percursors and causes in development and psychopathology* (pp. 169–198). Chichester, UK: Wiley.

Caplan, M. Z., & Hay, D. F. (1989). Preschoolers' responses to peers' distress and beliefs about bystander intervention. *Journal of Child Psychology and Psychiatry, 30,* 231–242.

Cassidy, J., Parke, R. D., Butkovsky, L., & Braungart, J. M. (1992). Family–peer connections: The roles of emotional expressiveness within the family and children's understanding of emotions. *Child Development, 63,* 603–618.

Cauce, A. M., Reid, M., Landesman, S., & Gonzales, N. (1990). Social support in young children: Measurement, structure, and behavioral impact. In B. R. Sarason, I. G. Sarason, & G. R. Pierce (Eds.), *Social support: An interactional view* (pp. 64–94). New York: Wiley.

Chapman, M., Zahn-Waxler, C., Cooperman, G., & Iannotti, R. (1987). Empathy and responsibility in the motivation of children's helping. *Developmental Psychology, 23,* 140–145.

Clark, R. A. (1994). Children's and adolescents' gender preferences for conversational partners for specific communicative objectives. *Journal of Social and Personal Relationships, 11,* 313–319.

Clinton, B. L., & Hancock, G. R. (1991). The development of an understanding of comforting messages. *Communication Reports, 4,* 55–63.

Costin, S. E., & Jones, D. C. (1992). Friendship as a facilitator of emotional responsiveness and prosocial interventions among young children. *Developmental Psychology, 28,* 941–947.

Cummings, E. M., Hollenbeck, B., Iannotti, R., Radke-Yarrow, M., & Zahn-Waxler, C. (1986). Early organization of altruism and aggression: Developmental patterns and individual differences. In C. Zahn-Waxler, E. M. Cummings, & R. Iannotti (Eds.), *Altruism and aggression: Biological and social origins* (pp. 165–188). New York: Cambridge University Press.

Cutrona, C. E., & Russell, D. W. (1990). Types of social support and specific stress: Toward a theory of optimal matching. In B. R. Sarason, I. G. Sarason, & G. R. Pierce (Eds.), *Social support: An interactional view* (pp. 319–366). New York: Wiley.

Cutrona, C. E., & Suhr, J. A. (1994). Social support in the context of marriage: An analysis of couples' supportive interactions. In B. R. Burleson, T. L. Albrecht, & I. G. Sarason (Eds.), *The communication of social support: Messages, interactions, relationships, and community* (pp. 113–135). Thousand Oaks, CA: Sage Publications.

Cutrona, C. E., Suhr, J. A., & MacFarlane, R. (1990). Interpersonal transactions and the psychological sense of support. In S. Duck with R. Silver (Eds.), *Personal relationships and social support* (pp. 30–45). London: Sage Publications.

Dakof, G. A., & Taylor, S. E. (1990). Victims' perceptions of support attempts: What is helpful from whom? *Journal of Personality and Social Psychology, 58,* 80–89.

Davis, M. H. (1983). Measuring individual differences in empathy: Evidence for a multidimensional approach. *Journal of Personality and Social Psychology, 44,* 113–126.

Delia, J. G., O'Keefe, B. J., & O'Keefe, D. J. (1982). The constructivist approach to communication. In F. E. X. Dance (Ed.), *Human communication theory: Comparative essays* (pp. 147–191). New York: Harper & Row.

Dlugokinski, E. L., & Firestone, I. J. (1974). Other-centeredness and susceptibility to charitable appeals: Effects of perceived discipline. *Developmental Psychology, 10,* 21–28.

Dodge, K. A. (1986). Social information-processing variables in the development of aggression and altruism in children. In C. Zahn-Waxler, E. M. Cummings, & R. Iannotti (Eds.), *Altruism and aggression: Biological and social origins* (pp. 280–302). New York: Cambridge University Press.

Dunn, J., Bretherton, I., & Munn, P. (1987). Conversations about feeling states between mothers and their young children. *Developmental Psychology, 23,* 132–139.

Dunn, J., Brown, J., & Beardsall, L. (1991). Family talk about feeling states and children's later understanding of others' emotions. *Developmental Psychology, 27,* 448–455.

Dunn, J., Brown, J., Slomkowski, C., Tesla, C., & Youngblade, L. (1991). Young children's understanding of other people's feelings and beliefs: Individual differences and their antecedents. *Child Development, 62,* 1352–1366.

Dunn, J., & Munn, P. (1986). Siblings and the development of prosocial behavior. *International Journal of Behavioral Development, 9,* 265–284.

Eagly, A. H. (1987). *Sex differences in social behavior: A social-role interpretation.* Hillsdale, NJ: Lawrence Erlbaum.

East, P. L. (1991). The parent–child relationship of withdrawn, aggressive, and sociable children: Child and parent perspectives. *Merrill-Palmer Quarterly, 37,* 425–443.

Edwards, R., Manstead, A. S. R., & MacDonald, C. J. (1984). The relationship between children's sociometric status and ability to recognize facial expressions of emotion. *European Journal of Social Psychology, 14*, 235–238.

Elicker, J., Englund, M., & Sroufe, L. A. (1992). Predicting peer competence and peer relationships in childhood from early parent–child relationships. In R. D. Parke & G. W. Ladd (Eds.), *Family–peer relationships: Modes of linkage* (pp. 77–106). Hillsdale, NJ: Lawrence, Erlbaum.

Eisenberg, N., Fabes, R. A., Schaller, M., Miller, P., Carlo, G., Poulin, R., Shea, C., & Shell, R. (1991). Personality and socialization correlates of vicarious emotional responding. *Journal of Personality and Social Psychology, 61*, 459–470.

Eisenberg, N., Fabes, R. A., Carlo, G., Troyer, D., Speer, A. L., Karbon, M., & Switzer, G. (1992). The relations of maternal practices and characteristics to children's vicarious emotional responsiveness. *Child Development, 63*, 583–602.

Eisenberg, N., Fabes, R. A., Carlo, G., Speer, A. L., Switzer, G., Karbon, M., & Troyer, D. (1993). The relations of empathy-related emotional and maternal practices to children's comforting behavior. *Journal of Experimental Child Psychology, 55*, 131–150.

Eisenberg, N., Cameron, E., Tryon, K., & Dodez, R. (1981). Socialization of prosocial behavior in the preschool classroom. *Developmental Psychology, 17*, 723–729.

Eisenberg, N., & Fabes, R. A. (1990). Empathy: Conceptualization, measurement, and relation to prosocial behavior. *Motivation and Emotion, 14*, 131–149.

Eisenberg, N., Fabes, R. A., Schaller, M., Carlo, G., & Miller, P. A. (1991). The relations of parental characteristics and practices to children's vicarious emotional responding. *Child Development, 62*, 1393–1408.

Eisenberg, N., & Lennon, R. (1983). Sex differences in empathy and related capacities. *Psychological Bulletin, 94*, 100–131.

Eisenberg, N., & Mussen, P. H. (1989). *The roots of prosocial behavior in children.* New York: Cambridge University Press.

Eisenberg-Berg, N., & Lennon, R. (1980). Altruism and the assessment of empathy in the preschool years. *Child Development, 51*, 552–557.

Eisenberg-Berg, N., & Mussen, P. (1978). Empathy and moral development in adolescence. *Developmental Psychology, 14*, 185–186.

Elliott, R. (1985). Helpful and nonhelpful events in brief counseling interviews: An empirical taxonomy. *Journal of Counseling Psychology, 32*, 307–322.

Fabes, R. A., Eisenberg, N., & Miller, P. A. (1990). Maternal correlates of children's vicarious emotional responsiveness. *Developmental Psychology, 26*, 639–648.

Farver, J. M., & Branstetter, W. H. (1994). Preschoolers' prosocial responses to their peers' distress. *Developmental Psychology, 30*, 334–341.

Feinberg, H. K. (1977). Anatomy of a helping situation: Some personality and situational determinants of helping in a conflict situation involving another's psychological distress. Unpublished doctoral dissertation. Amherst: University of Massachusetts, Department of Psychology.

Feshbach, N. D. (1975). The relationship of child-rearing factors to children's aggression, empathy and related positive and negative social behaviors. In J. deWit & W. W. Hartup (Eds.), *Determinants and origins of aggressive behavior* (pp. 427–436). The Hague: Mouton.

Garner, P. W., Jones, D. C., & Miner, J. L. (1994). Social competence among low-income preschoolers: Emotional socialization practices and social cognitive correlates. *Child Development, 65*, 622–637.

Goffman, E. (1967). *Interaction ritual: Essays on face-to-face behavior.* New York: Anchor Books.

Goldstein, A. P., & Michaels, G. Y. (1985). *Empathy: Development, training, and consequences.* Norwood, NJ: Lawrence Erlbaum.

Grodman, S. M. (1979). The role of personality and situational variables in responding to and helping an individual in psychological distress. Unpublished doctoral dissertation. Amherst: University of Massachusetts, Department of Psychology.

Grusec, J. E. (1982). The socialization of altruism. In N. Eisenberg (Ed.), *The development of prosocial behavior* (pp. 136–166). New York: Academic Press.

Grusec, J. E. (1991). Socializing concern for others in the home. *Developmental Psychology, 27*, 338–342.

Grusec, J. E., Kuczynski, L., Rushton, J. P., & Simutis, Z. M. (1978). Modeling, direct instructions, and attributions: Effects on altruism. *Developmental Psychology, 14*, 51–57.

Hay, D. F. (1993). Prosocial development. *Journal of Child Psychology and Psychiatry, 35,* 29–71.

Hay, D. F., Nash, A., & Pedersen, J. (1981). Responses of six-month-olds to the distress of their peers. *Child Development, 53,* 1071–1075.

Hoffman, M. L. (1975). Developmental synthesis of affect and cognition and its implications for altruistic motivation. *Developmental Psychology, 11,* 607–622.

Hoffman, M. L. (1977). Moral internalization: Current theory and research. In L. Berkowitz (Ed.), *Advances in experimental social psychology* (pp. 85–133). New York: Academic Press.

House, J. S. (1981). *Work, stress, and social support.* Reading, MA: Addison-Wesley.

Howe, N., & Ross, H. (1990). Socialization, perspective-taking, and the sibling relationship. *Developmental Psychology, 26,* 160–165.

Howes, C., & Eldridge, R. (1985). Responses of abused, neglected, and nonmaltreated children to the behaviors of their peers. *Journal of Applied Developmental Psychology, 6,* 261–270.

Howes, C., & Espinosa, M. P. (1985). The consequences of child abuse for peer interaction. *International Journal of Child Abuse and Neglect, 9,* 397–404.

Howes, C., & Farver, J. (1987). Toddlers' responses to the distress of their peers. *Journal of Applied Developmental Psychology, 8,* 441–452.

Iannotti, R. J. (1985). Naturalistic and structured assessments of prosocial behavior in preschool children: The influence of empathy and perspective taking. *Developmental Psychology, 21,* 46–55.

Kelly, G. A. (1955). *The psychology of personal constructs* (2 vols.). New York: W. W. Norton.

Kestenbaum, R., Farber, E. A., & Sroufe, L. A. (1989). Individual differences in empathy among preschoolers: Relation to attachment history. In N. Eisenberg (Eds.), *Empathy and related emotional responses: New directions for child development,* No. 44 (pp. 51–64). San Francisco: Jossey-Bass.

Klimes-Dougan, B., & Kistner, J. (1990). Physically abused preschoolers' responses to peers' distress. *Developmental Psychology, 26,* 599–602.

Koestner, K., Franz, C., & Weinberger, J. (1990). The family origins of empathic concern: A 26-year-longitudinal study. *Journal of Personality and Social Psychology, 58,* 709–716.

Kupersmidt, J. B., Coie, J. D., & Dodge, K. A. (1990). The role of poor peer relationships in the development of disorder. In S. R. Asher & J. D. Coie (Eds.), *Peer rejection in childhood* (pp. 274–307). Cambridge: Cambridge University Press.

Lazarus, R. S. (1991). *Emotion and adaptation.* New York: Oxford Press.

Lehman, D. R., Ellard, J. H., & Wortman, C. B. (1986). Social support for the bereaved: Recipients' and providers' perspectives on what is helpful. *Journal of Consulting and Clinical Psychology, 54,* 438–446.

Lehman, D. R., & Hemphill, K. J. (1990). Recipients' perceptions of support attempts and attributions for support attempts that fail. *Journal of Social and Personal Relationships, 7,* 563–574.

Lennon, R., & Eisenberg, N. (1987). Gender and age differences in empathy and sympathy. In N. Eisenberg & J. Strayer (Eds.), *Empathy and its development* (pp. 195–217). Cambridge: Cambridge University Press.

Main, M., & George, C. (1985). Responses of abused and disadvantaged toddlers to distress in agemates: A study in the day care setting. *Developmental Psychology, 21,* 407–412.

Mallinckrodt, B. (1992). Childhood emotional bonds with parents, development of adult social competencies, and availability of social support. *Journal of Counseling Psychology, 39,* 453–461.

Matthews, K. A., Batson, C. D., Horn, J., & Rosenman, R. H. (1981). "Principles in his nature which interest him in the fortune of others....": The heritability of empathic concern for others. *Journal of Personality, 49,* 237–247.

Mehrabian, A., & Epstein, N. (1972). A measure of emotional empathy. *Journal of Personality, 40,* 525–543.

Miller, P. A., Eisenberg, N., Fabes, R. A., Shell, R., & Gular, S. (1989). Mothers' emotional arousal as a moderator in the socialization of children's empathy. In N. Eisenberg (Ed.), *Empathy and related emotional responses: New directions for child development,* No. 44 (pp. 65–82). San Francisco: Jossey-Bass.

Parke, R. D., & Slaby, R. G. (1983). The development of aggression. In E. M. Hetherington (Ed.), *Handbook of child psychology,* Vol. 4, *Socialization, personality, and social development,* 4th ed. (pp. 547–642). New York: Wiley.

Payne, F. D. (1980). Children's prosocial conduct in structured situations and as viewed by others: Consistency, convergence, and relationships with person variables. *Child Development, 51,* 1252–1259.

Phinney, J., Feshbach, N., & Farver, J. (1986). Preschool children's responses to peer crying. *Early Childhood Research Quarterly*, *1*, 207–219.

Pierce, G., Sarason, I., & Sarason, B. (1990). Integrating social support perspectives: Working models, personal relationships, and situational factors. In S. Duck with R. Silver (Eds.), *Personal relationships and social support* (pp. 173–189). London: Sage Publications.

Radke-Yarrow, M., & Zahn-Waxler, C. (1986). The role of familial factors in the development of prosocial behavior: Research findings and questions. In D. Olweus, J. Block, & M. Radke-Yarrow (Eds.), *Development of antisocial and prosocial behavior* (pp. 189–216). Orlando, FL: Academic Press.

Radke-Yarrow, M., Zahn-Waxler, C., & Chapman, M. (1983). Children's prosocial dispositions and behavior. In E. M. Hetherington (Ed.), *Handbook of child psychology*, Vol. 4, *Socialization, personality, and social development*, 4th ed. (pp. 469–545). New York: Wiley.

Rehberg, H. R., & Richman, C. L. (1989). Prosocial behavior in preschool children: A look at the interaction of race, gender, and family composition. *International Journal of Behavioral Development*, *12*, 385–401.

Rheingold, H. L., & Emery, G. N. (1986). The nurturant acts of very young children. In D. Olweus, J. Block, & M. Radke-Yarrow (Eds.), *The development of antisocial and prosocial behavior* (pp. 75–96). New York: Academic Press.

Richman, C. L., Berry, C., Bittle, M., & Himan, K. (1988). Factors related to helping behavior in preschool-age children. *Journal of Applied Developmental Psychology*, *9*, 151–165.

Ritter, E. M. (1979). Social perspective taking ability, cognitive complexity, and listener adapted communication in early and late adolescence. *Communication Monographs*, *46*, 40–51.

Roberts, W., & Strayer, J. (1987). Parents' responses to the emotional distress of their children: Relation with children's competence. *Developmental Psychology*, *23*, 415–422.

Rotter, J. B. (1966). Generalized expectancies for internal versus external control of reinforcement. *Psychological Monographs*, *80* (Whole No. 609).

Rushton, J. P., Fulker, D. W., Neale, M. C., Nias, D. L. B., & Eysenck, H. J. (1986). Altruism and aggression: The heritability of individual differences. *Journal of Personality and Social Psychology*, *50*, 1192–1198.

Rushton, J. P., & Teachman, G. (1978). The effects of positive reinforcement, attributions, and punishment on model induced altruism in children. *Personality and Social Psychology Bulletin*, *4*, 322–325.

Russell, D. W., & Cutrona, C. (1991). Social support, stress, and depressive symptoms among the elderly: Test of process model. *Psychology of Aging*, *6*, 190–201.

Sagi, A., & Hoffman, M. L. (1976). Empathic distress in the newborn. *Developmental Psychology*, *12*, 175–176.

Samter, W., & Burleson, B. R. (1984). Cognitive and motivational influences on spontaneous comforting behavior. *Human Communication Research*, *11*, 231–260.

Samter, W., & Burleson, B. R. (June, 1990a). The role of affectively oriented communication skills in the friendships of young adults: A sociometric study. Paper presented at the International Communication Association convention. Dublin.

Samter, W., & Burleson, B. R. (1990b). Evaluations of communication skills as predictors of peer acceptance in a group living situation. *Communication Studies*, *41*, 311–326.

Samter, W., Burleson, B. R., Kunkel, A. W., & Werking, K. J. (July, 1994). Gender differences in beliefs about communication in intimate relationships: When gender differences make a difference— and when they don't. Paper presented at the International Communication Association convention. Sydney.

Silverstein, M., & Bengtson, V. L. (1994). Does intergenerational social support influence the psychological well-being of older parents? The contingencies of declining health and widowhood. *Social Science and Medicine*, *38*, 943–957.

Simner, M. L. (1971). Newborn's responses to the cry of another infant. *Developmental Psychology*, *5*, 136–150.

Strayer, F. F. (1981). The nature and organization of altruistic behavior among preschool children. In J. P. Rushton & R. M. Sorrentino (Eds.), *Altruism and helping behavior: Social, personality, and developmental perspectives* (pp. 331–348). Hillsdale, NJ: Lawrence Erlbaum.

Strayer, J. (1980). A naturalistic study of empathic behaviors and their relation to affective states and perspective-taking skills in preschool children. *Child Development*, *51*, 815–822.

Strayer, J., & Roberts, W. (1989). Children's empathy and role taking: Child and parental factors, and relations to prosocial behavior. *Journal of Applied Developmental Psychology, 10,* 227–239.

Tamborini, R., Salomonson, K., & Bahk, C. (1993). The relationship of empathy to comforting behavior following film exposure. *Communication Research, 20,* 723–738.

Thompson, R. A. (1987). Empathy and emotional understanding: The early development of empathy. In N. Eisenberg & J. Strayer (Eds.), *Empathy and its development* (pp. 119–145). Cambridge: Cambridge University Press.

Underwood, B., & Moore, B. (1982a). The generality of altruism in children. In N. Eisenberg (Ed.), *The development of prosocial behavior* (pp. 25–52). New York: Academic Press.

Underwood, B., & Moore, B. (1982b). Perspective-taking and altruism. *Psychological Bulletin, 91,* 143–173.

Walters, G., & Grusec, J. E. (1977). *Punishment.* San Francisco: Freeman.

Waters, E., & Sroufe, L. A. (1983). Social competence as a developmental construct. *Developmental Review, 3,* 79–97.

Waters, E., Wippman, J., & Sroufe, L. A. (1979). Attachment, positive affect, and competence in the peer group: Two studies in construct validation. *Child Development, 50,* 821–829.

Whiteman, M. (1967). Children's conceptions of psychological causality. *Child Development, 38,* 143–156.

Wood, J. (1994). *Who cares? Women, care, and culture.* Carbondale: Southern Illinois University Press.

Wortman, C. B., & Lehman, D. R. (1985). Reactions to victims of life crises: Support attempts that fail. In G. Sarason & B. R. Sarason (Eds.), *Social support: Theory, research, and application* (pp. 463–489). Dordrecht: Martinus Nijhoff.

Yarrow, M. R., Scott, P. M., & Waxler, C. Z. (1973). Learning concern for others. *Developmental Psychology, 8,* 240–260.

Yarrow, M. R., & Waxler, C. Z. (1976). Dimensions and correlates of prosocial behavior in young children. *Child Development, 47,* 118–125.

Zahn-Waxler, C., Iannotti, R., & Chapman, M. (1982). Peers and prosocial development. In K. H. Rubin & H. S. Ross (Eds.), *Peer relationships and social skills in childhood* (pp. 133–162). New York: Springer-Verlag.

Zahn-Waxler, C., Kochanska, G., Krupnick, J., & McKnew, D. (1990). Patterns of guilt in children of depressed and well mothers. *Developmental Psychology, 26,* 51–59.

Zahn-Waxler, C., & Radke-Yarrow, M. (1990). The origins of empathic concern. *Motivation and Emotion, 14,* 107–130.

Zahn-Waxler, C., Radke-Yarrow, M., & Brady-Smith, J. (1977). Perspective-taking and prosocial behavior. *Developmental Psychology, 13,* 87–88.

Zahn-Waxler, C., Radke-Yarrow, M., & King, R. A. (1979). Child rearing and children's prosocial initiations toward victims of distress. *Child Development, 50,* 319–330.

Zahn-Waxler, C., Radke-Yarrow, M., Wagner, E., & Chapman, M. (1992). Development of concern for others. *Developmental Psychology, 28,* 126–136.

Zahn-Waxler, C., Robinson, J., & Emde, R. (1992). The development of empathy in twins. *Developmental Psychology, 28,* 1038–1047.

7

Attachment, Social Competency, and the Capacity to Use Social Support

**HELEN M. COBLE, DIANA L. GANTT,
and BRENT MALLINCKRODT**

Much of the pioneering research on the stress-buffering effects of social support tended to view support primarily in terms of its perceived availability in the environment. Individual differences were often included in these models, not as independent variables, but only as dependent variables representing psychological or physical health symptoms of distress. In many of these studies, the capacity to benefit from available social support was accepted as a given. After a decade of research in which this paradigm predominated, however, researchers in the mid-1980s increasingly began to view social support as an interaction between individual difference variables and the environment (e.g., B. R. Sarason, Pierce, & I. G. Sarason, 1990; I. G. Sarason, B. R. Sarason, & Shearin, 1986). On the basis of this growing body of research, it appears that at least three conditions are necessary for an individual to derive benefit from social support for coping with a given stressful life event: (1) the environment must offer support of the functional types and from relationship sources that match the coping requirements of the event; (2) the individual must possess social skills necessary to engage in supportive relationships, establish intimacy, and recruit the specific types of social support needed for coping with the stressor; and (3) the individual must have the personality disposition and willingness to exercise these skills.

The first condition, availability of the correct functional type and source of

HELEN M. COBLE and BRENT MALLINCKRODT • Counseling Psychology Program, College of Education, University of Oregon, Eugene, Oregon 97503-5251. **DIANA L. GANTT** • Day Treatment Program, Providence Medical Center, Portland, Oregon 97213.

Handbook of Social Support and the Family, edited by Gregory R. Pierce, Barbara R. Sarason, and Irwin G. Sarason. Plenum Press, New York, 1996.

support, has been perhaps the most thoroughly examined of the three. Research suggests that there are functionally different types of social support, not all of which are beneficial in a given stressful life situation (Cutrona & Russell, 1990), and that some well-intentioned attempts to provide support may actually be harmful (Lehman, Ellard, & Wortman, 1986). Other studies suggest that support of a given type is most beneficial if provided from a particular relationship source. For example, support in the form of reassurance that one has the necessary skills to perform the tasks required in a job will likely be much more effective if it is provided by new coworkers or an on-the-job supervisor than if it is provided by one's spouse (LaRocco & Jones, 1978).

Although the availability of support is a necessary condition, it appears not to be sufficient to ensure that an individual will benefit from social support. For example, I. G. Sarason et al. (1986) found that conversation partners who rated themselves higher in social support were rated by independent judges as more socially skilled and interpersonally attractive. Certain basic skills, such as the ability to make appropriate eye contact, engage in mutually rewarding sustained conversation, and conform to the local cultural norms of communication, are probably crucial for the effective use of social support.

In recent years, three relatively independent streams of research, from social psychology, developmental psychology, and the study of interpersonal process in psychotherapy, have converged to suggest that there are a substantial number of persons who seem to possess many of the requisite basic social skills and who have readily available potentially supportive relationships, but who nevertheless fail to make use of these social resources. When requested to do so, these individuals can demonstrate minimally effective and sometimes high levels of basic social skills (for example, they can make appropriate personal self-disclosures to a therapist). They seem unable, however, to take the interpersonal risks involved in exercising these basic skills to recruit social support, especially the types of support typically provided in emotionally intimate relationships.

Perhaps nowhere is this difficulty more evident that in the case of clients in psychotherapy. For example, clients in group therapy are exposed to the same supportive milieu and typically must possess minimal basic social skills in order to be screened into the groups, but these clients differ markedly in their ability to use the social support that becomes available. It appears that support received from other group members is not sufficient in itself in many cases to produce therapeutic change. Mallinckrodt (1989) found that social support from persons outside a therapy group showed a much stronger relation to clients' symptom relief than support from fellow therapy-group members. Lasting therapeutic change occurs in many clients only when they learn to transfer new interpersonal skills acquired in the group to increase the satisfaction derived from their outside social relationships (Yalom, 1985).

Similarly, clients in individual therapy differ markedly in their ability to engage in a productive working relationship with their therapist (Horvath & Symonds, 1991). These differences cannot be explained entirely by differences in clients' basic social skills or the level of support offered by the therapist. Some of the differences may be associated with clients' generalized willingness to form emotionally intimate attachments. Growing empirical evidence supports the claim of Bowlby (1988) that clients' ability to form a productive therapeutic relationship is influenced by their childhood attachment to caregivers (Mallinckrodt, 1991; Mallinckrodt, Coble, & Gantt, 1995a; Mallinckrodt, Gantt, & Coble, 1995). For a review of literature concerning social competencies and interpersonal process in psychotherapy, see Mallinckrodt (in press).

In the remainder of this chapter, we will focus on the last two of the three necessary ingredients we have described, emphasizing the influence of early childhood attachment on individual differences in social skills, beliefs, and personality disposition. Our interest is colored by personal experience as therapists working with children and adults. We have seen some clients helped by the increased availability of social support alone, for example, following the experience of traumatic loss. We have seen others profit from the acquisition of basic social skills, especially those who have been institutionalized for lengthy periods. But we have also seen many clients with available support and basic social skills fail to make progress in therapy until they confront and overcome deep-seated fears regarding close personal attachments. We believe that these fears, together with beliefs about the self and others that interfere with developing intimate relationships—not the availability of social support per se, or the lack of basic social skills—pose the highest barrier to the benefits of social support for the greatest number of clients.

We use the term "social competencies" to encompass the last two of the three necessary conditions, that is, all the social skills that an individual must possess in order to make use of available social support and the belief structures and personality disposition required to make use of those skills. Note, therefore, that we use the term "competency" to refer to both a set of interpersonal relationship skills and the beliefs and personality disposition that prompt an individual to employ those skills to recruit social support.

A clinical example may illustrate the value of considering separately the two components of competency, skills and beliefs. Chester, an unmarried professional in his early 30s, began group therapy hoping to alleviate his chronic feelings of loneliness. After only a few sessions, Chester's behavior was markedly different toward different women in the group. With women he considered ineligible as potential romantic partners (i.e., married group members and the female therapist), he was warm and engaged in extended dialogue. With the female members of the group who were romantically unattached, however, Chester was withdrawn and occasionally hostile. Chester was later able to identify his belief that most women with whom he might become romantically involved would find him unappealing and that he had little to offer such a relationship. He found it much easier to talk to women committed to another relationship, because with them there was "no pressure, no expectation, and no chance of being disappointed." In fact, his social network included several such women he considered very close friends. In group sessions, and apparently with these female friends outside the group, Chester was able to engage in emotionally intimate relationships. However, it was his expectations about likely romantic partners and his low self-esteem—not any lack of basic social skills—that prevented him from establishing the type of relationship he desired.

The observation that many people possess adequate social skills and fail to use them to recruit readily available social support compels the question, what more is necessary than skills? Of course, researchers have yet to enumerate a comprehensive list of these social competencies, but among them may be important elements of self-concept and belief structure. For example, the belief that exercising social skills will lead to desired outcomes, "social self-efficacy," has been found to predict actual social behavior (Sherer & Adams, 1983) and perceived levels of social support (Mallinckrodt, 1992). A belief that seeking social support is an effective coping strategy also seems to be a requirement (Lazarus & Folkman, 1984). Persons who lack the higher-order social skills needed to use social support may have personality dispositions that prompt them to use coping strategies that do not rely on social support. Further, these dispositions toward social coping or problem-oriented coping may influence such basic decisions as career choice, because individuals are drawn to the social environment in the workplace that best matches their social skills and coping preferences (Wampold et al., 1995).

A capacity for intimacy and a willingness to engage in the interpersonal risk-taking and self-disclosure that are necessary to form close personal relationships is a likely requirement for making use of some of the most satisfying forms of social support (Duck, 1988). The capacity to trust others and allow oneself to become dependent on them also seems necessary and—if the relationship is to endure—requires a complex interplay of seeking to meet one's emotional needs, self-esteem, maintenance of personal boundaries, and the ability to regulate strong affect independently, to some degree, of the help-giving partner (Duck, 1988).

It is not necessary to generate an exhaustive list to be convinced that a person lacking one of these crucial higher-order social competencies may be unable to make use of available social support, despite possessing more basic skills such as the ability to engage in sustained conversation, make appropriate eye contact, and ask for help. Persons lacking higher-order social competencies may have relatively smaller social networks (Mallinckrodt, McCreary, & Robertson, 1995), but more typically they lack social support because of a general inability to recruit it from relationships that are available. Of course, this general difficulty also tends to leave them bereft of support in specific stressful situations, although we believe that individuals do vary in their ability to recruit different types of support. For example, some may be more adept at soliciting guidance or informational support, but have great difficulty obtaining the types of support provided from close emotional attachments. Hence, these individuals would presumably be more vulnerable to the types of stressors for which they require emotional rather than informational support.

The higher-order social competencies, such as the capacity to trust, depend on others, or develop emotional closeness, involve complex combinations of more basic social skills *and* the personality disposition and beliefs that create a willingness to use these skills. Of course, a lack of willingness to engage in close relationships or the belief that such connections are fraught with danger prevents some persons from fully developing the necessary component social skills. However, from our perspective working in therapy and research with relatively high-functioning individuals, when little interpersonal risk is involved, most of these clients can demonstrate quite competent levels of basic social skills, but many hold beliefs about themselves and the social world that create anxieties that interfere with their ability to recruit and use social support. The three streams of research we alluded to earlier—from social psychology, developmental psychology, and interpersonal process in psychotherapy—all suggest that early attachment experiences may have a profound impact on the development of social competencies.

OVERVIEW OF ATTACHMENT THEORY

Basic Concepts

John Bowlby and Mary Ainsworth were pioneers in the development of attachment theory. Bowlby (1969) proposed that attachment can be understood as both an emotional bond and a set of goal-directed behaviors that serve to maintain an infant's proximity to a caregiver and protect the infant from danger. The first attachment relationship is with the primary caregiver, most often the mother. Attachment relationships are established with the father and other persons as well, but the mother usually remains the primary attachment figure (Bowlby, 1977, 1988). Ainsworth contributed the concept of "secure base" to attachment theory (Bretherton, 1992). As a healthy attachment relationship develops, the child's emotional and physical needs are met and the child develops a felt sense of security. The child's accumulated experience that the caretaker is accessible and will be responsive if called upon for help provides a confident sense of secure base that facilitates exploration of both the physical and the social world. Paradoxically, if children can confidently rely early in their lives on the consistent responsiveness of caregivers when they become upset, they later explore more widely and they may actually retreat to the secure base of their caregiver less frequently (Bowlby, 1977, 1988). Thus, healthy emotional development is promoted by the combination of autonomous exploration and a sense of trust that nothing can sever the secure base attachment with the caregiver (Ainsworth, Blehar, Waters, & Wall, 1978).

The quality of an infant's attachment is manifested in the infant's response to physical absence of an attachment figure, as well as the attachment figure's ability to respond to and encourage the infant to explore, while providing a secure base (Bowlby, 1977). The Strange Situation protocol was developed by Ainsworth and her colleagues to assess the attachment relationship between infants (12–24 months old) and their mothers (Ainsworth & Wittig, 1969). The assessment is based on laboratory observation of an infant's attachment and exploratory behaviors through eight brief episodes that involve the introduction of a stranger and two separations from and reunions with mother. Assessment is completed on scales of proximity and contact seeking, contact maintenance, resistance, avoidance, searching behaviors, and interaction at a distance. Initial studies suggested three general categories of attachment, labeled "secure," "insecure–avoidant," and "insecure–ambivalent" (Ainsworth et al., 1978). Subsequently, a fourth group of infants who could not be easily placed into these categories was identified and labeled "disorganized–disoriented" by Main and her colleagues (Main & Solomon, 1986, 1990).

The *secure* attachment pattern is characterized by the infant's using mother as a secure base while freely exploring novel surroundings, becoming moderately upset at separation, greeting mother at reunion, and returning to exploration after reunion. The *insecure–avoidant* pattern is characterized by the infant's lack of proximity-seeking behavior (i.e., the infant ignores mother as she or he explores, indicating the absence of a secure base), showing little or no distress at separation, and ignoring or avoiding mother at reunion. *Insecure–ambivalent* attachment is characterized by the infant's maintaining close proximity to mother, lacking independent play or exploration, becoming upset at separation, being unable to be easily comforted at reunion, and showing a mixture of contact seeking and angry rejection at reunion (Ainsworth et al., 1978). The fourth group of infants presented diverse behaviors indicating *disorganization* and *disorientation*—for example, moving to a wall and leaning against it when frightened by a stranger, rising from and then falling to the floor at reunion, or freezing in place (Main & Solomon, 1986, 1990).

The validity of Ainsworth's laboratory classification was corroborated with extensive in-home observations of the infants and their mothers. Specific patterns of mothering behaviors were found to be related to the categories to which infants had been assigned on the basis of their observed behaviors in the Strange Situation (Ainsworth, Bell, & Stayton, 1971). Mothers of securely attached infants tended to enjoy physical contact and initiated frequent interactions with their infants. These mothers tended to display greater sensitivity to their babies' cues and to respond promptly and appropriately (Ainsworth et al., 1971; Ainsworth & Wittig, 1969).

Mothers of both avoidantly and ambivalently attached infants tended to be less sensitive to their babies' signals. In addition, mothers of avoidantly attached infants tended to interact with them less and were more likely to reject, interfere with, or interrupt their infants' attempts to communicate (Ainsworth et al., 1971; Ainsworth & Wittig, 1969). Consequently, these babies learned to deactivate the attachment system by playing independently and refraining from seeking contact at separation. This deactivation response probably stems from an approach–avoidance conflict involving anxieties aroused by separation, contrasted with fear of possible rejection if renewed contact with the attachment figure is sought (Ainsworth & Wittig, 1969; Kobak, Cole, Ferenz-Gillies, Fleming, & Gamble, 1993).

Mothers of ambivalently attached infants tended to be inconsistent (i.e., sometimes playful and affectionate and sometimes interfering or rejecting). Perhaps these infants have low frustration tolerance because their signals, which elicit inconsistent responses, have no predictable effect on caregivers' actions (Ainsworth & Wittig, 1969). Unlike the avoidantly attached infants, these infants' attachment behaviors are rewarded (albeit unpredictably). Thus, their attachment system, rather than being deactivated, may be "hyperactivated"; that is, the infants may become especially vigilant to cues of impending separation or rejection (Ainsworth et al., 1971; Kobak et al., 1993).

Another important aspect of attachment theory is the concept of internal representational models. An infant's representational models are formed through the experience of repeated interactions with primary attachment figures and the attachment figure's ways of communicating with and responding to the child. Through a developing schema of rules, perceptions, expectations, and beliefs about the self, others, and relationships, these models become established as influential cognitive structures and form a heuristic base for future relationships (Bowlby, 1977, 1988; Main, Kaplan, & Cassidy, 1985; Paterson & Moran, 1988; West, Sheldon, & Reiffer, 1989).

As an infant experiences success through coordinated emotional communication with the attachment figure, thereby receiving necessary care, the infant forms representations of the self as capable of performing effective goal-directed behavior (e.g., "If I ask for help, Mom will help me": "If I let him know that I'm scared, Dad will help me feel better"), of others as responsive and caring, and of relationships as flexible and capable of being influenced. Infants who experience repeated failure to achieve desired outcomes (i.e., a sense of comfort and felt security) within the attachment relationship are more likely to have representations of self as ineffective, of others as unreliable, and of relationships as unrewarding (Gianino & Tronick, 1988; Tronick, 1989). Thus, the consistency of caregivers' appropriate responses to an infant's goal-directed social behavior forms the basis for the adult sense of social self-efficacy.

These representations are termed "working models" because in early childhood they can be revised as new attachment patterns are encountered. Working models become increasingly resistant to change as development proceeds, however, because new information that does not fit into existing belief structures is difficult to assimilate and tends to be defensively excluded (Bowlby, 1988; Bretherton, 1985; Paterson & Moran, 1988). Thus, these beliefs about self and others become an increasingly dominant part of a child's interpersonal style as he or she brings working models to bear upon new relationships (Bowlby, 1988). Subsequent interaction patterns tend to be automatic, generalized, and inflexible, and to persist uncorrected despite subsequent disconfirming experiences (Bowlby, 1988; West et al., 1989).

Continuity of Attachment Patterns

A critical question for the study of adult social competencies and social support is the degree of developmental continuity with which attachment patterns are maintained. How much do attachment patterns formed in early childhood influence subsequent attachments? The Ainsworth Strange Situation has been the most widely used method of assessing attachment in infancy and early childhood. Classifications of infant attachment to mother, as assessed by the Strange Situation procedure, have proven to be stable from 12 months to 18 or 20 months in middle-class families with stable life circumstances (Connell, 1976; Main & Weston, 1981; Owen, Easterbrooks, Chase-Lansdale, & Goldberg, 1984; Waters, 1978). Less stability of attachment classification has been found in families that are disadvantaged socioeconomically or have experienced stressful life events or both (Egeland & Farber, 1984; Sroufe, Egeland, & Kreutzer, 1990; Thompson, Lamb, & Estes, 1982; Vaughn, Egeland, Sroufe, & Waters, 1979). Attachment classifications can be expected to be more stable in families that do not experience disruptive change that might affect maternal responsiveness (Main & Cassidy, 1988). Consistent with this expectation, Fagot and Pears (1995) found, in a longitudinal study of 96 families, that the number of children who were classified as insecure–resistant (ambivalent) increased from 10% at 18 months to 36% at 30 months of age. No child initially classified as insecure–resistant made a transition to secure attachment at 30 months, and every one of the children who moved in the opposite direction, that is, from secure attachment at 18 months to insecure–resistant at 30 months, came from a family that experienced a major transition in parental relationships (e.g., divorce).

Main and Cassidy (1988) developed a method for classification of attachment at age 6 that is similar to the Strange Situation but allows for the considerable development that occurs between 24 months and 6 years of age. Using this procedure, they compared the attachment of infants with both mother and father previously assessed at 12 months to the attachments of the same children at 6 years. They found that the reunion behaviors of 6-year-olds with their mothers could be reliably predicted from first-year classifications of attachment. Reunion behaviors with fathers were less predictable. A replication of this study completed with a German sample also found that first-year attachment to mother reliably predicted attachment classification of 6-year-olds (Grossman & Grossman, 1991 [cited in Main & Cassidy, 1988]).

Paralleling Ainsworth's in-home observations of infants, attachment classification of 6-year-olds was associated with specific maternal behaviors (Solomon, George, & Ivins, 1987). Avoidant attachment was related to maternal rejection, hostility, and discouragement of dependence. Secure attachment was related to maternal acceptance and encouragement of learning and competence. Ambivalent attachment was associated with overinvolvement, indulgence, and discouragement of independence. These studies suggest that attachment patterns are fairly stable from infancy through the first 6 years of life, either because caregiver behavior that originally gave rise to the pattern remains unchanged through this period or because attachment patterns established in infancy are fairly resistant to change. Probably both mechanisms serve to maintain continuity of attachment patterns, although developmental changes no doubt influence and modify these patterns (Bowlby, 1988).

We are aware of two longitudinal studies that, to date, have classified attachments in a cohort of infants and tracked the children for more than 10 years. One of these studies (Grossmann & Grossmann, 1991) involved a sample of German children originally assessed in 1977 and a second sample assessed for the first time in 1980. At an intermediate assessment of one sample of 40 children at 6 years of age, 87% retained the same attachment classification they exhibited as infants. At 10 years of age, their attachment patterns were not classified as to type, but quality of peer relations had a strong association with attachment in infancy. The other long-term longitudinal study (Elicker, Englund, & Sroufe, 1992) found similar, striking evidence of the consequences for peer relations of attachment patterns first observed in infancy. The findings of these studies are presented in more detail below in connection with our discussion of social competency in children. For now, we wish only to highlight these strong longitudinal connections over a span greater than 10 years as evidence for the continuity of attachment patterns.

Our review of published literature did not locate any longitudinal study that tracked attachment patterns over an interval longer than 10 years. Beyond this period, we must rely on the results of studies using retrospective methods with adults and adolescents. For example, Parker and his associates developed the Parental Bonding Instrument (PBI) (Parker, Tupling, & Brown, 1979) as a retrospective measure of attachment. The PBI asks adult respondents to rate each parent from their earliest memories through age 16 in terms of two qualities of the parental bond, care and overprotection. The care dimension taps memories of parental sensitivity and responsiveness; overprotection taps memories of parental interference with attempts to gain autonomy. Parker and his associates have conducted an impressive program of research to establish the validity of the PBI using the concurrent ratings of siblings, external raters, and mothers of the respondents themselves (for a review, see Parker, 1984).

Memories of a parenting style having low care coupled with high overprotection, a style termed "affectionless control," were reported significantly more often by depressed adults than by nondepressed controls (Parker, 1983; Parker, Kiloh, & Hayward, 1987). A second style, in which one parent is rated at least one standard deviation below the care-scale mean, was characteristic of 37% of a sample of depressed clients, but of only 3% of a normal control group. The Swedish Egna Minnen Betraffande Uppfostran ("My Memories of Upbringing" [Perris, Jacobsson, Lindstrom, von Knorring, & Perris, 1980]) is a retrospective measure assessing memories of parental rearing practices. A short form was found to have three factors, supportive, rejecting, and overinvolved, that were stable over a 4-year period and were predictive of adults' depression, social alienation, self-esteem, and life satisfaction (Winefield, Goldney, Tiggemann, & Winefield, 1989).

Unfortunately, retrospective methods like these may be least reliable for assessing psychosocial variables (Henry, Moffitt, Caspi, Langley, & Silva, 1994). Errors occur due to memory failure and the tendency to reconstruct the past to suit current needs (Yarrow, Campbell, & Burton, 1970). Self-report retrospective ratings of attachment to parents are susceptible to the influence of current mood or recent events (Richman & Flaherty, 1987). In an attempt to avoid conscious distortions, projective techniques have been used (Fishler, Sperling, & Carr, 1990) to assess object relations capacity from a psychodynamic perspective, which may be considered a generalized capacity for forming healthy attachments. Projective methods have also been used with adults to assess childhood attachment experience (e.g., Gacono & Meloy, 1991). Unfortunately, these studies, by their nature, can do little to conclusively establish the continuity of attachment patterns from childhood through maturity.

Long-term longitudinal studies that might furnish this evidence remain to be completed. However, this review identified a number of studies that do suggest continuity of attachment patterns from late infancy through the early school years, and two longer-term longitudinal studies suggest continuity through the beginning of adolescence. We find this evidence persuasive, but we hasten to emphasize that "continuity" does not imply that attachment patterns developed in infancy are invariant determinants of adult relationships. Attachment theory has never claimed this degree of determinism (Hazan & Shaver, 1994a,b). Rather, it suggests that early attachment establishes a foundation for future relationships that if confirmed by subsequent experience throughout childhood, becomes increasingly resistant to change. Eventually, the weight of this accumulated experience may make attachment patterns extremely difficult to modify, but Bowlby (1973) believed that the patterns are not firmly fixed until adolescence, and he later maintained (Bowlby, 1988) that intensive psychotherapy could modify attachment patterns throughout life. It has been argued (Mallinckrodt, 1995) that if Bowlby were wrong about this, therapists of adult clients would soon be out of a job.

Classification of Adult Attachment

A growing number of studies have attempted to bridge the gap in longitudinal research by developing systems for classifying attachment patterns in the close relationships of adults. The Adult Attachment Interview (AAI) (George, Kaplan, & Main, 1985; Main & Goldwyn, 1985) is designed to activate working models of attachment. Participants are asked to discuss attachment experiences in early childhood, but are not scored on the content of these memories. Instead, they are scored on variables such as coherence, anger, contradictions, memory for specific events, idealization, and thoughtfulness in their evaluation of childhood. Despite the subjectivity inherent in coding such data, the AAI has good reliability and discriminant validity (Bakersmans-Kranenburg & van IJzendoorn, 1993; Van IJzendoorn, Kranenburg, Zwart-Woudstra, Van Busschbach, & Lambermon, 1991).

Using the AAI, Main and her colleagues (Main & Goldwyn, 1985; Main et al., 1985) identified three styles of regulating the attachment system, labeled "dismissing," "free to evaluate," and "preoccupied," which parallel Ainsworth's infant classifications of avoidant, secure, and ambivalent. Dismissing strategies involve deactivation of the attachment system, observed as restricted attachment memories, diverting attention to other topics, idealizing parents, or devaluing attachment relationships (Kobak et al., 1993). Free-to-evaluate strategies are characterized by the ability to recall and flexibly evaluate even distressing memories of family life and to consider and resolve information about self and parents.

Preoccupied strategies are marked by hyperactivation of the attachment system, as indicated by easy recall of excessive or irrelevant information, difficulty in maintaining coherence in describing family life, and the inability to achieve a balanced perspective on self and parents (Kobak et al., 1993).

Kobak and Sceery (1988) found that adolescents rated as dismissing had significantly more difficulty recalling attachment memories and that those they could recall were characterized by parental rejection and lack of love. Adolescents who were rated as secure were able to easily recall attachment memories, reported memories coherently, and were successful at integrating negative events. Their memories were characterized by the absence of idealization of their parents. Adolescents who were categorized as preoccupied had no difficulty with recall, but reported memories with confusion and a lack of coherence.

Hazan and Shaver (1987) proposed three patterns of attachment in romantic relationships based on Ainsworth's categories. They developed a simple three-paragraph matching item to assess secure, ambivalent, and avoidant adult styles. Recent variations on this typology allow for ratings of all three styles, resulting in combinations of patterns (Brennan, Shaver, & Tobey, 1991). Hazan and Shaver (1987) found that the best predictor of adult attachment type was the participants' perceptions of their childhood relationship with their parents and of their parents' relationship with each other. Persons with a secure attachment style described their parents as having been more respectful and caring, not intrusive or demanding toward them as children, and more affectionate with each other.

Other research expanded the original three-paragraph measures into an 18-item instrument that assesses the underlying dimensions of "depend"—willingness to trust others and reliance on them to be available if needed; "close"—comfort with intimacy and emotional closeness; and "anxiety"—fears of abandonment (Collins & Read, 1990). These researchers found that persons with a secure style, classified on the basis of these underlying dimensions, perceived their parents as having been warm and not rejecting, but that persons with an anxious attachment style perceived their parents as having been cold or inconsistent.

A fourfold typology was introduced by Bartholomew (1990), based on the 2 × 2 combination of positive and negative internal working models of self and others. The "secure" attachment pattern reflects a positive model of self and others, the "preoccupied" pattern combines a negative model of self and a positive model of others, the "fearful" pattern features negative models of self and others, and the "dismissing" pattern indicates a positive model of self and a negative model of others. The Attachment Style Questionnaire (Feeney, Noller, & Hanrahan, 1994) is a 40-item self-report measure with five subscales: (1) confidence in self and others, (2) need for approval, (3) preoccupation with relationships, (4) discomfort with closeness, and (5) relationships as secondary to achievement. The first subscale measures secure attachment, whereas the other four tap varieties of insecure attachment. A three-factor solution suggests that subscales 2 and 3 combine to form an "anxious" attachment factor, and that 4 and 5 combine to form an "ambivalent" higher-order factor. However, factor analyses suggest that the five-subscale form of the ASQ provides a better fit for the data, and cluster analyses suggest that the five subscales can be used to classify subjects into groups that correspond closely to Bartholomew's four adult attachment types (Feeney et al., 1994).

Other survey measures developed to measure adult attachment style assess components of attachment anxiety (West & Sheldon-Keller, 1992) or trust, communication, and alienation (Armsden & Greenberg, 1987). Yet another classification scheme for adult attachment (Sperling & Berman, 1991) combines the bipolar dimensions of affiliation vs. nonaffiliation, aggression vs. nonaggression, and attachment security vs. insecurity. Bowlby (1977) himself described pathological adult attachment patterns of compulsive self-reliance, compulsive caregiving, compulsive careseeking, and angry withdrawal. A self-report instrument was designed to measure these patterns (West & Sheldon, 1988).

Although a great deal of thought and effort has been expended in developing systems to classify adult attachment patterns, as yet there has been no longitudinal research to conclusively associate adult attachment patterns with childhood attachment experiences. However, a considerable number of studies have examined among children and adults separately the associations between social competencies and attachment. We turn next to a review of this research.

ATTACHMENT AND SOCIAL COMPETENCIES

Social Competency in Children

It is widely believed that children learn to relate to others socially very early in life and that this learning takes place in the context of family ties. Even the youngest infants are active participants in the parent–child relationship. By 2 months, an infant is able to distinguish people from inanimate objects and responds by communicating greetings to people but acting on objects instrumentally (Brazelton, Koslowski, & Main, 1974; Trevarthen, 1974). When an infant is 3 months of age, parent–infant interactions are bidirectional; that is, each person in the dyad appraises the other's communications and uses this information to form contingent responses (J. F. Cohn & Tronick, 1987; Lester, Hoffman, & Brazelton, 1985). Tronick (1989) asserted that infants are able to communicate an emotional message that the caregiver uses to assist the infant toward success in her or his goal-directed activities. These infant communications were termed "other-directed regulatory behaviors" (Gianino & Tronick, 1988). Research suggests that infants expect a response to their crying by 3–4 months (Lamb & Malkin, 1986), implying that social expectations and intentions are evident by that time (J. F. Cohn & Tronick, 1983; Lamb, 1981). However, large individual differences have been found in the ability of mother–infant pairs to maintain coordinated interaction (Tronick & Cohn, 1989).

Considerable research suggests that social competencies of children are related to attachment patterns, especially to caregiver responsiveness. Many of these studies compared securely attached children to a combined group of the two insecure types (ambivalent and avoidant). We located only one study that examined the disorganized–disoriented pattern (D. A. Cohn, 1990). Despite inconsistencies and methodological problems, a number of studies suggest that securely attached infants and young children get along better with peers and are more sociable with unfamiliar adults than either the ambivalent or the avoidant type (for reviews, see Lamb, 1987; Main & Weston, 1981).

In studies of child–caregiver relationships, attachment patterns at 18 months predict infant–mother interaction at 24 months. Secure infants communicated more positive and less negative affect than insecure infants, and tended to be more attentive and less aggressive toward their mothers (Matas, Arend, & Sroufe, 1978). Compared to other patterns, secure attachment at 12 months also predicted higher levels of cooperation and compliance with mothers and less disobedience at 20 months (Londerville & Main, 1981). Insecure attachment was associated with more resistance to maternal control and significantly lower levels of reciprocal interaction at the later age (Bates, Maslin, & Frankel, 1985). Paralleling these findings, the mothers of insecurely attached 20-month-old infants were more adult-centered and used more coercive parenting methods than did mothers of securely attached infants. The insecurely attached infants assessed at 4 years were more aggressive and displayed more negative affect than the children who had been securely attached (Booth, Rose-Krasnor, & Rubin, 1991). Securely attached infants at 13 months and their caregivers tended to show better dyadic problem-solving competence, less negativism, and less aggression then other infant–caregiver dyads (Frankel & Bates, 1990). Securely attached infants at 24 months showed the highest levels of responsiveness to mother (Pierrehumbert, Iannotti, Cummings, & Zahn-Waxler, 1989). Infants with insecure attachment to both mother and a child-care provider were least able to engage in interactive play with familiar adults (Howes, Rodning, Galluzzo, & Myers, 1988).

Findings concerning the relation of attachment to quality of interaction with peers are somewhat more mixed. Infants with an unchanged secure attachment pattern between 12 and 18 months were found to have higher social competence with unfamiliar peers at 20–23 months; that is, secure infants were more sociable and cooperative with, and more oriented toward, the peer, and made more attempts to engage the peer than did insecurely attached infants (Pastor, 1981). Infants at 18 months of age classified as "B1" or "B2" subgroups (more securely attached), compared to "B3" and "B4" classifications (less securely attached), exhibited higher-quality peer interactions and spent more time interacting and being close to peers (Easterbrooks & Lamb, 1979).

In a study of the effects of child care, secure attachment to mothers at 12 months and relatively early enrollment in child care predicted higher levels of social competence with peers at 4 years of age (Howes, 1991). Among children with less secure maternal attachments at 4 years of age, those who had been enrolled in child care at an earlier age were more socially competent. In an intriguing series of observations, infants from each of the three attachment classifications were paired with securely attached infants who served as playmates (J. L. Jacobson & Willie, 1986; J. L. Jacobson, Wille, Tianen, & Aytch, April, 1983).

Secure–secure dyads, relative to ambivalent–secure or avoidant–secure dyads, exhibited the *least* positive interaction at 24 months of age, but the most positive at 36 months. However, Pierrehumbert et al. (1989) did find an association between secure attachment and responsiveness with peers at 24 months.

Other research examined attachment and the generalized social skills of children, typically after infancy. At age 3½, children with a secure attachment style were more successful at responding to environmental demands and creating or capitalizing on opportunities for growth (Waters, Wippman, & Sroufe, 1979). "Ego resiliency" and control were higher in securely attached 4- to 5-year-olds than in their counterparts (Arend, Gove, & Sroufe, 1979; Waters et al., 1979). Securely attached children at age 6 had more fluency of verbal discourse and emotional openness (Main et al., 1985). Securely attached children were shown to have higher nonverbal social competencies and more experiences interacting with peers (Lieberman, 1977) and to exhibit less dependency than children with insecure attachment patterns (Sroufe, Fox, & Pancake, 1983; Urban, Carlson, Egeland, & Sroufe, 1991).

Sex differences have been found in some studies, but not in others. At age 6, insecure boys were found to be less well liked and to like others less, to be less competent, and to start more fights than secure boys, with girls showing no differences (D. A. Cohn, 1990). Avoidant attachment predicted aggression and passive withdrawal for boys but not for girls at 42 months (Renken, Egeland, Marvinney, Mangelsdorf, & Sroufe, 1989). In another study, conversely, girls' but not boys' attachment history predicted results in all measured areas of peer competence (LaFreniere & Sroufe, 1985). Secure girls were seen as very well adjusted and adaptable socially, ambivalent girls as more withdrawn and submissive, and avoidant girls as assertive but also more negative and frequently rejected. Among a sample of children between 4 and 7 years old (Marcus & Mirle, 1990), boys and girls with positive attachment to their fathers showed fewer internalizing problems on the Child Behavior Checklist. Positive attachments to each parent predicted higher social competence for boys, but positive attachment to mother was negatively correlated with social competency for girls.

Several studies have shown no relation between attachment and social behaviors in children, but have found that attachment patterns predict the way a child is responded to by other children and adults (J. L. Jacobson & Wille, 1986; LaFreniere & Sroufe, 1985; Sroufe et al., 1983; Urban et al., 1991). This research indicated that avoidant children tended to be more alienated from others, elicited fewer positive responses from peers, and were rejected more often (J. L. Jacobson & Wille, 1986; LaFreniere & Sroufe, 1985). Further, avoidant children, together with ambivalent children, tended to receive more discipline and guidance (Sroufe et al., 1983). Ambivalent children tended to be more frequently involved in disruptive and anxiety-creating relationships (J. L. Jacobson & Wille, 1986).

A very small number of studies have examined attachment in adolescents. Some of the most dramatic findings were obtained from the longest-span longitudinal studies to date. Ten years after classifying the attachment of infants, Grossmann and Grossmann (1991) conducted intensive interviews with the children and parents. Infant attachment style significantly differentiated the way the 10-year olds coped with negative affect. Children whose infant attachment had been secure were more likely to acknowledge negative feelings like sadness or anger and were more likely to report "relationship-oriented" coping strategies such as seeking help from others when distressed. Peer relationships also showed marked contrasts. Children classified as secure infants, compared to those classified as avoidant and ambivalent, at age 10 were more likely to report having one (or a few) good friends who were reliable and trusted. To some degree the avoidant children, and even more so the ambivalent children, reported having either no close friends or very many good friends—whom they were then unable to name. These 10-year-olds were more likely to be rejected by peers than were children who had been classified as securely attached during infancy.

Similarly, Elicker et al. (1992) invited a subsample of children who had originally been assessed as infants in a study of "high-risk" families to participate in a summer camp at age 10–11. The children were interviewed and intensively observed in peer interactions outside their homes and away from their parents' influence. Attachment patterns first observed in infancy were strong predictors of relationships with peers. Children's self-ratings, and observational ratings by the professional staff camp counselors, indicated that those classified as secure in infancy were as young adolescents more emotionally healthy, socially competent, and self-assured. They spent more time with peers and less time along or with adults than did children classified as avoidant or ambivalent in infancy. Securely attached children also tended to be rated as more popular, sociable, and skilled in prosocial behavior. Interestingly, when these securely attached children befriended other children, the target children were most likely to also have been securely attached in infancy.

Cotterell (1992) found that the positive attachments to parents and to teachers among boys and girls aged 14–18 were related to positive self-esteem. A 3-year longitudinal study that sampled over 1200 adolescents found that a family history of alcoholism was associated with poorer attachment to parents and high levels of stress due to conflicts in relationships with others (Johnson & Pandina, 1991). During the adolescent transition of leaving home, attachment may interact in complex ways with family dysfunction or healthy structure to influence social competencies of young adults (Kenny & Donaldson, 1991). In this transition, it is especially important for adolescents to strike a healthy balance between individuation and continued connection to their family—a balance that is often difficult for their parents to achieve (Kenny, 1990).

To summarize the findings of these studies of attachment and social competency in children, results are mixed but generally support the conclusion that children with secure attachments to their caregivers, especially in the first 2 years of life, do develop a higher level of the social skills necessary to interact successfully with peers. This heightened level of social skill allows children to derive greater satisfaction from early peer interactions. These skills and experiences, in turn, almost certainly have far-reaching consequences for healthy adult development and form the foundation for the ability to develop socially supportive relationships throughout life, although as yet there are few longitudinal studies to support this conclusion as applied to adults. We turn now to studies of adult social competencies and attachment.

Social Competency in Adults

After developing classification systems and measures for adult attachment, researchers have investigated social competencies (or deficits) associated with each type or measure. We have summarized this research in Table 1. Note that this is not an exhaustive review of adult attachment research. Studies were not included in this review if they did not have a direct connection to the social competencies needed to derive benefits from social support.

Several studies have investigated the relationship between attachment and social self-efficacy. Armsden and Greenberg (1987) found that the quality of attachment to both parents and peers was moderately correlated with social self-concept. Further, attachment to peers and to parents each predicted 18–19% of the unique variance in self-esteem. Individuals with more secure attachments tended to have greater self-esteem and less self-concept confusion. Collins and Read (1990) found that persons with secure attachment reported more social self-confidence than persons with an anxious–ambivalent type, but found no significant effects for persons with the avoidant pattern. Using a four-category model that distinguishes between dismissing and fearful attachment, which have been grouped into a single "avoidant" type in three-category models, Bartholomew and Horowitz (1991) reported that individuals classified as having preoccupied and fearful types of attachment reported lower levels of self-confidence, but that individuals in both the secure and dismissing categories reported higher self-confidence. Feeney and Noller (1990) found that secure persons rated themselves as having more social self-esteem than either avoidant or anxious–ambivalent persons. Bringle and Bagby (1992) reported that secure persons had significantly higher self-esteem than those classified as avoidant. Kobak and Sceery (1988) found that persons with secure attachments were generally more socially competent than those with preoccupied attachments.

The ability to trust and develop intimacy in a relationship is a very important social competency for recruiting social support. Secure attachment in adults has been associated with greater social involvement, intimacy, closeness, affection, and commitment (Bartholomew & Horowitz, 1991; Collins & Read, 1990; Feeney & Noller, 1990; Hazan & Shaver, 1987, 1990; Hendrick & Hendrick, 1989; Simpson, 1990). Further, the capacity to trust implies a balance of control, interdependence, and reciprocity, which have been related to secure attachment as well (Bartholomew & Horowitz, 1991; Feeney & Noller, 1991; Simpson, 1990). Mikulincer and Nachshon (1991) found that secure attachment was related to more self-disclosure, greater disclosure flexibility, and greater personal comfort with others' disclosure. Results from a study by Lussier, Sabourin, and Lambert (1994) indicated that secure attachment was negatively associated with loneliness and positively associated with more successful coping strategies. Secure attachment has been associated, on one hand, with the capacity to depend on others, to seek

Table 1. Empirical Studies of Adult Attachment

Study	Sample	Attachment assessment[a]	Social competency measure(s)
	Assessment of dimensions thought to be related to attachment		
Armsden & Greenberg (1987)	93 College students	IPPA	Social self-concept
Bradford & Lyddon (1993)	157 College students	IPPA	Relationship satisfaction
Collins & Read (1990)	3 Samples: 406 and 118 college students and 71 couples[b]	AAS	Trust, intimacy, social self-confidence, relationship satisfaction
Flaherty & Richman (1986)	153 First-year medical students	PBI	Social support
Mallinckrodt (1991)	102 Clients	PBI	Social support
Mallinckrodt (1992)	253 College students	PBI	Social self-efficacy, attributional style, social support
Mallinckrodt, Coble, & Gantt (1995a)	84 Female clients	PBI, AAS	Social self-efficacy
Richman & Flaherty (1986)	211 First-year medical students	PBI	Locus of control, interpersonal dependency
I. G. Sarason et al. (1986)	251 College students	PBI	Social support, life satisfaction
B. R. Sarason et al. (1991)	210 College students, plus 67 of their mothers, 58 fathers, and 46 same-sex friends	PBI	Social support, loneliness, social reticence, perceptions of self and others, relationship quality
Sheldon & West (1990)	47 Outpatient clients	DSM-III-R Classification of Avoidant Personality Disorder	Desire for or fear of attachment, social skills
Wilkinson et al. (August, 1991)	114 Married couples	AAS	Marital satisfaction

(continued)

Table 1. (*Continued*)

Study	Sample	Attachment assessment[a]	Social competency measure(s)
		Continuous measures of attachment style	
Hendrick & Hendrick (1989)	391 College students	H&S, all styles rated for agreement	Intimacy, commitment, relationship satisfaction
Simpson (1990)	144 Dating couples[b]	3 Subscales derived from 13 items based on H&S paragraph measure	Intimacy, trust
Simpson et al. (1992)	83 Dating couples[b]	3 Subscales derived from 13 items based on H&S paragraph measure	Intimacy, trust
Sperling & Berman (1991)	130 College students	ASI, 4 style subscales	Desperate love
		Discrete attachment style categories	
Bartholomew & Horowitz (1991)	77 College students and friends; 69 college students	AI	Social self-confidence, intimacy, trust, caregiving
Bringle & Bagby (1992)	168 College students	H&S	Social self-esteem
D. A. Cohn et al. (1992)	27 Married couples	AAI	Marital satisfaction
Feeney & Noller (1990)	374 College students	H&S	Social self-esteem, intimacy, trust
Feeney & Noller (1991)	74 College students	H&S	Intimacy, trust, relationship quality
Feeney et al. (1993)	193 College students	H&S	Relationship history, attitudes, diary of interactions
Hazan & Shaver (1987)	620 Newspaper respondents, 108 college students	H&S	Intimacy, trust
Hazan & Shaver (1990)	670 Newspaper respondents	H&S	Intimacy
Kobak & Sceery (1988)	53 College students	AAI	Social competency, social support
Lussier et al. (August, 1994)	576 College students	H&S	Loneliness, self-attribution
Pistole (1989)	137 College students	H&S	Conflict management, relationship satisfaction
Wallace & Vaux (1993)	253 College students	H&S	Social support

Continuous measures and discrete categorization of attachment style

		CRQ, IPPA	Social support
Blain et al. (1993)	216 College students	CRQ, IPPA	Social support
Feeney & Noller (1992)	193 College students	H&S plus 15-item measure	Intimacy, relationship quality, reactions to dissolution
Kobak & Hazan (1991)	40 Married couples	H&S, Marital Q Set (Kobak, 1989)	Relationship satisfaction
Mikulincer et al. (1990)	80 College students	H&S, 3 subscales derived from 15-item measure	Trust, social identity
Mikulincer & Nachshon (1991)	352 College students	H&S, 3 subscales derived from 15-item measure	Intimacy, trust, reciprocity
Shaver & Brennan (1992)	242 College students	H&S, plus all styles rated for agreement	Intimacy, relationship satisfaction

[a](AAI) Adult Attachment Interview (George et al., 1985); (AAS) Adult Attachment Scale (Collins & Read, 1990); (ASI) Attachment Style Inventory (Sperling & Berman, 1991); (CRQ) Close Relationships Questionnaire (Bartholomew & Horowitz, 1991); (H&S) Hazan & Shaver (1987) 18-item measure; (IPPA) Inventory of Parent and Peer Attachment (Armsden & Greenberg, 1987); (PBI) Parental Bonding Instrument (Parker et al., 1979).

[b]These samples are comprised of college students and their dating partners.

support, and to use a close relationship as a secure base (Bartholomew & Horowitz, 1991; Collins & Read, 1990; Simpson, Rholes, & Nelligan, 1992) and, on the other hand, with the capacity to support giving, openness, and acceptance of one's relationship partner (Feeney & Noller, 1991; Hazan & Shaver, 1987; Simpson et al., 1992).

Ambivalent attachment was marked by greater anxiety (Collins & Read, 1990), obsessive preoccupation with and emotional dependence on another (Collins & Read, 1990; Feeney & Noller, 1990), a greater desire for reciprocity and union (Hazan & Shaver, 1987), and more loneliness and use of negative coping strategies (Lussier et al., 1994). High levels of anxiety and hypervigilance to separation interfere with the ability to trust (Mikulincer, Florian, & Tolmacz, 1990). Ambivalent individuals tend to be overly dependent, unassertive, or domineering, and tend to idealize their partners (Bartholomew & Horowitz, 1991; Feeney & Noller, 1990, 1991). Sperling and Berman (1991) found that dependent attachment is related to a "desperate love" style that is characterized by fear of rejection but an intense desire for reciprocation of love, and the sense that reciprocation would fill some sort of personal void. Richman and Flaherty (1986) found that remembrances of childhood maternal overprotection were related to a tendency to be cautious, guarded, and in greater need of external direction or support to be able to function adequately.

Avoidant attachment has been associated with lower levels of involvement, closeness, intimacy, and commitment (Bartholomew & Horowitz, 1991; Collins & Read, 1990; Shaver & Brennan, 1992; Simpson, 1990). Desire for distance and fear of intimacy have also been associated with avoidant attachment patterns (Feeney & Noller, 1991; Hazan & Shaver, 1987). Bartholomew and Horowitz (1991) found that dismissing or fearful persons are less likely to report the capacity to rely on others. Dismissing persons tended to be high in self-confidence but also hostile, whereas fearful persons tended to be unassertive and socially inhibited (Bartholomew & Horowitz, 1991). In studies of relationship dissolution, avoidant persons reported more relief and less emotional distress (Feeney & Noller, 1992; Simpson, 1990). Avoidant persons endorsed items relating to mistrust and less interdependence (Feeney & Noller, 1990; Simpson, 1990).

Investigators have assessed the quality of relationships associated with adult attachment styles by using observational and self-report methods. Individuals with avoidant attachments were more likely than those with secure or ambivalent attachments to report fewer social interactions of any kind, to report that they were not in love and had never been in love, and to report significantly lower levels of intensity in relationships in general (Hazan & Shaver, 1987; Feeney, Noller, & Patty, 1993). Pistole (1989) studied attachment styles and self-reported conflict management strategies. Secure individuals were more likely to use integrating (win–win) or compromising (win–lose/win–lose) strategies than were insecure couples. Ambivalent persons reported that they were more likely to use an obliging (lose–win) strategy.

Kobak and Hazan (1991) investigated attachment in connection with a problem-solving task completed by nondistressed married couples. Wives' attachment security was related to their tendency to be less rejecting. Husbands' perceptions of their wives' availability was related to both partners' ability to be less rejecting and offer more supportive validation when solving the problem. D. A. Cohn, Silver, Cowan, Cowan, and Pearson (1992) also studied attachment (secure vs. insecure) and its relation to married couples' interactions in an observed problem-solving task. In couples who were higher-functioning and had more positive interactions and less conflict, the husband was more likely to have a secure attachment style. There were no significant associations for wives, however. These researchers also compared the match of attachment styles within couples. Secure–secure couples exhibited the highest level of functioning, moderately positive interactions, and little conflict. Insecure–insecure couples exhibited the greatest conflict, lowest functioning, and least number of positive interactions. Secure–insecure dyads displayed the most positive interactions, reasonable functioning, and little conflict.

Relationship satisfaction has been significantly correlated with continuous measures of secure attachment and negatively correlated with continuous dimensions of avoidant and ambivalent attachment (Hendrick & Hendrick, 1989; Shaver & Brennan, 1992; Simpson, 1990). In comparing discrete attachment style categories, Pistole (1989) also found that secure persons report significantly greater satisfaction in their relationships than do either ambivalent or avoidant persons. Bradford and Lyddon (1993), however, in their study of college student adjustment, found that dimensions of attachment to parents or peers did not predict relationship satisfaction.

Several researchers have examined gender differences in attachment and relationship satisfaction within couples. Collins and Read (1990) studied dating couples and found that women's scores on the anxiety dimension of their attachment scale, and men's scores on the close dimension, were the best predictors of both their own and their partner's relationship satisfaction. In other research with nondistressed married couples, wives' and husbands' perceptions of their partner's availability was related to their own satisfaction and their ability to rely on their partner (Kobak & Hazan, 1991). Wilkinson, McCreary, and Weedon (August, 1994) found that women with secure adult attachment patterns reported generally greater relationship satisfaction than did ambivalent or avoidant women. Specially, secure women were more satisfied than ambivalent women regarding affection, problem-solving, time spent together, and sex. Secure women reported more satisfaction than avoidant women in relation to affection and sex. Further, men's attachment style predicted wives' marital satisfaction, but wives' attachment style did not predict their husbands' satisfaction.

An important new development in couples research suggests the disturbing possibility that adults with dysfunctional attachment patterns who are likely to abuse their children, or who fail to protect their children from abuse, are likely to seek one another as mates (Crittenden, Partridge, & Claussen, 1991). Crittenden (1992) suggests that the ethnological function of attachment extends beyond protection in childhood for a given generation, because the quality of an individual's attachment experience prepares him or her for the experience of becoming an attachment figure for the next generation. Since a review of the growing body of literature regarding the intergenerational transmission of attachment patterns is beyond the scope of this chapter, the aforecited two studies and other relevant studies are not included in Table 1. We note, however, that convincing evidence suggests that the quality of childhood attachment may have a strong influence on an individual's capacity to provide nurturance and social support to others, including her or his own children (see, for example, Crowell & Feldman, 1991; Crowell, O'Connor, Wollmers, Sprafkin, & Rao, 1992; Jacobvitz, Morgan, Kretchmar, & Morgan, 1991; Levine, Tuber, Slade, & Ward, 1991). Closing the causal intergenerational circle, other research suggests that the quality of available social support has a strong impact on the ability of otherwise distressed mothers to form healthy attachments to their infants (Crnic, Greenberg, & Slough, 1986; S. W. Jacobson & Frye, 1991; Knoiak-Griffin, 1989; Kurdek, 1988).

Research using the Attachment Style Questionnaire found that high confidence in self and others, and low levels of the four subscales measuring insecure attachment were related to retrospective ratings of families as having been high in intimacy and democratic parenting style, and low in conflict (Feeney et al., 1994). The experience of growing up in a dysfunctional family, particularly one in which one or both parents were psychologically unresponsive, has been associated retrospectively with adults' object relations deficits, especially insecure attachment (Hadley, Holloway, & Mallinckrodt, 1993). When family dysfunction takes the form of parental sexual abuse, damage to adult social competencies may be especially severe. Mallinckrodt, McCreary, and Robertson (1995) found that women who had been sexually abused by a family member, compared to women with no reported sexual abuse, reported more difficulties with intimacy, less willingness to form close attachments, and lower levels of social support. Eating disorder symptoms were also significantly associated with a history of incest. Women who reported eating disorder symptoms and incest, compared to those with no reported abuse or eating disorder symptoms, had smaller social networks and were significantly lower in social self-efficacy, emotional awareness, and willingness to depend on others.

Psychotherapy may furnish social support through a professional working relationship. A client's ability to form a productive working alliance in psychotherapy has been associated with the quality of parental bonds (Mallinckrodt, 1991; Mallinckrodt, Coble, & Gantt, 1995a). Clients with different attachment styles have been found to exhibit different patterns of interpersonal problems. These problem areas, in turn, were found to differ markedly in how amenable they were to change through brief dynamic psychotherapy (Horowitz, Rosenberg, & Bartholomew, 1993). Some retrospective evidence suggests that working models of self and others formed during early attachment experiences establish a template that influences clients' ability to form a working alliance with their therapists. Distinct patterns based on much earlier experiences may characterize a client's attachment to the therapist and form the basis for the phenomenon that psychodynamic theorists have labeled "transference" (Mallinckrodt, Gantt, & Coble, 1995).

To summarize, much of the research on adult attachment and social competency has been conducted only recently and is limited by difficulties in operational definition and measurement. Continuity of adult attachment patterns with patterns observed in infants and young children has often been assumed, but remains to be conclusively demonstrated. Regardless of the stability of attachment patterns over the life span, adult attachment styles do appear to have an important connection to the capacity to form intimate relationships. Indeed, adult attachment patterns are often defined largely in terms of differences in the capacity to form close relationships (e.g., Collins & Read, 1990; West & Sheldon, 1988). This capacity is also related to one's ability to recruit social support, especially the kinds of support typically provided in close personal attachments. The next section reviews studies that have empirically explored this question.

Social Support

Working models that guide an individual's social functioning organize incoming information about others and their capacity and willingness to provide support. Attachment theory predicts that those persons with a secure attachment style and positive working models of self and others should be more open to supportive relationships and more adept at mobilizing and utilizing social support. Those persons with more anxious styles, characterized by reluctance to trust and by fear and ambivalence toward others, should be less able to recruit and use social support.

Several studies have used the Parental Bonding Instrument (PBI) to measure attachment and social support. B. R. Sarason et al. (1991) found that persons who viewed their parents as caring and not overprotective were satisfied with many aspects of their social relationships. Representations of parents' care (i.e., emotional responsiveness) were associated with satisfaction with social support (I. G. Sarason et al., 1986). Flaherty and Richman (1986) found that parental warmth/care, but not overprotection, was correlated with perceived quality of social support, including nonfamilial relationships. In another study, maternal warmth was positively related to social support, but was unrelated 7 months later (Richman & Flaherty, 1987). High overprotection from either parent was associated with an external attribution style and interpersonal dependency. This intrusive, controlling parenting style was also negatively related to social support satisfaction, but only for women (Flaherty & Richman, 1986). Mallinckrodt (1992) also found that scores on the PBI Care scale were correlated with social support quality. However, using the same measures in a sample of psychotherapy clients, Mallinckrodt (1991) found that maternal overprotection was positively correlated with social support.

In a study of support-seeking and giving in a situation perceived as stressful, women at lower levels of anxiety with avoidant attachment style were able to seek support from their dating partner, but they sought less support as their anxiety increased (Simpson et al., 1992). They were, however, more responsive to support than secure women when it was offered. In addition, men with avoidant attachment styles offered less support to their partners than did men with secure styles. In other research that did not examine couples, for both men and women, higher reported social self-efficacy was associated with more perceived social support, whereas higher external attribution style for social outcomes was negatively associated with social support (Mallinckrodt, 1991).

Wallace and Vaux (1993) used the Hazan and Shaver (1987) paragraph method of classifying attachment styles to examine attachment and social network orientation. Network orientation was defined as a set of beliefs regarding the potential usefulness of the network to help with life problems. This orientation is assumed to affect willingness to use social support resources, and it overlaps conceptually with the working model of others. Wallace and Vaux found that persons with secure attachment styles were more positively oriented toward their support networks than were persons with either the ambivalent or the avoidant style. Examining the elements of independence and mistrust in network orientation, Wallace and Vaux found that persons with an avoidant attachment style scored highest on independence and that persons with an avoidant or ambivalent style were higher in mistrust than those with a secure style.

Research indicates that attachment style is associated with social behaviors that affect social support and with attitudes about the self and others that govern those behaviors. Adolescents categorized as low in secure attachment reported less willingness to share serious concerns with parents and less willingness to share both everyday and serious concerns with peers (Armsden & Greenberg, 1987). Persons with avoidant personality disorder, thought to be correlated with an avoidant attachment style, have indicated that they do not lack social skills, but instead have a fear of an attachment relationship (Sheldon & West, 1990). B. R. Sarason et al. (1991) found that perceptions of social support were positively related to beliefs about the self and others. Similarly, high social support was associated with a positive working model of self and others, but a negative model of self or others or both was related to a lower amount of perceived social support (Blain, Thompson, & Whiffen, 1993).

Any conclusions drawn from the small number of studies that have investigated social support and attachment must remain very tentative. The majority of the available findings do suggest that secure styles of adult attachment, positive working models of self and others, and recollections of one's parents as having been emotionally responsive and fostering autonomy are associated with higher levels of perceived social support in adults. The small number of studies also points out the great need for further research in this area.

CONCLUSIONS

We have suggested that the availability of social support in the environment and a basic level of social skills are not enough to ensure that an individual will benefit from social support. Higher-order social competencies are also necessary. These social competencies include complex skills, such as the ability to form emotionally intimate relationships; personality dispositions, such as a willingness to allow oneself to depend on others; and beliefs, such as the conviction that one is deserving of help, that there are many others available to provide supportive help, and that one's efforts to obtain this support have a good chance of succeeding. We have reviewed research suggesting that attachment experiences in early childhood have a strong influence on the development of social competencies in children and research suggesting that patterns of attachment evident in adults are also associated with social competencies needed to recruit and use social support.

Obviously, much more research is needed to more firmly establish these propositions. An equally critical need is for more longitudinal research on the continuity of attachment patterns. Although studies that follow a cohort from infancy through adulthood may be unfeasible for all but a few researchers, shorter-duration studies of 3–5 years using overlapping cohort age groups could nevertheless make a great contribution. Experimental and observational studies are needed in addition to studies using self-report methods. Although self-report methods are the most popular for exploring adult attachment, they are subject to response set bias and mood influences. Correlations from exclusively self-report methods may be inflated in some studies due to operationalization of constructs that amount to logical tautologies. When adult attachment styles are defined in terms of relationship-building skills, it should not be surprising that persons with such skills have more numerous and more satisfying relationships. Many of the studies reviewed in this chapter use category models to describe attachment. Until more research supports the existence of taxonomically distinct, discrete categories of attachment in adults (Mallinckrodt, Coble, & Gantt, 1995b), it may be more prudent to describe adult attachment in terms of continuous dimensions. The tendency to assign persons into discrete typologies creates a bias against discovering patterns that differ from conventional wisdom.

In addition to these methodological concerns, our review also points to some new directions for attachment research. Most previous studies have focused on relationships with a caregiver or intimate partner. However, other kinds of attachments are formed throughout the life span. These other attachments may provide supportive functions that influence the structure of working models and future social functioning. Clinicians have noted that some persons with very poor family histories are surprisingly emotionally healthy and socially well adjusted and that these persons typically have some positive alterative attachment figure, such as a sibling, grandparent, or perhaps even neighbor or teacher. The influence of these alternative attachment figures is a fertile area for exploration.

Finally, as therapists, we return to our concern about effective interventions. With the usual caveat that much more study is needed, considerable evidence suggests that social competencies training might be indicated, especially for young children whose attachment experiences have not provided them with the tools to develop quality peer relationships. If this intervention is provided early enough, rewarding experiences with others might prompt revisions in negative working models of others and self, with potentially far-reaching consequences for adult functioning. In some cases, however, social competencies training alone might not be helpful. When a child or adult client presents with problems of deficits in quality peer interactions or social support, careful assessment is required to determine which of the three necessary conditions we initially described might be deficient. Training in basic social skills will do little to help clients whose environments provide few potentially supportive relationships, nor will such training help clients who lack the higher-order social competencies and expectations about the social world needed to make use of the basic skills they are taught.

Research reviewed in this chapter suggests that a significant number of persons have adequate basic social skills, but hold beliefs about themselves and expectations about social reality that prevent them from making use of available potentially supportive relationships. Some may dismiss the value of social support entirely as a coping strategy. For persons with poor attachment experiences and low social competencies, the development of attachments to alternative caregiving figures (including therapists or members of facilitated peer groups) might prove to be an effective goal for therapy, especially for adults or for children when a direct family therapy intervention is not feasible. Therapists working to build the social competencies of adult clients need to know the degree to which the die has been cast by the client's early attachment experience and, with the scope available to them, how best to modify attachment patterns and social competencies. Our review of available research provided no definitive answer to this question. New investigations of the malleability of adult attachment patterns, and of the importance of alternative attachment figures, will have crucial implications for treatment.

REFERENCES

Ainsworth, M. D. S., Bell, S. M. V., & Stayton, D. J. (1971). Individual differences in Strange-Situation behaviour of one-year-olds. In H. R. Schaffer (Ed.), *The origins of human social relations* (pp. 17–57). London: Academic Press.

Ainsworth, M. D. S., Blehar, M. C., Waters, E., & Wall, S. (1978). *Patterns of attachment: A psychological study of the Strange Situation*. Hillsdale, NJ: Lawrence Erlbaum.

Ainsworth, M. D. S., & Wittig, B. A. (1969). Attachment and exploratory behavior of one-year-olds in a Strange Situation. In B. M. Foss (Ed.), *Determinants of infant behavior*, Vol. 4 (pp. 111–136). London: Methuen.

Arend, R., Gove, F. L., & Sroufe, L. A. (1979). Continuity of individual adaptation from infancy to kindergarten: A predictive study of ego-resiliency and curiosity in preschoolers. *Child Development*, *50*, 950–959.

Armsden, G. C., & Greenberg, M. T. (1987). The Inventory of Parent and Peer Attachment: Individual differences and their relationship to psychological well-being in adolescence. *Journal of Youth and Adolescence*, *16*, 427–454.

Bakermans-Kranenburg, M. J., & Van IJzendoorn, M. H. (1993). A psychometric study of the Adult Attachment Interview: Reliability and discriminant validity. *Developmental Psychology*, *29*, 870–879.

Bartholomew, K. (1990). Avoidance of intimacy: An attachment perspective. *Journal of Social and Personal Relationships*, *7*, 147–178.

Bartholomew, K., & Horowitz, L. M. (1991). Attachment styles among young adults: A test of a four-category model. *Journal of Personality and Social Psychology*, *61*, 226–244.

Bates, J. E., Maslin, C. A., & Frankel, K. A. (1985). Attachment security, mother–child interaction and temperament as predictors of behavior problem ratings at age three years. In I. Bretherton & E.

Waters (Eds.), Growing points of attachment theory and research. *Monographs of the Society for Research in Child Development, 50(1–2)*, Serial No. 209, 167–193.

Blain, M. D., Thompson, J. M., & Whiffen, V. E. (1993). Attachment and perceived social support in late adolescence: The interaction between working models of self and others. *Journal of Adolescent Research, 8*, 226–241.

Booth, C. L., Rose-Krasnor, L., & Rubin, K. H. (1991). Relating preschoolers' social competence and their mothers' parenting behaviors to early attachment security and high-risk status. Special Issue: Family–peer relationships. *Journal of Social and Personal Relationships, 8*, 363–382.

Bowlby, J. (1969). *Attachment and loss*, Vol. 1, *Attachment*. New York: Basic Books.

Bowlby, J. (1973). *Attachment and loss*, Vol. 2: *Separation—Anxiety and anger*. London: Hogarth Press.

Bowlby, J. (1977). The making and breaking of affectional bonds. I. Aetiology and psychopathology in the light of attachment theory. *British Journal of Psychiatry, 130*, 201–210.

Bowlby, J. (1988). *A secure base: Parent–child attachment and healthy human development*. New York: Basic Books.

Bradford, E., & Lyddon, W. J. (1993). Current parental attachment: Its relation to perceived psychological distress and relationship satisfaction in college students. *Journal of College Student Development, 34*, 256–260.

Brazelton, T. B., Koslowski, B., & Main, M. (1974). The origins of reciprocity: The early mother–infant interaction. In M. E. Lewis & L. A. Rosenblum (Eds.), *The effect of the infant on its caregiver* (pp. 49–76). New York: Wiley.

Brennan, K. A., Shaver, P. R., & Tobey, A. E. (1991). Attachment styles, genders and parental problem drinking. *Journal of Social and Personal Relationships, 8*, 451–466.

Bretherton, I. (1985). Attachment theory: Retrospect and prospect. In I. Bretherton & E. Waters (Eds.), Growing points of attachment theory and research. *Monographs of the Society for Research in Child Development, 50(1–2)*, Serial No. 209, 3–35.

Bretherton, I. (1992). The origins of attachment theory: John Bowlby and Mary Ainsworth. *Developmental Psychology, 28*, 759–775.

Bringle, R. G., & Bagby, G. J. (1992). Self-esteem and perceived quality of romantic and family relationships in young adults. *Journal of Research in Personality, 26*, 340–356.

Cohn, D. A. (1990). Child–mother attachment of six-year-olds and social competence at school. *Child Development, 61*, 152–162.

Cohn, D. A., Silver, D. H., Cowan, C. P., Cowan, P. A., & Pearson, J. (1992). Working models of childhood attachment and couple relationships. *Journal of Family Issues, 13*, 432–449.

Cohn, J. F., & Tronick, E. Z. (1983). Three-month-old infants' reaction to simulated maternal depression. *Child Development, 54*, 185–193.

Cohn, J. F., & Tronick, E. Z. (1987). Mother–infant face-to-face interaction: The sequence of dyadic states at 3, 6, and 9 months. *Developmental Psychology, 23*, 68–77.

Collins, N. L., & Read, S. J. (1990). Adult attachment, working models, and relationship quality in dating couples. *Journal of Personality and Social Psychology, 58*, 644–663.

Connell, D. B. (1976). Individual differences in attachment behavior: Long-term stability and relationships to language development. Unpublished doctoral dissertation. Syracuse, NY: Syracuse University.

Cotterell, J. L. (1992). The relation of attachments and support to adolescent well-being and school adjustment. *Journal of Adolescent Research, 7*, 28–42.

Crittenden, P. M. (1992). Quality of attachment in the preschool years. *Development and Psychopathology, 4*, 209–241.

Crittenden, P. M., Partridge, M. F., & Claussen, A. H. (1991). Family patterns of relationship in normative and dysfunctional families. *Development and Psychopathology, 3*, 491–512.

Crnic, K. A., Greenberg, M. T., & Slough, M. M. (1986). Early stress and social support influences on mothers' and high-risk infants' functioning in late infancy. Special Issue: Social support, family functioning, and infant development. *Infant Mental Health Journal, 7*, 19–33.

Crowell, J. A., & Feldman, S. S. (1991). Mothers' working models of attachment relationships and mother and child behavior during separation and reunion. *Developmental Psychology, 27*, 597–605.

Crowell, J. A., O'Connor, E., Wollmers, G., Sprafkin, J., & Rao, U. (1992). Mothers' conceptualizations of parent–child relationships: Relation to mother–child interaction and child behavior problem. *Development and Psychology, 3,* 431–444.

Cutrona, C. E., & Russell, D. W. (1990). Type of social and specific stress: Toward a theory of optimal matching. In B. R. Sarason, I. G. Sarason, & G. R. Pierce (Eds.), *Social support: An interactional view* (pp. 319–366). New York: Wiley.

Duck, S. (1988). *Relating to others.* Newbury Park, CA: Sage Publications.

Easterbrooks, M. A., & Lamb, M. E. (1979). The relationship between quality of infant–mother attachment and infant competence in initial encounters with peers. *Child Development, 50,* 380–387.

Egeland, B., & Farber, E. A. (1984). Infant–mother attachment: Factors related to its development and changes over time. *Child Development, 55,* 733–751.

Elicker, J., Englund, M., & Sroufe, L. A. (1992). Predicting peer competence and peer relationships in childhood from early parent–child relationships. In R. Parke & G. Ladd (eds.), *Family–peer relations: Modes of linkage* (pp. 77–106). Hillsdale, NJ: Lawrence Erlbaum.

Fagot, B. I., & Pears, K. (1995). Attachment: Infancy to preschool. Unpublished manuscript available from: Oregon Social Learning Center, 207 E. 5th Ave., Eugene, OR 97401.

Feeney, J. A., & Noller, P. (1990). Attachment style as a predictor of adult romantic relationships. *Journal of Personality and Social Psychology, 58,* 281–291.

Feeney, J. A., & Noller, P. (1991). Attachment style and verbal descriptions of romantic partners. *Journal of Social and Personal Relationships, 8,* 187–215.

Feeney, J. A., & Noller, P. (1992). Attachment style and romantic love: Relationship dissolution. *Australian Journal of Psychology, 44,* 69–74.

Feeney, J. A., Noller, P., & Hanrahan, M. (1994). Assessing adult attachment. In M. B. Sperling and W. H. Berman (Eds.), *Attachment in adults: Clinical and developmental perspectives* (pp. 128–154). New York: Guilford.

Feeney, J. A., Noller, P., & Patty, J. (1993). Adolescents' interactions with the opposite sex: Influence of attachment style and gender. *Journal of Adolescence, 16,* 169–186.

Fishler, P. H., Sperling, M. B., & Carr, A. C. (1990). Assessment of adult relatedness: A review of empirical findings from object relations and attachment theories. *Journal of Personality Assessment, 55,* 499–520.

Flaherty, J. A., & Richman, J. A. (1986). Effects of childhood relationships on the adult's capacity to form social supports. *American Journal of Psychiatry, 143,* 851–855.

Frankel, K. A., & Bates, J. E. (1990). Mother–toddler problem solving: Antecedents in attachment, home behavior, and temperament. *Child Development, 61,* 810–819.

Gacono, C., & Meloy, J. R. (1991). A Rorschach investigation of attachment and anxiety in antisocial personality disorder. *Journal of Nervous and Mental Disease, 179,* 546–552.

George, C., Kaplan, N., & Main, M. (1985). An attachment interview for adults. Unpublished manuscript. Berkeley: University of California.

Gianino, A., & Tronick, E. Z. (1988). The mutual recognition model: The infant's self and interactive regulation coping and defense capacities. In T. Field, P. McCabe, & N. Schneiderman (Eds.), *Stress and coping* (pp. 47–68). Hillsdale, NJ: Lawrence Erlbaum.

Grossmann, K. E., & Grossmann, K. (1991). Attachment quality as an organizer of emotional and behavioral responses in a longitudinal perspective. In C. M. Parkes, J. Stevenson-Hinde, & P. Marris (Eds.), *Attachment across the life cycle* (pp. 93–114). London: Tavistock/Routledge.

Hadley, J. A., Holloway, E. L., & Mallinckrodt, B. (1993). Common aspects of object-relations and self-representations in offspring from disparate dysfunctional families. *Journal of Counseling Psychology, 40,* 348–356.

Hazan, C., & Shaver, P. (1987). Romantic love conceptualized as an attachment process. *Journal of Personality and Social Psychology, 52,* 511–524.

Hazan, C., & Shaver, P. R. (1990). Love and work: An attachment-theoretical perspective. *Journal of Personality and Social Psychology, 59,* 270–280.

Hazan, C., & Shaver, P. R. (1994a). Attachment as an organizational framework for research on close relationships. *Psychological Inquiry, 5,* 1–22.

Hazan, C., & Shaver, P. R. (1994b). Deeper into attachment theory. *Psychological Inquiry, 5,* 68–79.

Hendrick, C., & Hendrick, S. S. (1989). Research on love: Does it measure up? *Journal of Personality and Social Psychology, 56*, 784–794.

Henry, B., Moffitt, T. E., Caspi, A., Langley, J., & Silva, P. A. (1994). On the "remembrance of things past": A longitudinal evaluation of the retrospective method. *Psychological Assessment, 6*, 92–101.

Horowitz, L. M., Rosenberg, S. E., & Bartholomew, K. (1993). Interpersonal problems, attachment styles, and outcomes in brief dynamic psychotherapy. *Journal of Consulting and Clinical Psychology, 61*, 549–560.

Horvath, A. O., & Symonds, B. D. (1991). Relation between working alliance and outcome in psychotherapy: A meta-analysis. *Journal of Counseling Psychology, 38*, 139–149.

Howes, C. (1991). A comparison of preschool behaviors with peers when children enroll in child-care as infants or older children. Special Issue: International perspective on day care for young children. *Journal of Reproductive and Infant Psychology, 9*, 105–115.

Howes, C., Rodning, C., Galluzzo, D. C., & Myers, L. (1988). Attachment and child care: Relationships with mother and caregiver. *Early Childhood Research Quarterly, 3*, 403–416.

Jacobson, J. L., & Wille, D. E. (1986). The influence of attachment pattern on developmental changes in peer interaction from the toddler to the preschool period. *Child Development, 57*, 338–347.

Jacobson, J. L., Wille, D. E., Tianen, R. L., & Aytch, D. M. (April, 1983). The influence of infant–mother attachment on toddler sociability with peers. Paper presented at the meeting of the Society for Research in Child Development. Detroit.

Jacobson, S. W., & Frye, K. F. (1991). Effect of maternal social support on attachment: Experimental evidence. *Child Development, 62*, 572–582.

Jacobvitz, D. B., Morgan, E., Kretchmar, M. D., & Morgan, Y. (1991). The transmission of mother–child boundary disturbances across three generations. *Development and Psychopathology, 3*, 513–527.

Johnson, V., & Pandina, R. J. (1991). Familial and personal drinking histories and measures of competence in youth. *Addictive Behaviors, 16*, 453–465.

Kenny, M. E. (1990). College seniors' perceptions of parental attachments: The value and stability of family ties. *Journal of College Student Development, 31*, 39–46.

Kenny, M. E., & Donaldson, G. A. (1991). Contributions of parental attachment and family structure to the social and psychological functioning of first-year college students. *Journal of Counseling Psychology, 38*, 479–486.

Knoiak-Griffin, D. (1989). Psychosocial and clinical variables in pregnant adolescents: A survey of maternity home residents. *Journal of Adolescent Health Care, 10*, 23–29.

Kobak, R. R. (1989). *The attachment interview Q-Sort.* Unpublished manuscript, University of Delaware.

Kobak, R. R., Cole, H. E., Ferenz-Gillies, R., Fleming, W. S., & Gamble, W. (1993). Attachment and emotion regulation during mother–teen problem solving: A control theory analysis. *Child Development, 64*, 231–245.

Kobak, R. R., & Hazan, C. (1991). Attachment in marriage: Effects of security and accuracy of working models. *Journal of Personality and Social Psychology, 60*, 861–869.

Kobak, R. R., & Sceery, A. (1988). Attachment in late adolescence: Working models, affect regulation, and representations of self and others. *Child Development, 59*, 135–146.

Kurdek, L. A. (1988). Social support of divorced single mothers and their children. *Journal of Divorce, 11*, 167–188.

LaFreniere, P. J., & Sroufe, L. A. (1985). Profiles of peer competence in the preschool: Interrelations between measures, influence of social ecology, and relation to attachment history. *Developmental Psychology, 21*, 56–69.

Lamb, M. E. (1981). Developing trust and perceived effectance in infancy. In L. P. Lipsitt & C. K. Rovee-Collier (Eds.), *Advances in infancy research* (pp. 101–127). Norwood, NJ: Ablex.

Lamb, M. E. (1987). Predictive implications of individual differences in attachment. *Journal of Consulting and Clinical Psychology, 55*, 817–824.

Lamb, M. E., & Malkin, C. M. (1986). The development of social expectations in distress-relief sequences: A longitudinal study. *International Journal of Behavioral Development, 9*, 235–249.

LaRocco, J. M., & Jones, A. P. (1978). Coworker and leader support as moderators of stress–strain relationships in work situations. *Journal of Applied Psychology, 63*, 629–634.

Lazarus, R. S., & Folkman, S. (1984). Stress appraisal and coping. New York: Springer.

Lehman, D. R., Ellard, J. H., & Wortman, C. B. (1986). Social support for the bereaved: Recipients' and providers' perspectives on what is helpful. *Journal of Consulting and Clinical Psychology, 54*, 438–446.

Lester, B., Hoffman, J., & Brazelton, T. B. (1985). The rhythmic structure of mother–infant interaction in term and preterm infants. *Child Development, 56*, 15–27.

Levine, L. V., Tuber, S. B., Slade, A., & Ward, M. J. (1991). Mothers' mental representations and their relationship to mother–infant attachment. *Bulletin of the Menniger Clinic, 55*, 454–469.

Lieberman, A. F. (1977). Preschoolers' competence with a peer: Relations with attachment and peer experience. *Child Development, 48*, 1277–1287.

Londerville, S., & Main, M. (1981). Security of attachment, compliance, and maternal training methods in the second year of life. *Developmental Psychology, 17*, 289–299.

Lussier, Y., Sabourin, S., & Lambert, V. (August, 1994). Attachment and cognitions: Comparisons between clinical and nonclinical college students. Paper presented at the 102nd Annual American Psychological Association Convention. Los Angeles.

Main, M., & Cassidy, J. (1988). Categories of response to reunion with the parent at age 6: Predictable from infant attachment classifications and stable over a 1-month period. *Developmental Psychology, 24*, 415–426.

Main, M., & Goldwyn, R. (1985). Adult attachment classification system. Unpublished manuscript. Berkeley: University of California.

Main, M., Kaplan, N., & Cassidy, J. (1985). Security in infancy, childhood, and adulthood: A move to the level of representations. *Monographs of the Society for Research in Child Development, 50*, 66–104.

Main, M., & Solomon, J. (1986). Discovery of an insecure–disorganized/disoriented attachment pattern. In T. B. Brazelton & M. Yogman (Eds.), *Affective development in infancy* (pp. 95–124). Norwood, NJ: Ablex.

Main, M., & Solomon, J. (1990). Procedures for identifying infants as disorganized/disoriented during the Ainsworth Strange Situation. In M. Greenberg, D. Cichetti, & M. Cummings (Eds.), *Attachment in the preschool years* (pp. 121–160). Chicago: University of Chicago Press.

Main, M. B., & Weston, D. R. (1981). The quality of the toddler's relationship to mother and to father: Related to conflict behavior and the readiness to establish new relationships. *Child Development, 52* 932–940.

Mallinckrodt, B. (1989). Social support and the effectiveness of group therapy. *Journal of Counseling Psychology, 36*, 170–175.

Mallinckrodt, B. (1991). Client's representations of childhood emotional bonds with parents, social support, and formation of the working alliance. *Journal of Counseling Psychology, 38*, 401–409.

Mallinckrodt, B. (1992). Childhood emotional bonds with parents, development of adult social competencies and the availability of social support. *Journal of Counseling Psychology, 39*, 453–461.

Mallinckrodt, B. (1995). Attachment theory and counseling: Ready to be a prime time player? *Counseling Psychologist, 23*, 501–505.

Mallinckrodt, B. (in press). Interpersonal relationship processes in individual and group psychotherapy. In S. Duck (Ed.), *Handbook of personal relationships* (2nd ed.). New York: Wiley.

Mallinckrodt, B., Coble, H. M., & Gantt, D. L. (1995a). Working alliance, client attachment, and social competencies for women in brief therapy. *Journal of Counseling Psychology, 42*, 79–84.

Mallinckrodt, B., Coble, H. M., & Gantt, D. L. (1995b). Toward differentiating client attachment from working alliance and transference: Reply to Robbins. *Journal of Counseling Psychology, 42*.

Mallinckrodt, B., Gantt, D. L., & Coble, H. M. (1995). Adult patterns of attachment in psychotherapy: Development of the Client Attachment to Therapist Scale. *Journal of Counseling Psychology, 42*, 307–317.

Mallinckrodt, B., McCreary, B. A., & Roberston, A. K. (1995). Cooccurrence of eating disorders and incest: The role of attachment, family environment, and social competencies. *Journal of Counseling Psychology, 42*, 178–186.

Marcus, R. F., & Mirle, J. (1990). Validity of a child interview measure of attachment as used in child custody evaluations. *Perceptual and Motor Skills, 70*, 1043–1054.

Matas, L., Arend, R. A., & Sroufe, L. A. (1978). Continuity of adaptation in the second year: The relationship between quality of attachment and later competence. *Child Development, 49*, 547–556.

Mikulincer, M., Florian, V., & Tolmacz, R. (1990). Attachment styles and fear of personal death: A case study of affect regulation. *Journal of Personality and Social Psychology, 58,* 273–280.

Mikulincer, M., & Nachshon, O. (1991). Attachment styles and patterns of self-disclosure. *Journal of Personality and Social Psychology, 61,* 321–331.

Owen, M. T., Easterbrooks, M. A., Chase-Lansdale, L., & Goldberg, W. A. (1984). The relations between maternal employment status and the stability of attachments to mother and father. *Child Development, 55,* 1894–1901.

Parker, G. (1983). Parental "affectionless control" as an antecedent to adult depression: A risk factor delineated. *Archives of General Psychiatry, 40,* 956–960.

Parker, G. (1984). The measurement of pathogenic parenting style and its relevance to psychiatric disorder. *Social Psychiatry, 19,* 75–81.

Parker, G., Kiloh, L., & Hayward, L. (1987). Parental representations of neurotic and endogenous depressives. *Journal of Affective Disorders, 13,* 75–82.

Parker, G., Tupling, H., & Brown, L. B. (1979). A parental bonding instrument. *British Journal of Medical Psychology, 52,* 1–10.

Pastor, D. L. (1981). The quality of mother–infant attachment and its relationship to toddlers' initial sociability with peers. *Developmental Psychology, 17,* 326–335.

Paterson, R. J., & Moran, G. (1988). Attachment theory, personality development, and psychotherapy. *Clinical Psychology Review, 8,* 611–636.

Perris, C., Jacobsson, L., Lindstrom, H., von Knorring, L., & Perris, H. (1980). Development of a new inventory for assessing memories of parental rearing behaviour. *Acta Psychiatrica Scandinavica, 61,* 265–274.

Pierrehumbert, B., Iannotti, R. J., Cummings, E. M., & Zahn-Waxler, C. (1989). Social functioning with mother and peers at 2 and 5 years: The influence of attachment. *International Journal of Behavioral Development, 12,* 85–100.

Pistole, M. C. (1989). Attachment in adult romantic relationships: Style of conflict resolution and relationship satisfaction. *Journal of Social and Personal Relationships, 6,* 505–510.

Renken, B., Egeland, B., Marvinney, D., Mangelsdorf, S., & Sroufe, L. A. (1989). Early childhood antecedents of aggression and passive-withdrawal in early elementary school. *Journal of Personality, 57,* 257–281.

Richman, J. A., & Flaherty, J. A. (1986). Childhood relationships, adult coping resources and depression. *Social Science and Medicine, 23,* 709–716.

Richman, J. A., & Flaherty, J. A. (1987). Adult psychosocial assets and depressive mood over time: Effects of internalized childhood attachments. *Journal of Nervous and Mental Disease, 175,* 703–712.

Sarason, B. R., Pierce, G. R., & Sarason, I. G. (1990). Social support: The sense of acceptance and the role of relationships. In B. R. Sarason, I. G. Sarason, & G. R. Pierce (Eds.), *Social support: An interactional view.* New York: Wiley.

Sarason, B. R., Pierce, G. R., Shearin, E. N., Sarason, I. G., Waltz, J. A., & Poppe, L. (1991). Perceived social support and working models of self and actual others. *Journal of Personality and Social Psychology, 60,* 273–287.

Sarason, I. G., Sarason, B. R., & Shearin, E. N. (1986). Social support as an individual difference variable: Its stability, origins, and relational aspects. *Journal of Personality and Social Psychology, 50,* 845–855.

Shaver, P. R., & Brennan, K. A. (1992). Attachment styles and the "Big Five" personality traits: Their connections with each other and with romantic relationship outcomes. *Personality and Social Psychology Bulletin, 18,* 536–545.

Sheldon, A. E. R., & West, M. (1990). Attachment pathology and low social skills in avoidant personality disorder: An exploratory study. *Canadian Journal of Psychiatry, 35,* 596–599.

Sherer, M., & Adams, C. H. (1983). Construct validation of the Self-Efficacy Scale. *Psychological Reports, 53,* 899–902.

Simpson, J. A. (1990). Influence of attachment styles on romantic relationships. *Journal of Personality and Social Psychology, 59,* 971–980.

Simpson, J. A., Rholes, W. S., & Nelligan, J. S. (1992). Support seeking and support giving within couples in an anxiety-provoking situation: The role of attachment styles. *Journal of Personality and Social Psychology, 62,* 434–446.

Solomon, J., George, C., & Ivins, B. (April, 1987). Mother–child interaction in the home and security of attachment at age 6. Paper presented at the biennial meeting of the Society for Research in Child Development. Baltimore.

Sperling, M. D., & Berman, W. H. (1991). An attachment classification of desperate love. *Journal of Personality Assessment, 56,* 45–55.

Sroufe, L. A., Egeland, B., & Kreutzer, T. (1990). The fate of early experience following developmental change: Longitudinal approaches to individual adaptation in childhood. *Child Development, 61,* 1363–1373.

Sroufe, L. A., Fox, N. E., & Pancake, V. R. (1983). Attachment and dependency in developmental perspective. *Child Development, 54,* 1615–1627.

Thompson, R. A., Lamb, M. E., & Estes, D. (1982). Stability of infant–mother attachment and its relationship to changing life circumstances in an unselected middle class sample. *Child Development, 53,* 144–148.

Trevarthen, C. (1974). Conversations with a two-month-old. *New Scientist, 62,* 230–235.

Tronick, E. Z. (1989). Emotions and emotional communication in infants. *American Psychologist, 44,* 112–119.

Tronick, E. Z., & Cohn, J. F. (1989). Infant–mother face-to-face interaction: Age and gender differences in coordination and the occurrence of miscoordination. *Child Development, 60,* 85–92.

Urban, J., Carlson, E., Egeland, B., & Sroufe, L. A. (1991). Patterns of individual adaptation across childhood. *Development and Psychopathology, 3,* 445–460.

Van IJzendoorn, M. H., Kranenburg, M. J., Zwart-Woudstra, H. A., Van Busschbach, A. M., & Lambermon, M. W. E. (1991). Parental attachment and children's socio-emotional development: Some findings on the validity of the Adult Attachment Interview in the Netherlands. *International Journal of Behavioral Development, 14,* 375–394.

Vaughn, B. E., Egeland, B. R., Sroufe, L. A., & Waters, E. (1979). Individual differences in infant–mother attachment at twelve and eighteen months: Stability and change in families under stress. *Child Development, 50,* 971–975.

Wallace, J. L., & Vaux, A. (1993). Social support network orientation: The role of adult attachment style. *Journal of Social and Clinical Psychology, 12,* 354–365.

Wampold, B. E., Ankarlo, G., Mondin, G., Trinidad, M., Baumler, B., & Prater, K. (1995). Social skills of and social environments predicted by different Holland types: A social perspective on person–environment fit models. *Journal of Counseling Psychology, 42,* 365–379.

Waters, E. (1978). The reliability and stability of individual differences in infant–mother attachment. *Child Development, 49,* 483–494.

Waters, E. W., Wippman, J., & Sroufe, L. A. (1979). Attachment, positive affect, and competence in the peer group: Two studies in construct validation. *Child Development, 50,* 821–829.

West, M., & Sheldon, A. E. R. (1988). Classification of pathological attachment patterns in adults. *Journal of Personality Disorders, 2,* 153–159.

West, M., Sheldon, A., & Reiffer, L. (1989). Attachment theory and brief psychotherapy: Applying current research to clinical interventions. *Canadian Journal of Psychiatry, 34,* 369–375.

West, M., & Sheldon-Keller, A. (1992). The assessment of dimensions relevant to adult reciprocal attachment. *Canadian Journal of Psychiatry, 37,* 600–606.

Wilkinson, P. L., McCreary, J. M., & Weedon, J. (August, 1994). Adult attachment style and marital dissatisfaction: A comparison of women and men. Paper presented at the 102nd Annual American Psychological Association Convention. Los Angeles.

Winefield, H. R., Goldney, R. D., Tiggemann, M., & Winefield, A. H. (1989). Reported parental rearing patterns and psychological adjustment: A short form of the EMBU. *Personality and Individual Differences, 10,* 459–465.

Yalom, I. D. (1985). *The theory and practice of group psychotherapy,* 3rd ed. New York: Basic Books.

Yarrow, M. R., Campbell, J. D., & Burton, R. V. (1970). Recollections of childhood: A study of the retrospective method. *Monographs of the Society for Research in Child Development, 35(5),* Serial No. 138.

8

Social Support as a Determinant of Marital Quality

The Interplay of Negative and Supportive Behaviors

CAROLYN E. CUTRONA

In relationships with others, negative behaviors (criticism, sarcasm, belittling the other) appear to have more impact on morale and satisfaction with the relationship than do positive behaviors (encouragement, comfort, assistance). For example, among caregivers of Alzheimer's patients, helpfulness of network members was unrelated to distress, but negative or disruptive behaviors by network members were significantly predictive of distress (Fiore, Becker, & Coppel, 1983; Keicolt-Glaser, Dyer, & Shuttleworth, 1988). A similar pattern of results was found among widows (Rook, 1984) and pregnant adolescents (Barrera, 1981). Within the marital relationship, when controlling for frequency of negative spouse behaviors, spouse supportiveness was not significantly related to depression among husbands (Schuster, Kessler, & Aseltine, 1990), although both negative and supportive spouse behaviors were significant predictors of depressive symptoms among wives in this study and in a study of women suffering from rheumatoid arthritis (Manne & Zautra, 1989). Vinokur and van Ryn (1993) found that perceived support from the spouse did not predict depressive symptoms beyond the variance explained by spousal criticism and other negative behaviors.

Why, then, is it worthwhile to pursue the study of social support within marriage? Would it be more fruitful to abandon the study of help-intended behaviors between husbands and wives and to concentrate exclusively on ways to curb destructive interactions? I contend that an exclusive focus on hurtful and noncooperative behavior within couples would be a serious mistake. Although

CAROLYN E. CUTRONA • Department of Psychology, Iowa State University, Ames, Iowa 50014.

Handbook of Social Support and the Family, edited by Gregory R. Pierce, Barbara R. Sarason, and Irwin G. Sarason. Plenum Press, New York, 1996.

negative behaviors may be the proximal cause of distress and the breakup of relationships, a long history of interactions contributes to relationship deterioration. In this chapter, I will argue that the nature and tone of these interactions can be significantly affected by the frequency and sensitivity of supportive acts by husbands and wives. Support within the marital relationship can promote a positive emotional tone and prevent the gradual acceleration of negative interactions that often precedes divorce. A new role is proposed for supportive behaviors. Whereas previous conceptualizations have emphasized the benefits gained by *individuals* from social support, I will argue that *relationships* gain similar benefits. These benefits include protection from stress-related deterioration, prevention of destructive behaviors, and promotion of a sense of cohesion and connectedness.

Four different mechanisms through which social support may contribute to the quality and survival of marital relationships will be described in this chapter. First, during times of severe stress, support from the spouse can prevent emotional withdrawal and isolation that can otherwise erode the marital relationship. Second, support from the spouse can prevent the onset of clinically significant depression and the aversive behaviors associated with depression that are damaging to relationships (e.g., self-pity, irritability, loss of motivation). Third, in the context of the inevitable disagreements that arise between couples, support-like behaviors can prevent conflicts from escalating in intensity to the point where they become destructive. Fourth, intense moments of emotional intimacy that strengthen the bond between partners are facilitated by supportive communications. This sense of trust and bonding can ease couples through times of potential problems. When the partner behaves in an unpleasant or inconsiderate way, attributions for his or her behavior are likely to be more benign when the relationship is characterized by trust and goodwill (Bradbury & Fincham, 1992; Fincham & Bradbury, 1990). These benign attributions ("He's really feeling stressed right now") prevent the occurrence of major blowups over minor transgressions.

Evidence in the literature for these four mechanisms will be summarized, followed by a discussion of the role that a lack of equity or disappointed expectations for social support may play in marital conflict. I will also describe preliminary data from an observational study of married couples that bears upon the interplay of negative and supportive behaviors in ongoing interactions.

PREVENTING STRESS-RELATED DETERIORATION

Under conditions of high stress (e.g., financial problems, death of a family member, serious illness), any marriage can show signs of distress. Compared to nonclinic couples, those who seek marital counseling report almost twice the frequency of stressful life events in the 3 years prior to initiating treatment and a significant increase in stress the year immediately preceding treatment initiation (Bird, Schuham, Benson, & Gans, 1981). Susceptibility to stress-related relationship deterioration is not limited to those who have a lifelong pattern of problems coping with stress. Couples who seek help for marital problems often score within the normal range on measures of neuroticism and other indices of adjustment (Libman, Takefman, & Brender, 1980).

Marital deterioration is not inevitable following adverse life events. Variability in the impact of traumatic events on the marital relationship can be illustrated by the bereavement literature. Some studies indicate that following the death of a child, marital stability is seriously diminished (Helmrath & Steinitz, 1978; Levav, 1982). High rates of marital breakup are reported following childhood cancer fatalities (Kaplan, Smith, Grobstein, & Fischman, 1973) and after the sudden death of a child by drowning (Nixon & Pearn, 1977). Conversely, a number of studies indicate that marital problems and divorces are not disproportionately common in couples whose child died of cancer (Lansky, Cairns, Hassanein, Wehr, & Lowman, 1978; Oakley & Patterson, 1966; Stehbens & Lascari, 1974). Studies have found that the death or serious illness of a family member may actually enhance communication and closeness among surviving members (Koch, 1985; McCubbin & Patterson, 1983; Shanfield & Swain, 1984). In the view of Lehman, Lang, Wortman, and Sorenson (1989), marital relationships appear to polarize following the death of a child—they either significantly worsen or significantly improve. Lehman and colleagues found significantly more divorces or separations among couples who suffered the loss of a child within the previous 4–7 years compared to nonbereaved controls. However, responses to the question "How do you feel your child's death affected your marriage?" were fairly evenly divided between those who felt their marriage had been weakened and those who felt it had been strengthened. Of the bereaved parents, 21% reported that after their child's death their marriage became somewhat or much worse and 29% reported that it became somewhat or much better.

It has been hypothesized that one mechanism through which marriage bestows its protective mental health function is by promoting a joint identity, a way of thinking of oneself as "part of a whole" (Gove, Hughes, & Style, 1983). Loss of this joint identity may be most likely during times of severe stress (Russell, 1988). In the Lehman et al. (1989) study, a common theme among parents whose marriages deteriorated following the death of a child was that one or both of the bereaved parents withdrew into their own private suffering rather than mourning together. Such withdrawal leaves each parent to cope individually with pain, anger, and grief. Emotional withdrawal, especially when it is more pronounced in one partner than in the other, can lead to considerable hurt, confusion, and resentment in the partner who desires more emotional contact (Christensen, 1988; Gottman & Levenson, 1986; Jacobson & Margolin, 1979). A pattern of emotional pursuit and flight may develop in which each partner becomes increasingly frustrated and angry at the other partner's behavior.

Couples who are able to provide support to one another during times of duress may be able to prevent significant emotional withdrawal by either partner. If highly stressed partners can maintain emotional contact with one another and weather adverse circumstances as "part of a whole" rather than in emotional isolation, their individual well-being and their relationship may sustain less damage. Sensitive and well-timed support from the spouse is an important component of maintaining emotional contact and reducing emotional isolation. When a stressor affects both parties emotionally, successful couples may adopt a strategy of "turn-taking," in which the individual who is momentarily most needy receives comfort from the other, who is secure in the knowledge that when his or her emotions become overwhelming, comfort will be forthcoming from the partner.

PREVENTING DEPRESSION

A second mechanism through which social support may prevent conflict and relationship deterioration in times of duress is through its impact on individual well-being. Distress may be less likely to turn into clinically significant depression if spousal support is available (Brown & Harris, 1978). Over time, the irritability, self-involvement, lack of motivation, and intense dysphoria that characterize prolonged clinical depression become highly aversive to spouse, family, and friends. A clear link between depression and marital distress has been documented (Coyne & Downey, 1991). Although marital problems sometimes play a causal role in depression, it appears that depression is often a causal factor in marital problems (Coyne & Downey, 1991). If sensitive and readily available support from the spouse is forthcoming, in the context of both major calamities and minor setbacks, the onset of clinical depression, with its damaging effects on relationships, may be avoided (Brown & Harris, 1978).

SUPPORT AND THE INTENSITY OF CONFLICT

Of course, not all conflict in relationships is caused by traumatic life events. Because of their high degree of interdependence, marital partners inevitably experienced some degree of conflict (Kelley, 1979). Relationships can break down at a variety of levels from a variety of causes. These causes include decreased liking for the partner, reduced satisfaction with the partner relative to other potential partners, unsatisfactory performance by the partner of role obligations, sexual problems, differences in desired intimacy, and dissatisfaction with the relative rewards and costs of maintaining the relationship (Duck, 1981).

Contributing to many of these problems are skill deficits on the part of one or both partners (Jacobson & Margolin, 1979). A survey of marital therapists revealed that poor communication was far and away the problem that therapists felt was most damaging to relationships (Geiss & O'Leary, 1981). A number of researchers have studied and compared the communication behaviors of distressed and nondistressed couples. A pattern of consistent differences has emerged. Compared to nondistressed couples, distressed couples display more negative affect (negative tone of voice, nonverbal inattention), more negative verbal behaviors (criticism, disagreement, sarcasm), less positive affect (smiling, positive tone of voice), and fewer positive verbal behaviors (approval, agreement, support) (Birchler, Weiss, & Vincent, 1975; Gottman, 1979; Margolin & Wampold, 1981;

Raush, Barry, Hertel, & Swain, 1974; Revenstorf, Vogel, Wegener, Hahlweg, & Schindler, 1980). In addition, individuals in distressed marriages are more likely to reciprocate negative behaviors than those in nondistressed marriages (Gottman, 1979; Margolin & Wampold, 1981). That is, if one partner makes a negative statement such as a criticism or complaint, there is a very high probability that the spouse will respond with a second negative behavior (e.g., whining, shouting, complaining). One effect of this pattern of negative reciprocation is an increasing spiral of emotional intensity in the conflicts of distressed couples (Gottman, Markman, & Notarius, 1977; Revenstorf et al., 1980). One reason that emotional intensity increases is that couples move from the original topic of disagreement (e.g., who should vacuum the rug) to an exchange of insults and accusations regarding the other's flaws (Raush et al., 1974). Kelly (1979) refers to this as escalation to the "dispositional level," in which the personal inadequacies and undesirable dispositions of the other, rather than specific actions or issues, are highlighted. For example, the argument over vacuuming may escalate to a heated exchange of accusations over irresponsibility, slovenliness, and exploitation ("If you weren't such a spoiled brat, you wouldn't treat me like your slave, and you'd help out around here more than once a year!"). According to Deutsch (1969), the hallmark of destructive conflict is this escalation, in which the conflict becomes independent of the original issues. Such conflicts may go beyond the "point of no return" in their bitterness and hurtfulness, such that the relationship is never again the same (Peterson, 1983).

What does this have to do with social support? Well-functioning couples rely on effective communication and problem-solving skills to resolve conflicts (Jacobson & Margolin, 1979). Among these skills are behaviors that fall under the rubric of social support. Research by Gottman and colleagues will be used to illustrate this point. Gottman (1979) observed the behavior of distressed and nondistressed couples as they tried to resolve an issue on which they disagreed. Differences in behavior, including the use of supportive communications, characterized distressed and nondistressed couples in all three stages of these problem-solving sessions. In the early stage of the interactions, distressed and nondistressed couples differed quite markedly in the way they laid out issues for discussion. Among the distressed, a pattern of "cross-complaining" was frequently observed. One partner would voice a complaint and the other would respond with a countercomplaint. This pattern of complaint and countercomplaint went on and on, gathering emotional intensity as both partners became more and more angry and frustrated.

By contrast, the nondistressed couples engaged in "validation sequences." One partner would voice a complaint and the other would validate the legitimacy of the expressed concern ("I can see why you were worried when I was out so late and didn't call"). Then the second partner would express a concern of his or her own and would receive the same kind of validation ("I know you think I'm a worrywort—I do always think that the worst is going to happen"). These validation sequences were much shorter than the countercomplaining exchanges of the distressed couples, and they did not escalate nearly as much in emotional intensity.

The validation statements used by the nondistressed couples appear to play a role in avoiding emotional escalation during conflict. These kinds of statements can easily be viewed as a type of social support. As described by Gottman (1979), they include expressions of sympathy, empathy, and understanding. They communicate a belief in the legitimacy of the other's feelings, thoughts, and actions. The ability (and willingness) to make such statements during disagreements appears to be a valuable asset in preventing the escalation of disagreements into highly destructive exchanges.

Gottman (1979) also observed differences in the verbal behavior of distressed vs. nondistressed couples during the second phase of the problem-solving sessions. During the "arguing" phase, members of distressed couples repeatedly summarized their own feelings, views, and positions on issues ("I just can't take it when you blab about our private life. I've told you over and over again—don't talk about me to your sister!"). By contrast, nondistressed spouses were more likely to summarize their *partner's* feelings, thoughts, and opinions ("You feel like I bad-mouth you to my sister all the time—and it makes you mad because you can't stand up for yourself and you don't think it's any of her business"). Summarizing the other's communications is a way to demonstrate understanding and to assure the other that she or he has been heard. In fact, summary statements, or "reflections," are a key component of some psychotherapeutic approaches (Rogers, 1951). Such communications convey empathy and appear to facilitate smooth resolution of conflict.

In the final phase of problem-solving sessions in the Gottman (1979) study, distressed couples engaged in a series of proposals and counterproposals that rarely converged on a mutually agreeable solution. Nondistressed couples engaged in the same kind of behavior, but very quickly agreed and settled on solutions that took the desires of both partners into account. It would appear that the ease with which they reached such compromises may be attributable, in part, to the more positive emotional tone that was maintained by the nondistressed couples. This more positive tone was maintained, in part, through the use of statements that validated and showed understanding of their partner's experience—social support. When individuals feel that their position has been given a fair hearing and that their feelings are understood, they are more willing to move from complaining to problem solution. If the discussion can be kept from deteriorating into inflammatory accusations that lead to intense hurt and anger, couples may be willing to compromise. Feeling less vulnerable, they may feel less need to protect themselves. Feeling less "wronged," they may feel less need to retaliate or punish the other with solutions that consider only their own well-being and desires.

The role of supportive behaviors in maintaining a positive or neutral emotional tone during interactions between husbands and wives appears to be critically important. Conflicts that arouse a high level of emotion—anger, fear, despair—can be highly destructive. Degree of physiological arousal during conflict significantly predicted deterioration of the marital relationship over a 3-year follow-up period in a study of Levenson and Gottman (1985). Gottman (1979) found that the *emotional tone* of couples' discussions discriminated better than the *content* of what was said in comparisons of distressed and nondistressed couples. The greatest differences were in nonverbal expressions of emotion (e.g., tone of voice, body language, lack of eye contact). The nondistressed could express their feelings in a neutral tone of voice—and could maintain this neutral tone even while disagreeing with their partners.

Fruzzetti and Jacobson (1990) argue that a high level of physiological arousal during conflict leads couples to withdraw from one another to avoid confrontation. As a result, problems are not resolved as they arise, leading to a stockpiling of hurts and resentments. When confrontations occur, their emotional intensity is very high. Thus, behavior strategies that promote open communication and a sense of being understood and listened to by one's partner are extremely important—not only during times of crisis, but also during the normal daily transactions that make up life with a partner.

INTIMACY AND SOCIAL SUPPORT

If intensely negative emotional exchanges lead to relationship deterioration, it is also possible that intensely positive emotional exchanges contribute to relationship survival. The role of social support in promoting such positive experiences will be considered next. Fruzzetti and Jacobson (1990) discuss the potentially powerful effects of intimate interactions on relationship maintenance. They define intimate interactions as those that "increase the understanding and vulnerability between partners and are accompanied by positive emotional arousal" (p. 127). They include interactions in which feelings about the relationship or the partner are expressed, or in which emotions are expressed by one partner and accepted and understood by the other. Intimate interactions are relationship-focused or self-revealing in content, not construed as an attack, and the importance of what is disclosed is appreciated by the listener, who responds in a positive, understanding or self-revealing way. Such interactions often develop into a series of empathic and self-revealing exchanges. Intimate conversations result in increased closeness, understanding, agreement in the interpretation of events, and a sense of "connectedness" (Fruzzetti & Jacobson, 1990).

Behaviors that fall under the rubric of social support appear to be critically important in facilitating intimate communication. Empathic statements that display concern and understanding of the other are an integral part of intimate exchanges between partners. Supportive responses to a partner's self-disclosures promote trust and appreciation and strengthen the commitment between partners— a commitment that may help the couple survive future conflicts. Jacobson and Margolin (1979) discuss a "bank account" model of marriage, in which happy couples "build up" positive experiences with their spouse—intimate exchanges, pleasant times together, acts of kindness by the partner. With such experiences "in the bank," small offenses are less likely to cause major blowups, because there is a large "balance" of goodwill and trust that is not depleted by a small "withdrawal." Thus, social support in the daily life of a couple can promote intimate exchanges, build trust, and, more generally, provide a positive emotional tone in the relationship. Supportive acts, by increasing the positive "balance" in the couple's relational "savings," may decrease a marital partner's sensitivity to the other's occasional acts of unkindness or thoughtlessness, because such transgressions occur within the context of a positive relationship. Negative acts are attributed to benign causes that are temporary or externally controlled (Bradbury & Fincham, 1992; Fincham & Bradbury, 1990). Thus, conflicts are less likely to escalate out of proportion to the problem. The goodwill engendered by supportive acts may actually prevent the occurrence of frequent and intense conflicts by virtue of the positive emotional tone that they establish in the relationship.

INEQUITY AND DISAPPOINTMENT
IN SUPPORT—ONE CAUSE OF CONFLICT

A major source of distress in marriage is unfulfilled expectations. According to Sager (1976), every individual enters marriage with an extensive set of expectations regarding how the other partner should behave and what that partner will provide (e.g., "He will love my mother"; "He will always be strong and protect me"; "She will always understand my moods"). According to Sager, these expectations are rarely articulated, and people are frequently unaware that they hold them. When the mate violates an expectation, however, intense emotions are evoked. One set of expectations concerns the partner's behavior during times of personal stress (e.g., "She will comfort me whenever I am sad or worried"). It seems likely that disappointed expectations for social support from the partner are a source of conflict in many relationships—that expectations for both tangible and emotional assistance in hard times are a particularly important part of the implicit marital contract. The following example illustrates this concept:

> After staying at work late to catch up on projects she couldn't finish because the day had been filled with demands and criticisms from her new supervisor, Sally was looking forward to pouring out her hurt, frustrations, and complaints to her husband, Jeff. She mentally went over how she would describe her day to him while she was driving home and had in mind a picture of how he would respond. This picture included his fetching her a glass of wine, listening attentively, and sharing her indignation over the injustices of the day. When she walked into the living room, Jeff lowered his newspaper just long enough to snap, "Where have you been? It's almost 7 o'clock! How am I supposed to eat dinner and get ready in time for my bowling league at 7:30? You never told me what you wanted for dinner, and I've been waiting here for you to get home!"

Scenes like this may not be unduly destructive if they occur infrequently. However, if a person feels that his or her mate is consistently inattentive to his or her needs during times of adversity, considerable resentment may build up.

There can be at least two different kinds of disappointments regarding social support from the spouse. The first concerns the relative levels of resources that one receives and provides to the other in a relationship. There is evidence that perceived discrepancies between inputs and outputs in marital relationships predict lower marital satisfaction and higher rates of divorce (Davidson, Balswick, & Halverson, 1983; Walster, Berscheid, & Walster, 1973; Austin & Walster, 1974). According to equity theory, people are happiest when they view a relationship as equitable—as one in which each person gives and receives the same level of rewards. Both receiving less than one gives ("underbenefit") and receiving more than one gives ("overbenefit") lead to distress. In the case of underbenefit, distress is in the form of anger, whereas being overbenefited leads to feelings of guilt, shame, or obligation (Walster et al., 1973).

A second kind of disappointment has less to do with equity than with specific expectations for what a spouse should provide. Spouses may view certain behaviors as their partner's responsibility, and these perceived responsibilities—emotional as well as instrumental—may differ for husband and wife. Thus, a husband may expect his wife to provide more nurturance than he provides to her, or a wife may expect her husband to provide an unemotional reaction to crises, even though she knows that her own reactions are intensely emotional. There is evidence that expectations for rewards play a significant role in reactions to the behavior of others (Austin & Walster, 1974), beyond considerations of equity.

PRELIMINARY INVESTIGATIONS OF CONFLICT AND SUPPORT

In my laboratory, we have begun to examine the interplay between negative behaviors and supportive behaviors in the marital relationship. A study of married couples whose supportive and negative behaviors were observed and recorded is presented below. The study examined: (1) the effect of supportive and negative behaviors on ratings of partner supportiveness and (2) the effects of inequity and disappointed expectations for social support on perceptions of the partner's supportiveness.

Method

Participants were 100 residents of university married student housing (50 couples) who responded to a recruitment letter inviting them to participate in a study of communication and problem solving (see also Cutrona & Suhr, 1992). Participants ranged in age from 19 to 47 (mean = 27.0) and had been married from less than 1 to 11 years (mean = 3.0). Couples were asked to spend an evening in the laboratory completing a battery of questionnaires and participating in an interaction exercise, which was videotaped. Questionnaires included measures of perceived social support from the spouse (Social Provisions Scale—Spouse Version) (Cutrona, 1989), marital adjustment (Dyadic Adjustment Scale) (Spanier, 1976), personality (Eysenck Personality Questionnaire) (Eysenck & Eysenck, 1975), and depressive symptoms (Beck Depression Inventory) (Beck, Ward, Mendelson, Mock, & Erbaugh, 1961). In the interaction exercise, partners took turns disclosing a current source of personal distress in their life to their spouse. Each problem was discussed for 10 minutes. After each 10-minute interaction, the discloser completed a postinteraction questionnaire concerning the supportiveness of his or her spouse during the interaction.

Videotapes of these interactions were later coded by trained observers using the Social Support Behavior Code (SSBC) (Cutrona, Suhr, & MacFarlane, 1990; Cutrona & Suhr, 1992; Suhr, 1990). The SSBC was designed to assess the frequency of occurrence of 23 individual behaviors that fall into five categories: information support (advice or factual input), tangible support (offering assistance or resources), emotional support (expressions of caring or empathy), esteem support (expressions of respect or confidence in the person's competence), and social network support (communicating similarity or belonging to a group of similar others). We have recently dropped the social network category because it occurs very rarely and shows lower interrater reliability than the other categories. The SSBC also assesses the frequency of negative behaviors (sarcasm, criticism, disagreement, interruption, complaint, refusal of request for help). The SSBC codes pertain to the content of verbal behaviors, with the single exception of the code for nonverbal expressions of affection (touching, hugging, holding hands), which is coded under emotional support. Mean interrater reliability (intraclass correlation) for the SSBC across the six major categories (five support and one negative behavior categories) is 0.77, $p < 0.001$ (Cutrona & Suhr, 1992).

The interaction task was designed to elicit supportive behaviors. As expected, many more supportive behaviors than negative behaviors were observed. As shown in Table 1, women made an average of 17.00 supportive statements and 2.72 negative statements per 10-minute segment. For men, these figures were 18.00 and 2.30, respectively. There were no significant differences between men and women in the mean number of supportive or negative behaviors displayed.

A note of caution should be introduced at this point. Because the interaction task was designed to elicit supportive behaviors, it is most informative about cooperative interactions between couples. It is unlikely to elicit the most destructive behaviors in couples' repertoires and may be less informative about the effects

Table 1. Mean Frequency of Supportive and Negative Behaviors Displayed in Listener Role

Type of behavior	Women ($N = 50$)		Mean ($N = 50$)	
	Mean	SD	Mean	SD
Support behaviors				
Information	9.44	6.11	8.80	5.29
Tangible	1.42	1.51	2.00	2.29
Emotional	3.24	3.00	3.72	4.16
Esteem	2.90	2.84	3.48	3.42
TOTAL	17.00	7.39	18.00	9.87
Negative behaviors	2.72	4.32	2.30	3.20

of negative behaviors than contexts in which couples are placed in competitive or adversarial roles. This point is important, because most of the research on marital interaction that uses observational methods has placed couples in situations that maximize the likelihood of conflict and minimize the probability that they will exhibit highly supportive behaviors (e.g., Gottman, 1979; Margolin & Wampold, 1981; Raush et al., 1974; Revenstorf et al., 1980). Thus, prior research may underestimate the potency of supportive behaviors and this study may underestimate the potency of negative behaviors.

Three primary questions were addressed in the study:

1. What are the relative contributions of supportive and negative behaviors to postinteraction ratings of partner supportiveness?
2. What are the effects of inequitable levels of support provided by husbands and wives?
3. What are the effects of violations of expectations for support from husband or wife?

Supportive and Negative Behaviors Predicting Ratings of Supportiveness

A multiple regression analysis was conducted to test the extent to which number of support behaviors and number of negative behaviors (coded by observers) predicted the discloser's postinteraction ratings of her or his partner's supportiveness. In addition, the discloser's personality (extraversion and neuroticism scores) and ratings of relationship quality (spouse support and marital adjustment scores) were entered into the regression equations. These variables were included to determine the extent to which factors outside the interaction contributed to peoples' evaluations of their partner's behavior in the listener role. For example, a person with a high level of neuroticism might be expected to evaluate the partner's behavior more negatively than a person with a low level of neuroticism (Watson & Clark, 1984). Similarly, a person who is very dissatisfied with his or her marriage would be expected to evaluate the partner's behavior negatively. Thus, four categories of predictors were tested: number of support behaviors received, number of negative behaviors received, personal characteristics, and relationship characteristics.

As shown in Table 2, number of supportive behaviors received from the spouse was a significant predictor of postinteraction partner supportiveness ratings. The more supportive behaviors displayed by the listener, the higher the discloser rated her or his partner's performance. Number of negative behaviors (sarcasm, criticism, disagreement, interruption, complaint, refusal of request for help) was not a significant predictor of postinteraction ratings of spouse support. Personal characteristics (especially depressive symptoms) and perceived quality of the marital relationship also contributed significantly to postinteraction ratings of partner supportiveness, as evidenced by the significant increment in R^2 that resulted when each of these groups of variables was entered into the regression equation.

Table 2. Multiple Regression Predicting Postinteraction
Ratings of Spouse Supportiveness[a]

Predictors	R^2 change	F change	Standardized beta[b]	r
Personal				
Extraversion			−0.04	0.07
Neuroticism			0.15	−0.21
Depression			−0.26[c]	−0.36
	0.13	4.87[d]		
Relationship				
Marital adjustment			0.25	0.49
Perceived spouse supportiveness			0.12	0.45
	0.15	9.53[d]		
Spouse support behaviors				
Information			0.08	0.11
Tangible			0.24[c]	0.24
Emotional			0.25[c]	0.38
Esteem			0.01	0.28
	0.13	5.05[d]		
Spouse negative behaviors	0.01	2.13	−0.12	−0.20

R^2 total = 0.42; $F(10,89)$ = 6.57; $p < 0.001$

[a]The number of participants was 100.
[b]Final beta weights, i.e., after all other variables have been entered into the equation.
[c]$p < 0.05$.
[d]$p < 0.01$.

Further analyses were conducted to determine whether men and women differed significantly in their patterns of results. A separate regression analysis was conducted to test for interactions between gender and each of the predictor variables. Results revealed two significant interactions with gender. The effect of perceived relationship quality (Social Provisions Scale [SPS]—Spouse Version) was significantly stronger for men than for women. Thus, men were more influenced than women by their assessment of their partner's supportiveness *before the interaction* in rating how supportive their wife had been during the interaction. The effect of extraversion was significantly stronger for women than for men. Extraverted women rated their spouse's performance in the listener role very positively—more so than did extraverted men. Neither the effects of supportive behavior nor those of negative behavior differed as a function of gender.

Thus, in the context of a cooperative interaction, negative behaviors occurred infrequently and had relatively little effect on individuals' evaluations of their partner's supportiveness. It appears that the *context* in which couples interact plays a major role in the salience of different classes of behaviors. In the context of a cooperative interaction, supportive behaviors were more salient determinants of interaction satisfaction than were negative behaviors. Prior research suggests that negative behaviors are more salient determinants of satisfaction in the context of conflict intractions (e.g., Gottman, 1979). Care must be taken to avoid overgeneralizing context-specific results to relationship satisfaction more generally.

A second factor to be considered in evaluating the results of this study is the relatively high level of marital satisfaction found among the participants. Mean scores for men and women on the Dyadic Adjustment Scale were 114.0 and 113.6, respectively—well above the suggested cutoff of 100 for distinguishing non-distressed from distressed couples. Research by Jacobson, Waldron, and Moore (1980) suggests that maritally distressed and nondistressed couples attend to different kinds of spouse behaviors. In a daily diary study, number of negative behaviors performed by the spouse was the best predictor of daily satisfaction with the marital relationship among maritally distressed couples. Among *nondistressed* couples, however, number of *positive behaviors* was the best predictor of daily satisfaction with the marital relationship. As described previously, when individuals have a history of positive experiences with their partner, they are less likely to react strongly to displeasing partner behaviors. Such displeasing behaviors are viewed as temporary deviations from a more general pattern of pleasing interactions. It is likely that such behaviors are attributed to temporary causes, perhaps causes that are not under the partner's control, such as a hard day at work or illness (Bradbury & Finchman, 1992; Fincham & Bradbury, 1990). In distressed couples, displeasing behaviors are viewed as deliberate or indicative of the partner's stable negative characteristics (greed, thoughtlessness, lack of sensitivity) (Fincham & O'Leary, 1983).

Lack of Equity in Support Behaviors Exchanged

The second question addressed was the extent to which equity in *number of support behaviors* given and received would be a determinant of satisfaction with spousal support. Number of support behaviors was assessed using observer SSBC scores. A difference score was computed between the number of support behaviors *received from the spouse* when disclosing a personal problem and the number of support behaviors *given to the spouse* when he or she disclosed a personal problem. Thus, positive scores reflect receiving more support than one gave (being over-benefited) and negative scores reflect receiving less support from the spouse than one gave (being underbenefited). According to equity theory, the highest level of satisfaction should occur when support received is equal to support given. Receiving more or less than one gives should lead to distress. To test this nonlinear prediction, the square of the support difference score (the quadratic term) was entered into a regression equation predicting postinteraction supportiveness ratings after the first-order difference score.

As shown in Table 3, the difference between number of support behaviors received and number given was a significant predictor of partner supportiveness ratings. The higher the level of support received relative to that given, the more supportive participants rated their spouse's behavior in the listener role. The quadratic term did not attain significance for men or women. Tests for gender differences revealed no significant interactions between gender and either the linear or the quadratic difference term. Thus, results suggest that a linear relationship best characterizes the association between relative number of support behav-

**Table 3. Multiple Regression Predicting Postinteraction Ratings
of Spouse Supportiveness from Difference
between Number of Support Behaviors Received and Number[a] Given**

Predictors	R^2 change	F change	Standardized beta[b]	r
Difference between support received and given	0.04	4.36[c]	0.21[c]	0.21[c]
Difference^2	0.01	<1	0.07	0.07
R^2 total = 0.05; $F(2,97)$ = 2.42; $p < 0.10$				

[a]The number of participants was 100.
[b]Final beta weights, i.e., after all other variables have been entered into the equation.
[c]$p < 0.05$.

iors given and received: The more support the partner provides relative to the amount given, the more supportive she or he is rated.

A final analysis was conducted to determine whether number of support behaviors received *relative to number given* was critical, or simply *absolute number* of support behaviors received from the spouse. In a regression equation predicting postinteraction supportiveness ratings, number of support behaviors received was entered, followed by the difference score. In this analysis, only absolute number of support behaviors received attained significance. The difference between amount of support given and received appears to be less influential than the absolute amount of support received from the spouse in the context of disclosing a personal problem.

Violated Expectations for Support from Partner

Observer counts of number of support behaviors do not take into account the relationship context in which they occur. An important aspect of this context is the *expectations* that each partner holds for the other. We wanted to examine the impact of receiving more or less support from the partner *than was expected*. No specific measure of support expectations was administered. However, the general measure of perceived social support from spouse (SPS—Spouse Version) that was administered before the interactions began was viewed as a reasonable approximation of support expectations. We reasoned that past experiences with the spouse would form the basis for responses to the SPS—the same data that would shape expectations for support from the partner in the interactions. To express the "expected support" and received support scores using the same metric, we standardized each and then computed a difference score between what was received from the spouse (standardized number of support behaviors coded by observers) and what was expected from the spouse (standardized preinteraction SPS score). Positive scores reflected receiving more than was expected; negative scores reflected receiving less than was expected.

The difference score was entered into a regression equation predicting postinteraction supportiveness ratings. Once again, we tested the prediction from equity theory that the highest level of satisfaction would occur when support received equals the expected level. To test this prediction, the square of the support expectations difference score (the quadratic term) was entered into the regression equation predicting postinteraction supportiveness ratings after the linear term. As shown in Table 4, the differences between expectation and support received did not attain significance. However, the square of the difference between expected and received support was a significant predictor of interaction satisfaction. To clarify the nature of the relation between the difference score and interaction satisfaction, the data were graphed in Figure 1. Support satisfaction was highest when support received equaled one's expectation level. Receiving either more or less than expected was associated with lower support satisfaction. The squared difference between expectation and support received retained significance when controlling for absolute number of support behaviors received from the spouse. Although it is not surprising that participants evaluated their partner's supportiveness negatively when they received *less* than they expected to receive, it is harder to explain why they evaluated their partner's performance negatively when they received *more* than they expected. It may be that individuals believe that they deserve a certain level of support and that receiving more makes them feel guilty (Austin & Walster, 1974). People who are overbenefited in this way may feel that they are then obliged to reciprocate by increasing their own level of support. Alternatively, receiving more than was expected may lead people to question the partner's motives—to make unstable, external attributions for the partner's behavior (Bradbury & Fincham, 1992; Fincham & Bradbury, 1990). They may attribute the partner's unexpectedly high level of supportiveness to a desire to "show off" in the presence of others or to "show them up" and embarrass them by behaving more supportively than they did.

Table 4. Multiple Regression Predicting Postinteraction Ratings of Spouse Supportiveness from Difference between Number of Support Behaviors Received and Number Expected[a]

Predictors	R^2 change	F change	Standardized beta[b]	r
Difference between support received and given	0.00	<1	0.04	−0.05
Difference^2	0.07	7.26[c]	−0.28[c]	−0.27[c]
R^2 total = 0.07; F (2,97) = 7.26; $p < 0.05$				

[a]The number of participants was 100.
[b]Final beta weights, i.e., after all other variables have been entered into the equation.
[c]$p < 0.01$.

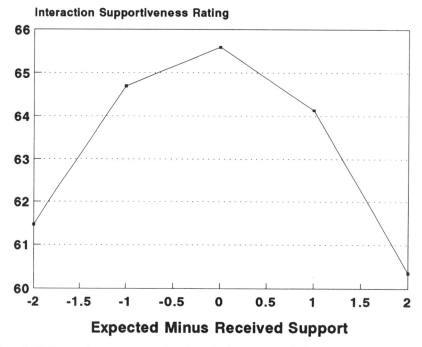

Figure 1. Difference between expected and received support predicting interaction satisfaction.

DISCUSSION

The utility of social support extends far beyond the narrow context of one person providing assistance to another in times of severe crisis. When disagreements arise between partners, supportive statements can prevent conflicts from escalating in emotional intensity. Expressing understanding of the other's point of view and recognizing the validity of the other's emotions are supportive acts that are used by happily married couples to moderate the intensity of conflicts. These behaviors allow both members of the couple to express their viewpoint freely, without intense anger, fear, or frustration. Lower levels of physiological arousal during conflict predict less decline in marital satisfaction over time (Levenson & Gottman, 1985). Fruzetti and Jacobson (1990) propose that couples who become intensely emotional during conflict begin to avoid topics that may lead to conflict because the conflict has become so aversive. Issues and problems that need to be discussed are not adequately resolved. A buildup of unresolved issues and resentments occurs. The next time a conflict arises, it is all the more intense because of these unexpressed frustrations. If supportive statements can keep the emotional intensity lower during disagreements, both members of the couple will feel freer to express themselves honestly, and problems can be dealt with as they arise.

Supportive communications can also increase the frequency of rewarding interactions that increase feelings of closeness. Fruzzetti and Jacobson (1990) describe the power of intimate conversations in building the strength of commitment to the relationship. These conversations include disclosures of personal feelings, goals, and dreams, as well as thoughts and emotions concerning the relationship. When such self-disclosures are met with support—expressions of caring, concern, and understanding—the discloser feels validated, and a mutual exchange of confidences often occurs. These moments of intimacy may form the "glue" that keeps relationships intact through difficult times. If the partner is associated with intensely positive experiences, then minor negative behaviors may not be as upsetting as they would be in a relationship without a history of shared positive experiences.

Supportive acts in the context of ordinary daily routines may also contribute to a general sense of trust and goodwill, which decreases the probability that minor offenses by the partner will be viewed as serious transgressions. Attributional processes may play a significant role in this process. If a spouse is generally viewed as trustworthy, caring, and helpful, an isolated act of thoughtlessness is less likely to be attributed to enduring negative characteristics or malevolent intentions. Instead, aversive behaviors will be viewed as stemming from temporary circumstances, perhaps circumstances beyond the partner's control (e.g., "He must have had a really bad day at work"), and they will not lead to intense anger and resentment (Bradbury & Fincham, 1992; Fincham & Bradbury, 1990).

Supportive acts may not only lower the probability of negative partner behaviors, such as angry outbursts, sarcastic comments, and criticisms, but also prevent emotional withdrawal during times of stress. If partners can maintain emotional contact with one another when one or both are suffering from physical illness, loss, or economic setback, neither will feel alone in his or her efforts to confront and deal with these problems. Emotional contact can be maintained through sensitively timed expressions of support—caring, understanding, offers of assistance. If the couple can confront adversity as a team rather than individually, they may evaluate problems as less overwhelming. In addition, such teamwork may avoid problems in the relationship that result from the withdrawal of one partner and the emotional pursuit of that partner by the other.

Thus far, I have discussed the role that supportive behaviors may play in preventing relationship deterioration. A related dynamic is the role that a lack of support may play in creating relationship problems. Receiving fewer support behaviors than were given was associated with lower postinteraction support ratings. It appears, however, that most of this effect was due to the absolute level of support received from the partner. The difference between support received and given did not predict postinteraction supportiveness ratings beyond the effect of number of support behaviors received. Lower levels of support from the spouse were associated with lower ratings, regardless of the difference between what was received and what was given.

A more important "measuring stick" for support appears to be the expectations that each partner brings to the interaction. It appears that discrepancies between levels of support provided and received affect partner evaluations less than discrepancies between *what is expected* and the support received. When controlling for number of behaviors received, the difference between support expected and received retained significance. Consistent with equity theory (Austin & Walster, 1974), support at the level of expectation was associated with the highest postinteraction supportiveness ratings. Support that fell short of or surpassed expectations was viewed less positively. People may feel guilty or uncomfortable when they receive more support than they expected. They may also feel pressured to increase the level of support they provide to the partner. In some cases, they may feel that the partner provided more support than was needed, thus suggesting personal weakness on their part. Alternatively, people may mistrust support that exceeds their expectations. They may attribute the partner's support efforts to selfish factors, such as trying to impress others or to gain something in return.

CLINICAL IMPLICATIONS

Most behaviorally oriented marital therapies focus on decreasing the frequency of aversive behaviors, such as criticisms, name-calling, and sarcasm. This focus is appropriate, given that distressed couples are more sensitive to negative than to positive partner behaviors (Jacobson et al., 1980). Furthermore, when individuals are still harboring a high degree of resentment toward their partner, they may be unwilling to engage in supportive behaviors. Even if they did engage in such behaviors, there is a good chance that the partner would view them as insincere and would suspect their spouse's motives. These findings suggest that if sessions devoted to building, practicing, and increasing the frequency of supportive communications were added to marital therapy, they would be most useful if introduced after basic conflict resolution strategies have been mastered and the frequency of aversive behaviors has decreased.

Alternatively, it might be best to teach the communication of social support as a *preventive* intervention. Supportive communications appear to function primarily as a method of affect regulation—that is, they appear to generate a general climate of goodwill, enhance positive emotions during self-disclosure, and prevent negative interactions from escalating in emotional intensity. Thus, it is probably most useful to teach support skills early in relationships to prevent the deterioration of goodwill and the occurrence of damaging high-intensity conflicts. Once goodwill and trust have eroded, it may be too late to restore them therapeutically. Marital therapists agree that one of the most difficult problems to reverse is the loss of love between partners (Geiss & O'Leary, 1981). Preventive interventions for dating couples or newlyweds that teach and emphasize the importance of supportive acts may allow some couples to maintain a generally positive emotional climate in their marriage and to avoid the erosion of love that is so difficult to reverse. The use of supportive communications in a variety of contexts should be discussed, demonstrated, and practiced. Couples should learn to communicate their support expectations and needs to one another and to negotiate methods for "turn-taking" when both are in need of support. The importance of maintaining emotional contact during times of stress and how to do so through supportive communications should be emphasized. The importance of sensitive and empathic responses to partner self-disclosures should be addressed as well. The communication of social support is not a simple task, and it should be taught explicitly, just as we teach methods of conflict resolution. As a noted marital therapist points out: "People don't get married to manage conflict. They get married for companionship, intimacy, and support" (Markman, personal communication). To assist persons in obtaining and retaining these resources is clearly an important goal.

RESEARCH AND THEORETICAL IMPLICATIONS

An important methodological point is that the context in which behaviors are studied strongly influences their importance. In situations that evoke negative behaviors, such as conflict interactions, negative behaviors are the most salient and influential. In situations that are conducive to positive behaviors, negative behaviors are much less influential and supportive acts are most salient. The quality of the relationship between marital partners also constitutes an important context. Those in unhappy relationships are more sensitive to their partner's displeasing behaviors than to their pleasing behaviors (Jacobson et al. 1980). Finally, the personalities of both spouses form another aspect of the context in which both positive and negative interactions take place. A depressed individual will react more negatively to his or her partner, regardless of the actual number or quality of support behaviors received from the partner. Similarly, an extraverted person is likely to evaluate her or his partner more positively than is someone low on extraversion (for a discussion of extraversion and positive emotionality, see Watson & Clark, 1983). Thus, researchers must take great care to specify the situational and relational contexts of their investigations (e.g., maritally dissatisfied couples who were asked to discuss an issue on which they disagreed). Care must be taken not to generalize results beyond the contexts to which they apply.

Theoretically, it is important to emphasize the interconnections between supportive and destructive behaviors, between intimacy and conflict. Neither positive nor negative behaviors can be adequately understood in isolation. Each affects the probability that the other will occur. A background of supportive acts can ease the sting of partner thoughtlessness. A background of coercive exchanges can undermine the best-intentioned supportive act. An intensely intimate self-disclosure that is met with validation and caring can strengthen a relationship so that it will later survive the strain of tragedy. Failure to provide the support that is needed during a crisis can lead to emotional withdrawal and the erosion of love.

Prior research has focused on the influence of social support on individual outcomes, such as adjustment and physical health. An exciting new direction is the study of the influence of social support on relationships. It may be that the benefits derived by individuals from supportive interactions are due primarily to the effects of these interactions on the quality, closeness, and trustworthiness of important relationships.

REFERENCES

Austin, W., & Walster, E. (1974). Reactions to confirmations and disconfirmations of expectancies of equity and inequity. *Journal of Personality and Social Psychology, 30,* 208–216.

Barrera, M. (1981). Social support in the adjustment of pregnant adolescents: Assessment issues. In B. H. Gottlieb (Ed.), *Social networks and social support* (pp. 69–96). Beverly Hills: Sage Publications.

Beck, A. T., Ward, C. H., Mendelson, M., Mock, J., & Erbaugh, J. (1961). An inventory for measuring depression. *Archives of General Psychiatry, 4,* 561–571.

Birchler, G. R., Weiss, R. L., & Vincent, J. P. (1975). Multimethod analysis of social reinforcement exchange between martially distressed and nondistressed spouse and stranger dyads. *Journal of Personality and Social Psychology, 31,* 349–360.

Bird, H. W., Schuham, A. I., Benson, L., & Gans, L. L. (1981). Stressful events and marital dysfunction. *Hospital and Community Psychiatry, 32,* 386–390.

Bradbury, T. N., & Fincham, F. D. (1992). Attributions and behaviors in marital interaction. *Journal of Personality and Social Psychology, 63,* 613–628.

Brown, G. W., & Harris, T. O. (1978). *Social origins of depression: A study of psychiatric disorder in women.* New York: Free Press.

Christensen, A. (1988). Dysfunctional interaction patterns in couples. In P. Noller & M. A. Fitzpatrick (Eds.), *Perspectives on marital interaction* (pp. 31–52). Clevedon, England: Multilingual Matters.

Coyne, J. C., & Downey, G. (1991). Social factors and psychopathology: Stress, social support, and coping processes. *Annual Review of Psychology, 42,* 401–425.

Cutrona, C. E. (1989). Ratings of social support by adolescents and adult informants: Degree of correspondence and prediction of depressive symptoms. *Journal of Personality and Social Psychology, 57,* 723–730.

Cutrona, C. E., & Suhr, J. A. (1992). Controllability of stressful events and satisfaction with spouse supportive behaviors. *Communication Research, 19,* 154–176.

Cutrona, C. E., Suhr, J. A., & MacFarlane, R. (1990). Interpersonal transactions and the psychological sense of support. In S. Duck & R. Silver (Eds.), *Personal relationships and social support* (pp. 30–45). London: Sage Publications.

Davidson, B., Balswick, J., & Halverson, C. (1983). Affective self-disclosure and marital adjustment: A test of equity theory. *Journal of Marriage and the Family, 45,* 93–113.

Deutsch, M. (1969). Conflicts: Productive and destructive. *Journal of Social Issues, 25,* 7–41.

Duck, S. (1981). Toward a research map for the study of relationship breakdown. In S. Duck & R. Gilmour (Eds.), *Personal relationships 3: Personal relationships in disorder* (pp. 1–29). New York: Academic Press.

Eysenck, H. J., & Eysenck, S. B. G. (1975). *Eysenck Personality Questionnaire.* San Diego: Educational and Industrial Testing Service.

Fincham, F. D., & Bradbury, T. N. (1990). Social support in marriage: The role of social cognition. *Journal of Social and Clinical Psychology, 9,* 31–42.

Fiore, J., Becker, J., & Coppel, D. B. (1983). Social network interactions: A buffer or a stress? *American Journal of Community Psychology, 11,* 423–439.

Fruzzetti, A. E., & Jacobson, N. S. (1990). Toward a behavioral conceptualization of adult intimacy: Implications for marital therapy. In E. A. Blechman (Ed.), *Emotions and the family: For better or worse* (pp. 117–135). Hillsdale, NJ: Lawrence Erlbaum.

Geiss, S. K., & O'Leary, D. (1981). Therapist ratings of frequency and severity of marital problems: Implications for research. *Journal of Marital and Family Therapy, 7,* 515–520.

Gottman, J. M. (1979). *Marital interaction: Experimental investigations.* New York: Academic Press.

Gottman, J. M., & Levenson, R. W. (1986). Assessing the role of emotion in marriage. *Behavioral Assessment, 8,* 31–48.

Gottman, J., Markman, H., & Notarius, C. (1977). The topography of marital conflict: A sequential analysis of verbal and nonverbal behavior. *Journal of Marriage and the Family, 39,* 460–477.

Gove, W. R., Hughes, M., & Style, C. B. (1983). Does marriage have positive effects on the psychological well-being of the individual? *Journal of Health and Social Behavior, 24,* 122–131.

Helmrath, T. A., & Steinitz, E. M. (1978). Death of an infant: Parental grieving and the failure of social support. *Journal of Family Practice, 6,* 785–790.

Jacobson, N. S., & Margolin, G. (1979). *Marital therapy: Strategies based on social learning and behavior exchange principles.* New York: Brunner/Mazel.

Jacobson, N. S., Waldron, H., & Moore, D. (1980). Toward a behavioral profile of marital distress. *Journal of Consulting and Clinical Psychology, 48,* 696–703.

Kaplan, D. M., Smith, A., Grobstein, R., & Fischman, S. E. (1973). Family mediation of stress. *Social Work, 18,* 60–69.

Kelley, H. H. (1979). *Personal relationships: Their structure and process.* Hillsdale, NJ: Lawrence Erlbaum.

Kiecolt-Glaser, J. K., Dyer, C. S., & Shuttleworth, E. C. (1988). Upsetting social interactions and distress among Alzheimer's disease family care-givers: A replication and extension. *American Journal of Community Psychology, 16,* 825–837.

Koch, A. (1985). "If only it could be me": The families of pediatric cancer patients. *Family Relations, 34,* 63–70.

Lansky, S. B., Cairns, N. U., Hassanein, R., Wehr, J., & Lowman, J. T. (1978). Childhood cancer: Parental discord and divorce. *Pediatrics, 62,* 184–188.

Lehman, D. R., Lang, E. L., Wortman, C. B., & Sorenson, S. B. (1989). Long-term effects of sudden bereavement: Marital and parent–child relationships and children's reactions. *Journal of Family Psychology, 2,* 344–367.

Levav, I. (1982). Mortality and psychopathology following the death of an adult child: An epidemiological review. *Israeli Journal of Psychiatry and Related Sciences, 19,* 23–28.

Levenson, R. W., & Gottman, J. M. (1985). Physiological and affective predictors of change in relationship satisfaction. *Journal of Personality and Social Psychology, 49,* 85–94.

Libman, E., Takefman, J., & Brender, W. (1980). A comparison of sexually dysfunctional, maritally disturbed and well-adjusted couples. *Personality and Individual Differences, 1(3),* 219–227.

Manne, S. L., & Zautra, A. J. (1989). Spouse criticism and support: Their association with coping and psychological adjustment among women with rheumatoid arthritis. *Journal of Personality and Social Psychology, 56,* 608–617.

Margolin, G., & Wampold, B. E. (1981). A sequential analysis of conflict and accord in distressed and nondistressed marital partners. *Journal of Consulting and Clinical Psychology, 49,* 554–567.

McCubbin, H. I., & Patterson, J. M. (1983). Family adaptation to crises. In H. I. McCubbin, A. E. Cauble, & J. M. Patterson (Eds.), *Family stress, coping, and social support* (pp. 26–47). Springfield, IL: Charles C Thomas.

Nixon, J., & Pearn, J. (1977). Emotional sequalae of parents and sibs following the drowning or near-drowning of a child. *Australian and New Zealand Journal of Psychiatry, 11,* 265–268.

Oakley, G. P., & Patterson, R. B. (1966). The psychological management of leukemic children and their families. *North Carolina Medical Journal, 27,* 186–192.

O'Leary, K. D., & Fincham, F. (1983). Assessment of positive feelings toward spouse. *Journal of Consulting and Clinical Psychology, 51,* 949–951.

Peterson, D. R. (1983). Conflict. In H. H. Kelley, E. Bersheid, A. Christensen, J. H. Harvey, T. L. Huston, G. Levinger, E. McClintock, L. A. Peplau, & D. R. Peterson (Eds.), *Close relationships* (pp. 360–396). New York: W. H. Freeman.

Rausch, H. L., Barry, W. A. Hertel, R. K., & Swain, M. A. (1974). *Communication, conflict, and marriage.* San Francisco: Jossey-Bass.

Revenstorf, D., Vogel, B., Wegener, K., Hahlweg, K., & Schindler, L. (1980). Escalation phenomenon in interaction sequences: An empirical comparison of distressed and nondistressed couples. *Behavioral Analysis and Modification, 4,* 97–115.

Rogers, C. R. (1951). *Client-centered therapy, its current practice, implications, and theory.* Boston: Houghton Mifflin.

Rook, K. S. (1984). The negative side of social interaction: Impact on psychological well-being. *Journal of Personality and Social Psychology, 46,* 1097–1108.

Russell, C. S. (1988). Marriages under stress: A research perspective. In E. W. Nunnally, C. S. Chilman, & F. M. Cox (Eds.), *Troubled relationships* (pp. 17–29). Newbury Park, CA: Sage Publications.

Sager, C. (1976). *Marriage contracts and couple therapy: Hidden forces in intimate relationships.* New York: Brunner/Mazel.

Schuster, T. L., Kessler, R. C., & Aseltine, R. H., Jr. (1990). Supportive interactions, negative interactions, and depressed mood. *American Journal of Community Psychology, 18,* 423–438.

Shanfield, S. B., & Swain, B. J. (1984). Death of adult children in traffic accidents. *Journal of Nervous and Mental Disease, 172,* 533–538.

Spanier, G. B. (1976). Measuring dyadic adjustment: New scales for assessing the quality of marriage and similar dyads. *Journal of Marriage and the Family, 38,* 15–28.

Stehbens, J. A., & Lascari, A. D. (1974). Psychological follow-up of families with childhood leukemia. *Journal of Clinical Psychology, 30,* 394–397.

Suhr, J. (1990). The development of the Social Support Behavior Code. Unpublished master's thesis, University of Iowa, Iowa City, IA.

Vinokur, A. D., & van Ryn, M. (1993). Social support and undermining in close relationships: Their independent effects on the mental health of unemployed persons. *Journal of Personality and Social Psychology, 65,* 350–359.

Walster, E., Berscheid, E., & Walster, G. W. (1973). New directions in equity research. *Journal of Personality and Social Psychology, 25,* 151–176.

Watson, D., & Clark, L. A. (1984). Negative affectivity: The disposition to experience aversive emotional states. *Psychological Bulletin, 96,* 465–490.

9

Parental Characteristics as Influences on Adjustment in Adulthood

GORDON PARKER and GEMMA L. GLADSTONE

INTRODUCTION

A long-standing assumption underpinning much psychiatric theorizing has been that developmental factors in childhood contribute to later adult social adjustment and behavior. More specifically, it has been argued that some developmental factors may dispose both to psychiatric conditions and to dysfunctional social and emotional relationships during adult life, either directly or by establishing a diathesis that makes the individual vulnerable to such consequences. Among the numerous developmental factors operating in the life of a child, parental behaviors and attitudes have been implicated as major influences, especially for younger children with limited social networks.

Clearly, a number of family influences could be considered. Diversities emerge from the structure of families (e.g., single- vs. two-parent; nuclear vs. extended families) and may produce alterations in members' roles and child–parent dynamics and, in turn, are likely to influence aspects of parenting. Although there are many such variable influences among families, fundamental dimensions of parenting have been identified, and these dimensions allow a firm base for empirical research to shape broad conclusions.

This chapter focuses upon parental influences as risk factors for adult psychopathology and upon their possible impact on later socialization patterns, at least as demonstrated empirically by one particular research approach, and where suffi-

GORDON PARKER and GEMMA L. GLADSTONE • Psychiatry Unit, Prince of Wales Hospital, Randwick 2031, Australia.

Handbook of Social Support and the Family, edited by Gregory R. Pierce, Barbara R. Sarason, and Irwin G. Sarason. Plenum Press, New York, 1996.

cient studies have been undertaken to allow some confidence about the consistency of findings.

FUNDAMENTAL DIMENSIONS OF PARENTING

Various studies seeking to distinguish core dimensions of parenting have been reasonably consistent in refining two constructs underlying parental attitudes and behaviors (Arrindell et al., 1986; Parker, Tupling, & Brown, 1979; Roe & Siegelman, 1963). First, a "care" dimension of parenting has emerged consistently as the principal construct, and a second dimension of "control" or "protection" has usually been generated. Just as these two fundamental dimensions have been identified as primary elements in parent–child relationships, they have also been defined as elements common to all significant interpersonal relationships. Thus, Hinde (1979) has argued that "care" and "protection" dimensions underpin all important relationships, whether parent–child, intimate–intimate, teacher–pupil, or therapist–patient.

THE PARENTAL BONDING INSTRUMENT

In order to examine the influence of aberrant parenting on the psychological and social functioning of recipients, Parker et al. (1979) developed the Parental Bonding Instrument (PBI). The PBI was designed to measure perceived characteristics of parenting through the retrospective accounts of individuals. Questions are completed using a 1–4 Likert-type scale varying from "very like" to "very unlike," with subjects requested to rate both their mother and father as they remembered them in their first 16 years. Of the items on the PBI, 12 are identified as Care items (defined, at one pole, by affection, emotional warmth, empathy, and closeness and at the other pole by emotional coldness, indifference, and neglect) and 13 as Protection or control items (defined, at one pole, by items that suggest control, overprotection, prevention of independence, and intrusion and at the other pole by the allowance of autonomy and independency). The former items allow a maximum Care scale score of 36 and the latter items a maximum Protection scale score of 39. In the initial formulation study, respondents' scores on these two dimensions correlated negatively, with overprotection thus associated with a deficiency (rather than a sufficiency) of care. On the basis of data obtained from a normative general practice study (Parker et al., 1979), cutoff scores for "high" and "low" care and protection were derived. Suggested cutoff scores for mothers were 27.0 (care) and 13.5 (protection) and for fathers 24.0 (care) and 12.5 (protection). The authors argued that when used together (i.e., applying the cut-off score decisions), the two scales allow four broad styles of parenting to be examined. The first quadrant was termed "optimal parenting" and is defined by the combination of high care scores and low overprotection scores; the second quadrant, "affectionate constraint," is defined by the combination of high care and high protection scores; the third, "affectionless control," is a style identified by the combination of low care and high overprotection scores; and the final quadrant, known as "neglectful parenting," is formed when low care scores and low protection scores combine.

Cubis, Lewin, and Dawes (1989) administered the PBI to a community sample of Australian adolescents and identified three (rather than two) PBI dimensions. They argued for the existence of two protection factors, "perceived social control" and "personal intrusiveness," along with the original care factor. The "perceived social control" factor was characterized by items describing predominantly the social domain of the recipient (e.g., "Lets me go out as often as I want"; "Tries to control everything I do"; "Lets me do things I like doing"). By contrast, the "personal intrusiveness" factor was characterized by items describing the personal and emotional domain (e.g., "Tends to baby me"; "Does not want me to grow up"; "Tries to make me dependent on him [her]"). This subdivision may well have some utility in empirical studies examining for various consequences of parental overprotection.

Sociodemographic Issues

In the initial development study (Parker et al., 1979), normative PBI data were obtained and the potential influences of several variables were assessed. In this study, 410 Australian subjects completed the PBI along with questionnaires that included demographic items. Subjects scored their mothers as significantly more caring and somewhat more protective than their fathers. The respondent's sex, however, did not influence parental ratings of care and protection. Analogous findings were also evident in samples of both clinical and nonclinical subjects (see Parker, 1983a,b; Truant, Donaldson, Herscovitch, & Lohrenz, 1987). Subjects' age and social class were also examined in the developmental study as possible influences upon PBI scores; however, only a weak positive correlation was observed linking higher social class with higher maternal care scores. This outcome was also found in the normative data obtained from an Oxford, England, sample (see Parker, 1983a), together with the finding that fathers were perceived as more protective of daughters than of sons. Parker (1983a) also examined the influence of family size (number of siblings) by administering the PBI to 252 postgraduate students. He found a nonsignificant trend for only children to score their mothers as more protective than did children with siblings. The original development study (Parker et al., 1979) found no association between age of respondent and parental care and protection scores. Cubis et al. (1989), however, detected a trend for their adolescent subjects to score parents as less caring and more controlling overall, compared to the responses given by other adult samples. These authors also noted that while their male and female adolescent subjects returned similar Care scale scores, females tended to rate mothers as more caring than males. On the "perceived social control" subscale of the Protection scale, mothers were judged as less controlling by female subjects than by males, while on the "personal intrusiveness" subscale, females scored fathers as more intrusive than did males. When the "Protection" scale scores were aggregated, however, sex differences failed to be significant. Rey, Bird, Kopec-Schrader, and Richards (1993) also found significant differences in parental care and protection scores as a function of subjects' age and sex. Older subjects scored their mothers and fathers as less caring than younger subjects, although they did not score their parents as more controlling. Females scored their fathers, but not their mothers, as more overprotective than did males.

It is important to know whether cultural variations influence the way the PBI is both scored and interpreted, and two relevant studies have been reported. First, Parker and Lipscombe (1979) found that Greek female adolescents living in Australia scored their mothers and fathers as significantly more overprotective than did a comparison group of Australian females. Second, Kitamura and Suzuki (1993) administered their translated version of the PBI to Japanese high school students and to the students' parents. The authors found the PBI factor structures to be similar to those derived from Australian samples, arguing for cross-cultural consistency in fundamental parental characteristics. Additionally, students' scores on the Care scale correlated negatively with their scores on the Protection scale, challenging the oft-put view that overprotection is an expression of care—in that the opposite appears to be the case.

Modified Versions of the Parental Bonding Instrument

Some researchers have introduced and experimented with modified versions of the PBI. Thus, Parker (1983a), noting that some respondents were experiencing difficulty interpreting five statements in the PBI that risked double negative responses, deleted the five relevant items, resulting in a revised version. He reported that the new instrument's consensual and predictive validity coefficients were significantly weaker compared to the original version, while the reliability of the instrument remained unaffected. Gamsa (1987) took the same five items and altered the nature of the statements from negative to positive. For example, "Did not help me as much as I needed" was changed to "Helped me as much as I needed," "Did not talk with me very much" was changed to "Talked to me often," and "Did not want me to grow up" was reworded to "Wanted me to grow up." Gamsa first administered the original PBI to student subjects and then, 5 months later, instructed them to complete the new version. No significant differences were found between mean scores on the two versions of the PBI, and as scores on the two measures were highly positively correlated, it appeared that the modification did not alter the nature of the original factors. The mean values obtained for both maternal and paternal scores were all consistent with normative data obtained by Parker et al. (1979). Gamsa (1987) has argued that such a modification has the potential to reduce confusion experienced by some subjects, noting that a total of 14 requests were made by subjects for help in completing the unmodified PBI. Some researchers have modified the PBI in order to reduce the time and effort required to complete the questionnaire.

Although any shortened version of the PBI is intended to make the completion of its items simpler, it must also preserve the structure and psychometric properties of the original version. Moreover, although short versions of the instrument would probably simplify the administration procedure in normative subject samples, it has been argued that it may be unwise to replace the 25-item version in clinical populations. Klimidis, Minas, and Ata (1992) developed a brief current form of the PBI (the PBI-BC), seeking to investigate perceptions of current parental styles. Their 8-item version (derived from the original instrument) inquires into parental characteristics as perceived by adolescents over a previous 3-month period. Their subject group included adolescents who had recently immigrated or who had refugee status. In part, the authors wanted to assess the potential impact that these current experiences may have upon subjects' evaluations of parental attitudes and behaviors. In terms of the new measure's factor structure, the authors found that is was closely replicative of the original version (Parker et al., 1979) and that the scales of the PBI-BC had reasonably high internal consistency. Their findings also highlighted significant cultural differences in parental ratings (e.g., female subjects who were recent immigrants tended to rate fathers as more overprotective than did male immigrants and nonimmigrant female subjects).

Todd, Boyce, Heath, and Martin (1994) also produced a shortened version of the PBI as part of a questionnaire booklet containing shortened versions of the Intimate Bond Measure (IBM) (Wilhelm & Parker, 1987) and the Interpersonal Sensitivity Measure (IPSM) (Boyce & Parker, 1989). In their study, 2000 paris of twins between 18 and 26 years of age completed a 7-item version of the PBI containing 3 Care and 4 Protection items together with IBM and IPSM short forms. In order to investigate whether their modified PBI was a valid measure of the fundamental constructs captured by the full-length version, they compared scores on the short form with scores obtained on the full-length version sent to a subset of twins 12 months later. The authors found that scores obtained from the subset sample were generally consistent with those obtained from the full sample on most subscale scores. Relatively high Pearson correlation coefficients were observed between the full-length and the shortened version of the PBI ($r = 0.61$–0.70).

Similarly, in a study examining the relationship between adult depression and parental bonding in a large nonclinical sample of female twins, Neale et al. (1994) used a 7-item short form of the PBI. Positively and negatively weighted items for each factor were included in the short form (item numbers being 3, 4, 5, 7, 16, 19, and 23). Interestingly, they found that factor analysis showed that item number 7 ("Liked me to make my own decisions") loaded more strongly on a Care factor than on a Protection factor.

Parker, Hadzi-Pavlovic, Greenwald, and Weissman (1995) examined the relationship between low parental care and lifetime depression in a community sample of subjects. The authors chose one central item (number 6: "Was affectionate to me") from the Care scale of the PBI to measure parental care and one central measure from the Protection scale (number 9: "Tried to control everything I did") to measure parental control. Both items were selected on the basis of their strong factor loadings in the original PBI development studies (Parker et al.,

1979). The authors did not anticipate that the single Care measure would reflect the full PBI measure; however, when scores on the single Care item were intercorrelated with full PBI care scale scores (in an independent data base of depressed patients), the two measures were highly correlated ($r = 0.83$). Thus, support has been demonstrated for several condensed versions of the PBI.

Reliability of the Parental Bonding Instrument

In regard to the internal consistency of the PBI measure, Parker et al. (1979) established that both the Care and the Protection scale had high split-half reliability (0.88 and 0.74, respectively) when tested in a nonclinical population sample. A number of other clinical and nonclinical studies have confirmed the high internal consistency of scores on the Care and Protection PBI scales (Arrindell, Hanewald, & Folk, 1989; Brewin, Firth-Cozens, Furnham, & McManus, 1992; Leigh, Robins, Welkowitz, & Bond, 1989; Richman & Flaherty, 1986). Overall, examinations of internal consistency have shown moderate homogeneity for scores on the Protection scale (as anticipated for a scale that seeks to reflect somewhat overlapping constructs of protection, control, encouragement of dependency, and infantilization) and excellent homogeneity for scores on the Care scale of the PBI.

The PBI was devised so that adult respondents could provide information on the nature of parenting received during their first 16 years. Subjects are required to rate retrospective memories of parental style, so that responses are based on recollections of *perceived* parental attributes. Whether or not such recalled perceptions about parents match actual past parental characteristics is a question of interest and will be addressed to some degree later in a discussion on validity. However, this issue has little relevance to questions about the consistency of PBI scores over time. That is, if the PBI is a reliable measure of respondents' accounts about parents (whether those accounts match or contrast with reality), high test–retest reliability should be observed between scores over time.

Various studies have assessed the short-term test–retest reliability of the PBI. In the original nonclinical sample (Parker et al., 1979), the test–retest reliability agreement was 0.76 for the Care scale and 0.63 for the Protection scale over a 3-week interval. Subsequently, researchers have administered the PBI to clinically depressed patients during their depressive episode and at follow-up (when improved) some weeks later and found significant reliability. Thus, Whisman and Kwon (1992) administered the PBI to students with varying degrees of depressive symptoms on two occasions with a 3-month interval. They found a test–retest reliability agreement of 0.86 for the Care scale and 0.85 for the Protection scale of the PBI. Plantes, Prusoff, Brennan, and Parker (1988) also observed excellent test–retest reliability of PBI scores, when a group of depressives (mostly nonmelancholic) rated their parents first when depressed and subsequently some 4–6 weeks later when improved. The reliability agreements for scores completed by all subjects (depressives and controls) were: 0.94 for maternal care, 0.93 for maternal protection, 0.90 for parental care, and 0.96 for paternal protection. Such studies are extremely important in preempting concerns that any anomalous PBI reports from depressed subjects may reflect state-dependent biases emerging from the depressed mood and therefore be invalid.

Additionally, Parker, Fairley, Greenwood, Jurd, and Silove (1982) administered the PBI to a group of patients with schizophrenia shortly after they were admitted and subsequently when they were judged to have improved. On both testing occasions, their PBI scores suggested lower parental care and higher parental protection than matched nonclinical controls. The authors reported that patients' scores at the two assessment periods were strikingly similar. The correlation coefficients were: 0.77 for maternal care, 0.73 for maternal protection, 0.58 for paternal care, and 0.69 for maternal protection. However, when Warner and Atkinson (1988) administered the PBI to a group of schizophrenic patients on two occasions with a 3-week interval, they reported higher test–retest coefficients, ranging from 0.79 to 0.88. It has been suggested that these subjects' scores were significantly more consistent due to greater stability of the patients' condition and reduced schizophrenic symptoms.

More recently, longer-term test–retest reliability PBI data have become available. Gotlib, Mount, Cordy, and Whiffen (1988) studied women in the postpartum period and then at a mean period of 30 months later, administering only the maternal component of the PBI. These authors noted that maternal care and protection scores were significantly stable over time. Wilhelm and Parker (1990) examined the test–retest reliability of the PBI over a 10-year period with data obtained from a cohort of teachers college students. They found mean PBI scores to be relatively consistent over time and observed moderate to high test–retest reliability coefficients. Maternal care received a correlation coefficient of 0.63; maternal protection. 0.68; paternal care, 0.72; and paternal protection, 0.56. The authors concluded that the PBI is a reliable measure over an extended period and confirmed it to be an accurate measure of perceived parenting.

Validity of the Parental Bonding Instrument

The extent to which a test successfully measures the constructs that it was designed to measure equates the extent to which that measure is a valid instrument.

As noted earlier, the PBI is a subjective measure, relying upon self-reports provided by respondents, and aims to assess the phenomenological perception of parental qualities, attitudes, and child-raising behaviors. These parental qualities, attitudes, and behaviors encapsulate the two principal dimensions of parental characteristics, parental care and parental protection or control, with item statements worded to invite subjective assessment by the recipient (e.g., "Appeared to understand my problems and worries"; "Could make me feel better when I was upset"). It may well be the case that disparities exist between what an individual perceives to be true and what actually existed or occurred in previous years within the "reality" of the parent–child relationship. At one level, this has not been a concern to the PBI researchers. As it is impossible for respondents to escape the frame of subjective interpretation in any such measure, any disparities between that which was "perceived" and that which was "actual" may be quite irrelevant if the value and meaning of phenomenological experiences are respected (i.e., the way we respond to the world is determined more by our perceptions than by any "reality").

However, in circumstances in which, for instance, depressed subjects falsely perceive their parents as uncaring, a causal link may lie between perception and outcome, but it cannot then be claimed that there is a causal link between insufficient *actual* parental care and depression. Thus, in addition to testing the validity of the PBI as a measure of *perceived* parenting, it is also important to know the extent to which it measures *actual* parenting. The latter issue may be difficult to pursue because the effect of any "real" parental style will invariably be mediated by a child's unique reactions, coping style, and cognitive schemata, as well as by any inherited diathesis to psychological dysfunction. We now consider some validity studies examining the validity of the PBI as a measure of both "perceived" and "actual" parenting.

Perceived Parenting Validity Studies. In the original PBI development study, Parker et al. (1979) examined the degree to which PBI care and overprotection scores correlated with subjects' responses during a semistructured interview. Two separate examiners questioned subjects about parental care and overprotection during interviews and found high correlations between interview ratings of "parental care" and PBI Care scale scores ($r = 0.77$ and 0.78). However, lower intercorrelations were obtained for intercorrelations of the Protection scale ($r = 0.48$ and 0.50) with the interviewer's ratings of overprotection. The authors argued that these lower coefficients may have reflected subjects' greater difficulty in interpreting and responding to inquires about parental overprotection (Parker et al., 1979; Parker, 1983a).

I. G. Sarason, B. R. Sarason, and Shearin (1986) gave the PBI and the Social Support Questionnaire (SSQ) (a measure of the number of and satisfaction with available support figures) to a large group of college students. They found the PBI care ratings to be positively related to SSQ ratings and PBI overprotection ratings to be inversely related to SSQ ratings. Similarly, B. R. Sarason, Shearin, Pierce, and I. G. Sarason (1987) gave the PBI and a number of self-report measures of social support to a group of subjects to complete. They found that scores on the SSQ correlated positively with maternal care ($r = 0.43$ to 0.63) and paternal care (0.40 to 0.48) and negatively with maternal protection (-0.21 to -0.32) and paternal protection (-0.17 to -0.26). The authors compared PBI scores with scores on the Inventory Schedule for Social Interactions (ISSI), a 52-item structured interview assessing perceived availability and adequacy of attachment and social integration (see Henderson, Byrne, & Duncan-Jones, 1981), and found that PBI maternal care was clearly linked with ISSI "availability of attachment" ($r = 0.38$) and "availability of social integration" ($r = 0.41$), while PBI paternal care showed similar links ($r = 0.33$ and $r = 0.33$, respectively). The authors also found that ISSI "availability of social integration" was negatively correlated with maternal ($r = -0.35$) and paternal ($r = -0.51$) protection. The extent to which parents were encapsulated (alone or in combination with other attachment figures) in such attachment measures remains unestablished and problematic and therefore limits any close interpretation. While it might be argued that these results offer some support for the concurrent validity of the PBI as a measure of perceived parenting, findings may also reflect a general response bias influencing perceptions and ratings of all interpersonal relationships.

In a study by Birtchnell (1988), depressive and control subjects were interviewed about their early relationships with their parents and in addition completed the PBI. The information gained from interview was consistent with PBI scores, in that depressed subjects reported significantly less maternal care and greater maternal protection than controls; however, this trend was not significant for fathers. Rodgers (in press) also compared the qualitative accounts (obtained at interview) with the PBI scores from 3262 subjects of 43 years average age. During the interview, subjects were asked about any mistreatment experienced in childhood and were encouraged to comment freely. Rodgers found overall consistency between PBI scores and subjects' retrospective accounts. The majority of those who reported mistreatment also rated parents as low on care and high on control, while those reporting no mistreatment and a happy unbringing rated parents high on caring. Subjects who reported an unhappy upbringing produced very low care scores and high control scores; those whose accounts reflected neglectful parenting also produced very low PBI care scores and significantly less high control scores. Overall, the PBI appears to be of satisfactory reliability and validity as a measure of perceived parental characteristics.

Actual Parenting Validity Studies. Several relevant studies have been reported. In a mixed clinical and nonclinical sample, subjects and their nominated siblings completed the PBI for themselves and on the basis of their observations of their parents' attitudes and behaviors toward the other sibling (Parker, 1981, 1983a). The mean coefficients of agreement between subjects' PBI scores and siblings' corroborative reports were moderate: 0.62 for PBI care and 0.47 for PBI protection. Parker (1986) gave the PBI to a group of 78 monozygotic (MZ) and dizygotic (DZ) twins, with subjects rating their parents in the orthodox way. It was expected that PBI scores for the MZ twins would be highly correlated, because of presumed similarities in parenting and shared genes leading to similar perceptional and attributional styles in MZ twins. However, the mean correlation coefficients for the PBI scales were strikingly similar for the two groups: 0.70 for the MZ and 0.71 for the DZ twins. These values far exceeded those obtained earlier (Parker, 1983a) for siblings scoring parents, and while they are supportive of the validity of the PBI, they failed to highlight the anticipated differential MZ and DZ data.

Mackinnon, Henderson, and Andrews (1991) conducted a similar study using 672 twins from the Australian National Health and Medical Research Council Twin Registry and found weaker associations for DZ twins. These authors found that agreement in PBI scale scores was generally high between female co-twins, with the mean correlation coefficient being higher for MZ ($r = 0.69$) than for DZ ($r = 0.56$) twins. Mean agreement coefficients for male twins were significantly lower (MZ = 0.56, DZ = 0.10), and though the very low agreement between DZ male twins is puzzling, the authors argued that the scales may have been affected by competition or comparisons made by males with their twin brothers.

In another study using a nonclinical group, subjects were instructed to score themselves on trait and state depression measures and their mothers on the PBI (Parker, 1981, 1983a). The mothers also scored themselves on the PBI (i.e., as they judged they had related to that child in the child's first 16 years). Although there were moderate levels of agreement between subjects and their mothers (0.44 for care and 0.55 for protection), there was a tendency for mothers to score themselves as more caring and less protective than they were rated by their children. This trend was also observed in the validation study by Kitamura and Suzuki (1993) using their Japanese version of the PBI. As noted earlier, however, the study by Kitamura and Suzuki showed that mothers considered overprotection to be synonymous with care. Parker also found that when PBI scores were intercorrelated with subjects' depression scores, higher depression was associated with lower maternal care and with higher maternal protection, whether judged by the mother or the subject. Thus, for those subjects who were more depressed, both the subjects and their mothers rated the maternal care as less and the maternal protection as more, with agreement arguing against subjects' scores being distorted by depression or by a response bias. In the same study, mothers who were judged as most overprotective on the PBI were subsequently assessed by an interviewer blind to PBI scores. Those discriminated on the PBI as overprotective mothers were judged at interview (on the basis of their own descriptions of themselves as parents) to have been significantly more overprotective, controlling, infantilizing, dependency-inducing, and indulging in their earlier parenting years.

APPLIED STUDIES

While the relevance of anomalous parenting (as measured by the PBI) has been examined in relation to a large number of adult psychiatric disorders and socialization patterns, we will review only a few and will limit consideration to areas addressed by a number of studies so that some synthesis can be attempted. At the broadest level, research findings (Parker, 1983a) suggest that high levels of controlling parenting, together with low levels of parental care, result in an increased risk of developing neurotic disorders in adulthood, but that anomalous parenting is not distinctly overrepresented in those who develop psychotic conditions such as manic–depressive psychosis or schizophrenia, indicating that any parental contribution may vary considerably across separate psychiatric disorders. As noted earlier, this review will focus on disorders that have been considered in multiple studies, but will also focus on ones in which anomalous parenting has been strongly imputed or quantified.

Depression

Various nonclinical studies have examined for links between PBI scores and trait depression scores. Consistent but not significant trends have been observed linking higher depression levels with low parental care and with parental over-protection (see Howard, 1981; Merskey et al., 1987; Parker, 1983b; Parker & Hazdi-Pavlovic, 1984; Richman & Flaherty, 1986). There now exist a number of studies examining PBI scores returned by those with clinical depression. Studies using patients with separate depressive disorders have indicated that PBI scores vary in relation to broad depressive type, suggesting some degree of specificity to the parental deprivation hypothesis. Parker (1979a) gave the PBI to patients with bipolar disorder (i.e., manic–depressive illness) and to control subjects matched by age and sex. He found no significant differences in scores on the PBI Care and Protection scales between the two groups. Joyce (1984) also compared bipolar depressives with control patients attending a general practice and similarly found no differences in PBI scores. Parker, Kiloh, and Hayward (1987) studied a group of patients with unipolar (major) depression and observed that endogenous (or melancholic) depressives also returned PBI scores similar to those of age- and sex-matched controls. Thus, studies that have examined the presumed categorical "melancholic" (or endogenous depressive) "type" have been unable to show evidence of an overrepresentation of anomalous parenting in the reports of such patients (by PBI measurement).

Mackinnon, Henderson, and Andrews (1993) studied 922 adult twins, ages 18–65, of whom some were diagnosed formally with some type of depressive disorder. Included in the 468 female subjects were 15 given a diagnosis of dysthymia, 21 with a major depressive episode, and 21 with both. The numbers of male subjects assigned to those categories were 5, 12, and 5, respectively. The authors conducted a logistic regression analysis with PBI scores from this mixed sample and found support for the view that depressive adults report the experience of having received poorer parenting than do adult normals. An interactive pattern of low care and high protection was not significantly predictive of adult depression for their community sample. Rather, the care dimension alone (low care) exhibited a strong relationship with adult depression, with the protection dimension failing to add strength to the predictive validity of low care.

Various case–control studies of neurotic depressives in Australia have consistently established anomalous PBI scores (i.e., low care/high protection) to be overrepresented (Hickie et al., 1990; Parker, 1979a; Parker et al., 1987). In a study of 125 neurotic depressives, Parker (1983b) found that depressives scored their mothers and fathers as both less caring and more protective than did subjects in the control group. He also noted an effect of sex of parent linked with sex of child, whereby female depressives reported a greater decrement in maternal rather than paternal care, and a greater excess of maternal rather than paternal protection, when compared with routine controls. Male depressives reported a greater decrement in paternal than in maternal care, but a similar excess of maternal and paternal protection. In the same study, a discriminant function analysis established that low paternal and maternal care were the two strongest discriminators between the depressives and the controls. This finding was replicated to some extent in a United States study by Plantes et al. (1988), in which a similar depressive group reported significantly less parental care and greater parental protection, in comparison to a control group.

Parker and Hadzi-Pavlovic (1992) gave the PBI to 65 melancholic and 84 nonmelancholic depressed patients. In light of previous findings, the authors anticipated "anomalous parenting" to be a differential risk factor relevant to nonmelancholic (nonendogenous) depression, but less relevant to melancholia (endogenous depression). They again found support for their specificity hypothesis, whereby nonmelancholic depressives were significantly more likely to report low parental care than were their matched controls. The scores returned by melancholic depressives failed to indicate any increased chance of anomalous parenting. The authors also found evidence for additive and "compensatory" effects between the perceived parenting styles of both mother and father on the risk for nonmelancholic depression. Thus, if both parents were rated negatively (e.g., affectionless control/neglectful parenting), the risk was increased considerably. On the other hand, if one parent was rated positively (e.g., optimal parenting), this was observed to "compensate" somewhat for the poor style projected by the anomalous parent, and in such instances, the risk of depression was reduced.

Parker (1993) gave the PBI to 123 depressed subjects in a study examining the relationship among anomalous parenting, cognitive style, personality, and depression. Subjects also completed a state depression questionnaire and a collection of personality measures. It was anticipated that a "low care/high protection" style of parenting might dispose to a vulnerable cognitive style, then acting as a diathesis to adult depression. Findings included low parental care being significantly linked with high scores on the Dysfunctional Attitudes Scale (Form A) and with low self-esteem scores. Parental overprotection was also linked significantly with low self-esteem. The results indicated that anomalous parenting (particularly low care) did not directly influence subjects' mood state, but was associated with a general dysfunctional attitude style and lower evaluations of the self, supporting the view that anomalous parenting is unlikely to dispose directly to depression, but establishes a vulnerability or diathesis.

Kendler, Kessler, Neale, Heath, and Eaves (1993) conducted a study to develop an exploratory, causal model for predicting the 1-year prevalence of depression in a population base sample of 680 female–female twin pairs. Subjects were assessed three times at intervals of greater than 1-year and completed a set of health, lifestyle, and personality questionnaires, and additionally were assessed by personal interview. A number of predictor variables (for depression) were considered, including "parental warmth." The authors assessed the last by using an empirically derived subscale of the PBI (the 7-item short-form version) and by averaging the care scores given for the mother and father across each twin pair. Other predictor variables included: genetic factors, childhood parental loss, life traumas, neuroticism, social support, history of major depression, recent difficulties, and recent stressful life events. These authors reported that the best-fitting model accounted for 50% of the variance in the threat of major depression over two periods of 1-year assessments, with parental warmth having an intermediate effect as a predictor variable. The presence of recent stressful life events was the single most powerful risk factor for major depression in the model. Genetic background was the second largest risk factor for major depression, and 60% of this effect was direct. The remaining 40% was indirect, mediated predominantly by a history of prior depressive episodes, stressful life events, life traumas and neuroticism.

In conclusion, the numerous PBI studies indicate some consistency in linking "affectionless control" parenting with both nonclinical depression and non-melancholic depression, but no increased chance of developing melancholia (the more "biological" type of depression), with such specificity a helpful caveat. Additionally, the studies suggest that such parenting establishes a diathesis to depression, while studies to be reported shortly indicate that such a vulnerability is distinctly susceptible to modification by subsequent social attachments and other variables.

Anxiety and Anxiety-Related Disorders

There have been several studies that have explored for possible links between PBI scores and measures of trait anxiety in nonclinical populations. The Costello and Comrey (1967) trait anxiety measure, designed to assess any predisposition to develop anxious-affective states, has been used in many of these studies. So far, studies have consistently identified trends linking low parental care and high parental protection with higher trait anxiety levels. Low care and higher anxiety have been more strongly observed in ratings made about mothers than in ratings made about fathers (Parker, 1979b, 1986; Merskey et al., 1987).

In a study in which their brief current version of the PBI was used (i.e., the 8-item form), Klimidis, Minas, and Ata (1992) assessed 631 Australian adolescents' experiences with obsessions, compulsions, and ruminations. They found that higher obsession and rumination scores were linked significantly with low paternal and maternal care and with high paternal protection. However, higher compulsion scores were linked with both higher maternal and paternal protection scores, but not with paternal care scores. In a further study, Cavedo and Parker (1994) examined the relationship between perceived parental bonding and obsessionality using 344 nonclinical subjects. Subjects completed the PBI along with two measures of obsessionality: the Maudsley Obsessional–Compulsive Inventory and the Leyton Obsessionality Inventory. The authors found that higher PBI protection scores were linked with higher scores on both the obsessionality measures. Both maternal and paternal high protection scores were linked with higher obsessionality scores for female subjects, but only high paternal protection scores were linked with higher obsessionality scores for male subjects. Links with PBI care scale scores, however, were less clear.

Further studies examining the relationship between anxiety and dimensions of parenting (i.e., care and protection) have been conducted with clinically diagnosed patients. Faravelli, Panichi, Pallanti, Grecu, and Rivelli (1991) administered the PBI to two groups: (1) 32 outpatients diagnosed with panic disorder (PD) (of whom 6 had no phobic avoidance, 4 mild agoraphobia, 7 moderate avoidance, and 15 severe agoraphobia) and (2) a group of controls. Overall, patients with PD reported significantly less parental care and more parental protection. Only 3% of PD patients reported optimal maternal bonding, compared to 25% of controls. Leon and Leon (1990) compared a group of normal controls with patients previously diagnosed with PD and generalized anxiety disorder (GAD). Parenting quadrant assignments showed that there was an over-representation of parents identified as low care/high protection ("affectionless control") among the anxiety patients. Similarly, in reporting the results of a meta-analysis, Gerlsma, Emmelkamp, and Arrindell (1990) argued that parental "affectionless control" was significantly evident and over-represented in the reports of patients with anxiety disorders.

Silove, Parker, Hadzi-Pavlovic, Manicavasagar, and Blaszcynski (1991) compared PBI scores from 80 clinically anxious patients with those of a group of controls matched by age and sex. Patients included those with PD and GAD. Logistic regression analyses revealed that GAD patients had a much greater risk of assigning mothers, and both parents to anomalous parenting quadrants, including the quadrant of "affectionless control." Scores achieved by PD patients, however, exhibited a distinctive pattern whereby they were more likely to report "affectionate constraint" (high care/high protection) by mothers. In regard to these findings, the authors suggested that one aberrant parental style ("affectionless control") may be of most relevance to the pathogenesis of GAD, whereas "affectionate constraint" may be a secondary parental response to a primary childhood manifestation of PD (e.g., school phobia). Such suggested specificity requires further study respecting the possible clinical and etiological differences between PD and GAD.

In a clinical study on obsessive–compulsive disorder (OCD), Hafner (1988) undertook a postal survey of 81 subjects who attended a self-help support group and who met DSM-III-R criteria for the disorder. Subjects with OCD reported significantly lower parental care scores (mother and father) and significantly higher parental protection scores (mother and father) than did control subjects.

Phobic Disorders

Various studies have indicated that patients with phobic disorders often recall experiencing a deficiency of parental warmth and care during their childhood, whereas overprotection has been reported to a lesser degree. Parker (1979a) assessed 40 English agoraphobic patients and 41 patients with social phobia as well as a matched group of controls with the PBI and found that social phobics reported significantly less parental care and more overprotection than controls. However, patients with agoraphobia differed from controls only in that they reported less maternal care.

Silove (1986) studied 33 patients with agoraphobia attending an inpatient therapy program and 31 control subjects. He found that 13 of the agoraphobics and 8 of the controls reported a significant separation before the age of 16 (e.g., death of parent, divorce, permanent separation), although this difference was not statistically significant. Agoraphobic subjects produced lower care and higher protection PBI scores for both parents than did controls, unlike the findings in the previous study (Parker, 1979a), wherein agoraphobic patients produced very low maternal care scores only. Silove argued that their data revealed a trend for persons with agoraphobia to report excessive major early losses in childhood.

Some studies have used the Egna Minnen Betraffande Uppfostram ("My Memories of Upbringing") (see Arrindell, Emmelkamp, Monsma, & Brilman, 1983; Arrindell, Kwee, et al., 1989) as a measure of memories about personal upbringing, to investigate the relationship between perceived parental rearing practices and the experience of phobic disorders. In the first study, Arrindell et al. (1983) found that when compared to controls, social phobics and height phobics perceived both their mother and their father as lacking in warmth, as rejecting, and as overprotective. In the second study, Arrindell, Kwee, et al. (1989) also found that social phobics rated both parents as having been rejecting, emotionally cold, and overprotective. Interestingly, both studies found that agoraphobics perceived both parents as lacking in emotional warmth, but only their mothers as having been rejecting. Such studies suggest that nuances of anomalous parenting may have differential effects on the base disturbance (i.e., anxiety) and on some of its consequences and manifestations (e.g., phobic avoidance behaviors).

Eating Disorders

Much theorizing on the nature of eating disorders (especially anorexia nervosa and bulimia nervosa) has argued for the somewhat deterministic role of anomalous parenting (e.g., enmeshment, overprotection and control). Recently, these assumptions have been tested using the PBI, with somewhat variable results.

In a study by Gomez (1984), 10 anorexia nervosa (AN) patients' scores on the PBI were compared with scores obtained from a control group. Gomez found that the AN patients scored their mothers as significantly less caring and more protective compared to controls, while both groups rated their fathers similarly. Palmer, Oppenheimer, and Marshall (1988) also compared the scores of 35 English AN patients with unmatched normative data published in Australia and found that the AN patients reported significantly less maternal care only. Russell, Kopec-Schader, Rey, and Beumont (1992) administered the PBI to three adolescent groups: (1) AN patients, (2) a group of matched normals, and (3) a group referred for psychiatric assessment without anorectic symptoms. In contrast to the findings just mentioned, the authors found that the AN patients rated their mothers and fathers as more caring and less protective than the nonanorectic referred group and rated their parents similarly to the nonclinical control group on both the Care and Protection scales.

Russell et al. (1992) also compared the scores of 20 bulimia nervosa (BN) patients with the scores from 20 control subjects and found that the BN patients rated their fathers as less caring than did the control group, with this being the only significant finding. Pole, Waller, Stewart, and Parkin-Feigenbaum (1988) administered the PBI to 56 BN outpatients and 30 control subjects. After aggregating the maternal and paternal PBI scale scores, the authors found that 75% of bulimics reported the experience of low care, compared to 47% of controls. The "optimal parenting" quadrant was the one that most clearly distinguished bulimics from controls, with only 5.4% of bulimics as against 43.8% of controls so assigning their parents. Bulimics were observed to perceive their mothers as significantly less caring than controls, and while they also reported low paternal care, a trend toward the perception of overprotection from fathers was also observed.

In a study by Kent and Clopton (1992), the relationship between bulimia and various family variables was examined, with the PBI being administered to three groups of subjects: (1) 24 subjects who met DSM-III-R requirements for bulimia, (2) 24 subclinical bulimics, and (3) 24 symptom-free subjects (controls). The authors found that contrary to past investigations (Palmer et al., 1988; Calam, Waller, Slade, & Newton, 1990), no significant differences were observed in either care or protection scores among the three groups.

In a study by Fichter, Quadflieg, and Brandl (1993), patients with binge eating disorders (BED), BN, and obesity were administered the PBI as part of an investigation of recurrent overeating. The authors found that BED patients had significantly higher scores on the Protection scale of the PBI for their mothers only, compared to patients with BN. There were no differences in scores between the BN and obesity groups and the BED and obesity groups. Furthermore, there were no significant differences among groups regarding control by fathers, care by mothers, or care by fathers.

Studies that have compared eating disorder patients as a group with control subjects have identified significant trends whereby patients with eating disorders tend to rate parents as less caring and somewhat more protective than do control groups (Calam et al., 1990; Steiger, Van der Feen, Goldstein, & Leichner, 1989). Findings like these tend to suggest some degree of homogeneity among eating disorder patients in regard to the two fundamental parenting dimensions. However, as present research has failed to find a clear picture of perceived low parental care and overprotection, further research in this relatively new area of examination needs to be pursued.

This subject of eating disorders has been considered for two principal reasons. First, it is commonly put that those with eating disorders, and particularly those with AN, have an "enmeshed" family structure. If so, we would anticipate clear evidence of a greater level of overprotection. Failure to support this view clearly and consistently raises an issue that must be considered whenever anomalous parenting is quantified in a clinical sample (i.e., is it an antecedent or a consequence?). It is possible, then, that much of the family enmeshment described in those with an eating disorder may be a consequence of the family distress about their adolescent child—and have no or little relationship to onset of the disorder (i.e., not be a cause). In many research studies, it may therefore be important to have subjects rate their parents both *before* and *after* onset of the disorder, to examine evidence for and against any anomalous parenting being an antecedent (and possible causal) factor or not.

Early Socialization

A variety of research using the PBI has given support to the claim that anomalous parenting (e.g., low caring and high overprotection) may instigate a disposition to experience a range of neurotic disorders, including depression, in adult life. Even though poor parental bonding could be conceptualized as creating an initial weakness or tendency for later psychological problems, it is unlikely in most cases that such developmental diatheses be permanent and durable, especially in the face of positive "compensatory" life events. It seems intuitively reasonable to propose that meaningful positive events (e.g., a secure, intimate relationship) may modify the effect of poor parental style and attenuate any existing vulnerability to reactive psychopathology in adulthood (e.g., nonmelancholic depression).

Parker and Hadzi-Pavlovic (1984) conducted a study to assess the extent to which an intimate relationship could modify the effect of poor parental bonds upon depression for a group of adult women. The subjects were 79 women (a large proportion of whom were married), with a mean age of 33 years, whose natural mothers had died when the women were between 8 and 12 years old and whose fathers had remarried in the following few years. Subjects completed PBI forms for their mothers, their stepmothers, and their fathers; the Zung (1965) depression scale, to measure state depression; and the Costello and Comrey (1967) scale, to measure trait depression. The authors derived their own self-report scale of "marital affection," using three items that appear to reflect care ("supportive," "loving," and "understanding") and one item that appeared to oppose care ("critical"). The possibility of a distinct depressive episode was assessed by using the probe question from the Schedule for Affective Disorders and Schizophrenia lifetime depression scale. Of the 79 women, 59 (75%) responded positively to this probe, suggesting a distinct depressive episode at some time in their life.

A distinct depressive episode was reported by most (91%) of the subjects who had produced low care scores for both their stepmother and their father. The experience of a depressive episode was slightly less likely for subjects scoring one parent "low" and one "high" on care and even less likely for subjects reporting "high" care for both parents. If lack of care and overprotection were parental anomalies placing a child at high risk of depression, then any amelioration of such presumed negative (causal) effects would be associated with variation (i.e., reduction) in the likelihood of depression. Parker and Hadzi-Pavlovic (1984) found evidence to support this claim. After they entered marital affection scores into a regression analysis, they found that low parental care was no longer a significant predictor and that low marital affection was the only significant predictor of state depression scores.

Interestingly, they found that subjects who experienced affectionate and caring relationships with their husbands (regardless of the level of parental care received) were, overall, significantly less likely to express symptoms of depression compared to subjects who perceived and reported little or no marital affection. Specifically, subjects who reported "low" care from stepmothers and fathers, but "high" affection from husbands, scored 30% higher on the trait and only 6% higher on the state depression measure than those who reported "high" parental care and "high" marital affection. Moreover, these women rated themselves as significantly less depressed (16% on the trait and 20% on the state measure) than those women who reported "high" parental care but "low" affection from their husbands. The authors suggested that the study offered support for the proposition that close affectionate bonding in adult life may modify the effects of parental deprivation. These findings were optimistic, in suggesting that favorable human experiences can attenuate or reduce vulnerability to disorder. It is important that this study showed that recent relationships were more salient definers of depression levels for these women than were past relationships.

Another important issue relating to the experience of anomalous parenting during childhood can be conceptualized in terms of a "continuity hypothesis," whereby poor parental bonding may predispose the individual to the establishment and maintenance of unsatisfactory social and intimate bonds in adulthood. While there has been some PBI-based research pointing to a significant association between deficits in perceived parenting style and unsatisfactory bonds in adulthood, a number of studies have failed to establish a link or pattern between the quality of parenting received in childhood and the quality of social support and relationships during adulthood.

Flaherty and Richman (1986) examined the relationship between medical students' perceptions of their relationships with their parents (using the PBI) and the perceived quality of their current social support networks. Subjects completed the Social Support Network Inventory (assessing the five most important members in the respondents' social networks and taping into aspects of availability, support, and reciprocity). The authors found that perceived parental care and affectivity in childhood were significantly related to adult social support levels, whereas parental overprotection was not significantly related. Those who rated their mothers or fathers or both high in affection manifested significantly higher mean scores for ratings of both social support and nonfamilial relationships. Flaherty and Richman argued that parental affectivity (but not overprotection) can be conceived as significantly related to the capacity of individuals to form subsequent supportive relationships.

Parker and Barnett (1988) gave the PBI and the Interview Schedule for Social Interactions (ISSI) to 129 women within 3 weeks of hospital discharge after giving birth to their first child and gave the ISSI again 12 months later. Subjects' care ratings (for mothers) on the PBI were significantly linked with their ratings of availability of close meaningful relationships and the availability of extended social support figures on the ISSI on both testing occasions. Subsequently, subjects' "neuroticism" ratings were partialed out (because they were thought to reflect a "plaintive-set" response bias), leaving a significant link only between maternal care ratings and ratings of current availability of close relationships.

Like the studies just mentioned, other research has highlighted the nexus between subjects' remembrance of high care (particularly maternal) during childhood and their positive perceptions of current (adult) social support (Henderson, Duncan-Jones, Byrne, & Scott, 1980; I. G. Sarason et al., 1986; B. R. Sarason et al., 1987). In part, these findings might be explained by the mothers' continuous contribution of "care" to their adult child's social domain, so resulting in a general "maternal care" response bias.

As the previously discussed findings of Parker and Hadzi-Pavlovic suggest, the experience of a positive intimate relationship and the presence of a trusted confidant would seem to have a reparative capacity, even against earlier detrimental experiences. One study (Quinton, Rutter, & Liddle, 1984) has demonstrated that selection of a nonaberrant spouse (who provided emotional support and favorable living conditions) produced a significant "protective" effect against further emotional problems for subjects who were earlier raised without a significant parent figure (i.e., children raised institutionally).

Wilhelm and Parker (1988) developed an instrument to measure the qualities of intimate bonds. The Intimate Bond Measure (IBM) is an adult self-report measure assessing the key dimensions of care and control. A series of studies have examined links between PBI and IBM ratings, to investigate whether perceived levels of parental care and control relate to similar levels of perceived care and control in adult intimate relationships. If significant links are established between several self-report measures, it is necessary to examine whether exposure to certain parental characteristics does establish a pattern for adult interpersonal relationships or whether a general response bias is operating, with all interpersonal relationships judged in response to that bias, so determining associations and suggested links.

Hickie et al. (1990) gave the PBI and the IBM to a group of 136 depressive patients and observed that a correlation matrix showed no link between parental care and partner care ratings and only weak links between parental overprotection and partner control ratings. However, a small group of subjects who gave "very low" parental care ratings (less than 10 for either parent) also returned very poor care ratings for their partners (less than 10). Hickie, Parker, Wilhelm, and Tennant (1991) also gave the PBI and the IBM to 69 nonmelancholic depressives who had been in an intimate cohabiting relationship for at least 12 months. After correlation of the PBI and IBM care ratings, only one significant association was observed: Female patients who gave their mothers high care ratings gave their intimate partner lower care ratings ($r = -0.40$).

Results from both studies by Hickie and colleagues of patients with clinical depression failed to find any apparent link between exposure to anomalous parenting and adverse attachment experiences to an intimate in adulthood, despite a current dysfunctional intimate relationship being associated with a greater risk for nonmeloncholic depression.

The lack of "developmental continuity" observed by Hickie et al. (1990, 1991) is consistent with findings reported by Truant, Herscovitch, and Lohrenz (1987) and Truant, Herscovitch, Donaldson, and Lohrenz (1990). These studies examined the relationship between childhood bonding and separation experiences and quality of marriage for both normative and clinical subjects. First, Truant, Herscovitch, and Lohrenz (1987) examined this issue with 124 general practice patients, tested with a questionnaire package containing the PBI and the Locke–Wallace Short Marital Adjustment Test (see Locke & Wallace, 1959). The authors found that when all subjects were considered, ratings of maternal and paternal care and overprotection on the PBI were not significantly linked with their ratings of marital quality. However, when the variables of "previous marriages" and "emotional illness" were removed from further analyses, significant correlations were observed for a select subgroup. This subgroup consisted mainly of females who had experienced childhood parental separation, and for them, poor marital quality was significantly positively correlated with low PBI care. The authors concluded that their findings reflect an interactive model in which the quality of childhood relationships is associated with (but not necessarily determinant of) the quality of marriages, particularly when poignant adverse experiences (i.e., separation) have occurred and when the effects of separation experiences can be modified by the quality of care before, during, and after the separation.

In a second study (Truant et al., 1990), no associations were found between childhood experiences (as measured by the PBI) and adult marital quality in either the sample of psychiatric outpatients or the sample of general practice patients. Subjects who had experienced a major separation in childhood scored higher on a measure of emotional illness (Crown-Crisp Experimental Index) and were more likely to have experienced a psychiatric illness. Interestingly, the clinical and control groups did not differ in the number of separation experiences they reported, nor did their reports differ significantly in relation to the nature and length of their separation.

CONCLUDING COMMENTS

Overall, investigations into the relationship between childhood experiences and later adult psychopathology suggest that negative parenting styles (unless they involve extreme rejection) will not causally ensure adult emotional and psychiatric dysfunction. Instead, most of the PBI research indicates that anomalous parenting acts by creating a diathesis to some disorders (which may act independently or in conjunction with genetic determinants) and that any such diathesis is susceptible to modification by a range of socialization and interpersonal experiences that have the capacity to "undo" the risk variable. Such a broad conclusion is similar to the view now generally accepted about the later influence of parental death on a young child. For example, Birtchnell (1980) observed that the loss of a mother (through death) during childhood was not on its own associated with later adult psychopathology. Rather, there was a significant association between psychopathology and poor quality of substitute mothering after loss.

Consequently, Birtchnell argued that direct and unmodified causal relationships are unlikely to prevail in the realm of human development.

Similarly, investigations of the relationship between childhood experiences and later social and intimate relationships have illustrated that, overall, the effects of inadequate attachments in childhood are not immutable. The task of the clinician and the researcher is now to pursue identification of those factors that most efficiently reduce the risk of adult psychopathology in those who have experienced significant parental deprivation in their earlier years.

REFERENCES

Alnaes, R., & Torgersen, S. (1990). Parental representations of inpatients with major depression, anxiety disorders and mixed conditions. *Acta Psychiatrica Scandinavica, 81,* 518–522.

Arrindell, W. A., Emmelkamp, P. M. G., Monsma, A., & Brilman, E. (1983). The role of perceived parental rearing practices in the aetiology of phobic disorders: A controlled study. *British Journal of Psychiatry, 143,* 183–187.

Arrindell, W. A., Hanewald, G. J. F. P., & Fold, F. M. (1989). Cross-national constancy of dimensions of parental rearing style: The Dutch version of the Parental Bonding Instrument (PBI). *Journal of Personality and Individual Differences, 10,* 949–956.

Arrindell, W. A., Kwee, M. G. T., Methorst, G. J., Van Der Ende, J., Pol, E., & Moritz, B. J. M. (1989). Perceived parental rearing style of agoraphobics and socially phobic inpatients. *British Journal of Psychiatry, 155,* 526–535.

Arrindell, W. A., Perris, C., Perris, H., Eisemann, M., Van der Ende, J., & Von Knorring, L. (1986). Cross-national invariance of dimensions of parental rearing behavior: Comparisons of psychometric data of Swedish depressives and healthy with Dutch target ratings on the EMBU. *British Journal of Psychiatry, 148,* 305–309.

Birtchnell, J. (1980). Women whose mothers died in childhood: An outcome study. *Psychological Medicine, 10,* 699–713.

Birtchnell, J. (1988). Depression and family relationships—a study of young, married women on a London housing estate. *British Journal of Psychiatry, 153,* 758–769.

Boyce, P. M., & Parker, G. (1989). Development of a scale to measure interpersonal sensitivity. *Australian and New Zealand Journal of Psychiatry, 23,* 341–351.

Brewin, C. R., Firth-Cozens, J., Furnham, A., & McManus, C. (1992). Self-criticism in adulthood and recalled childhood experience. *Journal of Abnormal Psychology, 101,* 561–566.

Calam, R., Waller, G., Slade, P., & Newton, T. (1990). Eating disorders and perceived relationships with parents. *International Journal of Eating Disorders, 9,* 479–485.

Cavedo, L. C., & Parker, G. (1994). Parental Bonding Instrument: Exploring for links between scores and obsessionality. *Social Psychiatry and Psychiatric Epidemiology, 29,* 79–82.

Costello, C. G., & Comrey, A. L. (1967). Scales for measuring depression and anxiety. *Journal of Psychology, 66,* 303–313.

Cubis, J., Lewin, T., & Dawes, F. (1989). Australian adolescents' perceptions of their parents. *Australian and New Zealand Journal of Psychiatry, 23,* 35–47.

Faravelli, C., Panichi, C., Pallanti, S., Grecu, L. M., & Rivelli, S. (1991). Perceptions of early parenting in panic and agoraphobia. *Acta Psychiatrica Scandinavica, 84,* 6–8.

Fichter, M. M., & Noegel, R. (1990). Concordance for bulimia nervosa in twins. *International Journal of Eating Disorders, 9,* 255–263.

Fichter, M. M., Quadflieg, N., & Brandl, B. (1993). Recurrent overeating: An empirical comparison of binge eating disorder, bulimia nervosa, and obesity. *International Journal of Eating Disorders, 14,* 1–16.

Flaherty, J. A., & Richman, J. A. (1986). Effects of childhood relationships on the adult's capacity to form social supports. *American Journal of Psychiatry, 143,* 851–855.

Gamsa, A. (1987). A note on the modification of the Parental Bonding Instrument. *British Psychological Society, 60,* 291–294.

Gerlsma, C., Emmelkamp, P. M. G., & Arrindell, W. A. (1990). Anxiety, depression and perception of early parenting: A meta-analysis. *Clinical Psychology Review, 10,* 251–277.

Gomez, J. (1984). Learning to drink: The influence of impaired psychosexual development. *Journal of Psychosomatic Research, 28,* 403–410.

Gotlib, I. H., Mount, J. H., Cordy, N. I., & Whiffen, V. E. (1988). Depression and perceptions of early parenting: A longitudinal investigation. *British Journal of Psychiatry, 152,* 24–27.

Hafner, R. J. (1988). Obsessive–compulsive disorder: A questionnaire survey of a self-help group. *International Journal of Self Psychiatry, 34,* 310–315.

Henderson, S., Byrne, D. G., & Duncan-Jones, P. (1981). *Neurosis and the social environment.* Sydney: Academic Press.

Henderson, S., Duncan-Jones, P., Bryne, D. G., & Scott, R. (1980). Measuring social relationships: The Interview Schedule for Social Interactions. *Psychological Medicine, 10,* 723–734.

Hickie, I., Parker, G., Wilhelm, K., & Tennant, C. (1991). Perceived interpersonal risk factors of non-endogenous depression. *Psychological Medicine, 21,* 399–412.

Hickie, I., Wilhelm, K., Parker, G., Boyce, P., Hadzi-Pavlovic, D., Brodaty, H., & Mitchell, P. (1990). Perceived dysfunctional intimate relationships: A specific association with the non-melancholic depressive subtype. *Journal of Affective Disorders, 19,* 99–107.

Hinde, R. A. (1979). *Toward understanding relationships.* London: Academic Press.

Howard, J. (1981). The expression and possible origins of depression in male adolescent delinquents. *Australian and New Zealand Journal of Psychiatry, 15,* 311–318.

Joyce, P. R. (1984). Parental bonding in bipolar affective disorder. *Journal of Affective Disorders, 7,* 319–324.

Kendler, K. S., Heath, A., Martin, N. G., & Eaves, L. J. (1986). Symptoms of anxiety and depression in a volunteer twin population. *Archives of General Psychiatry, 43,* 213–221.

Kendler, K. S., Kessler, R. C., Neale, M. C., Heath, A. C., & Eaves, L. J. (1993). The prediction of major depression in women: Toward an integrated etiologic model. *American Journal Psychiatry, 150,* 1139–1148.

Kent, J. S., & Clopton, J. R. (1992). Bulimic women's perceptions of their family relationships. *Journal of Clinical Psychology, 48,* 281–292.

Kitamura, T., & Suzuki, T. (1993). A validation study of the Parental Bonding Instrument in a Japanese population. *Japanese Journal of Psychiatry and Neurology, 47,* 29–36.

Klimidis, S., Minas, I. H., & Ata, A. W. (1992). The PBI-BC: A brief current form of the Parental Bonding Instrument for adolescent research. *Comprehensive Psychiatry, 33,* 374–377.

Klimidis, S., Minas, I. H., Ata, A. W., & Stuart, G. W. (1992). Construct validation in adolescents of the brief current form of the Parental Bonding Instrument. *Comprehensive Psychiatry, 33,* 378–383.

Leigh, I. W., Robins, C. J., Welkowitz, J., & Bond, R. N. (1989). Toward greater understanding of depression in deaf individuals. *American Annals of the Deaf, 134,* 249–254.

Leon, C. A., & Leon, A. (1990). Panic disorder and parental bonding. *Psychiatric Annals, 20,* 503–508.

Locke, H., & Wallace, K. M. (1959). Short marital adjustment and prediction tests: Their reliability and validity. *Marriage and Family Living, 21,* 251–255.

Mackinnon, A. J., Henderson, A. S., & Andrews, G. (1991). The Parental Bonding Instrument: A measure of perceived or actual parental behavior. *Acta Psychiatrica Scandinavica, 83,* 153–159.

Mackinnon, A. J., Henderson, A. S., & Andrews, G. (1993). Parental affectionless control as an antecedent to adult depression: A risk factor refined. *Psychological Medicine, 23,* 135–141.

Merskey, H., Lau, C. L., Russell, E. S., Brooke, R. I., James, M., Laprano, S., Neilsen, J., & Tilsworth, R. H. (1987). Screening for psychiatric morbidity: The pattern of psychological illness and pre-morbid characteristics in four chronic pain populations. *Pain, 30,* 141–157.

Neale, M. C., Walters, E., Heath, A. C., Kessler, R. C., Perusse, D., Eaves, L. J., & Kendler, K. S. (1994). Depression and parental bonding: Cause, consequence, or genetic covariance. *Genetic Epidemiology, 11(6),* 457–461.

Palmer, R. L., Oppenheimer, R., & Marshall, P. D. (1988). Eating-disordered patients remember their parents: A study using the Parental-Bonding Instrument. *International Journal of Eating Disorders, 7,* 101–106.

Parker, G. (1979a). Reported parental characteristics of agoraphobics and social phobics. *British Journal of Psychiatry, 135*, 555–560.

Parker, G. (1979b). Reported parental characteristics in relation to trait depression and anxiety levels in a non-clinical group. *Australian and New Zealand Journal of Psychiatry, 13*, 260–264.

Parker, G. (1981). Parental reports of depressives: An investigation of several explanations. *Journal of Affective Disorders, 3*, 131–140.

Parker, G. (1983a). *Parental overprotection: A rick factor in psychosocial development.* New York: Grune & Stratton.

Parker, G. (1983b). Parental affectionless control as an antecedent to adult depression. *Archives of General Psychiatry, 40*, 956–960.

Parker, G. (1986). Validating an experiential measure of parental style: The use of a twin sample. *Acta Psychiatrica Scandinavica, 73*, 22–27.

Parker, G. (1989). The Parental Bonding Instrument: Psychometric properties reviewed. *Psychiatric Developments, 4*, 317–335.

Parker, G. (1992). Early environment. In E. S. Paykel (Ed.), *Handbook of affective disorders* (pp. 171–183). New York: Churchill Livingstone.

Parker, G. (1993). Parental rearing style: Examining for links with personality vulnerability factors for depression. *Social Psychiatry and Psychiatric Epidemiology, 28*, 97–100.

Parker, G., & Barrett, B. (1988). Perceptions of parenting in childhood and social support in adulthood. *American Journal of Psychiatry, 145*, 479–482.

Parker, G., Barnett, E. A., & Hickie, I. B. (1992). From nurture to network: Examining links between perceptions of parenting received in childhood and social bonds in adulthood. *American Journal of Psychiatry, 149*, 877–885.

Parker, G., Fairley, J. A., Greenwood, J., Jurd, S., & Silove, D. (1982). Parental representations of schizophrenics and their association with onset and course of schizophrenia. *British Journal of Psychiatry, 141*, 573–581.

Parker, G., & Hadzi-Pavlovic, D. (1984). Modification of levels of depression in mother-bereaved women by parental and marital relationships. *Psychological Medicine, 14*, 125–135.

Parker, G., & Hadzi-Pavlovic, D. (1992). Parental representations of melancholic and non-melancholiac depressives: Examining for specificity to depressive types and for evidence of additive effects. *Psychological Medicine, 22*, 657–665.

Parker, G., Hadzi-Pavlovic, D., Greenwald, S., & Weissman, M. (1995). Low parental care as a risk factor to lifetime depression in a community sample. *Journal of Affective Disorder, 33*, 173–180.

Parker, G., Kiloh, L., & Hayward, L. (1987). Parental representations of neurotic and endogenous depressives. *Journal of Affective Disorders, 13*, 75–82.

Parker, G., & Lipscombe, P. (1979). Parental characteristics of Jews and Greeks in Australia. *Australian and New Zealand Journal of Psychiatry, 13*, 225–229.

Parker, G., Tupling, H., & Brown, L. B. (1979). A Parental Bonding Instrument. *British Journal of Medical Psychology, 52*, 1–10.

Plantes, M. M., Prusoff, B. A., Brennan, J., & Parker, G. (1988). Parental representations from depressed outpatients from a U.S. sample. *Journal of Affective Disorders, 15*, 149–155.

Pole, R., Waller, D. A., Stewart, S. M., & Parkin-Feigenbaum, L. (1988). Parental caring versus overprotection in bulimia. *International Journal of Eating Disorders, 7*, 601–606.

Quinton, D., Rutter, M., & Liddle, C. (1984). Institutional rearing, parental difficulties and marital support. *Psychological Medicine, 14*, 107–124.

Rey, J. M., Bird, K. D., Kopec-Schrader, E., & Richards, I. N. (1993). Effects of gender, age and diagnosis on perceived parental care and protection in adolescents. *Acta Psychiatrica Scandinavica, 88*, 440–446.

Richman, J. A., & Flaherty, J. A. (1986). Childhood relationships, adult coping resources and depression. *Social Science and Medicine, 23*, 709–716.

Rodgers, B. (1994). Long term consequences of controlling and uncaring parenting (submitted).

Roe, A., & Siegelman, M. (1963). A parent–child questionnaire. *Child Development, 34*, 355–369.

Russell, J. D., Kopec-Schrader, E., Rey, J. M., & Beumont, P. J. V. (1992). The Parental Bonding Instrument in adolescent patients with anorexia nervosa. *Acta Psychiatrica Scandinavica, 86*, 236–239.

Sarason, B. R., Shearin, E. N., Pierce, G. R., & Sarason, I. G. (1987). Interrelations of social support measures: Theoretical and practical implications. *Journal of Personality and Social Psychology, 52,* 813–832.

Sarason, I. G., Sarason, B. R., & Shearin, E. N. (1986). Social support as an individual difference variable: Its stability, origins and relational aspects. *Journal of Personality and Social Psychology, 50,* 854–855.

Silove, D. (1986). Perceived parental characteristics and reports of early parental deprivation in agoraphobic patients. *Australian and New Zealand Journal of Psychiatry, 20,* 365–369.

Silove, D., Parker, G., Hadzi-Pavlovic, D., Manicavasagar, V., & Blaszczynski, A. (1991). Parental representations of patients with panic disorder and generalised anxiety disorder. *British Journal of Psychiatry, 159,* 835–841.

Steiger H., Van der Feen, J., Goldstein, C., & Leichner, P. (1989). Defence styles and parental bonding in eating-disordered women. *International Journal of Eating Disorders, 8,* 131–140.

Todd, A. L., Boyce, P. M., Heath, A. C., & Martin, N. G. (1994). Shortened versions of the interpersonal sensitivity measure, Parental Bonding Instrument and intimate bond measure. *Journal of Personality and Individual Differences, 16,* 323–329.

Truant, G. S., Donaldson, L. A., Hersovitch, J., & Lohrenz, J. G. (1987). Parental representation in two Canadian groups. *Psychological Reports, 61,* 1003–1008.

Truant, G. S., Herscovitch, J., Donaldson, L. A., & Lohrenz, J. G. (1990). Separation experiences in childhood and adult marital quality. *Canadian Journal of Psychiatry, 35,* 153–157.

Truant, G. S., Herscovitch, J., & Lohrenz, J. G. (1987). The relationship of childhood experience to the quality of marriage. *Canadian Journal of Psychiatry, 32,* 87–92.

Warner, R., & Atkinson, M. (1988). The relationship between schizophrenic patients' perception of their parents and the course of their illness. *British Journal of Psychiatry, 153,* 344–353.

Whisman, M. A., & Kwon, P. (1992). Parental representations, cognitive distortions, and mild depression. *Cognitive Therapy and Research, 16,* 557–568.

Wilhelm, K., & Parker, G. (1988). The development of a measure of intimate bonds. *Psychological Medicine, 18,* 225–234.

Wilhelm, K., & Parker, G. (1990). Reliability of the Parental Bonding Instrument and Intimate Bond Measure scales. *Australian and New Zealand Journal of Psychiatry, 24,* 199–202.

Zung, W. W. K. (1965). A self-rating depression scale. *Archives of General Psychiatry, 12,* 63–70.

10

Compensatory Processes in the Social Networks of Older Adults

KAREN S. ROOK and TONYA L. SCHUSTER

Changes in the composition, functions, or health-related effects of a person's social network can occur at any point in life, but such changes have aroused special interest among gerontologists for several reasons. First, older adults experience many life events and role transitions (e.g., retirement, bereavement, and residential relocation) that lead to network disruptions and reconfigurations (e.g., Lopata, 1979). Second, the financial and physical limitations that some older adults experience tend to restrict their social network involvement. Third, basic aging processes may produce shifts in the motivations for social contact and in preferences for social partners, resulting in a realignment of social network ties (e.g., Carstensen, 1991). Fourth, the onset of chronic health problems in later life may alter the psychosocial and material resources needed from the social network, and this alteration in turn may precipitate transformations in the functions performed by specific network members (e.g., Felton, 1990; Miller & McFall, 1991; Penning, 1990; Stoller & Pugliesi, 1988) and in the extent to which formal service providers become involved to supplement or supplant the efforts of network members (Noelker & Bass, 1989). Fifth, ample theory and research suggest that features of social network involvement have important consequences for human health and well-being (House, Umberson, & Landis, 1988), thus lending some urgency to efforts to understand how older adults respond to changes in their social networks.

For all these reasons, gerontologists have a keen interest in compensatory

KAREN S. ROOK and TONYA L. SCHUSTER • School of Social Ecology, University of California at Irvine, Irvine, California 92717.

Handbook of Social Support and the Family, edited by Gregory R. Pierce, Barbara R. Sarason, and Irwin G. Sarason. Plenum Press, New York, 1996.

processes in older adults' social networks. The notion that older adults' trans-actions with members of their social networks undergo transformations in re-sponse to changing patterns of needs and resources is widely accepted. Moreover, such transformations are generally assumed to play an important role in reducing older adults' vulnerability to adverse mental and physical health outcomes. Yet despite the wide acceptance of these ideas, the literature on compensatory processes in older adults' social networks remains underdeveloped in some re-spects. Terminology is highly variable and inconsistent, with terms that describe theoretically distinct phenomena often used interchangeably. Theoretical models exist that might guide our thinking about these issues, but their implications for social network compensation have rarely been contrasted. Similarly, the methodo-logical approaches that researchers have adopted to examine compensatory processes in older adults' social networks have seldom been examined critically (see Carstensen, Hanson, & Freund, 1995, for a recent exception). The goal of this chapter is to contribute to an integration and evaluation of relevant work on compensatory processes in older adults' social networks. Specifically, we wish to examine theory and empirical evidence that bear on two related issues: (1) how older adults seek to compensate for social network disruptions and losses and (2) the extent to which such efforts succeed in preserving their well-being.

We begin by examining work on the issue of "relationship specialization," or the idea that particular categories of social network members perform particular functions (e.g., Weiss, 1974). Some theorists believe, for example, that older adults' friends and family members provide distinctive kinds of social support, with family members more often providing instrumental support and friends more often providing emotional support and companionship (see the review by Crohan & Antonucci, 1989). Other theorists have proposed different forms of relationship specialization (e.g., Litwak, 1985), while still other theorists question whether such specialization occurs (e.g., Cantor, 1979). These different theoreti-cal positions provide a basis for deriving alternative predictions regarding the nature of older adults' responses to deficiencies in their social networks. If normative patterns of relationship specialization tend to characterize older adults' social networks, they are likely to direct, or even constrain, older adults' efforts to compensate for social network disruptions and losses. For example, older adults' efforts to find substitutes for network members who once provided support may be shaped by prevailing norms regarding who can appropriately be asked to provide emotional support, instrumental support, or companionship. Alternatively, if little normative relationship specialization occurs, then substitu-tion processes may be both less predictable and less constrained.

We will complement this analysis of work that bears on the nature and form of substitution processes with a review of work that bears on the outcomes, or effects, of network substitutions. This review leads us into a consideration of the extent to which older adults' efforts to compensate for network disruptions and losses actually succeed, as gauged by evidence of their apparent effects on emotional or physical health. Thus, two related but distinct kinds of compensatory processes will be distinguished (cf. Backman & Dixon, 1992)—substitution (the "replacement" of missing network ties or functions) and compensation (evidence that the substituted network ties or functions have effects equivalent to those that they replace). The terms "substitution" and "compensation," although often used interchangeably in the literature, represent related but distinct processes (Backman & Dixon, 1992; East & Rook, 1992). Making this distinction provides a framework for organizing the available theory and research and, more important, reminds us that network "replacements" do not necessarily yield the same health-related benefits as the network ties or functions that were missing. We will review contrasting theoretical positions on the possibility of compensatory effects and will examine the scant empirical evidence that bears directly on this issue.

We will consider, as well, two kinds of compensatory processes that do not entail creating new network ties or realigning existing ties. One process involves a psychological redefinition of social needs and aspirations; the other process involves the substitution of nonsocial activities and investments for the missing social activities and ties. Theorists take different positions regarding the viability of such compensatory processes, with some suggesting that such processes seldom can "make up for" significant social deficits or losses and others arguing that at least some degree of compensation may be possible.

Thus, our analysis in the chapter is organized around a set of sequentially related questions: (1) What theories and evidence exist to suggest that normative patterns of relationship specialization characterize older adults' social networks? (2) What do different models of relationship specialization suggest about the kinds of network substitutions that may occur in later life following network disruptions or losses? (3) To what extent do these substitutions actually compensate for missing network ties or functions? (4) To what extent can other processes compensate for missing network ties or functions? A concluding section discusses the methodological approaches that seem most likely to advance our understanding of substitution and compensation processes in older adults' social networks.

A few qualifications should be noted regarding the scope of our review. In discussing substitution and compensation processes in older adults' social networks, we do not presume that all such processes reflect older adults' own initiatives; some may reflect initiatives taken by members of older adults' networks (cf. Salthouse, 1995). The proactive vs. reactive nature of older adults' role in this process may well have important implications (cf. Lawton, 1989), but must await analysis in future work. In addition, most, but not all, of the work we will review has focused on older adults. Some of the theoretical models we discuss, for example, were developed specifically with reference to the elderly, whereas others were developed without reference to a particular age group. We will attempt to make these variations clear as we present relevant work. Finally, we attempt to note throughout the review instances in which the models offered or the empirical evidence reported may not apply to particular subgroups of older adults, but it is doubtful that we have succeeded in doing justice to the enormous heterogeneity that exists in the elderly population. We hope, however, that our efforts to review the existing literature will facilitate more systematic consideration of subgroup variations in future research.

RELATIONSHIP SPECIALIZATION AND SUBSTITUTION
IN THE SOCIAL NETWORKS OF OLDER ADULTS

Considerable empirical evidence suggests that the relationships comprising older adults' informal support systems become specialized in the forms of support they provide. Evidence of relationship specialization is particularly robust in work that has compared the functions performed by older adults' family members and friends. Relationship specialization has been documented in studies that have employed quite diverse measures of relationship functions, ranging from simple measures of the frequency of interaction to specific assessments of emotional support, instrumental support, and companionship. The normative pattern of specialization appears to be one in which older adults' family members provide a broad array of support, while their friends provide everyday companionship and emotional intimacy. Antonucci (1990, p. 214) concluded in a recent review of the literature that "the role of family and friendship support relationships appear to be different, though at times overlapping."

Older adults' family members represent the backbone of the informal support system, particularly with respect to their role in promoting physical health and forestalling institutionalization (e.g., Coe, Wolinsky, Miller, & Prendergast, 1984; Pearlman & Crown, 1992). Yet studies consistently have suggested that friendships contribute more to older adults' morale and psychological well-being than do family relationships (see the reviews by Crohan & Antonucci, 1989; Larson, Mannell, & Zuzanek, 1986; Ward, 1985). In an early demonstration of this surprising pattern, Spakes (1979) found that both the number of close friends and degree of satisfaction with the frequency of friend contacts were related to older adults' life satisfaction, whereas neither of the corresponding measures of family involvement was related to life satisfaction. Similarly, Wood and Robertson (1978) found that involvement (number and frequency of activities) both with grand-children and with friends was significantly related to elderly respondents' life satisfaction, but the association with friend involvement was substantially greater. More generally, evidence suggests that older adults' friends often have positive effects on their well-being and much less often have negative effects, but the opposite seems to be true for family relations (Crohan & Antonucci, 1989).

These paradoxical findings that point to differential effects of family and friend relationships have been interpreted on a largely ad hoc basis (Dean, Kolody, & Wood, 1990). Explanations have focused on differences in companion-ability that presumably arise from fundamental differences between friendship and kinship in voluntarism and homophily. Family and friend relationships in later life appear to be governed by different norms, values, and expectations (Crohan & Antonucci, 1989). Antonucci (Antonucci, 1985; Antonucci & Jackson, 1987) argued that people use different standards to judge these relationships because of the obligatory nature of family relationships and the voluntary nature of friendships. From this perspective, the provision of support by family members constitutes obligatory behavior, which dilutes its positive impact; the failure of family members to provide support represents a failure to meet obligations and therefore evokes negative reactions. The provision of support by friends, in contrast, constitutes more altruistic behavior, which enhances its positive impact; the failure of friends to provide support does not necessarily violate expectations and therefore does not inevitably evoke negative reactions.

Moreover, the voluntary nature of friendships is sustained by and facilitates the mutual gratification that derives from companionate interaction. Larson et al. (1986) provided evidence that friends appear to be most important to older adults as a source of enjoyment and, as such, tend to have their greatest impact on older adults' mood states. Family members contribute to well-being and adaptive functioning in a broader sense. As Adams (1967, p. 70) noted, "It is kin whom you confide in and count on, it is friends whom you enjoy."

Such enjoyment is fostered, as well, by homophily with friends. Older adults' friends tend to be highly homogeneous in terms of age, sex, and (to some extent) socioeconomic status (Crohan & Antonucci, 1989). Friendships in old age thus revolve around common cohort experiences, interests, and lifestyles, as well as an equal ability to exchange assistance. Friends share more in common than do family members and help to embed older persons in a network of ties based on common interests and values. Thus, social integration is an important aspect of friendship support. Lee and Ishii-Kuntz (1987) provided evidence that the effects of loneliness on morale are mediated by feelings of social integration, which suggests another mechanism that may account for the superiority of friends as sources of well-being in later life. Homophily of status and power also contributes to the greater benefit of friend support by avoiding the status asymmetries and feelings of dependency that can be engendered by family support (cf. Rook, 1990). Finally, interaction with peers may represent a critically important context for reaffirming self-worth in old age (Crohan & Antonucci, 1989; Felton & Berry, 1992; Rook, 1990), by providing opportunities for appropriate social comparison as well as opportunities to feel needed and to feel competent in the friend role.

To summarize, most explanations for the differential associations of kinship and friendship with well-being in later life emphasize voluntarism and homophily. These explanations are rich in detail and insightful in their own right, but they cannot adequately account for the full spectrum of relationship specialization that may be present in older adults' informal support networks. Although the distinction between family and friends may lie at the core of most such specialization, more elaborate theoretical models have been developed that subsume this distinction and that specifically address the processes of support network activation and substitution in the changing social networks of older adults. These models are addressed in the following section.

Theoretical Perspectives on Relationship Specialization and Substitution

Theorists hold divergent views regarding the extent and form of relationship specialization that occurs within older adults' social networks. Some theorists believe, for example, that network members can readily perform more or less interchangeable functions, whereas other theorists believe that only certain categories of network members are likely or able to perform particular functions. These differing views, in turn, lead to different predictions regarding the possibility of network replacements or realignments, should disruptions occur in the existing pattern of support exchanges. Some theorists believe that such substitutions are entirely feasible and pose little difficulty; others believe that substitutions may be constrained or even impossible. Those who believe that at least some degree of substitution can occur differ, moreover, regarding the form that such substitutions might take. This section examines the contrasting perspectives of several theorists who have written more extensively about these issues concerned with later life.

Cantor (1979) contrasted four alternative models that describe the processes by which different relationships within older adults' social networks are mobilized for particular needs. Each model grew out of specific assumptions about the extent and nature of relationship specialization that occurs in older adults' social networks and the attendant prospects for substitution of functions within the network. These four models, and a fifth model developed by Weiss (1974), are described below, and their key points of differentiation are summarized in Table 1.

Additive Model. In the additive model, each network member is capable of performing any of a wide range of support tasks that, added together, increase the sum total of support available to an elderly person. Because different types of relationships are functionally equivalent in this model, relationship specialization does not occur. Moreover, substitution does not become an issue, because any network member presumably can take over the tasks formerly performed by another network member.

Asymmetric Model. In contrast, in the asymmetric model, one network member dominates in providing all forms of support; no other network member is involved or considered appropriate. Thus, relationship types are not functionally

Table 1. Theoretical Models of Relationship Specialization and Substitution within Informal Social Networks

Model	Degree of specialization	Basis for specialization	Possibility of substitution
Additive	None	None	Substitution of any network member possible
Assymetric	Complete	None	Quite limited
Hierarchical–compensatory	Modest	Support recipient preferences	Hierarchical substitution possible
Task-specific[a]	Substantial	Efficiency of task performance	Somewhat limited
Functional-specificity	Substantial	Suitability for support provision	Somewhat limited

[a]The task-specific model addresses, as well, specialization and substitution between informal and formal caregivers.

equivalent, relationship specialization is complete in an "all-or-none" sense, and substitution is more problematic.

Neither the additive nor the asymmetric model has received much empirical support.

Hierarchical-Compensatory Model.   The model developed and most preferred by Cantor (1979) is the hierarchical-compensatory model. In this model, the support system is viewed as helping older people to fulfill three critical needs, for companionship, everyday assistance, and crisis assistance (Cantor & Little, 1985). Who provides which types of support in this model is based on the primacy of the relationship between the older person and the social network member, with primary members being preferred as a source of multiple forms of support and companionship. Thus, the degree of relationship specialization is modest in this model because primary network members represent the preferred source of all forms of support. Moreover, these preferences are believed to follow a predictable order, such that kin generally are the most preferred support providers, followed by friends and neighbors, and then by formal organizations (e.g., health care organizations). According to the model, when the initially preferred support provider is absent or inaccessible, other support providers will be chosen as substitutes in an order that follows a normatively defined hierarchy of preferences. This model corresponds fairly closely to a similar model of family support provision to older adults suggested by Shanas (1979), who proposed that support from the family follows a principle of substitution, with the spouse, children, and more distant relatives providing support in serial order.

Task-Specific Model.   In this fourth model, preferences receive minimal attention, and emphasis is placed on the nature of the support tasks to be performed. Litwak and colleagues (Litwak, 1985; Litwak & Figueira, 1968; Dono et al., 1979) argued that the structural aspects of two basic forms of social organization— primary groups and service bureaucracies—influence the particular kinds of tasks that each could perform most effectively. Bureaucratic structures are characterized by technical expertise, whereas primary groups are characterized by diffuse role relations, face-to-face contact (proximity), affectivity, and long-term duration. Bureaucratic structures overall are superior in performing tasks that require technical skills, whereas primary groups are superior in performing tasks that require proximity, ongoing commitment, or face-to-face contact. According to Litwak's task-specific model, each kind of social group will handle most effectively the tasks that match their structurally produced form of competence.

Moreover, the primary groups—kin, friends, neighbors, and spouses—differ in key respects that make them differentially suited to providing particular kinds of support to older adults. The most distinctive feature of kinship, for example, is the permanency of group membership, thus making kin best suited to tasks that involve long-term commitment and intimacy (emotional succor). Friendship is distinguished by its voluntary nature, affectivity, and similarity, thus making friends particularly well suited to providing companionship. The distinctive characteristic of the neighborhood is the geographic proximity of its members, making neighbors well equipped to handle tasks that require face-to-face contact and immediate responses during an emergency. The martial dyad, in contrast, would be characterized as high on all these dimensions (e.g., duration, affectivity, geographic proximity), and it accordingly functions in all task areas, limited only by human resources (such as time, energy, and knowledge). Thus, in the task-specific model, specialization occurs not only between informal support networks and formal service providers but also among the primary groups that comprise the support network.

Litwak addressed the issue of substitution by proposing what he termed "functional substitutability." He suggested that when individuals do not have the full range of primary groups, they may lack some important support services unless they can locate (atypical) groups or relationships that have at least some of the same structural properties as those of the missing primary groups. Thus, in a strict sense, no substitution can occur for tasks that ordinarily flow from a group characterized by particular structural form. A limited possibility of substitution, however, hinges on the availability of a group with a "variant" structure (Litwak's term), which will necessarily have an altered (variant) form of task competence.

This model, like Cantor's hierarchical-compensatory model, has been highly influential in the gerontological literature and has been examined in a number of empirical investigations. This empirical work is discussed in a separate section.

Functional-Specificity Model. Though this related theoretical model was not developed to apply specifically to older adults, it deals comprehensively with the issues addressed by the other models and thus warrants consideration here. Weiss (1974) argued that most research on social relationships has tacitly incorporated the "fund of sociability" assumption, in which relationships are seen as relatively undifferentiated in the resources, or social provisions, they offer. Social interaction, from this perspective, is distributed nonsystematically over a variety of relationships so as to achieve a constant quantity (or fund), with few implications stemming from the pattern of social provisions derived from particular individuals. Weiss contended that empirical evidence largely has failed to support this position.

Weiss offered, as an alternative, the functional-specificity model, in which individuals' requirements for key social provisions can be met only within certain kinds of relationships. Because of this necessary relationship specialization, people require a mix of different relationships in order to obtain the diverse social provisions that are essential to well-being. In Weiss's view, the specialization of relationships is probably always incomplete, but certain types of relationships fairly consistently offer particular provisions.

Weiss proposed that six universal social needs can be met through the provisions of social relationships, with each provision ordinarily derived from a particular type of relationship: (1) attachment, or a sense of security and closeness (provided by the marital relationship or other intimate relationships); (2) social integration, or a cohesive group of relationships that form a basis for shared social activities and interests; (3) opportunity for nurturance, or the opportunity to develop a sense of commitment and to feel needed by nurturing others (as in child-rearing); (4) reassurance of work, or the affirmation of the individual's competence in a social role (e.g., in the role of worker); (5) reliable alliance, or the expectation that assistance will be forthcoming from others when needed (provided primarily by kin); and (6) guidance, or the availability of trustworthy advice in stressful situations.

The absence of an essential relational provision would be signaled by distress that is specific to the missing provision (Weiss, 1973, 1974). For example, the absence of an attachment figure is believed to result in feelings of insecurity, vigilance to threat, and desperate longing. The absence of social integration, in contrast, is believed to produce boredom and feelings of social marginality.

Given the view of Weiss (1973, 1974) that particular social provisions stem most effectively from particular kinds of social relationships, the possibility of substitution is limited. His position is strongest with regard to the need for attachment and the need for social integration. In his view, the anxiety and longing experienced by those who lack an attachment figure cannot be compensated for by participation in group ties (social integration) and, conversely, the boredom and marginality of those who lack group ties cannot be compensated for by an attachment figure. Empirical work on Weiss's model is discussed in a subsequent section.

Overview of Theoretical Perspectives. As indicated in Table 1, these theoretical models reflect different positions on the issue of relationship specialization and offer different predictions about the possibility of substitution should network deficits exist or losses occur. Despite these differences, there are some notable points of overlap among the models.

First, proponents of each model appear to view the marital relationship as performing multiple functions. In Cantor's hierarchy, the marital relationship is not considered separately, but presumably it would be high in primacy and, therefore, would represent a preferred source of most forms of support. In Litwak's model, the marital dyad is viewed as having the structural characteristics necessary to function effectively in performing a variety of support tasks. Similarly, Weiss suggests that the marital relationship may be an exception to the more common tendency for relationships to become specialized in terms of their provisions. More important, although these models share a common focus on the issue of relationship specialization, each model emphasizes different aspects and implications of such specialization. Cantor's hierarchical-compensatory model deals with older adults' *preferences* for who provides support; relationships become "specialized" on the basis of their primacy (or importance) to an older person. Presumably, well-being is enhanced more by provisions that stem from the preferred provider (or from a hierarchically specified substitute) than by those that stem from other sources. Litwak, in contrast, deals with the *efficiency* of informal social networks and formal service providers with regard to specific support tasks; from this perspective, particular categories of support providers can most efficiently perform particular kinds of tasks. Litwak does not clearly specify the outcome of this matching of tasks and primary groups, but more efficient provision of support to older adults presumably leads to better health outcomes, as suggested by a study of longevity conducted by Litwak and Messeri (1989). Unlike Cantor and Litwak, Weiss emphasizes how different social network members function to meet a set of *universal social needs*. Although he is less concerned with specifying precisely who can best satisfy particular needs, he emphasizes that some types of relationships are best suited, or even required, to fulfill some needs. Thus, like Litwak, Weiss sees the relationship specialization that occurs within the network as arising from a match between the type of relationship and the type of need to be met, although this match is not based on structural characteristics that produce efficiency. Well-being, in Weiss's view, is enhanced when all social needs are met.

These models address, as well, the issue of substitutability among relationships, and they suggest notably different predictions regarding the possibility of network substitution and compensation. For Cantor, substitution follows a widely preferred (or normative) hierarchy of kin, nonkin, and formal organizations; older adults turn to the next person in the preference hierarchy if the first choice is not available. For Litwak, in contrast, possibilities for substitution are sharply limited, given that particular support functions can be performed most effectively by groups with well-matched structural characteristics; substitution occurs only in the relatively rare instances when groups with atypical structural features can be identified. Thus, Litwak's model generally predicts that when an older person lacks social network ties with ideal structural characteristics for providing a particular kind of support, that type of support is likely to remain missing. Weiss's position on the possibility of substitution is strongest regarding the needs for attachment and social integration, which usually must be met through, respectively, an intimate relationship and group ties. Weiss acknowledges that overlapping functions are sometimes performed by different network members. In general, however, when a particular type of relationship (such as an attachment figure) is not available, the associated need is likely to remain unfulfilled, resulting in a particular form of emotional distress.

The differentiated roles of specific social network relationships clearly loom large in theorists' efforts to make predictions about relationship specialization and substitution. Given this, it is important to comment on the various reasons for which particular kinds of relationships may be missing in an older adult's social network. A social tie may be absent because it was never formed, such as a spouse among lifelong single people or children among childless individuals. Alternatively, a social tie may exist but may be unavailable as a source of support because of geographic distance, such as when children live far away from parents. Further, a social tie may once have existed but may no longer exist for reasons such as death or residential relocation. Finally, a social network member may no longer be able to perform the support functions that were once performed because of his or her own life circumstances or because the older person's support needs have become overwhelming. In such cases, the social tie itself is intact, but specific support functions cannot be fulfilled. Given that social network substitution is a dynamic process, our analysis in the sections that follow concentrates on older adults' responses to the *loss* of network ties or functions or both. As Connidis and Davies (1990) noted, it makes little sense to discuss the issue of substitution among individuals who never had a particular kind of social tie. This does not mean that the networks of the never married, for example, are static or less resourceful than those of other individuals (cf. Connidis & Davies, 1990). Because our interest is in understanding the processes by which older adults may seek to replace missing network ties or functions, we will focus our discussion, where the existing research permits us to do so, on older adults whose social networks once included such ties or functions.

Empirical Work on Specialization and Substitution

Our discussion of empirical work on specialization and substitution in older adults' social networks is organized in terms of the contrasting theoretical models we reviewed above. We begin by reviewing studies that have examined the hierarchical-compensatory model, the task-specific model, or the functional-specificity model. Then we turn to studies that have attempted to compare these different models.

As will become apparent, researchers have used somewhat different criteria and assessment approaches for drawing inferences about specialization and substitution. We provide a brief overview of these inferential strategies before describing specific studies. Cantor, as noted earlier, believed that support providers function as "generalists" rather than "specialists." She was therefore less interested in specialization than in substitution (or what she termed "compensation"). This orientation led Cantor to emphasize older adults' preferences for support providers. Evidence that these preferences followed the predicted hierarchical order was interpreted as indicating that substitution is possible and occurs in an orderly fashion. Others have reasoned that if substitutions follow a predictable hierarchy and are stimulated by the absence of a typically preferred support provider, then unmarried older adults should rely on different support providers than do married older adults (e.g., Connidis & Davies, 1990; Dykstra, 1993; Peters, Hoyt, Babchuk, Kaiser, & Iijima, 1987). Researchers similarly have tested Cantor's notion of hierarchical substitution by comparing older adults who have no children with those who have children (e.g., Connidis & Davies, 1992). If the patterns of support provision differ between these groups, substitution is inferred to have occurred. The latter kind of comparison addresses substitution in the context of presumed network deficits, rather than network losses per se.

Unlike Cantor, Litwak believed that specialization does occur and approached this issue by assessing who performed which support tasks for older adults, irrespective of their preferences. Litwak held little hope for substitution if structurally qualified primary groups were unavailable to provide specific kinds of support, and he accordingly searched for evidence that the tasks ordinarily performed by one kind of relationship cannot readily be assumed by another kind of relationship.

Much of the empirical work on Weiss's functional-specificity model has been conducted with young adults, but those studies that have been conducted with older adults generally have examined predictions about relationship specialization by examining whether particular social network members more often function as sources of certain social provisions than do other network members. This work, like work that has examined Litwak's perspective, has emphasized who actually provides various types of support, regardless of the elderly support recipient's preferences.

We will discuss the implications of these different empirical strategies in a subsequent section. For example, although substitution is a dynamic process that can best be evaluated through longitudinal designs, most studies of substitution have made use of cross-sectional designs.

Empirical Work on the Hierarchical-Compensatory Model.   The initial empirical evidence for Cantor's hierarchical-compensatory model was derived from a study of 1552 elderly inner city residents of New York (Cantor, 1979). The elderly individuals were asked to indicate to whom they would turn (other than a spouse) for instrumental and emotional support in ten hypothetical scenarios that posed various problems and needs. In almost all scenarios, respondents preferred kin (particularly children) over other network members, even when there was no evidence of a current relationship between the respondents and their kin (as reflected in low rates of contact or great geographic distance). The one area in which a substantial proportion of the elderly respondents indicated that they would turn to friends or neighbors as readily as to kin was for relief from loneliness. Additionally, among respondents without children, friends and neighbors emerged as the single most important sources of support, followed by other relatives, and then by "no one."

On the basis of these data, Cantor concluded that only when family members, particularly children, are unavailable do friends, neighbors, and other sources of support (e.g., formal organizations) become important, and this substitution occurs only for certain well-defined tasks (such as providing companionship and short-term emergency service). Even though friends and neighbors play a significant role in providing relief from loneliness and in providing emergency aid, Cantor concluded that their most important function is to serve as substitutes when kin and children are not available.

Chatters, Taylor, and Jackson (1986) replicated Cantor's initial findings in a nationally representative sample of older African-Americans. In this sample, kin (children) were generally nominated before friends as preferred support providers. Although this study did not examine ethnic differences, it is in line with the few available studies that have revealed similarities across ethnic groups in patterns of relationship specialization (e.g., Cantor, 1979; Litwak, 1985).

Empirical Work on the Task-Specific Model.   Litwak (1985) tested his model with data from a 1978 survey of 1818 older adults, about one fourth of whom resided in institutional settings and three fourths in noninstitutional settings in

New York or Florida. The study revealed that different primary groups (neighbors, friends, modified extended family, spouses) typically did provide the types of services and support (such as watching the house, providing companionship, providing care during illness, and housecleaning) that corresponded to their hypothesized structural competence. Litwak also presented evidence that substitutability for each of these tasks was limited. Thus, in this sample, older people who lacked a particular type of primary group were much more likely than those who had ties to the particular primary group to lack the corresponding type of service or support. For example, many more respondents without friends (45%) reported having no one with whom to share leisure activities than did respondents with friends (10%). Substitution appeared to be possible only when the older person could locate an atypical group with the same structural characteristics as the missing primary group. For example, although Litwak did not consistently differentiate children from other kin in his analyses, he did find that other kin were significantly more likely to provide certain services for older adults who did not have children or whose children were unavailable than were other kin of older adults whose children were available.

Empirical Work on the Functional-Specificity Model. An extensive test of Weiss's model with an elderly sample was conducted by Simons (1983, 1984), who focused on three key social needs, for assistance/security, intimacy, and reassurance of worth. Data from a survey of 299 aged persons living in the Midwest yielded a number of findings that supported Weiss's predictions about specialization. Relationships with spouses and children (but not with siblings, friends, or groups) were related to feelings of security. Having a confidant relationship (with a spouse or close friend) was associated with less loneliness, but social interaction with adult children and siblings was unrelated to loneliness. Feelings of uselessness were inversely related to the frequency of group participation and contact with friends, but were unrelated to contact with others. Thus, this study offered some evidence of relationship specialization insofar as contact with kin and contact with nonkin appeared to offer different psychological benefits to the elderly study participants.

A comparison of the distinctive roles of kin vs. nonkin formed the central focus of another recent study of Weiss's functional-specificity model (Felton & Berry, 1992). The researchers assessed who provided each of six types of social support to 82 elderly residents of New York City. They found that kin and nonkin were equally important as sources of attachment, reassurance of worth, and reliable alliance, but were differentially important as sources of other types of social support. Kin, for example, more often provided guidance and opportunities for nurturance, whereas nonkin more often provided companionship. These findings thus support the view that at least some degree of relationship specialization occurs in older adults' social networks.

Felton and Berry (1992) investigated, further, whether receiving support from particular sources had psychological consequences, as hypothesized by Weiss (1974). These researchers found that most types of social support were valuable to the elderly respondents, regardless of their source. Nevertheless, some distinctive effects emerged. Reassurance of worth appeared to contribute more to well-being when provided by nonkin than when provided by kin, whereas instrumental assistance appeared to contribute more to well-being when provided by kin than when provided by nonkin. Thus, the findings of Felton and Berry (1992) suggested that older people feel better when kin meet their instrumental needs and friends meet their emotional needs: "The data give us no reason to think that [Cantor's] substitution hierarchy dictates, for all social support functions, what sources of support will be most satisfying" (p. 96). The findings raise the possibility that esteem-enhancing forms of social support are more valuable when derived from nonkin and that stress-reducing forms of support are more valuable when provided by kin. The authors expand on Crohan and Antonucci (1989) to suggest "that family are most likely to perform, and are best at performing, compensatory functions or functions that offset stressful circumstances and the negative emotions that tend to accompany them, whereas nonkin are best at enhancing esteem and are more likely than kin to do so" (p. 96).

Studies Comparing Alternative Models. The evidence on specialization and substitution that emerged from these studies hinges not only on the way that the researchers conceptualized these processes but also on the manner in which support functions were assessed. For example, Cantor assessed who would be tapped most often as a source of support (thus emphasizing the frequency of support provision by different network members), whereas Litwak focused on the type of support provided by different network members (thus emphasizing type rather than amount of support provided). Such conceptual and methodological differences make it difficult to compare the empirical evidence for each model.

Despite these difficulties, some researchers have undertaken comparative studies. For example, several researchers have attempted to compare Cantor's and Litwak's models. Not surprisingly, such studies find evidence for and against both models (e.g., Penning, 1990; Peters et al., 1987; Seeman & Berkman, 1988). All these studies took the approach of evaluating who provided which types of support to the elderly participants—the "who" and "what" aspects of support provision highlighted by Cantor, Litwak, and Weiss. Spouses, children, and then friends consistently emerge as the most frequent sources of support in this empirical work, as Cantor would predict on the basis of the hierarchy of preferences. This work does not necessarily favor Cantor's model over others, however, because most studies have yielded evidence, as well, that different network members often perform different support tasks or functions, as both Litwak and Weiss would predict. Thus, with regard to the issue of relationship specialization, the comparative studies do not conclusively favor one model over the others.

Connidis and Davies (1990) sought to integrate Cantor's hierarchical-compensatory model and Litwak's task-specific model by developing predictions about who served as confidants vs. companions in a sample of 400 older adults. Their findings were consistent with the task-specific model in that spouses and friends performed somewhat different tasks, with spouses more often serving as confidants and friends more often serving as companions. Subgroup comparisons based on marital and parental status revealed a number of differences in who provided companionship and confidant support. Among never-married older adults, friends alone served as companions, whereas among married older adults with children, both the spouse and friends served as companions. The unmarried women were unique in their reliance on siblings as both companions and confidants.

In a subsequent study, Connidis and Davies (1992) compared widowed elderly parents to married elderly parents and found that friends, other relatives, and children are more likely to serve as confidants of widowed parents than of married parents. A similar pattern of substitution for the role of companion appeared to occur if the widowed parents' children lived nearby: "Significant differences between the widowed and the married suggested that the previously married substitute the loss of a spouse with children and friends for confiding, and with children, friends, and other relatives for companionship" (p. 120).

Analyses of patterns of support provision in a sample of 160 older adults revealed that spouses provided the most emotional and instrumental support, followed by children, friends, siblings, and other relatives (Peters et al., 1987). This order is consistent with the notion of a preference hierarchy, although other studies have failed to find evidence of such a hierarchical ordering (e.g., Dykstra, 1993). Moreover, further analyses within these categories of social network members also yielded evidence consistent with the task-specific model in that the extent of assistance provided varied with the particular tasks involved.

Mixed evidence has emerged regarding hierarchical substitution (or the compensatory component of Cantor's model). Peters et al. (1987) found that unmarried older adults received no more support from children than did married older adults, a finding that they construed as challenging Cantor's model. Group differences in support receipt as a function of marital status or parental status have failed to emerge in several other studies as well (Connidis & Davies, 1992; Dykstra, 1993; Penning, 1990). For example, Dykstra (1993) assessed the support provided by close network members in a sample of 165 older adults in the Netherlands and compared cohabiting older adults and never-married older adults to determine whether the supportiveness of particular relationships varies with the presence or absence of a spouselike relationship. The results indicated that the never married did not receive more support from siblings, other relatives, or friends than did the cohabiting. Johnson and Troll (1992) similarly found little evidence that older adults who do not have children obtain support from other relatives.

Seeman and Berkman (1988) incorporated both Cantor's hierarchical-compensatory and Weiss's functional-specificity models in a large community sample of older adults. In a challenge to Cantor's views regarding the primacy of particular support providers, comparisons of specific types of ties showed that neither spouses nor children represented the primary sources of emotional or instrumental support. Ties with children, for example, were most strongly related to aspects of instrumental support, whereas ties with close friends and relatives were more strongly related to aspects of emotional support. This pattern of specialization is more consistent with Litwak's task-specific model. Further analyses, however, suggested that support provision varied as a function of the older

adults' marital status in a manner that was consistent with Cantor's notion of
compensatory substitution. The results of this study thus are consistent with some
aspects of both the hierarchical-compensatory and the task-specific models.

The results discussed thus far are based on cross-sectional studies and so
provide only a snapshot of substitution processes that may follow network disruptions and losses, such as bereavement or retirement. Ferraro (1984), in his review
of widowhood and social participation in later life, noted considerable overall
stability in social participation, even though older widowed persons "experience a
shifting or realignment of relationships" (p. 464) that favors what he calls a
compensation model. Stylianos and Vachon (1993) recently completed a thorough review of the role of social support in bereavement, including longitudinal
evidence. They concluded on the basis of a variety of studies that although family
(especially child) support is crucial in the initial stages of bereavement, friends
(frequently new friends) become increasingly important as an individual adapts to
the new role of widowed person. The relatively greater importance of friends, as
well as children, to the widowed does not correspond to Cantor's hierarchy.

Overview of Empirical Work on Specialization and Substitution.

The evidence
we have reviewed suggests that some degree of specialization occurs in older
adults' relationships, but offers fewer insights about the consequences of specialization. Despite Cantor's premise that the support network is directed toward
fulfilling critical needs, she presented no evidence on the efficacy of her hypothesized pattern of specialization, and despite Litwak's emphasis on "efficiency," he
presented no evidence on the efficacy of his task-specific pattern of specialization.
Weiss's model invites more explicit attention to implications for well-being in that
he predicts better psychological outcomes for certain patterns of relationship
specialization than for others. Modest evidence supports Weiss's view that patterns
of relationship specialization have implications for well-being (e.g., Dean et al.,
1990; Felton & Berry, 1992; Simons, 1983/1984), and as noted earlier, a larger body
of evidence (not guided by these theoretical models) suggests that interactions
with kin vs. friends exhibit dissimilar associations with well-being in later adulthood (e.g., Arling, 1976; Elwell & Maltbie-Crannell, 1981; Larson et al., 1986; Wood
& Robertson, 1978). The extent to which different patterns of relationship specialization affect well-being in later life and the reasons for such effects warrant
greater empirical attention, as does the central issue of how patterns of relationship specialization may influence substitution processes following a network
disruption or loss.

With respect to the empirical evidence on substitution, Cantor's hierarchy of
preferences is upheld only in the ordering of most frequent support providers,
while Litwak's task-specific model is upheld more generally. Although the literature is not altogether consistent, most evidence suggests that the patterns of
support provision to married vs. unmarried older adults do not differ substantially, with the exception of support from children. Thus, across studies, alternative configurations of support activation in line with the hierarchy suggested by
Cantor emerge infrequently. Among widowed older adults, support from both

children, and perhaps even more importantly from friends, appears to increase following the death of the spouse. Nevertheless, the ordering of this substitution does not correspond neatly to Cantor's hierarchical-compensatory model.

In evaluating the evidence for substitution in older adults' informal social networks, it is important to bear in mind that researchers' strategies for assessing social support and services strongly influence the conclusions that emerge. An emphasis on the source of support, without a corresponding emphasis on the quantity or quality of support, may exaggerate the evidence of substitution. Johnson and Catalano (1983) noted that, as compared with the support provided by spouses and adult children, the support provided by more distant relatives is often more perfunctory. The perfunctory quality of such support will be missed in measures that emphasize only the source of support. Similarly, reports of social contact and instrumental assistance tell us little about the extent to which older adults' needs for expressive forms of support are met (Johnson & Catalano, 1983). Johnson and her colleagues (Johnson, 1983; Johnson & Catalano, 1983) argued, further, that many researchers appear to assume that older adults derive social contact and aid through interactions with social network members that are largely positive in nature. Yet transactions involving aid, particularly long-term aid, hold the potential for strain and conflict, including the resurrection of long-dormant interpersonal problems (Johnson, 1983; Johnson & Catalano, 1983). The potential for conflict increases as more distant family members (e.g., nieces, nephews) are called upon to take over the support functions previously performed by others, with the costs of such arrangements sometimes exceeding the rewards (Johnson, 1983). Thus, without careful consideration of our assessment strategies, we may greatly overestimate both the extent and the adequacy of substitutions that occur in older adults' social networks.

SPECIALIZATION AND SUBSTITUTION
BETWEEN INFORMAL AND FORMAL CAREGIVERS

Our central aim in this chapter is to consider specialization and substitution processes in older adults' informal social networks. Such networks, however, do not represent the sole source of needed support and services in later life. Considerable interest has focused on the links between informal and formal support providers. Formal sources of care become particularly important in discussions of provision of support to older adults who are frail or childless or both (e.g., Choi, 1994). For this reason, we undertake a brief discussion of theoretical views on the nature of the links between informal and formal caregivers. The questions we examined in the preceding section have direct parallels here—specifically, to what extent do informal and formal caregivers specialize in providing different kinds of support to older adults and to what extent can formal caregivers substitute for informal caregivers in providing support? Noelker and Bass (1989) contrasted five theoretical models that provide somewhat different answers to these questions. We rely heavily upon their analysis in laying out alternative theoretical models here. Five models are described below, one of which (Litwak's task-specific model) was discussed earlier in a different context. Key dimensions on which these models differ are summarized in Table 2.

Kin Independence Model

The kin independence model describes an arrangement in which kin caregivers attempt to meet an older person's needs for support without the involvement of formal service providers; that is, kin caregivers function independently of formal caregivers (Noelker & Bass, 1989). Evidence suggests that family members provide the vast majority of the assistance given to elderly individuals and that relatively few of these families make use of formal service providers (e.g., Stone, Cafferata, & Sangl, 1987). Noelker and Bass (1989) investigated the patterns of informal and formal caregiving in a sample of 519 families in which an older person was receiving care. They found that 42% of the families exhibited a pattern of caregiving that conformed to the kin independence model. Noelker and Bass (1989) did not address whether kin caregivers and formal caregivers specialize in providing fundamentally different forms of support, but they presumably view the possibilities for substitution as limited in this model because they contrasted it with a substitution model (discussed below).

Supplementation Model

The supplementation model refers to those situations in which informal caregivers (typically spouses and family members) turn to formal caregivers (e.g., visiting nurses, homemaker services, home meal delivery services) to provide additional assistance with or respite from tasks that are emotionally or physically draining. The formal caregivers thus supplement the efforts of informal caregivers rather than provide specialized services (Noelker & Bass, 1989). Because the

Table 2. Theoretical Models of Task Specialization and Substitution between Informal and Formal Caregivers

Model	Basis for specialization	Degree of specialization	Possibility of substitution
Kin independence	Not addressed	Not addressed	Limited
Supplementation	None	None	Substitution of formal caregiver for informal caregiver possible
Substitution	Not addressed	Not addressed	Substantial
Supervision	Not addressed	Not addressed	Not applicable
Task-specific[a]	Efficiency of task performance	Substantial	Limited

[a]The task-specific model addresses, as well, specialization and substitution within older adults' informal social networks.

two kinds of caregivers perform essentially the same tasks, relationship specialization is absent and substitution should be feasible. This model has received some empirical support, although it appears to be less common than other models that describe the links between informal and formal caregiving systems (Noelker & Bass, 1989).

Substitution Model

According to the substitution model, formal caregivers will substitute for family members in providing needed services under certain conditions (Noelker & Bass, 1989). As in Cantor's hierarchical-compensatory model, such substitution usually occurs when the family is unavailable to perform the needed support tasks or when family ties do not exist. Noelker and Bass (1989) questioned this model, noting that family members often supervise and subsidize the work of the formal caregivers rather than relinquish their support-providing role entirely (see Archbold, 1982). Modified forms of substitution have been documented in some studies, with service providers taking over at least some tasks that family members cannot perform but sharing other tasks with family members (Noelker & Bass, 1989). Somewhat greater evidence of substitution emerges when elderly individuals who have no spouse or children are contrasted with elderly individuals who have these family ties; formal service use tends to be greater among the former group (Cicirelli, 1981) (though see Choi, 1994).

Supervision Model

Family members sometimes function as supervisors of service provision by formal caregivers (Logan & Spitze, 1994; Noelker & Bass, 1989), as Sussman (1977) observed two decades ago when he pointed out that family members often play an important role in mediating older adults' transactions with complex service bureaucracies, such as Medicare or Social Security. The notion that family members often help to procure or supervise services for older adults has enjoyed a good deal of popularity, but has a modest empirical base. Noelker and Bass (1989) noted in this regard that empirical evidence suggests that family members appear to obstruct older adults' access to services at least as often as they facilitate such access.

Task-Specific Model

As noted earlier, the task-specific model of Litwak and colleagues (Litwak, 1985; Litwak & Figueira, 1968; Dono et al., 1979) postulates that informal and formal caregivers have different kind of expertise and accordingly perform different kinds of support functions. Thus, the informal and formal caregiving systems represent dual realms of specialization and can be viewed as providing complementary services (Litwak & Szelinyi, 1969; Noelker & Bass, 1989). This model has received a fair amount of empirical support.

Overview of Models

As Table 2 indicates, these models offer somewhat different predictions about the extent to which informal and formal caregivers perform specialized support functions for older adults, although the models are less clear about the bases for specialization. They also offer different predictions about the possibility that formal caregivers can substitute for informal caregivers in performing particular support functions. Empirical work designed to test competing models is sparse, although studies that examine individual models can be identified. Moreover, as has been true of investigations of the theoretical models that describe specialization and substitution within older adults' informal social networks, investigations of the models discussed here may be unlikely to yield evidence that clearly favors one model over another. Older adults' transactions with informal support providers and formal caregivers may be characterized by a hybrid mix of models, and as Noelker and Bass (1989) have noted, different models may be ascendant at different points in time in an older person's life.

Efforts to integrate the models presented in Tables 1 and 2 seem well worthwhile, although such an integration is beyond the scope of this chapter. For example, the kin independence model in Table 2 might be elaborated by merging it with the hierarchical-compensatory model in Table 1 to develop predictions about the order in which kin (e.g., adult children, siblings, other relatives) would be likely to assume responsibility for providing support to an elderly family member. Similarly, some of the models in Table 1 could be elaborated by merging them with models in Table 2 to accommodate the possibility that the onset of significant disability and other changes over time can cause an older person's needs to exceed the support-giving capacity of the informal network, thereby increasing the likelihood that informal caregivers will attempt to enlist the assistance of formal caregivers.

A further refinement of the models presented in Tables 1 and 2 would involve efforts to make predictions about specialization and substitution not only between but also within broad categories of caregivers, such as informal vs. formal service providers or family vs. friends. Most of the models in these tables treat the potential caregivers within these broad categories as essentially interchangeable. For example, friends who might be available to provide some of the companionship once provided by a spouse are treated as functionally equivalent, even though one friend might be much better suited than another to this task. Clear differences may exist, as well, among an older adult's children with respect to their capacity and readiness to perform important support functions. Support from formal service providers may be preferable, in some cases, to support from particular members of older adults' informal support networks. Yet attention to these differences within as well as between broad categories of potential supporters appears to be largely absent from the theoretical models outlined in Tables 1 and 2.

The extent to which formal service providers and organizations (e.g., churches, senior citizen centers) function, independently or in conjunction with informal social networks, to meet the support needs of elderly individuals is likely to assume increased importance in future years, as the number of older adults who are unmarried, childless, or very old continues to grow (Choi, 1994). In seeking to understand the potential links between formal and informal caregiving, we must be careful to avoid assuming that a low level of formal service use means that informal caregivers are meeting all support needs; a low level of formal service use can coincide with a low level of informal caregiving. In addition, we should not assume that efforts to substitute formal services for missing informal services emerge in an uncomplicated fashion from the simple recognition that needed forms of support are missing. Knowledge of the array of available services, attitudes about the appropriateness of using such services, and sociodemographic factors influence the receptivity of older adults and their family members to formal service provision (Choi, 1994). We should be careful, as well, not to assume that formal services make the same contribution to older adults' well-being as the informal services they have come to replace. The issue of compensatory effects is addressed in the next section.

COMPENSATION

Theoretical Perspectives on Compensation

The work discussed thus far has examined theoretical perspectives and empirical work on the possibility of "substitutions" in response to disruptions or losses in older adults' social networks, but it did not address the critically important question of whether such substitutions actually succeed in preserving older adults' well-being. Few theorists have written about the issue of compensation in the context of older adults' social ties (though see Carstensen, Hanson, & Freund, 1995; Ferraro & Farmer, 1995), perhaps because researchers often simply assume that network substitutions do have compensatory effects (Backman & Dixon, 1992). Indeed, we found it difficult to locate formal theoretical positions on this issue, but we can contrast several different kinds of compensatory processes that might follow the disruption or loss of social network ties in later life. We describe these processes briefly and discuss several different methodological strategies that researchers have used (or could use) in their search for compensatory effects.

Compensation via Establishment of New Ties or Realignment of Existing Ties. First, as most of our analysis has suggested, older adults may respond to social network disruptions or losses by seeking to develop new social ties or to realign existing social ties. For example, an older person who has lost a close friend because of the friend's death or residential relocation may seek to compensate either by establishing a new friendship or by seeking to obtain additional support and companionship from existing friendships. In suggesting this possibility, we do not wish to imply that long-term relationships, such as long-term friendships or marital relationships, can be "replaced" by other social ties (cf. Kahn and Antonucci's view of the difficulty of replacing long-term, core network members [Kahn &

Antonucci, 1980]). A close relationship that has spanned many decades—prototypic of many of the close relationships of the elderly—not only may have evolved idiosyncratic interaction patterns and satisfactions that cannot easily be replicated but also may serve as a repository of shared memories and experiences that cannot be duplicated (Baumeister & Leary, 1995). Thus, the meaning and personal significance of such long-term relationships go well beyond what might be suggested by everyday exchanges of support and companionship. Nonetheless, evidence suggests that older adults do seek to reorganize their social lives following a network loss (e.g., Bankoff, 1981; Ferraro, Mutran, & Barresi, 1984; Stylianos & Vachon, 1993), and the creation of new social ties or modification of existing ties may help to preserve well-being (Morgan, 1988). This buttressing of well-being, even if imperfect, can be construed as a form of compensation.

Compensation via Redefinition of Social Needs or Aspirations. Implicit in the discussion of compensation thus far is the notion that older adults' social needs and aspirations remain essentially unchanged following a social network disruption or loss. Yet it is plausible that, for some older adults, a reassessment of social needs may occur after such network changes. For some, this may entail a psychological redefinition of personal needs for companionship and support. Well-being would be preserved in this fashion not by creating new social ties or reconfiguring existing ties, but rather by modifying one's social aspirations so as to narrow the gap between aspirations and opportunities (or between aspirations and resources). In other literatures, this has been referred to as an accommodative strategy of coping (Brandstadter & Renner, 1990) or a form of secondary control (Heckhausen & Schulz, 1995). This process of redefining needs and aspirations may be stimulated, in part, by lack of success in efforts to change the situation (Brandtstater & Renner, 1990). For example, a lonely older person who has tried unsuccessfully to find new companions or to increase contacts with existing companions may be compelled at some point to accept more modest aspirations for companionship.

Weiss (1974) has questioned whether such a psychological redefinition of social needs actually can preserve well-being in the face of a true network deficit. He suggested that lonely individuals rarely succeed in alleviating the distress of loneliness by attempting to define away their needs for social contact. Baumeister and Leary (1995) similarly concluded from an extensive review of work on the adaptive significance of social bonds that the need for strong, stable social bonds is universal and fundamental to human functioning, with undesirable consequences stemming from deprivation of this need. Denial of this need, in their view, is difficult.

Other theorists, however, have noted that shifts in the desire or motivations for social contact may be relatively common in later adulthood. Carstensen (1991), for example, has argued that the salience of particular motivations for social contact changes in later adulthood, leading older adults to restrict their social contacts to those that offer the greatest prospects for emotional rewards. In Carstensen's view, this voluntary reduction of social contact that reflects increased selectivity in the choice of interaction partners is adaptive rather than problematic for older adults. In a related vein, other work has suggested that the tendency to adjust personal goals as a means of coping with losses and obstacles increases across the life course (Brandtstater & Renner, 1990). Given that such age-related tendencies may exist, it is plausible that some older adults compensate for network losses by reevaluating their social needs and desires.

Compensation via Development of New Nonsocial Activities or Renewal of Existing Nonsocial Activities.   Another kind of compensatory process that might follow a social network loss involves establishing new nonsocial activities and pastimes or renewing existing pastimes. Whether nonsocial activities can compensate for social activities has been debated occasionally in the literature on loneliness (e.g., Rook & Peplau, 1982; Young, 1982), without much consensus. It is clear, however, that such nonsocial activities can help to elevate mood and, indeed, have been prescribed as a component of some treatments for depression (e.g., Lewinsohn & Amenson, 1978). Some older adults, therefore, may seek to compensate for social network losses by increasing their involvement in gratifying nonsocial activities. For example, an older person whose social network has shrunk considerably and who lacks promising opportunities for establishing or renewing social ties may turn to hobbies, reading, or other solitary activities that provide alternative satisfactions. Nonsocial "substitutions," in this sense, are conceptually analogous to the social "substitutions" discussed earlier.

Overview of Alternative Perspectives.   These different perspectives highlight three different strategies that older adults might use, singly or in combination, to compensate for deficiencies in their social networks. The strategies are not exhaustive, but they illustrate that compensatory activities take a variety of different forms. The strategies we have discussed vary, for example, in their emphasis on behavioral vs. cognitive processes and in their emphasis on social vs. nonsocial domains. Older adults' choice of strategies may mirror their choice of coping strategies in other life contexts or may be constrained by aspects of their current life situation, such as their health or financial resources (Ferraro et al., 1984; Morgan, 1988).

By invoking the term "strategies," we do not wish to imply that older adults necessarily pursue any of these activities in a conscious or planful way, although they may do so at times. Some compensatory behaviors that occur in response to social network disruptions or losses may occur without deliberation or even awareness (Dixon & Backman, 1995; Salthouse, 1995). For example, an elderly individual who has become lonely after a good friend moved away may attempt to extend contacts with neighbors and casual acquaintances in a largely unconscious effort to replace some of the companionship that has been lost. Thus, much, but not all, compensatory behavior is likely to be planful (Backman & Dixon, 1992). Nor do we wish to imply that these strategies necessarily yield beneficial outcomes. Compensatory behaviors are not always successful (Carstensen et al., 1995; Dixon & Backman, 1992), and the lack of success may itself require an adaptive response

(Dixon & Backman, 1992). Compensatory activities and compensatory outcomes represent logically related but nonetheless distinct phenomena (Backman & Dixon, 1992). Whether compensatory activities have beneficial effects is an empirical question that requires a convincing methodological approach.

Empirical Work on Compensation

Most of the empirical work that has sought to examine compensatory processes and outcomes in older adults' social networks has focused on social substitutions for network deficits or losses. Thus, our discussion cannot shed much light on compensation that occurs through the psychological redefinition of social needs or through investment in nonsocial activities. Moreover, the body of work on the effects of compensatory processes in older adults' social networks is small, because few of the studies that have analyzed specialization or substitution have included an outcome measure. Those that have, however, illustrate somewhat different approaches to this issue.

Cross-Sectional Approaches.   Cross-sectional approaches to this issue have been most common among the relatively few studies that have assessed compensatory effects empirically. One cross-sectional approach has involved comparing the well-being of those who have sustained a network loss *and* who (presumably) have established a "replacement" tie with those who have not sustained a network loss. If no group differences in well-being exist, then the "replacement" tie can be inferred to have compensated for the lost tie (cf. East & Rook, 1992). This approach takes what might be described as a strong position on compensation, in that compensation is viewed as having occurred only when people who have sustained a network loss fare as well on some outcome of interest (e.g., depression or loneliness) as do people who have not sustained a loss.

The second cross-sectional approach reflects a more moderate position on compensation. This approach focuses only on those who have sustained a network loss and examines whether, within this group, those who have established a "replacement" tie fare better than those who have not established a replacement tie. This approach allows for the possibility that, overall, those who have sustained a network loss may continue to be worse off than those who have not sustained a network loss. A partial degree of compensation can be inferred if the replacement ties boost the well-being of those in the loss group. These strong and moderate positions on compensation are conceptually analogous to the strong and moderate versions of the social support–stress buffering hypothesis that have been discussed widely in the literature on life stress (cf. Cohen & Wills, 1985).

A study by Dykstra (1993) illustrates this second cross-sectional approach to compensation. Dykstra (1993) examined whether the association between loneliness and the level of support provided by others varied according to the availability of a partner. She found that among the divorced or widowed, greater support from children and friends was significantly related to less loneliness. Among those who were living with a partner, neither support from friends nor support from children predicted loneliness (after the portion of variance accounted for by the partner was controlled). Dykstra (1993) concluded that emotional support from children and friends compensated for the support provided by the lost spouse among formerly married older adults.

Simons (1983/1984) also investigated substitution and compensation in a cross-sectional study of older adults that focused on three of the social provisions proposed by Weiss (1974): security, intimacy, and reassurance of worth. Simons found, as predicted, that an older person's siblings or confidant relationships can contribute to a sense of security in the absence of a spouse or interaction with adult children; friends and group ties did not have this compensatory effect. Regarding the need for intimacy, Simons expected that a confidant relationship with a friend would compensate for the absence of a spouse, but he obtained only limited support for this prediction. Finally, regarding reassurance of worth, he found that older persons who do not participate in groups and organizations feel more useful if they experience more interaction with friends; interaction with kin, in contrast, did not contribute to feelings of usefulness. Thus, in Simons's study, compensation appeared to require the match between provisions and providers that Weiss emphasized (see also Felton & Berry, 1992). Simons concluded that his findings demonstrate the importance of diversity in the social networks of the aged: "Although some substitution of relationships may take place, no single type of relationship ... was able to satisfy all three of the psychological desires considered in the present study" (p. 137).

Longitudinal Approaches.   Longitudinal approaches to the investigation of compensatory effects would entail assessing the well-being of a sample of older adults both before and after a network loss occurred. A compensatory effect would be inferred if the pre–post decline in well-being is smaller among those who have established a replacement social tie than among those who have not established such a tie. This finding would constitute moderate evidence of compensation; strong evidence would require that no significant pre–post declines in well-being occur among those who have established a replacement tie. Because compensatory processes, by definition, occur over time, prospective longitudinal approaches hold the greatest promise of extending our understanding. Moreover, several researchers have noted that social network substitutions and compensatory effects undergo changes themselves over time; for example, widowed people appear to emphasize different types and sources of support at different points in the course of their bereavement (e.g., Bankoff, 1981; Ferraro, 1984; Schuster & Butler, 1989).

Overview of Empirical Work.   Empirical evaluations of older adults' "compensatory" responses to social network losses and disruptions are both difficult to locate and complicated by formidable methodological challenges. Our discussion has not addressed the considerable complexities that surround efforts to identify and pin down empirically those actions by older adults that truly represent compensatory adjustments to a social network deficiency of some sort (see Carstensen et al., 1995; Ferraro & Farmer, 1995; and Salthouse, 1995, for a discussion of methodological requirements for causal inference). How do researchers decide, for example, whether renewed contact with an infrequently seen friend constitutes a compensatory response to loss or a mere coincidence? How should we attempt to document the internal shifts in social needs and aspirations that may characterize some older adults' efforts to grapple with social network deficiencies? How can we anticipate the time period during which such compensatory adjustments may emerge, in order to plan a synchronized assessment strategy? Given that not all network losses and disruptions are likely to lead to compensatory behavior (Ferraro & Farmer, 1995), how should we conceptualize and categorize the relevant network events so as to avoid an undifferentiated and potentially misleading search for compensatory effects? These questions highlight some of the issues—challenging but also intriguing—that will require our attention if we are to advance our understanding of compensatory processes in older adults' social networks.

CONCLUSION

In closing, we offer two general recommendations to researchers who share our interest in understanding how older adults expand or realign their social networks in response to network disruptions and losses.

First, we urge researchers to make conceptual distinctions among relationship specialization, substitution, and compensation. The degree of specialization that has characterized an older person's social network prior to some loss or disruption may influence the perceived need to find substitutes for missing social ties or functions as well as judgments about the viability of potential substitutes. Thus, relationship specialization represents an important antecedent condition that shapes substitution processes.

Substitution, in contrast, refers to the processes by which older adults seek to replace or "make up for" needed social ties or functions that they have lost from their social networks. Although such substitution efforts often will revolve around the creation of new social ties or reconfiguration of existing ties, our analysis suggests that it may be useful to consider, as well, substitution efforts that involve the creation or revitalization of nonsocial activities.

Compensation is the cousin process to substitution, in that it refers to the outcome of substitution efforts—the extent to which substitution efforts actually have compensatory effects. The strongest case for compensation would be established by demonstrating that an older person's well-being does not decline following a social network loss if substitutes have been found for the missing ties or functions. A somewhat weaker but nonetheless persuasive case for compensation would be established by demonstrating that among older adults who have experienced a social network loss, those who establish a substitute tie fare better than those who do not (even though the preloss levels of well-being perhaps cannot be recovered).

This leads to our second general recommendation: that researchers think carefully about the kinds of research designs, assessment procedures, and data analyses that will be needed to document substitution and compensation processes in older adults' lives (cf. Carstensen et al., 1995). The conclusions we derive about these processes will be influenced strongly by the manner in which social support is conceptualized and assessed (e.g., whether we focus on needs, preferences, or actual patterns of support provision and whether we assess a broad or narrow range of support functions and services). Similarly, the particular subgroups of older adults included in our studies (e.g., whether we focus on married or unmarried individuals or on the young-old or old-old) will influence the evidence we obtain regarding relationship specialization and substitution. The cross-sectional vs. longitudinal design of the study will influence our ability to make confident inferences about causal links between compensatory behaviors and compensatory outcomes of interest. The evidence that we muster for compensatory processes will depend, as well, on the types of outcomes assessed and the nature of the statistical analyses undertaken (e.g., within- vs. between-person comparisons). We hope that our discussion of these issues has helped to suggest some directions for extending research on compensatory processes in older adults' social networks.

REFERENCES

Adams, B. (1967). Interaction theory and the social network. *Sociometry, 30,* 64–78.

Antonucci, T. C. (1985). Personal characteristics, social support, and social behavior. In E. Shanas & R. H. Binstock (Eds.). *Handbook of aging and the social sciences,* 2nd ed. (pp. 94–128). New York: Van Nostrand Reinhold.

Antonucci, T. C. (1990). Social supports and social relationships. In R. H. Binstock & L. K. George (Eds.), *Handbook of aging and the social sciences,* 3rd ed. (pp. 205–226). New York: Academic Press.

Antonucci, T. C., & Jackson, J. S. (1987). Social support, interpersonal efficacy, and health: A life course perspective. L. L. Carstensen & B. A. Edelstein (Eds.), *Handbook of clinical gerontology* (pp. 291–311). New York: Pergamon Press.

Archbold, P. G. (1982). All-consuming activity: The family as caregiver. *Generations, 7,* 12.

Arling, G. (1976). The elderly widow and her family, neighbors and friends. *Journal of Marriage and the Family, 38,* 757–768.

Backman, L., & Dixon, R. A. (1992). Psychological compensation: A theoretical framework. *Psychological Bulletin, 112,* 259–283.

Baltes, P. B., & Baltes, M. M. (1990). Psychological perspectives on successful aging: The model of selective optimization and compensation. In P. B. Baltes & M. M. Baltes (Eds.), *Successful aging: Perspectives from the behavioral sciences* (pp. 1–34). Cambridge, UK: Cambridge University Press.

Bankoff, E. A. (1981). Effects of friendship support on the psychological well-being of widows. *Research in the Interweave of Social Roles: Friendship, 2,* 109–139.

Baumeister, R. F., & Leary, M. R. (1995). The need to belong: Desire for interpersonal attachment as a fundamental human motivation. *Psychological Bulletin, 117,* 497–529.

Brandstadter, J., & Renner, G. (1990). Tenacious goal pursuit and flexible goal adjustment: Explication and age-related analysis of assimilative and accommodative strategies of coping. *Psychology and Aging, 5,* 58–67.

Cantor, M. H. (1979). Neighbors and friends: An overlooked resource in the informal support system. *Research on Aging, 1,* 434–463.

Cantor, M. H., & Little, V. (1985). Aging and social care. In R. H. Binstock & E. Shanas (Eds.), *Handbook of aging and the social sciences* (pp. 745–781). New York: Van Nostrand-Reinhold.

Carstensen, L. L. (1991). Socioemotional and selectivity theory: Social activity in life-span context. *Annual Review of Gerontology and Geriatrics, 11*, 195–217.

Carstensen, L. L., Hanson, K. A., & Freund, A. M. (1995). Selection and compensation in adulthood. In R. A. Dixon & L. Backman (Eds.), *Compensating for psychological deficits and declines: Managing losses and promoting gains* (pp. 107–126). Mahwah, NJ: Lawrence Erlbaum.

Chatters, L. M., Taylor, R. J., & Jackson, J. S. (1986). Aged blacks' choices for an informal helper network. *Journal of Gerontology, 41*, 94–100.

Choi, N. G. (1994). Patterns and determinants of social services utilization: Comparison of the childless elderly and elderly parents living with or apart from their children. *Gerontologist, 34*, 353–362.

Cicirelli, V. G. (1981). Kin relationships of childless and one-child elderly in relation to social services. *Journal of Gerontological Social Work, 4*, 19–33.

Coe, R. M., Wolinsky, F. D., Miller, D. J., & Prendergast, J. M. (1984). Complementary and compensatory functions in social network relationships among the elderly. *Gerontologist, 24*, 396–400.

Cohen, S., & Wills, T. A. (1985). Stress, social support, and the buffering hypothesis. *Psychological Bulletin, 98*, 310–357.

Connidis, I. A., & Davies, L. (1990). Confidants and companions in later life: The place of family and friends. *Journal of Gerontology, 45*, 141–149.

Connidis, I. A., & Davies, L. (1992). Confidants and companions: Choices in later life. *Journal of Gerontology, 47*, S115–S122.

Crohan, S., & Antonucci, T. C. (1989). Friends as a source of social support in old age. In R. G. Adams & R. Blieszner (Eds.), *Older adult friendships: Structure and process* (pp. 129–146). Newbury Park, CA: Sage Publications.

Dean, A., Kolody, B., & Wood, P. (1990). Effects of social support from various sources on depression in elderly persons. *Journal of Health and Social Behavior, 31*, 148–161.

Dixon, R. A., & Backman, L. (1995). Concepts of compensation: Integrated, differentiated, and Janus-faced. In R. A. Dixon & L. Backman (Eds.), *Compensating for psychological deficits and declines: Managing losses and promoting gains* (pp. 3–19). Mahwah, NJ: Lawrence Erlbaum.

Dono, J. E., Falbe, C. M., Kail, B. L., Litwak, E., Sherman, R. H., & Siegel, D. (1979). Primary groups in old age: Structure and function. *Research on Aging, 1*, 403–433.

Dykstra, P. A. (1993). The differential availability of relationships and the provision and effectiveness of support to older adults. *Journal of Social and Personal Relationships, 10*, 355–370.

East, P. L., & Rook, K. S. (1992). Compensatory patterns of support among children's peer relationships: A test using school friends, nonschool friends, and siblings. *Developmental Psychology, 28*, 163–172.

Elwell, F., & Maltbie-Crannell, A. D. (1981). The impact of role loss upon coping resources and life satisfaction of the elderly. *Journal of Gerontology, 36*, 223–232.

Felton, B. J. (1990). Coping and social support in older people's experiences of chronic illness. In M. A. P. Stephens, J. H. Crowther, S. E. Hobfoll, & D. L. Tennenbaum (Eds.), *Stress and coping in later-life families* (pp. 153–171). New York: Hemisphere.

Felton, B. J., & Berry, C. A. (1992). Do the sources of the urban elderly's social support determine its psychological consequences? *Psychology and Aging, 7*, 89–97.

Ferraro, K. F. (1984). Widowhood and social participation in later life: Isolation or compensation? *Research on Aging, 6*, 451–468.

Ferraro, K. F., & Farmer, M. M. (1995). Social compensation in adulthood and later life. In R. A. Dixon & L. Backman (Eds.), *Compensating for psychological deficits and declines: Managing losses and promoting gains* (pp. 127–145). Mahwah, NJ: Lawrence Erlbaum.

Ferraro, K. F., Mutran, E., & Barresi, C. M. (1984). Widowhood, health, and friendship support in later life. *Journal of Health and Social Behavior, 25*, 245–259.

Heckhausen, J., & Schulz, R. (1995). A life-span theory of control. *Psychological Review, 102*, 284–304.

House, J. S., Umberson, D., & Landis, K. (1988). Structures and processes of social support. *Annual Review of Sociology, 14*, 293–318.

Johnson, C. L. (1983). Dyadic family relations and social support. *Gerontologist, 23*, 377–383.

Johnson, C. L., & Catalano, D. J. (1983). A longitudinal study of family supports to impaired elderly. *Gerontologist, 23*, 612–625.

Johnson, C L., & Troll, L. (1992). Family functioning in late late life. *Journal of Gerontology: Social Sciences, 47*, S66–S72.

Kahn, R. L., & Antonucci, A. (1980). Convoys over the life course: Attachment, roles, and social support. In P. B. Baltes & O. G. Brim (Eds.), *Life-span development and behavior,* Vol. 3 (pp. 253–286). New York: Academic Press.

Larson, R., Mannell, R., & Zuzanek, J. (1986). Daily well-being of older adults with family and friends. *Psychology and Aging, 1*, 117–126.

Lawton, M. P. (1989). Environmental proactivity and affect in older people. In S. Spacapan & S. Oskamp (Eds.), *The social psychology of aging* (pp. 135–163). Newbury Park, CA: Sage Publications.

Lee, G. R., & Ishii-Kuntz, M. (1987). Social interaction, loneliness, and emotional well-being among the elderly. *Research on Aging, 9*, 459–482.

Lewinsohn, P. M., & Amenson, C. S. (1978). Some relations between pleasant and unpleasant mood-related events and depression. *Journal of Abnormal Psychology, 87*, 644–654.

Litwak, E. (1985). *Helping the elderly: The complementary roles of informal networks and formal systems.* New York: Guilford Press.

Litwak, E., & Figueira, J. (1968). Technological innovations and theoretical functions of primary groups and bureaucratic structures. *American Journal of Sociology, 73*, 468–481.

Litwak, E., & Messeri, P. (1989). Organizational theory, social supports, and mortality rates: A theoretical convergence. *American Sociological Review, 54*, 49–67.

Litwak, E., & Szelinyi, I. (1969). Primary group structures and their functions. *American Sociological Review, 34*, 54–64.

Logan, J. R., & Spitze, G. (1994). Informal support and the use of formal services by older Americans. *Journal of Gerontology: Social Sciences, 49*, S25–S34.

Lopata, H. Z. (1979). *Women as widows: Support systems.* New York: Elsevier.

Miller, B., & McFall, S. (1991). Stability and change in the informal task support network of frail older persons. *Gerontologist, 31*, 735–745.

Morgan, D. L. (1988). Age differences in social network participation. *Journal of Gerontology: Social Sciences, 55*, S129–S137.

Noelker, L. S., & Bass, D. M. (1989). Home care for elderly persons: Linkages between formal and informal caregivers. *Journal of Gerontology: Social Sciences, 44*, S63–S70.

Pearlman, D. N., & Crown, W. H. (1992). Alternative sources of social support and their impacts on institutional risk. *Gerontologist, 32*, 527–535.

Penning, M. J. (1990). Receipt of assistance by elderly people: Hierarchical selection and task specificity. *Gerontologist, 30*, 220–227.

Peters, G. R., Hoyt, D. R., Babchuk, N., Kaiser, M., & Iijima, Y. (1987). Primary-group support systems of the aged. *Research on Aging, 9*, 392–416.

Rook, K. S. (1990). Social relationships as a source of companionship: Implications for older adults' psychological well-being. In B. R. Sarason, I. G. Sarason, & G. R. Pierce (Eds.), *Social support: An interactional view* (pp. 219–250). New York: Wiley.

Rook, K. S., & Paplau, L. A. (1982). Perspectives on helping the lonely. In L. A. Peplau & D. Perlman (Eds.), *Loneliness: A sourcebook of current theory, research and therapy* (pp. 357–378). New York: Wiley.

Salthouse, T. (1995). Refining the concept of psychological compensation. In R. A. Dixon & L. Backman (Eds.), *Compensating for psychological deficits and declines: Managing losses and promoting gains* (pp. 127–145). Mahwah, NJ: Lawrence Erlbaum.

Schuster, T. L., & Butler, E. W. (1989). Bereavement, social networks, social support, and mental health. In D. A. Lund (Ed.), *Older bereaved spouses: Research with practical applications* (pp. 55–68). New York: Hemisphere.

Seeman, T. E., & Berkman, L. F. (1988). Structural characteristics of social networks and their relationship with social support in the elderly: Who provides support. *Social Science and Medicine, 26*, 737–749.

Shanas, E. (1979). The family as a social support system in old age. *Gerontologist, 19*, 169–174.

Simons, R. L. (1983/1984). Specificity and substitution in the social networks of the elderly. *International Journal of Aging and Human Development, 18*, 121–139.

Spakes, P. R. (1979). Family, friendship and community interaction as related to life satisfaction of the elderly. *Journal of Gerontological Social Work, 1,* 279–293.

Stoller, E. P., & Pugliesi, K. L. (1988). Informal networks of community-based elderly: Changes in composition over time. *Research on Aging, 10,* 499–516.

Stone, R. G., Cafferata, G. L., & Sangl, J. (1987). Caregivers of the frail elderly: A national profile. *Gerontologist, 27,* 616–626.

Stylianos, S. K., & Vachon, M. L. S. (1993). The role of social support in bereavement. In M. S. Stroebe, W. Stroebe, & R. O. Hansson (Eds.), *Handbook of bereavement: Theory, research, and intervention* (pp. 397–410). New York: Cambridge University Press.

Sussman, M. B. (1977). Family, bureaucracy and the elderly individual: An organizational/linkage perspective. In E. Shanas & M. B. Sussman (Eds.), *Family, bureaucracy, and the elderly* (pp. 2–20). Durham, NC: Duke University Press.

Ward, R. A. (1985). Informal networks and well-being in later life: A research agenda. *Gerontologist, 25,* 55–61.

Weiss, R. S. (1973). *Loneliness: The experience of emotional and social isolation.* Cambridge: MIT Press.

Weiss, R. S. (1974). The provisions of social relationships. In Z. Rubin (Ed.), *Doing unto others* (pp. 17–26). Englewood Cliffs, NJ: Prentice-Hall.

Wood, V., & Robertson, J. (1978). Friendship and kinship interaction: Differential effect on the morale of the elderly. *Journal of Marriage and the Family, 40,* 367–373.

Young, J. E. (1982). Loneliness, depression and cognitive therapy. In L. A. Peplau & D. Perlman (Eds.), *Loneliness: A sourcebook of current theory, research and therapy* (pp. 379–405). New York: Wiley.

11

What Is Supportive about Social Support?

On the Psychological Needs for Autonomy and Relatedness

RICHARD M. RYAN and JESSICA A. SOLKY

The close connection between personal well-being and the availability of rich, intimate personal relationships has become increasingly evident to psychological theorists. Clearly, there are relationships that heal, that soothe, that foster growth, that facilitate health, and that provide satisfactions essential to a sense of well-being.

The literature on social support has contributed to this perspective by demonstrating that having vs. not having a network of supportive others conduces to better adjustment and health. It has been well established that increased social support can be a buffer against psychological distress, and such support has been linked with positive mental health outcomes such as lower rates of depressive symptoms, milder temperament, lower stress, decreased loneliness, and a more positive self-image (Cohen, Sherrod, & Clark, 1986; Lepore, 1992; Pierce, Sarason, & Sarason, 1991; Reis & Franks, 1994; Sarason et al., 1991; Windle, 1992).

Given that social support has been associated with positive mental health outcomes, pinpointing the critical elements that separate supportive from nonsupportive relationships becomes a next crucial step. Specifically, which qualities of interpersonal relationships render them supportive and thus enhancing of the psychological or physical well-being of the participants?

In this chapter, we hypothesize that for social contacts to enhance psychological well-being, they must be characterized by *autonomy support*. Relationships

RICHARD M. RYAN and JESSICA A. SOLKY • Department of Psychology, University of Rochester, Rochester, New York 14627.

Handbook of Social Support and the Family, edited by Gregory R. Pierce, Barbara R. Sarason, and Irwin G. Sarason. Plenum Press, New York, 1996.

lacking in autonomy support, conversely, are suggested not just to fail to enhance but often to undermine well-being. In addition, we explore the role of *involvement*, defined as the dedication of time or resources within a relationship, as an aspect of social support. We review evidence suggesting that the meaning and psychological effects of involvement and tangible supports vary in accord with the degree of autonomy support that characterizes a relationship.

A second purpose of this chapter is to examine the link between social supports and *human needs*. We argue that social supports enhance psychological well-being because they fulfill critical and basic psychological needs and that explicating these needs can lead to increased understanding of how social supports function. In particular, we suggest that social contacts that are autonomy-supportive typically satisfy basic psychological needs for autonomy, relatedness, and competence, and accordingly foster enhanced self-regard, self-regulation, vitality, and feelings of connectedness with others. Conversely, relationships lacking in autonomy support, while quite obviously unfulfilling with respect to autonomy needs, are also insufficiently satisfying of relatedness needs as well, and thereby fail to produce many of the beneficial effects typically expected from social supports.

SOCIAL SUPPORTS AND PSYCHOLOGICAL NEEDS

Organismic theories of personality and development have historically emphasized the role of specific human needs in energizing behavior and giving salience to particular outcomes (e.g., Deci & Ryan, 1985b; Maslow, 1970; Murray, 1938; White, 1963). However, theorists have tended to use the term *need* in two distinct senses. The first sense reflects a quite general definition of psychological needs, in which needs are equated with nearly any motive force, including acquired desires and wants. Such theories identify not only widely recognized needs, such as affiliation or autonomy, but also quite narrow needs, such as needs for acquisitions, status and power, and dominance, among others. Thus, the concept of need is employed in these theories in much the same way as it is colloquially used in statements such as "I need a new car" or "I need to meet some new people." In this usage, the concept of need could refer to just about any form of motive, wish, want, or goal. The Murray (1938) conceptualization of psychological needs stands as a primary example of this approach.

This quite general or loose definition of needs is problematic, however, when we see that sometimes (indeed often) desires and wants may do harm to the self or organism and thus may run against the grain of another fundamental use of the term *need*. In this latter usage, one that applies across the biological sciences, a need is defined in terms of the *nutriments or conditions essential to an entity's development and health*. Thus, an organism *needs* food, *needs* water, and *needs* shelter to thrive and, ultimately, to survive. With regard to psychological development, a number of theorists have argued that there are correspondents to the bodily needs for food, water, and shelter (e.g., Bowlby, 1979; Maslow, 1970; White, 1959).

Self-determination theory (Deci & Ryan, 1985b, 1991; Ryan, 1993), which is the framework we employ, is among such theories. It assumes three needs to be essential in accounting for the nurturance and growth of the human psyche: the psychological needs for autonomy, competence, and relatedness. The theory assumes that mental health and self-actualization are realized only to the extent that these three needs are fulfilled, whereas it will be plagued by conflict and pathology when either inner or outer conditions thwart satisfaction of these needs (Ryan, Deci, & Grolnick, 1995). From this perspective, varied contexts, relationships, and behaviors can be examined for their adequacy as instruments for fulfilling human needs and personal development.

Applying this perspective to the concept of social support suggests that the positive psychological effects of social support may derive from the capacity of social support systems to satisfy one or more of these basic psychological needs. Most obvious is that social supports help people feel connected, valued, and cared for, and thus satisfy the need for relatedness. Pursuing what is perhaps a less obvious point, however, we additionally hypothesize that unless interpersonal interactions convey to the individual respect and support for his or her autonomy, neither relatedness nor autonomy needs will feel fulfilled.

The *need for autonomy* refers to the fundamental human propensity to have one's behavior emanate from the self, that is, to feel volitional and self-determined. The need for autonomy is reflected in what deCharms (1968) described as our primary need to be the "origin" of our behavior, as opposed to being a "pawn" to external forces or a mere cog in a chain of events. More specifically, people's need for autonomy includes being agentic, self-expressive, and spontaneous in their actions. Deci and Ryan (1985b, 1987, 1991) have argued that the functional effects of autonomy go beyond mere instrumentality and efficacy. Indeed, they have demonstrated that even behavior that is efficacious with regard to specified outcomes and rewards can have deleterious psychological consequences if it is perceived as coming from sources and forces external to the self.

The *need for relatedness* refers to the basic human need or propensity to be securely connected to and esteemed by others and to belong to a larger social whole. That relatedness represents a fundamental human psychological need has been long recognized within a variety of theoretical traditions (Baumeister & Leary, 1995).

The need for relatedness has often been cast in opposition to the need for autonomy, particularly by theorists who equate autonomy with independence, individualism, or detachment. However, when autonomy is defined in terms of volition and being an "origin" of one's actions (rather than as independence), then relatedness and autonomy not only are not opposing needs, but also are typically mutually facilitative. For instance, an individual within an interaction who does not experience autonomy support typically will not feel *related to*, and accordingly will not derive supportive benefits from, that interaction. By contrast, relationships that entail respect and support for one's autonomy augment the felt quality of interpersonal connectedness, as well as the expected psychological benefits of social support. Furthermore, we suggest that among the reasons that social supports facilitate psychological well-being is that when social supports are autonomy-supportive, they encourage affective expression and self-disclosure, aid reflective choicefulness, contribute to self-initiative and self-esteem, and thus ultimately facilitate greater self-regulation and integration. We turn now to a consideration of why this is so.

AUTONOMY SUPPORT IN THE CONTEXT OF RELATIONSHIPS

Comparative examination of everyday social interactions readily reveals that some are merely impersonal transactions and some are truly relationships. For example, casual interactions with airline attendants, hotel clerks, and taxi drivers may do little, because of their superficial and role-bound nature, to enhance one's psychic well-being. Typically, such interactions do not represent relationships, nor do they function as social supports. By contrast, contacts of the same duration with one's spouse, best friend, or sibling would be more likely, in many cases, to provide an individual some real psychological meaning and benefit. If, however, one's contacts with a spouse, sibling, or friend were cold, impersonal, or superficial, those interactions would offer no more social support than contacts with atten-dants, clerks, and taxi drivers. And, conversely, contacts with a stranger can occasionally resonate deeply and thereby feel supportive of one's self. Thus, it is not by their formal role status that others provide us with psychological benefits or supports, but rather by *what they do* in the context of our interactions. It is only when interactions with others entail a certain set of dynamic qualities that these interactions bestow supportive benefits upon us. The question is what differenti-ates interactions that represent real supports from interactions that are simply social contacts.

One answer is that in a relationship, something of our *self* is revealed, acknowledged, or encouraged in some way. The reason that friend, spouse, and sibling would typically yield more social support than attendant, driver, and clerk is that they know us and address us in a more intimate way, so we may feel more acceptance, security, and, along with these, more freedom to be ourselves. Indeed, it is the capacity of others, whatever their formal relationship to us, to authen-tically contact us, and to draw out and support our real feelings, sensibilities, and choices, that usually underlies the sense of support and nurturance they provide. This brings us to a hypothesis that has organized most of the research we shall review: Unless there is perceived support for the self afforded within relationships, the functional enhancements expected from social supports will not be evidenced.

The concept of *autonomy support* (Deci & Ryan, 1987; Ryan, 1993) concerns this central issue of contact and encouragement of the self in the context of interpersonal interactions. Autonomy support refers to the readiness of a person to assume another's perspective or internal frame of reference and to facilitate self-initiated expression and action. Autonomy support thus typically entails ac-knowledgment of the other's perceptions, acceptance of the other's feelings, and an absence of attempts to control the other's experience and behavior. In supporting another's autonomy, we care for the true self of the other, by heeding and facilitating its expression and exercise.

Of course, the notion of autonomy support grows directly from the meaning of autonomy itself. Autonomy refers to self-regulation and governance. An autonomous behavior is one that is volitional or self-endorsed. Autonomous behavior is also *authentic* in the technical and spiritual senses of that term—it "proceeds from its author" (Wild, 1965). In attributional language, autonomy is described as behavior that has an *internal perceived locus of causality* or that emanates from the self of the actor (deCharms, 1968; Ryan & Connell, 1989). By contrast, behavior that is coerced, controlled, or subtly cajoled lacks autonomy. It follows from this that autonomy-supportive relationships will tend to foster more authentic self-expression and less sense of being contingently valued, controlled, or pressured to be certain ways. This formulation also suggests why one might feel more securely connected to those who relate to one in autonomy-supportive ways.

RESEARCH ON AUTONOMY SUPPORT

Thus far, we have argued that autonomy support is a critical element in relationships that yield supportive effects. Furthermore we suggest that autonomy-supportive relationships are not simply beneficial as buffers during episodes of stress (Cohen & Wills, 1985), but rather are more generally facilitative of psychological development and integration (Ryan, 1993). We now turn to a review of research that demonstrates the functional impact of autonomy support in multiple relationship contexts, from relationships with parents, teachers, and healthcare providers to relationships with friends and lovers. The review is organized quasi-developmentally beginning with research on autonomy support in early caregiving relationships and proceeding toward adult intimate relationships. The review not only shows the life-span relevance of autonomy support, but also illustrates the manifold effects of autonomy-supportive relationships on personality functioning and social adjustment. Autonomy support appears not only to facilitate individual well-being but also to enhance the strength and felt closeness of relationships within which it occurs.

PARENTS AS A CHILD'S FIRST SOCIAL SUPPORT

According to both attachment and object relations theorists (e.g., Bowlby, 1969; Winnicott, 1965) and those who have recently elaborated these frameworks (e.g., Bretherton, 1987; Stern, 1985), infants are innately prepared to engage in social relations. Similarly, contemporary motivational perspectives on development suggest that the need for relatedness is present from birth (Connell & Wellborn, 1990; Deci & Ryan, 1991). In all these approaches, however, the likelihood that an infant will establish a good foundational relationship is thought to depend very much on how the infant is received and responded to by caregivers.

Among the elements required to ensure a strong, secure relatedness to others is the provision of autonomy support by caregivers. This requirement has been recognized in several theoretical frameworks, though perhaps with different constructs.

Within attachment theory, the issue of autonomy support is considered an aspect of caregiver *sensitivity*, defined as the provision of contingent, appropriate, and consistent responses to the child's signals and needs (Ainsworth, Blehar, Waters, & Wall, 1978; Lamb & Easterbrooks, 1981). The construct of sensitivity thus conveys that a caregiver responds to the child's initiations in ways that are empathic and attuned to the child's needs. This definition of sensitivity overlaps considerably with the more life-span-oriented concept of autonomy support, because what one is being "sensitive to" are the child's expressed needs and autonomous initiations and strivings. Indeed, Bretherton (1987) described sensitivity in terms of "maternal respect for the child's autonomy" (p. 1075).

Sensitivity facilitates a child's well-being, competence, and initiative, all of which represent examples of the psychological benefits often associated with the concept of social support in later development. Numerous studies have supported this link between sensitive, autonomy-supportive caregiving and well-being. Specifically, sensitivity has been shown to foster greater curiosity, effectance, and ego resiliency (Arend, Gove, & Sroufe, 1979; Waters, Wippman, & Sroufe, 1979), increased self-initiation (Stevenson & Lamb, 1981; Watson, 1966), improved learning (Lewis & Coates, 1980; Yarrow, Rubenstein, & Pederson, 1975), and greater resourcefulness and adjustment (Brody, 1956).

In a study illustrative of this point, Frodi, Bridges, and Grolnick (1985) examined the proposition that maternal autonomy support in infancy would facilitate mastery motivation and the development of agency and competence. In a short-term longitudinal study, these investigators examined the relations between maternal autonomy support vs. control and (1) infant persistence and competence in a mastery situation and (2) the infants' affect during exploration. They found evidence that, at both 12 and 20 months, maternal autonomy support facilitated these developmental outcomes. Furthermore, indices of sensitivity derived from traditional attachment procedures were highly correlated with ratings of maternal autonomy support derived from self-determination theory. Grolnick, Frodi, and Bridges (1984) also reported relations between mothers' tendencies to support their infants' autonomy and the mastery motivation of those infants during their second year of life. Results of their study showed that children of mothers who were identified as more controlling were less persistent in independent problem solving and exploration than were children of mothers who evidenced greater levels of autonomy support.

In a related study in a somewhat older group, Deci, Driver, Hotchkiss, Robbins, and Wilson (1993) videotaped interactions between mothers and their 5- to 7-year-olds in a free-play situation. Maternal vocalizations during the interactive-play period were coded as being controlling, autonomy-supportive, or neutral. A hidden camera also recorded the child's behavior following dyadic free play, after the mother had left her child alone in the room. The amount of time the child spent playing with the target task while alone in the room, as well as the child's ratings of liking for the task, were used as measures of the child's intrinsic motivation for that activity. Results revealed negative relations between maternal controllingness and both measures of intrinsic motivation. These and related studies suggest that parental autonomy support contributes to a child's inner security, which is in turn reflected in the child's ability and willingness to be a curious investigator of the surrounding world. These studies thus show how autonomy support may foster feelings not only of autonomy but also of greater competence and relatedness.

Object relations theories also emphasize the issue of autonomy support, which is highlighted within, for example, the idea of Winnicott (1965) of responsive, nonimpinging, "good enough" mothering. According to object relations approaches, warm, empathic, and responsive parenting both facilitates self-development and leads to the construction of facilitative *object representations*, which, like the *working models* construct of attachment theory (Bretherton, 1987), are internalized schemata for understanding and organizing behavior in social contexts.

Ryan, Avery, and Grolnick (1985) investigated the importance of perceived autonomy within children's object representations using a projective method developed by Urist (1977) that assesses *mutuality of autonomy* (MOA). Derived from object-relational (Winnicott, 1965) and self-psychological (Kohut, 1971) theories, the MOA assessment places one's internalized schemata of relationships along a dimension ranging from those characterized by reciprocal dialogue and autonomy to those characterized by unifocal power and overwhelming control. Thus, the MOA construct inherently assumes that the quality of one's relatedness is to a great degree a function of the autonomy supportiveness that characterizes it.

Operationally, MOA scores are obtained by rating Rorschach percepts involving interacting figures for the relative dominance and imbalance vs. mutuality and balance entailed in their interaction. For example, seeing an elephant stomping on a bug involves a projection of an imbalanced, dominating relationship, whereas seeing two people cooking a meal together involves a projection of balanced, mutuality-oriented actions. It is presumed that these projections are indicative of individual differences in the nature of subjects' internalized representations or "working models" of relationships, such that those low in MOA see relationships in general to be characterized by control, dominance, and power imbalances. In support of this view, Ryan et al. (1985) found that, within their sample made up of largely minority, urban children, lower MOA was associated with less perceived control, poorer school grades, and, most relevantly, worse interpersonal and classroom adjustment as rated by teachers.

Avery and Ryan (1988) studied urban children's object representations of parents. They used a projective technique (Blatt, Quinlan, Chevron, & McDonald, 1982) in which each parent is described in an open-ended manner, and this description is later rated along a number of discrete dimensions, the majority of which load on a global factor called *nurturance*. Nurturance represents an atmosphere of psychological care and support. As expected, nurturance was predictive of a variety of school-adjustment and self-esteem outcomes. In order to determine what elements contribute to nurturant representations, Avery and Ryan also had the children complete a self-report scale (Grolnick, Ryan, & Deci, 1991) that assessed the dimensions of parental autonomy support and involvement. They found that the parent representations rated as nurturant were those that were rated in children's self-reports as high in autonomy support and involvement. Thus, it seems that nurturant, "good enough" parents are those perceived to be involved (dedicating time and resources to the child) and supportive of their child's autonomy.

One of the significant ways in which parents represent social supports for their children is through helping them negotiate extrafamilial challenges, such as school and friendships. Grolnick and Ryan (1989) studied how parents support their children's school involvement through an in-depth interview study with parents of rural elementary schoolchildren. The interview was done separately with each parent and focused on how the parent reacted to the child's school-related experiences or attempted to promote academic motivation. Among the dimensions assessed were parental autonomy support and involvement. *Autonomy support* was gauged by a summary of three different indices derived from the interviews. The first concerned the parent's expressed value for autonomy or volition, as opposed to obedience and compliance. A second rating concerned the democratic vs. authoritarian character of the home—the extent to which everyone participated in family decisions vs. one adult figure made the decisions. A third and final rating concerned actual discipline techniques—whether they were coercive and punitive in nature vs. minimally controlling and whether they involved acknowledgment and information provision (for a description of autonomy-supportive discipline, see Koestner, Ryan, Bernieri, & Holt, 1984). These three ratings were shown to form one autonomy-support factor.

Involvement was rated from two indices: time spent with the child and knowledge of the child on a day-to-day level. Involvement in this context thus represents a form of tangible support.

Results showed important outcomes to be associated with both variables. Autonomy support per se was significantly associated with children's having more volition with respect to school achievement, greater perceived competence, and better grades and standardized achievement test outcomes. Involvement, specifically maternal involvement, predicted better achievement, teacher-rated competence, and some aspects of adjustment.

In a subsequent study, Grolnick et al. (1991) hypothesized that parental influences on school adjustment and achievement worked largely through their impact on the child's "inner resources" of perceived autonomy, competence, and control. They tested a model of achievement behaviors in which perceived parental autonomy support and involvement (measured through the child's self-report) facilitated greater self-perceptions of control, competence, and personal autonomy in the student with respect to school activities. These inner resources were in turn expected to predict achievement outcomes. Results confirmed that autonomy support and involvement both facilitated perceived autonomy, control, and competence, which in turn predicted achievement outcomes. Again, this research shows how the perceived qualities within the relationship predict its functional impact on child outcomes, particularly the sense of agency and confidence a child carries into the world outside the family.

Although it seems clear that autonomy support promotes greater competence and initiative, it is equally important to note that it also strengthens the security of the very relationships within which it occurs; furthermore, it generally facilitates the development of "working models" or "internal representations" of relationships that foster adaptive functioning in subsequent interpersonal contexts (Ryan, 1993). That is, one should feel more loved and connected to others insofar as others have historically cared for and supported one's self. Recent research by Sarason et al. (1991) provided evidence congruent with this formulation. They found that subjects who reported that their parents had been affectionate and caring toward them during childhood (facilitating relatedness) and not overprotective or domineering (facilitating perceived autonomy) perceived themselves as young adults to have more satisfying social support systems. Furthermore, such students also tended to perceive other students as having good social supports. Sarason and coworkers concluded that responsive, supportive interactions in childhood contribute to a sense of (1) oneself as loved and cared for by important others, (2) oneself as worthy of the positive regard of others, and (3) others as available and willing to provide support.

In another quite recent study, Dresner and Grolnick (1994) examined how the autonomy and interpersonal relatedness of college women was influenced by their parental object representations. The women's current relationships were classified as being caring, respectful, and intimate, or alternatively as being either superficial or enmeshed (Levitz-Jones & Orlofsky, 1985; Orlofsky, Marcia, & Lesser, 1973). Results indicated that whereas women whose relationships were caring and intimate had parental representations that were accepting and autonomy-supportive, the women with more superficial relationships had object representations that were nonaccepting and overcontrolling, and the women with enmeshed relationships had representations that were nonaccepting but idealized. Furthermore, women who were high in autonomy orientation (Deci & Ryan, 1985a) had parental representations that were autonomy-supportive, while those not displaying high autonomy had representations that were overly controlling.

The controlling vs. autonomy-supportive parenting environment not only contributes to the personal well-being of children but also profoundly impacts the value a child eventually places on relationships themselves. In a study of late adolescents, Kasser, Ryan, Zax, and Sameroff (1995) found that young adults who perceived their parents as warm, nurturant, and autonomy-supportive were likely to have stronger values for affiliation and generativity. Subjects who expressed particularly high values for material success, in contrast, tended to describe their parents as less autonomy-supportive and warm. Further, the latter subjects were less likely to report a willingness to utilize their parents as supportive resources. Additional maternal interview data corroborated this pattern. Kasser and colleagues suggested that cold, controlling, uninvolved parents have children whose needs have been ignored and that, as a result, the adolescents look to satisfy their sense of self-worth more through external sources such as financial success than through contact with others.

In all these studies, the effects of relationships with parents differ in accord with the experienced *quality* of the relationship. Relationships with parents characterized by autonomy support conduce to greater sense of self in the forms of autonomy, competence, and relatedness, and thus truly represent a critical form of social support in development.

Furthermore, autonomy support from parents in early life engenders in the child a more positive set of expectations concerning the self-in-relationships that continues to enhance well-being across the life span. As the research reviewed above suggests, it seems that children whose parents have been the most nurturant and autonomy-supportive are more likely to enter into relationships with a set of positive expectations concerning others. Having experienced that others can care for and respect them, they are more willing to engage and express themselves (see, for example, Hodgins, Koestner, & Duncan, in press; Emmons & Colby, 1994). In turn, this openness makes it easier for others to positively relate to them and to be more autonomy-supportive. Conversely, children who have been poorly nurtured, experiencing neglect or excessive control, are likely to enter into new relationships more defensively, guardedly, and perhaps defiantly. As a result, others are less open to them, less nurturant, and more likely to be controlling.

Similarly, parents and other adults who treat others in ways that are controlling and unempathic are typically those who themselves did not receive autonomy support during their development and thus lack the developmental basis for understanding or supporting others. They are in a certain sense doing to others what has been done to them. In this transactional viewpoint, then, there is a tendency for autonomy-support/control dynamics in one's developmental context to reproduce themselves in one's adult relationships and in one's style of caregiving toward the next generation.

BETWEEN TEACHER AND CHILD

Parents are obviously the first and most pervasive relationship anyone has. Accordingly, the quality of parent–child relationships has been theorized to have significant impacts on personality development and to predispose a child to specific expectations concerning relationships with others. Yet as children become increasingly admitted to the extrafamilial universe, they enter into relationships with other influential figures whose qualities and style may be more or less supportive of psychological well-being. Teachers are such influential figures.

To study the effects of different relational qualities between teachers and students, Deci, Schwartz, Sheinman, and Ryan (1981) created an assessment of teachers' propensities to be autonomy-supportive vs. controlling. Prior to the school year, teachers read vignettes of problem situations in school and rated various alternative approaches to these problems that varied in their controlling vs. autonomy-supportive character. For example, a student, Jimmy, is portrayed in one vignette as recently becoming listless in class and late with assignments. A controlling approach might be to tell Jimmy that his recent attitude is unacceptable and convey the idea that failure to turn in future assignments will result in negative consequences. By contrast, an autonomy-supportive teacher might begin, not by telling him what he must do, but rather by asking Jimmy, "What's going on?" In addition to attempting to draw out and understand Jimmy's perspective, the teacher would also try to engage *his* participation in thinking about and solving his school problems.

Deci and coworkers used this teacher-orientation measure as a predictor of student motivation and self-esteem over the following academic year. It was found that more autonomy-supportive teachers facilitated greater intrinsic or mastery motivation in their students, as reflected in their students' greater desire for challenges, independent mastery, and curiosity relative to students of controlling teachers. Students in classrooms of autonomy-oriented teachers also expressed greater perceived competence or confidence in their abilities. Most pertinent to the role of teachers as "social supports," however, it was found that children whose teachers were oriented more toward autonomy support evidenced higher self-esteem. Thus, autonomy support affected not only motivation but also feelings of confidence and general self-worth. Interestingly, students also reported feeling more warmth from those teachers who endorsed an autonomy-oriented approach.

Ryan and Grolnick (1986) examined children's perceptions of teachers using the deCharms (1976) origin climate survey, which assesses the degree to which teachers are autonomy-supportive vs. controlling. Parallel to the Deci et al. (1981) findings, they found that children who perceived their teachers to be more autonomy-supportive had greater intrinsic motivation, perceived competence, and self-esteem compared to those who experienced their classroom climate to be more controlling. Students also saw more autonomy-supportive teachers as warmer and as liking them more than teachers who were less autonomy-supportive. Ryan and Grolnick additionally had these children write projective stories about a "neutral" classroom scene. They found that children who saw their own classroom teacher as autonomy-supportive were more likely to tell stories involving more agentic children and more supportive teachers, whereas children who perceived their own teacher to be low in autonomy support told stories with more aggression, "pawnlike" student protagonists, and authoritarian teachers. These projective results show the match between the perceived world and children's internalized representational schemata. In both perceptions and "working models," autonomy support is a dimension of significance.

AUTONOMY WITHIN ADULT RELATIONSHIPS

The connection between autonomy and intimacy in adult relationships is interesting in two ways. On one hand, autonomy support is assumed to still matter as much as it does in more "uneven" relationships such as teacher–child or parent–child dyads. In addition, it is important in adult relationships for each individual to see the other as relating to him or her out of volition or autonomy. To feel that we are truly cared for, we want to know that our partners relate to us freely and willingly. Indeed, ultimately, the best-quality adult relationships are herein argued to be those that entail mutuality of autonomy. Recent studies have begun to examine these dynamic issues.

Rempel, Holmes, and Zanna (1985) investigated the construct of *trust* in intimate relationships. They characterized trust in terms of one's attributions of one's partner's reliability and one's willingness to put oneself at risk in relating to that partner (e.g., self-disclosing, depending on promises). They also argued that trust is marked by feelings of confidence and security within the relationship. Studying 47 dating or married couples, Rempel and coworkers assessed the associations among feelings of love and trust and perceptions of one's own and one's partner's motives for being in the relationship. The three types of motives they measured for relationship participation were *extrinsic* (parental approval, social recognition), *instrumental* (e.g., personal gain, enjoyment of the partner's appearance, wit, sensitivity), and *intrinsic* (mutual satisfaction, empathic concern, valuing the relationship in and of itself). They found that trust in the relationship was positively associated with the perception that one's partner was involved in the relationship for intrinsic reasons. Feelings of love were associated with self-reports of both intrinsic and instrumental motivations for being in the relationship. Finally, people who intrinsically valued the relationship and their partner's qualities were more likely to have faith that the relationship would endure.

In another analysis of intimate relationships, Blais, Sabourin, Boucher, and Vallerand (1990) argued that the motivational style of each partner for engaging in and maintaining their relationship is an individual-difference variable that aids in understanding the quality of the couple's relationship. Accordingly, they examined perceived autonomy in relationships as a predictor of couple satisfaction and happiness, hypothesizing that more autonomous orientations should lead to more adaptive behaviors and, in turn, more positive affective experiences. It was also proposed that when one is more autonomously related, one is more likely to view relationship problems as challenges rather than annoyances, to experience less distress, and to be more inclined to work through and positively cope with such problems. As predicted, the quality of relationships (perceptions of adaptive behaviors and dyadic happiness) was positively related to self-reports of autonomous motivation for living together and negatively related to heteronomous or controlled motivation. It seems that adults' self-determination for involvement in a relationship is a marker of, if not a determinant of, the quality of the relationship.

It seems clear, then, that relationships characterized by mutual autonomy are those that breed the greatest subjective satisfaction. It is also true that, as with children, when adults feel that their autonomy is supported, a number of additional psychological benefits may accrue. Grow and Ryan (1994) recently completed a study of adults in a nursing home facility that shows that this is true even as one approaches the final stages of development. In this study, residents of a nursing home were assessed to determine both the quantity and the quality of their social support systems. Specifically, they were asked to report on the amount of contact they had with relatives and friends, as well as how autonomy-supportive and affectionate these contacts were. The perceived autonomy support of nursing home staff was also measured. Results revealed that whereas the quantity of social contacts was not strongly predictive of either psychological or physical health ratings, both the perceived support for autonomy and the level of affection variables (reflecting relational qualities) did predict these outcomes. Furthermore, staff autonomy support was also associated with residents' well-being. It seems that humans never cease being affected by the degree to which others care for and respect their autonomy in the context of relationships, bespeaking the idea that there are, indeed, basic and enduring psychological needs for autonomy and relatedness (Ryan, 1991, 1993).

DIFFERENTIATING AUTONOMY SUPPORT FROM SUPPORT FOR "INDEPENDENCE"

We have shown that autonomy is a critical quality of relationships that can influence perceived closeness, personal motivation, and psychological well-being across the life span. Autonomy support, however, is only one aspect of the social support phenomenon. In particular, reviews of the many ways in which others can be socially supportive have also pointed to the importance of *tangible supports* as a form of psychological aid (Cobb, 1979; House, 1981). Examples of tangible supports include financial assistance, material goods, and volunteering time, help, or guidance.

It seems intuitively true that, on average, persons who are in need will benefit when others around them show a readiness to provide tangible supports. However, the effects of tangible supports may depend heavily on the extent to which they are provided in a context of autonomy support vs. being used in ways that feel like controls, pressures, or messages of incompetence. That is, tangible supports, aside from their practical functions, tend to take on a dynamic meaning within relationships. We specifically hypothesize that the psychological impact of tangible support or involvement changes under autonomy-supportive vs. controlling circumstances. Furthermore, we suggest that one's willingness to rely on others for tangible supports depends in part upon the perceived quality of one's relationships with providers.

Some Dynamic Considerations

Tangible supports can be helpful in two distinct ways: They can straightforwardly assist one with a problem and therefore represent practical or functional support (Cohen & Wills, 1985), and they can demonstrate caring or love, and therefore represent a form of psychological support. Sometimes these two impacts co-occur, and sometimes they compete. That is, tangible supports can be offered either in a way that feels supportive and respectful of one's autonomy or in a way that threatens autonomy, sense of competence, or other needs so as to feel psychologically unsupportive even if practically useful.

As an example, imagine a parent taking new furniture to a young couple who have just decided to move in together. The furniture may tangibly help the starting couple both materially (it saves them money) and physically (it's a concrete comfort). Thus, *tangible* or practical social support has clearly occurred. However, this material gift may also represent a *psychological* support to the couple if, for instance, it is taken to mean that the parent respects and supports the couple's relationship and their decision to live together. In this way, acts of tangible support can convey important messages of encouragement and acceptance, which may bolster the receiver's well-being.

Tangible support can be controlling, however, rather than autonomy-supportive. A gift offered irrespective of the couple's needs, tastes, or desires is one example. Thus, a couple who want to make it on their own, or who want a specific style of apartment, may feel impinged upon or controlled by a gift of furniture from a parent. They may read into the gift pressures toward certain values or lifestyles, or they may simply feel unresponded to in terms of their own identities and tastes. These examples simply illustrate that the impact of tangible support will differ considerably depending upon the intended or perceived meaning behind the giving of goods, guidance, or resources. It is the message rather than the object that defines the degree to which the tangible support is also psychologically supportive.

A study by Weiss and Grolnick (April, 1991) shows how the psychological effects of tangible inputs and guidance can vary as a function of whether they occur within the context of autonomy-supportive vs. controlling relationships. Specifically, Weiss and Grolnick focused on parental *involvement* (which, as previously noted, is conceptualized within self-determination theory as parents' dedication of time and resources to their child) and its relationship to adolescents' internalizing and externalizing symptomatology (Achenbach & Edelbrock, 1987). Adolescents rated their mothers and fathers on dimensions of involvement and autonomy support, and they completed a self-report profile of symptoms. Analyses indicated that parents who were perceived to be *both* highly involved and autonomy-supportive had children who reported very low levels of either internalizing or externalizing symptoms, as would be expected. However, there were also significant interactions between parental involvement and autonomy support on both types of symptoms, indicating that the combination of low autonomy support and high involvement was associated with the *highest* level of symptoms. It seems that sometimes more help from parents can yield less psychological benefit, if the help is offered within a context of control. This finding suggests again that the relational dynamics of autonomy support moderate the impact of the tangible aids provided within social support systems.

Such dynamics highlight a critical conceptual issue that warrants attention within the social support literature, namely, *the distinction between independence and autonomy*, the meanings of which are often equated. Independence generally means relying on oneself for the fulfillment of needs or wants. The opposite of independence is dependence, which is in evidence when one relies on others for specific provisions (Ryan & Lynch, 1989; Ryan, 1993). In contrast to independence, autonomy refers to self-regulation and volition in one's activities, an issue that is orthogonal to one's degree of reliance. The opposite of autonomy is not dependence, but rather heteronomy—the state of being coerced or controlled by forces external to the self. Concretely, one may feel autonomous in relying on others or unwillingly dependent on others; one can also be willingly self-reliant or, alternatively, forced into caring for oneself.

It follows from this distinction that the impact of tangible supports may differ in accord with one's relative willingness to be in a circumstance of reliance and, further, that much of one's willingness to rely on another may depend upon the extent to which the other's offerings are perceived to be responsive to and respectful of the self vs. being a vehicle of control. It is these complex dynamics between autonomy and dependence that can help explain why it is often the case that people reject help and support from others or accept help but feel diminished by it. Understanding that autonomy and dependence are not necessarily antithetical also helps explain how support and help that are willingly and noncontingently given can have positive psychological implications as well as practical ones.

The persistent confusion between the concepts of autonomy and independence (the dictionary definitions of which indeed overlap) has led to a number of debates and competing formulations, particularly within the developmental literature. Therein, a number of authors appear to make the claim that as development proceeds, children optimally relinquish their reliance on parents and move toward self-reliance. While this view may sound reasonable on the surface, the building evidence suggests that it is quite a misinformed view of the general case.

Ryan and Lynch (1989) argued that adolescents, in particular, are prone to turn away from tangible support or guidance from adults if the psychological quality of the relationship in which tangible supports are offered is poor. To demonstrate this point, Ryan and Lynch showed within varied adolescent samples that a low degree of reliance on parents for help or guidance was negatively correlated with indices of adjustment such as self-esteem, perceived competence, and lovability. Furthermore, they found that the typical familial context associated with such nonreliance is one lacking in cohesion and characterized by insecure attachments. They argued that adolescents who indicate less willingness to turn to their parents for support, guidance, or help were not "independent" in any positive sense of that term, but rather suffered from *detachment*. They further questioned the overall developmental formulation that suggests that increasing nonreliance on parents is in any sense optimal. Instead, they argued that the developmental task of adolescence is not to become independent from parents, but rather to develop mutuality and autonomy within interdependencies (see also Ryan, 1993).

A recent study of adolescents by Ryan, Stiller, and Lynch (1994) supported this formulation. These investigators found that compared to their peers who reported a willingness to seek support from parents, teachers, or friends, students who indicated that they do not turn to others for help with emotional or school-related problems were *more* likely to experience poorer school adjustment, motivation, self-esteem, and identity integration. Thus, contrary to the idea that independence is invariantly positive, these authors argued that it can also be a sign of alienation from social supports. And among the most salient reasons for feeling such alienation and detachment from others is the perception that the others do not support one's autonomy or care for one's true self.

In sum, we suggest that tangible support has differing meanings and functional significance within autonomy-supportive and non-autonomy-supportive relationships. While the very construct of social support has highlighted the benefits of human interdependency, the psychological meaning of receiving tangible help or guidance from others is moderated by the extent to which such help competes with vs. supports one's feelings of agency and freedom. We have further argued that in ideal relationships, one need not feel diminished by being dependent, but instead may be encouraged and vitalized by responsive, facilitative, and caring others.

CONCLUSIONS

In this chapter, we have examined autonomy support as an element within relationships that is critical to their functioning as a psychological support for the individual. Autonomy support was defined as the support for an individual's self-regulation, and it involves respect for another's feelings, values, and perspective. Autonomy-supportive relationships stand in contrast to relationships in which others take an evaluative and judgmental stance or otherwise control, pressure, or impinge upon one's behavior and experience.

Our review of the literature has shown that in a straightforward sense, autonomy-supportive relationships enhance personal well-being. Autonomy support does not just buffer one from negative outcomes during distress, but actually facilitates development, expression, and integration of the self. Thus, autonomy support has been linked with varied indices of psychological development and integration, such as increased self-esteem, self-confidence, achievement, volition, and vitality. Autonomy support also appears to facilitate feelings of security and connectedness within the relationships in which it occurs, more positive views of others, and greater valuing of affiliation and community.

These positive outcomes have been analytically addressed within the current formulation to be a function of the fact that when autonomy is supported in relationships, fundamental human psychological needs are satisfied, specifically the needs for autonomy, relatedness, and competence. Autonomy support demonstrates a valuing of and confidence in the other person, and hence facilitates a depth and richness to perceived relatedness and competence that is unmatched under conditions of controlling and coercive forms of "support." More obviously, autonomy support facilitates the perception of oneself as an origin of behavior, enlivening one's sense of agency and heightening feelings of vitality.

The impact of other dimensions of social support, such as tangible support, was also argued to be dynamically tempered by their association with autonomy-supportive vs. more controlling contexts. Indeed, it was highlighted that within relationships of dependency, providers can either enhance a person's sense of autonomy, relatedness, and competence or actually undermine satisfaction of these needs depending upon how they convey their help to the dependent. The offering of material goods or advice with strings attached or with pressure toward specified outcomes can lead to "support" that backfires in its psychological effects. By contrast, if tangible support is given in a context of respect for autonomy, it is likely to be experienced as nurturance, and thus to strengthen both well-being and one's relational connectedness.

REFERENCES

Achenbach, T., & Edelbrock, C. (1987). Mutual for the Youth Self Report. Unpublished manuscript. Burlington: University of Vermont.

Ainsworth, M. D. S., Blehar, M. C., Waters, E., & Wall, S. (1978). *Patterns of attachment*. Hillsdale, NJ: Lawrence Erlbaum.

Arend, R., Gove, F., & Sroufe, L. A. (1979). Continuity of adaptation from infancy to kindergarten: A predictive study of ego-resiliency and curiosity in preschoolers. *Child Development, 50*, 950–959.

Avery, R. R., & Ryan, R. M. (1988). Object relations and ego development: Comparison and correlates in middle childhood. *Journal of Personality, 56*, 547–569.

Baumeister, R., & Leary, M. R. (1995). The need to belong: Desire for interpersonal attachments as a fundamental human motivation. *Psychological Bulletin, 117*, 497–529.

Blais, M. R., Sabourin, S., Boucher, C., & Vallerand, R. J. (1990). Toward a motivational model of couple happiness. *Journal of Personality and Social Psychology, 59*, 1021–1031.

Blatt, S. J., Quinlan, D. M., Chevron, E. S., & McDonald, C. (1982). Dependency and self-criticism: Psychological dimensions of depression. *Journal of Consulting and Clinical Psychology, 50*, 113–124.

Bowlby, J. (1969). *Attachment*. New York: Basic Books.

Bowlby, J. (1979). *The making and breaking of affectional bonds*. London: Tavistock Publications.

Bretherton, I. (1987). New perspectives on attachment relations: Security, communication and internal working models. In J. Osofsky (Ed.), *Handbook of infant development* (pp. 1061–1100). New York: Wiley.

Brody, D. S. (1956). *Patterns of mothering*. New York: International Universities Press.

Cobb, S. (1979). Social support and health through the life course. In M. W. Riley (Ed.), *Aging from birth to death: Interdisciplinary perspectives* (pp. 93–106). Washington, DC: American Association for the Advancement of Science.

Cohen, S., Sherrod, D. R., & Clark, M. S. (1986). Social skills and the stress-protective role of social support. *Journal of Personality and Social Psychology, 50*, 963–973.

Cohen, S., & Wills, T. A. (1985). Stress, social support, and the buffering hypothesis. *Psychological Bulletin, 98*, 310–357.

Connell, J. P., & Wellborn, J. G. (1990). Competence, autonomy and relatedness: A motivational analysis of self-system processes. In M. R. Gunnar & L. A. Sroufe (Eds.), *The Minnesota symposium on child psychology*, Vol. 22, *Self-processes in development* (pp. 43–77). Hillsdale, NJ: Lawrence Erlbaum.

deCharms, R. (1968). *Personal causation: The internal affective determinants of behavior*. New York: Academic Press.

deCharms, R. (1976). *Enhancing motivation: Change in the classroom*. New York: Irvington.

Deci, E. L., Driver, R. E., Hotchkiss, L., Robbins, R. J., & Wilson, I. M. (1993). The relation of mothers' controlling vocalizations to children's intrinsic motivation. *Journal of Experimental Child Psychology, 55*, 151–162.

Deci, E. L., & Ryan, R. M. (1985a). The general causality orientation scale: Self-determination in personality. *Journal of Research in Personality, 19*, 109–134.

Deci, E. L., & Ryan, R. M. (1985b). *Intrinsic motivation and self-determination in human behavior.* New York: Plenum Press.

Deci, E. L., & Ryan, R. M. (1987). The support of autonomy and the control of behavior. *Journal of Personality and Social Psychology, 53*, 1024–1037.

Deci, E. L., & Ryan, R. M. (1991). A motivational approach to self: Integration in personality. In R. Dienstbier (Ed.), *Nebraska symposium on motivation*, Vol. 38, *Perspectives on motivation* (pp. 237–288). Lincoln: University of Nebraska Press.

Deci, E. L., Schwartz, A. J., Sheinman, L., & Ryan, R. M. (1981). An instrument to assess adults' orientations toward control versus autonomy with children: Reflections on intrinsic motivation and perceived competence. *Journal of Educational Psychology, 73*, 642–650.

Dresner, R., & Grolnick, W. S. (1994). Constructions of early parenting, intimacy, and autonomy in young women. Unpublished manuscript. Worcester, MA: Clark University.

Emmons, R. A., & Colby, P. M. (1994). Emotional conflict and interpersonal processes: Linking ambivalence and repression to social support. Unpublished manuscript. Davis: University of California.

Frodi, A., Bridges, L., & Grolnick, W. S. (1985). Correlates of mastery-related behavior: A short term longitudinal study of infants in their second year. *Child Development, 56*, 1291–1298.

Grolnick, W., Frodi, A., & Bridges, L. (1984). Maternal control styles and the mastery motivation of one-year-olds. *Infant Mental Health Journal, 5*, 72–82.

Grolnick, W. S., & Ryan, R. M. (1989). Parent styles associated with children's self-regulation and competence in school. *Journal of Educational Psychology, 81*, 143–154.

Grolnick, W. S., Ryan, R. M., & Deci, E. L. (1991). The inner resources for school achievement: Motivational mediators of children's perceptions of their parents. *Journal of Educational Psychology, 83*, 508–517.

Grow, V. M., & Ryan, R. M. (1994). Autonomy and relatedness as predictors of health, vitality, and psychological well-being for elderly individuals in a nursing home facility. Unpublished manuscripts. Rochester, NY: University of Rochester.

Hodgins, H. S., Koestner, R., & Duncan, N. (1996). On the compatibility of autonomy and relatedness. *Personality and Social Psychology Bulletin, 22*, 227–237.

House, J. S. (1981). *Work, stress, and social support.* Reading, MA: Addison-Wesley.

Kasser, T., Ryan, R. M., Zax, M., & Sameroff, A. J. (1995). The relations of maternal and social environments to late adolescents' materialistic and prosocial values. *Developmental Psychology, 31*, 907–914.

Koestner, R., Ryan, R. M., Bernieri, F., & Holt, K. (1984). Setting limits on children's behavior: The differential effects of controlling versus informational styles on intrinsic motivation and creativity. *Journal of Personality, 52*, 233–248.

Kohut, H. (1971). *The analysis of self.* New York: International Universities Press.

Lamb, M. E., & Easterbrooks, M. A. (1981). Individual differences in parental sensitivity: Origins, components, and consequences. In M. E. Lamb & L. R. Sherrod (Eds.), *Infant social cognition: Empirical and theoretical considerations* (pp. 127–154). Hillsdale, NJ: Lawrence Erlbaum.

Lepore, S. J. (1992). Social conflict, social support, and psychological distress: Evidence of cross-domain buffering effects. *Journal of Personality and Social Psychology, 63*, 857–867.

Levitz-Jones, E. M., & Orlofsky, J. L. (1985). Separation–individuation and intimacy capacity in college women. *Journal of Personality and Social Psychology, 49*, 156–169.

Lewis, M., & Coates, D. (1980). Mother–infant interaction and infant cognitive performance. *Infant Behavior and Development, 3*, 95–105.

Maslow, A. H. (1970). *Motivation and personality*, 2nd ed. New York: Harper & Row.

Murray, H. A. (1938). *Explorations in personality.* New York: Oxford University Press.

Orlofsky, J. L., Marcia, J. E., & Lesser, I. (1973). Ego identity status and the intimacy versus isolation crisis of young adulthood. *Journal of Personality and Social Psychology, 27*, 211–219.

Pierce, G. R., Sarason, I. G., & Sarason, B. R. (1991). General and relationship-based perceptions of social support: Are two constructs better than one? *Journal of Personality and Social Psychology, 61*, 1028–1039.

Reis, H. T., & Franks, P. (1994). The role of intimacy and social support in health outcomes: Two processes or one? *Personal Relationships, 1*, 185–197.

Rempel, J. K., Holmes, J. G., & Zanna, M. P. (1985). Trust in close relationships. *Journal of Personality and Social Psychology, 49*, 95–112.

Ryan, R. M. (1991). The nature of the self in autonomy and relatedness. In J. Strauss & G. R. Goethals (Eds.), *The self: Interdisciplinary approaches* (pp. 208–238). New York: Springer-Verlag.

Ryan, R. M. (1993). Agency and organization: Intrinsic motivation, autonomy and the self in psychological development. In J. Jacobs (Ed.), *Nebraska symposium on motivation: Developmental perspectives on motivation*, Vol. 40 (pp. 1–56). Lincoln: University of Nebraska Press.

Ryan, R. M., Avery, R. R., & Grolnick, W. S. (1985). A Rorschach assessment of children's mutuality of autonomy. *Journal of Personality Assessment, 49(1)*, 6–12.

Ryan, R. M., & Connell, J. P. (1989). Perceived locus of causality and internalization: Examining reasons for acting in two domains. *Journal of Personality and Social Psychology, 57*, 749–761.

Ryan, R. M., Deci, E. L., & Grolnick, W. S. (1995). Autonomy, relatedness, and the self: Their relation to development and psychopathology. In D. Cicchetti & D. J. Cohen (Eds.), *Manual of developmental psychopathology: Vol. 1. Theory and methods* (pp. 618–655). New York: Wiley.

Ryan, R. M., & Grolnick, W. S. (1986). Origins and pawns in the classroom: Self-report and projective assessments of individual differences in children's perceptions. *Journal of Personality and Social Psychology, 50*, 550–558.

Ryan, R. M., & Lynch, J. (1989). Emotional autonomy versus detachment: Revisiting the vicissitudes of adolescence and young adulthood. *Child Development, 60*, 340–356.

Ryan, R. M., Stiller, J., & Lynch, J. H. (1994). Representations of relationships to teachers, parents, and friends as predictors of academic motivation and self-esteem. *Journal of Early Adolescence, 14*, 226–249.

Sarason, B. R., Pierce, G. R., Shearin, E. N., Sarason, I. G., Waltz, J. A., & Poppe, L. (1991). Perceived social support and working models of self and actual others. *Journal of Personality and Social Psychology, 60*, 273–287.

Stern, D. N. (1985). *The interpersonal world of the infant.* New York: Basic Books.

Stevenson, M. B., & Lamb, M. E. (1981). The effects of social experience and social style on cognitive competence and performance. In M. E. Lamb & L. R. Sherrod (Eds.), *Infant social cognition: Empirical and theoretical considerations* (pp. 375–394). Hillsdale, NJ: Lawrence Erlbaum.

Urist, J. (1977). The Rorschach test and the assessment of object relations. *Journal of Personality Assessment, 41(1)*, 3–9.

Waters, E., Wippman, J., & Sroufe, C. A. (1979). Attachment, positive affect, and competence in the peer group: Two studies in construct validation. *Child Development, 50*, 821–829.

Watson, J. S. (1966). The development and generalization of contingency awareness in early infancy: Some hypotheses. *Merrill-Palmer Quarterly, 12*, 123–135.

Weiss, L. A., & Grolnick, W. S. (April, 1991). The roles of parental involvement and support for autonomy in adolescent symptomatology. Paper presented at the Biennial Meeting of the Society for Research in Child Development. Seattle.

White, R. W. (1959). Motivation reconsidered: The concept of competence. *Psychological Review, 66*, 297–333.

White, R. W. (1963). *Ego and reality in psychoanalytic theory.* New York: International Universities Press.

Wild, J. (1965). Authentic existence: A new approach to "value theory." In J. M. Edie (Ed.), *An invitation to phenomenology: Studies in the philosophy of experience* (pp. 59–78). Chicago: Quadrangle.

Windle, M. (1992). Temperament and social support in adolescence: Interrelations with depressive symptoms and delinquent behaviors. *Journal of Youth and Adolescence, 21*, 1–21.

Winnicott, D. W. (1965). *The maturational process and the facilitating environment.* New York: International Universities Press.

Yarrow, L. J., Rubenstein, J. L., & Pederson, F. A. (1975). *Infant and environment: Early cognitive and motivational development.* New York: Wiley (Halsted).

12

The Impact of Marital and Social Network Support on Quality of Parenting

RONALD L. SIMONS and CHRISTINE JOHNSON

Several decades of research have demonstrated a link between quality of parenting and child development (Baumrind, 1993; Maccoby, 1992; Maccoby & Martin, 1983). These studies suggest that a parenting style characterized by warmth, inductive reasoning, appropriate monitoring, and clear communication fosters a child's cognitive functioning, social skills, moral development, and psychological adjustment. In contrast, parenting practices involving hostility, rejection, and coercion have been shown to increase the probability of negative developmental outcomes such as delinquency, psychopathology, academic failure, and substance abuse. These findings point to the importance of studies concerned with identifying the determinants of parental behavior. This chapter presents our model for integrating theory and research on this topic. The model identifies social support as an important cause of variations in quality of parenting.

We begin by reviewing studies showing that life stress, an antisocial personality, emotional distress, or having experienced harsh parenting during childhood increases the probability that an adult will engage in inept parenting. We then develop hypotheses regarding the manner in which both marital and social network support operate to reduce the risk to parenting posed by these factors. These hypotheses identify direct, indirect, and moderating effects of support on parenting. We argue that marital support and social network support influence parental behavior in quite different ways and that the impact of marital support varies by gender of parent. Findings from research on the determinants of

RONALD L. SIMONS and CHRISTINE JOHNSON • Department of Sociology and the Center for Family Research in Rural Mental Health, Iowa State University, Ames, Iowa 50011.

Handbook of Social Support and the Family, edited by Gregory R. Pierce, Barbara R. Sarason, and Irwin G. Sarason. Plenum Press, New York, 1996.

parenting are used to evaluate the validity of the ideas presented. We end the chapter with a consideration of the treatment implications of our theoretical model.

HAZARDS TO COMPETENT PARENTING

Past studies have provided considerable evidence that certain socioenvironmental, biographical, and psychological characteristics tend to increase the probability that adults will engage in inept parenting. Figure 1 presents the major risk factors identified by this research, along with the relationships that are posited to exist among them. As we will see in the next section, there is reason to believe that parenting is buffered against these risk factors by social support. In order to see how social support can affect such buffering, we must first clarify the nature of these risk factors and the manner in which they affect parenting. Thus, this section briefly discusses each of the relationships depicted in Figure 1.

Personality and Emotional Well-Being

An arrow in Figure 1 indicates a relationship between a person's personality/emotional state and that person's quality of parenting. This arrow represents a summary of two lines of research. First, past research has established that certain personality characteristics increase the probability of inept parenting. The attribute that has been most closely related to low-quality parenting is that of antisocial behavior trait. Antisocial behavior involves actions that are deemed risky, inappropriate, shortsighted, or insensitive by the majority of people in the society. Thus, individuals display an antisocial trait to the extent that they engaged in delinquent behavior during late childhood and early adolescence and continue as adults to participate in deviant actions such as interpersonal violence, substance use, sexual promiscuity, traffic violations, and the like. Logic would suggest that antisocial persons are likely to lack the motivation or skill necessary for competent parenting. Consonant with this idea, several studies have reported an association between antisocial behavior trait and quality of parenting (Capaldi & Patterson, 1991; Laub & Sampson, 1988; Patterson & Capaldi, 1991; Simons, Beaman, Conger, & Chao, 1993).

In addition to this personality effect, past research has established that a person's style of parenting is influenced by his or her emotional state. Several studies have reported a relationship between psychological depression and reduced quality of parenting (Colletta, April, 1981; Conger, McCarthy, Young, Lahey, & Kropp, 1984; Grossman, Eichler, & Winickoff, 1980; Orraschel, Weissman, & Kidd, 1980; Radke-Yarrow, Richters, & Wilson, 1988; Weissman & Paykel, 1974). This relationship would be expected, as one of the primary symptoms of depression is a diminished interest in activities and situations previously experienced as rewarding (Willner, 1985). Social relationships and events seem to lose their reinforcing value, and the person often becomes cantankerous if pressed or

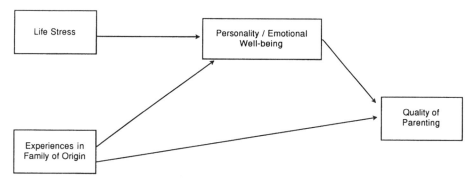

Figure 1. Impact of childhood experiences, life stress, and personality/emotional well-being on quality of parenting.

required to participate. Consequently, as persons become depressed, they are likely to become more disinterested and irritable in their approach to parenting.

Life Stress

Another arrow in Figure 1 indicates that life stress indirectly influences quality of parenting through its impact on the parent's personality/emotional well-being. Several studies have reported a link between life stress and reduced quality of parenting. There is evidence, for example, that unemployment and labor market shrinkage are associated with an increased incidence of child abuse (Light, 1973; Stenberg, Catalano, & Dooley, 1981), that job dissatisfaction is related positively to severity of punishment and inversely to involvement and use of inductive reasoning (Kemper & Reichler, 1976; McKinley, 1964), and that family economic hardship reduces parental involvement and increases the probability of harsh, explosive discipline (Caspi & Elder, 1988; Conger et al., 1984; Conger, Elder, Lorenz, Simons, & Whitbeck, 1992; Simons, Lorenz, Conger, & Wu, 1992).

Although there is strong support for the idea that life stress exerts a disruptive influence on parenting, one might expect the effect of stress on parenting to be indirect through its impact on the parent's emotional state. Evidence from both laboratory and survey research indicates that aversive events promote negative thoughts and memories, psychomotor tension, and a tendency to be depressed and irritable in interactions with others (Berkowitz, 1989). Thus, the frustration produced by economic hardship is likely to foster a depressed psychological state that operates, in turn, to decrease warmth and involvement with others, including one's children. Studies that have investigated this mediation hypothesis have found that indeed the impact of life stress on parenting is indirect through its effect on the parent's emotional well-being (Conger et al., 1992; Simons, Beaman, Conger, & Chao, 1993; Simons, Whitbeck, Melby, & Wu, 1994).

Parenting Experiences in Family of Origin

The last factor presented in Figure 1 concerns the manner in which the parent was parented as a child. A variety of studies have reported that individuals who were subjected to harsh treatment by their parents during childhood are at risk for following similar practices with their own offspring (Egeland, Jacobvitz, & Papatola, 1987; Herrenkohl, Herrenkohl, & Toedter, 1983; Straus, 1983). One arrow proceeding from this box in Figure 1 indicates that much of the effect of harsh treatment during childhood is indirect through its impact on the parent's personality/emotional state.

This indirect effect appears to operate in two ways. First, children raised by harsh or neglectful parents often develop antisocial characteristics (Patterson, Reid, & Dishion, 1992; Sampson & Laub, 1993; Simons, Wu, Conger, & Lorenz, 1994). Thus, individuals who received little parental nurturance or support during childhood are at risk for becoming antisocial adults, and we have already seen that persons with antisocial tendencies are at risk for inept parenting. Consonant with this line of reasoning, Simons, Wu, Johnson, and Conger (1995) found that much of the association between childhood abuse and harsh parenting of one's own children was indirect through antisocial behavior trait.

Second, there is evidence that exposure to inept parenting during childhood influences quality of parenting as an adult through its effect on emotional well-being. Rejecting or uninvolved parents tend to dispense feedback that lowers a child's feelings of self-worth and to furnish a set of unpredictable, aversive contingencies that promote perceptions of low self-efficacy (Skinner, 1985). Low self-esteem and perceptions of helplessness have, in turn, been linked to depression (Abramson, Seligman, & Teasdale, 1978; Beck, 1976). Therefore, one would expect a childhood history of exposure to harsh, rejecting parenting to be positively associated with depression. Several studies have found such an association to obtain (Abraham & Whittock, 1969; Jacobson, Fasman, & DiMascio, 1975; Lyons-Ruth, Cornell, Gruneboum, Botein, & Zoll, 1984; Whitbeck et al., 1992). This pattern of findings suggests that, at least in part, persons raised by abusive or neglectful parents are at risk for being poor parents themselves because they suffer from feelings of depression and irritability. A recent paper by Simons, Beaman, et al. (1993) provides support for this idea.

Although much of the effect of childhood abuse on adult parenting may be indirect through the parent's personality or emotional state, there appears to be, as another arrow in Figure 1 indicates, a direct effect as well. Two recent studies reported that individuals subjected to severe physical discipline as children continued to demonstrate an elevated risk for utilizing similar parenting strategies with their own offspring even after controlling for the effects of personality and emotional well-being (Simons, Whitbeck, Conger, & Wu, 1991; Simons, Beaman, et al., 1993). Thus, in addition to increasing the probability of antisocial tendencies and depression, it seems that childhood exposure to rejection, neglect, or physical abuse teaches parenting scripts that children grow up to enact with their own offspring.

While the socioenvironmental, biographical, and psychological factors presented in Figure 1 increase the risk for inept parenting, parents often have access to coping resources that operate to counter these deleterious influences. The coping resource most often cited is that of social support. Social support, whether from a spouse or from friends and relatives, is viewed as a protective mechanism that combats the effect of hazardous factors and promotes high-quality parenting (Belsky, 1984; Cicchetti & Rizley, 1981; Cochran & Brassard, 1979). The next two sections of this chapter attempt to identify the specific ways in which social support influences parenting. Spouse and social network support are considered separately, as these two types of support are expected to bolster parenting through quite different avenues.

SPOUSE SUPPORT AND QUALITY OF PARENTING

The construct most often considered in studies of the determinants of parenting is quality of the marital relationship. A variety of studies have reported an association between marital satisfaction and skillful parenting (Belsky, Gilstrap, & Rovine, 1984; Easterbrooks & Emde, 1988; Engfer, 1988; Feldman, Nash, & Aschenbrenner, 1983; Meyer, 1988; Pederson, 1982; Simons, Whitbeck, Conger, & Melby, 1990). This relationship has been shown to hold for both mothers and fathers, in various countries, and for parents of infants, toddlers, and preschoolers (Belsky, 1990). A recent study by Cox, Owen, Lewis, and Henderson (1989) reported that the influence of marital quality upon parenting remains after controlling for the effects of parents' psychological characteristics.

Although there is strong evidence that characteristics of the marital relationship are associated with quality of parenting, the processes that link the two remain to be identified. Theorizing about such mechanisms has been hindered, in part, by the variety of definitions and measures used in research on marital quality. Some investigators, for example, use dyadic measures, whereas others emphasize the importance of obtaining separate assessments for each spouse; some obtain global reports of relationship satisfaction, whereas others strive to assess the specific behaviors that each spouse directs toward the other.

We believe that spouse support might best be defined as the extent to which a person receives high levels of warmth, encouragement, and assistance in interactions with the partner. This definition is consistent with the definition of social support used in studies concerned with stress and coping (Cobb, 1976; Cohen & Wills, 1985; House, 1981; Wills, 1990). Indeed, we view spouse support as social support provided by a spouse.

Direct Effects

So defined, marital support might be expected to influence quality of parenting in several ways. First, a supportive spouse is likely to provide advice and assistance to the other spouse regarding the tasks and responsibilities of parenting. This resource should enable a parent to perform his or her parenting duties more competently. This function is depicted in Figure 2 by arrow F, which links

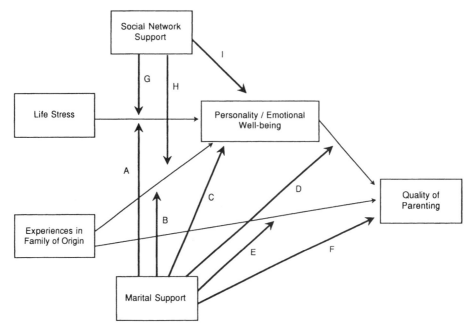

Figure 2. Model of the direct, indirect, and moderating influences of social network and marital support on quality of parenting.

marital support to quality of parenting. Two recent studies have reported evidence for this direct effect of spouse support on parenting (Simons, Lorenz, Wu, & Conger, 1993; Simons, Whitbeck, Melby, & Wu, 1994).

Indirect Effects

Besides this direct effect, Jay Belsky (Belsky, 1984; Belsky & Vondra, 1989) has argued that marital support influences quality of parenting through its impact on psychological well-being. Expressions of warmth and caring from a spouse are strongly rewarding. A variety of studies have found high marital support to be associated with low levels of psychological distress, as depicted by arrow C in Figure 2 (Campbell, Converse, & Rogers, 1976; Glenn & Weaver, 1981; Lee, 1978; Lewinsohn, Hoberman, & Rosenbaum, 1988; Merikangas, Prusoff, Kupfer, & Frank, 1985). Thus, the evidence suggests that spouse support affects quality of parenting indirectly through its impact upon the partner's emotional well-being.

Moderating Effects

Finally, in addition to these direct and indirect influences, spouse support might be expected to operate as a protective factor that buffers parenting against the various potentially disruptive influences. Some researchers have suggested, for example, that spouse support operates as a coping resource that reduces the threat that life stress poses for parenting (Belsky & Vondra, 1989; Cicchetti & Rizley, 1981). Consonant with this hypothesis, Elder, Liker, and Cross (1984) found that marital support had a buffering effect for fathers in their study of families of the Great Depression, and Simons, Lorenz, et al. (1992) found this effect for mothers in their study of rural families in Iowa. In these two studies, the relationship between life stress and problematic parenting was significantly lower for individuals with a supportive spouse.

Although these studies provide substantiation for the idea that spouse support may protect parenting from the threat posed by life stress, they do not provide information about the manner in which this moderating influence is achieved. Figure 2 identifies two possible avenues. First, spouse support is likely to reduce the association between economic strain and psychological distress (arrow A). Given the emotional intensity and frequency of interaction in marital relationships, a person's mate should be a particularly potent source of support and assistance during difficult times (Fincham & Bradbury, 1990; Recs, 1990). In keeping with this contention, several studies have reported that supportive social relationships serve to moderate the relationship between stressful events and psychological distress (Kessler, Price, & Wortman, 1985; Thoits, 1985). Thus, there is reason to believe that a marital partner will be less likely to become emotionally distressed in the face of aversive events when the other partner is a source of understanding, advice, and assistance.

Second, spouse support may buffer parenting against the threat posed by stressful events by reducing the relationship between emotional distress and parental behavior (arrow D). Supportive spouses most likely provide increased encouragement, advice, and assistance with parenting when they perceive their mates to be emotionally upset. This likelihood suggests that the presence of a supportive spouse may reduce the probability that a person's emotional distress will spill over into his or her parenting. Two recent studies provide support for this idea. Simons, Lorenz, et al. (1993) found that the association between depression and parental uninvolvement was significantly lower for mothers high on spouse support, and Simons, Whitbeck, Melby, and Wu (1994) found the same moderator pattern for the relationship between hostility and harsh parenting. Thus, at least in the case of mothers, it appears that there are two avenues whereby spouse support serves to buffer the disruptive effects of life stress: by tempering the effect of aversive events on emotional well-being and by reducing the impact of emotional distress on quality of parenting.

Just as there are two ways in which marital support buffers parenting against life stress, so there appear to be multiple means whereby support from a spouse reduces the threat posed by having been raised by dysfunctional parents. Figure 2 identifies three avenues through which such protection might be expressed. First, supportive spouses may have a moderating effect in that they may model, cue, and reinforce parenting practices that counter the ineffectual parenting scripts that their mates learned in their families of origin (arrow E). Consistent with this hypothesis, Quinton and Rutter (1988) have reported that girls raised in a deprived environment are less likely to engage in inept parenting if they have a supportive mate. Similarly, Egeland, Jacobvitz, and Sroufe (1988) found that involvement in an emotionally satisfying marital relationship significantly decreases the probability that abused mothers will engage in similar parenting practices with their own children.

Spouse support might also reduce the risk to parenting posed by childhood exposure to dysfunctional parents by decreasing the likelihood that such a family environment will result in antisocial tendencies, a protective influence represented by arrow B. Several studies have shown that individuals who experienced harsh, uninvolved, or inconsistent parenting during childhood are at risk for antisocial behavior during adolescence and early adulthood (Sampson & Laub, 1993; Widom, 1989). Further, a recent paper by Simons, Wu, Johnson, and Conger (1995) reported that, at least in part, the effect of childhood exposure to inadequate parenting on subsequent use of inept parenting practices with one's own children is indirect through antisocial behavior trait: Parental rejection and inconsistency increase the probability that an individual will develop a general antisocial orientation, which in turn increases the likelihood that the individual will be an inept parent.

Few studies have investigated the possibility that a supportive spouse might moderate antisocial tendencies acquired in one's family of origin. Two panel studies, however, provide support for this idea. Sampson and Laub (1990, 1993) recently examined three decades of panel data for a group of several hundred males who had been adjudicated delinquent during adolescence. They found that strong attachment to a spouse significantly increased the chances that a man would discontinue involvement in antisocial behavior. Marital status had little predictive value; rather, it was high quality of the marital relationship that increased the probability of a conventional lifestyle. Similarly, Werner and Smith (1992), in their Kauai Longitudinal Study, found that high quality of the marital relationship reduced the probability that persons who were delinquent during adolescence would continue to be antisocial as adults. Consonant with the findings of Sampson and Laub, marital status per se had no moderating influence. These studies suggest that a supportive spouse may protect parenting by reducing the likelihood that experiences in one's family of origin will result in an adult pattern of antisocial behavior.

Finally, spouse support may buffer parenting by diminishing the likelihood that a person with antisocial tendencies will engage in dysfunctional parenting. Earlier, we noted that arrow D in Figure 2 indicates that marital support serves to reduce the probability that a mate's negative emotional state will spill over into his or her approach to parenting. In addition, this arrow suggests that a supportive spouse may prevent an antisocial partner from expressing this behavior trait toward their children. We are not aware of any studies that have tested this hypothesis. It seems likely, however, that a supportive spouse may be able to soothe and caution a drunken or angry mate who threatens to strike out at the children.

Summarizing, there are a variety of ways in which marital support may impact quality of parenting. These avenues include direct, indirect, and moderating influences. Thus, it appears that the level of support received from a spouse is a major determinant of parental behavior. The next section considers the manner in which social network support affects quality of parenting.

SOCIAL NETWORK SUPPORT AND QUALITY OF PARENTING

Social network support refers to warmth, encouragement, and assistance provided by friends, neighbors, and extended family. Several prominent behavioral scientists have contended that social network support, like marital support, serves to increase parental nurturance and reduces the probability of harsh or rejecting parenting practices (Belsky, 1984; Belsky & Vondra, 1989; Cicchetti & Rizley, 1981; Garbarino, 1977; Garbarino & Crouter, 1978). A few studies have found support for this idea. Powell (1980), for example, reported that mothers who had regular contact with friends were more responsive to their children than mothers who had less frequent interaction with friends. Colletta (1981) found that teenage mothers were less likely to engage in harsh punishment if they had supportive contact with friends and relatives. Further, findings by Jennings, Stagg, and Connors (1985) indicated that mothers were more nurturing and less controlling when they were satisfied with the emotional support they were receiving from their social network.

Although support from friends, relatives, and neighbors has been linked to quality of parenting, Belsky (Belsky, 1984; Belsky & Vondra, 1989) has argued that such support is likely to be secondary to that of the marital relationship. Consistent with this view, studies that have examined the relative importance of marital vs. other kinds of support have found that quality of the marital relationship is more strongly related to variations in parental behavior than is social network support (Crnic, Greenberg, Ragozin, Robinson, & Basham, 1983; Friedrich, 1979; Wandersman & Unger, 1983).

While these studies do indicate that social network support is secondary to marital support as a determinant of quality of parenting, they fail to identify the reasons for the primacy of the marital relationship. Belsky and Vondra (1989) have suggested that the marital relationship is more fundamental because individuals typically invest much more time and emotional energy in their marriage than in other relationships. While this suggestion is undoubtedly true, we believe that structural considerations also limit the extent to which relationships with friends serve to influence parental behavior. The marital partner is available within the home to provide encouragement and assistance with the everyday tasks of parenting, whereas friends and relatives are not.

These dissimilarities between marital and other close relationships suggest important differences in the way spouse and social network support are likely to influence parenting. These differences are depicted in Figure 2. In the previous section, we discussed seven means whereby marital support might affect quality of parenting. Consonant with the hypothesis that the marital partner impacts parenting more than friends, relatives, and neighbors, Figure 2 identifies only three avenues of influence for social network support. The remainder of this section is concerned with comparing and contrasting the various ways that social network support differs from marital support in its effect on parental behavior.

Direct Effects

First, although Figure 2 shows a direct path from marital support to quality of parenting (arrow F), no such path is shown for social network support. This difference is a function of the structural considerations just mentioned. Although a supportive spouse furnishes advice and assistance that helps the other spouse parent more competently, friends and relatives, while they may occasionally help with child care, are simply not available in the household to provide assistance with the everyday tasks and responsibilities of parenting.

Indirect Effects

Social network support would be expected, however, to influence parental behavior indirectly through its impact upon emotional well-being (arrow I). Several studies have reported that support from friends and relatives diminishes feelings of depression (Kessler et al., 1985). Although there is evidence that a supportive social network operates to reduce depression, this effect is likely to be smaller than that of spouse support. Given the intensity and frequency of inter-action with the marital partner, one would expect the level of support and assistance provided by the partner to influence emotional well-being to a greater degree than quality of interaction with friends and relatives. Consistent with this argument, past studies have found that quality of the marital relationship is a stronger predictor of depression than is satisfaction with less intimate relation-ships (Brown & Harris, 1978; Leaf, Weissman, Myers, Tischler, & Holzer, 1984). These findings suggest that path I is more influential than path C.

Moderating Effects

Thus far, we have argued that social network support is secondary to marital support, as it does not directly affect parenting and its indirect effect through emotional well-being is likely to be less consequential than that of the marital relationship. In addition, one would expect social network support to be a less potent *buffer* of parenting than support from a spouse. Figure 2 depicts several ways in which this is likely to be the case.

First, as noted earlier, studies have reported that supportive social relation-ships may moderate the relationship between stressful events and depression. Figure 2 suggests that both marital and spouse support might serve this function. Given differences in frequency and intensity of interaction, however, spouse support is more likely to produce this buffering effect than is support from friends and relatives (i.e., arrow A is expected to have a greater effect than arrow G).

Second, while we argued that spouse support may moderate the effect of emotional disturbance on parenting (arrow D), social network support is not expected to display this effect. One spouse may encourage or assist the other, distressed spouse with tasks relating to parenting and thereby reduce the probability that the distressed spouse's emotional state will spill over into her or his parenting. Friends and relatives, on the other hand, are not usually available in the household to provide advice and assistance with the everyday tasks and responsibilities of parenting. Therefore, although friends and relatives may offer understanding and encouragement that moderates the effect of stressors upon emotional well-being, there is little reason to expect that they will be able to lessen the disruptive influence of emotional distress on parenting. Simons, Lorenz, et al. (1993) found support for this contention. Although marital support moderated the impact of emotional distress on quality of parenting, social network support did not.

By the same logic, there is no reason to believe that social support from friends can moderate the relationship between having been exposed to harsh parenting as a child and the probability of using similar parenting practices with one's own offspring. Although a supportive spouse may model, cue, and reinforce parenting practices that counter the ineffectual parenting scripts that their mates learned in their families of origin (arrow E), friends and relatives are rarely present when parents discipline their children. Further, it is considered culturally inappropriate for a friend to provide unsolicited advice regarding parenting practices.

While it is unlikely that friends and relatives can moderate parenting scripts acquired in the family of origin, arrow H in Figure 2 indicates that they may reduce the probability that childhood exposure to inept parenting will result in a general antisocial lifestyle. This suggestion is bolstered by recent studies that have reported that supportive relationships with friends and relatives reduce the probability that persons raised in a high-risk family environment will display behavior problems during adolescence and adulthood (Simons, Whitbeck, & Wu, 1994; Werner & Smith, 1992).

Although Belsky and Vondra (1989) assert that the marital partner is the primary support system for parenting, they contend that the social network becomes the principal parental support system when marital support is absent. Thus, they view social network support as a more critical determinant of quality of parenting for single than for married parents. We believe this to be true in a limited sense. Compared to persons married to a supportive spouse, single parents (or married parents who receive little warmth and assistance from their marital partners) are more dependent upon their social network for social support. Understanding, assistance, and companionship provided by friends and relatives should be more consequential for the emotional well-being of such persons than for individuals who have access to a supportive spouse (Emerson, 1981; Homans, 1974). Thus, the association between social network support and emotional well-being (arrow I) should be stronger for persons low compared to those high on spouse support. Simons, Lorenz, et al. (1993) found some support for this idea.

While social network support may become a more salient determinant of emotional well-being when marital support is low or absent, it is unlikely that it can compensate or substitute to any significant degree for the other functions served by a supportive spouse. There is no reason to believe, for example, that social network support may exert a direct effect on parenting when the spouse is missing. Friends and relatives are so rarely present in the household that even under conditions of low spouse support, it is unlikely that they will be able to provide sufficient assistance to contribute significantly to the quality of everyday parental behavior. Consistent with this contention, a recent study of single-parent families reported that the impact of social network support on quality of parenting was limited to an indirect effect through parents' emotional well-being (Simons, Beaman, et al., 1993). And Simons, Lorenz, et al. (1993) failed to find any evidence that social network support directly influences the parenting practices of married persons who lack a supportive relationship with their spouses.

Our conclusion that social network support has little impact upon quality of parenting is contrary to the claim made by many that absence of social network support (or social isolation) is a major cause of child maltreatment (Garbarino & Stocking, 1980; Helfer & Kempe, 1976; Whittaker & Garbarino, 1983). While this assertion is frequently made, it should be noted that there is actually little research support for the contention. Unfortunately, studies on this topic have been plagued with conceptual and methodological difficulties. The evidence that exists, however, fails to find an association between lack of social network support and physical abuse of children. Further, while there is some evidence that neglectful parents are socially isolated, the isolation appears to be a consequence of the parents' personality characteristics (Seagull, 1987). These findings are consistent with the arguments and research findings that we have presented regarding the limited role of social network support as a determinant of parental behavior.

While we believe that social network support exerts much less influence on quality of parenting than marital support, this assertion needs to be qualified. It may well be that friends and relatives who live with the parent have the potential to exercise on parenting practices an influence similar to that of a marital partner. We have argued that the marital relationship is a primary source of support for parental behavior because of the frequency and intensity of interaction that characterizes such relationships. If this is true, a comparable effect would be expected from other adults who share a residence with the parent. Thus, a close friend or relative who lives with the parent (e.g., lover, grandmother) and assists in the rearing of the child might fulfill the same supportive functions as a spouse. This consideration is important given the increasing number of nontraditional families in our society. There is a need for research that examines the manner in which support provided by such individuals influences parental behavior.

GENDER DIFFERENCES

Although the marital relationship is an important support for the parenting of both mothers and fathers, there is evidence of gender differences in the way spouse support impacts parental behavior. These differences appear to be rooted in culturally based role definitions. Marital couples tend to acknowledge a division of labor whereby the husband is recognized as the expert in some areas and the wife in others. In most marriages, parenting is fundamentally the wife's domain (LaRossa, 1986). Men are usually much less involved than their wives in the daily care and supervision of the children (Lamb, 1977; Parke, 1981; Pleck, 1985; Rexroat & Shehan, 1987), and they tend to see themselves as cast in a supporting role in which their responsibility is to provide assistance to the primary parent, the mother (Barnett & Baruch, 1988; LaRossa, 1986; Nock & Kingston, 1988; Simons, Beaman, et al., 1992). The parenting duties of the husband tend to center around playing with the child and enforcing discipline.

Given this division of labor, husbands often defer to their wives in matters pertaining to parenting. As a consequence, husbands tend to be influenced by their wives' ideas about children and parenting. Two recent studies (Simons et al., 1990; Simons, Beaman, et al., 1993) have reported an association between a wife's parenting beliefs and her husband's parental behavior. Indeed, these studies found that the wife's beliefs were often better predictors of the husband's parenting practices than were his own beliefs about parenting. These findings indicate that wives are a major determinant of the level and quality of their husbands' involvement in parenting. Presumably, the closer and more supportive the marital relationship, the more the husband will be influenced by his wife's parenting views.

This culturally based division of labor regarding parenting also suggests gender differences in the way spouse support serves to buffer the impact of emotional distress on parental behavior. Men are usually much less involved than their wives in the daily care and supervision of the children (Belsky et al., 1984; Clarke-Stewart, 1980; Ehrensaft, 1983; Lamb, 1977; Parke, 1981). Most of the burdens of child care fall on the mother, who is expected to discharge her parenting responsibilities regardless of the stressors or emotional distractions with which she may be confronted. A supportive husband, however, will be sensitive to his wife's emotional state and provide increased assistance with parenting during times of stress. One would expect this assistance to lessen the probability that the wife's negative emotional state will disrupt her parenting.

Whereas the wife's involvement in parenting is normatively obligated, the husband's level of participation is more a matter of choice. To the extent that fathers are involved in parenting, their behavior tends to center upon playing with the child and enforcing discipline. Hence, during times of emotional distress, the husband might be expected to withdraw from parenting. Given the culturally prescribed voluntary nature of the husband's involvement in parenting, the supportive wife is likely to allow this choice. Thus, the supportive husband may assist his distressed wife with culturally obligated parenting tasks, thereby reducing the impact of her emotional state upon her parenting behaviors, but the supportive wife may permit her distressed husband to retreat from parental involvement until he feels better. In other words, while husband support may serve to moderate the association between the wife's emotional distress and quality of her parenting (arrow D in Figure 2), the reverse probably does not hold true: The supportive wife likely does not moderate the association between husband distress and quality of his parenting because she allows him to withdraw from parenting responsibilities. This idea is corroborated by recent studies reporting that marital support reduces the association between emotional distress and quality of parenting for mothers, but not for fathers (Simons, Lorenz, et al., 1992, 1993; Simons, Whitbeck, Melby, & Wu, 1994).

Thus, while there are various avenues whereby marital support enhances quality of parenting for both mothers and fathers, it also appears that there are gender differences in the way a supportive spouse influences the other spouse's parenting. Given cultural norms regarding parenting responsibilities, husbands tend to conform to the parenting beliefs of a supportive wife, and a supportive husband reduces the probability that a wife's emotional distress will spill over into her parenting.

TREATMENT IMPLICATIONS

Human service professionals often face the task of improving the quality of parenting provided by parents. This situation occurs when parents are neglecting or abusing their children or when children are displaying externalizing or internalizing problems that might be ameliorated through a change in parental behavior. Although a number of strategies for enhancing quality of parenting have been developed, outcome studies suggest that the most effective procedures involve teaching parents the specific skills associated with competent parenting (Kazdin, 1984; Patterson, 1982). Unfortunately, researchers have established that contextual factors often nullify treatment effects.

Several studies have reported an increased probability of treatment failure among high-stressed or disadvantaged families (Dumas, 1984; Dumas & Wahler, 1983). Although these parents may demonstrate short-term improvement in childrearing techniques, their parenting practices often return to baseline levels within a few weeks (Dumas, 1990; Wahler & Dumas, 1987). Such results indicate that parental behavior is not simply a reflection of skills and beliefs regarding parenting. Rather, a parent's behavior toward his or her child is shaped by a variety of socioenvironmental factors. On the basis of this finding, some practitioners have argued that parent intervention programs need to include a consideration of contextual factors (Dumas, 1990). But which of the various determinants of parental behavior should be targeted? The answer to this question requires that we identify factors that both exert a strong effect upon parental behavior and are amenable to practitioner influences.

Our review in this chapter indicated that childhood abuse, aversive events and circumstances, emotional distress, and antisocial tendencies tend to increase the probability of dysfunctional parenting. It would be very difficult to address such factors as part of an intervention concerned with improving quality of parenting. In most cases, a therapist charged with the task of teaching parenting skills will not have the expertise, time, or energy required to address these contextual influences.

In recent years, great enthusiasm has developed among human service professionals regarding the use of naturally existing social support networks to prevent or treat social problems. Consonant with this trend, some child welfare experts have contended that intervention programs for inept parenting should target the informal social support networks of parents (Garbarino & Stocking, 1980; Helfer & Kempe, 1976; Whittaker & Garbarino, 1983). Considerations of practicality aside, the arguments and evidence presented in this chapter suggest that this approach is likely to have little effect.

Although social network support appears to have little impact on parental behavior, we have seen that marital support contributes to quality of parenting in a number of ways. First, a supportive spouse often directly effects the mate's parenting by offering advice, cues, and encouragement. Second, support provided by a spouse can influence parenting indirectly through its impact on the marital partner's emotional well-being. Finally, spouse support may moderate the extent to which an abusive childhood, an antisocial personality, or psychological distress results in destructive parenting practices. Whereas a practitioner may be helpless to modify these risks for dysfunctional parenting, a supportive spouse may serve to limit their effects.

Spouse support is not only a powerful determinant of parental behavior, but also would seem to be more amenable to practitioner influence than most of the other factors that have been found to affect parental behavior. Parent training often involves both parents, so issues of marital support could easily be included as an additional component of treatment. In cases in which intervention is directed toward only one of the parents, the other parent might be invited to attend sessions concerned with enhancing marital support. When available, live-in lovers, friends, or relatives might be substituted in the case of single parents.

Presumably, marital support interventions would focus upon the different avenues of influence identified in Figure 2. The spouses might be taught, for example, to cue and reinforce each other to use parenting strategies learned in treatment rather than continue to follow the dysfunctional practices acquired in childhood. Further, the partners might be encouraged to provide each other with extra encouragement and assistance with parenting tasks during times of emotional distress. Techniques that have been developed for improving a couple's communication and problem-solving skills might be used as a basis for designing strategies for teaching spouses to enhance the quality of each other's parenting. Research on determinants of parental behavior suggests that expanding the focus of parent training to include a consideration of marital support may well magnify the effectiveness of such interventions.

REFERENCES

Abraham, M., & Whittock, F. (1969). Childhood experience and depression. *British Journal of Psychiatry*, *115*, 883–888.

Abramson, L., Seligman, M., & Teasdale, J. (1978). Learned helplessness in humans: Critique and reformulation. *Journal of Abnormal Psychology*, *87*, 49–74.

Barnett, R. C., & Baruch, G. K. (1987). Determinants of fathers' participation in family work. *Journal of Marriage and the Family, 49,* 29–40.

Baumrind, D. (1993). The average expectable environment is not good enough: A response to Scarr. *Child Development, 64,* 1299–1317.

Beck, A. T. (1976). *Cognitive therapy and emotional disorder.* New York: International Universities Press.

Belsky, J. (1984). The determinants of parenting: A process model. *Child Development, 55,* 83–96.

Belsky, J. (1990). Child care and children's socioemotional development. *Journal of Marriage and the Family, 52,* 885–903.

Belsky, J., Gilstrap, B., and Rovine, M. (1984). The Pennsylvania Infant and Family Development Project. I. Stability and change in mother–infant and father–infant interaction in a family setting at 1-to-3-to-9 months. *Child Development, 55,* 692–705.

Belsky, J., & Vondra, J. (1989). Lessons from child abuse: The determinants of parenting. In D. Cicchetti & V. Carlson (Eds.), *Child maltreatment: Theory and research on the causes and consequences of child abuse and neglect* (pp. 153–202). New York: Cambridge University Press.

Berkowitz, L. (1989). Frustration–aggression hypothesis: Examination and reformulation. *Psychological Bulletin, 106,* 59–73.

Brown, G. W., & Harris, T. D. (1978). *Social origins of depression: A study of psychiatric disorder in women.* New York: Free Press.

Campbell, A., Converse, P. E., & Rogers, W., (1976). *The quality of American life.* New York: Russell Sage Foundation.

Capaldi, D. M., & Patterson, G. R. (1991). Relation of parental transitions to boys' adjustment problems. I. A linear hypothesis. II. Mothers at risk for transitions and unskilled parenting. *Developmental Psychology, 27,* 489–504.

Caspi, A., & Elder, G. H., Jr. (1988). Emergent family patterns: The inter-generational construction of problem behavior and relationships. In R. A. Hinde & J. Stevenson-Hinde (Eds.), *Relationships within families* (pp. 218–240). New York: Oxford University Press.

Cicchetti, D., & Rizley, R. (1981). Developmental perspectives on the etiology, intergenerational transmission and sequelae of child maltreatment. *New Directions for Child Development, 11,* 31–56.

Clarke-Stewart, K. A. (1980). The father's contribution to children's cognitive and social development in early childhood. In F. Pedersen (Ed.), *The father–infant relationship* (pp. 111–146). New York: Praeger.

Cobb, S. (1976). Social support as a moderator of life stress. *Psychosomatic Medicine, 38,* 300–314.

Cochran, M. M., & Brassard, J. A. (1979). Child development and personal social networks. *Child Development, 50,* 601–616.

Cohen, S., & Wills, T. A. (1985). Stress, social support, and the buffering hypothesis. *Psychological Bulletin, 98,* 310–357.

Colletta, N. D. (April, 1981). The influence of support systems on the maternal behavior of young mothers. Paper presented at the biennial meeting of the Society for Research in Child Development. Boston.

Conger, R. D., Elder, G. H., Jr., Lorenz, F. O., Simons, R. L., & Whitbeck, L. B. (1992). A family process model of economic hardship and influences on adjustment of early adolescent boys. *Child Development, 63,* 526–541.

Conger, R. D., McCarthy, J. A., Young, R. K., Lahey, B. B., & Kropp, J. P. (1984). Perception of child, child-rearing values, and emotional distress as mediating links between environmental stressors and observed maternal behavior. *Child Development, 55,* 2234–2247.

Cox, M., Owen, M. R., Lewis, J. M., & Henderson, V. K. (1989). Marriage, adult adjustment, and early parenting. *Child Development, 60,* 1015–1024.

Crnic, K. A., Greenberg, M. T., Ragozin, A. S., Robinson, N. M., & Basham, R. (1983). Effects of stress and social support on mothers and premature and full-term infants. *Child Development, 54,* 209–217.

Dumas, J. E. (1984). Child, adult-interactional, and socioeconomic setting events as predictors of parent training outcome. *Education and Treatment of Children, 7,* 351–364.

Dumas, J. E. (1990). Contextual effects in mother–child interaction: Beyond an operant analysis. In E. A. Blechman (Ed.), *Emotions and the family* (pp. 155–179). Hillsdale, NJ: Lawrence Erlbaum.

Dumas, J. E., & Wahler, R. G. (1983). Predictors of treatment outcome in parent training: Mother insularity and socioeconomic disadvantage. *Behavioral Assessment, 5*, 301–313.

Easterbrooks, M. A., & Emde, R. N. (1988). Marital and parent–child relationships: The role of affect in the family system. In R. A. Hinde & J. Stevenson-Hinde (Eds.), *Relationships within families: Mutual influences* (pp. 83–103). New York: Oxford University Press.

Egeland, B., Jacobvitz, D., & Papatola, K. (1987). Intergenerational continuity of abuse. In R. J. Gelles & J. B. Lancaster (Eds.), *Child abuse and neglect: Biosocial dimensions* (pp. 255–176). New York: Aldine.

Egeland, B., Jacobvitz, D., & Sroufe, L. A. (1988). Breaking the cycle of abuse. *Child Development, 59*, 1080–1088.

Ehrensaft, D. (1983). When women and men mother. In J. Trebilcot (Ed)., *Mothering: Essays in feminist theory* (pp. 41–61). Totowa, NJ: Rowan & Allanheld.

Elder, G. H., Jr., Liker, J. K., & Cross, C. E. (1984). Parent–child behavior in the Great Depression: Life course and intergenerational influences. In P. B. Baltes & O. G. Brim (Eds.), *Life span development and behavior*, Vol. 6 (pp. 109–158). New York: Academic Press.

Emerson, R. M. (1981). Social exchange theory. In M. Rosenberg & R. H. Turner (Eds.), *Social psychology: Sociological perspectives* (pp. 30–65). New York: Basic Books.

Engfer, A. (1988). The interrelatedness of marriage and the mother–child relationship. In R. A. Hinde & J. Stevenson-Hinde (Eds.), *Relationships within families: Mutual influences* (pp. 104–118). New York: Oxford University Press.

Feldman, S. S., Nash, S. C., & Aschenbrenner, B. (1983). Antecedents of fathering. *Child Development, 54*, 1628–1636.

Fincham, F. D., & Bradbury, T. N. (1990). Social support in marriage: The role of social cognition. *Journal of Social and Clinical Psychology, 9*, 31–42.

Friedrich, W. N. (1979). Predictors of the coping behavior of mothers of handicapped children. *Journal of Consulting and Clinical Psychology, 47*, 1140–1141.

Garbarino, J. (1977). The price of privacy in the social dynamics of child abuse. *Child Welfare, 56*, 565–575.

Garbarino, J., & Crouter, A. C. (1978). Defining the community context of parent–child relations. *Child Development, 49*, 604–616.

Garbarino, J., & Stocking, S. (1980). *Protecting children from abuse and neglect: Developing and maintaining effective support systems for families.* San Francisco: Jossey-Bass.

Glenn, N. D., & Weaver, C. N. (1981). The contribution of marital happiness to global happiness. *Social Forces, 43*, 161–168.

Grossman, F., Eichler, L., & Winickoff, S. (1980). *Pregnancy, birth, and parenthood: Adaptations of mothers, fathers, and infants.* San Francisco: Jossey-Bass.

Helfer, R. E., & Kempe, C. H. (1976). *Child abuse and neglect: The family and the community.* Cambridge, MA: Ballinger.

Herrenkohl, E. C., Herrenkohl, R. C., & Toedter, L. J. (1983). Perspectives on the intergenerational transmission of abuse. In D. Finkelhor, R. J. Gelles, G. T. Hotaling, & M. A. Straus (Eds.), *The dark side of families: Current family violence research* (pp. 305–316). Beverly Hills: Sage Publications.

Homans, G. C. (1974). *Behavior: Its elementary forms.* New York: Harcourt Brace Jovanovich.

House, J. C. (1981). *Work stress and social support.* Reading, MA: Addison-Wesley.

Jacobson, S., Fasman, J., & DiMascio, A. (1975). Deprivation in the childhood of depressed women. *Journal of Nervous and Mental Diseases, 160*, 5–13.

Jennings, K. D., Stagg, V., & Connors, R. (April, 1985). Social support and mothers' interactions with their preschool children. Paper presented at the biennial meeting of the Society for Research in Child Development. Toronto.

Kazdin, A. E. (1984). Treatment of conduct disorders. In J. B. W. Williams & R. L. Spitzer (Eds.), *Psychotherapy research: Where are we and where should we go?* (pp. 3–27). New York: Guilford Press.

Kemper, T., & Reichler, M. (1976). Father's work integration and frequencies of rewards and punishments administered by fathers and mothers to adolescent sons and daughters. *Journal of Genetic Psychology, 129*, 207–219.

Kessler, R. C., Price, R. H., & Wortman, C. B. 1985. Social factors in psychopathology: Stress, social support, and coping processes. *Annual Review of Psychology, 36*, 531–572.

Lamb, M. E. (1977). *The role of the father in child development.* New York: Wiley.

LaRossa, R. (1986). *Becoming a parent.* Beverly Hills: Sage Publications.

Laub, J. H., & Sampson, R. J. (1988). Unraveling families and delinquency: A reanalysis of the Guecks' data. *Criminology, 26,* 355–379.

Leaf, P. J., Weissman, M. M., Myers, J. K., Tischler, G. L., & Holzer, D. E. (1984). Social factors related to psychiatric disorder: The Yale Epidemiologic Catchment Area Study. *Social Psychology, 19,* 53–61.

Lee, G. R. (1978)., Marriage and morale in later life. *Journal of Marriage and the Family, 40,* 131–139.

Lewinsohn, P. M., Hoberman, H. M., & Rosenbaum, M. (1988). A prospective study of risk factors for unipolar depression. *Journal of Abnormal Psychology, 97,* 251–264.

Light, R. (1973). Abused and neglected children in America: A study of alternative policies. *Harvard Educational Review, 43,* 556–598.

Lyons-Ruth, K., Cornell, D., Gruneboum, M., Botein, M., & Zoll, D. (1984). Maternal family history, maternal caretaking and infant attachment in multiproblem families. *Journal of Preventative Psychiatry, 2,* 403–425.

Maccoby, E. (1992). The role of parents in the socialization of children: An historical overview. *Developmental Psychology, 28,* 1006–1017.

Maccoby, E., & Martin, J. A. (1983). Socialization in the context of the family: Parent–child interaction. In P. Mussen (Ed.), *Handbook of child psychology* (pp. 1–101). New York: Wiley.

McKinley, D. (1964). *Social class and family.* New York: Free Press.

Merikangas, K. R., Prusoff, B. A., Kupfer, D. J., & Frank, E. (1985). Marital adjustment in major depression. *Journal of Affective Disorders, 9,* 5–11.

Meyer, H. J. (1988). Marital and mother–child relationships: Developmental history, parent personality, and child difficulties. In R. A. Hinde & J. Stevenson-Hinde (Eds.), *Relationships within families: Mutual influences* (pp. 181–192). New York: Oxford University Press.

Orraschel, H., Weissman, M. M., & Kidd, K. K. (1980). Children and depressed parents; the childhood of depressed parents; depression in children. *Journal of Affective Disorders, 2,* 1–16.

Nock, S., & Kingston, P. (1988). Time with children: The impact of couples' work-time commitments. *Social Forces, 67,* 59–85.

Parke, R. D. (1981). *Fathers.* Cambridge, MA: Harvard University Press.

Patterson, G. R. (1982). *Coercive family process.* Eugene, OR: Castalia.

Patterson, G. R., & Capaldi, D. M. (1991). Antisocial parents: Unskilled and vulnerable. In P. A. Cowan & E. M. Hetherington (Eds.), *Family transitions* (pp. 195–218). Hillsdale, NJ: Lawrence Erlbaum.

Patterson, G. R., Reid, J. B., & Dishion, T. J. (1992). *Antisocial boys.* Eugene, OR: Castalia.

Pederson, F. (1982). Mother, father and infant as an interactive system. In J. Belsky (Ed.), *In the beginning: Readings on infancy.* New York: Columbia University Press.

Pleck, J. H. (1985). *Working wives/working husbands.* Beverly Hills: Sage Publications.

Powell, D. R. (1980). Personal social networks as a focus for primary prevention of child maltreatment. *Infant Mental Health Journal, 1,* 232–239.

Quinton, D., & Rutter, M. (1988). *Parenting breakdown: The making and breaking of inter-generational links.* Brookfield, VT: Avebury.

Radke-Yarrow, M., Richters, J., & Wilson, W. E. (1988). Child development in a network of relationships. In R. A. Hinde & J. Stevenson-Hinde (Eds.), *Relationships within families: Mutual influences* (pp. 48–67). New York: Oxford University Press.

Recs, H. T. (1990). The role of intimacy in interpersonal relationships. *Journal of Social and Clinical Psychology, 9,* 15–30.

Rexroat, C., & Shehan, C. (1987). The family life cycle and spouses' time in household. *Journal of Marriage and the Family, 49,* 737–750.

Sampson, R. J., & Laub, J. H. (1990). Crime and deviance over the life course: The salience of adult social bonds. *American Sociological Review, 55,* 609–627.

Sampson, R. J., & Laub, J. H. (1993). *Crime in the making: Pathways and turning points through life.* Cambridge, MA: Harvard University Press.

Seagull, E. A. W. (1987). Social support and child maltreatment: A review of the evidence. *Child Abuse and Neglect, 11,* 41–52.

Simons, R. L., Beaman, J., Conger, R. D., & Chao, W. (1992). Gender differences in the intergenerational transmission of parenting beliefs. *Journal of Marriage and the Family, 54,* 823–836.

Simons, R. L., Beaman, J., Conger, R. D., & Chao, W. (1993). Childhood experience, conceptions of parenting, and attitudes of spouse as determinants of parental behavior. *Journal of Marriage and the Family, 55*, 385–398.

Simons, R. L., Lorenz, F. O., Conger, R. D., & Wu, C. (1992). Support from spouse as mediator and moderator of the disruptive influence of economic strain on parenting. *Child Development, 63*, 526–541.

Simons, R. L., Lorenz, F. O., Wu, C., & Conger, R. D. (1993). Martial and spouse support as mediator and moderator of the impact of economic strain upon parenting. *Developmental Psychology, 29*, 368–381.

Simons, R. L., Whitbeck, L. B., Conger, R. D., & Melby, J. N. (1990). Husband and wife differences in determinants of parenting: A social learning/exchange model of parental behavior. *Journal of Marriage and the Family, 52*, 375–392.

Simons, R. L., Whitbeck, L. B., Conger, R. D., & Wu, C. (1991). Intergenerational transmission of harsh parenting. *Developmental Psychology, 27*, 159–171.

Simons, R. L., Whitbeck, L. B., Melby, J. N., & Wu, C. (1994). Economic pressure and harsh parenting. In R. D. Conger & G. H. Elder (Eds.), *Families in troubled times: Adapting to change in rural America* (pp. 207–222). New York: Adline.

Simons, R. L., Whitbeck, L. B., & Wu, C. (1994). Resilient and vulnerable adolescents. In R. D. Conger & G. H. Elder (Eds.), *Families in troubled times: Adapting to change in rural America* (pp. 223–234). New York: Adline.

Simons, R. L., Wu, C., Conger, R. D., & Lorenz, F. O. (1994). Two routes to delinquency: Differences between early and late starters in the impact of parenting and deviant peers. *Criminology, 32*, 247–275.

Simons, R. L., Wu, C., Johnson, C., & Conger, R. D. (1995). A test of theoretical perspectives on the intergenerational transmission of domestic violence. *Criminology, 33*, 141–172.

Skinner, E. A. (1985). Action, control judgements, and the structure of control experience. *Psychological Rev, 92*, 39–58.

Stenberg, L., Catalano, R., & Dooley, D. (1981). Economic antecedents of child abuse and neglect. *Child Development, 52*, 975–985.

Straus, M. A. 1983. Ordinary violence, child abuse, and wife-beating: What do they have in common? In D. Finkelhor, R. J. Gelles, G. T. Hotaling, & M. A. Straus (Eds.), *The dark side of families: Current family violence research* (pp. 213–234). Beverly Hills: Sage Publications.

Thoits, P. A. (1985). Social support and psychological well-being: Theoretical possibilities. In I. G. Sarason & B. R. Sarason (Eds.), *Social support: Theory, research and applications* (pp. 39–50). Boston: Martinus Nijhoff.

Wahler, R. G., & Dumas, J. E. (1987). Stimulus class determinants of mother–child coercive interchanges in multi-distressed families: Assessment and intervention. In J. D. Burchard & S. N. Burchard (Eds.), *Prevention of delinquent behavior* (pp. 190–219). Newbury Park, CA: Sage Publications.

Wandersman, L., & Unger, D. G. (April, 1983). Interaction of infant difficulty and social support in adolescent mothers. Paper presented at the biennial meeting of the Society for Research in Child Development. Detroit.

Weissman, M. M., & Paykel, E. S. (1974). *The depression of women: A study of social relations.* Chicago: University of Chicago Press.

Werner, E. E., & Smith, R. S. (1992). *Overcoming the odds: High risk children from birth to adulthood.* Ithaca, NY: Cornell University Press.

Whitbeck, L. B., Hoyt, D. R., Simons, R. L., Conger, R. D., Elder, G. H., Lorenz, F. O., & Huck, S. (1992). Intergenerational continuity of parental rejection and depressed affect. *Journal of Personality and Social Psychology, 63*, 1036–1045.

Whittaker, J. K., & Garbarino, J. (1983). *Social support networks: Informal helping in the human services.* New York: Aldine.

Widom, C. S. (1989). Does violence beget violence? A critical examination of the literature. *Psychological Bulletin, 106*, 3–28.

Willner, P. (1985). *Depression: A psychobiological synthesis.* New York: Wiley.

Wills, T. A. (1990). Social support and the family. In E. A. Blechman (Ed.), *Emotions and the family* (pp. 75–98). Hillsdale, NJ: Lawrence Erlbaum.

13

The Mutual Influence of Family Support and Youth Adaptation

CHRISTINE TIMKO and RUDOLF H. MOOS

Research on the family environment has demonstrated that levels of family support bear strong relationships to the adaptation of children and adolescents. The purpose of this chapter is to examine the mutual influence of family support and youth adaptation and to suggest mechanisms that may explain why these reciprocal relations occur. We begin the chapter by describing the concept and measurement of the family environment. Next, we present a conceptual model of the mutual influence of the family environment and family members' adaptation and review studies of family support and youth functioning. We then focus on possible mechanisms by which family support and youth adaptation exert their mutual influence. We conclude by suggesting directions for future research.

THE FAMILY ENVIRONMENT

Just as individuals have unique personalities, so do family environments. The Family Environment Scale (FES) was developed by Moos and Moos (1994) to measure the social climate of the family. As shown in Table 1, the 10 FES subscales assess three underlying sets of dimensions: relationship, personal growth (or goal orientation), and system maintenance. The relationship and system maintenance dimensions primarily reflect internal family functioning, whereas the personal growth dimensions primarily reflect the linkages between the family and the larger social context.

CHRISTINE TIMKO and RUDOLF H. MOOS • Center for Health Care Evaluation, Department of Veterans Affairs Health Care System, and Stanford University Medical Center, Palo Alto, California 94304.

Handbook of Social Support and the Family, edited by Gregory R. Pierce, Barbara R. Sarason, and Irwin G. Sarason. Plenum Press, New York, 1996.

Table 1. Family Environment Scale: Subscales and Descriptions

	Relationship dimensions
1. Cohesion	Degree of commitment, help, and support family members provide for one another
2. Expressiveness	Extent to which family members are encouraged to express their feelings directly
3. Conflict	Amount of openly expressed anger and conflict among family members

	Personal growth dimensions
4. Independence	Extent to which family members are assertive, are self-sufficient, and make their own decisions
5. Achievement orientation	Extent to which activities (such as school and work) are cast into an achievement-oriented or competitive framework
6. Intellectual–cultural orientation	Level of interest in political, intellectual, and cultural activities
7. Active–recreational orientation	Participation in social and recreational activities
8. Moral–religious emphasis	Emphasis on ethical and religious issues and values

	System maintenance dimensions
9. Organization	Degree of importance of clear organization and structure in planning family activities and responsibilities
10. Control	Extent to which set rules and procedures are used to run family life

The Cohesion, Expressiveness, and Conflict subscales measure relationship dimensions and are the primary focus of this chapter. These subscales assess the level of commitment and support family members provide for one another, the extent to which family members express their feelings directly, and the amount of openly expressed anger and conflict among family members.

The relationship dimensions of the FES are conceptually related to the construct of perceived social support (Lakey & Cassady, 1990; Lakey & Heller, 1988; I. G. Sarason, B. R. Sarason, & Shearin, 1986) in that an individual's ratings reflect a set of stable and organized beliefs about the availability of support, the quality of relationships, and the extent to which members are cared for and valued. The relationship dimensions are also related, although less closely, to the construct of enacted or received social support (Lakey & Cassady, 1990; Lakey & Heller, 1988). That is, family cohesion, expressiveness, and lack of conflict also reflect the supportive behaviors that family members provide for one another on an ongoing basis and in times of particular need. Although we focus on the relationship dimensions here, it is important to recognize that the effects of family support cannot be fully understood in isolation from the other dimensions of the family environment that are assessed on the FES. For example, the family's emphasis on aspects of personal growth, such as independence and achievement, and on system maintenance, including organization and control, may be most beneficial in the context of high levels of family support.

The FES can be used in two main forms: the Real Form (Form R), which asks family members to describe their current family, and the Ideal Form (Form I), which focuses on family members' preferences about the family environment. Each FES subscale is internally consistent and has adequate test–retest reliability, and intercorrelations among the subscales are low to moderate. Detailed normative data on normal and distressed families are available in the FES manual (Moos & Moos, 1994).

In addition to the relationship dimensions of the FES, we rely in this chapter on the Family Adaptability and Cohesion Scales (FACES) and their modifications, FACES II and FACES III (Olson, 1991; Olson et al., 1982; Olson, Sprenkle, & Russell, 1979). In these scales, family cohesion assesses the degree to which a family member feels connected and bonded to, or separated and autonomous from, other family members; there are also measures of family adaptability and communication. The FACES instruments are designed to be administered twice to family members to obtain measurements of the perceived family (i.e., How would you describe your family now?) and the ideal family (i.e., How would you like your family to be?). The subscales are internally consistent, and normative FACES data were obtained from a national sample.

CONCEPTUAL FRAMEWORK: THE FAMILY ENVIRONMENT AND FAMILY MEMBERS' ADAPTATION

Moos and Moos (1994) developed a conceptual model that focuses on the family environment and its associations with youth and adult adaptation. As shown in Figure 1, the conceptual model suggests that the family environment and family members' adaptation mutually influence each other. More specifically, the personal characteristics, coping skills, and well-being of each adult (Panel 1) and child (Panel II) family member can affect the quality of family relationships, the family's emphasis on personal growth goals, and the family's focus on system maintenance (Panel IV). For example, when a child or parent has a behavioral, emotional, or substance abuse disorder, the family environment is likely to be affected. Another key set of factors that also influence the family climate includes acute life crises and ongoing stressors and resources from settings outside the family, such as school and work (Panel III). Moreover, when a life crisis such as a child's serious illness occurs, other family members' personality characteristics and coping skills can alter the influence of the crisis on the family.

In turn, the family environment shapes the sets of factors that shape it. Thus, a supportive family (Panel IV) can affect adults' coping skills and functioning (Panel V) and children's cognitive and emotional development, self-confidence, and well-being (Panel VI). The family environment can influence both dysfunctional and other family members' well-being; for example, a cohesive family can

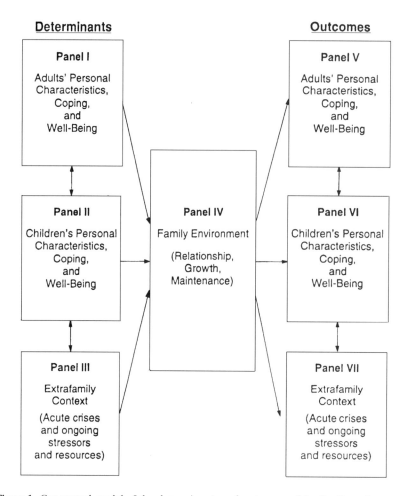

Figure 1. Conceptual model of the determinants and outcomes of the family environment.

foster an alcoholic father's remission (Panel V) and his children's adaptation (Panel VI). By its protective influence, the family environment can reduce the ongoing stressors and enhance the social resources that are associated with extrafamily context factors (Panel VII). Finally, the model shows that children's adaptation is influenced by parental functioning directly, as well as indirectly through the parents' influence on the family environment.

In the following sections, we draw on this conceptual framework to review research that used the FES or FACES to examine family support and youth adaptation. To focus the review, we selected studies of families having a child or parent with a behavior, substance abuse, or psychiatric disorder. Most of the studies covered here examined the influence of family support (Panel IV) on youth functioning (Panel VI). Fewer studies have examined the influence of youth functioning (Panel II) on family support (Panel IV), or the links among parent functioning (Panel I), family support (Panel IV), and youth adaptation (Panel VI).

FAMILIES OF YOUTHS WITH BEHAVIOR, SUBSTANCE ABUSE, OR PSYCHIATRIC PROBLEMS

Our selective review of studies of families having a psychiatrically impaired or substance-abusing family member focuses on two issues. The first is how family support in the distressed families compares to that in normative families; the second issue concerns how variations in family support are related to various outcomes among children and adolescents. The review covers studies of youths with behavior, substance abuse, or psychiatric problems and then moves on to studies of adult family members and their effects on family support and child outcomes.

In the studies of youths, family support is usually assessed on the basis of the children's perceptions of the family, although mothers' and fathers' ratings are sometimes used. The youth outcomes in these studies are quite varied; they involve children's self-reports of feelings and behavior, parent and teacher reports of the child's behavior, clinician reports of children's psychological states, and children's, mothers', and therapists' ratings of the youths' treatment outcomes. Although most of these studies examine associations between family support and youth adaptation using a cross-sectional research design, some use a longitudinal design to predict youth functioning from family support assessed on a prior occasion.

Youths with Behavior Problems or Conduct Disorders

Compared with normative families, families of youths with behavior problems or conduct disorders tend to be less cohesive and expressive and more conflictual, according to mothers, fathers, and offspring (Fox, Rotatori, Macklin, Green, & Fox, 1983; LeFlore, 1988; McGee, Silva, & Williams, 1983, 1984; McGee, Williams, & Silva, 1984, 1985; Morris et al., 1988). In one study, both children's and parents' reports of more family conflict were related to the child's having more parent- and teacher-reported behavior problems and lower perceived self-competence (Jaycox & Repetti, 1993). Lower family cohesion and higher conflict have also been associated with more frequent delinquent behavior among boys (Tolan & Lorion, 1988). In a longitudinal study, mothers' ratings of family support (i.e., a composite of cohesion, expressiveness, and conflict) when their child was age 7 and age 9 were related to the number of disorders the child had at age 11; when family support was low, children were more likely to have multiple behavioral and emotional disorders than to have one or no disorder (Williams, Anderson, McGee, & Silva, 1990).

Youths with Substance Abuse Problems

A. S. Friedman and Utada (1992) asked both adolescent drug abuse treatment clients and their mothers to complete the FES and the FACES-II. The adolescent clients had lower scores on cohesion and expressiveness, and higher scores on conflict, in comparison to adolescent norms; mothers also saw less cohesion and expressiveness in comparison to parental norms. In related work, A. S. Friedman, Tomko, and Utada (1991) found that low levels of family conflict reported by adolescent drug abuse treatment clients at treatment intake were associated with better treatment outcomes 15 months later, according to both clients and their mothers.

In another longitudinal study (Andrews, Hops, Ary, Lichtenstein, & Tildesley, 1991), adolescent girls who used marijuana or hard drugs reported more family conflict than did adolescent girls who abstained from substance use. The more conflict mothers saw in their relationships with their daughters, the more likely were the daughters to begin using alcohol in the subsequent year. Similarly, when adolescent boys perceived their families as less cohesive, they were more likely to begin using hard drugs during the next year. Consistent with these results, cross-sectional studies found that high family conflict was associated with more alcohol use and more physical distress symptoms from drinking in varied samples of students (Baer, Garmezy, McLaughlin, Pokorny, & Wernick, 1987; Smith, Rivers, & Stahl, 1992).

Youths with Psychiatric Problems

Using the FACES, Kiser et al. (1988) found that children and adolescents in a psychiatric day treatment program, as well as their parents, judged their families to be less cohesive than did youth and parents in a nonclinical sample. Similarly, studies using the FES found that adolescents referred to or using psychiatric clinics or other mental health services saw their families as less cohesive and expressive and more conflictual than did matched controls (Dixon, 1986; Tyerman & Humphrey, 1981). Consistent with these findings, college students who requested psychological counseling reported less supportive family relationships than did a normative sample of students. In addition, among students requesting therapy, more supportive family relationships were related to longer stays in therapy, and to more success in dealing with problems, according to therapists' ratings (Oxenford & Nowicki, 1982).

Among children hospitalized for psychiatric problems, those who attempted suicide tended to see their families as less cohesive and expressive and more conflictual than those who did not make an attempt (Asarnow & Carlson, 1988; Asarnow, Carlson, & Guthrie, 1987). In addition, less cohesion and expressiveness and more conflict were related to more suicidal behavior among child psychiatric inpatients (Campbell, Milling, Laughlin, & Bush, 1993), to more depression among adolescent psychiatric inpatients (Barrera & Garrison-Jones, 1992), and to suicidal ideation and depression among junior high and high school students (Friedrich, Reams, & Jacobs, 1982; Meneese & Yutrzenka, 1990).

Summary of Studies on Youths

The studies just reviewed demonstrate that children and adolescents with behavior, substance abuse, or psychiatric problems are likely to have families that are less supportive than normative families. In addition, lower levels of family support are associated with more dysfunction, while more support is associated with better outcomes among the offspring. Longitudinal research suggests that low family support is predictive of poor subsequent child functioning and is detrimental to treatment success.

Although the evidence of an association between family support and youth adaptation is considerable, much of this research is ambiguous as to the direction of influence, or assumes that family environment is a determinant of child and adolescent outcomes. Rather than emphasize the unidirectional influence of family support on offspring, we conceptualize youth adaptation in the context of the family, with child functioning and family environment in a mutual influence network (see Figure 1). Therefore, we next consider studies of how variations in family members' adaptation impact family support.

YOUTH ADAPTATION AND FAMILY SUPPORT

Because relatively few studies have examined family environment as an outcome, this section focuses on varied samples of families. In their longitudinal study of children in special education programs, Nihira and Mink examined the reciprocal influence of the child and the home environment. While there were clear effects of the home environment on child development, there was also strong support for the idea that the child's adaptation can alter the family climate. When the children were more socially competent and self-sufficient initially, the home environment changed to become more harmonious 3 years later (Nihira, Meyers, & Mink, 1983). In addition, better child self-esteem (rated by the children and their teachers) was associated with subsequent increased levels of family cohesion and expressiveness (Nihira, Mink, & Meyers, 1985).

Mink and Nihira (1987) found that youth adaptation influenced family support most strongly in two types of families: control-oriented (i.e., high demands are made on the child and family relations are somewhat discordant) and child-oriented (i.e., the family behaves positively toward the child while focusing on achievement as well as intellectual and recreational activities). Specifically, in control-oriented families, children's greater engagement in maladaptive behaviors predicted less cohesion and more conflict 1 year later. In child-oriented families, poorer psychological adjustment among children predicted less cohesion and more conflict.

Halverson and Wampler (1993) conducted a longitudinal study of family and child functioning among families with preschool children, using assessments by mothers, fathers, teachers, and laboratory observers. More externalizing behavior among boys at baseline predicted less family cohesion at a 1-year follow-up. In contrast, girls' baseline externalizing behavior was unrelated to subsequent levels of family cohesion, possibly because parents interpreted such behavior by girls as reflecting assertiveness and competence. In these families, baseline family cohesion did not predict boys' or girls' externalizing behavior 1 year later.

The relationship between adolescents' alcohol and drug abuse treatment outcomes and family functioning following treatment was examined by Stewart and Brown (1993). In contrast to families of adolescents who continued their substance abuse, families of consistently abstinent teenagers showed gradual and steady increases in cohesion and expressiveness. By the 2-year posttreatment follow-up, the abstinent group was higher on these dimensions, and was also lower on conflict. These results support the hypothesis that family support is in part a reaction to adolescent functioning.

Other longitudinal research by Liem and Liem (1988) examined family support and depression among men who had recently lost their jobs. Cross-lagged panel correlations showed that depression among the men predicted poor family cohesion 1 year later more strongly than poor cohesion predicted the men's subsequent depression. That is, depression among the men was more a determinant of low family cohesiveness than a reaction to poor family support.

These findings lend credence to the conceptualization of the relationship between family members' adaptation and family support as a reciprocal or interactive process. Next, we review studies of families having adult members with psychiatric or substance abuse problems. Our purpose is to examine the extent to which the parents' dysfunction impairs family support, which in turn impairs the functioning of the offspring.

FAMILIES OF PARENTS WITH PSYCHIATRIC OR SUBSTANCE ABUSE PROBLEMS

In the studies of adults, family support was assessed primarily by mothers and fathers, but offsprings' ratings were also used. The youth outcomes in these studies included emotional, behavior, and physical health indices, and consisted of parental or youth ratings. Most of these studies examined associations among parental functioning, family support, and youth adaptation cross-sectionally; few used a longitudinal design.

Parents with Psychiatric Problems

Like families having a child with a psychiatric disorder, families in which a parent has a psychiatric disorder or is in psychiatric treatment or counseling are less supportive in comparison to normative families. In a sample of parents of children with or without psychiatric disorders, mothers and fathers who had psychiatric diagnoses reported less family cohesion and more conflict than did mothers and fathers without psychiatric diagnoses (Hibbs, Hamburger, Kruesi, & Lenane, 1993). Similarly, among families receiving counseling, FES scores calculated from ratings made by the mother, father, and adolescent child showed that these families had less cohesion and expressiveness and more conflict than did families that showed no evidence of problems warranting treatment (Scoresby & Christensen, 1976). Families having a member with a dependent personality disorder had less cohesion and expressiveness than did families making up a normal control group (Head, Baker, & Williamson, 1991). In an exception to these reports, however, S. Friedman (1990) found that families with an adult who was diagnosed as having panic disorder with agoraphobia had less conflict than did normative families; it is possible that family members were attempting to protect the distressed family member from further anxiety.

Moos and his colleagues conducted a longitudinal study of the families of men and women with unipolar depression. At treatment intake (Billings & Moos, 1983), both the depressed patients and their spouses reported less family cohesion and expressiveness and more conflict than did nondepressed case controls and their spouses. In comparison to children of controls, children of depressed parents had substantially more physical and psychological problems, including more depression and anxiety. They also had more academic, school discipline, and peer interaction problems. Within the families of depressed patients, and within the control families, a supportive family environment was associated with fewer psychological and physical problems among the children. Taken together, the findings suggest that the less supportive family milieu found among families of depressed parents is a mediator of the effects of parental depression on child functioning.

A 1-year follow-up of these families (Billings & Moos, 1986) found that when parents' depression had not remitted, family cohesion and expressiveness were lower, and conflict was higher, in comparison to control families. In contrast, support in families of parents whose depression had remitted was similar to that of control families, and was higher than that of nonremitted-parent families. Family cohesion and expressiveness increased over the year among remitted-parent families, underscoring the influence that family members' functioning has on family support.

The 1-year follow-up also found that children of parents whose depression had not remitted showed more psychological dysfunction, physical health problems, and behavior difficulties than did children of control parents. Children of parents whose depression had remitted also continued to display more dysfunction than children of controls, especially in psychological symptoms and behavior problems. Children's dysfunction in families of remitted parents was less severe, however, than that observed for children of nonremitted parents.

Analyses combining the control, remitted-parent, and nonremitted-parent groups at the 1-year follow-up found that more family support was associated with fewer child health problems. In addition, family environments that were less supportive at the time of parents' intake into the study were associated with poorer levels of functioning among the children 1 year later. Again, as a whole, these results indicate that parental depression may reduce family support and thereby interfere with children's health and development.

Alcoholic Parents

In families with an alcoholic parent, both parents and children report less family cohesion and expressiveness, and more family conflict, than do members of normative families (Casey, Griffin, & Googins, 1993; Clair & Genest, 1987; Filstead, McElfresh, & Anderson, 1981; Jarmas & Kazak, 1992; Petersen-Kelley, 1985; Tarter, Kabene, Escallier, Laird, & Jacob, 1990). Additionally, more family cohesion and expressiveness and less conflict are associated with less proneness to depression, more self-esteem, and better mood states among offspring of alcoholic parents; more cohesion and less conflict are also associated with less anxiety (Clair & Genest, 1987, 1992). Furthermore, when family cohesion is weaker and conflict is stronger, adolescents are more concerned and distressed about parental drinking (Dinning & Berk, 1989).

As they found for depressed parents, Moos and Billings (1982) found that the remission status of an alcoholic parent is important for family support and youth adaptation. In comparison to matched non-problem-drinking families, families of relapsed alcoholics with children living at home were lower on cohesion and expressiveness. However, families of remitted alcoholics did not differ on support from matched controls. Children in families of relapsed alcoholics had more emotional problems, especially depression and anxiety, than children in control families. In contrast, children of recovered alcoholics were less depressed than children of controls. Generally, children living in supportive families had fewer emotional problems.

Summary of Studies on Parents

Compared with normative families, families having a parent with psychiatric or substance abuse problems tend to be less supportive, and this lack of family support is linked to more psychological, behavior, and health problems among children. When psychiatric and substance abuse patients improve enough to be considered remitted, family support tends to increase and children's dysfunction tends to decrease. Thus, parental functioning appears to influence youth adaptation in part indirectly, through its effects family support. We next consider mechanisms by which family support and youth adaptation exert their mutual influence.

MECHANISMS BY WHICH FAMILY SUPPORT AND YOUTH ADAPTATION EXERT THEIR MUTUAL INFLUENCE

We propose that a supportive family environment is reflective of more specific aspects of adaptive family functioning, which affect and are affected by youth adaptation. As Jacob and Leonard (1994) suggest, an unsupportive family environment is associated with disruptive parental behavior, and this disruption explains the relationship between the lack of family support and adverse child outcomes. The family environment literature suggests three major mechanisms that link family support to youth adaptation: parental interactions with the child, marital interactions, and the extent to which family routines are maintained. We consider each of these mechanisms in turn.

Parental Interactions with the Child

The impact of parenting on child outcomes has long been recognized; inadequate parenting can have severely damaging and wide-ranging effects on children's cognitive, emotional, and social development (Maccoby & Martin, 1983; Martin, 1987). In addition, a growing number of studies are demonstrating the impact of children's functioning on child–parent interactions. For example, children's symptoms of maladjustment are a cause as well as a consequence of depressed mothers' critical and hostile parenting (Conrad & Hammen, 1989; Downey & Coyne, 1990). In their longitudinal study of children in special education programs, Nihira et al. (1983) found that parenting behavior was higher on pride, affection, warmth, and quality when the child was more socially competent; that is, the youths' adjustment influenced important aspects of parenting behavior.

Associations between varied aspects of parenting and family support have been observed in concurrent studies. For example, in a study of families of children with severe communication disorders, Bristol (1987) reported an association between more family cohesion (as perceived by mothers) and higher-quality parenting (rated by an in-home observer). Similarly, according to mothers, more enjoyment of their children and of their parental role is related to more family support (Corse, Schmid, & Trickett, 1990).

In a combined group of mothers of children with or without psychiatric problems, those with less family cohesion and more family conflict scored higher on a measure of expressed emotion, which reflected being more critical of and overinvolved with the child (Hibbs et al., 1993). College students' ratings of their mothers and fathers as more overprotective and intrusive, and as less caring, were associated with lower ratings of family cohesion (B. R. Sarason, Shearin, Pierce, & I. G. Sarason, 1987). A. S. Friedman and Utada (1992), who found that adolescent drug abuse clients in treatment scored lower on family support than did those in a normative sample, also found that these clients reported having less communication (both positive and negative) with each parent. In contrast, more agreement between parents and children about how the child would react to different school and home situations, as well as children's perceptions that their mothers' and fathers' beliefs were similar to their own, were related to high family scores on cohesiveness and expressiveness (Alessandri & Wozniak, 1989).

Another concurrent study found that in comparison to fathers of well-behaved boys, fathers of aggressive boys saw less family support (i.e., less cohesion and expressiveness and more conflict) and were also less effective in solving problems with their sons (Morris et al., 1988). Specifically, in interactions with their sons, fathers of aggressive boys engaged in fewer positive solution behaviors and more negative solution behaviors. They had the same number of positive child-referent cognitions as the fathers of well-behaved boys, but nearly 8 times as many negative child-referent cognitions; they also had fewer positive and more negative family-referent cognitions.

In contrast to studies that focused mainly on parenting–family support relationships, a few concurrent studies have also examined youth adaptation along with parent–child interactions and family climate. Scalf-McIver and Thompson (1989) used daughters' responses to find that less family cohesion and more family conflict, perceptions that mothers and fathers had been inconsistent with affection during the growing-up years, and daughters' depression and bulimic symptomatology were all interassociated. In the study by Jaycox and Repetti (1993), mothers' and fathers' descriptions of the parent–child relationship as having a "negative emotional tone" were related to both more family conflict and more child behavior problems.

Marital Interactions

In addition to the child–parent relationship, the quality of the marital relationship may mediate between family support and youth adaptation. Poor quality of the marital relationship has been clearly demonstrated to be predictive of problems in child adjustment (Grych, Seid, & Fincham, 1992), and difficult children also have a negative effect on marital adjustment (Hetherington, 1991), although findings are less consistent on this direction of influence (Martin, 1987).

Varying indicators of the quality of marital interactions have been found to be associated with family support in cross-sectional studies. In a study of mothers of children with autism, severe communication disorders, or behavioral problems, Bristol (1984) found that mothers who reported more family cohesion and expressiveness also reported better marital adjustment and happiness. Similarly, Fife, Norton, and Groom (1987) studied families in which a child had leukemia; when family cohesion was stronger, fathers were more satisfied with their marriages. More family support (i.e., more cohesion and expressiveness and less conflict) was also related to more marital satisfaction among mothers of children who were mentally retarded (Friedrich, Cohen, & Wilturner, 1987). These associations between family support and marital adjustment hold in samples of normative married couples as well (Schaefer & Olson, 1980; Waring, McElrath, Lefcoe, & Weisz, 1981).

Feldman, Wentzel, Weinberger, and Munson (1990) investigated relationships among parents' marital satisfaction, family support, and child outcomes. They conceptualized the marital subsystem as playing a central role in providing cohesion and stability for the entire family. This being the case, the quality of the marriage can have a pervasive effect on family life as a whole as well as on individual outcomes of family members. Feldman and colleagues found that more marital satisfaction on the part of mothers and fathers was related to observers' ratings of more family warmth (i.e., affection and caring) and less family hostility (i.e., open hostility and put-downs) and to composites created from child, teacher, parent, and peer ratings of the children's functioning. Specifically, when parents were more satisfied, children were less distressed (e.g., anxious and depressed) and more restrained (e.g., considerate and responsible) and performed better in school. These results held when parental functioning and child-rearing indices were controlled in analyses.

To our knowledge, only the study by Halverson and Wampler (1993) has examined marital quality and family and child functioning over time. They found that among boys, more externalizing behavior at baseline was related to poorer concurrent marital quality, which predicted less family cohesion 1 year later. The predictive relationship between poor marital quality and low family cohesion was also found for girls.

Family Routines

The third mechanism that may explain the mutual influence of family support and youth adaptation has been identified in research on children of alcoholic parents. Wolin and his colleagues (Wolin, Bennett, & Noonan, 1979; Wolin, Bennett, Noonan, & Teitelbaum, 1980) found that families that maintained their family routines and rituals throughout the children's upbringing, even in the face of a parent's alcohol problems, evidenced less transmission of alcoholism when the children became adults. Families in which routines were substantially disrupted by a parent's alcohol problems were more likely to have adult children with alcohol problems.

The maintenance of family routines and rituals taps into the family's shared sense of identity and may be an important mediator between family support and child outcomes. Low family support may involve families' spending less time and placing less importance on family routines and tasks, which in turn may impact negatively on the children. Additionally, raising children with psychiatric, behavior, or substance abuse problems may interfere with the family's carrying out daily routines as well as special celebrations and thus reduce family cohesion and increase conflict.

Jensen, James, Boyce, and Hartnett (1983) provided some support for these ideas in their examination of the routinization of ongoing, daily family life in relation to the family environment. Family routines were defined as observable and repetitive behaviors that involved family members and occurred with predictable regularity (e.g., children do regular household chores; parents take certain actions when children get out of line; family eats dinner together most nights). As expected, families that performed routines more frequently had more cohesion and less conflict.

Fiese and Kline (1993) also found associations between family routines and family support. College students' ratings of engaging in more family rituals, assessed across seven settings ranging from dinnertime to religious celebrations, were related to more family cohesion. As the Wolin studies did, Fiese and Kline's study also found evidence for connections between family rituals and the out-comes of offspring. Students who attributed more meaning to family rituals had more self-esteem and less anxiety.

Because family routines and rituals involve assigning roles to family members to plan and prepare shared activities, it is important to note that more engage-ment in these activities should be related to the system maintenance dimensions of the FES, as well as to the relationship dimensions (Table 1). The system maintenance dimensions of organization and control overlap conceptually with family routinization in that they emphasize clear structure in family activities and responsibilities and the use of set rules and procedures to run family life. In fact, both Jensen et al. (1983) and Fiese and Kline (1993) found positive relation-ships between frequency of performing family routines and Organization and Control scores.

Taken together, these studies support the idea that child–parent inter-actions, marital interactions, and family routines mediate the relationship be-tween family support and youth adaptation. However, studies designed to ade-quately test this hypothesis have not yet been conducted. Therefore, we conclude the chapter by describing directions for future research on the relationship between family support and youth functioning and its mediators.

DIRECTIONS FOR FUTURE RESEARCH

While there can be little doubt that there is an association between family support and youth adaptation, studies are needed that focus on the direction, as well as the strength, of this association. Specifically, prospective, longitudinal research is needed in which family support and youth adaptation are assessed on multiple occasions. This research should be based on conceptual models that depict how family environment and child outcomes influence each other and how these influences change over time. Studies incorporating multiple follow-ups might also assess mothers' and fathers' functioning in order to probe the recipro-cal causal links between parental well-being, family environment, and children's outcomes (Billings & Moos, 1986).

Efforts have been made to conduct such longitudinal studies in order to examine chronic illness among children and adolescents in the context of child and family functioning. Moos and Timko and their colleagues conducted a longitudinal study of youth with juvenile rheumatic disease (JRD), using a concep-tual model in which the child's chronic illness impacts the family environment and the family environment affects the course of treatment and the child's psychosocial outcomes. Compared with JRD patients who had mild functional disability, those with moderate or severe disability reported less supportive family relationships at baseline, but not 1 year later (Timko, Stovel, Moos, & Miller, 1992a). These results suggest that a long-term illness such as JRD may be most disruptive to family relationships when it is newly diagnosed and seen to interfere with the youth's normal functioning; subsequently, as the ramifications of the disease are understood and accepted, family support is likely to improve.

Cross-sectional results showed that adolescent patients who perceived their fathers as more supportive had fewer symptoms of depressed mood; less support from mothers was associated with engaging in more deviant behaviors and having less social competence (Timko, Stovel, Baumgartner, & Moos, 1995). Longitudinal findings showed that more family support was related to patients having more good friends; in addition, when mothers were functioning better, particularly when they had stronger feelings of mastery over illness-related stressors, patients were less emotionally distressed and engaged in more social activities (Timko, Stovel, Moos, & Miller, 1992b).

More family support at baseline was related to mothers having fewer symptoms of depressed mood 1 year later; further, when patients' disease-related and psychosocial functioning was better initially, mothers showed less depression and personal strain at the 1-year follow-up (Timko, Stovel, & Moos, 1992). Finally, mothers' and fathers' better functioning at baseline predicted patients having less JRD-related pain, more social competence, and fewer behavior problems 4 years later (Timko, Baumgartner, Moos, & Miller, 1993). Consistent with these results, Varni and his colleagues found family support to be associated with better functional status, less pain, and fewer behavior problems among children with JRD (Thompson, Varni, & Hanson, 1987; Varni, Wilcox, & Hanson, 1988; Varni, Wilcox, Hanson, & Brik, 1988).

More family support is also associated with better outcomes for young diabetic patients. Varni, Babani, Wallander, Roe, and Frasier (1989) found that lack of family support predicted diabetic children's internalizing problems, such as anxiety and distress, and externalizing problems, such as acting out and troublesome behavior. Hauser et al. (1990) focused on family climate as a predictor of treatment adherence among youths with diabetes in a 4-year longitudinal study. In analyses of the 1-year data, high cohesion as perceived by parents, and low conflict as perceived by both parents and children, were related to better adherence to the treatment regimen as rated by clinicians. In addition, high initial cohesion (rated by parents and children) and low conflict (rated by children) were associated with better adherence to the treatment regimen over 4 years. Although Hauser and his colleagues have focused on how family environment at the time of disease onset contributes to short-term and subsequent adherence, they note that the child's early nonadherence may lead to family conflicts and disruptions in family coherence. Generally, this ongoing research on diabetic patients and their families is intended to identify specific mechanisms such as treatment adherence that link family life to the individual's disease-related and psychosocial outcomes.

Explanatory Mechanisms

The need for longitudinal studies that are based on integrated conceptual frameworks is especially apparent in attempting to determine and understand the mechanisms by which family support and youth adaptation exert their mutual influence. Although research has demonstrated associations between parenting and child outcomes, and between parenting and family support, only longitudinal studies can reveal concurrent and predictive relationships among all these factors. Similarly, while some evidence is available regarding the interplay among marital interactions, child functioning, and family climate, we know of only one longitudinal study that is investigating the directions of these relationships over time (Halverson & Wampler, 1993). Research on family rituals, child well-being, and family support is at an early stage, so far consisting of only a few cross-sectional studies.

We recognize that in discussing child–parent interactions, marital interactions, and family rituals, we have greatly oversimplified these complex, multidimensional concepts. Therefore, although there is evidence that these mechanisms help to explain associations between family support and youth adaptation, it is unclear exactly what aspects of parental interactions and family routines are the strongest mediating variables. Identifying the dimensions of parenting, marital interactions, and family rituals that best explain the reciprocal influence between family support and child functioning should be a goal of subsequent research.

While we have focused on mediators between family support and youth adaptation, it is possible that these same mechanisms—that is, parent–child interactions, marital interactions, and family rituals—also help to explain relationships between parental functioning and family support. Furthermore, it is likely that these mechanisms influence each other. For example, marital satisfaction may provide parents with the emotional resources that are necessary to engage in warm and consistent interactions with their children (Feldman et al., 1990). Similarly, families in which parent–child interactions are generally positive may be more likely to engage in family routines and celebrations.

Future research to explain relationships between family support and youth adaptation should also explore other possible mediators. These mediators may include children's interactions with their siblings, as well as the children's coping responses. Jenkins (1992) found that children living in disharmonious homes were more likely to have a poor (i.e., hostile and aggressive) relationship with one of their siblings than were children in harmonious homes. In addition, the poorer the quality of sibling relationships, the more likely the children were to have symptoms of emotional and behavioral problems. Furthermore, children in disharmonious homes who did manage to have a close relationship with a sibling had much lower levels of emotional and behavioral problems than did children in disharmonious homes who had no such positive relationships.

Jenkins described two pathways by which the relationships among disharmony at home, sibling relationships, and child outcomes may occur. Children in disharmonious homes may develop a poor internalized image of themselves due to their involvement in hostile family relationships. Alternatively, children's emotional and behavior problems may prevent children from reaching out and developing close relationships with siblings, which in turn may produce hostility.

To determine the direction of effects, Jenkins suggested an intervention study in which the treatment is designed to improve the relationship between disturbed children and their siblings in disharmonious homes.

Regarding coping, youths who use more approach and less avoidance coping tend to be better adjusted (Ebata & Moos, 1991), and adolescents who appraise their family environment as high on cohesion and lower on conflict tend to rely more heavily on active, and less on emotionally based, coping responses (Stern & Zevon, 1990). These results suggest that youths' greater reliance on approach coping may help to explain the association between stronger family support and better youth adaptation. Consistent with this suggestion, in a 2-year longitudinal study of the transition to college, initial parental support was associated with students' subsequent psychological adjustment directly and indirectly, through students' use of approach coping (Valentiner, Holahan, & Moos, 1994). Valentiner and colleagues speculated that parents' support may foster self-efficacy in off-spring, which in turn aids their offspring in planning and executing more active coping strategies. According to our model, it is also likely that better youth functioning is associated with more reliance on adaptive coping strategies, which impacts positively on family support.

Stressors and Resources

Another potential avenue for future research is to examine family support and youth adaptation in relation to acute and chronic family stressors, such as a parent's loss of employment, or economic deprivation. As our conceptual model (Figure 1) specifies, life stressors have an influence on the family environment, and the family climate affects how well family members adapt to crises and to ongoing difficult situations.; For example, Liem and Liem (1988) found that families in which the father had recently become unemployed had less cohesion and more conflict than families in which the father had not lost his job. Silbereisen and Walper (1988) similarly found that financial hardship was predictive of lower family support, which in turn predicted less self-esteem and more behavior problems among adolescent family members. However, when family support remained high despite economic deprivation, adolescents tended not to interact with others who engaged in deviant behavior; when family support was low in these economically deprived families, teenagers had more contact with deviant peers and adults.

The work of Schneewind (Schneewind, 1987; Schneewind, Beckman, & Engfer, 1983) also illuminates how chronic stressors affect the family climate, which in turn affects adolescents' coping styles and personal orientations. He found that the combination of an impoverished ecological context (i.e., lack of money and of adequate living space) with the father working in a boring and restrictive job fostered a nonstimulating and controlling family climate. These ongoing ecological and work factors were also associated with the father's authoritarianism and the son's development of an external control orientation and an inability to find alternative ways to reach his goals. In contrast, a positive ecological context was related to a more expressive family climate and more social activities among the children.

The family's social resources represent another potentially important determinant and outcome of family support and youth adaptation (Figure 1). Daniels and Moos (1988) found, for example, that when fathers had better relationships at work, the quality of family relationships was more positive and children had fewer adjustment problems. In addition, mothers who engaged in more activities with friends had higher self-esteem, which was associated with better family relationships and better child functioning. A study of abusive mothers found these women to have low levels of family support, as well as little support from friends, coworkers, and community members (Corse et al., 1990). While these studies focus on associations among parents' social resources, family climate, and child adaptation, the children's relationships with peers, schoolmates, teachers, and others also bear important connections to youth and family functioning.

Multiple Informants

Turning to a methodological issue, it is important that future studies of family support and youth adaptation, no matter what their specific focus, use multiinformant designs. Conclusions about relationships between family support and child outcomes that are based on the viewpoint of one family member or another individual may be discrepant from those that are drawn with data obtained from alternate perspectives. Achieving a comprehensive understanding of the association between family climate and the functioning of children, and of the mediators of that association, will involve obtaining information about each component from several sources, including offspring, parents, teachers, and independent observers (Moos & Billings, 1982).

CONCLUSION

An understanding of the effects that family support and children have on each other over time is needed to determine what strategies to employ in helping children and families adapt to each other. The identification of common causal processes among children and parents with different disorders could lead to the formulation of generic family intervention programs. Given the risk that unsupportive family climates pose to children, and the risk that disruptive child behavior poses to families, such programs could play a substantial preventive role in reducing the incidence of children's and families' dysfunction.

ACKNOWLEDGMENTS

Preparation of this chapter was supported by NIAAA Grants AA02863 and AA06699 and by VA HSR&D Service funds.

REFERENCES

Alessandri, S. M., & Wozniak, R. H. (1989). Perception of the family environment and intrafamilial agreement in belief concerning the adolescent. *Journal of Early Adolescence, 9,* 67–81.

Andrews, J. A., Hops, H., Ary, D., Lichtenstein, E., & Tildesley, E. (1991). The construction, validation, and use of a Guttman scale of adolescent substance use: An investigation of family relationships. *Journal of Drug Issues, 21,* 557–572.

Asarnow, J. R., & Carlson, G. A. (1988). Suicide attempts in preadolescent child psychiatry inpatients. *Suicide and Life Threatening Behavior, 18,* 129–136.

Asarnow, J. R., Carlson, G. A., & Guthrie, D. (1987). Coping strategies, self-perceptions, hopelessness, and perceived family environments in depressed and suicidal children. *Journal of Consulting and Clinical Psychology, 55,* 361–366.

Baer, P. E., Garmezy, L. B., McLaughlin, R. J., Pokorny, A. D., & Wernick, M. J. (1987). Stress, coping, family conflict, and adolescent alcohol use. *Journal of Behavioral Medicine, 10,* 449–466.

Barrera, M., & Garrison-Jones, C. (1992). Family and peer social support as specific correlates of adolescent depressive symptoms. *Journal of Abnormal Child Psychology, 20,* 1–16.

Billings, A., & Moos, R. H. (1983). Comparisons of children of depressed and nondepressed parents: A social–environmental perspective. *Journal of Abnormal Child Psychology, 11,* 463–485.

Billings, A., & Moos, R. (1986). Children of parents with unipolar depression: A controlled 1-year follow-up. *Journal of Abnormal Child Psychology, 14,* 149–166.

Bristol, M. (1984). Family resources and successful adaptation to autistic children. In E. Schopler & G. Mesibov (Eds.), *The effects of autism on the family* (pp. 289–310). New York: Plenum Press.

Bristol, M. (1987). Mothers of children with autism or communication disorders: Successful adaptation and the double ABCX model. *Journal of Autism and Developmental Disorders, 17,* 469–486.

Campbell, N. B., Milling, L., Laughlin, A., & Bush, E. (1993). The psychosocial climate of families with suicidal pre-adolescent children. *American Journal of Orthopsychiatry, 63,* 142–145.

Casey, J., Griffin, M., & Googins, B. (1993). The role of work for wives of alcoholics. *American Journal of Drug and Alcohol Abuse, 19,* 119–131.

Clair, D. J., & Genest, M. (1987). Variables associated with the adjustment of offspring of alcoholic fathers. *Journal of Studies on Alcohol, 48,* 345–355.

Clair, D. J., & Genest, M. (1992). The Children of Alcoholics Screening Test: Reliability and relationship to family environment, adjustment, and alcohol-related stressors of adolescent offspring of alcoholics. *Journal of Clinical Psychology, 48,* 414–420.

Conrad, M., & Hammen, C. (1989). Role of maternal depression in perceptions of child maladjustment. *Journal of Consulting and Clinical Psychology, 57,* 663–667.

Corse, S. J., Schmid, K., & Trickett, P. K. (1990). Social network characteristics of mothers in abusing and nonabusing families and their relationships to parenting beliefs. *Journal of Community Psychology, 18,* 44–59.

Daniels, D., & Moos, R. H. (1988). Exosystem influences on family and child functioning. *Journal of Social Behavior and Personality, 3,* 113–133.

Dinning, W. D., & Berk, L. A. (1989). The Children of Alcoholics Screening Test: Relationship to sex, family environment, and social adjustment in adolescents. *Journal of Clinical Psychology, 45,* 335–339.

Dixon, M. A. (1986). Families of adolescent clients and nonclients: Their environments and help-seeking behaviors. *Advances in Nursing Science, 8,* 75–88.

Downey, G., & Coyne, J. C. (1990). Children of depressed parents: An integrative review. *Psychological Bulletin, 108,* 50–76.

Ebata, A. T., & Moos, R. H. (1991). Coping and adjustment in distressed and healthy adolescents. *Journal of Applied Developmental Psychology, 12,* 33–54.

Feldman, S. S., Wentzel, K. R., Weinberger, D. A., & Munson, J. A. (1990). Marital satisfaction of parents of preadolescent boys and its relationship to family and child functioning. *Journal of Family Psychology, 4,* 213–234.

Fiese, B. H., & Kline, C. A. (1993). Development of the Family Ritual Questionnaire: Initial reliability and validation studies. *Journal of Family Psychology, 6,* 290–299.

Fife, B., Norton, J., & Groom, G. (1987). The family's adaptation to childhood leukemia. *Social Science and Medicine, 24*, 159–168.

Filstead, W., McElfresh, O., & Anderson, C. (1981). Comparing the family environments of alcoholic and "normal" families. *Journal of Alcohol and Drug Education, 26*, 24–31.

Fox, R., Rotatori, A., Macklin, F., Green, H., & Fox, T. (1983). Socially maladjusted adolescents' perception of their families. *Psychological Reports, 52*, 831–834.

Friedman, A. S., Tomko, L. A., & Utada, A. (1991). Client and family characteristics that predict better family therapy outcome for adolescent drug abusers. *Family Dynamics of Addiction Quarterly, 1*, 77–93.

Friedman, A. S., & Utada, A. (1992). The family environments of adolescent drug abusers. *Family Dynamics of Addiction Quarterly, 2*, 32–45.

Friedman, S. (1990). Assessing the marital environment of agoraphobics. *Journal of Anxiety Disorders, 4*, 335–340.

Friedrich, W. N., Cohen, D. S., & Wilturner, L. S. (1987). Family relations and marital quality when a mentally handicapped child is present. *Psychological Reports, 61*, 911–919.

Friedrich, W. N., Reams, R., & Jacobs, J. H. (1982). Depression and suicidal ideation in early adolescence. *Journal of Youth and Adolescence, 11*, 403–407.

Grych, J. H., Seid, M., & Fincham, F. (1992). Assessing marital conflict from the child's perspective: The Children's Perception of Interparental Conflict Scale. *Child Development, 63*, 558–572.

Halverson, C. F., & Wampler, K. S. (1993). The mutual influence of child externalizing behavior and family functioning: The impact of a mild congenital risk factor. In R. E. Cole & D. Reiss (Eds.), *How do families cope with chronic illness?* (pp. 71–93), Hillsdale, NJ: Lawrence Erlbaum.

Hauser, S. T., Jacobson, A. M., Lavori, P., Wolfsdorf, J. I., Herskowitz, R. D., Milley, J. E., Bliss, R., Wertlieb, D., & Stein, J. (1990). Adherence among children and adolescents with insulin-dependent diabetes mellitus over a four-year longitudinal follow-up: Immediate and long-term linkages with the family milieu. *Journal of Pediatric Psychology, 15*, 527–542.

Head, S. B., Baker, J. D., & Williamson, D. A. (1991). Family environment characteristics and dependent personality disorder. *Journal of Personality Disorders, 5*, 256–263.

Hetherington, E. M. (1991). The role of individual differences and family relationships in children's coping with divorce and remarriage. In P. A. Cowan & M. Hetherington (Eds.), *Family transitions* (pp. 165–194). Hillsdale, NJ: Lawrence Erlbaum.

Hibbs, E. D., Hamburger, S. D., Kruesi, M. J. P., & Lenane, M. (1993). Factors affecting expressed emotion in parents of ill and normal children. *American Journal of Orthopsychiatry, 63*, 103–112.

Jacob, T., & Leonard, K. (1994). Family and peer influences in the development of adolescent alcohol abuse. In R. Zucker, G. Boyd, & J. Howard (Eds.), *The development of alcohol problems: Exploring the biopsychosocial matrix of risk*. Washington, DC: NIAAA.

Jarmas, A. L., & Kazak, A. E. (1992). Young adult children of alcoholic fathers: Depressive experiences, coping styles, and family systems. *Journal of Consulting and Clinical Psychology, 60*, 244–251.

Jaycox, L. H., & Repetti, R. L. (1993). Conflict in families and the psychological adjustment of preadolescent children. *Journal of Family Psychology, 7*, 344–355.

Jenkins, J. (1992). Sibling relationships in disharmonious homes: Potential difficulties and protective effects. In F. Boer & J. Dunn (Eds.), *Children's sibling relationships: Developmental and clinical issues* (pp. 125–138). Hillsdale, NJ: Lawrence Erlbaum.

Jensen, E. W., James, S. A., Boyce, W. T., & Hartnett, S. A. (1983). The Family Routines Inventory: Development and validation. *Social Science and Medicine, 17*, 201–211.

Kiser, L. J., Nunn, W. B., Millsap, P. A., Heston, J. D., McDonald, J. C., Trapp, C. A., & Pruitt, D. B. (1988). Child and adolescent day treatment: Population profile. *International Journal of Partial Hospitalization, 5*, 287–305.

Lakey, B., & Cassady, P. B. (1990). Cognitive processes in perceived social support. *Journal of Personality and Social Psychology, 59*, 337–343.

Lakey, B., & Heller, K. (1988). Social support from a friend, perceived support, and social problem solving. *American Journal of Community Psychology, 16*, 811–824.

LeFlore, L. (1988). Delinquent youths and family. *Adolescence, 23*, 629–642.

Liem, R., & Liem, J. H. (1988). Psychological effects of unemployment on workers and their families. *Journal of Social Issues, 44*, 87–105.

Maccoby, E. E., & Martin, J. A. (1983). Socialization in the context of the family: Parent–child interaction. In E. M. Hetherington (Ed.), *Handbook of child psychology*, Vol. 4, *Socialization: Personality and social development* (pp. 1–102). New York: Wiley.

Martin, B. (1987). Developmental perspectives on family theory and psychopathology. In T. Jacob (Ed.), *Family interaction and psychopathology* (pp. 163–202). New York: Plenum Press.

McGee, R., Silva, P. A., & Williams, S. (1983). Parents' and teachers' perceptions of behavior problems in seven year old children. *The Exceptional Child, 30*, 151–161.

McGee, R., Silva, P. A., & Williams, S. (1984). Perinatal neurological, environmental, and developmental characteristics of seven-year-old children with stable behaviour problems. *Journal of Child Psychology and Psychiatry, 25*, 573–586.

McGee, R., Williams, S., & Silva, P. A. (1984). Background characteristics of aggressive, hyperactive, and aggressive/hyperactive boys. *Journal of the American Academy of Child Psychiatry, 23*, 280–284.

McGee, R., Williams, S., & Silva, P. A. (1985). Factor structure and correlates of ratings of inattention, hyperactivity, and antisocial behavior in a large sample of nine-year-old children from the general population. *Journal of Consulting and Clinical Psychology, 53*, 480–490.

Meneese, W. B., & Yutrzenka, B. A. (1990). Correlates of suicidal ideation among rural adolescents. *Suicide and Life Threatening Behavior, 20*, 206–212.

Mink, I. T., & Nihira, K. (1987). Direction of effects: Family life styles and behavior of TMR children. *American Journal of Mental Deficiency, 92*, 57–64.

Moos, R., & Billings, A. (1982). Children of alcoholics during the recovery process: Alcoholic and matched control families. *Addictive Behaviors, 7*, 155–163.

Moos, R. H., & Moos, B. S. (1994). *Family Environment Scale manual.* Palo Alto, CA: Consulting Psychologists Press.

Morris, P. W., Horne, A. M., Jessell, J. C., Passmore, J. L., Walker, J. M., & Sayger, T. V. (1988). Behavioral and cognitive characteristics of fathers of aggressive and well-behaved boys. *Journal of Cognitive Psychotherapy: An International Quarterly, 2*, 251–265.

Nihira, K., Meyers, C. E., & Mink, I. T. (1983). Reciprocal relationship between home environment and development of TMR adolescents. *American Journal of Mental Deficiency, 88*, 139–149.

Nihira, K., Mink, I. T., & Meyers, C. E. (1985). Home environment and development of slow learning adolescents: Reciprocal relations. *Developmental Psychology, 21*, 784–794.

Olson, D. H. (1991). Three-dimensional (3-D) circumplex model and revised scoring of FACES III. *Family Process, 30*, 74–79.

Olson, D. H., McCubbin, H. I., Barnes, H., Larsen, A., Muxen, M., & Wilson, M. (1982). *Family inventories: Inventories used in a national survey of families across the family life cycle.* St. Paul, MN: Family Social Science.

Olson, D. H., Sprenkle, D. H., & Russell, C. S. (1979). Circumplex model of marital and family systems. I. Cohesion and adaptability dimensions, family types, and clinical applications. *Family Process, 18*, 3–28.

Oxenford, C., & Nowicki, S. (1982). Perceived family climate of students deciding to pursue counseling. *Journal of American College Health, 30*, 224–226.

Petersen-Kelley, A. (1985). Family environment and Alateens: A note on alcohol abuse potential. *Journal of Community Psychology, 13*, 75–76.

Sarason, B. R., Shearin, E. N., Pierce, G. R., & Sarason, I. G. (1987). Interrelations of social support measures: Theoretical and practical implications. *Journal of Personality and Social Psychology, 52*, 813–832.

Sarason, I. G., Sarason, B. R., & Shearin, E. N. (1986). Social support as an individual difference variable: Its stability, origins, and relational aspects. *Journal of Personality and Social Psychology, 5*, 845–855.

Scalf-McIver, L., & Thompson, K. (1989). Family correlates of bulimic characteristics in college females. *Journal of Clinical Psychology, 45*, 467–472.

Schaefer, M. T., & Olson, D. H. (1980). Assessing intimacy: The PAIR inventory. *Journal of Marital and Family Therapy, 7*, 47–60.

Schneewind, K. A. (1987). Die Familienklimaskalen. In M. Cierpka (Ed.), *Familiendiagnostik* (pp. 320–342). Heidelberg: Springer.

Schneewind, K., Beckman, M., & Engfer, A. (1983). *Eltern und Kinder: Umwelteinflüsse auf das familiäre Verhalten.* Stuttgart, Federal Republic of Germany: Kohlhammer.

Scoresby, A. L., & Christensen, B. (1976). Differences in interaction and environmental conditions of clinic and non-clinic families: Implications for counselors. *Journal of Marriage and Family Counseling, 2,* 63–71.

Silbereisen, R. K., & Walper, S. (1988). A person–process–context approach. In M. Rutter (Ed.), *Studies of psychosocial risk: The power of longitudinal data* (pp. 96–113). New York: Cambridge University Press.

Smith, P. D., Rivers, P. C., & Stahl, K. J. (1992). Family cohesion and conflict as predictors of drinking patterns: Beyond demographics and alcohol expectancies. *Family Dynamics of Addiction Quarterly, 2,* 61–69.

Stern, M., & Zevon, M. A. (1990). Stress, coping, and family environment: The adolescent's response to naturally occurring stressors. *Journal of Adolescent Research, 5,* 290–305.

Stewart, M. A., & Brown, S. A. (1993). Family functioning following adolescent substance abuse treatment. *Journal of Substance Abuse, 5,* 327–339.

Tarter, R. E., Kabene, M., Escallier, E. A., Laird, S. B., & Jacob, T. (1990). Temperament deviation and risk for alcoholism. *Alcoholism: Clinical and Experimental Research, 14,* 380–382.

Thompson, K. L., Varni, J. W., & Hanson, V. (1987). Comprehensive assessment of pain in juvenile rheumatoid arthritis: An empirical model. *Journal of Pediatric Psychology, 12,* 241–255.

Timko, C., Baumgartner, M., Moos, R. H., & Miller, J. J. (1993). Parental risk and resistance factors among children with juvenile rheumatic disease: A four-year predictive study. *Journal of Behavioral Medicine, 16,* 571–588.

Timko, C., Stovel, K., Baumgartner, M., & Moos, R. H. (1995). Acute and chronic stressors, social resources, and functioning among adolescents with juvenile rheumatic disease. *Journal of Research on Adolescence, 5,* 361–385.

Timko, C., Stovel, K., & Moos, R. H. (1992). Functioning among mothers and fathers of children with juvenile rheumatic disease: A longitudinal study. *Journal of Pediatric Psychology, 17,* 705–724.

Timko, C., Stovel, K., Moos, R. H., & Miller, J. J. (1992a). Adaptation to juvenile rheumatic disease: A controlled evaluation of functional disability with a one-year follow-up. *Health Psychology, 11,* 67–76.

Timko, C., Stovel, K., Moos, R. H., & Miller, J. J. (1992b). A longitudinal study of risk and resistance factors among children with juvenile rheumatic disease. *Journal of Clinical Child Psychology, 21,* 132–142.

Tolan, P. H., & Lorion, R. P. (1988). Multivariate approaches to the identification of delinquency proneness in adolescent males. *American Journal of Community Psychology, 16,* 547–561.

Tyerman, A., & Humphrey, M. (1981). Dimensions of the family environment in adolescence. *Journal of Adolescence, 4,* 353–361.

Valentiner, D. P., Holahan, C. J., & Moos, R. H. (1994). Social support, appraisals of event controllability, and coping: An integrative model. *Journal of Personality and Social Psychology, 66,* 1094–1102.

Varni, J. W., Babani, L., Wallander, J. L., Roe, T., & Frasier, D. (1989). Social support and self-esteem effects on psychological adjustment in children and adolescents with insulin-dependent diabetes mellitus. *Child and Family Behavior Therapy, 11,* 1–17.

Varni, J. W., Wilcox, K. T., & Hanson, V. (1988). Mediating effects of family social support on child psychological adjustment in juvenile rheumatoid arthritis. *Health Psychology, 7,* 421–431.

Varni, J. W., Wilcox, K. T., Hanson, V., & Brik, R. (1988). Chronic musculoskeletal pain and functional status in juvenile rheumatoid arthritis: An empirical model. *Pain, 32,* 1–7.

Waring, E. M., McElrath, D., Lefcoe, D., & Weisz, G. (1981). Dimensions of intimacy in marriage. *Psychiatry, 44,* 169–175.

Williams, S. M., Anderson, J., McGee, R., & Silva, P. A. (1990). Risk factors for behavioral and emotional disorder in preadolescent children. *Journal of the American Academy of Child and Adolescent Psychiatry, 29,* 413–419.

Wolin, S. J., Bennett, L. A., & Noonan, D. L. (1979). Family rituals and the recurrence of alcoholism over generations. *American Journal of Psychiatry, 136,* 589–593.

Wolin, S. J., Bennett, L. A., Noonan, D. L., & Teitelbaum, M. A. (1980). Disrupted family rituals: A factor in the intergenerational transmission of alcoholism. *Journal of Studies on Alcohol, 41,* 199–214.

III

Stress, Clinical Problems, and Support Needs for Families

14

The Relation of Family Support to Adolescents' Psychological Distress and Behavior Problems

MANUEL BARRERA, JR., and SUSAN A. LI

Adolescence is a developmental period that presents special considerations in the study of socially supportive relationships within the family. Perhaps the most significant consideration concerns the growing influence of peers in the lives of adolescents (Petersen & Hamburg, 1986). Puberty, sexuality, and the emergence of romantic involvements add important dimensions to adolescent peer relationships (Brooks-Gunn, 1991; Steinberg, 1981). Also, some have asserted that adolescence, particularly late adolescence, is a time in which autonomy needs are more pronounced than needs for dependence on parents (see White, Speisman, & Costos, 1983). In some cases, adolescents might adopt strategies for the development of autonomy that include less reliance on the support of family members and greater self-reliance or reliance on peers. We might question, then, the role of supportive relationships with parents and other family members during this developmental period in which autonomy and the emergence of peer relationships appear to be so influential. Comparisons to peer relationships are potentially valuable perspectives for understanding the role of parents and families in providing social support and for understanding the impact of these provisions. While the focus of this chapter is on family support during adolescence, one of our special interests in conducting this review was to contrast the contributions of adolescents' supportive relationships with peers and those of relationships with family members.

MANUEL BARRERA, JR., and SUSAN A. LI • Department of Psychology, Arizona State University, Tempe, Arizona 85287-1104.

Handbook of Social Support and the Family, edited by Gregory R. Pierce, Barbara R. Sarason, and Irwin G. Sarason. Plenum Press, New York, 1996.

In addition to bringing changes in social relationships with peers and family members, adolescence may also see the development of psychopathology and behavior problems. Problems associated with alcohol, drugs, and sexuality often make their initial appearance during adolescence. As a society, we have critical concerns about adolescent behavior problems such as teen pregnancy, crime, sexually transmitted diseases, and drug abuse that have significant consequences for young people, their families, and communities (Scales, 1990). Depression becomes more prominent than it was during childhood and arguably increases in prevalence as adolescents approach young adulthood. Eating disorders such as anorexia and bulimia, as well as suicidal behavior, also achieve prominence during adolescence. Thus, problems associated with both internalizing and externalizing dimensions of psychological disorder are well represented in adolescence.

This chapter brings together the interests in understanding adolescents' socially supportive relationships with family members and in understanding adolescents' experience with behavior problems and psychological disorder. Consistent with the spirit of the book, our specific goal in this chapter is to take a critical look at research that has tried to identify the relation between family support and adolescents' psychological disorder. In doing this, we explore several specific questions:

1. Nature of adolescents' social support: Who provides social support to adolescents and what types of support are provided? How does the support provided by family members compare to support from peers?
2. Determinants of adolescents' family social support: Which factors aid or impair a family's ability to provide support?
3. Relation of family support to psychological distress and problem behavior: Is there an association between family support and indicators of psychological disorder? How does this association compare to that found for support that adolescents receive from peers?
4. Implications for theory and action: How do these findings inform the development of theory about adolescents' social support or interventions designed to prevent or remediate adolescents' distress and behavior problems?

Despite our intent to feature the concept of *family* support, we found that many of the best studies on adolescents' social support assessed *parental* support to the exclusion of support from other family members. There may in fact be good reasons to consider separately the contributions of parents and those of other family members (Barrera, Chassin, & Rogosch, 1993). Unfortunately, in contrast to the considerable attention that has been paid to adolescent–parent relationships, few studies have assessed adolescents' relationships with siblings, grandparents, or other relatives. For example, research on adolescents' relationships with siblings has been identified as a gap in the literature (Clark-Lempers, Lempers, & Ho, 1991). Nevertheless, we have included research on parental support in this review even if support from other family relationships was not assessed.

In addition to the focus on parental support, there are many studies that have quantified family support in the aggregate, oftentimes using popular measures of perceived social support such as subscales of the Family Environment Scale (Moos, Insel, & Humphrey, 1972) or the Perceived Social Support—Family scale (PSS-Family) (Procidano & Heller, 1983). An advantage of the PSS is that it has a companion subscale, the PSS-Friends, which has been used in several studies that compared the support that adolescents perceived from family and peers (e.g., DuBois, Felner, Brand, Adan, & Evans, 1992; Windle, 1992). In the end, the research reviewed herein consists largely of two types, studies that used measures of perceived social support that are referenced to the "family" and those that assessed parental support.

NATURE OF ADOLESCENTS' SOCIAL SUPPORT: CONTRASTING FAMILY SUPPORT WITH OTHER SOURCES OF SUPPORT

Before questions of the mental health consequences of family support for adolescents are considered, it is instructive to place family support in a context of social support that is received from other sources, particularly peers. In fact, there is a long history of research on the relative influence of parents and peers that helps us understand whom adolescents consult when they need help and which types of troubles result in support seeking (Greenberg, Siegel, & Leitch, 1983; Richardson, Galambos, Schulenberg, & Peterson, 1984). Research that contrasts family members with other potential support providers reveals a unique role of the family in supplying adolescents with social resources.

Studies suggest that during preadolescence and early adolescence, parents (particularly mothers) are greater sources of support than peers. In a study of 199 5th- and 6th-graders, students rated parents, siblings, grandparents, and friends on various relationship qualities (Furman & Buhrmester, 1985). The pattern of findings differed somewhat for boys and girls, but mothers and fathers were the most prominent providers of affection, enhancement of worth, and instrumental aid. Furthermore, relationships with parents were rated as more important and satisfying than relationships with grandparents, friends, and siblings. Siblings, in fact, were perceived as the greatest source of conflict. There is an obvious caution reflected in these results for those who would like to characterize support provided by "the family." Aggregating across family members could mask distinct differences between parents and siblings in the amount of support and conflict that an adolescent receives from his or her family (also see Richardson et al., 1984). The data of Furman and Buhrmester (1985) also showed that friends were prominent sources of intimacy. Friends were rated the highest for companionship of all those relationships that Furman and Buhrmester considered. Through the eyes of these young adolescents, parents were the most active providers of both emotional and tangible support, while friends occupied very predictable roles as social companions. These findings are consistent with those of Levitt, Guacci

Franco, and Levitt (1993), who assessed the family and peer support of an ethnically diverse sample of 7-, 10-, and 14-year-olds. Family support was dominant across all three age groups, but peer support increased with age. Whereas family members were most commonly listed in the inner circle of intimate support providers, peers were more likely to be named with those network members who were regarded as outside the most intimate circle of support providers.

In a subsequent cross-sectional study, Furman and Buhrmester (1992) explored changes in the supportive provisions of key relationships that might occur as children move through adolescence. They examined subjects from four developmental periods: preadolescence (4th grade), early adolescence (7th grade), middle adolescence (10th grade), and late adolescence (college). Consistent with their earlier findings for 5th- and 6th-graders (Furman & Buhrmester, 1985), they found that 4th-graders rated parents as the most active providers of support. Seventh-grade students saw parents as similar to same-sex friends in supplying support, and 10th-graders rated parents somewhat lower than same-sex friends. Finally, college students viewed mothers, same-sex friends, and romantic partners as comparable in support provision. Graphs of these data showed a U-shaped curve for parents' provision of support that was highest for 4th-graders, declined to a nadir for 10th-graders, and increased slightly for college students. Comparable data for same-sex friend support showed an *inverted* U-shaped curve that had its highest points at the 7th and 10th grades. It also was interesting that *conflict* with parents was a mirror image of the curve for parental support (i.e., an inverted U-shaped curve). It reached its highest points during early and middle adolescence, when parental support was at its lowest points.

The shift to greater reliance on friends during early and middle adolescence and the corresponding decrease in perceptions of parental support might be explained by several mechanisms. First, the nature of stressors and the personal concerns that adolescents confront during some phases of adolescence might favor peers as the sources of advice and understanding. For instance, issues such as sexuality, physical appearance, and other changes associated with puberty might be more readily discussed with peers than with parents (Sebald, 1989). Conflict with parents might be a stressor that adolescents bring to their peers for commiseration and problem solving. Also, achieving autonomy from the family would be facilitated by a decrease in reliance on parents and an increase in association with other adolescents who are also seeking greater independence (see Richardson et al., 1984).

In fact, there is support for some of these proposed mechanisms. Adolescents appear to seek out social support from parents and peers for different personal concerns (Sebald, 1989) and are likely to favor advice from parents or peers depending on the issue (Brittain, 1963). Sebald (1989) reported data from questionnaires administered to high school students in which he asked adolescents to indicate whose advice they sought for 18 issues (e.g., future occupation, dating, personal problems). Adolescents showed a willingness to consult parents on issues such as how to spend money, selection of courses, occupational choices, and college attendance. They expressed a very low likelihood of consulting parents on questions concerning clubs, dress, social events, hobbies, reading materials, and dating. Virtually the opposite picture emerged for peers. Peers were very unlikely to be sources of advice on careers, courses, and college, but very likely to be sources of advice on social activities, elements of teen culture (e.g., dress, magazines, hobbies), and dating partners. In the one item related to substance use ("participating in drinking parties"), teens reported that they were more likely to seek the advice of friends than of parents. This same study showed that there was an apparent gender difference in the preferred source of "advice on personal problems." Boys' ratings were relatively balanced between parents and peers concerning whom they would consider more important to consult, but girls strongly preferred peers over parents. Collectively, these results are both reassuring and alarming. Parents were viewed as valuable sources of advice for critically important issues concerned with careers, academic preparation, and finances, but peers were prime sources of advice on dating, alcohol use, and even personal problems.

These results are consistent with the conclusion drawn by Greenberg et al. (1983), who cited studies conducted in the 1960s and 1970s. Parents influence big-picture decisions such as educational and occupational goals, but peers influence lifestyle choices such as music and clothing selections. In many cases, however, lifestyle choices also include activities that are closely connected to problem behaviors such as the use of drugs and alcohol. The majority of adolescents are not likely to nominate parents as the initial resource for getting help with problems associated with drugs or alcohol (Windle, Miller-Tutzauer, Barnes, & Welte, 1991) or even more general personal problems (Sebald, 1989).

Conclusion

With few exceptions, research on the sources of adolescents' social support has a justifiable focus on parents and peers. Both sources of support are prominent throughout adolescence, but general statements can be made about how adolescents see the relative frequency of supportive provisions from parents and peers across different stages of adolescence. The greater reliance on parents that occurs during preadolescence gives way to greater reliance on peers during middle adolescence and finally to a more balanced involvement, encompassing supportive exchanges with both parents and peers in late adolescence and young adulthood. It is also apparent that parents and peers are consulted for different problems and life decisions. There is a substantial history of research that shows the influence of parents on adolescents' choices about work and education. Peers, on the other hand, are consulted for lifestyle choices and for issues connected with sexuality, the use of drugs and alcohol, and more general problems. If parents and peers are asked to provide support for different problems, what implications are there for interpreting the relations of family and peer support to mental health criteria? This question will be revisited later in the chapter.

DETERMINANTS OF SOCIAL SUPPORT WITHIN THE FAMILY

Several theoretical models have been proposed to identify factors that influence the support parents provide to their children (Abidin, 1992; Belsky, 1984; Webster-Stratton, 1990). These determinants of supportive parenting include parents' intrapersonal characteristics as well as influences from the broader social context surrounding parental behavior. Supportive parental behaviors within the context of the family are affected by factors such as the current psychological functioning of the parent (including diagnosable psychopathology), parental social support networks, marital relations, and life stress. In general, events that tax a parent's resources, create stress, and impair the parent's ability to function in the parental role are likely to have adverse effects on social support to adolescents.

Parental Psychopathology

There is substantial evidence to suggest that parents' psychopathology negatively affects their provision of social support. In particular, the effects of parents' depression on their supportive parenting have been given considerable attention. Specifically, maternal affectional involvement and responsiveness, and family cohesion, are lower in families with a depressed parent than in comparison families (Billings & Moos, 1983; Downey & Coyne, 1990; Goodman & Brumley, 1990; Zahn-Waxler, Denham, Iannotti, & Cummings, 1992). In studies using adolescent samples, decrements in social support associated with both paternal and maternal affective disorder have been identified. Almeida and Galambos (1991) found a negative relation between paternal depression and fathers' acceptance of their adolescent children. This result was consistent with those from another study that found that children of depressed parents reported less family cohesion and parental caring than did children of nondepressed parents (Fendrich, Warner, & Weissman, 1990; Kaslow, Warner, John, & Brown, 1992). In one of our own studies that focused on fathers' social support (Li, Barrera, & Chassin, August, 1994), we found that paternal affective disorder was a significant predictor of fathers' reports of their inconsistent support to their adolescent children. From these studies, there appears to be a negative relation between parental depression and supportive parenting.

In addition to parental depression, parental alcoholism impairs family social support. Studies have found that alcoholic families exhibit decreased family cohesion and expressiveness in comparison to nonalcoholic families (Barry & Fleming, 1990; Filstead, McElfresh, & Anderson, 1981). These decrements in family cohesion include aspects such as lower family support and decreased feelings of togetherness in alcoholic families (Barry & Fleming, 1990). As the alcoholism status of the family changes, supportive family functioning also changes. Family cohesion in recovered alcoholic families is similar to cohesion in nonalcoholic families (Moos & Billings, 1982; Moos, Finney, & Chan, 1981; Moos & Moos, 1984). In contrast, families with relapsed alcoholics show significantly less cohesion than recovered or nonalcoholic families.

There is mixed evidence for the influence of parental alcoholism on parental social support behaviors. Barrera et al. (1993) found no relation between parental alcoholism and adolescents' reports of father, mother, sibling, and chum support. Li et al. (August, 1994) found that paternal alcoholism diagnosis was a significant predictor of both father and mother report of paternal inconsistent support, but not adolescent report. Similarly, in a study of 4th-, 5th-, and 6th-graders, Roosa, Tein, Groppenbacher, Michaels, and Dumka (1993) found that in contrast to their expectations, parental problem drinking was not related to preadolescents' reports of maternal acceptance and communication. It appears that the influence of parental alcoholism and depression on supportive parenting is found consistently for parents' reports of support, but is found inconsistently when parental support is assessed from the adolescents' perspective.

Although the studies reviewed above did not find effects for adolescents' report, significant effects for adolescents have been noted. In a study of adolescent children of alcoholics, adolescents with alcoholic fathers rated their families as more unreliable, and less affectionate, loving, trusting, secure, warm, and understanding, than did adolescents with nonalcoholic fathers (Callan & Noller, 1986). Holden, Brown, and Mott (1988) found that adolescents with an alcoholic parent were significantly more likely to receive support from nonparent family members and to report less support from parents. In general, these adolescents received less support from multiple resources (including parents) than did adolescents without an alcoholic parent. Benson and Heller (1987) reported findings from a sample of adult daughters of alcoholic/problem-drinking, disturbed, and normal fathers. Current family support and consistent love and affection in relationships with father and mother were more impaired for daughters with alcoholic/problem-drinking fathers than for daughters with normal fathers. Subjects who had two alcoholic parents reported the most problematic relationships. Retrospective reports of support in early adolescence by these subjects were not significantly different across the groups, but the number of intimate others at age 14 was significantly lower for daughters with two alcoholic parents. Findings from these studies support the conclusion that at least two forms of parental psychopathology are significant predictors of supportive parental behavior. It is likely that other forms of parental psychopathology would have detrimental effects on parental support as well.

Supports and Stressors

In addition to parental psychopathology, contextual aspects of the parent's environment influence parental support. There is evidence to suggest that the amount of social support received by the parent affects support provided to the adolescent. Although the following study used a sample of young children, mothers' reports of perceived competence in the parenting role were significantly negatively related to three separate measures of the mothers' social support (Quittner, Glueckauf, & Jackson, 1990). Spouse support as a predictor of the quality of parenting has also been assessed in studies of young children (Bristol,

Gallagher, & Schopler, 1988). A study of 7th-graders by Simons, Lorenz, Wu, and Conger (1993) found that spouse support but not social network support had a direct effect on supportive parenting for fathers and mothers, and that both spouse support and social network support had indirect effects on parenting through the parent's depression.

General life stress events such as the death of a spouse, financial stress, family conflict, and divorce may also affect parental social support. In the area of bereavement, S. G. West, Sandler, Pillow, Baca, and Gersten (1991) found that death of a spouse predicted the nature of the surviving parent's report of family cohesion. As seen in other studies, parental death was not significantly related to the child's report of parental warmth with the surviving parent. Similarly, terminal illness can affect parental behavior. Parents with a terminally ill spouse and children between ages 7 and 16 reported decreased confidence in their emotional sensitivity and responsiveness to their child's needs (Siegel et al., 1990). Many diverse stressors can affect supportive parental behavior. In the study of Simons et al. (1993), economic pressure had indirect effects on supportive parenting through parental depression and spousal support. Fauber, Forehand, Thomas, and Wierson (1990) found that marital conflict was significantly related to parental acceptance/rejection of adolescent children in both intact and recently divorced families. In the Roosa et al. (1993) study, negative life events including family conflict significantly predicted decreased supportive parenting. Negative life events are also related to decreased family cohesion (Moos & Moos, 1984).

In addition to these stressors, changes in family composition can affect levels of support within the family. Adolescents whose parents are recently divorced experience poorer parenting (characterized by significantly more conflict, less problem solving, and less positive communication) than adolescents in intact families (Forehand, Thomas, Wierson, Brody, & Fauber, 1990). Pink and Wampler (1985) found that family cohesion was lower in step-parent families, especially within the male parent–adolescent relationship. Smith (1991) found that levels of family cohesion were similar for remarried and intact first-marriage families except when there was an adolescent child in the remarried family. In that study, lower reports of family cohesion were found in remarried families with adolescents. Thus, family composition in conjunction with the child's developmental age appears to significantly affect the supportive environment of the family. Studies of stress and support suggest that relations between the two constructs are complex (Barrera, 1988), and stress and support, when considered in tandem, have a significant influence on supportive parenting behavior (Simons et al., 1993; Webster-Stratton, 1990).

The determinants reviewed in this section had direct effects on parental support as well as indirect effects through the parent's mental health and perceived parenting competence. In summary, there is evidence to suggest that a number of individual characteristics (depression, alcoholism) as well as contextual factors (support, stress) determine the support that adolescents receive from parents and other family members.

RELATION OF FAMILY SUPPORT TO DISTRESS
AND PROBLEM BEHAVIOR

Internalizing Disorders: Depression and Self-Esteem

Depression.   Attachment theory is one of the conceptual bases that underlie our understanding of the influence of social support on psychological disorder. From attachment theory, both the failure to form adequate social bonds and the loss of intimate relationships would render a person susceptible to depression. It is predictable, then, that the relation between social support and depression is one of the best-established findings, particularly with adults (Barnett & Gotlib, 1988; Barrera, 1986). For adolescents, an association between depression and family support has been found for psychiatric inpatients (Barrera & Garrison-Jones, 1992), pregnant adolescents (Cutrona, 1989), a predominantly African-American urban sample (Maton, 1990), a multiethnic group sample in which teachers rated children's depressed mood (Levitt et al., 1993), and general adolescent samples (Baron & MacGillivray, 1989; Feldman, Rubenstein, & Rubin, 1988; Harter, Margold, & Whitesell, 1992; Kobak, Sudler, & Gamble, 1992; Licitra-Kleckler & Waas, 1993; Papini, Roggman, & Anderson, 1991; Slavin, 1991; Slavin & Rainer, 1990). These demonstrations have involved several different types of social support measures, including perceptions of family climate (Barrera & Garrison-Jones, 1992), perceptions of parenting (Baron & MacGillivray, 1989), perceptions of parental approval (Harter et al., 1992), collaterals' reports of support (Cutrona, 1989), and behavioral observations of problem-solving tasks (Kobak et al., 1992).

Cognitive models of depression include the idea that a negative view of the world is one defining feature of depression that influences the other manifestations of the syndrome, including strained social relationships. In light of these models, findings based entirely on self-report data are open to the alternative interpretation that the relation between family support and depression is spurious because negative cognitive distortions are ubiquitous and cause both depression and perceptions of poor family social support. Research that has included non-self-report measures of family support strengthens our confidence that the relation between depression and family support is not simply an artifact of self-report bias. In short, the relation of family support to depression has been found for a variety of samples, a variety of support measures, and a variety of reporters.

Not surprisingly, most of the research on the relation of family social support to adolescent depression symptoms has been cross-sectional. The past several years, however, have seen the publication of notable prospective studies that included specific depression measures (Slavin, 1991; Slavin & Rainer, 1990; Windle, 1992) and others in which depression was part of a larger construct of psychological distress (DuBois, Felner, Meares, & Krier, 1992; Dubow, Tisak, Causey, Hryshko, & Reid, 1992). Slavin (1991) found prospective effects of family support on depressive symptoms over a 6-month interval in one study, but found prospective effects only for girls over an 8-month interval in a second study of 233 high school sophomores, juniors, and seniors (Slavin & Rainer, 1990). Similarly, in a study of 277 high school sophomores and juniors, Windle (1992) found a prospective effect for family support (PSS-Family) on depression (Center for Epidemiological Studies—Depression scale [CES-D]) over a 6-month interval, but like the findings of Slavin and Rainer (1990), this finding was observed for girls only. The similarity of the prospective effects found by Windle (1992) and Slavin and Rainer (1990) is impressive in that the two studies did not use the same measures of family support or depression. It should be noted, however, that neither study assessed formally the interaction between gender and family social support. In both studies, separate analyses were conducted for males and females. Nevertheless, the most persuasive findings that link family social support and depression indicate that this relationship holds for adolescent girls, but not for boys.

Self-Esteem. The esteem-enhancing qualities of social support and the ability of social support to promote a resilient self-concept in individuals are viewed as central mechanisms of the effectiveness of support as a stress buffer (Cobb, 1976; Cohen & Wills, 1985; Thoits, 1986). Certainly, for children and adolescents, the family is a prime source of information for determining that one is a person of value who is esteemed by others (Sandler, Miller, Short, & Wolchik, 1989). Similar to research on the other prominent internalizing problem, depression, there is ample evidence that family social support is related to self-esteem and self-concept. The esteem-enhancing qualities of parental support (Greenberg et al., 1983) are found for both mothers' and fathers' provisions of support to their adolescent children (Barrera, Li, & Chassin, 1993; Hoffman, Ushpiz, & Levy-Shiff, 1988). In two cross-sectional studies reported by Maton (1990) and another by Rowlison and Felner (1988), the PSS-Family scale was related to measures of self-esteem. Finally, Levitt et al. (1993) examined interactions between family social support and several demographic variables in the prediction of positive self-concept. Family social support was related positively to self-concept for Anglos and Hispanics, but not for African-American children and adolescents. Also, family social support was related to self-concept for girls, but not for boys.

Popular theory and measures conceptualize self-concept as consisting of distinct components that correspond to domains such as scholastic competence, social competence with peers, and physical abilities (Harter, 1982). Research by Cauce and her colleagues examined the relation of family support to several aspects of self-concept. In one study that assessed self-concept with the Self-Appraisal Inventory (Frith & Narikawa, 1972), family support was related to scholastic self-concept, but not to peer acceptance (Cauce, Felner, Primavera, & Ginter, 1982). In a separate study that used the Harter (1982) Perceived Social Competence Scale for Children, family support was significantly correlated with peer competence and physical competence, but not with school competence (Cauce, Hannan, & Sargeant, 1992). Although family support was related to some aspect of self-concept for adolescents in both studies, there were inconsistent findings for peer and scholastic self-concepts, perhaps because different self-concept measures were used in the two studies.

Problem Behaviors: Externalizing Symptoms and Substance Use

Unlike theories linking social support and depression that emphasize affective reactions to loneliness and the loss of social ties, the theoretical mechanisms linked to adolescents' problem behaviors (such as externalizing behaviors and substance use) emphasize the importance of family support as a condition for proper socialization. Hypothetically, adolescents who have a positive bond with prosocial parents will be in a better position to regulate their own behavior than will adolescents who are estranged from or only loosely connected to their parents. Also, adolescents who have a close, supportive relationship with their parents and other family members will be less likely to affiliate with deviant peers who are prime agents for introducing other adolescents to alcohol and substance use.

Externalizing Symptoms.   Poor family support has been associated with delinquency, crime, school and family offenses (Licitra-Kleckler & Waas, 1993), and general problem behavior (Taylor, Casten, & Flickinger, 1993). Findings from our own longitudinal study of adolescent children of alcoholic and nonalcoholic parents showed that support from both fathers and mothers was related to externalizing symptoms (Barrera et al., 1993; Stice, Barrera, & Chassin, 1993). However, these effects were observed most prominently in cross-sectional analyses with adolescents' reports of both parental support and externalizing symptoms. Prospective effects of parental support on externalizing symptoms were not significant, nor were effects significant when externalizing symptoms were measured with parental reports. Stice and Barrera (1995) conducted additional analyses on these data to explore the possibility of reciprocal relations between externalizing symptoms and parental support. Structural equation modeling was conducted on two waves of panel data that were separated by a 1-year interval. Results showed that adolescents' reports of externalizing symptoms at the first assessment were prospectively related to parental support at the second assessment. The reverse, however, was not true. Parental support was not prospectively related to externalizing symptoms. Of course, these results merit replication in an independent sample, but they issue a caution in the interpretation of cross-sectional relations between externalizing symptoms and support. Consistent with other studies that concluded that children's behavior influences parenting practices (cf. Lytton, 1990), it is possible that adolescents' conduct problems result in the withdrawal of parental support.

In contrast to the results from our own research, there have been two longitudinal studies that found prospective effects for family social support as measured by the PSS-Family scale (DuBois et al., 1994; Windle, 1992). Windle (1992) assessed nearly 300 high school sophomores and juniors in two assessment periods 6 months apart. He found significant cross-sectional relations between family support and delinquency at both time periods. More important, he found that female subjects' time 1 scores on PSS-Family were related prospectively to delinquency problems at time 2, even after delinquency problems at time 1 were entered into the regression analyses (Windle, 1992). This effect was not found for males. The research design and data analytical strategy used by DuBois et al. (1994) were similar to Windle's in several respects. In the research of DuBois and colleagues, there were slightly more than 300 7th- and 8th-graders who were assessed twice over a 7-month interval. These researchers found prospective effects for family support in a regression analysis in which family social support was entered in a final step following the inclusion of the time 1 criterion, socio-economic status variables, and major and minor stress events. In this regression model, family social support accounted for approximately 2% of the variance in delinquency scores. Although this effect is not large, it is notable that it was found despite moderate stability of conduct problems ($r = 0.48$) and the correlation of family social support with other predictors such as parental education, major stress events, and daily hassles.

The DuBois et al. (1994) study ended with analyses that tested the possibility of reciprocal effects of conduct problems and family support. Psychological distress at time 1 was prospectively related to family support at time 2, but conduct problems at time 1 were not prospectively related to family support at time 2. It is not completely apparent why these findings were not consistent with those reported by Stice and Barrera (1995). The zero-order correlations between time 1 support and time 2 externalizing (conduct) problems were virtually identical in the two studies ($r = -0.27$ in DuBois et al. [1994] and $r = -0.28$ in Stice and Barrera [1995]). The zero-order correlation of time 1 externalizing symptoms on time 2 parental support was $r = -0.42$ in Stice and Barrera (1995), but it was not reported in DuBois et al. (1994). These two studies did differ in their sampling and use of measures. Approximately half the subjects in Stice and Barrera (1995) were adolescent children of alcoholics. It is possible that the magnitude of the externalizing symptoms they reported or special qualities of these symptoms increased their influence on subsequent provisions of parental social support. Future research might consider if there are certain characteristics of externalizing symptoms or characteristics of adolescents with externalizing disorders that have an adverse influence on future supportive exchanges between family members and adolescents.

Alcohol Use. Similar to research on depression, there is a large body of literature on the association between family support and adolescent alcohol use (for reviews, see Foxcroft & Lowe, 1991; Glynn, 1981). Much of this literature is concerned with parenting that uses constructs such as "nurturance," "cohesion," "warmth," "attachment," "closeness," and "affection," rather than the term "social support." In a meta-analysis of 28 studies, Foxcroft and Lowe (1991) found overwhelming evidence (23 of 28 studies) of an association between family support and adolescent alcohol use. Somewhat surprisingly, there was more evidence showing a relation between family *support* and alcohol use than there was for a relation between family *control* and alcohol use. They reviewed 16 studies that investigated family control and adolescents' alcohol use, and 7 of these studies failed to show a significant negative relation to alcohol use. In contrast to the linear effects found for social support, they speculated that control might have curvilinear effects on alcohol use. Both extremely high and extremely low levels of control might be associated with adolescent alcohol use.

Since Foxcroft and Lowe's review, more studies have shown the association between family support and adolescents' alcohol use (Holden et al., 1988; Stice et al., 1993; Wills & Vaughan, 1989; Windle, 1992). As described previously, Windle (1992) provided prospective analyses of the relation of family social support to a number of criteria, including alcohol consumption and problems due to alcohol consumption. In cross-sectional analyses of the data from girls at both the first and second assessment (6 months later), family support was significantly related to both alcohol use and problems. In the prospective analysis, family support was related only to alcohol problems. It also was interesting that this significant prospective effect was found in a regression model that included support from peers, stressful events, and the interaction of stress with both peer and family support. None of these other predictors was related to alcohol problems, and significant effects were found only for girls.

A longitudinal study of 454 adolescents and their parents showed significant relations between parental support and adolescents' alcohol use (Stice et al., 1993). The sample had an elevated risk for alcohol use in that approximately half the adolescents were from homes in which at least one parent was alcoholic (see Chassin, Rogosch, & Barrera, 1991). Adolescents and their parents were interviewed in their homes during two annual assessments. In cross-sectional analyses at time 1 and time 2, parental support was related to a measure of adolescents' alcohol use. In longitudinal analyses that adjusted for both time 1 parental support and adolescents' alcohol use, time 2 parental support was related to time 2 alcohol use. True prospective effects of time 1 parental support on time 2 alcohol use were also marginally significant. The data from Windle (1992) and Stice et al. (1993) are the most convincing evidence to date that social support from parents and the larger family influences adolescents' problematic alcohol use.

Substance Use.   On an outcome that is highly related to alcohol use, many studies show that family support is related to adolescents' substance use (Barrera et al., 1993; Brook, Whiteman, Gordon, & Cohen, 1986; Chassin, Presson, Sherman, Montello, & McGrew, 1986; DuBois et al., 1994; Licitra-Kleckler & Waas, 1993; Stice & Barrera, 1995; Stice et al., 1993; Wills & Vaughan, 1989). Glynn (1981) provided a valuable review that not only contrasted the influence of parents and peers, but also contrasted these influences for the various stages of substance use that Kandel (1975) identified. Studies reviewed by Glynn did not always use the term *social support,* but many dealt with highly related constructs such as attachment, positive involvement, and positive family relationships. He concluded that despite some exceptions, parental involvement, attachment to parents, and a strong family orientation appeared to lower the risk of substance use.

The relation between parental support and adolescent substance use sometimes emerges in complex ways. For example, in the research by Brook et al. (1986), there was not a significant zero-order correlation between fathers' support and their adolescent daughters' marijuana use. There was some evidence, however, that father support interacted with a variable that captured adolescents' orientation toward parents or peers. For those adolescent daughters who had a parent orientation, those who had supportive fathers used less marijuana than those who had unsupportive fathers. Wills and Vaughan (1989) looked for interactions between parental support and peer influences on the smoking behavior of adolescents. Parental support appeared to buffer the deleterious effects of having friends who smoke. Parental support showed its strongest relations to subjects' smoking when subjects reported the greatest amount of smoking among their peers. This is a familiar version of the buffering hypothesis that is sometimes expressed as the prediction that social support will have its greatest effect for those who are exposed to the risk factor (i.e., the stressor).

Additional support for the influence of family support on illicit drug use comes from the longitudinal research reported by DuBois et al. (1994). Family support measured by the PSS-Family scale during an initial assessment was related to reports of illicit substance use 7 months later ($r = -0.13$, $p < 0.05$). However, family support was not significantly related to this criterion when the regression model included reports of illicit substance use at the initial assessment, sociodemographic variables, and stress. Apparently, family support correlation with stress, initial substance use, and perhaps other predictors was sufficient to account for the prospective effect of time 1 family support on time 2 substance use.

Stice and Barrera (1995) conducted analyses to determine possible reciprocal effects between parental support and substance use. The lack of parental support might create conditions that result in adolescents' increased use of substances, but adolescents' use of substances also might result in a withdrawal of support by parents. The substance use measure included in these analyses was a composite of alcohol and illicit drug use over a 3-month period. To evaluate reciprocal effects, time 1 and time 2 measures of both substance use and parental support were included in structural equation models that estimated the prospective relation of (1) parental support to adolescents' substance use and (2) adolescents' substance use to parental support. The results of these analyses were consistent with a model in which there were reciprocal effects between parental support and substance use. Time 1 parental support was negatively related to time 2 substance use and time 1 substance use was negatively related to time 2 parental support. Additional analyses indicated that these two effects were essentially equal in magnitude. This study illustrated a principle that is often overlooked in research on the relation of social support to mental health criteria. Psychological distress and behavior problems can be both outcomes and causes of disturbed family support. As described earlier, this same study (Stice & Barrera, 1995) suggested that adolescents' externalizing symptoms best fit a model in which they were antecedents, rather than a consequence, of poor parental support.

Studies That Have Included Both Internalizing and Externalizing Criteria

It is obvious from the preceding discussion that there is considerable evidence to suggest that family support is related to a broad range of criteria that include internalizing disorders (e.g., depression) and externalizing disorders (e.g., delinquency and substance use). Yet we might ask, "Is family support more highly related to certain forms of adolescent psychological disorder and problem behavior than to others?" This question has implications for both theory and intervention. If family support shows a particularly strong association with some disorders but not with others, we might clarify the unique role of family support in the etiology of a particular disorder. Some theoretical models of depression, for example, postulate a special role for social support (e.g., Billings & Moos, 1982). However, if social support fits models of depression as well models for externalizing disorders, then any disorder-specific role for social support would be misleading. Determining which disorders are related to family support and which are not also has implications for intervention. Rather than regarding social support as a panacea, it is instructive to identify those outcomes that are likely to change as a result of family support manipulations and those that are not likely to change.

One approach to addressing this question is to look at studies that concurrently examined several criteria with the same sample and the same research procedures. Table 1 summarizes the results of eight studies that contained at least one measure of internalizing and externalizing symptoms. None of these studies contained a formal test that contrasted internalizing and externalizing symptoms on the strength of their relations to family support.

From visual inspection of the data in Table 1, there do not appear to be obvious differences between internalizing symptoms and narrowly defined conduct disorder symptoms. Studies by Barrera et al. (1993), DuBois et al. (1994), Feldman et al. (1988), and Windle (1992) found that internalizing and externalizing symptoms had comparable relations to family social support. For example, in their prospective study of 300 7th- and 8th-graders, DuBois et al. (1994) assessed a composite of psychological distress measures (depression, anxiety, and self-esteem), conduct problems, and a number of additional behavior problems (tobacco and alcohol use, illicit drug use, grades, absences from school, and school suspensions) over a 7-month interval. Regression analyses of each time 2 criterion used predictors that were assessed at time 1, which included the time 1 criterion, sociodemographic variables, major and small life stress events, family support, and school personnel support. Family support showed small but statistically significant relations to two criteria, psychological distress (i.e., internalizing) and conduct problems (i.e., externalizing). Furthermore, the relation of family support to these criteria were virtually identical (about 2% of the variance).

It is rare to find research that gives some indication of the generalizability of findings to ethnic minority populations. A study by Taylor et al. (1993) was conducted with a sample of 125 African-American 9th- to 12th-graders from single- and two-parent households. This study is relevant not only because it provided data on the relation of kinship support to depression and problem behaviors (e.g., drug use, vandalism, and physical assault), but also because it estimated a simple mediational model that included authoritative parenting as a mediator of the effects of kinship support on adolescents' psychosocial adjustment. Kinship support was related only to problem behavior in single-parent households; kinship

Table 1. Relation of Family Support to Internalizing and Externalizing Symptoms[a]

Study	Social support measure	Internalizing	Externalizing
Barrera & Garrison-Jones (1992)	Family Resources Index	Depression: $r = -0.28*$ Anxiety: NS	Conduct disorder: NS
Barrera et al. (1993)	Mother's support Father's support	Self-esteem: $sr^2 = 0.12*$ Self-esteem: $sr^2 = 0.13*$	Externalizing: $sr^2 = 0.07*$ Externalizing: $sr^2 = 0.06*$
DuBois et al. (1992)	PSS-Family	Psychological distress (composite) Time 1: $r = -0.42*$ Time 2: $r = -0.63*$	GPA Time 1: $r = 0.14$ Time 2: $r = 0.11$
DuBois et al. (1994)	PSS-Family for all criteria	Psychological distress (composite) Time 1: $r = -0.34*$ Time 2: $r = -0.29*$	Conduct problems Time 1: $r = -0.27*$ Time 2: $r = -0.27*$ Tobacco/alcohol Time 1: $r = -0.26*$ Time 2: $r = -0.22*$ Illicit drug use Time 1: $r = -0.10$ Time 2: $r = -0.13*$ GPA Time 1: $r = 0.14*$ Time 2: $r = 0.15*$ School absences Time 1: $r = -0.06$ Time 2: $r = -0.08$ School suspensions Time 1: $r = 0.05$ Time 2: $r = -0.15*$

Study	Measure	CDI	Aggression (restraint)
Feldman et al. (1988)	Family cohesion	$r = -0.64*$	$r = 0.40*$
	Mother's good communication	$r = -0.46*$	$r = 0.58*$
	Father's good communication	$r = -0.42*$	$r = 0.28*$
Licitra-Kleckler & Waas (1993)	PSS-Family	Depression: beta $= -0.39*$	School/family offenses: beta $= -0.28*$ Drugs: beta $= -0.20*$ Delinquency: beta $= -0.16*$ Crime: beta $= -0.25*$
Taylor et al. (1993)	Kinship support	Just one-parent families CES-D: $r = 0.01$ NS	Problem behavior: $r = -0.38*$
Windle (1992)	PSS-Family	Results for just girls Depression Time 1: beta $= -0.38*$ Time 2: beta $= -0.24*$ Prospective: beta $= -0.17*$	Deliquency Time 1: beta $= -0.17*$ Time 2: beta $= -0.32*$ Prospective: beta $= -0.20*$ Alcohol problems Time 1: beta $= -0.17*$ Time 2: beta $= -0.27*$ Prospective: beta $= -0.25*$ Alcohol consumption Time 1: beta $= -0.29*$ Time 2: beta $= -0.15*$ Prospective: NS

^{a}Measures: (CDI) Children's Depression Inventory; (CES-D) Center for Epidemiological Studies—Depression scale; (GPA) grade point average; (PSS-Family) Perceived Social Support—Family scale.
*Indicates statistically significant effect.

support was not related to depression in single-parent households or to either criterion in two-parent households. Analyses were consistent with the hypothesis that authoritative parenting mediated the relation of kinship support to problem behavior. The findings of Taylor and colleagues are unusual, however, in that they did not show significant relations between family social support and depression.

The most apparent pattern that emerges from Table 1 is that the relations of family support to school problems and illicit drug use are somewhat lower than those to internalizing and conduct disorder symptoms. The weak effects for these criteria could be due to their infrequent occurrence in general samples or to the family's limited influence in the school environments of adolescents. Otherwise, the comparability of the relations of family support to internalizing and externalizing criteria suggests that family support exerts its influence through several possible mechanisms that could include self-esteem enhancement, identification with prosocial adults, parental opportunities for monitoring and rule enforcement, and antidepressive attachments to family members. It is also apparent from these studies that the relations of family support to internalizing and externalizing criteria are often small (e.g., 2% of the variance in criteria), particularly in prospective analyses that simultaneously consider the effects of demographic characteristics, stress, and preexisting symptoms. Reliable measures and samples of several hundred participants are required to detect effects of this magnitude.

Specificity of Family Support

Is family support more highly related to psychological distress and problem behaviors than support from other network members, particularly peers? Numerous writers have addressed the roles of parents and peers in adolescent development (see Youniss & Smollar, 1985). Youniss and Smollar (1985) noted that parents are more likely than peers to offer guidance that has a future orientation (such as the importance of good school performance) and to assert authority to assist their children in avoiding trouble. Friendships, on the other hand, emphasize a present-oriented acceptance rather than change or rule conformity. Youniss and Smollar (1985) wrote (p. 142):

> Friends are helpful, cooperative, and willing to sacrifice self-gain for the other's welfare. This support differs from that given by parents in a key way.... When one friend has a problem, the other is likely to deal with that problem as it is presented and is unlikely to offer an analysis or solution from an external frame of reference.

From this analysis, we might expect peers to be less effective than parents in resolving problems or in enforcing standards for appropriate conduct. Support from friends, however, might be as effective as or more effective than support from family members in promoting self-acceptance and the sense of well-being that comes with the knowledge that one is loved and respected by others.

The Weiss (1974) theory of sociability also underscores the importance of contrasting support from family members and friends. Weiss hypothesized that support received from specific relationships serves specific mental health functions. For example, in adults, the kinds of support provided by same-sex friends are not identical to those provided by a spouse. The loss of a spouse through death or divorce, or the failure of support provisions within an intact marriage, may create needs that cannot be met through the provisions of even the best of friends. There are obvious applications of this hypothesis to adolescents. The lack of support from parents might create needs and deficits that are manifested in particular forms of psychological disorder. Similarly, lack of support from peers might result in other needs that would have somewhat distinct consequences.

Table 2 presents results from 20 studies that included both peer and family support. The results of 7 studies showed that social support from both parents and peers is related to mental health outcomes, particularly self-esteem and depression. However, when there were sizable differences between family and peer support's relationships to criteria, almost without exception, family social support showed the strongest relations to mental health outcomes. This was true when the criterion was depression (e.g., Armsden, McCauley, Greenberg, Burke, & Mitchell, 1990; Barrera & Garrison-Jones, 1992; Slavin, 1991; Slavin & Rainer, 1990; Windle, 1992) or externalizing symptoms and substance use (Barrera et al., 1993; Chassin et al., 1986; Licitra-Kleckler & Waas, 1993; Wills & Vaughan, 1989; Windle, 1992). Perhaps the most provocative findings came from those studies that showed family and peer support to have *opposite* relations to psychological distress and problem behavior criteria (Barrera & Garrison-Jones, 1992; Chassin et al., 1986; Wills & Vaughan, 1989) or that suggested deleterious effects of peer support (Cauce et al., 1982, 1992).

In our own research, we contrasted parental support with support from same-sex best friends in a cross-sectional study of 296 adolescents, of whom 145 had alcoholic parents and 151 did not (Barrera et al., 1993). Five criteria were examined: adolescents' reports of self-esteem, externalizing symptoms, and substance use, and mother and father reports of externalizing. Support from mothers and fathers was significantly related to adolescents' reports of self-esteem, externalizing, and substance use. In contrast, support from best friends was related only to self-esteem. This pattern of findings follows directly from the theoretical discussion of Youniss and Smollar (1985) on the functions of parents and friends. If friends serve primarily a validation function that is marked by acceptance, their support should be related to self-esteem. If parents serve a validation function but also function as agents who correct, enforce rules, and solve problems from a perspective that is external to the adolescent, then we would expect their support to be related positively to self-esteem and negatively to problem behavior.

A study of 277 adolescents by Windle (1992) addressed two topics considered in this chapter: (1) differential effects of family and peer support and (2) effects of family support on different criteria (depressive symptoms, delinquent activity, alcohol problems, and alcohol consumption). This was a complex study that included two assessment periods, examined interactions between support and stress, and reported the results separately for boys and girls.

For boys, there was very limited evidence of the relation of family social support to depression, delinquency, or alcohol involvement. Of the 16 regression

Table 2. Relation of Family Social Support to Psychological Distress and Problem Behavior: Comparisons to Peer Support[a]

Study	Criteria	Family social support (SS)	Peer social support (SS)
Armsden et al. (1990)	Depression		
	Kiddie-SADS		
	Parent report	Parent attachment: $r = -0.43*$	Peer attachment: $r = -0.04$
	Child report	Parent attachment $r = -0.56*$	Peer attachment: $r = -0.30*$
	CDI	Parent attachment: $r = -0.53*$	Peer attachment: $r = -0.34*$
Barrera et al. (1993)	Self-esteem	Mother SS: %var = 11.8*	Best friend SS %var = 10.4*
		Father SS: %var = 12.6*	
	Externalizing	Mother SS: %var = 6.8*	Best friend SS: %var = 0.4
		Father SS: %var = 6.0*	
Barrera & Garrison-Jones (1992)	Depression	Family Relationship Index (from FES): $r = -0.28*$	Peer Multiplexity (from ASSIS): $r = 0.28*$ (opposite)
Cauce et al. (1982)		Family support:	Informal support (peers and nonfamily adults): F = 5.92* (note: inverse relation)
	GPA	NS	F = 4.14*
	School absences	NS	F = 5.22* (interaction with sex, positive effect for boys)
	Peer self-concept	NS	
	Scholastic self-concept	F = 5.93*	NS
Cauce et al. (1992)		Family support	Peer support
	Anxiety	$r = -0.05$	$r = 0.18*$ (opposite)
	General competence	$r = 0.23*$	$r = -0.08$
	School competence	$r = 0.04$	$r = -0.21*$ (opposite)
	Peer competence	$r = 0.32*$	$r = 0.19*$
	Physical competence	$r = 0.23*$	$r = 0.08$
Chassin et al. (1986)	Change from nonsmoker to smoker	Parental support: $t = -2.89*$	Peer support: $t = 1.54$

Study	Measure	Parental support	Peer support
DuBois et al. (1992)	Change from tried smoking to more frequent smoking	Parental support: $t = -4.56*$	Peer support: $t = 3.04*$ (opposite)
	Psychological distress	PSS-Family	PSS-Friends
	Time 1	$r = -0.42*$	$r = -0.31*$
	Time 2	$r = -0.63*$	$r = -0.34*$
	GPA		
	Time 1	$r = 0.14$	$r = 0.22*$
	Time 2	$r = 0.11$	$r = 0.23*$
Dubow et al. (1991)	Time 2 criteria	Time 1 predictors	Time 1 predictors
	Teacher-rated problems	Parent SS: $r = -0.13$	Peer SS: $r = -0.17*$
	Teacher-rated competence	Parent SS: $r = 0.21*$	Peer SS: $r = 0.18*$
	GPA	Parent SS: $r = 0.16*$	Peer SS: $r = 0.25*$
	Parent-rated problems	Parent SS: $r = 0.18*$	Peer SS: $r = 0.08$
Feldman et al. (1988)	Depression	Family cohesion: $r = -0.64*$; Mother's good communication: $r = -0.46*$; Father's good communication: $r = -0.42*$	Peer support: $r = -0.56*$
	Restraint of aggression	Family cohesion: $r = 0.40*$; Mother's good communication: $r = 0.58*$; Father's good communication: $r = 0.28*$	Peer support: $r = 0.34*$
Greenberg et al. (1983)	Self-esteem	Affect toward parents: $r = 0.38*$	Affect toward peers: $r = 0.22*$
	Life satisfaction	Affect toward parents: $r = 0.29*$	Affect toward peers: $r = 0.21*$
Harter et al. (1992)	Depression	Mother's support: $r = 0.62*$; Father's support: $r = 0.60*$	Classmate's support: $r = 0.62*$; Close friend's support: $r = 0.61*$
Hoffman et al. (1988)	Self-esteem	Mother's support: beta $= 0.39*$; Father's support: beta $= 0.25*$	Peer support: beta $= 0.23*$

(Continued)

Table 2. (*Continued*)

Study	Criteria	Family social support (SS)	Peer social support (SS)
Licitra-Kleckler & Waas (1993)	Delinquency	PSS-Family Beta = -0.28^*	Perceived SS-Friend Beta = 0.06
	School/family offenses	Beta = -0.20^*	Beta = 0.06
	Drugs	Beta = -0.16^*	Beta = 0.05
	Delinquency	Beta = -0.25^*	Beta = -0.04
	Serious crime	Beta = -0.39^*	Beta = -0.32^*
	Depression		
Maton (1990)	Study 1	PSS-Family	Perceived SS-Friend
	Self-esteem	$r = 0.27^*$	$r = 0.32^*$
	Life satisfaction	$r = 0.35^*$	$r = 0.33^*$
	Depression	$r = -0.10$	$r = -0.20^*$
	Study 2		
	Self-esteem	$r = 0.36^*$	$r = 0.21^*$
	Life satisfaction	$r = 0.27^*$	$r = 0.36^*$
	Depression	$r = -0.40^*$	$r = -0.06$
Rowlison & Felner (1988)	Self-concept	PSS-Family $r = 0.44^*$	Perceived SS-Friends $r = 0.32^*$
	Anxiety	$r = -0.38^*$	$r = -0.16^*$
	Depression	$r = -0.45^*$	$r = -0.20^*$
	Somatization	$r = -0.28^*$	$r = -0.10^*$
	GPA	$r = 0.15^*$	$r = 0.26^*$
	School absences	$r = -0.12^*$	$r = -0.05$
	Maladjustment		
	Teacher raters	$r = -0.10^*$	$r = -0.13^*$
	Parent raters	$r = -0.21^*$	$r = -0.08$
Slavin (1991)	Depression	Perceived family support	Perceived friend support
	Time 1	$r = -0.25^*$	$r = -0.03$
	Time 2	$r = -0.33^*$	$r = -0.11^*$
	Prospective (T1–T2)	$r = -0.20^*$	$r = 0.01$

		Perceived family support	Perceived friend support
Slavin & Rainer (1990)	Depression		
	Results for girls (N = 166)		
	Time 1	r = −0.44*	r = −0.20*
	Time 2	r = −0.39*	r = −0.10
	Prospective	r = −0.36*	r = −0.22*
	Results for boys (N = 124)		
	Time 1	r = −0.23	r = −0.14
	Time 2	r = −0.23	r = 0.09
	Prospective	r = −0.14	r = −0.08
Wills & Vaughan (1989)	Smoking	Parental support: beta = −0.15*	Peer support: beta = 0.11* (opposite)
	Alcohol use	Parental support: beta = −0.13*	Peer support: beta = 0.11* (opposite)
Windle (1992)		PSS-Family	Perceived SS-Friends
	Results for girls only		
	Depression		
	Time 1	Beta = −0.38*	NS
	Time 2	Beta = −0.24*	Beta = −0.19*
	Prospective	Beta = −0.17*	NS
	Delinquency		
	Time 1	Beta = −0.17*	NS
	Time 2	Beta = −0.32*	NS
	Prospective	Beta = −0.20*	NS
	Alcohol problems		
	Time 1	Beta = −0.17*	Beta = 0.20*
	Time 2	Beta = −0.27*	NS
	Prospective	Beta = −0.25*	NS
	Alcohol consumption		
	Time 1	Beta = −0.29*	NS
	Time 2	Beta = −0.15*	NS
	Prospective	NS	NS

aMeasures: (ASSIS) Arizona Social Support Interveiw Schedule; (CDI) Children's Depression Inventory; (FES) Family Environmental Scale; (GPA) grade point average; (PSS-Family) Perceived Social Support—Family scale; (SADS) Schedule for Affective Disorders and Schizophrenia.
*Indicates statistically significant effect.

analyses, only the time 1 cross-sectional analysis of delinquency activities showed a main effect for family support. Friendship support showed a somewhat different pattern in that there were relations between it and depressive symptoms at time 1 and time 2, but not in the prospective analyses. The real difference between family and friendship support was found in their interactions with stress. There was some evidence of stress buffering for family support when the criterion was alcohol problems. In contrast, the interactions between stress and friendship support showed paradoxical effects. For boys who experienced many stressful life events, high friendship support was related *positively* to depression and alcohol problems/consumption. This pattern was consistent with the reports of other studies that suggest a detrimental aspect of peer support, perhaps because some peers who provide support are themselves deviant.

The findings for girls reinforced even more clearly the conclusion that family support is more strongly related to psychological distress and problem behavior than is friendship support. Family support was significantly related to all four criteria in each of the two cross-sectional analyses. More important, family support was related to three of the four criteria in the prospective analysis in which time 2 criteria were regressed on time 1 predictors. None of these effects was significant for the prospective analyses of friendship support. Not only were there very few significant effects for friendship support in the cross-sectional analyses, but also there was some indication that friendship support was *positively* related to alcohol problems and delinquent activity. These latter effects are quite similar to those reported by Wills and Vaughan (1989), who discussed how support from adolescents' peers can promote deviance (also see Wills, 1990).

A rather clear conclusion emerges from this research. In many cases in which self-esteem and depression were the criteria, family and peer social support showed comparable relations to mental health outcomes. When differences were found, however, family support showed stronger and more consistent relations to psychological distress and behavior problems than did friendship (peer) support. Friendship support did appear to have a self-esteem-enhancing function, but at times it also showed positive relations to distress and deviant behavior such as substance use.

IMPLICATIONS FOR THEORY AND FUTURE RESEARCH

Some of the most fascinating questions that emerge from this literature concern the contrast between family and peer support. Future research should promote an understanding of peer support and those conditions that are associated with its negative effects. These conditions might include factors that lie outside the family's direct influence, but parents and family are likely to influence how peer support functions in the lives of adolescents (Barrera & Garrison-Jones, 1992; Wills, 1990; Wills & Vaughan, 1989). Rather than considering peer support separate from family support, it would be instructive to conduct research that explores the possible influences between them (Blain, Thompson, & Whiffen,

1993; Cooper & Cooper, 1992). There are two key questions that could be addressed. First, what role does family social support play in determining the structure and function of peer support? For example, does family support deter adolescents from associating with deviant peers? The control aspects of parenting (such as parental monitoring) appear to deter associations with deviant peers (e.g., Chassin, Pillow, Curran, Molina, & Barrera, 1993), but the supportive aspects of parenting and family life have not received comparable attention. A second question concerns ways that family support might moderate peers' influence on problem behavior. The study by Wills and Vaughan (1989) stands out here as an example of this type of research. They found that the relation of peer support to adolescents' smoking was greatest at low levels of support from adults and that the negative effects of peer smoking were moderated by parental support. Few studies have reported these interactions that inform us about the interrelations between peer and parental support.

In general, the research on family support has not been closely tied to theory testing or directed at the question of how family support works to affect psychological distress and problem behavior. As one indicator of this lack, it is revealing that path analyses and structural equation models have not been applied extensively to the study of adolescents' family and parental support. Other than some attempts to place supportive parenting and kinship support within a broader network of variables (Miller, Cowan, Cowan, Hetherington, & Clingempeel, 1993; Roosa et al., 1993; Taylor et al., 1993), researchers have not made extensive use of analytical strategies that could test models of the antecedents and consequences of family support. On the other hand, there have been several excellent longitudinal studies that have advanced the literature beyond the limited sophistication of cross-sectional studies (Chassin et al., 1986; DuBois et al., 1992, 1994; Dubow et al., 1991; Slavin, 1991; Slavin & Rainer, 1990; Stice & Barrera, 1995; Windle, 1992). Some of these studies contain implicit models that include familiar variables such as stress (DuBois et al., 1992; Dubow et al., 1991) and that tested for stress-buffering effects. The application of modeling techniques to longitudinal research would add still greater sophistication to the knowledge base on family support.

There is much more that could be done by way of increasing the role of theory in research on family support. Although it is approaching the mundane because of its long history and its frequency of inclusion in research, stress continues to be a relevant construct for understanding adolescents' psychological distress and problem behavior (Petersen & Hamburg, 1986) as well as the functioning of family support. There are ways to strengthen the connections between stress and theories of adolescent development. Beyond the assessment of stressors that, at times, might focus on uncontrollable occurrences of unrelated events, there are transitions and "developmental tasks" that could form the basis of stress constructs. The theory of optimal matching (Cutrona & Russell, 1990) and the support specificity hypothesis (Cohen & McKay, 1984) both call for detailed explications of an individual's needs and the availability of support that specifically addresses these needs. If these theories were adopted as frameworks for conceptualizing future research on adolescents' family social support, more studies would assess the developmental demands of adolescence and how well family support meets these demands.

Despite the importance of peer involvement during adolescence, support from parents and other family members shows associations with psychological distress and problem behavior outcomes that suggest a role for family support in interventions. Family therapy and parent training interventions routinely include components that are designed to develop appropriate levels of family cohesion and appropriate expressions of parental support. What is not so obvious is that family support shows relations to internalizing disorders as well as to externalizing disorders. Intuitively, the linkages of family support to depression and self-esteem are clearer than its linkages to externalizing disorder and substance use. Pragmatically, parental control techniques have clearer links to the treatment of externalizing disorders and substance use than does parental support. However, research findings indicate the potential value of family support interventions directed at reducing externalizing problems and substance use.

There are important qualifiers to this suggestion. One conclusion from the review by Glynn (1981) on family influences on adolescent substance use was the following (p. 375):

> *The most effective family influences appear to be those which are developed in advance of adolescence* [emphasis added]. Satisfactory family relationships and climate, emotional support, and moderation in the use of alcohol are influences which appear to delay or diminish adolescent initiation into drug use. These influences are developed over a long period of time.

This is a realistic conclusion, but a discouraging one for those who would like to develop interventions for the rapid deployment of family social support during adolescence. A long history of supportive exchanges within a family probably influences mechanisms and leads to consequences that are different from those that result from just a brief and recent history of family support.

A second qualifier follows from the report by Stice and Barrera (1995). Their findings showed prospective effects of parental social support on substance use, but their models suggested that adolescents' externalizing symptoms influenced parental support more than parental support influenced externalizing symptoms. The Glynn (1981) hypothesis might also fit the findings of Stice and Barrera (1995) concerning externalizing problems. It is possible that the prospective influence of parental support on externalizing symptoms primarily comes before adolescence. If this hypothesis received greater substantiation, it would point toward the development of interventions that used parental support as a prevention strategy. Designing preventive interventions that make effective use of social support has been somewhat elusive (Gottlieb, 1988), but the findings reviewed in this chapter suggest that there is merit in continuing efforts to formulate interventions that are based on social support from parents and other family members.

ACKNOWLEDGMENTS

Dr. Barrera's work on this chapter was supported by grant DA05227 from the National Institute on Drug Abuse. Ms. Li was supported by an American Psychological Association Minority Fellowship Award and a predoctoral fellowship from a National Institute of Mental Health Research Training Grant (MH18387).

REFERENCES

Abidin, R. R. (1992). The determinants of parenting behavior. *Journal of Clinical Child Psychology, 21,* 407–412.

Almeida, D. M., & Galambos, N. L. (1991). Examining father involvement and the quality of father–adolescent relations. *Journal of Research on Adolescence, 1,* 155–172.

Armsden, G. C., McCauley, E., Greenberg, M. T., Burke, P. M., & Mitchell, J. R. (1990). Parent and peer attachment in early adolescent depression. *Journal of Abnormal Child Psychology, 18,* 683–697.

Barnett, P. A., & Gotlib, I. H. (1988). Psychosocial functioning and depression: Distinguishing among antecedents, concomitants, and consequences. *Psychological Bulletin, 104,* 97–126.

Baron, P., & MacGillivray, R. G. (1989). Depressive symptoms in adolescents as a function of perceived parental behavior. *Journal of Adolescent Research, 4,* 50–62.

Barrera, M., Jr. (1986). Distinctions between social support concepts, measures, and models. *American Journal of Community Psychology, 14,* 413–445.

Barrera, M., Jr. (1988). Models of social support and life stress: Beyond the buffering hypothesis. In L. H. Cohen (Ed.), *Life events and psychological functioning: Theoretical and methodological issues* (pp. 211–236). Newbury Park, CA: Sage Publications.

Barrera, M., Jr., Chassin, L., & Rogosch, F. (1993). Effects of social support and conflict on adolescent children of alcoholic and nonalcoholic fathers. *Journal of Personality and Social Psychology, 64,* 602–612.

Barrera, M., Jr., & Garrison-Jones, C. (1992). Family and peer social support as specific correlates of adolescent depressive symptoms. *Journal of Abnormal Child Psychology, 20,* 1–16.

Barrera, M., Jr., Li, S. A., & Chassin, L. (1993). Ethnic group differences in vulnerability to parental alcoholism and life stress: A study of Hispanic and non-Hispanic Caucasian adolescents. *American Journal of Community Psychology, 21,* 15–35.

Barry, K. L., & Fleming, M. F. (1990). Family cohesion, expressiveness, and conflict in alcoholic families. *British Journal of Addiction, 85,* 81–87.

Belsky, J. (1984). The determinants of parenting: A process model. *Child Development, 55,* 83–96.

Benson, C. S., & Heller, K. (1987). Factors in the current adjustment of young adult daughters of alcoholic and problem drinking fathers. *Journal of Abnormal Psychology, 96,* 305–312.

Billings, A. G., & Moos, R. H. (1982). Psychosocial theory and research on depression: An integrative framework and review. *Clinical Psychology Review, 2,* 213–237.

Billings, A. G., & Moos, R. H. (1983). Comparisons of children of depressed and nondepressed parents: A social–environment perspective. *Journal of Abnormal Child Psychology, 11,* 463–486.

Blain, M. D., Thompson, J. M., & Whiffen, V. E. (1993). Attachment and perceived social support in late adolescence: The interactions between working models of self and others. *Journal of Adolescent Research, 8,* 226–241.

Bristol, M. M., Gallagher, J. J., & Schopler, E. (1988). Mothers and fathers of young developmentally disabled and nondisabled boys: Adaptation and spousal support. *Developmental Psychology, 24,* 441–451.

Brittain, C. V. (1963). Adolescent choices and parent–peer cross-pressures. *American Sociological Review, 28,* 385–391.

Brook, J. S., Whiteman, M., Gordon, A. S., & Cohen, P. (1986). Some models and mechanisms for explaining the impact of maternal and adolescent characteristics on adolescent stage of drug use. *Developmental Psychology, 22,* 460–467.

Brooks-Gunn, J. (1991). How stressful is the transition to adolescence for girls? In M. E. Colten & S. Gore (Eds.), *Adolescent stress: Causes and consequences* (pp. 131–149). New York: Aldine de Gruyter.

Callan, V. J., & Noller, P. (1986). Perceptions of communicative relationships in families with adolescents. *Journal of Marriage and the Family, 48,* 813–820.

Cauce, A. M., Felner, R. D., Primavera, J., & Ginter, M. A. (1982). Social support in high risk adolescents: Structural components and adaptive impact. *American Journal of Community Psychology, 10,*
417–428.

Cauce, A. M., Hannan, K., & Sargeant, M. (1992). Life stress, social support, and locus of control during early adolescence: Interactive effects. *American Journal of Community Psychology, 20,* 787–798.

Chassin, L., Pillow, D. R., Curran, P. J., Molina, B. S. G., & Barrera, M., Jr. (1993). Relation of parental
alcoholism to early adolescent substance use: A test of three mediating mechanisms. *Journal of
Abnormal Psychology, 102,* 3–19.

Chassin, L., Presson, C., Sherman, S. J., Montello, D., & McGrew, J. (1986). Changes in peer and parent
influence during adolescence: Longitudinal versus cross-sectional perspectives on smoking initiation. *Developmental Psychology, 22,* 327–334.

Chassin, L., Rogosch, F., & Barrera, M., Jr. (1991). Substance use and symptomatology among adolescent children of alcoholics. *Journal of Abnormal Psychology, 100,* 449–463.

Clark-Lempers, D. S., Lempers, J. D., & Ho, C. (1991). Early, middle and late adolescents' perceptions
of their relationships with significant others. *Journal of Adolescent Research, 6,* 296–315.

Cobb, S. (1976). Social support as a moderator of life stress. *Psychosomatic Medicine, 38,* 300–314.

Cohen, S., & McKay, G. (1984). Social support, stress, and the buffering hypothesis: A theoretical
analysis. In A. Baum, S. E. Taylor, & J. E. Singer (Eds.), *Handbook of psychology and health,* Vol. 4
(pp. 253–267). Hillsdale, NJ: Lawrence Erlbaum.

Cohen, S., & Wills, T. A. (1985). Stress, social support, and the buffering hypothesis. *Psychological
Bulletin, 98,* 310–357.

Cooper, C. R., & Cooper, R. G., Jr. (1992). Links between adolescents' relationships with their parents
and peers: Models, evidence, and mechanisms. In R. D. Parke & G. W. Ladd (Eds.), *Family–peer
relationships: Modes of linkage* (pp. 135–158). Hillsdale, NJ: Lawrence Erlbaum.

Cutrona, C. E. (1989). Ratings of social support by adolescents and adult informants: Degree of
correspondence and prediction of depressive symptoms. *Journal of Personality and Social Psychology,
57,* 723–730.

Cutrona, C. E., & Russell, D. W. (1990). Type of social support and specific stress: Toward a theory of
optimal matching. In B. R. Sarason, I. G. Sarason, & G. R. Pierce (Eds.), *Social support: An interactional view* (pp. 319–366). New York: Wiley.

Downey, G., & Coyne, J. C. (1990). Children of depressed parents: An integrative review. *Psychological
Bulletin, 108,* 50–76.

DuBois, D. L., Felner, R. D., Brand, S, Adan, A. M., & Evans, E. G. (1992). A prospective study of life
stress, social support, and adaptation in early adolescence. *Child Development, 63,* 542–547.

DuBois, D. L., Felner, R. D., Meares, H., & Krier, M. (1994). Prospective investigation of the effects of
socioeconomic disadvantage, life stress, and social support on early adolescent adjustment.
Journal of Abnormal Psychology, 103, 511–522.

Dubow, E. F., Tisak, J., Causey, D., Hryshko, A., & Reid, G. (1991). A two-year longitudinal study of
stressful life events, social support, and social problem-solving skills: Contributions to children's
behavioral and academic adjustment. *Child Development, 62,* 583–599.

Fauber, R., Forehand, R., Thomas, A. M., & Wierson, M. (1990). A mediational model of the impact of
marital conflict on adolescent adjustment in intact and divorced families: The role of disrupted
parenting. *Child Development, 61,* 1112–1123.

Feldman, S. S., Rubenstein, J. L., & Rubin, C. (1988). Depressive affect and restraint in early adolescents: Relationships with family structure, family process and friendship support. *Journal of Early
Adolescence, 8,* 279–296.

Fendrich, M., Warner, V., & Weissman, M. M. (1990). Family risk factors, parental depression, and
psychopathology in offspring. *Developmental Psychology, 26,* 40–50.

Filstead, W. J., McElfresh, O., & Anderson, C. (1981). Comparing the family environments of alcoholic
and normal families. *Journal of Alcohol and Drug Education, 26,* 24–31.

Forehand, R., Thomas, A. M., Wierson, M., Brody, G., & Fauber, R. (1990). Role of maternal functioning and parenting skills in adolescent functioning following parental divorce. *Journal of
Abnormal Psychology, 99,* 278–283.

Foxcroft, D. R., & Lowe, G. (1991). Adolescent drinking behaviour and family socialization factors: A meta-analysis. *Journal of Adolescence, 14,* 255–273.

Frith, S., & Narikawa, O. (1972). *Attitudes toward school.* Los Angeles: Instructional Objectives Exchange.

Furman, W., & Buhrmester, D. (1985) Children's perceptions of the personal relationships in their social networks. *Developmental Psychology, 21,* 1014–1024.

Furman, W., & Buhrmester, D. (1992). Age and sex differences in perceptions of networks of personal relationships. *Child Development, 63,* 103–115.

Glynn, T. J. (1981). From family to peer: A review of transitions of influence among drug-using youth. *Journal of Youth and Adolescence, 10,* 363–383.

Goodman, S. H., & Brumley, H. E. (1990). Schizophrenic and depressed mothers: Relational deficits in parenting. *Developmental Psychology, 26,* 31–39.

Gottlieb, B. H. (Ed.) (1988). *Marshaling social support: Formats, processes, and effects,* Newbury Park, CA: Sage Publications.

Greenberg, M. T., Siegel, J. M., & Leitch, C. J. (1983). The nature and importance of attachment relationships to parents and peers during adolescence. *Journal of Youth and Adolescence, 12,* 373–386.

Harter, S. (1982). The Perceived Competence Scale for Children. *Child Development, 53,* 87–97.

Harter, S., Margold, D. B., & Whitesell, N. R. (1992). Model of psychosocial risk factors leading to suicidal ideation in young adolescents. *Development and Psychopathology, 4,* 167–188.

Hoffman, M. A., Ushpiz, V., & Levy-Shiff, R. (1988). Social support and self-esteem in adolescence. *Journal of Youth and Adolescence, 17,* 307–316.

Holden, M. G., Brown, S. A., & Mott, M. A. (1988). Social support network of adolescents: Relation to family alcohol abuse. *American Journal of Drug and Alcohol Abuse, 14,* 487–498.

Kandel, D. B. (1975). Stages in adolescent involvement in drug use. *Science, 190,* 912–914.

Kaslow, N., Warner, V., John, K., & Brown, R. (1992). Intrainformant agreement and family functioning in depressed and nondepressed parents and their children. *American Journal of Family Therapy, 20,* 204–217.

Kobak, R. R., Sudler, N., & Gamble, W. (1991). Attachment and depressive symptoms during adolescence: A developmental pathway analysis. *Development and Psychopathology, 3,* 461–474.

Levitt, M. J., Guacci-Franco, N., & Levitt, J. L. (1993). Convoys of social support in childhood and early adolescence: Structure and function. *Developmental Psychology, 29,* 811–818.

Li, S. A., Barrera, M., Jr., & Chassin, L. (August, 1994). Paternal inconsistent support and adolescent mental health. Poster presented at the American Psychological Association Convention. Los Angeles.

Licitra-Kleckler, D. M., & Waas, G. A. (1993). Perceived social support among high-stress adolescents: The role of peers and family. *Journal of Adolescent Research, 8,* 381–402.

Lytton, H. (1990). Child and parental effects in boys' conduct disorder: A reinterpretation. *Developmental Psychology, 26,* 683–697.

Maton, K. I. (1990). Meaningful involvement in instrumental activity and well-being: Studies of older adolescents and at risk urban teen-agers. *American Journal of Community Psychology, 18,* 297–320.

Miller, N. B., Cowan, P. A., Cowan, C. P., Hetherington, E. M., & Clingempeel, W. G. (1993). Externalizing in preschoolers and early adolescents: A cross-study replication of a family model. *Developmental Psychology, 29,* 3–18.

Moos, R. H., & Billings, A. G. (1982). Children of alcoholics during the recovery process: Alcoholic and matched control families. *Addictive Behaviors, 7,* 155–163.

Moos, R. H., Finney, J. W., & Chan, D. A. (1981). The process of recovery from alcoholism. I. Comparing alcoholic patients and matched community controls. *Journal of Studies on Alcohol, 42,* 383–401.

Moos, R. H., Insel, P. M., & Humphrey, B. (1972). *Family, work, and group environment scales: Combined preliminary manual.* Palo Alto, CA: Consulting Psychologists Press.

Moos, R. H., & Moos, B. S. (1984). The process of recovery from alcoholism. III. Comparing functioning in families of alcoholics and matched control families. *Journal of Studies on Alcohol, 4,* 111–118.

Papini, D. R., Roggman, L. A., & Anderson, J. (1991). Early-adolescent perceptions of attachment to mother and father: A test of the emotional-distancing and buffering hypotheses. *Journal of Early Adolescence, 11,* 258–275.

Petersen, A. C., & Hamburg, B. A. (1986). Adolescence: A developmental approach to problems and psychopathology. *Behavior Therapy, 17,* 480–499.

Pink, J. E. T., & Wampler, K. S. (1985). Problem areas in stepfamilies: Cohesion, adaptability, and the stepfather–adolescent relationship. *Family Relations, 34,* 327–335.

Procidano, M., & Heller, K. (1983). Measures of perceived social support from friends and family: Three validation studies. *American Journal of Community Psychology, 11,* 1–24.

Quittner, A. L., Glueckauf, R. L., & Jackson, D. N. (1990). Chronic parenting stress: Moderating versus mediating effects of social support. *Journal of Personality and Social Psychology, 59,* 1266–1278.

Richardson, R. A., Galambos, N. L., Schulenberg, J. E., & Peterson, A. C. (1984). Young adolescents' perceptions of the family environment. *Journal of Early Adolescence, 4,* 131–153.

Roosa, M. W., Tein, J. Y., Groppenbacher, N., Michaels, M., & Dumka, L. (1993). Mothers' parenting behavior and child mental health in families with a problem drinking parent. *Journal of Marriage and the Family, 55,* 107–118.

Rowlison, R. T., & Felner, R. D. (1988). Major life events, hassles, and adaptation in adolescence: Confounding in the conceptualization and measurement of life stress and adjustment revisited. *Journal of Personality and Social Psychology, 55,* 432–444.

Sandler, I. N., Miller, P., Short, J., & Wolchik, S. A. (1989). Social support as a protective factor for children in stress. In D. Belle (Ed.), *Children's social networks and social supports* (pp. 277–307). New York: Wiley.

Scales, P. (1990). Developing capable young people: An alternative strategy for prevention programs. *Journal of Early Adolescence, 10,* 420–438.

Sebald, H. (1989). Adolescents' peer orientation: Changes in the support system during the past three decades. *Adolescence, 24,* 937–946.

Siegel, K., Raveis, V. H., Bettes, B., Mesagno, F. P., Christ, G., & Weinstein, L. (1990). Perceptions of parental competence while facing the death of a spouse. *American Journal of Orthopsychiatry, 60,* 567–576.

Simons, R. L., Lorenz, F. O., Wu, C. I., & Conger, R. D. (1993). Social network and marital support as mediators and moderators of the impact of stress and depression on parental behavior. *Developmental Psychology, 29,* 368–381.

Slavin, L. A. (1991). Validation studies of the PEPSS, a measure of perceived emotional support for use with adolescents. *Journal of Adolescent Research, 6,* 316–335.

Slavin, L. A., & Rainer, K. L. (1990). Gender differences in emotional support and depressive symptoms among adolescents: A prospective analysis. *American Journal of Community Psychology, 18,* 407–421.

Smith, T. A. (1991). Family cohesion in remarried families. *Journal of Divorce and Remarriage, 17,* 49–66.

Steinberg, L. D. (1981). Transformation in family relations at puberty. *Developmental Psychology, 17,* 833–840.

Stice, E. M., & Barrera, M., Jr. (1995). A longitudinal examination of the reciprocal relations between perceived parenting and adolescents' substance use and externalizing behaviors. *Developmental Psychology, 31,* 322–334.

Stice, E. M., Barrera, M., Jr., & Chassin, L. (1993). Relation of parental support and control to adolescents' externalizing symptomatology and substance use: A longitudinal examination of curvilinear effects. *Journal of Abnormal Child Psychology, 21,* 609–629.

Taylor, R. D., Casten, R., & Flickinger, S. M. (1993). Influence of kinship social support on the parenting experiences and psychosocial adjustment of African-American adolescents. *Developmental Psychology, 29,* 382–388.

Thoits, P. A. (1986). Social support as coping assistance. *Journal of Consulting and Clinical Psychology, 54,* 416–423.

Webster-Stratton, C. (1990). Stress: A potential disrupter of parent perceptions and family interactions. *Journal of Clinical Child Psychology, 19,* 302–312.

Weiss, R. S. (1974). The provisions of social relationships. In Z. Rubin (Ed.), *Doing unto others.* Englewood Cliffs, NJ: Prentice-Hall.

West, S. G., Sandler, I., Pillow, D. R., Baca, L., & Gersten, J. (1991). The use of structural equation modeling in generative research: Toward the design of a preventive intervention for bereaved children. *American Journal of Community Psychology, 19*, 459–480.

White, K. M., Speisman, J. C., & Costos, D. (1983). Young adults and their parents: Individuation to mutuality. In H. D. Grotevant & C. R. Cooper (Eds.), *Adolescent development in the family* (pp. 61–76). San Francisco: Jossey-Bass.

Wills, T. A. (1990). Multiple networks and substance abuse. *Journal of Social and Clinical Psychology, 9*, 78–90.

Wills, T. A., & Vaughan, R. (1989). Social support and substance use in early adolescence. *Journal of Behavioral Medicine, 12*, 321–339.

Windle, M. (1992). A longitudinal study of stress buffering for adolescent problem behaviors. *Developmental Psychology, 28*, 522–530.

Windle, M., Miller-Tutzauer, C., Barnes, G. M., & Welte, J. (1991). Adolescent perceptions of help-seeking resources for substance abuse. *Child Development, 62*, 179–189.

Wyman, P. A., Cowen, E. L., Work, W. C., & Parker, G. R. (1991). Developmental and family milieu correlates of resilience in urban children who have experienced major life stress. *American Journal of Community Psychology, 19*, 405–425.

Youniss, J., & Smollar, J. (1985). *Adolescent relations with mothers, fathers, and friends.* Chicago: University of Chicago Press.

Zahn-Waxler, C., Denham, S., Iannotti, R. J., & Cummings, E. M. (1992). Peer relations in children with a depressed caregiver. In R. D. Parke & G. W. Ladd (Eds.), *Family and peer relationships: Modes of linkage* (pp. 317–344). Hillsdale, NJ: Lawrence Erlbaum.

15

Social Support in Postdivorce Families

An Attachment Perspective

INGE BRETHERTON, REGHAN WALSH, and MOLLY LEPENDORF

Raising children in a postdivorce family can be an especially demanding and complex task (Emery, 1988). Even though many of the most severe stresses associated with the divorce process are substantially attenuated within 2 years (Hetherington, 1989), parents and children in postdivorce families continue to face challenges related to coparental negotiations and conflict about child-rearing and child support, as well as financial stresses, task overload, and relationship adjustment (Wallerstein & Blakeslee, 1989). How family members, especially divorced parents, cope with these challenges is likely to be affected by a number of risk and protective factors. One potential protective factor is social support, but there have been remarkably few studies of how and to what extent close family members, friends, and professionals facilitate or perhaps even hinder parents' postdivorce adjustment.

Since epidemiological studies first revealed relationships between individuals' physical and mental health and their embeddedness in a social network (e.g., Cobb, 1976), the definition and study of social support has undergone many changes. Initially, a number of researchers treated social support as a unitary construct, evaluating aspects that were easily assessed and quantified such as the size of an individual's social network, frequency of contact with, and interconnection among network members (for a review, see Sarason, Sarason, & Pierce, 1990). Better predictors of mental health than network size and frequency of contact,

INGE BRETHERTON, REGHAN WALSH, and MOLLY LEPENDORF • Department of Child and Family Studies, University of Wisconsin–Madison, Madison, Wisconsin 53706.

Handbook of Social Support and the Family, edited by Gregory R. Pierce, Barbara R. Sarason, and Irwin G. Sarason. Plenum Press, New York, 1996.

however, turned out to be individuals' *perception* of and *satisfaction* with their social network (e.g., Henderson, 1981; Sarason, Pierce, Bannerman, & Sarason, 1993). It is not so much the number of people available and how often they provide help that appears to matter as it is how potential and actual sources of help are perceived by the recipient.

A further refinement was the examination of the *different forms* of support that network members provide. Since Weiss (1974) articulated the distinct provisions of social relationships, four categories of social support have been repeatedly identified by researchers: emotional support, companionship, instrumental or tangible support, and informational support or advice (e.g., Cohen & Willis, 1985; Cutrona & Russell, 1990; Kahn & Antonucci, 1980). In addition, there has been growing evidence that specific forms of support may be perceived as differentially helpful depending on an individual's expertise or personal relationship with the support provider (Sarason et al., 1993). As the latter researchers claim about one of their own studies (p. 1082):

> The results ... reinforce the view that it is not just the receipt of supportive behavior alone, but the supporter's positive view of the individual as expressed in the positive qualities of the relationship, that may be important in establishing, not only global perceptions of support, but support's beneficial effects.... In such situations, the characteristics of the relationship are important both in the support provided ... and in the way the support is interpreted by the recipient.

This statement links research on social support with the literature on attachment, as highlighted in the following statement by John Bowlby (1978):

> Evidence is accumulating that human beings of all ages are happiest and able to deploy their talents to best advantage when they are confident that, standing behind them, there are one or more trusted persons who will come to their aid should difficulties arise. The person so trusted, also known as an attachment figure (Bowlby, 1969), can be considered as providing his (or her) companion with a secure base from which to operate.... Looked at in this light healthy personality functioning at every age reflects, first, an individual's ability to recognize suitable figures willing and able to provide him with a secure base, and, second, his ability to collaborate with such figures in mutually rewarding relationships. (pp. 101, 104)

According to attachment theory, the perceived availability of trustworthy attachment figures enables individuals to better explore solutions for stressful situations or to avert such situations before they arise (see also Cobb, 1976). That is, perceived available support (Sarason, Sarason, & Pierce, 1990) may lower the need for actual support because it potentiates an individual's coping ability. Moreover, when circumstances require actual support, secure attachment relationships are the context in which such support is most likely to be perceived as welcome and helpful. In the absence of a trusting relationship, some forms of support may have self-esteem lowering rather than enhancing effects (Sarason, Pierce, & Sarason, 1990).

It is unclear, however, to what extent attachment theory is applicable to support from individuals such as friends, neighbors, coworkers, and professionals who do not strictly fit the definition of attachment figure. According to Weiss

(1974), interaction with close friends cannot substitute for a marital partner (attachment figure) because friends do not have the same loneliness-allaying capacity that a committed partner supplies. On the other hand, Weiss also found that friends provide a sense of social (community) integration that cannot be supplied by a marital partner. Nevertheless, qualities inherent in secure attachment relationships such as trustworthiness, reliability, and empathy are also likely to be an important factor in how support is negotiated between receiver and provider in relationships that do not qualify as attachments, and hence how effective received help is in enhancing the receiver's and perhaps even the giver's well-being in such relationships.

In our study of social support as experienced by mothers in postdivorce families we combined ideas from the literatures on attachment and social support. Much has been written about how emotionally open or defensive communication patterns in attachment situations affect an individual's representation or working model of self (Bretherton, 1990). However, the particular ways in which adults in attachment and attachment-like relationships actually negotiate help-seeking and support-giving have been mapped out in much more detail by researchers in the stress/coping and social support tradition. These researchers have studied the various forms of support offered and sought, the support-related stresses engendered, and most importantly, the effects of stressful life events on the transactions of careseekers and careproviders (see Coyne, Ellard, & Smith, 1990).

Although spousal support is one of the most important sources of help in married families (Wan, Jaccard, & Ramey, in press), we expected that, in postdivorce families, the mother's parents, other relatives, and close friends would play a more prominent support role. However, because social ties may have costs as well as benefits, we wanted to examine both positive and stressful aspects of the mother's relationships with specific network members, including the child's father. Finally, we speculated that a mother's belief in a benign, controllable world would enable her to better mobilize her social network when needed. For this reason we also collected data on the mother's locus of control beliefs and planfulness. Mental health (depression) and reported stressful life events served as outcome variables.

METHOD

Participating Families

This chapter is based on findings from 50 divorced mothers with preschool children. Forty-two families were identified through public court records; the other 8 were recruited through local preschools. Mothers who were employed outside the home or pursuing a degree (or both), had been legally separated or divorced for at least 2 years and had at least one child aged 4.5 to 5 years of age were eligible for the study. Overall, 44% of the mothers recruited through courts and who fulfilled study criteria volunteered to participate. Note that some of the mothers whom we could not contact by telephone and who did not respond to our letter of invitation may have been ineligible rather than reluctant to participate. Thus the actual number of eligible but nonparticipating mothers may have been lower than 56%.

The mothers' age ranged from 23 to 41 years, with a mean of 32 years. All had graduated from high school, 34% had also attended college, and 34% had obtained bachelor or higher degrees. Mothers' average income (including child support) was at the $23–24,000 level (range $6,000–80,000). The few mothers with incomes below the poverty level received various forms of assistance from parents and others (most of them were students working part-time). All but two of the fathers were employed. Fifteen mothers had one child, 26 had two children, and 9 had more than two children. Mothers had primary physical custody in 45 cases, and shared physical custody with the fathers in 5 cases. Mothers had sole legal custody in 15 cases; for the other 35 cases, legal custody was joint.

The fathers' education level was very similar to the mothers' ($r(49) = .53, p < .0001$). Mothers' and father's occupation level (categorized according to Hollingshead, 1978) were also significantly correlated, $r(49) = .30, p < .05$). The fathers of all but 5 children lived within easy reach (less than 10 miles away). Seventy-five percent of the children in the study saw their fathers at least every 2 weeks (usually over the weekend). Children with out-of-state fathers visited with him only a few times per year. Two fathers with drug/alcohol problems were restricted to supervised visits, though altogether 11 fathers were reported to have serious drinking or drug problems. Some of these fathers did not have regular contact with their children. One child had not seen his father since the age of 6 months although there was telephone contact between the parents.

Assessments

A questionnaire and a structured social network interview were used to assess social support. Both instruments were based on the notions that social support is not a unitary construct (i.e., that advice or informational support, emotional support, companionship, and tangible help should be treated as separate support categories), and that contributions by different network members or member categories should be assessed separately. In order to evaluate the mothers' relationship to the child's father at the time of divorce, the mothers filled out the Marital Autonomy and Relatedness Inventory. A personality inventory (including scales for locus of control, planfulness, and impulsivity) was also administered to assess the mothers' belief system and stress-related personality characteristics. The Beck Depression Inventory and the Family Inventory of Life Events and Changes served as outcome variables.

Sources of Help Questionnaire (SOHQ).   The SOHQ was developed by Wan et al. (in press). Mothers used a 5-point scale to rate the helpfulness of their parents (the child's maternal grandparents), relatives, close friends, coworkers, church or temple, doctors, counselors/therapists, and books from 1 (not at all helpful) to 5 (extremely helpful). Separate ratings were made for the provision of (1) informational support (specifically, parenting advice), (2) emotional support, (3) tangible help, and (4) companionship. Also rated was the frequency of contact in relation to parenting advice and rearing children from 1 (not at all) to 5 (once a week or more). Overall satisfaction with help from each source was evaluated via a 10-point scale (ranging from −5 to +5). Mothers were asked only to rate network members who were available (e.g., if their parents had died, or they were not in contact with relatives, they were to indicate this circumstance rather than give a low rating).

The introduction to the questionnaire read as follows:

> When parents have problems or need perspectives on raising their children or managing their family, they frequently turn to other people for advice help and support. We would like to find out whom you contact for help and advice related to your family, how often you contact them and how satisfied you are with the help that they provide. We will ask you to do separate ratings for each of four types of help.

For the purposes of this questionnaire, informational support was defined as advice on parenting; emotional support as listening, reassuring, and showing care; tangible help as running errands, babysitting, financial assistance, or other forms of physical or material help; and companionship as sharing time in leisure and recreational activities, offering a sense of friendship, and participating in shared activities.

On the basis of a factor analysis of data from their initial validation study for the SOHQ, Wan et al. (in press) had concluded that separate assessments of the four different forms of help were useful. Although ratings for different forms of help tend to be significantly correlated, in their study, some social network members specialized in particular types of help.

Social Network Interview (SNI). This second assessment of social support was adapted from Cochran, Larner, Riley, Gunnarsson, and Henderson (1990). The structured SNI provides detailed quantitative and qualitative information about many aspects of the mother's and the child's social network.

Initially, the mother was asked to name all the people (relatives, neighbors, friends, coworkers, organizational contacts, professionals) who were important to her. Systematic information about types of help, proximity, and frequency of contacting was obtained for each of the persons named, but is not reported in this chapter. The next step was to identify the most important members of the overall network (the primary network members), and then to specify why they were most important. Mothers were also requested to list network members who caused stress but were nevertheless important to them, and to provide reasons why they perceived the particular network member as stress-provoking. Finally the mothers were asked to list and discuss members of the child's social network and to report how the child responded to parental dating or parental involvement with a new partner.

On the basis of verbatim transcriptions of the audiorecorded SNI, we categorized the reasons a mother supplied for placing the child's father and her partners, parents, other relatives, and friends in her primary network and/or for naming them as sources of stress. For ex-husbands and partners, we included in our analysis any additional comments made while the mother talked about the child's social network and described the child's reactions to parental dating.

Mother's comments were first sorted into positive and negative statements. Because mothers did not use identical descriptive categories across all their network members, a variety of positive (support) and negative (stress) categories were then developed separately for the different types of network members. This task was undertaken by a coder who had no knowledge of other data from the study whose coding was verified by two additional researchers. Disagreements were resolved by discussion.

These categorized statements from the SNI were used in two ways: descriptively, to present a more vivid picture of how postdivorce mothers experience their social network, and quantitatively, to compare the SNI data with other measures. Quantitative SNI measures of support and stress were computed by summing across the number of different positive and negative categories that had been generated from the mother's comments about the child's father, the mother's parents, her other relatives, close friends, and new partners (boyfriends and fiancés).

Marital Autonomy and Relatedness Inventory (MARI).   The MARI (Schaefer & Edgerton, 1979) has scales for love, rejection, autonomy, and controllingness, as well as for agreement/disagreement about child rearing. Respondents rate their partners. Hence, in this study, the love and rejection scales pertain to the mothers' ratings of the fathers' considerate and rejecting behavior toward them. Mothers were asked to fill out the MARI in terms of how they perceived spousal behavior around the time of permanent separation (e.g., the rejection scale assessed how rejected the mother felt by the child's father at that time).

The Beck Depression Inventory (BDI).   The BDI is a 21-item, self-administered measure with well-established reliability (Beck, Ward, Mendelson, Mock, & Erbaugh, 1961; Beck & Beamesderfer, 1974). The inventory was designed to assess both symptoms and severity of depression.

Mothers' Personality Inventory: Locus of Control, Planfulness, and Impulsiveness. This 200-item composite questionnaire includes 5-point rating scales for internal and external locus of control (from Levenson, 1974), with external locus of control divided in to belief in powerful others and belief in luck. The questionnaire also contains scales for planfulness (Eysenck & Eysenck, 1977; Jackson, 1977), impulsiveness and risk-taking (Eysenck & Eysenck, 1977), and social desirability (Crowne & Marlowe, 1980). We considered planfulness an important variable because of findings by Rutter (1987) that this personality characteristic is stress-buffering.

Family Inventory of Life Events and Changes (FILE).   The FILE (McCubbin & Patterson, 1991) is a 71-item yes/no inventory of stressful, family-related events/ changes in the prior 12 months, including intrafamily, marital, family-care, and finance and business strains, as well as work–family transitions, illness and losses through death, transitions in and out of the family, and family legal violations. The questionnaire is scored in terms of the number of events checked "yes" by the respondent.

Procedure

This study of social support was part of a larger investigation of attachment in postdivorce families that included laboratory and home observations in addition to the instruments described above. The SNI was administered to the mothers at a place of her choice (work, home, university). This interview took about 2 hours and was audiotaped. After the interview, the mother was given a packet of questionnaires that included a detailed demographic inventory and the SOHQ for completion at home. She returned these materials at the beginning of a subsequent session at the university. On this occasion, the mother was given a second packet of questionnaires which included the MARI, the BDI, and the FILE. This packet was returned during a home observation after which the mother received the third packet of questionnaires, including the Personality Inventory (Locus of Control, Planfulness, and Impulsiveness). The mother returned this third set of questionnaires during a final wrap-up session.

RESULTS AND DISCUSSION

Mothers' mean SOHQ ratings of their personal and formal/professional sources of support are reported first, followed by correlations of these ratings with demographic variables and the intercorrelations among the support ratings, controlling for maternal age and education. Descriptive findings obtained from the SNI are presented next, followed by correlations of the SOHQ and quantified SNI ratings. Finally we report correlations of the social support variables with the MARI, the BDI, and the FILE.

Ratings from the Sources of Help Questionnaire

Mothers' SOHQ ratings (means and standard deviations) of supporters' perceived helpfulness are presented in Table 1. Because mothers were asked not to rate unavailable sources, the number of mothers who provided ratings for a particular source of help varied. The number of mothers who rated each source of support appears in parentheses after each source of help listed in Table 1. Significant differences among the four types of support, based on Tukey's HSD test, are indicated for each source.

Most strikingly, mothers rated the fathers' helpfulness as substantially lower than that of all other network members. Aggregated over the different types of helpfulness, the father's mean helpfulness rating was 1.7. The lowest ratings were, not surprisingly, for companionship and emotional support whereas mothers

Table 1. Means and Standard Deviations of Perceived Helpfulness Ratings by Source, Type of Support, Frequency of Contact with the Source, and Overall Satisfaction with Support: Data from the Sources of Help Questionnaire

Sources of help	Parenting advice	Types of support		Frequency of contact	Overall satisfaction (-5 to $+5$)
		Emotional support	Tangible help	Companionship	
Child's father (48)	1.9[a] (1.1)	1.6[b] (1.0)	1.9[a] (1.1)	1.4[b] (1.0)	3.3 (1.5)	-2.0 (3.2)
Mother's parents (48)	3.6[b] (1.2)	3.6[b] (1.3)	3.7[b] (1.5)	4.0[a] (1.3)	3.6 (1.6)	2.7 (2.8)
Relatives (48)	3.1[b] (1.2)	3.4 (1.2)	3.0[b] (1.4)	3.5[a] (1.4)	3.1 (2.4)	2.2 (2.4)
Close friends (50)	3.6[b] (1.0)	4.2[a] (1.0)	3.3[c] (1.3)	3.9[b] (3.9)	4.0 (1.1)	2.9 (2.0)
Coworkers/students (48)	2.6[b] (1.1)	3.1[a] (1.0)	2.0[c] (1.0)	2.7[b] (1.1)	3.1 (1.4)	1.9 (2.0)
Church (37)	2.2[a] (1.3)	2.2[a] (1.3)	1.4[b] (1.0)	1.9[a] (1.1)	1.8 (1.2)	.53 (2.7)
Child's teacher (44)	3.0[a] (1.0)	2.3[b] (1.1)	1.1[c] (1.2)	1.3[c] (1.0)	2.7 (3.6)	1.9 (2.1)
Doctor (48)	2.9[a] (1.1)	2.4[b] (1.2)	1.1[c] (.03)	1.3[c] (1.0)	1.9 (1.0)	1.4 (2.5)
Counselor (40)	3.4[a] (1.4)	3.5[a] (1.4)	1.2[b] (1.0)	1.6[b] (1.2)	2.6 (1.5)	2.4 (2.5)
Books (45)	3.2[a] (1.1)	2.7[b] (1.0)	1.0[c] (.02)	1.3[c] (1.3)	2.4 (1.1)	1.4 (1.9)

Note. Numbers in parentheses after each source of help refer to the number of mothers who provided ratings for the particular source. Within sources of help, means with superscript $a > b > c$ ($p < .05$, significance tested with Tukey's HSD post hoc test).

found the father's parenting advice and tangible support significantly more helpful, though the means were still very low. In addition the mean overall *satisfaction* rating (on a scale from −5 to +5) for support received from the child's father was the only negative mean among all ratings.

For the mothers' parents, on the other hand, the mean helpfulness ratings were all above 3, with the mean rating for companionship significantly greater than the ratings for parenting advice, emotional support, and tangible help. The mean overall satisfaction rating was well in the positive range. For relatives, means for both companionship and emotional support were significantly higher than those for parenting advice and tangible help. The results for close friends were similar, except that tangible help was rated lower than parenting advice. With respect to coworkers, parenting advice and emotional support were rated as significantly more helpful than tangible help and companionship.

Within-subjects ANOVAs for the overall satisfaction ratings of fathers, maternal grandparents, relatives, friends, and coworkers were highly significant (F 4,40 = 34.4, $p < .0001$). Tukey's HSD post-hoc tests for support satisfaction showed that mean ratings for the child's father were significantly lower than those for all the other sources included in this analysis.

The contrast between the very low ratings for father helpfulness (with respect to the four separate categories of help and the overall satisfaction rating) and the much higher ratings for the mothers' parents, relatives, close friends, and coworkers was especially intriguing when compared with corresponding analyses of the frequency with which mothers contacted a source for help in child-related matters. Although the within-subjects ANOVA for frequency of contacting a source was highly significant (F 4,40 = 3.8, $p < .005$), Tukey's HSD post hoc tests showed that the father contact ratings did not differ from contact ratings for other support sources. However, friends were contacted significantly more often than relatives and coworkers.

The findings regarding the child's father are especially striking when contrasted with findings from the Wan et al. (in press) standardization sample based on married families. In these families, spouses received the highest helpfulness ratings (with means in the range of 4.5 for the different types of helpfulness). Because we had failed to anticipate the high proportion of mothers (64%) who had boyfriends and fiances who were involved in the children's lives, we had not requested mothers to rate new partners as a separate category. However, for those six mothers who entered ratings for their boyfriends or fiancés under the category "other," helpfulness was rated very highly (M = 4.6 for the overall satisfaction ratings). Of these rated partners, 3 lived with the mother. Overall, 22% of the 32 partners lived with the mother.

Regarding the perceived helpfulness of the mothers' formal network, that is, of professionals and organizations, church support (rated by 74% of the mothers) received the lowest ratings in all categories, and especially for overall support satisfaction. Some mothers in the study commented that they felt judged by ministers or members of the congregation. By contrast, mothers appeared quite satisfied with the parenting advice and emotional support of mental health professionals (these sources would not be expected to provide tangible help and companionship). The child's teachers (rated by 88% of the mothers) and books (rated by 90%) were evaluated as very helpful in terms of parenting advice. Within types of support, the pattern of findings for teachers and mental health professionals resembled that for coworkers, that is, parenting advice and emotional support were rated significantly more highly than tangible help and companionship.

Some researchers question the usefulness of ratings by support type. In this study, the variability of ratings is much greater for the formal/professional sources of support than for the personal sources, suggesting that separate ratings are especially informative with respect to the formal network. However, despite the fact that the mean differences among types of support were smaller for the informal than the formal network, many were statistically significant. At the same time, the intercorrelations among types of support within each informal support source were very high. For the six correlations among types of help, the mean correlation coefficients (all significant at $p < .001$) were $r(47) = .72$ for fathers, $r(47) = .75$ for the mothers' parents, $r(49) = .73$ for relatives, $r(49) = .56$ for close friends, and $r(47) = .53$ for coworkers. The corresponding mean intercorrelations for the formal network were high only for church ($r(36) = .68$, lowest $p < .002$). For the child's teacher, doctors, counselors/therapists, and books, only two to three of the six coefficients were significant (mean coefficients = .42, .36, .38, and .18, respectively).

Correlations of the Sources of Help Questionnaire with Demographic Variables

Parental socioeconomic status and maternal age were significantly correlated with a number of the social support ratings. More educated mothers rated themselves as more satisfied with overall support from the child's father ($r(47) = .30$, $p < .02$), but none of the correlations of maternal education with the four types of father helpfulness were significant.

The four types of support (parenting advice, emotional support, tangible help, and companionship) as well as frequency of contact for the mother's parents were negatively correlated with mother's age, father education, and father occupation. Correlation coefficients ranged from $r(47) = -.27$, $p < .05$, to $-.45$, $p < .001$, excepting one nonsignificant correlation between father education and grandparental emotional support. In other words, mothers who were younger and had less educated ex-spouses in lower status jobs rated their own parents as more helpful for each of the four types of support (parenting advice, emotional support, tangible help, and companionship), though the correlations with the overall satisfaction ratings only reached conventional levels of significance with father occupation ($r(47) = -.34$, $p < .01$). Similarly, emotional support, companionship and frequency of help from relatives were negatively correlated with maternal education ($r(49) = -.26$, $-.23$, and $-.35$, respectively; $p < .05$). That is, less educated mothers rated their relatives as more helpful in several respects, but the overall satisfaction rating for relatives was not correlated with demographic variables. Ratings of supportiveness by close friends were not correlated with any of the demographic variables, except for emotional support, which was negatively correlated with maternal income (mothers who were less well off received more emotional support from friends).

Helpfulness by coworkers (including costudents) was not related to demographic variables except for parenting advice which was positively related to maternal income and occupation. Overall satisfaction with counselor helpfulness was related to father education ($r(39) = .32$, $p < .05$). Finally, and not surprisingly, overall satisfaction ratings with books were related to mother education, and to father education and occupation ($r(43) = .32$, .31, and .29, respectively; p for all r's $< .05$). Overall, it was striking that maternal income was correlated with few of the social support variables.

With the exception of maternal occupation and age, all demographic variables were significantly intercorrelated, with $r(49)$ ranging from .31, $p < .01$, to .59, $p < .0001$). Given these intercorrelations and the relatively small sample size, we controlled only for maternal age and education in all subsequent computations.

Intercorrelations among Sources of Help

Table 2 presents the correlations among overall support satisfaction scores for the child's father, maternal grandparents, other relatives, close friends, and member of the formal/professional network as well as books. The number of mothers on which the correlation coefficients are based varies as a function of the number of mothers who provided a response for the particular source of help. This number appears in parentheses following each source.

Interestingly, there were no significant correlations between mothers' ratings of satisfaction with support from the child's father and support from her parents, relatives, friends, or coworkers. On the other hand, ratings of the father were negatively correlated with ratings of the formal/professional sources of support (teachers, counselors, doctors, and books) suggesting that mothers who were least satisfied with help from the child's father tended to gain a sense of support from formal sources.

Support satisfaction ratings for sources other than the father (both personal and formal/professional were significantly intercorrelated. Correlations were consistently higher within than between the personal and formal/professional sources of help, and although the correlations between ratings of the personal and formal sources were somewhat lower, they were still statistically significant. These findings make the divergence between mothers' ratings of the child's father and the rest of the network even more striking. On the one hand, there is an underlying consistency in mothers' satisfaction with perceived help from all sources other than the child's father which argues in favor of Barbara Sarason's view of social support as a personality characteristic. On the other hand, the findings regarding the child's father suggest that support satisfaction can be very relationship-specific.

Table 2. Partial Correlations among Ratings of Satisfaction with Various Sources of Support (Controlling for Mother's Age and Education)

Source of help	1	2	3	4	5	6	7	8	9
1. Child's father (48)									
2. Mother's parents (48)	-.14								
3. Relatives (48)	.12	.51***							
4. Friends (50)	-.00	.28*	.55***						
5. Workmates (48)	-.19	.33*	.52***	.67***					
6. Church (37)	-.43**	.43**	.51***	.33*	.48**				
7. Child's teacher (45)	-.29*	.21+	.28*	.49***	.51***	.29*			
8. Counselor/therapist (40)	-.47**	.22+	.31*	.12	.33*	.62***	.38*		
9. Doctor (48)	-.31*	.29*	.52***	.37**	.59***	.59***	.61***	.61***	
10. Books (42)	-.37**	.31*	.26+	.21	.47***	.61***	.20	.71***	.54***

Note. Numbers in parentheses after each source of help refer to the number of mothers providing ratings, hence not all coefficients have the same df.

$+p < .10$, $*p < .05$, $**p < .01$, $***p < .001$.

Social Network Interview

Network Members.   The great majority of mothers (84%) listed the child's father as a member of their extended social network (in many cases exclusively as a source of stress). However, 24% also placed him in their primary network.

Overall, 92% percent of the mothers nominated one or both of their own parents as members of their overall network and 82% included one or both parents in their primary network (14% of the mothers had divorced parents). In addition, 70% of the mothers named relatives other than parents as members of their primary network. The vast majority of these relatives were siblings. Mothers identified 40 sisters and 18 brothers as primary network members, but nominated only 3 of their grandmothers, 2 aunts, 2 uncles, and 1 sister-in-law in this category.

Further, 94% of the mothers named friends (including neighbors and coworkers who had become friends) as members of their primary networks. As previously noted, 64% of the mothers included a partner (termed "boyfriends" or "fiancés") as a network member. In 8 cases, these men were nominated as members of the mothers' primary network.

The Child's Father.   In line with the low ratings of paternal support on the SOHQ, most mothers mentioned considerably more reasons why they considered the child's father stressful than why they considered him supportive ($M = 3.2$ vs. $M = .9$, respectively, $t(49) = 5.07$, $p < .0001$). The most common source of stress (36%) was the father's perceived lack of interest in the children even during visitation, such as:

> "His dad doesn't do much with him."

> "He just plops them down in front of the TV."

Along the same lines, 15 mothers thought that the father did not spend enough time with the children in order to develop a close relationship:

> "I wish that he would see her more often. He only takes her when he's supposed to—he never plans for anything more, like on a vacation or going camping."

> "His dad really hangs out with the adults. If he has something planned, it doesn't matter if the kids are there or not."

Thirty percent of the mothers were upset about problems related to the payment of child support:

> "When I took him back to family court and I told him I wanted his support reviewed, he immediately quit his two part-time jobs."

In addition, mothers reported difficulties with the transition between maternal and paternal residences, fathers' negative comments about the mother to the children or directly to the mother herself:

> "At the beginning of the divorce he was calling me 'Mommy Dearest,' telling the children I'm Mommy Dearest and a bad person."

Inability to trust the father and fathers' lack of respect for the mother were additional stresses.

As far as supportive behaviors by the father were concerned, 28% of the mothers mentioned that both parents were working on improving communication in order to provide the best for their children:

> "We're both committed to working to provide the best thing for the children."

Sixteen percent of the mothers emphasized that they tried to be polite or get along with the child's father:

> "We don't expect it to be perfect, so we get along,"

and 12% mentioned that they could ask the child's father for both tangible help and/or emotional support:

> "I wouldn't hesitate if I was broken down somewhere to call and ask him to pick me up."

> "... when I can't handle it anymore and (I) vent all the frustrations on him and he listens."

The Mothers' Parents.   Mothers generated far more positive than negative statements about their parents ($M = 3.5$ vs. $M = 1.6$, $t(47) = 4.27$, $p < .0001$). Some of the most common reasons why the mothers' parents were considered important were the provision of child care (52%) and emotional support (46%). In addition, 32% of the mothers made strong statements about the degree to which they could rely on their parents, such as:

> "She would do anything for me."

> "He is always there for me."

> "My mom would bend over backwards for me."

> "I can always count on my mom."

> "Whatever I need, they're there."

Other reasons for placing maternal parents in the primary network was the existence of a special bond or close relationship (36%), feeling comfortable with calling on parents when needed (32%), parents helping out financially (28%), providing other instrumental help (22%), parents being fond of the children (16%), their supportiveness regarding the divorce (16%), being good role models for the children or the mother (14%), and mothers providing support to their parents (6%).

The most common source of stress was parents being judgmental about the divorce (24%):

> "You made your bed, now lie in it."

> "My mother would say things like: 'It's not like he ever hit you.'"

> "This is totally against anything that they believe in.... People don't get divorced."

About a quarter of the mothers (24%) also felt stressed by their parents' irritating behavior toward themselves or their children:

"Just sometimes somebody gets in your personal space and usually it's my mom."

"They are stressful because they say hurtful things to (child) ... hurtful things."

Parental put-downs of the mother were another not uncommon problem (16%):

"I'm not what my mother wanted."

"He will not approve of my discipline."

"If I did lose my job my mother would probably curl up and die."

Other mothers mentioned past problems that still cause conflict in the relationship (16%):

"alcoholic ... so I never really forgave her."

"old history."

Several mothers commented that accepting help carried obligations or was conditional (12%):

"... they would expect things in return ... they would expect to be able to give advice."

"The obligation stress."

"She makes me feel like I can't say or be critical at all."

A few mothers mentioned that the parent was too controlling (12%):

"You kind of feel like you reverted back in a way to having to listen to what mom and dad say all of a sudden."

Others noted that their parents provided less help or emotional support than they had hoped (12%) or that they felt stressed by problems in their parents' lives (12%). Very few mothers (4%) complained that they received no help with childcare or finances. Only two mothers discussed problems in making contact with their parents, and one mother felt that her efforts to seek help were rejected outright.

Other Relatives. As noted above, the great majority of relatives identified as primary network members were the mothers' sisters and brothers. About a quarter of the mothers (24%) initially explained that the sibling was an important network member simply because she or he was "family" or "my sister," though most subsequently provided more detailed justifications. The most common of these was that the relationship was a close one (34%):

"Very special to me."

"We would be best friends if we weren't sisters."

and/or that the sibling was "always there" when needed (32%):

"Always willing to help when needed."

"She stuck it out with me."

Additionally, 24% of the mothers mentioned good communication and sharing of confidences:

"... from 'How are you?' to deep problems."

"I can feel free to talk with them about anything."

"There are times when I go to her before (fiancé) even."

" 'Cause I never told my parents all the problems I was having, I used to confide in my sister."

While 8 mothers said that the sibling was emotionally supportive:

"Someone to tell you you are doing a pretty good job."

Other mothers commented that they and the sibling were in a similar situation (N = 8) and that the sibling helped with childcare (16%). The remainder in descending order of frequency were that the sibling or other relative cared about the children, had an attractive personality, had a personality similar to the mother's, had a good relationship with the mother in childhood ("we stood up for each other as children"), provided financial help, provided material help, was nonjudgmental, gave good advice, had children the same age, provided companionship, had similar interests or values, needed support from the mother, made frequent contact, and kept the family together. Only one mother mentioned proximity as an important reason for including a relative in her primary network.

Siblings and other relatives were infrequently listed as stressful members of the network. Each of the following issues were mentioned by only 1 of the mothers: that she and her sister did not share interests, that the sister was hard on her in childhood, that the sister mothered her too much, that she could not trust her sister to keep information in confidence, and that she was bothered by the sibling's personality.

Friends.   As regards friends, 44% of the mothers mentioned the length of relationship (often since high school):

"... very good friend for more than 10 years."

"... friends for 15 years."

"... really good friends since grade school."

Twenty-one mothers pointed to the friend's emotional support:

"She just understood and was a shoulder at that time, still is."

whereas 34% mothers commented on shared circumstances:

"She's gone through all the things I've gone through."

"We are in much similar circumstances."

"She's been through a lot of grief, like me."

Many mothers mentioned good and open communication (32%):

"We just know how each other feels."

"We can talk about anything."

"Deals more with my personal life ... she knows pretty much everything that's going on that way."

Fourteen mothers mentioned the friend's attractive personality:

"Fun, caring."

"Easygoing, down-to-earth."

"Concerned, caring."

"Extremely generous."

and just over a quarter (26%) reported that the friend had a good relationship with her children, that the mothers had a close relationship or special bond with the friend (24%), that they had similar personalities, values, or goals (22%), appreciated the friend's advice (20%), companionship (18%), and proximity (18%), that distance did not interfere with the relationship (16%), that the friend had always been there for them (16%) and that the friend "listened" (14%) and was like family (12%), and that she and the friend had been through a lot together (22%). Other reasons mentioned by 10% of the mothers each was that the friend could be counted on when needed, that the friend made the mother feel that *she* was needed, that there was frequent contact, and that the mother trusted the friend. A few mothers (8% or less) stated that the friend was supportive during the divorce, that the friend knew the mother very well, that the friend and mother were mutually supportive, and that the friend and mother helped each other materially. Only one mother mentioned a friend under the rubric of stress, presumably because in contrast to parents, relationships with friends are chosen and can be terminated. Indeed, several mothers mentioned that they did not have time for friends who were not supportive and worthwhile. Parents and relatives may also be more stressful because they feel freer to criticize that individuals who are not family members.

Maternal Partners. Mothers provided many positive reasons why their partners were important to them but mentioned few stresses ($M = 4.4$ vs. $M = 1.1$, $t(31) = 6.3$, $p < .0001$). Of the 32 mothers who discussed partners as members of their social network, 71% commented that the child liked, loved, or felt positively toward the partner:

"They (children) are fond of (partner), once in a while they call him daddy."

"(Child) has got him wrapped around her little finger."

"(Child) wants to have him as part of the family."

and 37% commented that the partner was interacting well with the children:

"He is so good with the kids."

"... a lot of effort to try and accommodate with the children."

Mothers also mentioned that partners helped with child care and children's activities (32%):

"Roughhousing, watch cartoons, go a lot of places, the zoo."

"Plays with (child) and took care of her."

"(Partner) fixes (child's) bike if it needs fixing."

"Wrestles around on the floor, reads to them, go for walks together."

"He built a tree-house for the boys, and (child) loves to play in that."

"They play catch in the backyard ... and helping him ride the bike ... trying to get (child) to try new things."

Overall, 75% of the 32 partners were mentioned positively in one or more of the three child-related categories.

As regards the partners' relationship to the mother, 14 mothers noted that the partners provided support, often described as emotional or esteem support:

"My own needs, my own time, my own support."

"boosting my ego."

"takes up all the slack."

A substantial number of mothers (26%) praised the partner's positive personality characteristics, an alternative way of talking about the partner's style of relating to her:

"Very honest and hardworking, very caring."

"I didn't know a man could have so much compassion."

"He's very funny."

"He has a great sense of humor, and I didn't know how much I would value that."

Having similar interests or values (16%) was also commonly mentioned as was having a positive relationship (14%):

"We click on every level."

"Real close to him, we get along well."

Being a good listener, open communication, and support with divorce and post-divorce issues were each mentioned by 10% of the mothers. Fewer than 10% of the mothers mentioned the following qualities or behaviors: that the partner understood her situation (8%), was "someone to do things with" (6%), offered good advice (6%), and was "always there" (i.e., ready to provide support; 6%). Two mothers mentioned help with chores ("fixes everything"). Other positive statements, made by 1 mother each were: a long history together and financial support. All but 1 of the 32 mothers with partners made one or more statements about positive relations with him.

In all, 59% of the 32 mothers discussed stressful aspects of their partner relationships. Of these, 3 mothers mentioned difficulties in trusting the partner, and 2 mothers each discussed the following partner-related problems: doubts about continuing the relationship, the partner not having a positive relationship with the child, disagreements about childrearing, disagreements about daily routines, the partner living too far away, interfering in the mother's relationship with the child, and the partner's problems with an ex-spouse or girlfriend:

"He's having marital problems—he's separated from his wife. I'm seeing him and I'm thinking about that a lot."

One mother each reported that the partner was not a positive influence in her life, was not a good role model for the child, or had a problem with alcohol.

Intercorrelations of the Sources of Help Questionnaire and Social Network Interview

As previously noted, positive SNI scores were derived by summing across the number of positive/supportive categories into which the mothers' statements about a particular primary network member had been placed. Negative SNI scores were generated by summing across negative/stressful categories.

The quantified positive SNI scores derived from statements about the child's father were positively related and corresponding negative SNI scores were negatively related to the mothers' ratings of the child's father on the SOHQ (this was the case both for the four types of support and for overall satisfaction with support). Table 3 presents only the correlations of SNI scores with overall satisfaction of father support from the SOHQ. The findings suggest that, in rating their perceptions of father helpfulness on the SOHQ, mothers had weighed positive against negative factors.

Furthermore, in line with the already reported within-SOHQ correlations for the various sources of help, SNI scores generated for the child's father were not related to SOHQ ratings of the mothers' parents, nor were SNI statements about the mothers' parents related to SOHQ ratings of the child's father. However, when the within-SNI scores were compared, a significant negative correlation emerged between negative SNI scores concerning the child's father and positive SNI scores concerning the mothers' parents ($r(43) = -.30$, $p < .05$, controlling for mother's age and education). That is when a mother perceived the child's father as more stress-provoking, she perceived her own parents more positively.

Similarly, positive SNI scores generated from maternal statements about partners were negatively correlated with SOHQ ratings of the child's father. In other words, mothers with partners who, judging from the SNI, felt more positively about their new partners were less satisfied with the support they received from the child's father, according to their SOHQ responses. The ex-spouse/partner

Table 3. Partial Correlations of Helpfulness and Satisfaction Ratings from the Sources of Help Questionnaire and Problem and Support Summary Scores from the Social Network Interview (Controlling for Mother's Age and Education)

SNI support/problems	SOHQ satisfaction with father's support	SOHQ satisfaction with maternal grandparents' support
Child's father—support	.49***	
Child's father—problems	−.45***	
Mother's parents—support		.43**
Mother's parents—problems		−.26*
Mother's partner—support	−.34*	
Mother's partner—problems		.26+

Note. Only coefficients with $p < .10$ are shown. Not all coefficients have the same df (e.g., only 32 mothers had new partners).
$+p < .10$, $*p < .05$, $**p < .01$, $***p < .001$.

correlations could be explained in a variety of ways: (1) when the mother has a boyfriend or fiancé who is involved with the children, a father may become less involved, (2) a mother who has a new partner may have a tendency to idealize the partner and devalue the child's father, or (3) a mother under these circumstances may call on the father less.

Note also, that there was a trend for mothers' SOHQ ratings of their parents' support to be positively correlated with SNI-derived scores of partner problems, and for positive SNI scores concerning the mothers' parents to be negatively correlated with positive statements about her partner ($r(26) = -.26$, $p < .10$, controlling for mothers' age and education).

Although these findings suggest that there may be compensatory or trade-off factors at work, the negative father–maternal parent as well as the negative father–boyfriend correlations must be treated with caution. Much further research is necessary before drawing firm conclusions.

Correlations of the Sources of Help Questionnaire and the Social Network Interview with Other Relationship and Personality Variables

Relationship and personality variables based on the MARI, Personality Inventory, BDI and FILE were significantly correlated with mothers' scores from the SOHQ and SNI (controlling for mothers' age and education). However, the correlational patterns varied by network member.

The Child's Father.   Interestingly, none of the maternal SOHQ ratings of the child's father nor the corresponding SNI support and stress scores were related to mothers' self-reported depression (BDI) or to the number of stressful events she checked on the FILE. These father measures were, however, systematically and meaningfully related to several MARI scales (see Table 4).

When mothers rated themselves as more satisfied with support by the child's father on the SOHQ, they also tended to evaluate him more favorably on the love and child-rearing agreement scales and less negatively on the rejection and child-rearing leniency scales of the MARI. These correlations were obtained despite the fact that the mean ratings on the love scale were quite low, while those for rejection and controllingness were quite high, reversed from what we previously noted in responses by married parents (Bretherton, Winn, Page, MacFie, & Walsh, 1993).

There are two (not mutually exclusive) ways to explain these findings: (1) There is continuity between the ex-spousal relationship as experienced at the time of permanent separation and the present, or (2) the perception of the current relationship colors ratings of the past relationship. Whichever interpretation is favored, perceived father helpfulness is related to variations in the perceived quality of the ex-spousal relationship including coparental agreement/disagreement.

Interestingly, the MARI scales of rejection, controllingness, and paternal leniency were also moderately correlated with mothers' belief in chance, whereas belief in powerful others was only related to rejection. Planfulness was related only

Table 4. Partial Correlations between Father Ratings from the Sources of Help Questionnaire, Support and Problem Measures from the Social Network Interview, and the Marital Autonomy and Relatedness Scale (Controlling for Mother's Age and Education)

| | MARI scales | | | | | |
	Love	Rejection	Autonomy	Control	Parenting agreement	F more lenient
SOHQ satisfaction with F (48)	.36**	−.48***			.51***	−.39**
SNI F supportive (48)	.57***	−.47***	.30*	−.21+	.47***	
SNI F stressful (48)		.26*		.30*	−.37**	
Locus of Control, Chance (50)		.26*		.28*	−.24*	.29*
Locus of Control, Power (50)		.26*				
Planfulness (50)			.28*			

Note. Only coefficients with $p < .10$ are shown. Numbers in parentheses after social support and personality variables refer to the number of mothers who gave responses.
$+p < .10$, $*p < .05$, $**p < .01$, $***p < .001$.

to autonomy. Mothers who report a more negative ex-spousal and coparental relationship, then, are also somewhat more likely to profess a belief that life is controlled by fate or luck.

Other Sources of Help. In contrast, perceived helpfulness from sources other than the child's father were significantly related to the BDI and the FILE. Note that twelve of the 50 mothers had scores above 10 on the BDI (recommended by Schwab, Bialow, & Holzer, 1967, as the cutoff score for clinically significant depression). The mean BDI score was 6.5, and mothers checked a mean of 12 stressful events on the FILE (Range 5–23). This number is substantially above the norm of 9.2 for married women (McCubbin & Patterson, 1991).

Of the four types of SOHQ-rated helpfulness, only companionship support by the mothers' parents, relatives, friends, coworkers, and church/temple was significantly (negatively) correlated with the BDI (see Table 5). The correlations with the overall satisfaction ratings from the SOHQ were also significant, but lower (they are not displayed here). Correlations obtained with companionship ratings of the mothers' own parents, relatives, and friends were highest, whereas correlations for coworkers and church/temple were lower, but still significant. Mothers who were less depressed and who experienced fewer stressful life events also rated books as more helpful.

In contrast, the SOHQ-rated frequency of support by coworkers, counselors, and doctors, as well as parenting advice from counselors, was *positively* correlated with the number of stressful life events mothers reported on the FILE. Doctors' frequency of support was also correlated positively with the BDI.

Regarding the SNI variables, mothers who evaluated the support relationship

**Table 5. Partial Correlations between Measures
from the Sources of Help Questionnaire, the Beck Depression
Inventory, the Social Network Interview,
and the Family Inventory of Life Events and Changes
(Controlling for Mother's Age and Education)**

Social support/stress measures	BDI	FILE
Sources of Help Questionnaire ratings		
Mother's parents' companionship (48)	−.40*	−.21+
Relatives' companionship (48)	−.48***	−.24+
Friends' companionship (50)	−.41**	−.22+
Coworkers' companionship (48)	−.30*	
Coworkers' frequency of support (48)		.29*
Church companionship (37)	−.32*	
Counselor/therapist's frequency of support (40)		.50**
Counselor/therapist's informational support (40)		.41**
Doctor's frequency of support (48)	.31*	.29*
Books support satisfaction (42)	−.52**	−.38*
Social Network Interview		
Statements about mother's parents—support (48)		−.33*
Statements about mother's parents—stress (48)	.35**	
Marital Autonomy and Relatedness Scale		
Child's father controlling mother (50)		.28*
Child's father more lenient than mother (50)	.23+	.31*

Note. Only coefficients with $p < .10$ are shown. Numbers in parentheses after social support/
stress measures refer to the number of mothers who provided ratings or information.
$+p < .10$, $*p < .05$, $**p < .01$, $***p < .001$.

with grandparents more negatively had higher scores on the BDI (were more depressed), whereas mothers who made more positive statements about the child's grandparents reported fewer stressful life events. With respect to the child's father, none of the helpfulness ratings from the SOHQ nor the positive or negative SNI statements were correlated with the BDI or FILE. However, two variables from the MARI were of interest. Mothers who rated the child's father as more controlling toward them and as overly lenient toward the children tended to have higher scores on the FILE. The correlation of father leniency with the BDI did not reach significance.

Given that the data are not longitudinal, the interpretation of the findings shown in Table 5 is somewhat problematic. Negative correlations between support satisfaction and depression have been obtained in many studies. They have often been taken as evidence that individuals who are satisfied with the support they receive become less depressed or are buffered against depression. The reverse, however, could also be the case; that is, mothers who are less depressed may receive more effective and willing help from supporters or may ask for or accept such help more readily. Alternatively, depressed mothers may view support (given or offered) in a less positive light, though as Wan et al. (in press) note, the causal direction in the depression–support correlations may well be bidirectional. If this interpretation is correct, our findings could represent a benign (stress-buffering) circle whereby support both counteracts and prevents depression.

That lower maternal depression scores in this study are most strongly correlated with companionship support is especially interesting. Some studies report that companionship support makes important contributions to self-esteem. Individuals who choose to spend leisure time (a commodity in short supply) together signal nonverbally that they have high regard for each other (Rook, 1990). Companionship may also enhance mental health because it does not put the recipient in a one-down position, as emotional, tangible, and informational help may do, especially if the supporter's motivation is based on feelings of obligation rather than caring.

On the other hand, the *positive* correlations of SOHQ ratings of support frequency from coworkers, doctors, and counselors with the FILE measure suggest that mothers may seek out these sources in response to a pile-up of negative life events. Hence, our data could be interpreted as simultaneously representing the buffering effects of companionship support by members of the primary social network and stress-related responses to temporary crises that call for more frequent help from the professional and work-related network.

Unfortunately, regression analyses that would allow us to untangle these influences are not advisable, given the relatively small sample size and the varying number of mothers making SOHQ ratings for different sources of help. However, inspection of the correlations among variables related to the BDI and FILE listed in Table 5 supports the argument that two somewhat independent influences may be at work. First, the companionship support ratings for the informal network (the child's maternal grandparents, relatives, friends, and coworkers) are significantly intercorrelated (mean r = .40, range .19 to .59). Mothers who rated one source of companionship as helpful tended to appreciate the companionship of other sources as well. However, these companionship ratings are, by and large, not correlated with the frequency and support ratings for formal network sources (mean r = .12, range .26 to .02). Only the frequency (not helpfulness) of coworker support is significantly correlated with frequency of support from doctors, supporting a stress-related interpretation. Within the formal network, the only significant within-network correlations are between ratings of satisfaction with support from books and the two counseling ratings (frequency and informational support), presumably because counselors recommend books. Finally, also supporting a stress-based interpretation of the positive correlations between counseling and the BDI and FILE is the finding that mothers who rate the child's father as more controlling of them and overly lenient with children on the MARI have significantly more frequent contact with counselors (r (37) = .30, p < .03, and .32, p < .03, respectively). Frequent contact with doctors is also significantly correlated with father leniency (r (45) = .30, p < .03). On the other hand, the two MARI ratings listed on Table 5 are not correlated with the SOHQ companionship ratings of the mothers' parents, other relatives and friends. However, mothers who rated the father as controlling of them on the MARI tended to find church companionship more helpful (r (36) = .38, p < .01).

Correlations of the Beck Depression Inventory, the Family Inventory of Life Events, and Changes and Maternal Personality Variables

Maternal self-reports of depression and stress were also positively related to external locus of control (powerful others and chance), but there were no correlations with internal locus of control. In addition, both planfulness and impulsiveness were related to the BDI and FILE (see Table 6). Mothers who rated themselves as more planful and less impulsive had significantly lower depression scores and checked fewer negative life events.

These findings can be interpreted in two ways: (1) Mothers who believe that they have less control over their lives may unwittingly create more stressful life events by not taking charge, or (2) stressful events affect maternal belief systems. The two interpretations, though contradictory at first sight, are not necessarily mutually exclusive.

Mothers who describe themselves as more planful provide significantly more positive and fewer negative reasons for regarding new partners as important (SNI), and mothers who perceive the partner more positively are also less likely to rate themselves as impulsive. That is, although lack of supportiveness by the child's father or the partner is not related to depression (as had been expected), the father and partner variables are related to control beliefs and planfulness. Note also that of the two MARI scales that are negatively correlated with the FILE, one is perceived controllingness by the child's father.

Interestingly, in view of our interpretation of BDI and FILE correlations with companionship ratings of the mothers' parents, relatives, and friends presented in Table 5, belief in powerful others and chance was negatively related to how helpful mothers found the companionship of these sources of support (mean $r = -.28$, $p < .02$). With respect to the formal network, frequency of help from doctors was positively correlated with belief in chance and with impulsiveness

Table 6. Partial Correlations of Maternal Beliefs and Personality with the Beck Depression Inventory and the Family Inventory of Life Events and Changes (Controlling for Mother's Age and Education)

Maternal beliefs and personality	BDI	FILE
Locus of control		
Powerful others	.39**	.26*
Chance	.41**	.42**
Internal	—	—
Planfulness	−.24*	−.31*
Impulsiveness	.24*	.35**

Note. Only coefficients with $p < .10$ are shown. All 50 mothers provided ratings.
$+p < .10$, $*p < .05$, $**p < .01$.

$(r(45) = .27, p < .03$, and $.37, p < .01$, respectively). Similarly, frequency of contact with counselors/therapists (though not their helpfulness) was positively correlated with self-rated impulsiveness and negatively with planfulness $(r(37) = -.33, p < .02$, and $.35, p < .02)$. Ratings of overall satisfaction with books was negatively correlated with belief in chance $(r(41) = -.33, p < .02)$, but positively with impulsiveness $(r(41) = .26, p < .05)$, with the latter correlation probably due to reading assignments made by counselors (remember that frequency of counselor support was related with impulsiveness also). Finally, belief in chance was correlated with the MARI ratings of father controllingness and lenience with children $(r(49) = .35, p < .01$, and $.29, p < .02$, respectively). These correlational patterns support our earlier argument regarding the beneficial effects of companionship support from the informal network, and the stress-related effects of frequent help from coworkers, doctors, and counselors. While they also show that locus of control beliefs play a powerful role in mental health and the perception of stress, we cannot assume that the effect is unidirectional. As far as parenting is concerned, postdivorce mothers (and fathers) often have less control, so that life may affect belief as much as belief affects life.

CONCLUDING REMARKS

The five major findings of this study concern the ex-spousal/coparental relationship, trade-off effects within the support network when viewed as a whole, links between support satisfaction and relationship quality, the differential provisions of specific sources of help, and correlations between social support and depression/stress. After considering each of these topics, we will conclude with suggestions for integrating ideas from the attachment, social support, and coping literatures.

With respect to the first topic, our findings show that ex-spouses have a unique place in divorced mothers' social networks. The fact that they elicited extremely low ratings on the SOHQ and a preponderance of negative statements during the SNI was especially striking given mothers' primarily positive evaluations of their new partners (boyfriends and fiancés). In our view, mothers' generally negative stance toward the child's father as a source of help has a number of related causes. First, special problems are inherent in combining an ex-spousal with a continuing coparental relationship. Ex-spouses commonly use highly negative attributions about the former partner as part of their attempt to dissolve the emotional bond (Vaughan, 1990; Weiss, 1974), but these processes conflict with their coparenting task.

In addition, the divorced mothers in our sample had set high standards for the quality of parenting they expected from the fathers of their children. In most of these families, the mothers were primarily responsible for childrearing and appeared to feel that the father should make up in quality what he did not provide in quantity. We suspect (based on their comments during the SNI) that the mere act of caring for the children on weekends was not seen as particularly supportive by many mothers for two reasons: (1) because such care is regarded as the father's obligation and (2) because mothers were concerned about and had little control over the quality of care the children received. Only a minority of mothers reported fairly amicable relations and communication with the child's father. Nevertheless, that a significant number of mothers had managed to negotiate cooperative coparenting suggests that we need to examine more specifically the processes through which families arrive at more positive interparental relations.

In contrast to the low mean rating of father support, partners' assistance in caring for children was considered very helpful, perhaps because partners do not have an obligation to provide it. It is also noteworthy, however, that most mothers made it very clear that they were not interested in a partner who did not also try to relate positively to their child or children. In addition, mothers were highly positive about the partners' emotional and companionship support, expressed sometimes in terms of the partner's personality (compassionate or fun), in terms of the mother's feelings about him ("I can trust him," "I enjoy being with him"), and in terms of the father's behavior ("He listens"). Interestingly, financial support as a positive partner quality was mentioned only once.

Second, related to the father/partner findings, but applicable more generally, our data suggest that it is worth looking for trade-off effects in the perceived overall functioning of a social network. The importance of some members may wax and wane depending on the availability of and relationship quality with others. Whereas assessments of perceived support from the child's father and the child's maternal grandparents were not correlated, both father and to some extent grandparent helpfulness ratings tended to decrease when the mother had a steady partner who was supportive. This finding was not dependent on whether the partner actually lived with the mother (few did). Also suggestive of trade-off effects are the negative correlations between helpfulness by the child's father and those of various formal network members.

The question has been raised whether social support ratings are affected by stresses in the relationship between helpseekers and providers. Correlations between SOHQ ratings and SNI scores in this study provide strong support for such a link. Both negative and positive SNI statements about fathers and the mothers' parents related to the corresponding SOHQ ratings, but in opposite directions. This corroborates the findings of Sarason et al. (1993) that the quality of the relationship between helpseekers and providers plays a crucial role in whether support is welcomed and seen as effective.

Third, the suggestion of Sarason et al. (1993) that the ability to successfully enlist social support operates like a personality trait received only limited support. Variations in perceived father helpfulness were not correlated with maternal ratings of other network members' helpfulness, and there was a trend for partner problems to be correlated with variations in perceived helpfulness by the mother's parents. Moreover, the fact that father helpfulness was related to the MARI, whereas helpfulness by the other network members was not, demonstrates that the ability to elicit effective support is, at least in this study, relationship-specific.

Fourth, our findings indicate that provisions offered by the various sources of help differ within and across relationship categories. For relatives and close friends both companionship and emotional support, and for the child's maternal grandparents just companionship support received significantly higher ratings than the other types of support. At the same time, for these three sources of help all ratings were relatively high (above the scale midpoint). Overall satisfaction and frequency of support ratings were highest for the mothers' parents and her close friends. Concerning coworker ratings, emotional support received the highest scores, while across the formal network (church, child's teacher, doctor, counselor, and books) parenting advice and emotional support were (not surprisingly) rated more highly than tangible help and companionship. Furthermore, for the entire formal network, ratings for tangible help and companionship were also low in an absolute sense (all were below 2 on a 5-point scale). From the SNI, moreover, we discovered further evidence suggesting that it may be useful to distinguish among different types of emotional support. Emotional support provided by the mothers' parents was more often seen as unconditional (always being there) and frequently expressed in very intense terms ("She would bend over backwards …"). In contrast, the emotional support provided by friends (and often also by siblings) tended to be based on shared life situations or long-term confiding relationships. These exploratory findings deserve further examination in future studies.

Finally, the contrasting positive and negative correlations of the various support measures with depression and stressful life events suggest—though they cannot fully confirm—that social networks may concurrently fulfill both a maintenance/preventive function and a crisis management function. Companionship support from parents, relatives, close friends, coworkers, and church contacts was related to lower depression scores and fewer stressful life events. On the other hand, frequency of help from coworkers, doctors, and counselors was related to a higher number of stressful life events. Many studies have reported negative correlations between social support and depression, though a few found the opposite effect. We suspect that these apparent contradictions are due to the different functions that support may fulfill (preventive and/or interventive). Because we assessed network support in terms of mothers' personal versus formal network members, and by types as well as frequency of support, we saw concurrent indications of preventive and interventive functions of social support in the same sample. This interpretations was supported by intercorrelations among the variables related to the BDE and FILE, as well as by the fact that the companionship support from informal network members was negatively related and frequency of support from coworkers and counselors was positively related to belief in chance. In addition, we were able to show that stresses in postdivorce mothers' interpersonal relationships with parents and ex-spouses were positively related to depression, that is, stressful relationships interfered with mental health and hence undermined the effectiveness of such support as was given.

Overall, our findings highlight the usefulness of the social support literature in examining the function of different types of adult attachment relationships, that is, those between adult children and their parents, between adult siblings, between friends, and between ex-marital partners. Recent work on adult attachment has been almost exclusively limited to investigating individuals' general styles of relating to others, not on the quality of *relationships between adults*. Furthermore, the study of adult attachment relations has been limited to romantic partners, and has not included close friends and adult parent–child relations. In addition, attachment theorists have not sufficiently investigated the costs of social support for the support provider, or the network context within which the support occurs.

Aside from the seminal work by Weiss (1974), ex-spousal relationships as well as the contradictions inherent in ex-spousal/coparental relationships have not been studied from an attachment perspective. We believe that further analysis of how recipients and providers in attachment or attachment-like relationships negotiate support in stressful situations can shed light on our understanding of how and under what conditions attachment relations succeed and do not succeed in fulfilling the stress-buffering function proposed by Bowlby. To examine this question more closely in postdivorce families is important, not only with respect to the parents' mental health, but in regard to their ability to provide security and support to their children.

ACKNOWLEDGMENTS

This study was funded by a grant from the National Institutes of Health (RO1 HD26766). Additional support was provided by the University of Wisconsin Research Committee and the Waisman Center. We would like to express our deep gratitude to the mothers and children who gave of their time to participate in this study.

REFERENCES

Beck, A. T., & Beamesderfer, A. (1974). Assessment of depression: The depression inventory. In P. Pichot (Ed.), *Psychological measurements in psychopharmacology: Modern problems in pharmacopsychiatry*, Vol. 7 (pp. 151–169).

Beck, A. T., Ward, C. H., Mendelson, M., Mock, J., & Erbaugh, J. (1961). An inventory for measuring depression. *Archives of General Psychiatry, 4*, 561–569.

Bowlby, J. (1969). *Attachment and loss, Vol. I: Attachment.* New York: Basic Books.

Bowlby, J. (1979). *The making and breaking of affectional bonds.* London: Tavistock Publications.

Bretherton, I. (1990). Open communication and internal working models: Their role in the development of attachment relationships. In R. A. Thompson (Ed.), *Socioemotional development: Nebraska symposium on motivation 1988* (pp. 59–113). Lincoln, NE: University of Nebraska Press.

Bretherton, I., Biringen, Z., Ridgeway, D., Maslin, C., & Sherman, M. (1989). Attachment: The parental perspective. *Infant Mental Health Journal, 10*, 203–220.

Bretherton, I., Winn, L., Page, T., MacFie, J., & Walsh, R. O. (1993, March). *Concordance of preschoolers' family stories with parental reports of family climate, family stress and child temperament.* Paper presented at the biennial meetings of the Society for Research in Child Development, New Orleans.

Cobb, S. (1976). Social support as a moderator of life stress. *Psychosomatic Medicine, 38*, 300–314.

Cochran, M., Larner, M., Riley, D., Gunnarsson, L., & Henderson, C. R. (1990). *Extending families.* New York: Cambridge University Press.

Cohen, S., & Wills, T. A. (1985). Stress, social support, and the buffering hypothesis. *Psychological Bulletin, 98,* 310–357.

Coyne, J. C., Ellard, J. H., & Smith, D. A. F. (1990). Social support, interdependence, and the dilemmas of helping. In B. R. Sarason, I. G. Sarason, & G. R. Pierce (Eds.), *Social support: An interactional view* (pp. 129–149). New York: Wiley.

Crowne, D. P., & Marlowe, D. (1980). *The approval motive.* Westport, CT: Greenwood Press.

Cutrona, C. E., & Russell, D. W. (1990). Type of social support and specific stress: Toward a theory of optimal matching. In B. R. Sarason, I. G. Sarason, & G. R. Pierce (Eds.), *Social support: An interactional view* (pp. 319–366). New York: Wiley.

Emery, E. R. (1988). *Marriage, divorce and children's adjustment.* Newbury Park, CA: Sage Publications.

Eysenck, S. B. G., & Eysenck, H. J. (1977). The place of impulsiveness in a dimensional system of personality description. *British Journal of Social and Clinical Psychology, 16,* 57–68.

Henderson, S. (1981). Social relationships, adversity, and neurosis: An analysis of prospective observations. *British Journal of Psychiatry, 138,* 191–198.

Hetherington, E. M. (1989). Coping with family transitions: Winners, losers, and survivors. *Child Development, 60,* 1–14.

Hollingshead, A. B. (1978). *The four-factor index of social status.* Unpublished manuscript, Yale University.

Jackson, D. N. (1977). Reliability of the Jackson personality inventory. *Psychological Reports, 40,* 613–614.

Kahn, R. L., & Antonucci, T. C. (1980). Convoys over the life-course: Attachment, roles and social support. In P. B. Baltes & O. G. Brim (Eds.), *Life-span development and behavior* (pp. 253–286). New York: Academic Press.

Levenson, H. (1981). Differentiating among internality, powerful others, and chance. *Research with the Locus of Control Construct, 1,* 15–63.

McCubbin, H. I., & Patterson, J. (1991). FILE family inventory of life events and changes. In H. I. McCubbin & A. I. Thompson (Eds.), *Family assessment inventories for research and practice (2nd ed.)* (pp. 81–95). Madison, WI: University of Wisconsin–Madison.

Pierce, G. R., Sarason, B. R., & Sarason, I. G. (1990). Investigating social support perspectives: Working models, personal relationships, and situational factors. In S. Duck (Ed.), *Personal relationships and social support* (pp. 173–189). Newbury Park, CA: Sage Publications.

Rook, K. S. (1990). Social relationships as a source of companionship: Implications for older adults' psychological well-being. In B. R. Sarason, I. G. Sarason, & G. R. Pierce (Eds.), *Social support: An interactional view* (pp. 219–250). New York: Wiley.

Rutter, M. (1987). Psychosocial resilience and protective mechanisms. *American Journal of Orthopsychiatry, 57,* 316–331.

Sarason, B. R., Pierce, G. R., Bannerman, A., & Sarason, I. (1993). Investigating the antecedents of perceived social support: Parents' views of and behavior towards their children. *Journal of Personality and Social Psychology, 65,* 1071–1085.

Sarason, B. R., Sarason, I. G., & Pierce, G. R. (1990). The road to theory in the field of social support. In B. R. Sarason, I. G. Sarason, & G. R. Pierce (Eds.), *Social support: An interactional view* (pp. 1–25). New York: Wiley.

Sarason, B. R., Pierce, G. R., & Sarason, I. G. (1990). Social support: The sense of acceptance and the role of relationships. In B. R. Sarason, I. G. Sarason, & G. R. Pierce (Eds.), *Social support: An interactional view* (pp. 97–128). New York: Wiley.

Schaefer, E. S., & Edgerton, M. (1979). *Short report on the Marital Relatedness and Autonomy Inventory (MARI).* Unpublished manuscript, University of North Carolina.

Schwab, J. J., Bialow, M., & Holzer, C. E. (1967). Diagnosing depression in medical in-patients. *Journal of Clinical Psychology, 23,* 94–96.

Vaughan, D. (1986). *Uncoupling: Turning points in intimate relationships.* New York: Oxford University Press.

Wallerstein, J. S., & Blakeslee, A. (1989). *Second chances: Men, women, and children a decade after divorce.* New York: Ticknor & Fields.

Wan, C. K., Jaccard, J., and Ramey, S. L. (in press). Relationship between social support and life satisfaction as a function of family structure: An analysis of four types of support. *Journal of Marriage and the Family.*

Weiss, R. S. (1974). The provisions of social relationships. In Z. Rubin (Ed.), *Doing unto others* (pp. 17–26). Englewood Cliffs, NJ: Prentice-Hall.

16

Social Support and Pregnancy

A Comprehensive Review
Focusing on Ethnicity and Culture

CHRISTINE DUNKEL-SCHETTER, LYNDA M. SAGRESTANO,
PAMELA FELDMAN, and CHRISTINE KILLINGSWORTH

In the 1970s, following the publication of influential papers by authors such as Caplan (1974), Cassel (1976), and Cobb (1976), investigators began to study social support (Norbeck, 1988). One oft-cited early study highlighted the potential importance of social support in pregnancy by considering social support as an element of "psychosocial assets" and showing that pregnant women with a combination of high life stress and few psychosocial assets experienced more pregnancy complications than did women with low life stress and a higher level of psychosocial assets (Nuckolls, Cassel, & Kaplan, 1972). Since then, a number of studies have attempted to clarify the role of social support in pregnancy outcomes.

Social support in pregnancy is a particularly promising area of investigation because pregnancy and birth are clearly biopsychosocial events. Psychosocial factors such as stress or social support have been shown to significantly influence pregnancy outcomes, independent of biomedical factors or variables (Lobel, 1994; Elbourne & Oakley, 1991). These and other socioenvironmental influences are now recognized by scientists in multiple disciplines as potent variables in understanding maternal and infant health. In addition, pregnancy is more easily studied than many health events. It is of standard and reasonably short duration, and it has a number of objectively defined and reliably measured outcomes, such as infant birthweight or neonatal complications. Research on pregnancy is also

CHRISTINE DUNKEL-SCHETTER, LYNDA M. SAGRESTANO, PAMELA FELDMAN, and CHRISTINE KILLINGSWORTH • Department of Psychology, University of California at Los Angeles, Los Angeles, California 90024-1563.

Handbook of Social Support and the Family, edited by Gregory R. Pierce, Barbara R. Sarason, and Irwin G. Sarason. Plenum Press, New York, 1996.

optimized by the large numbers of women who become pregnant and deliver infants.

Although the role of social support in pregnancy outcomes has been empirically investigated, little attention has been paid to theoretical frameworks or conceptual issues that might guide research on this issue. In particular, the roles of the couple, the family, and the woman's sociocultural context have received relatively little systematic research attention. Insomuch as pregnancy generally evolves in the context of a continuing relationship between a man and a woman, each of whom has a social network, it is inherently an event involving families. Furthermore, the couple and their families exist in a cultural milieu, wherein cultural values and norms influence their attitudes and behavior. Nevertheless, pregnancy is too often conceptualized as though the woman were an isolated individual.

This chapter reviews past research on social support during pregnancy in two sections: (1) research on social support and birth outcomes and (2) research linking social support to maternal emotions and behavior in pregnancy. With these reviews as an empirical basis clearly documenting the importance of support in pregnancy, a third section of the chapter examines ethnic and cultural issues integral to understanding social support processes in pregnancy.

Though there is a growing awareness of the importance of culture to fully understanding psychological processes in general (Markus & Kitayama, 1991), research on pregnancy has not yet incorporated theoretical approaches that conceptualize cultural variables.

There are well-established differences between ethnic groups in the United States in birth outcomes. For example, the rate of low-birthweight births among African-Americans is twice that of European-Americans with births to Latina women giving birth in the United States often falling in the middle (National Center for Health Statistics, 1992). Social support is one of many possible mediators of this ethnic difference. Although it is important to distinguish culture and ethnicity, ethnic differences in birth outcomes may be clues to cultural influences in pregnancy that are worthy of direct consideration. Thus, it is critical in research on social support and pregnancy to integrate ethnic and cultural perspectives into one's approach.

Our emphasis in this chapter is on Latino or Hispanic culture because our work has focused on this group in particular. Latinos are currently the largest group of immigrants to the United States, and they constitute a near majority of the population in southern California where our research is conducted. Although there is little empirical research on ethnicity and support in pregnancy per se, we include that which is available in this chapter. We conclude the chapter with a call to integrate a cultural perspective with research on close relationships in the study of social support in pregnancy.

EFFECTS OF SOCIAL SUPPORT DURING PREGNANCY AND BIRTH ON BIRTH OUTCOMES

Historically, social support research has suffered from definitional problems. At present, the term "social support" is still defined in a variety of ways, but principally either as *available* or *perceived support* or as *enacted* or *received support* (Dunkel-Schetter & Bennett, 1990). Our approach to the study of social support in pregnancy emphasizes the latter of these—the support that is actually provided to women during the prenatal period or during labor (Collins, Dunkel-Schetter, Lobel, & Scrimshaw, 1993). Three types of support arise most often in the research literature: (1) emotional support, (2) informational support, and (3) instrumental or tangible support, the latter including task and material forms of assistance (Dunkel-Schetter, Folkman, & Lazarus, 1987; Schwarzer, Dunkel-Schetter, & Kemeny, 1994). A variety of measures are used to assess these various support concepts. This variety will be evident in the literature reviewed and, as will be seen throughout the chapter, contributes to an inability to formulate generalizations about the effects of support.

Studies on social support in pregnancy and during birth can be divided into three categories: (1) correlational studies that examine the relation between a woman's prenatal social support and her pregnancy outcomes; (2) intervention studies that investigate the benefits of social support programs made available to women throughout their pregnancies; and (3) studies of social support interventions that focus on the presence of a supportive companion during labor and delivery. We review each of these three literatures in detail, and we highlight methodological issues to be addressed in future studies.

Correlational Studies on Prenatal Social Support

Correlational studies generally assess various aspects of a pregnant woman's social support network and their relation to her pregnancy and birth outcomes. Life events, used to measure stress levels, are often assessed as well, in order that interactions between stress and social support can be investigated (e.g., Magni, Rizzardo, & Andreoli, 1986; Norbeck & Anderson, 1989a). Some studies prospectively compare the outcomes of high-risk subgroups to those of low-risk subgroups (e.g., Kemp & Hatmaker, 1989; Lightfoot, Keeling, & Wilton, 1982; Williamson & LeFevre, 1992). Others retrospectively compare the characteristics of women with poor outcomes to those of women with good outcomes (e.g., Berkowitz & Kasl, 1983; Magni et al., 1986). Still others concentrate specifically on subgroups considered to be at high risk for poor birth outcomes, such as pregnant teenagers (e.g., Barrera & Balls, 1983; Boyce, Schaefer, & Uitti, 1985; Turner, Grindstaff, & Phillips, 1990). In general, inconsistencies in the definition and measurement of social support, and in outcome measures, make the results of this line of research mixed or difficult to interpret. It appears, however, that some types and sources of social support may lead to better pregnancy outcomes. Moreover, social support appears to affect different subgroups of women in different ways.

One important finding of this line of research is that different functional aspects of received social support (as opposed to "perceived support," or support perceived to be available) have different effects on pregnancy outcomes. Norbeck and Tilden (1983) measured the three most commonly cited functional aspects of received support—informational, emotional, and tangible—as well as life stress and "emotional disequilibrium" (anxiety, depression, and low self-esteem) in a group of women at low risk for pregnancy complications. They found an interaction between tangible support and life stress; women who reported low tangible support and high stress during pregnancy experienced more infant and gestation complications (e.g., premature labor, low Apgar scores), and women who reported low tangible support and low stress during pregnancy experienced more labor and delivery complications (e.g., prolonged labor, cesarean delivery). Psychological support, a combination of emotional and informational support, had an indirect effect on pregnancy outcomes; it was found to be inversely associated with emotional disequilibrium, which, in turn, was associated with infant complications. In general, evidence suggests that tangible support and emotional support are most likely to be beneficial in pregnancy (see also Boyce et al., 1985; Collins et al., 1993; Pascoe, Chessare, Baugh, Urich, & Ialongo, 1987; Williamson & LeFevre, 1992), whereas the benefits of informational support are likely to be dependent on who is the provider and the context in which it is offered (for a discussion, see Dunkel-Schetter, Blasband, Feinstein, & Herbert, 1992). It should be noted that the majority of participants in this study were European-American (61%), although it included smaller numbers of African-Americans, Latinas, and Asian-Americans.

Other aspects of received support, such as its source, quantity, and quality, also seem to affect outcomes differently. One group of researchers (Collins et al., 1993) measured received social support, satisfaction with received support, amount of support from different sources (i.e., the baby's father, health care providers), and network resources (number of kin and friends, father's presence in the home), and compared them in relation to birth outcomes. In this study, more received support was associated with higher Apgar scores and better labor progress. Greater *satisfaction* with support predicted additional variance in Apgar scores and also predicted less postpartum depression. Women who received support from the baby's father specifically suffered less postpartum depression. Also, those with a greater number of network resources had babies with higher birthweights. Thus, like the study of Norbeck and Tilden (1983), this study found different effects for different functional aspects of social support. These findings are often difficult to interpret. Why, for instance, should task and informational support be associated with Apgar scores (i.e., physician ratings of the infant's status moments after birth) but the combination of task and material support be associated with labor difficulties? The answer may lie in a better understanding of the mechanisms through which social support works (Collins et al., 1993).

Complicating matters are indications that different subgroups of women appear to respond differently to social support (Andresen & Telleen, 1992; Collins et al., 1993; Oakley, 1988; Olds, Henderson, Tatelbaum, & Chamberlin, 1986; Sarason & Sarason, 1993). Pregnant teenagers, for example, are one subgroup that appears to be especially affected by the quality and quantity of their social support networks. In one prospective study (Barrera & Balls, 1983), pregnant teenagers with small social networks and a higher incidence of negative life events gave birth to infants with lower Apgar scores. Among teenagers who were less satisfied with the support they received, a greater number of negative life events also predicted more birth complications. More recently, Turner et al. (1990) found that family support is especially crucial to the pregnancy and psychological outcomes of teenagers. Specifically, the Canadian teenagers in this study who reported higher levels of family support had babies with higher birthweights and experienced less postpartum depression. Furthermore, low–socioeconomic status (SES) teenagers showed these effects regardless of stress level, whereas higher-SES teenagers showed these effects only when their life stress level was high.

Another prospective study also supported the importance of the family to pregnant teenagers (Boyce et al., 1985). In this study, teenagers who perceived their family and friends to be more helpful had fewer neonatal complications. Those who reported higher levels of "permanence and continuity" also experienced fewer neonatal complications. According to the researchers, assessing teenagers' sense of permanence and continuity captured a form of subjective experience rarely measured in studies of social support and health. Boyce et al. (1985) define the sense of permanence as "the belief or perception that certain central, valued elements of life experience are stable and enduring" (p. 1280). Thus, there are a handful of studies on pregnant teenagers showing that low social support combined with low SES or high life stress or both is associated with adverse psychological and infant outcomes in this age group.

Ethnic group membership and cultural differences also seem to moderate the effects of social support. One study, for example, found that African-American women who received more support from their partners and mothers had fewer pregnancy complications and fewer preterm births (Norbeck & Anderson, 1989a). In contrast, European-American women who reported both high stress and high support from their mothers actually had longer labors, and those who reported high stress and high support from their relatives were more likely to require a cesarean delivery. Interestingly, no effects were found for Latina women, leading the investigators to propose that this group of recent immigrants may possess characteristics that protect them from pregnancy complications. Other studies have also reported different effects for different ethnic groups (e.g., Berkowitz & Kasl, 1983; Casper & Hogan, 1990), as well as for women living in different cultures (Thorpe, Dragonas, & Golding, 1992). However, there are few studies directly investigating ethnic and cultural differences in support beliefs, expectations, and norms during pregnancy. Further research in this area may reveal mediators of ethnic differences in pregnancy outcomes (for a discussion, see Jacobson, 1986).

In summary, correlational research on social support in pregnancy presents a complex set of findings. Different dimensions of social support (e.g., function, quality, quantity, and source) appear to have distinct effects on the physical and psychological outcomes of pregnancy. Moreover, characteristics of the support recipient (e.g., her context, age, ethnicity, and stress level) appear to influence the effects of social support. Clarification of the role of different dimensions of social support, the context in which it is provided, and characteristics of its recipients and providers needs to be accomplished in a more systematically rigorous manner. Interestingly, these are issues that have been raised previously regarding social support in general (Cohen & Syme, 1985; Sarason & Sarason, 1993). It is also important to realize that social support may not always be beneficial. In one study, family enmeshment (an extreme form of cohesion) was negatively related to birthweight (Ramsey, Abell, & Baker, 1986; see also Norbeck & Anderson, 1989a).

Prenatal Social Support Interventions

Interventions implemented to improve the social support of pregnant women typically involve home visits by a midwife, nurse, or social worker who provides some combination of emotional support (e.g., Bryce, Stanley, & Garner, 1991; Spencer, Thomas, & Morris, 1989), informational support (e.g., Olds et al., 1986; Piechnik & Corbett, 1985; Sokol, Woolf, Rosen, & Weingarden, 1980), and instrumental assistance (e.g., Spencer et al., 1989). Some interventions include telephone contact available 24 hours a day or a special support office reserved for the use of pregnant women in a particular program (e.g., Heins, Nance, McCarthy, & Efird, 1990; Oakley, Rajan, & Grant, 1990; Villar et al., 1993). Others attempt to strengthen the woman's existing social network by requiring a support person (often her partner, a family member, or a friend) to be present at each home visit (e.g., Olds et al., 1986; Villar et al., 1993). Interventions of this type have been invoked most often for women who are socially or medically at high risk for poor pregnancy outcomes (e.g., Bryce et al., 1991; Forde, 1993; Heins et al., 1990; Oakley et al., 1990; Olds et al., 1986; Sokol et al., 1980; Spencer et al., 1989; Villar et al., 1993). Studies of these interventions are often experimental or quasi-experimental and tend to evaluate the interventions in terms of improvements in labor, delivery, and infant outcomes.

Methodological inconsistencies in this area of research have resulted in somewhat uneven findings (Oakley, 1985, 1988). Nonetheless, some studies evaluating social support interventions have found important benefits. In one study, Oakley et al. (1990) randomly assigned working-class British women with a history of low-birthweight babies to one of two groups: (1) an intervention group that received regular home visits from a midwife or (2) a control group that received standard prenatal care only. The midwives visited women in the intervention group at 14, 20, and 28 weeks, called or briefly visited between these scheduled visits, and were on call to the women 24 hours a day to supply as much support as they requested. Midwives did not provide clinical care, but instead provided emotional and informational support by encouraging the women to discuss any topic they wished. Delivery records indicated that women in the intervention group had significantly larger babies. Infants in both groups required resuscitation at about the same rate, but babies of mothers in the intervention group required less invasive methods of resuscitation. Intervention mothers were less likely to require antenatal hospital admission, more likely to have spontaneous onset of labor and spontaneous vaginal deliveries, and less likely to use epidural anesthesia. In addition, mothers and babies in the intervention group were healthier.

Other investigators, however, have not found such impressive effects. Heins et al. (1990) randomly assigned women at high risk for low-birthweight babies to an intervention or control group. Mothers in the intervention group were visited every 1–2 weeks by nurses or nurse midwives who offered emotional and informational support; they assessed and educated women on risks associated with nutrition, substance abuse, stress, activity level, and social support. In addition, they taught women the signs and symptoms of preterm labor and offered 24-hour telephone support. Overall, the birth outcomes of the two groups (measured in terms of birthweight and incidence of preterm birth) did not differ. One subgroup, however, did seem to benefit. African-American women with high-risk scores at the beginning of their pregnancies had a lower incidence of very-low-birthweight babies. These results suggest the possibility that interventions may be more effective for some at-risk subgroups of pregnant women than for others.

One group that appears to benefit from additional support is teenage mothers, especially those who are very young. Piechnik and Corbett (1985) found that nonwhite adolescents under the age of 15 who received support from a multidisciplinary team gave birth to larger babies than control adolescents of the same age and race. Similar findings were reported by Olds et al. (1986). In this study, women considered high risk based on their meeting at least one of three criteria—under 19 years old, single-parent status, or low SES—were randomly assigned to a control group or to an intervention group that received home visits from nurses who provided parent education, information about community services, and enhancement of the women's existing support networks. Among the benefits reported for the intervention group was the finding that nurse-visited young adolescents under age 17 had babies of higher birthweight than young adolescent controls. In addition to offering evidence that younger women may benefit more from additional social support, these studies also suggest that the effectiveness of support interventions may differ depending on a woman's ethnic group (Heins et al., 1990; Piechnik & Corbett, 1985). In both of these studies, the young, ethnic-minority women benefited significantly from additional support, whereas the young European-American women did not.

Many studies do not obtain significant results because of methodological problems that exist in research on interventions. Specifically, the studies that do not show results sometimes suffer from small sample sizes (e.g., Blondel, Breart, Llado, & Chartier, 1990) or insufficient statistical power to detect differences (e.g., Bryce et al., 1991; Spencer et al., 1989), or they employ weak manipulations (e.g., Blondel et al., 1990). Others do not use random assignment (e.g., Forde, 1993; Larsson, Spangberg, Theorell, & Wager, 1987; Piechnik & Corbett, 1985; Sokol et al., 1980) or have differential attrition. For example, one study reported that almost 60% of the women randomly assigned to the intervention group refused the intervention (Spencer et al., 1989). Another study began the intervention so late in the pregnancy that some mothers received no home visits, and some women in the control group received home visits who shouldn't have (Blondel et al., 1990). Unfortunately, these methodological weaknesses are common in studies that fail to show benefits of supportive interventions.

In addition, studies seeking to determine the effects of social support interventions on high-risk groups sometimes use such broad criteria for defining risk that the rate of perinatal complications reported for their "high-risk" group hardly differs from the rate reported for the general population (e.g., Spencer et al., 1989). Thus, some studies that profess to study women with high-risk pregnancies are not actually doing so, and the potential benefits of interventions aimed at this group may be underestimated. On the other hand, selection of truly "at-risk" subgroups may be more difficult than it seems. For instance, one researcher found that assessment of poor psychosocial conditions using a questionnaire was not sufficient to identify women most likely to benefit from additional support (Forde, 1993). His method of assessing risk, based on a "subjective and intuitive combination of all accessible clinical information" (p. 131), is probably too unwieldy or ambitious for most applications, but it points to a possible weakness in this line of research that should be corrected. In sum, this area of research requires further systematic investigation before we can confidently identify which, if any, risk factors differentiate women most likely to benefit from additional support.

Finally, differences in the definitions and operationalizations of social support reduce the likelihood of seeing consistent results in this line of research. For instance, although both emotional and instrumental support have been found to be helpful in many circumstances, and information or advice is often helpful when it comes from a credible source, one group of researchers actually discouraged their midwives from providing instrumental or informational support because doing so was not part of the intervention protocol and they feared it would interfere with other aspects of the support intervention (Bryce et al., 1991). Interventions offered in other studies vary in the support components included, but not in a way that allows us to systematically evaluate the differences or effects.

To summarize, studies assessing social support interventions have reported many benefits for mothers receiving the intervention, including improvements in birth outcomes (Heins et al., 1990; Oakley et al., 1990; Olds et al., 1986; Piechnik & Corbett, 1985; Sokol et al., 1980), specifically, lower perinatal mortality (Sokol et al., 1980); less utilization of labor and delivery interventions such as epidural anesthesia or oxytocin (Oakley et al., 1990); and better infant health (Oakley et al., 1990). Other benefits of interventions include improvements in maternal health, health habits, and knowledge (Oakley et al., 1990; Olds et al., 1986; Villar et all., 1993); more utilization of community services (Olds et al., 1986); and more satisfaction with maternity care (Blondel et al., 1990; Larsson et al., 1987). However, methodological flaws weaken the conclusions that can be drawn from this line of research. Future studies must use adequate sample sizes, sound research designs, and interventions that have sufficient impact, lest benefits that might otherwise emerge go unnoticed. When investigating women at high risk for pregnancy complications, investigators must ensure that the criteria used to select high-risk groups appropriately differentiate them from low-risk pregnant women. In addition, further research is needed to determine which elements of social support interventions are most effective and under what circumstances (e.g., in what subgroups) benefits are most likely to occur. The suggestion made by several researchers, that the type of support needs to match the stressor for maximal impact, seems critical here (Cohen & McKay, 1984; Dunkel-Schetter et al., 1992). Psychological and behavioral outcomes also need to be assessed more frequently, coincident with a focus on birth outcomes (Elbourne, Oakley, & Chalmers, 1989).

Social Support during Labor and Delivery

The presence of a supportive person during labor and childbirth seems to have an unambiguously and consistently positive effect on perinatal outcomes. In one recent study (Kennell, Klaus, McGrath, Robertson, & Hinkley, 1991), women admitted to a United States hospital in active labor were randomly assigned to one of three groups. The first group received continuous support from volunteers known as *doulas* trained to assist during labor and delivery and to use various support techniques. The doulas offered emotional and informational support by soothing and touching the women, explaining events to them, and, when necessary, translating medical instructions. The second group received no support, but was unobtrusively observed while receiving routine hospital care. The third group served as a control group and received routine hospital care only. The results confirmed the benefits of social support during labor and delivery. Women in the supported group had shorter labors and were less likely to use epidural anesthesia, less likely to receive medication to augment labor, and less likely to require cesarean or forceps deliveries. The infants of mothers in the supported group benefited as well; they were less likely to require prolonged hospital stays or special tests. Interestingly, women in the observed group showed some positive effects as well, leading Kennell et al. (1991) to speculate that a laboring woman may benefit simply from feeling less "alone and needy" (p. 2201).

As this study suggests, the positive effects of support during labor do not require that the support provider be someone with whom the woman has had a close relationship. In fact, positive effects have been observed whether the support person was a family member, a friend, the woman's husband, or a complete stranger. Pascoe (1993) compared duration of labor for three groups of women: (1) those who received no support during labor; (2) those who were supported by a relative or friend; and (3) those who were supported by a trained birth companion who had not met the woman before admission to the hospital. The mean duration of labor for the latter two groups was almost identical. In this study, the labors of supported women averaged 10½ hours, as compared to 16 hours for unsupported women. The significant difference in labor duration remained even after the analyses controlled for maternal age, education, marital status, race, amniotomy, and labor induction.

Perhaps the most impressive finding of this line of research is that the presence of a companion who is not trained, skilled, knowledgeable, or even familiar to the pregnant woman but simply offers emotional support is sufficient for very dramatic results to occur. For instance, in a study of Guatemalan women randomly assigned to either a supported labor group or an unsupported labor group, the supported women developed fewer problems during labor (including those requiring cesarean section or labor augmentation), were less likely to have infants who had to be transferred to the neonatal intensive care unit, and had shorter labors (Klaus, Kennell, Robertson, & Sosa, 1986). As in the previously mentioned study by Kennell et al. (1991), the untrained female support volunteers were strangers to the women and simply sat with them, rubbed their backs, held their hands, and provided explanation and encouragement. Other studies have shown similarly positive results with a stranger acting as the support person (Sosa, Kennell, Klaus, Robertson, & Urrutia, 1980; Wolman, Chalmers, Hofmeyr, & Nikodem, 1993).

In sum, the presence of a supportive companion during labor and delivery— whether someone trained or not trained, familiar to the laboring woman or not— has been shown to decrease the duration of labor (Kennell et al., 1991; Klaus et al., 1986; Pascoe, 1993; Sosa et al., 1980), to reduce perinatal complications (Kennell et al., 1991; Klaus et al., 1986; Pascoe, 1993; Sosa et al., 1980), and to lead to better infant outcomes among women from different cultural and racial backgrounds, including Guatemalans, European-Americans, African-Americans, and American Latinas (Kennell et al., 1991; Klaus et al., 1986). Evidence suggests that support during labor and delivery may also improve psychological and behavioral outcomes of pregnancy; supported women may experience decreased postpartum depression and anxiety and increased self-esteem in the weeks following delivery (Wolman et al., 1993). They may also have more positive interactions with their infants in the hours following delivery (Sosa et al., 1980).

This research domain may benefit from an examination of the long-term behavioral and psychological consequences of support during labor and delivery for mothers, children, and their families (Kennell et al., 1991). In addition, Kennell et al. (1991) note a need to investigate how support offered by husbands or partners differs from support provided by trained volunteers or professional labor coaches. Finally, the mechanisms through which support during labor and delivery works have yet to be elucidated (Kennell et al., 1991; Klaus et al., 1986; Pascoe, 1993). In the meantime, serious consideration should be given to implementing labor support programs for women (Kennell et al., 1991), given the gains that can be attained with what is a simple and low-cost intervention (Kennell et al., 1991; Pascoe, 1993).

Conclusion: Review of Research on Social Support and Birth Outcomes

The three research areas just reviewed—correlational studies of prenatal social network support, prenatal social support interventions, and social support during labor—comprise a broad and complex body of research. We have noted differences in how various dimensions of social support influence pregnancy outcomes and how subgroups of women respond differently to social support. The findings of the studies reviewed are generally positive; social support seems to be beneficial. In some subgroups especially (e.g., young women and members of particular ethnic groups), the presence and involvement of supportive others is associated with better outcomes for mother and baby. Social support from partners and family members may be particularly important to pregnant women (Casper & Hogan, 1990; Kemp & Hatmaker, 1989; Norbeck & Anderson, 1989a,b; Ramsey et al., 1986; Turner et al., 1990). It is important to note, however, that support from family members may also have negative consequences, although this question has received little or no attention in pregnancy research (e.g., Lightfoot et al., 1982; Norbeck & Anderson, 1989a; for a discussion of support type/provider interactions, see Dunkel-Schetter et al., 1992). This area deserves close examination.

Methodological problems exist, however, that make it difficult to draw more specific conclusions. In particular, inconsistencies in outcome measures used from one study to the next complicate our ability to summarize findings across studies. Some researchers group together outcomes that may actually be heterogeneous (Norbeck & Tilden, 1983). More problematic, however, are inconsistencies in the way social support has been defined, measured, and operationalized (Barrera & Balls, 1983; Collins et al., 1993; Norbeck & Tilden, 1983). Each group of researchers tends to use different measurement instruments, some of which are more refined or validated than others (Norbeck & Tilden, 1983; Sarason & Sarason, 1993). In addition, a number of social support dimensions have been found to have effects that are distinct and independent of each other, for instance, the quality vs. quantity of support, or different functional types of support (Collins et al., 1993). Researchers studying social support in pregnancy need to be aware of these distinctions and to make use of them if there is to be consistency across studies and investigators. There is a profusion of instruments, but the field would benefit greatly if researchers relied only on psychometrically sound instruments. Use of more objective measures, rather than relying solely on self-reports, would also benefit the field. Empirical investigations are needed in areas that have been underresearched, in particular studies of three issues: (1) the characteristics of the support provider, the support recipient, and the stress context in which support is offered (Collins et al., 1993; Norbeck & Anderson, 1989b); (2) mechanisms through which social support works to improve birth outcomes (Collins et al., 1993; Oakley, 1985); and (3) consideration of simultaneous effects of social support on psychological and medical outcomes (Collins et al., 1993). Also largely ignored in this body of literature—or studied in only a rudimentary way—are close relationship issues, the role of the family, and the woman's sociocultural background. Social support is too often studied as though it were a process that occurs entirely within the individual instead of as an interpersonal exchange (Collins et al., 1993). We return to this topic at the end of the chapter.

ASSOCIATIONS OF PRENATAL SOCIAL SUPPORT
WITH MATERNAL EMOTIONS AND BEHAVIOR DURING PREGNANCY

Pregnancy researchers have been concerned with examining not only the relationship between social support and birth outcomes, but also the impact of social support on psychological and physical health during pregnancy. Pregnancy can be a challenging and stressful period for women due to fluctuations in their appearance, physiology, emotional well-being, and close relationships (Gjerdingen, Froberg, & Fontaine, 1991). Support is believed to play an important role in mitigating the physical and emotional strain women often experience during pregnancy. It has also been found to bolster positive health behaviors and lifestyle changes. Studies in several areas suggest ways in which support aids women in coping physically and psychologically during pregnancy. These areas of research examine the effects of social support on stress, anxiety and depression, utilization of prenatal care, and health behaviors during pregnancy, and may shed light on some of the mechanisms linking social support to birth outcomes.

Social Support and Prenatal Stress, Anxiety, and Depression

Several studies have shown that social support, in general, is related to lower levels of stress, anxiety, and depression during pregnancy (Albrecht & Rankin, 1989; MacDonald, Peacock, & Anderson, 1992; Norbeck & Anderson, 1989b; O'Hara, 1986; Tietjen & Bradley, 1985; Tilden, 1983; Zuckerman, Amaro, Bauchner, & Cabral, 1989). However, most of the studies were cross-sectional, making it difficult to infer causality. In a study of low-income Latina, African-American, and European-American women in mid- to late pregnancy, Norbeck and Anderson (1989b) found both direct and buffering effects of prenatal support (measured in both functional and structural terms) on anxiety (Norbeck, Lindsey, & Calieri, 1981, 1983). Overall support accounted for a significant share of the variance in anxiety in both mid- and late pregnancy. In addition, individuals high in stress and low in spousal support were most likely to experience anxiety during pregnancy. Unlike other studies in this area, this study was longitudinal and the findings were obtained after controlling for marital status and ethnicity. Tilden (1983) reported similar findings for the relationship between support (emotional, informational, and tangible) and emotional disequilibrium, a composite index of state anxiety, trait anxiety, depression, and self-esteem, in a multiethnic sample of 141 women of whom 60% were European-American, 15% African-American, 11% Latina, 4% Filipino, 4% Japanese, and 5% other ethnicities. Consistent with Norbeck and Anderson (1989b), there was not a significant statistical interaction between support and life event stress in effects on emotional disequilibrium.

In a sample of 47 predominantly European-American women, Albrecht and Rankin (1989) found that social support was related to state and trait anxiety. In this study, support was measured as intimacy, nurturance, social integration, self worth, and guidance. Overall support was strongly negatively correlated with trait anxiety and marginally negatively correlated with state anxiety. These negative correlations may suggest either that anxious individuals perceive less support in their relationships or that lack of support leads to greater anxiety. These analyses did not control for income, marital status, or other potential confounding variables. Overall, these studies suggest that overall support is related to state and trait anxiety; yet more controlled investigations are necessary to draw causal inferences.

Thorpe et al. (1992) compared the impact of support on emotional well-being in a sample of 200 Greek and 156 British pregnant women. Emotional well-being was a composite index of depression, anxiety, and somaticism. Social support was predictive of the emotional well-being of British women. However, it did not predict the well-being of Greek women during pregnancy. For Greek women, stress (in the form of life events) was associated with emotional well-being. Social relationships appeared to be a source of stress for Greek women in this study, in that they reported stress in the families with whom they typically lived. The authors also indicated that social support may be appreciated less in Greece because Greek culture is a traditional one in which support is expected or assumed. This study points to the role of culture in understanding the relationship between support and emotional well-being.

Zuckerman et al. (1989) examined the effects of different types of support on depressive symptoms. In a low-income multiethnic sample, they measured tangible, emotional, and self-esteem support, as well as network members' feelings toward the woman's pregnancy. Total support and emotional support were negatively related to reports of depressive symptoms. Depression was also associated with women's perceiving their partners or families as unhappy with the pregnancy. These findings are consistent with the pattern of results from other studies on support and psychological functioning and thus further suggest that support facilitates greater psychological well-being during pregnancy. Like the other findings, however, the cross-sectional nature of these findings does not permit causal inferences to be made about the relation between support and indicators of psychological well-being.

Another set of findings has shown that marital status and spousal support are associated with lower levels of anxiety and depression (Hobfoll & Leiberman, 1987; Kalil, Gruber, Conley, & Syntiac, 1993; MacDonald et al., 1992; O'Hara, 1986; Tietjen & Bradley, 1985). In a study of 1431 white British pregnant women, MacDonald et al. (1992) observed that marital status is linked to life event stress and depression. They compared married women to cohabiting women, women living with other adults, and women on their own. Unmarried pregnant women tended to be less educated, of lower SES, younger, and more dependent on state support than married women. Married women were significantly less depressed during pregnancy than women in the other three groups, with women on their own experiencing the highest levels of depression. Those who lived on their own also experienced the most stressful life events, whereas married women had the least. Women living on their own during pregnancy were more likely to move, become homeless, have partners who were convicted or imprisoned, and have problems in their relationships with partners. Thus, women living alone during pregnancy (in Britain at least) are at greater risk of experiencing stress and depression than those living with others and, in particular, compared to married women.

The findings on marital status and psychological strain may be a function of the support women have received from their spouses during pregnancy. Several studies suggest that support from the spouse plays an important role in reducing stress, anxiety, and depression during pregnancy, compared to other sources of support. For example, one prospective study of 546 pregnant women found that women with supportive husbands had lower state and trait anxiety in each trimester (Kalil et al., 1993). Women with emotional confidantes, particularly female friends and relatives, had lower levels of anxiety as well.

In a prospective study of 99 predominantly European-American women, O'Hara (1986) measured the instrumental and emotional support women received from their spouses and confidantes. Depressed women reported significantly less support from their spouses, in particular instrumental support, and greater support from their confidantes, than nondepressed women. Support from spouses, particularly instrumental support, was negatively related to depression, whereas support from confidantes was positively related to depression in this sample. Tietjen and Bradley (1985) also found that spousal support, measured in terms of both amount of and satisfaction with support, was negatively related to prenatal depression. Satisfaction was also negatively associated with prenatal stress and anxiety. Support from network members, in contrast, was not significantly related to any indicators of well-being or adjustment.

The results of these studies suggest at least two potential relations between spousal support and depression. Depressed women may have more difficulty obtaining spousal support, or lack of spousal support may place women at greater risk of depression during pregnancy. There is some support for the latter relation in a large survey study addressing the support–adjustment relation (Kessler, Kendler, Heath, Neale, & Eaves, 1992). In this study, spousal support buffered the effects of stress on depression.

Two studies have attempted to understand how the relation between support and psychological adjustment differs for high- vs. low-risk women (Kemp & Hatmaker, 1989; Mercer & Ferketich, 1988). Kemp and Hatmaker (1989) found no differences in social support and anxiety between the two groups, yet found that satisfaction with partner support was associated with lower levels of anxiety in low-risk women only. For high-risk women, partner support was negatively correlated with norepinephrine levels, a presumed biochemical indicator of stress.

Mercer and Ferketich (1988) also found that support has different implications for high- vs. low-risk women. Consistent with the previous study, social support was associated with lower prenatal anxiety for low-risk women, yet not for high-risk women. Support was also a predictor of prenatal depression for low-risk women only. Thus, the findings from these two studies consistently reveal that for low-risk women, higher support is associated with greater psychological well-being. However, the relationship between support and well-being is not as clear for high-risk women. Mercer and Ferketich (1988) found that high-risk women reported more prenatal life event stress, anxiety, and depression, as well as more social support. These findings differ from those of Kemp and Hatmaker (1989), who observed no differences in social support and anxiety between high- and low-risk women. The results may be discrepant because the Mercer and Ferketich (1988) sample comprised older, middle- and upper-middle-class European-Americans whereas the Kemp and Hatmaker sample (1989) was composed of low-income African-Americans. Further research should be conducted to clarify these relations in high-risk women of different ethnic groups.

To summarize, it appears that support in general during pregnancy may be associated with greater psychological well-being. Marital status and spousal support are particularly important, in that they are strongly related to less stress, anxiety, and depression even when other sources of support are available. Some mixed results were obtained in these studies though, probably due to the differences between studies in sample size and ethnic composition and in conceptualization and measurement of social support. Furthermore, demographic variables are not always controlled in these studies. For instance, social support has been shown to be greater for middle-class women and lower for working-class women (Quine, Rutter, & Gowen, 1993), but social class is rarely considered. In addition, all the studies except one (Norbeck & Anderson, 1989b) were cross-sectional and thus cannot speak to the issues of causality. Strengths of these studies, however, are the use of multiethnic samples and largely the same measures of stress and anxiety.

Social Support and Prenatal Care

Another line of research has investigated the role of social support in the utilization of prenatal care (Giblin, Poland, & Ager, 1990; Higgins, Murray, & Williams, 1994; St. Clair, Smeriglio, Alexander, & Celentano, 1989; Zambrana, Dunkel-Schetter, & Scrimshaw, 1991; Zambrana, Scrimshaw, & Dunkel-Schetter, in press). Insomuch as prenatal care is predictive of better birth outcomes, it may be an important mediator of the association between prenatal support and birth outcomes. Theorists have proposed that social support can help women overcome obstacles to obtaining care such as lack of money to pay for care, lack of transportation, and problems getting time off work, as well as psychological obstacles such as the desire to not be pregnant and fear of seeking care. These obstacles may be particularly relevant for low-income women from ethnic and immigrant groups, who often initiate prenatal care much later in pregnancy (Brown, 1988). This points to the importance of considering ethnic and socioeconomic differences in prenatal care, as well as the role of support in reducing these barriers. The following studies examine the impact of support from the baby's father and family on utilization of prenatal care by different ethnic groups.

Several studies have found that support from the baby's father has a strong influence on utilization of prenatal care among women of different ethnic groups (Giblin et al., 1990; Sable, Stockbauer, Schramm, & Land, 1990; Zambrana et al., 1991; Zambrana et al., in press). In a study with a sample of 107 Mexican-immigrant, Mexican-American, and African-American women, Zambrana et al. (1991a) found that a woman's having a relationship with the baby's father was the strongest predictor of initiation of care, whereas support from friends and family was not associated with utilization. Zambrana et al. (in press) conducted a larger study of 525 Mexican-American, 764 Mexican-immigrant, and 255 African-American women. For Mexican immigrants and Mexican-Americans, initiation of care was significantly and positively associated with living with the baby's father. In contrast, living with the baby's father bore no relation to initiation of care by African-Americans, and living with relatives was associated with slower initiation of care.

Others have also found that support from the baby's father contributed to prenatal care utilization in large samples of low-income women. Giblin et al.

(1990) assessed support comprehensively by asking about sources and types of support in a sample of 300 predominantly African-American women. After demographics, health behaviors, and other support factors were controlled, "intimacy" and "comfort," involving tangible and emotional support received from the baby's father, were the only significant support variables to predict prenatal care initiation. Given that this study measured support receipt from the baby's father as compared to cohabitation with him (Zambrana et al., in press), or to the existence of a relationship with him (Zambrana et al., 1991a), and not with a single-item measure of support (Sable et al., 1990), we can assert with greater confidence that support from the baby's father is related to prenatal care for African-American as well as Latina women. Sable et al. (1990) obtained similar findings in a sample of 1464 women. Support from the baby's father was a stronger predictor of prenatal care than was support from others. Women were shown to have greater risk of receiving inadequate care if they were African-American, single, less educated, poor, having unwanted pregnancies, and higher parity. Thus, support from the baby's father appears to be particularly beneficial to low-income African-American women, who tend to obtain inadequate care.

Support from the family appears to influence prenatal care significantly less than support from the father, even among low-income groups who might depend more on their families for help with child care, transportation, and expenses (St. Clair et al., 1989; St. John & Winston, 1989; Zambrana et al., 1991a). Zambrana et al. (1991a) found that family support was not related to prenatal care among 107 African-American, Mexican-American, and Mexican-immigrant women. In a survey study with 733 women, 20% of whom were Native American or African-American, St. John and Winston (1989) found that family support was marginally related to use of prenatal care. The family's feelings about the pregnancy, however, moderated obstacles to care such as difficulty in paying, not wanting the pregnancy, and personal inconveniences in utilization of prenatal care. The direction of the statistical interactions suggested that for a woman who faced great obstacles to receiving care, the family's happiness with her pregnancy had the strongest effects on her receiving care. Although the family's feelings are not synonymous with social support receipt, they do reflect to some extent the nature of the woman's social environment during pregnancy. These findings reveal that aspects of the woman's environment can reduce obstacles to care, although family support alone cannot account for differences in utilization of prenatal care.

St. Clair et al. (1989) also had mixed findings on the role of family support in the timing and use of prenatal care in a sample of predominantly single African-American women. They hypothesized that women who had more structural support during pregnancy would seek prenatal care later and have fewer prenatal visits. Structural support was measured in terms of density and closeness of the social network. They found, however, that women with larger networks of relatives and more frequent contact with friends initiated prenatal care earlier and had more prenatal visits; network size was the strongest predictor of prenatal care utilization. Women who sought care later reported stronger emotional intimacy with their relatives. Emotional intimacy with relatives was also a significant predictor of the amount and timing of prenatal care. Given that these results were mixed, it is difficult to draw conclusions on family support from these findings.

In conclusion, the studies on prenatal care revealed that having a relationship with and receiving support from the baby's father were instrumental to obtaining adequate care for large multiethnic samples of different socioeconomic backgrounds. For Mexican-American, Mexican-immigrant, and African-American women, living with the baby's father and perceiving him as supportive were related to utilization of prenatal care. In studies that employed both functional and structural measures of support, family support did not appear to have as strong an impact on prenatal care utilization as spousal support. Limitations of these studies on prenatal care were that they relied on single-item measures of social support, did not control for demographics or structural barriers to care before assessing the role of support, and did not test for interaction effects between social support and obstacles to care in prenatal care utilization. Nonetheless, they are especially important because they studied large groups of ethnic-minority women in an attempt to explain differences in utilization of care in pregnancy.

Social Support and Health Behaviors during Pregnancy

Few studies have explored the relationship between social support and health behaviors such as drinking, smoking, and substance use during pregnancy (Aaronson, 1989; Albrecht & Rankin, 1989; Giblin et al., 1990; MacDonald et al., 1992). Given that the measures and methodologies of these studies differ, it is also difficult to draw any firm conclusions from the literature. Nevertheless, conducting research in this area can provide insight into possible avenues of prevention given the established relationship between substance use and a range of poor birth outcomes. Alcohol use has been associated with birth defects and fetal alcohol syndrome, and cigarette use has been linked to low birthweight, spontaneous abortion, and premature delivery (Archie, 1992).

In a study of 529 white and middle-class pregnant women, Aaronson (1989) measured the impact of social support on cigarette, alcohol, and caffeine use. She employed a measure of overall social support, the Personal Resources Questionnaire (PRQ; Brandt & Weinert, 1981), as well as measures of how family members felt about abstinence from substance use and how many people in the home drank, smoked, or consumed caffeine. The latter two sets of measures were significant predictors of use of all three substances, but the measure of general social support was not. This study suggests that attitudes of others toward substance use, as well as the patterns of use or nonuse of substances by others, contributes to use or abstinence in pregnant women. Overall support, however, does not appear to reduce substance use. In contrast, Albrecht and Rankin (1989) found that overall support (as measured with the PRQ) and alcohol use were significantly negatively correlated in 47 predominantly European-American women. Thus, social support appears to play a role in reducing substance use in pregnant women; however, which types of support will be the most effective in doing so is still left unclear.

In their study of 1431 white British pregnant women, MacDonald et al. (1992)

investigated the relations between marital status and health behaviors during pregnancy. They measured cigarette, alcohol, and caffeine use at three time points and measured consumption during the week prior to the interview. They found that significantly fewer married women smoked during pregnancy compared to cohabiting women and those living with other adults. Women on their own were most likely to be smokers and to smoke heavily. In terms of alcohol use, women living with other adults abstained from drinking alcohol during pregnancy as compared to married women and others. Women on their own were also the most frequent drinkers. There were no major differences in caffeine consumption among these groups. One major strength of this study was its use of longitudinal measures of health behaviors; however, support was not measured and cannot be inferred from marital status.

Giblin et al. (1990) conducted one of the few studies that examined support and health behaviors in a sample of African-American women. They factor analyzed items assessing different types of social support, and three factors emerged: intimacy (relationship with the baby's father), comfort (tangible and emotional support received), and security (feelings of safety and stability). They found that use of street drugs was negatively correlated with all three factors, and smoking and drinking were not correlated with any of them. The authors proposed that the use of drugs may lead to greater social isolation rather than the reverse causal direction. There may also be a third variable operating here, with demographics such as low income and ethnicity producing a spurious correlation between social support and drug use. By controlling for these factors, future studies can draw stronger conclusions about the relationship between support and health behaviors.

In conclusion, several steps by future researchers would benefit future research on the link between social support and health behaviors during pregnancy. First, longitudinal studies with prospective designs would enable researchers to assess the substance use over time and to observe fluctuations in use that might occur during pregnancy. Second, the use of standard measures of social support and substance use would be preferable to the variety of ad hoc measures found in the previous studies. Reliability of self-reports of use of substances is a constant concern requiring extra care in measurement. Urine screening and blood tests for substances including tobacco, alcohol, and drugs are more reliable and can identify the degree of underreporting, although they are expensive to conduct and can raise ethical issues that must be addressed fully. Third, more statistical controls are necessary, given that studies on social support and prenatal care have obtained markedly different results when they controlled for demographic variables (e.g., St. John & Winston, 1989). Finally, studies should include large samples of women of diverse SES and ethnic backgrounds in order to understand how the relationship between support and substance use differs in various populations.

Conclusion: Review of Research on Prenatal Social Support and Emotions and Behavior

The studies reviewed in this section examined the relations among social support measures, various indicators of psychological adjustment, and important behaviors during pregnancy. Support in general was associated with less stress, anxiety, and depression. Marital status and support from the baby's father were also related to the adjustment and behavior of women during pregnancy. Support from the baby's father tends to mitigate stress, anxiety, and depression and to improve prenatal care utilization in women from several ethnic groups. Family support and support from others is not as clearly related to positive adjustment, prenatal care, or health behaviors. In sum, it appears that general support and spousal support contribute most to positive attitudes and behavior during pregnancy.

IMPORTANCE OF CULTURE IN UNDERSTANDING
SOCIAL SUPPORT IN PREGNANCY

The foregoing literature review indicates that researchers are beginning to understand some of the significant benefits of support in pregnancy. However, we need to take a more sophisticated theoretical approach incorporating cultural variables to better understand racial and ethnic differences that have emerged in research. Cultural differences influence the definition and perception of social support, or the way individuals "give, get, accept, or reject it" (Jacobson, 1986, p. 259). Such differences may lead to profound disparities in the impact of apparently similar forms of support. According to Vaux (1985), "Social support processes are interwoven with the fabric of society and are undoubtedly related to macrosystem phenomena. That is, the extent, composition, and context of our social relationships are determined to some degree by cultural blueprints" (p. 90).

In particular, it is useful to consider value orientations as they shape the nature of close relationships in different cultures. In order to gain an understanding of the interaction between culture and support, it is important to compare support processes systematically across cultures that tend toward different value orientations. Therefore, in the following sections, we will discuss cultural issues, especially culturally variant value orientations, and how cross-cultural differences in value orientations affect close relationships, and potentially social support processes.

Background on the Study of Culture

Before we attempt to examine cultural differences in social support, it is important to conceptually distinguish among the three concepts of race, ethnicity, and culture, as these terms are often incorrectly used or used interchangeably. *Race* is defined by physical characteristics, usually common to an inbred, geographically isolated population, and is arguably arbitrary (Betancourt & Lopez, 1993; Jones, 1991; Zuckerman, 1990). If one considers the three conventionally distinguished "races" (Caucasoid, Negroid, Mongoloid), there is more within-group variability than between-group variability in behavior, indicating that racial groups are more alike than different (Zuckerman, 1990). Relying on race as a category can result in people's assuming that members of a group are more similar to each other than to members of another group (Allen & Wilder, 1979; Holtz & Miller, 1985; Miller & Brewer, 1986) and viewing members of groups more in conventional stereotypes (Wilder & Shapiro, 1991). *Ethnicity* refers to groups with common nationality, culture, or language (Betancourt & Lopez, 1993). As groups come into increasing contact, however, these distinctions become increasingly blurred. Culture is often conceptualized as the human-made part of the environment, or as a system of meanings that emerge in adaptive interaction and are learned, socially shared, and transmitted from one generation to another (Betancourt & Lopez, 1993; Triandis, 1994). Finally, *acculturation* refers to the process by which an individual who has moved from one culture into another incorporates the beliefs and customs of the second culture into his or her existing structure of beliefs and customs (Berry, 1990; Mendoza & Martinez, 1981; Padilla, 1980). Thus, acculturation tends to diffuse the influence of a person's original culture.

Differences that emerge between racial and ethnic groups are often attributed to cultural differences. This is a false assumption, however, as race and ethnicity are not interchangeable with culture. Much research in cross-cultural psychology has focused on identifying differences among groups, but has failed to identify the specific aspect of cultures or the mechanisms that may influence the behavior (Betancourt & Lopez, 1993). As a result, our knowledge of culture in psychology mainly consists of documentation of group differences in behavior, but little understanding of the underlying elements of cultures that lead to such differences. This situation is analogous to trends in early research on gender. Instead, we must identify those aspects of culture that may influence the behavior of people with different racial and ethnic backgrounds, and study why such differences in behavior affect a variety of outcomes, including experiences in pregnancy.

One way of conceptualizing the differences among cultures is by examining *value orientations*. A value orientation refers to the priorities or preferences for particular goals, such as familism and tradition in Mexican-American culture and autonomy and achievement in European-American culture. Specific cultures, and the individuals in that culture, usually express the particular value orientations of the culture, which functions as a group ideology and guides individual behavior (Kluckhohn, 1951; Schwartz, 1990, 1992; Schwartz & Bilsky, 1987; Triandis, 1989, 1994). Two value orientations that have received considerable attention in the literature are individualism and collectivism.

Individualism has been described as an orientation that values the independent, autonomous, self-sufficient individual who has a unique set of internal attributes and acts according to these attributes. In an individualistic culture, personal goals are placed above group goals as a means of self-actualization (Hui & Triandis, 1986; Markus & Kitayama, 1991; Triandis, 1989, 1994; Triandis et al., 1986). The United States and other English-speaking countries have been found to be particularly high on individualism (Hofstede, 1980). In contrast, *collectivism* has been described as an orientation that values the interdependent individual— one who views the self in relation or connection to the group and subordinates personal goals to the goals of the group in the pursuit of the common interest of the collectivity (Hui & Triandis, 1986; Markus & Kitayama, 1991; Triandis, 1994; Triandis et al., 1986). The countries of East Asia and Latin America have been found to be high on collectivism (Hofstede, 1980; Marin & Triandis, 1985).

Although cultures may exhibit similar patterns of attitudes and behavior due to these contrasting value orientations, most cultures incorporate different degrees of both individualism and collectivism. Given that humans are both individuals and members of groups, no one culture is entirely collectivist or individualist. Individualism and collectivism represent ideal patterns of social relations for different cultures. Individualism and collectivism have been viewed as "idealized cultural scripts" that lie on a continuum as end points for development and socialization (Greenfield, 1994). For example, individuals in some cultures may place greater importance on a few ingroups (e.g., the family and the organization in Japan), whereas others consider only one ingroup as extremely important (e.g., the family in Hispanic cultures) (Triandis, 1994).

In addition, individualism or collectivism can be viewed not only as a cultural variable expressed at the societal level, but also as an individual variable expressed as a personality attribute. Individuals in a society will differ in the degree to which they conform to the societal standard of individualism or collectivism. Therefore, individualism and collectivism can be viewed as individual variables in addition to being societal-level variables (Markus & Kitayama, 1991; Triandis, Bontempo, & Villareal, 1988; Triandis, McCusker, & Hui, 1990). Individualism refers to the aforementioned value orientation as expressed at the societal level. Corresponding to this value orientation is a personality attribute often found in individuals of individualist cultures referred to as *idiocentrism*. Similarly, the personality attribute that corresponds to cultural collectivism is referred to as *allocentrism*. Research indicates that within cultures, individuals who are allocentric tend to receive more social support than those who are idiocentric (Triandis, 1989, 1994). By making this distinction, we can then also consider the case of the allocentric person in an individualistic culture or of the idiocentric person in a collectivist culture (Triandis et al., 1990). This consideration becomes increasingly important as individuals from collectivist cultures immigrate to individualistic cultures and experience being allocentric in a society that values individualism. For example, a pregnant woman who has recently immigrated from Mexico to the United States may experience stress from having an allocentric orientation in an individualistic culture. However, she may receive more support from others in her cultural group than pregnant women who are not from a collectivist culture.

We wish to emphasize that there are advantages and disadvantages to both individualism and collectivism. Although a collectivist orientation stressing interdependence among members of the ingroup may lead to higher levels of social support for allocentric individuals, this support often comes at the expense of expressing one's individual needs and goals, which may change over time when one lives in an individualistic culture. In contrast, idiocentric individuals in an individualistic culture benefit from the expression of individual needs and goals, but at the expense of ties to an interdependent network of family and friends. These issues may be of special importance during pregnancy.

Social Support and Culture

Like research in other areas, most social support research has not addressed the question of value orientations, but rather has separated individuals according to ethnic or racial background and made inferences about cultural differences. In order to understand the differences that do emerge, however, it is necessary to focus on value orientations. There is evidence to suggest that social support varies among cultures and ethnic groups as a function of collectivist vs. individualist value orientation. Given that the nature of our social relationships arises from the ways in which our cultures are structured and the norms that guide them, it is not surprising that these orientations are linked to cultural and ethnic differences.

The relationship between culture and social support becomes more complex when we consider individuals who immigrate to new countries. For immigrants, the interaction between these two variables is compounded by factors such as the stress of being a minority, isolation from one's own culture, language difficulties, and generation gap from ancestral country. Our ability to generalize from the ancestral culture may be limited depending upon whether the migration was voluntary or involuntary, the number of family members that immigrated, available community support, ability to maintain language, economic pressures, social pressures to alter traditional values, and urbanization. It is important, however, not to underestimate the possible influence of ancestral culture on patterns of social support in groups that have migrated. Much of the research indicates some stability in the norms and values regarding social support between Africans and African-Americans, between Asians and Asian-Americans, and between Latin Americans living in the United States and those living in their native country (Greenfield, 1994).

Given that immigrants come to their host countries under varied conditions, acculturation is another cultural variable that needs to be measured on an individual level. Measures of acculturation usually involve assessment of language preference and years since immigrating, as well as other variables. These measures allow researchers to assess the degree to which immigrants maintain the values and normative behavior of their ancestral cultures and accommodate to those of the new culture. In the following studies, some ethnic differences emerge in social support during pregnancy that are consistent with previous research on Latino culture. A few of the findings are paradoxical, however, contradicting common assumptions about Latino culture. Differences in acculturation may account for these inconsistencies; that is, acculturation may operate as a modifier of the relationship between ethnicity and social support. For this reason, we believe that measures of acculturation must be incorporated into future studies of ethnicity and social support to clarify the issues.

Latin Cultures and Social Support

Early research on Hispanics in the United States and anthropological research in Latin America has indicated that a strong interdependent orientation exists in Latin cultures (Marin & Triandis, 1985). The collective orientation of Latinos involves one primary group or collective—the extended family (Knouse, 1991). This is called *familism*, which places the family and community life as the primary source of identity and support, with values and behaviors reflecting the importance of the family for the individual as well as the relative emphasis and priority given to the needs of the family (O. Ramirez & Arce, 1981; Roland, 1988; Rothman, Gant, & Hnat, 1985; Zuniga, 1992). In the Mexican-American community, familism is characterized by an extended family system involving relatively strong and extensive bonds beyond the nuclear family, including grandparents, uncles, aunts, cousins, siblings, godparents, and friends (Chilman, 1993; O. Ramirez & Arce, 1981; Valle & Bensussen, 1985; Vega, 1990; Zuniga, 1992). Families usually live in nuclear households, with networks of families interconnected, resulting in clusters of interdependent nuclear families (Keefe, 1984; O. Ramirez & Arce, 1981; Sena-Rivera, 1979; Vega, 1990). Mexican-Americans have been shown to exhibit higher levels of familism than African-Americans or European-Americans (Keefe, Padilla, & Carlos, 1978; Mindel, 1980).

Traditionally, the Mexican-American family has been characterized as patriarchal. Although the ideal of patriarchy still exists in most families, the stereotype of a male-dominated family and rigid sex and age grading is no longer accurate (Baca-Zinn, 1980; O. Ramirez & Arce, 1981). Sex roles are not as rigidly defined, although fathers are regarded as more dominant and concerned with matters outside the home, whereas mothers are more concerned with matters within the home (Baca-Zinn, 1980; Chilman, 1993; Ybarra, 1982). Research suggests that the stereotype of *machismo* (absolute patriarchy, flamboyant masculinity, and sexual virility) is an exaggerated misrepresentation of the actual Latino male sex role (Mirande, 1977; Valdez, 1980; Ybarra-Soriano, 1977). That role is better defined in terms of respect, honesty, loyalty, responsibility, and courage (Alvirez & Bean, 1976; R. Ramirez, 1979). Furthermore, as more Latina women are working outside the home, more egalitarian family patterns are emerging, reflected by joint decision making and fathers contributing more at home (Baca-Zinn, 1980; Chilman, 1993; Cromwell & Ruiz, 1979; Mirande, 1979; O. Ramirez & Arce, 1981; Ybarra, 1982). Latino couples reporting more egalitarian roles also report more marital satisfaction (Bean, Curtis, & Marcum, 1977; Chilman, 1993).

The primary source of emotional support for Latinos often comes from within the extended family network (Keefe, Padilla, & Carlos, 1979). One study suggests that Hispanics are more willing to sacrifice for the family, exhibit strong feelings of attachment, loyalty, and solidarity with family members, and tend to socialize more with family and friends than with coworkers (Knouse, 1991). They emphasize personal cooperation and help and exhibit more positive behaviors in interpersonal situations than do European-Americans (Triandis et al., 1984). Furthermore, Latinos tend to have less extensive friendship networks than European-Americans, yet have deeper friendships with people of similar ethnic backgrounds. These friendships are an important source of social support.

Social support from the extended family plays a particularly important role in the process of immigration and acculturation. Latinos tend to migrate toward kin networks to ensure links to their national and international community. Support can be critical to adaptation in terms both of developing relations with members of the host country and of accessing ethnic networks (Salgado de Snyder, 1987). Immigration results ipso facto in a strong reduction in interpersonal relationships, especially with those who are most supportive of the immigrants' beliefs and values. Thus, immigrants may lose support when it is most valuable (Baptiste, 1993; Salgado de Snyder, 1987). Some researchers have argued, however, that Mexicans experience a relatively stress-free migration due to available social support in the United States (Guendelman, 1988; Sabogal, Marion, Otero-Sabogal, Marin, & Perez-Stable, 1987). Nonetheless, research indicates that recent immigrants report less available support from friends and relatives and are less satisfied than Mexican-Americans and European-Americans and at higher risk for psychopathology (Vega & Kolody, 1985). Furthermore, women high in ethnic loyalty report having less social support, lower self-esteem, lower satisfaction with social support, and higher acculturative stress (Salgado de Snyder, 1987).

As Mexican-Americans undergo the process of acculturation, conflict arises over how to accommodate traditional Mexican values and American values. The brunt of this struggle falls mainly on first- and second-generation Mexican-Americans. Furthermore, the longer a family is in the United States, the more it must use the English language. Second-generation Mexican-Americans may lose their facility in Spanish, thus resulting in conflict and weaker ties to the family unit (Chilman, 1993; Rothman et al., 1985). In addition, acculturation may alter traditional support networks among Hispanic immigrant groups. Some researchers have argued that as Mexican-Americans become more acculturated and develop more extensive friendship networks, their degree of familism will decrease. However, support for this contention is mixed (Knouse, 1991; Sabogal et al., 1987; Triandis, Marin, Betancourt, & Chang, 1982), and Zuniga (1992) argues that one of the last value stances immigrants give up is their sense of familism and family loyalty. We believe that the concepts of acculturation and of individualism–collectivism are key to understanding social support patterns in Latino cultures.

Research on Ethnic and Cultural Differences in Social Support in Pregnancy

Pregnancy offers a unique opportunity to examine how the social networks of different cultures and ethnic groups respond to a woman during an important transition in her life, one that is often very challenging psychologically and physically. Because it is universal across cultures, and thus has relevance to all women, pregnancy differs from other culture-specific events. It also carries some symbolic value, in that it involves planning for the arrival of a new and unique member of the social system, which may carry different meanings in individualist vs. collectivist cultures. This event reflects the way a network responds to the inclusion of a new member and the changes in social structure that come with it. Thus, the social support provided during this event provides some insight into the nature of the culture; at the same time, knowledge of the values and practices of the culture will allow us to make some predictions about social support during pregnancy. We have just discussed differences in social support in Latino populations and now will examine how these differences generalize to support during pregnancy.

Studies have revealed ethnic differences in social support receipt, satisfaction, need for support, and sources of support during pregnancy. Some studies have been conducted with solely or mostly Latina pregnant women (Engle, Scrimshaw, Zambrana, & Dunkel-Schetter, 1990; Scrimshaw, Engle, Arnold, & Haynes, 1987; Scrimshaw, Zambrana, & Dunkel-Schetter, in press; Zambrana, Dunkel-Schetter, Collins, & Scrimshaw, 1994; Zayas & Busch-Rossnagel, 1992). Three studies have measured support receipt during pregnancy with comparisons of Latinas, African-Americans, and European-Americans (Dunkel-Schetter, Lobel, Collins, & Scrimshaw, 1994; Norbeck & Anderson, 1989a; Wasserman, Rauh, Brunelli, Garcia-Castro, & Necos, 1990). Insomuch as our focus is mainly on Latinas and comparative work, this section of the review may be incomplete with respect to studies of other groups.

Social Support during Pregnancy among Latinas

A few studies have concentrated primarily on the Latina pregnant population and have begun to address differences in social support due to acculturation for this group (Engle et al., 1990; Scrimshaw et al., 1987, in press; Zambrana, Dunkel-Schetter, Collins, & Scrimshaw, 1994; Zayas & Busch-Rossnagel, 1992). They generally find that both the baby's father and female relatives provide the most support during pregnancy, yet there are some differences between Mexican-Americans and Mexican immigrants. Mexican-Americans receive more family support and Mexican immigrants receive more spousal support. Most research in this area has failed to measure support comprehensively by assessing all types of support, satisfaction with support, needs for support, and sources of support. Future research on support for Latina women could benefit from assessing social support in this multidimensional manner.

Spousal Support. Latina women are generally more likely to be married and to live with the baby's father than women from other ethnic groups. Studies of Latinas during pregnancy suggest that partners and spouses are critical sources of support to women of different national origins and ages. The role of the father as a major provider of support during pregnancy has been reported in studies of Mexican-American women (Lantican & Corona, 1992), as well as Puerto Rican, Central American, and South American women (Zayas & Busch-Rossnagel, 1992). Zayas and Busch-Rossnagel (1992) also found that 50% of both adolescent and older Latina mothers reported that the baby's father was supportive and involved in their pregnancies. Thus, support from the baby's father appears to be an important resource for Latina women in these descriptive studies; however, there are no comparison data to suggest that spousal support for Latinas differs from that for pregnant women of other ethnic groups.

In a study on acculturation and psychosocial mediators of birth outcomes in Mexican women, Zambrana, Dunkel-Schetter, Collins, and Scrimshaw (1994) found that acculturation affected the amount of support from the baby's father. Based on interviews with 911 Mexican-American and Mexican-immigrant low-income pregnant women, the results indicated that Mexican-immigrant women were more likely to live with and be married to the baby's father than were Mexican-American women. Mexican-American women received less support from the baby's father and were more likely to experience stress than Mexican-immigrant women. This study also found that for both Mexican-American and Mexican-immigrant women, support from the baby's father was associated with significantly less stress, less substance use, and more positive attitudes toward pregnancy. More acculturated women reported more drug and alcohol use, felt more negative about their pregnancies, and experienced more stressful life events such as being fired from a job or being arrested.

The UCLA Birth Project was conducted with 291 low-risk primiparous women of Mexican origin, a majority of whom were recent immigrants. Significant associations between support from the baby's father and behaviors in pregnancy were reported in several papers (Scrimshaw et al., in press; Engle et al., 1990). For example, support from the baby's father was significantly positively related to the initiation of prenatal care and the number of prenatal visits (Scrimshaw et al., in press). Scrimshaw et al. (1987) also showed that support from the baby's father was related positively to duration of breast feeding. Thus, support from the baby's father appears to be linked to at least some healthier attitudes and behaviors during pregnancy for unacculturated Latinas.

Family Support.   Studies that focus on support for pregnant Latinas reveal that the family, particularly female relatives, is a critical source of support in pregnancy. In a study by Lantican and Corona (1992), 42 Filipino and 42 Mexican-American women having their first birth completed the Norbeck Social Support Questionnaire (Norbeck et al., 1981, 1983), which involved ranking different sources of support. Mothers and sisters were listed as the major sources of affection, affirmation, and aid. Similar findings were obtained in a study of pregnant Latinas of mixed backgrounds and ages (Zayas & Busch-Rossnagel, 1992). For 24% of older women in the sample and 40% of adolescents, mothers provided support during pregnancy. Female relatives and friends were also found to be supportive of half of older women and two thirds of teens. Neither of these studies provides comparative data on ethnic differences. However, they are consistent with the finding of Norbeck and Anderson (1989a) that suggests that Latinas receive more support from their mothers as compared to African-Americans and European-Americans. Latinas also prefer to have their mothers or sisters with them during labor and delivery (Scrimshaw et al., in press). Since many studies do not ask specifically about support from female relatives during pregnancy, they may conceal these cultural variations in reliance on different sources of support.

Although Mexican-American women are less likely to live with and receive support from the baby's father than are Mexican immigrants (Zambrana, Dunkel-Schetter, Collins, & Scrimshaw, 1994), they are more likely to receive support from their families. While immigrants often rely heavily on their spouses when they first arrive, their family network builds over time with the arrival of other relatives from Mexico and births in their own family. The UCLA Birth Project findings showed that support from family was associated with less prenatal and postnatal anxiety (Engle et al., 1990). Family support was also associated with less desire for pain medication during labor, expectations for a more active role during labor, and greater knowledge of childbirth. In particular, support from female family members is presumably associated with these aspects of labor and childbirth, given that these members are preferred companions during childbirth and have more knowledge than male relatives. Thus, family support from female relatives is a critical resource during pregnancy and delivery particularly for Mexican-American women.

Comparative Studies on Ethnic Differences in Social Support

Norbeck and Anderson (1989a) conducted a comparative study with 208 low-income Latina, African-American, and European-American women to measure psychosocial predictors of pregnancy outcomes. Although the study was primarily concerned with the relationship between social support and pregnancy outcomes, exploratory descriptive analyses revealed different patterns of social support among women of these ethnic groups. A multidimensional measure of social support, the aforementioned Norbeck Social Support Questionnaire (Norbeck et al., 1981, 1983), was employed to assess the amount of emotional and tangible support received, as well as sources of support including the spouse or partner, mother, other relatives, and friends. Latinas reported the lowest levels of emotional and tangible support, whereas the means were somewhat higher for African-Americans and highest for European-Americans. Latinas also indicated receiving the least support from relatives and the least support from friends, and they had the smallest support network compared to African-Americans and European-Americans. In contrast, Latinas received greater spousal support and support from their mothers than women in the other two groups. These findings should be regarded as tentative, given that significance tests were not used to test ethnic differences in social support.

The lack of overall support received by Latinas in the Norbeck and Anderson (1989a) study may be related to the finding that they reported experiencing much less stress than European-American and African-American women during pregnancy. The authors proposed that because the lives of these women improved with immigration, they perceived less stress than they had preimmigration. However, acculturation was not factored in; thus, its impact on levels of stress or perceptions of support is unknown. An alternative explanation is that Latinas may underreport levels of support as compared to individuals from other cultures because such support is expected in more traditional cultures (Thorpe et al., 1992) and is not as salient. In other words, the frame of reference or the threshold for perceiving and reporting instances of support may be different in different cultures. We have also considered the possibility that individuals from collectivist cultures do indeed *receive* less support but perceive that they have more. These possibilities merit investigation.

The UCLA Psychosocial Factors in Pregnancy Project, conducted by Dunkel-Schetter, Scrimshaw, and Lobel (Dunkel-Schetter et al., 1994; Lobel, Dunkel-Schetter, & Scrimshaw, 1991), involved a sample of 136 Latina, 53 African-American, and 52 European-American low-income pregnant women who were interviewed many times during their pregnancies. Measures of social support comparable to those in the preceding study were employed. Material, task, emotional, and informational types of support received were assessed (Collins et al., 1993). Subjects were asked who provided each type of support, how much they needed of each type, and how satisfied they were with each type of support received. The following results of tests of ethnic differences in social support have not been published previously.

Consistent with the findings of Norbeck and Anderson (1989a), Latina women received the least total support compared to African-American and European-American women in this study, and these differences were particularly strong for material and task help. European-Americans received the most total support and African-Americans received intermediary levels. However, African-American women received the most material support during pregnancy, followed by European-Americans and then Latinas. There were no ethnic differences found in emotional and informational support received or in levels of stress. Although it may appear that Latinas' networks were not providing an adequate amount of overall support, they reported significantly less need for support. Latinas also reported a marginally higher level of satisfaction with overall support (in particular informational support) than the other two groups. These findings suggest that Latinas may be receiving less overall support due to their having less need for support and their feelings of greater satisfaction with support received than women of other ethnic groups.

The findings from the UCLA Psychosocial Factors in Pregnancy Project on ethnic differences in total or overall support may also be related to ethnic differences in coping strategies used during late pregnancy. This study measured the extent to which pregnant women used planful problem solving, information seeking, visualization, and distancing to cope with the anxiety of impending childbirth. Latinas were the most likely to use distancing and the least likely to use information-seeking strategies compared to African-Americans and European-Americans. These findings suggest an additional factor in understanding the social support results reported above—specifically, that Latinas may be receiving somewhat less support during pregnancy due to their different attitudes and ways of coping with childbirth. In trying to understand the various patterns of support in different groups, it may be important to consider differences among different ethnic groups in attitudes toward pregnancy and toward methods of coping with the many stresses involved.

Consistent with the findings of Norbeck and Anderson (1989a), the results from the UCLA Psychosocial Factors in Pregnancy Project indicate that the baby's father was identified as the major provider of support to Latinas. Latinas reported the highest levels of emotional support from the baby's father, followed by European-Americans and then African-American women. The findings on spousal support may be related to the finding that Latinas were significantly more likely to be married to and living with the baby's father, whereas African-American women were least likely to be married to or cohabiting with the father. African-American women received support primarily from relatives, whereas European-Americans depended on friends, relatives, and the baby's father for different types of support. A measure of satisfaction with health care provider support (emotional support, information, and overall care received) was also employed. Latinas reported the highest levels of satisfaction with health care provider support, followed by African-Americans and European-Americans.

The UCLA Psychosocial Factors in Pregnancy Project also included structural measures of support, including number of friends and relatives, frequency of contact with both, and satisfaction with relationships with friends and family (Collins et al., 1993). No ethnic differences were shown in family network size, frequency of contact with family members, or satisfaction with family relationships. However, Latinas reported the largest friendship networks and the most frequent contact with friends. This apparent conflict with other studies showing that Latinas rely more on family and less on friends may be due to having a more acculturated sample. Further investigation in this and other studies on acculturation will aid in our understanding of how support is related to acculturation and more directly to cultural norms and values.

Wasserman et al. (1990) investigated differences in support receipt among adolescent and adult mothers of Latina and African-American descent. They measured types of general support including guidance, tangible, emotional, and social support, as well as prenatal support, or support specifically related to the needs of pregnant women. Whereas the Latinas in the UCLA Psychosocial Factors in Pregnancy Project (Dunkel-Schetter et al., 1994) were of mixed national origins and acculturation levels, Latinas in this sample were primarily first-generation immigrants and were from either the Dominican Republic or Puerto Rico. Wasserman et al. (1990) hypothesized that Latinas, due to their low level of acculturation, would receive less support and have smaller social networks than African-Americans. Consistent with this hypothesis, the findings revealed that Latina women reported significantly less guidance, emotional support, and tangible support than African-American women. Differences were not found, however, in prenatal support or assistance in obtaining prenatal care. These findings again reveal that Latinas are likely to receive less support than African-American and presumably European-American women. However, the degree to which acculturation may account for these differences could not be determined, given that it was not measured directly.

In conclusion, differences in amount of support receipt and in sources of support are evident in both comparative studies of Latinas, African-Americans, and European-Americans and studies of Latinas who differ in levels of acculturation. Overall support appears to be lower for Latinas compared to other ethnic groups; however, they sometimes report less stress, less need for support, and greater satisfaction with the support they receive. They may also be less anxious about pregnancy in particular, given more positive attitudes toward pregnancy in Latina women (Zambrana, Dunkel-Schetter, Scrimshaw, & Collins, 1995). In general, Latina women are more likely to be married to the baby's father and to receive more support from the baby's father than women in other minority ethnic groups. However, whereas Mexican immigrants report greater support from the baby's father, Mexican-Americans receive support from their families. Support from both the baby's father and the family is associated with positive attitudes and healthy behaviors in pregnancy. Thus, differences in support provision may vary due not only to ethnicity, but also to acculturation, which points to the importance of understanding the influence of culture in the provision of support.

In the previous sections, we outlined ethnic and racial differences in social support. Although the studies discussed did not include measures of culture, we can speculate about the ethnic differences that emerged on the basis of information about levels of acculturation and the value orientation of Latino cultures. For example, within Latina samples, both spousal support and family support were valued by, and were beneficial to, Mexican-immigrant and Mexican-American women. However, the Mexican immigrants received more spousal support, whereas the Mexican-Americans received more family support. This distinction may suggest that immigrants experience a reduction in the size of their social networks, but that their social networks grow as their time in the Untied States grows longer. Despite these changes during the acculturation process, familism appears to be valued by both groups.

When Latinas were compared to women of other ethnic and racial backgrounds, they were found to receive less social support than European-American and African-American women, yet to indicate less need for support and greater satisfaction with received support. Several explanations may account for this difference. First, Latinas may perceive their lives in the Untied States as better than their lives in Mexico and therefore experience less stress and need less social support. Second, Latinas may underreport their levels of received support, as compared to individuals from other cultures, because support is expected in collectivistic cultures and Latinas' thresholds for recognizing support may therefore be higher than those of women from other cultural groups. Third, Latinas report having smaller social networks than women from other groups and therefore may have less opportunity to receive support. Finally, it could be that other variables such as attitudes, ways of coping, or health behaviors mediate or modify the relations between ethnicity and social support during pregnancy. These competing explanations warrant investigation.

CONCLUSION

Social support during pregnancy appears to exert beneficial influences on the behavior, emotions, and outcomes of pregnant women. However, precise specification of these effects, particularly specification of the circumstances under which they are strongest, must await future research with clearer conceptualization of critical concepts, psychometrically sound measures, and rigorous research designs. This line of research has advanced to the point where different questions can now be asked: Who most needs social support during pregnancy? Which types of support are most beneficial to which groups of women? Who is best able to provide social support to women of different ethnic and cultural groups? Do women experiencing different stressors in pregnancy require different supportive interventions? How are supportive interventions best delivered? The benefits to finding answers to these questions are threefold. First, a greater understanding of support in pregnancy can contribute to advancement of basic scientific research on social support and health in general. Second, such information may contribute to efforts to reduce rates of adverse physical and psychological outcomes for mothers and infants. Finally, reduction of adverse outcomes such as low birthweight may provide cost savings in medical care during labor and delivery and in pediatrics.

In this chapter, we emphasized the need for focusing on ethnic and cultural issues integral to social support processes during pregnancy. However, there is also a pressing need to integrate research on social support in pregnancy with existing knowledge of close relationships, particularly the marital relationship. Researchers of close relationships have highlighted the need to integrate these two bodies of work (Duck, 1990; Kelley et al., 1983). We wholeheartedly agree with this recommendation with respect to research on pregnancy in particular. The understanding of culture and the understanding of close relationships are inextricably tied by the concept of interdependence (Kelley et al., 1983). The level of interdependence valued in a particular culture is a primary determinant of the level of interdependence in relationships within that culture. This being the case, behavior in close relationships is influenced by culturally determined value orientations (Dion & Dion, 1993). Embracing the concept of *embedded contextualism*, and striving to understand the individual within the context of the family (or close relationship), and the individual and family within the context of their culture, will aid in the research process (Szapocznik & Kurtines, 1993).

Furthermore, research on close relationships indicates that support in different role relationships may be associated with different outcomes. For example, information or emotional support provided by a parent to a pregnant teen may be received differently than these forms of support from a peer. However, these social roles alone do not capture important aspects of relationships, including quality, level of intimacy, commitment, and satisfaction. Such qualitative aspects of relationships undoubtedly influence the nature of supportive interactions in important ways as well, and deserve further attention.

In conclusion, we believe that the study of pregnancy offers a superb venue for social support research to explore issues concerning the family. Yet only by blending knowledge from research in health psychology, cultural psychology, and close relationships can we hope to progress.

ACKNOWLEDGMENTS

All authors contributed equally to this chapter. We would like to thank Dr. Patricia Greenfield and Dr. Nancy Collins for helpful contributions to the development of this work. National Institute of Mental Health training grant MH15750 provided funding for Dr. Sagrestano, Ms. Feldman, and Ms. Killingsworth as trainees in the Health Psychology Program at UCLA. Research reported in the chapter was funded by a March of Dimes grant to the first author. In addition, Dr. Dunkel-Schetter's research collaborations and NIH grants with Calvin Hobel, M.D. (R01 HD29553), Curt Sandman, Ph.D., and Pathik Wadhwa, Ph.D., M.D. (R01 HD210413), and with Ruth Zambrana, Ph.D., and Susan Scrimshaw, Ph.D. (HS/HD 05518), have contributed to the development of this work.

REFERENCES

Aaronson, L. S. (1989). Perceived and received support: Effects on health behavior during pregnancy. *Nursing Research, 38(1)*, 4–9.

Albrecht, S. A., & Rankin, M. (1989). Anxiety levels, health behaviors, and support systems of pregnant women. *Maternal–Child Nursing Journal, 18(1)*, 49–60.

Allen, V. L., & Wilder, D. A. (1979). Group categorization and attribution of belief similarity. *Small Group Behavior, 10*, 73–80.

Alvirez, D., & Bean, F. D. (1976). The Mexican American family. In C. H. Mindel & R. W. Habenstein (Eds.), *Ethnic families in America: Patterns and variations.* New York: Elsevier.

Andresen, P. A., & Telleen, S. L. (1992). The relationship between social support and maternal behaviors and attitudes: A meta-analytic review. *American Journal of Community Psychology, 20*, 753–774.

Archie, C. (1992). Licit and illicit drug use in pregnancy. In N. Hacker & J. G. Moore (Eds.), *Essentials of Obstetrics and Gynecology*, 2nd ed. Philadelphia: W. B. Saunders.

Baca-Zinn, M. (1980). Gender and ethnic identity among Chicanos. *Frontiers, 5*, 18–24.

Baptiste, D. A. (1993). Immigrant families, adolescence, and acculturation: Insights for therapists. *Marriage and Family Review, 19*, 341–363.

Barrera, M., & Balls, P. (1983). Assessing social support as a prevention resource: An illustrative study. *Prevention in Human Services, 2*, 59–74.

Bean, F. D., Curtis, R. L., Jr., & Marcum, J. P. (1977). Familism and marital satisfaction among Mexican Americans: The effects of family size, wife's labor force participation, and conjugal power. *Journal of Marriage and the Family, 39*, 759–767.

Berkowitz, G. S., & Kasl, S. V. (1983). The role of psychosocial factors in spontaneous preterm delivery. *Journal of Psychosomatic Research, 27*, 283–290.

Berry, J. W. (1990). Psychology of acculturation. In J. W. Berry, J. G. Draguns, & M. Cole (Eds.), *Nebraska Symposium on Motivation* (pp. 201–234), Lincoln: University of Nebraska Press.

Betancourt, H., & Lopez, S. R. (1993). The study of culture, ethnicity, and race in American psychology. *American Psychologist, 48*, 629–637.

Blondel, B., Breart, G., Llado, J., & Chartier, M. (1990). Evaluation of the home-visiting system for women with threatened preterm labor: Results of a randomized controlled trial. *European Journal of Obstetrics & Gynecology and Reproductive Biology, 34*, 47–58.

Boyce, W. T., Schaefer, C., & Uitti, C. (1985). Permanence and change: Psychosocial factors in the outcome of adolescent pregnancy. *Social Science and Medicine, 21*, 1279–1287.

Brandt, P. A., & Weinert, C. (1981). The PRQ: A social support measure. *Nursing Research, 30*, 277–280.

Brown, S. S. (Ed.). (1988). *Reaching mothers, reaching infants.* Washington, DC: National Academy Press.

Bryce, R. L., Stanley, F. J., & Garner, J. B. (1991). Randomized controlled trial of antenatal social support to prevent preterm birth. *British Journal of Obstetrics and Gynaecology, 98,* 1001–1008.

Caplan, G. (1974). Support systems. In G. Caplan (Ed.), *Support systems and community mental health: Lectures on concept development* (pp. 1–40). New York: Behavioral Publications.

Casper, L. M., & Hogan, D. P. (1990). Family networks in prenatal and postnatal health. *Social Biology, 37,* 84–101.

Cassel, J. (1976). The contribution of the social environment to host resistance. *American Journal of Epidemiology, 104,* 107–123.

Chilman, C. S. (1993). Hispanic families in the United States. In H. P. McAdoo (Ed.), *Family ethnicity: Strength in diversity.* Newbury Park, CA: Sage Publications.

Cobb, S. (1976). Social support as a moderator of life stress. *Psychosomatic Medicine, 38,* 300–314.

Cohen, S., & McKay, G. (1984). Social support, stress, and the buffering hypothesis: A theoretical analysis. In A. Baum, J. E. Singer, & S. E. Taylor (Eds.), *Handbook of psychology and health,* Vol. 4 (pp. 253–263). Hillsdale, NJ: Lawrence Erlbaum.

Cohen, S., & Syme, S. L. (1985). Issues in the study and application of social support. In S. Cohen & S. L. Syme (Eds.), *Social support and health* (pp. 3–22). San Diego: Academic Press.

Collins, N. L., Dunkel-Schetter, C., Lobel, M., and Scrimshaw, S. C. M. (1993). Social support in pregnancy: Psychosocial correlates of birth outcomes and postpartum depression. *Journal of Personality and Social Psychology, 65(6),* 1243–1258.

Cromwell, R. E., & Ruiz, R. A. (1979). The myth of macho dominance in decision making with Mexican and Chicano families. *Hispanic Journal of Behavioral Sciences, 1,* 355–373.

Dion, K. K., & Dion, K. L. (1993). Individualistic and collectivistic perspectives on gender and the cultural context of love and intimacy. *Journal of Social Issues, 49,* 53–69.

Duck, S. W. (Ed.) (1990). *Personal relationships and social support.* London: Sage Publications.

Dunkel-Schetter, C., & Bennett, T. L. (1990). Differentiating the cognitive and behavioral aspects of social support. In B. R. Sarason, I. G. Sarason, & G. R. Pierce (Eds.), *Social support: An interactional view* (pp. 267–296). New York: Wiley.

Dunkel-Schetter, C., Blasband, D., Feinstein, L. G., & Herbert, T. L. (1992). Elements of supportive interactions: When are attempts to help effective? In S. Spacapan & S. Oskamp (Eds.), *Helping and being helped in the real world* (pp. 83–114). Newbury Park, CA: Sage Publications.

Dunkel-Schetter, C., Feinstein, L. G., & Call, J. (1986). UCLA Social Support Inventory. Unpublished manuscript. UCLA.

Dunkel-Schetter, C., Folkman, S., & Lazarus, R. S. (1987). Correlates of social support receipt. *Journal of Personality and Social Psychology, 53(1),* 71–80.

Dunkel-Schetter, C., Lobel, M., Collins, N., Scrimshaw, S. C. M., & Hobel, C. (1995). Psychosocial risk factors in prenatal public-clinic patients associated with birth outcomes. Unpublished manuscript. UCLA.

Elbourne, D., & Oakley, A. (1991). An overview of trials of social support during pregnancy. In H. Berendes, S. Kessel, & S. Yaffee (Eds.), *Advances in the prevention of low birthweight: An international symposium* (pp. 203–223). Washington, DC: National Center for Education in Maternal and Child Health.

Elbourne, D., Oakley, A., & Chalmers, I. (1989). Social and psychological support during pregnancy. In I. Chalmers, M. Enkin, & M. J. N. C. Keirse (Eds.), *Effective care in pregnancy and childbirth,* Vol. 1, *Pregnancy* (pp. 221–236). Oxford: Oxford University Press.

Engle, P. L., Scrimshaw, S. C., Zambrana, R. E., and Dunkel-Schetter, C. (1990). Prenatal and postnatal anxiety in Mexican women giving birth in Los Angeles. *Health Psychology, 9(3),* 285–299.

Forde, R. (1993). Clinical assessment of pregnant women's psychosocial conditions, prematurity, and birthweight. *Scandinavian Journal of Primary Health Care, 11,* 130–134.

Giblin, P. T., Poland, M. L., & Ager, J. W. (1990). Effects of social supports on attitudes, health behaviors and obtaining prenatal care. *Journal of Community Health, 15(6),* 357–368.

Gjerdingen, D. K., Froberg, D. G., & Fontaine, P. (1991). The effects of social support on women's health during pregnancy, labor and delivery, and the postpartum period. *Family Medicine, 23(5),* 370–375.

Greenfield, P. M. (1994). Independence and interdependence as developmental scripts: Implications for theory, research, and practice. In P. M. Greenfield & R. R. Cocking (Eds.), *Cross-cultural roots of minority child development*. Hillsdale, NJ: Lawrence Erlbaum.

Guendelman, S. (1988). Sociocultural factors in Hispanic pregnancy outcomes. In C. J. Morton & R. G. Hirsch (Eds.), *Developing public health social work programs to prevent low birthweight and infant mortality: High risk populations and outreach*. Washington, DC: Public Health Social Work Institute.

Heins, H. C., Nance, N. W., McCarthy, B. J., & Efird, C. M. (1990). A randomized trial of nurse-midwifery prenatal care to reduce low birthweight. *Obstetrics & Gynecology, 75*, 341–345.

Henneborn, W. J., & Cogan, R. (1975). The effect of husband participation on reported pain and probability of medication during labor and birth. *Journal of Psychosomatic Research, 19*, 215–222.

Higgins, P., Murray, M. L., & Williams, E. M. (1994). Self-esteem, social support, and satisfaction differences in women with adequate and inadequate prenatal care. *Birth, 21(1)*, 26–33.

Hobfoll, S. E., & Lieberman, J. R. (1987). Personality and social resources in immediate and continued stress resistance among women. *Journal of Personality and Social Psychology, 52(1)*, 18–26.

Hofstede, G. (1980). *Culture's consequences*. Beverly Hills: Sage Publications.

Holtz, R., & Miller, N. (1985). Assumed similarity and opinion certainty. *Journal of Personality and Social Psychology, 48*, 890–898.

Hui, C. H., & Triandis, H. C. (1986). Individualism and collectivism: A study of cross-cultural researchers. *Journal of Consulting and Clinical Psychology, 20*, 296–309.

Jacobson, D. E. (1986). Types and timing of social support. *Journal of Health and Social Behavior, 27*, 250–264.

Jones, J. M. (1991). Psychological models of race: What have they been and what should they be? In J. D. Goodchilds (Ed.), *Psychological perspectives on human diversity in America* (pp. 5–46). Washington, DC: American Psychological Association.

Kalil, K. M., Gruber, J. E., Conley, J., & Syntiac, M. (1993). Social and family pressures on anxiety and stress during pregnancy. *Pre and Perinatal Psychology Journal, 8(2)*, 113–118.

Keefe, S. E. (1984). Real and ideal extended familism among Mexican Americans and Anglo Americans: On the meaning of "close" family ties. *Human Organization, 43*, 65–70.

Keefe, S. E., Padilla, A. M., & Carlos, M. L. (1978). *Emotional support systems in two cultures: A comparison of Mexican Americans and Anglo Americans*, Occasional Paper No. 7. Los Angeles: Spanish Speaking Mental Health Research Center, UCLA.

Keefe, S. E., Padilla, A. M., & Carlos, M. L. (1979). The Mexican-American extended family as an emotional support system. *Human Organization, 38*, 144–152.

Kelley, H. H., Berscheid, E., Christensen, A., Harvey, J. H., Huston, T. L., Levinger, G., McClintock, E., Peplau, L. A., & Peterson, D. R. (1983). *Close relationships*. New York: W. H. Freeman.

Kemp, V. H., & Hatmaker, D. D. (1989). Stress and social support in high-risk pregnancy. *Research in Nursing and Health, 12*, 331–336.

Kennell, J., Klaus, M., McGrath, S., Robertson, S., & Hinkley, C. (1991). Continuous emotional support during labor in a U.S. hospital. *Journal of the American Medical Association, 265*, 2197–2201.

Kessler, R. C., Kendler, K. S., Heath, A., Neale, M. C., & Eaves, L. J. (1992). Depressed mood and adjustment to stress: A genetic epimediologic investigation. *Journal of Personality and Social Psychology, 62(2)*, 257–273.

Klaus, M., Kennell, J., Robertson, S., & Sosa, R. (1986). Effects of social support during parturition on maternal and infant morbidity. *British Medical Journal, 293*, 585–587.

Kluckhohn, C. (1951). Values and value-orientations in the theory of action: An exploration in definition and classification. In T. Parsons & E. Shils (Eds.), *Toward a general theory of action*. Cambridge, MA: Harvard University Press.

Knouse, S. B. (1991). Social support for Hispanics in the military. *International Journal of Intercultural Relations, 15*, 427–444.

Lantican, L. S. M., & Corona, D. F. (1992). Comparison of the social support networks of Filipino and Mexican-American primigravidas. *Health Care for Women International, 13*, 329–338.

Larsson, G., Spangberg, L., Theorell, T., & Wager, J. (1987). Maternal opinion of psychosocial support: Evaluation of an antenatal programme. *Journal of Advanced Nursing, 12*, 441–449.

Lightfoot, E. C., Keeling, B., & Wilton, K. M. (1982). Characteristics distinguishing high-anxious and medium-/low-anxious women during pregnancy. *Journal of Psychosomatic Research, 26*, 345–350.

Lobel, M. (1994). Conceptualizations, measurement, and effects of prenatal maternal stress on birth outcomes. *Journal of Behavioral Medicine, 17(3)*, 225–272.

Lobel, M., Dunkel-Schetter, C., & Scrimshaw, S. C. M. (1992). Prenatal maternal stress and prematurity: A prospective study of socioeconomically disadvantaged women. *Health Psychology, 11(1)*, 32–40.

MacDonald, L. D., Peacock, J. L., & Anderson, H. R. (1992). Marital status: Association with social and economic circumstances, psychological state and outcomes of pregnancy. *Journal of Public Health Medicine, 14(1)*, 26–34.

Magni, G., Rizzardo, R., & Andreoli, C. (1986). Psychosocial stress and obstetrical complications. *Acta Obstetricia et Gynecologica Scandinavica, 65*, 273–276.

Marin, G., & Triandis, H. C. (1985). Allocentrism as an important characteristic of the behavior of Latin Americans and Hispanics. In R. Diaz-Guerrero (Ed.), *Cross-cultural and national studies in social psychology* (pp. 85–104). Amsterdam: Elsevier.

Markus, H. R., & Kitayama, S. (1991). Culture and the self: Implications for cognition, emotion, and motivation. *Psychological Review, 98(2)*, 224–253.

Mendoza, R. H., & Martinez, J. L. (1981). The measurement of acculturation. In A. Baron, Jr. (Ed.), *Explorations in Chicano psychology* (pp. 71–82). New York: Praeger.

Mercer, R. T., & Ferketich, S. L. (1988). Stress and social support as predictors of anxiety and depression during pregnancy. *Advances in Nursing Science, 10(2)*, 26–39.

Miller, N., & Brewer, M. (1986). Categorization effects on ingroup and outgroup perception. In J. F. Dovidio & S. L. Gaertner (Eds.), *Prejudice, discrimination, and racism* (pp. 209–230). Orlando, FL: Academic Press.

Mindel, C. H. (1980). Extended familism among urban Mexican Americans, Anglos, and blacks. *Hispanic Journal of Behavioral Sciences, 2*, 21–34.

Mirande, A. (1977). The Chicano family: A reanalysis of conflicting views. *Journal of Marriage and the Family, 39*, 747–756.

National Center for Health Statistics (1992). *Health, United States, 1991.* Hyattsville, MD: U.S. Public Health Service.

Norbeck, J. S. (1988). Social support. In J. J. Fitzpatrick, R. M. Taunton, & J. Q. Benoliel (Eds.), *Annual review of nursing research*, Vol. 6. New York: Springer.

Norbeck, J. S., & Anderson, N. J. (1989a). Psychosocial predictors of pregnancy outcomes in low-income black, Hispanic, and white women. *Nursing Research, 38(4)*, 204–209.

Norbeck, J. S., & Anderson, N. J. (1989b). Life stress, social support, and anxiety in mid- and late-pregnancy among low income women. *Research in Nursing and Health, 12*, 281–287.

Norbeck, J. S., Lindsey, A. M., & Carrieri, V. L. (1981). The development of an instrument to measure social support. *Nursing Research, 30*, 264–269.

Norbeck, J. S., Lindsey, A. M., & Carrieri, V. L. (1983). Further development of the Norbeck Social Support Questionnaire. *Nursing Research, 32*, 4–9.

Norbeck, J. S., & Tilden, V. P. (1983). Life stress, social support, and emotional disequilibrium in complications of pregnancy: A prospective, multivariate study. *Journal of Health and Social Behavior, 24*, 30–46.

Nuckolls, K. B., Cassel, J., & Kaplan, B. H. (1972). Psychosocial assets, life crises, and the prognosis of pregnancy. *American Journal of Epidemiology, 95*, 431–441.

Oakley, A. (1985). Social support in pregnancy: The "soft" way to increase birthweight. *Social Science and Medicine, 21*, 1259–1268.

Oakley, A. (1988). Is social support good for the health of mothers and babies? *Journal of Reproductive and Infant Psychology, 6*, 3–21.

Oakley, A., Rajan, L., & Grant, A. (1990). Social support and pregnancy outcome. *British Journal of Obstetrics and Gynaecology, 97*, 155–162.

O'Hara, M. W. (1986). Social support, life events, and depression during pregnancy and the puerperium. *Archives of General Psychiatry, 43*, 569–573.

Olds, D. L., Henderson, C. R., Tatelbaum, R., & Chamberlin, R. (1986). Improving the delivery of prenatal care and outcomes of pregnancy: A randomized trial of nurse home visitation. *Pediatrics, 77,* 16–28.

Padilla, A. (1980). *Acculturation: Theory, models, and some new findings.* Boulder, CO: Westview.

Pascoe, J. M. (1993). Social support during labor and duration of labor: A community-based study. *Public Health Nursing, 10,* 97–99.

Pascoe, J. M., Chessare, J., Baugh, E., Urich, L., & Ialongo, N. (1987). Help with prenatal household tasks and newborn birthweight: Is there an association? *Developmental and Behavioral Pediatrics, 8,* 207–212.

Piechnik, S. L., & Corbett, M. A. (1985). Reducing low birthweight among socioeconomically high-risk adolescent pregnancies. *Journal of Nurse-Midwifery, 30,* 88–98.

Quine, L., Rutter, D. R., & Gowen, S. (1993). Women's satisfaction with the quality of the birth experience: A prospective study of social and psychological predictors. *Journal of Reproductive and Infant Psychology, 11,* 107–113.

Ramirez, O., & Arce, C. H. (1981). The contemporary Chicano family: An empirically based review. In A. Baron, Jr. (Ed.), *Explorations in Chicano psychology.* New York: Praeger.

Ramirez, R. (1979). Machismo: A bridge rather than a barrier to family and marital counseling. In P. P. Martin (Ed.), *La Frontera perspective: Providing mental health services to Mexican Americans* (pp. 61–62). Tucson: La Frontera Center.

Ramsey, C. N., Abell, T. D., & Baker, L. C. (1986). The relationship between family functioning, life events, family structure, and the outcome of pregnancy. *Journal of Family Practice, 22,* 521–527.

Roland, A. (1988). *In search of self in India and Japan.* Princeton, NJ: Princeton University Press.

Rothman, J., Gant, L. M., & Hnat, S. A. (1985). Mexican-American family culture. *Social Science Review, 59,* 197–215.

Sable, M. R., Stockbauer, J. W., Schramm, W. F., and Land, G. H. (1990). Differentiating the barriers to adequate prenatal care in Missouri, 1987–1988. *Public Health Reports, 105,* 549–555.

Sabogal, F., Marin, G., Otero-Sabogal, R., Marin, B. V., & Perez-Stable, E. J. (1987). Hispanic familism and acculturation: What changes and what doesn't? *Hispanic Journal of Behavioral Sciences, 9,* 397–412.

Salgado de Snyder, V. N. (1987). The role of ethnic loyalty among Mexican immigrant women. *Hispanic Journal of Behavioral Sciences, 9,* 287–298.

Sarason, B. R., & Sarason, I. G. (1993). Assessment of social support. In S. A. Schumaker & C. M. Czajkoriski (Eds.), *Social support and cardiovascular disease* (pp. 41–63). New York: Plenum Press.

Schwartz, S. H. (1990). Individualism–collectivism: Critique and proposed refinements. *Journal of Cross-Cultural Psychology, 21,* 139–157.

Schwartz, S. H. (1992). Universals in the content and structure of values: Theoretical advances and empirical tests in 20 countries. In M. Zanna (Ed.), *Advances in experimental social psychology,* Vol. 25. New York: Academic Press.

Schwartz, S. H., & Bilsky, W. (1987). Toward a universal psychological structure of human values. *Journal of Personality and Social Psychology, 53,* 550–562.

Schwarzer, R., Dunkel-Schetter, C., & Kemeny, M. (1994). The multidimensional nature of received social support in gay men at risk of HIV infection and AIDS. *American Journal of Community Psychology, 22(3),* 319–339.

Scrimshaw, S. C. M., Engle, P. L., Arnold, L., & Haynes, K. (1987). Factors affecting breastfeeding among Mexican women in Los Angeles. *American Journal of Public Health, 77(4),* 467–470.

Scrimshaw, S. C. M., Zambrana, R., & Dunkel-Schetter, C. (in press). Issues in Latino women's health: Myths and challenges. In S. Ruzek, V. Oleson, & A. Clarke (Eds.), *Women's health: The dynamics of diversity.* Philadelphia: Temple University Press.

Sena-Rivera, J. (1979). Extended kinship in the United States: Competing models and the case of la familia Chicana. *Journal of Marriage and the Family, 41,* 121–129.

Sokol, R. J., Woolf, R. B., Rosen, M. G., & Weingarden, K. (1980). Risk, antepartum care, and outcome: Impact of a maternity and infant care project. *Obstetrics & Gynecology, 56,* 150–156.

Sosa, R., Kennell, J., Klaus, M., Robertson, S., & Urrutia, J. (1980). The effect of a supportive companion on perinatal problems, length of labor, and mother–infant interaction. *New England Journal of Medicine, 303,* 597–600.

Spencer, B., Thomas, H., & Morris, J. (1989). A randomized controlled trial of the provision of a social support service during pregnancy: The South Manchester Family Worker Project. *British Journal of Obstetrics and Gynaecology, 96,* 281–288.

St. Clair, P. A., Smeriglio, V. L., Alexander, C. S., & Celentano, D. D. (1989). Social network structure and prenatal care utilization. *Medical Care, 27(8),* 823–831.

St. John, C., & Winston, T. J. (1989). The effect of social support on prenatal care. *Journal of Applied Behavioral Science, 25(1),* 79–98.

Szapocznik, J., & Kurtines, W. M. (1993). Family psychology and cultural diversity: Opportunities for theory, research, and application. *American Psychologist, 48,* 400–407.

Taylor, S. E., Peplau, L. A., & Sears, D. O. (1994). *Social psychology.* Englewood Cliffs, NJ: Prentice-Hall.

Thorpe, K. J., Dragonas, T., & Golding, J. (1992). The effects of psychosocial factors on the emotional well-being of women during pregnancy: A cross-cultural study of Britain and Greece. *Journal of Reproductive and Infant Psychology, 10,* 191–204.

Tietjen, A. M., & Bradley, C. F. (1985). Social support and maternal psychosocial adjustment during the transition to parenthood. *Canadian Journal of Behavioral Science, 17(2),* 109–121.

Tilden, V. P. (1983). The relation of life stress and social support to emotional disequilibrium during pregnancy. *Research in Nursing and Health, 6,* 167–174.

Triandis, H. C. (1989). Self and social behavior in differing cultural contexts. *Psychological Review, 96,* 269–289.

Triandis, H. C. (1990) Cross-cultural studies of individualism and collectivism. In J. W. Berry, J. G. Draguns, & M. Cole (Eds.), *Nebraska symposium on motivation* (pp. 41–133). Lincoln: University of Nebraska Press.

Triandis, H. C. (1994). *Culture and social behavior.* New York: McGraw-Hill.

Triandis, H. C., Bontempo, R., Betancourt, H., Bond, M., Leung, K., Brenes, A., Georgas, J., Hui, C. H., Marin, G., Setialdi, B., Sinha, J. B. P., Verma, J., Spangenberg, J., Touzard, H., & De Montmollin, G. (1986). The measurement of etic aspects of individualism and collectivism across cultures. *Australian Journal of Psychology, 38,* 257–267.

Triandis, H. C., Bontempo, R., & Villareal, M. J. (1988). Individualism and collectivism: Cross-cultural perspectives on self–ingroup relationships. *Journal of Personality and Social Psychology, 54,* 323–338.

Triandis, H. C., Hui, C. H., Albert, R. D., Leung, S., Lisansky, J., Diaz-Loving, R., Plascencia, L., Marin, G., Betancourt, H., & Loyola-Cintron, L. (1984). Individual models of social behavior. *Journal of Personality and Social Psychology, 46,* 1389–1404.

Triandis, H. C., Marin, G., Betancourt, H., & Chang, B. (1982). *Acculturation, biculturism, and familism among Hispanic and mainstream Navy recruits.* Technical Report No. 15. Champaign: University of Illinois, Department of Psychology.

Triandis, H. C., McCusker, C., & Hui, H. C. (1990). Multimethod probes of individualism and collectivism. *Journal of Personality and Social Psychology, 59(5),* 1006–1020.

Turner, R. J., Grindstaff, C. F., & Phillips, N. (1990). Social support and outcome in teenage pregnancy. *Journal of Health and Social Behavior, 31,* 43–57.

Valdez, R. (Winter, 1980). The Mexican American male: A brief review of the literature. *Newsletter of the Mental Health Research Project* (pp. 4–5). San Antonio: I.D.R.A.

Valle, R., & Bensussen, G. (1985). Hispanic social networks, social support, and mental health. In W. Vega & M. Miranda (Eds.), *Stress and Hispanic mental health.* DHHS Publication No. 85-1410. Rockville, MD: National Institute of Mental Health.

Vaux, A. (1985). Variations in social support associated with gender, ethnicity, and age. *Journal of Social Issues, 41(1),* 89–110.

Vega, W. A. (1990). Hispanic families in the 1980s: A decade of research. *Journal of Marriage and the Family, 52,* 1015–1024.

Vega, W. A., & Kolody, B. (1985). The meaning of social support and the mediation of stress across cultures. In W. A. Vega & M. Miranda (Eds.), *Stress and Hispanic mental health.* Washington, DC: DHHS Publication No. 85-1410. Rockville, MD: National Institute of Mental Health.

Villar, J., Farnot, U., Barros, F., Victora, C., Langer, A., & Belizan, J. M. (1993). A randomized trial of psychosocial support during high-risk pregnancies. *New England Journal of Medicine, 327,* 1266–1271.

Wasserman, G. A., Rauh, V. A., Brunelli, S. A., Garcia-Castro, M., & Nekos, B. (1990). Psychosocial attributes and life experiences of disadvantaged minority mothers: Age and ethnic variations. *Child Development, 61,* 566–580.

Wilder, D. A., & Shapiro, P. (1991). Facilitation of outgroup stereotypes by enhanced ingroup identity. *Journal of Experimental Social Psychology, 27,* 431–452.

Williamson, H. A., & LeFevre, M. (1992). Tangible assistance: A simple measure of social support predicts pregnancy outcome. *Family Practice Research Journal, 12,* 289–295.

Wolman, W., Chalmers, B., Hofmeyr, G. J., & Nikodem, V. C. (1993). Postpartum depression and companionship in the clinical birth environment: A randomized, controlled study. *American Journal of Obstetrics and Gynecology, 168,* 1388–1393.

Ybarra, L. (1982). When wives work: The impact on the Chicano family. *Journal of Marriage and the Family, 44,* 169–178.

Ybarra-Soriano, L. (1977). Conjugal role relationships in the Chicano family. Unpublished Ph.D. dissertation. Berkeley: University of California.

Zambrana, R. E., Dunkel-Schetter, C., & Scrimshaw, S. C. M. (1991). Factors which influence use of prenatal care in low-income racial–ethnic women in Los Angeles County. *Journal of Community Health, 16(5),* 283–295.

Zambrana, R. E., Dunkel-Schetter, C., Scrimshaw, S. C. M., & Collins, N. (1996). Mediators of ethnic-associated differences in preterm delivery and infant birthweight. Unpublished manuscript.

Zambrana, R. E., Hernandez, M., Dunkel-Schetter, C., & Scrimshaw, S. C. M. (1991). Ethnic differences in the substance use patterns of low-income pregnant women. *Family and Community Health, 13(4),* 1–11.

Zambrana, R. E., Scrimshaw, S. C. M., Collins, N., & Dunkel-Schetter, C. (1996). Prenatal health behaviors and psychosocial factors in pregnant women of Mexican origin: The role of acculturation. Unpublished manuscript.

Zambrana, R. E., Scrimshaw, S. C. M., & Dunkel-Schetter, C. (in press). Prenatal care and medical risk in low-income primiparous Mexican-origin and African American women. *Families, Systems, and Health.*

Zayas, L. H., & Busch-Rossnagel, N. A. (1992). Pregnant Hispanic women: A mental health study. *Families in Society, 73(9),* 515–521.

Zuckerman, M. (1990). Some dubious premises in research and theory on racial differences: Scientific, social, and ethical issues. *American Psychologist, 45,* 1297–1303.

Zuckerman, B., Amaro, H., Bauchner, H., & Cabral, H. (1989). Depressive symptoms during pregnancy: Relationship to poor health behaviors. *American Journal of Obstetrics and Gynecology, 160(5),* 1107–1111.

Zuniga, M. E. (1992). Families with Latino roots. In E. W. Lynch & M. J. Hanson (Eds.), *Developing cross-cultural competence.* Baltimore: Paul H. Brookes.

17

Social Support and Social Coping in Couples

STEVAN E. HOBFOLL, REBECCA P. CAMERON, HEATHER A. CHAPMAN, and ROBERT W. GALLAGHER

INTRODUCTION

Traditionally, coping has been viewed as a process by which individuals confront and resolve (or fail to confront and resolve) challenges and obstacles. Rarely have the interpersonal context and consequences of coping been considered. As a result, the psychological literature on coping has demonstrated an individualistic, androcentric bias. The problem-solving coping strategies traditionally employed by men have been judged more efficacious than the emotion-focused and social-resource-based strategies traditionally employed by women. These gender differences have been used to explain women's higher rates of certain mental illnesses, such as depression, and mental health care utilization, but often from the perspective of victim blaming (Rosario, Shinn, Morch, & Huckabee, 1988). The benefits of traditionally feminine coping behaviors and the costs of traditionally male coping behaviors to families and to society have been largely ignored (Solomon & Rothblum, 1986). Integration of the coping literature and the social support literature offers an opportunity to contextualize coping behavior as a multidimensional interpersonal phenomenon (Fondacaro & Moos, 1987).

Coping in Couples

Consideration of the interpersonal process aspects of coping and the impact of gendered styles is most readily begun at the level of the marital or heterosexual-

STEVAN E. HOBFOLL, REBECCA P. CAMERON, HEATHER A. CHAPMAN, and ROBERT W. GALLAGHER • Applied Psychology Center, Kent State University, Kent, Ohio 44242.

Handbook of Social Support and the Family, edited by Gregory R. Pierce, Barbara R. Sarason, and Irwin G. Sarason. Plenum Press, New York, 1996.

couple relationship, in which individual and shared goals would optimally be combined and balanced. Ideally, couples and families act to meet mutual goals, including economic, emotional, and social goals, and to allow individuals in the family opportunities for meeting personal goals. This endeavor requires communication, cooperation, and compromise. Because of the high degree of cooperation needed to attain these ideals, there are many opportunities for gendered behavior patterns and differential expectations to interfere with effective coping.

The pursuit of individual goals within the couple may not be well coordinated. Men and women may not find each others' goals understandable or their strategies for achieving these goals compatible. Men have been traditionally encouraged to adopt individualistic, problem-focused approaches and to isolate themselves in response to stress (Hobfoll, 1991). In contrast, women are typically socialized to be communally oriented and have therefore been accorded responsibility for the emotional well-being of their families (Barnett, 1993). Indeed, psychological theory as well as lay conceptualizations are replete with examples of wives and mothers assuming and being given responsibility for their husbands' and children's psychological outcomes and, by extension, their professional outcomes (Baruch, Biener, & Barnett, 1987; Chodorow, 1989; Strickland, 1992). Women's focus on the affective well-being of their loved ones and close relationships frequently conflicts with men's avoidance of these issues, typically resulting in a conflict pattern characterized by the term "demand–withdraw." In this interaction, one partner, typically the female, desires more intimacy. In seeking greater involvement, this partner encroaches on the other's (typically the male's) need for distance, causing him to withdraw, and initiating a vicious cycle that can be difficult to break (Christensen, 1988; Fruzzetti & Jacobson, 1990; Jacobson, 1989).

Cultural Differences

Just as communal and individualistic coping styles are divided in accordance with traditional gender roles in Western cultures, entire cultures can be contrasted in their valuation of and emphasis on communal vs. individualistic strategies. Examining these cultural differences may help us illustrate these distinctions. Whereas Western, Eurocentric cultures highly value individuality and independence, Afrocentric and Asian cultures value communality and interdependence (Markus & Kitayama, 1991; McGoldrick, Preto, Hines, & Lee, 1991) and offer us a view of alternative, although also restrictive, models of successful coping. An example can be found in the examination by Weisz, Rothbaum, and Blackburn (1984) of the socialization patterns of American and Japanese children. These researchers assert that Japanese socialization is characterized by an emphasis on learning to conform to social roles, to cooperate, and to be carefully attuned to others, minimizing direct conflict.

In contrast, American socialization values the development of individuality, such that one is not considered fully mature until one has rejected the possibility of conforming to family and society and has developed an individually validated personal ethos (Sampson, 1977). There are trade-offs inherent in either style. Western patterns promote individual freedoms, but also foster alienation. Non-Western patterns promote group cohesion and empathy, but require subordination of one's individuality (Weisz et al., 1984). These East–West differences are similar to male–female differences discussed in the literature.

Gender, Coping, and Conflict

Just as an understanding of the differences between cultures provides insight into cross-cultural conflicts, an understanding of gender-role differences provides insight into conflict within couples. Men and women cope, not in isolation, but within the context of their relationships. Thus, coping has interpersonal as well as individual effects. The social support literature documents the benefits men receive from sharing their partners' social coping resources (Shumaker & Hill, 1991). Some of the more extreme consequences of individualistic coping styles, such as workaholism, child support nonpayment, and domestic violence, result in high costs to women and children.

Thus, whereas men show less depression in the aftermath of coping with a particular stressor, it may be that their success stems from having delegated their emotional burdens, as well as family task responsibilities, to their partners. When viewed from this perspective, the potential consequences to partners of particular coping styles and behaviors become apparent. Although some literature has focused on the impact of gender-role socialization on marital functioning (Goldner, 1985; Miller, 1976; Vetere, 1992), this work could be expanded and enriched by incorporating coping theory. Much familial conflict can be seen to be the result of conflicts between two people socialized to focus on different needs and to utilize discrepant strategies to meet those needs (Block, 1983; Hobfoll & Stokes, 1988; Noller, 1988).

Integration of Individualist and Collectivist Concepts

In response to the traditional, gender-biased values interlaced into psychological theory, a feminist voice emerged in psychology in the 1970s, pointing out the inherent value of communal styles and validating the differences in women's experience and sense of self (Chodorow, 1978; Gilligan, 1982; Miller, 1976; Riger, 1992). At times, this literature risks subscribing to either/or, extreme views of optimal functioning just as traditional, androcentric literature has done (Baber & Allen, 1992; Guisinger & Blatt, 1994; Riger, 1992; Yoder & Kahn, 1993). The increasing representation of women in psychology presumably will lead to continuing reexamination of theories rooted in and limited by gender bias. According to Denmark (1994), however, attempts to integrate feminist approaches into teaching, research, and practice still often meet with indifference or outright hostility.

Fortunately, a new paradigm is emerging in recent theory, proposing the view that communality and individuality can be seen as complementary rather than incompatible aspects of human functioning (e.g., Guisinger & Blatt, 1994). Guisinger and Blatt (1994) suggest that both individuality and relatedness are important facets of human experience. Further, they suggest that this duality is dialectical in nature. Individuality permits mature connectedness, and connectedness is essential to a healthy self. These authors offer evidence from anthropology, evolutionary biology, and psychology for the existence of innate prosocial tendencies, and they suggest that prosocial and individualistic orientations become integrated in late adolescence. This balanced perspective holds much promise, both as a basis for theories that better approximate the "truths" of human functioning and as an impetus toward social and policy reform (Guisinger & Blatt, 1994).

Before proceedings, we consider it necessary to clarify our use of gender as an organizing principle regarding coping. We offer generalizations about gendered styles, but recognize that there is risk in any generalization based on biological grouping and affirm the axiom that within-group variability is generally higher than between-group variability (Jacklin, 1989; Riger, 1993). As we will develop further in our discussion of the Multiaxial Model of Coping, the truly important distinctions may be between traditional and nontraditional gender-role orientations and between men and women within the traditional orientations. Traditional gender roles are still salient, however, and gender-based distinctions are therefore not entirely outmoded. The changes that have arisen in gender roles since the 1960s, and the current controversy about women's roles in particular, provide a fascinating but complex context of change for examining the utility of the full range of human coping potential.

AUTONOMY AND COMMUNALITY

Traditional Conceptualizations of Coping

Reflecting cultural biases, optimal psychological development in Western culture has been conceptualized as growth toward a highly differentiated, autonomous self (Guisinger & Blatt, 1994; Sampson, 1977). These individualistic values permeate psychological theory and empiricism, limiting our ability to conceptualize from a communal perspective. Naturally, coping research to date reflects individualistic premises, but in doing so, it affirms a narrow view of human possibility. Under the old paradigm, women ought to strive to be more like men— that is, more autonomous and problem-focused—in order to function better and suffer fewer psychological problems. However, women who do so risk disapproval and guilt for failing to fulfill their roles as nurturers and caretakers. These communal roles are necessary to maintain social connections, but have not been accorded the status that could make them more rewarding (Solomon & Rothblum, 1986).

Similarly, men and women risk career limitations when they demonstrate a commitment to full participation in family life (e.g., missing work due to a child's illness) or attempt to utilize communal strategies in the workplace (Robinson & Barret, 1986; Strober, 1988). Women's cooperative styles in the workplace have been found to foster productivity by emphasizing collaborative rather than competitive work relationships. Unfortunately, facilitating *overall* productivity is not often rewarded in the workplace, whereas the appearance of making an independent contribution is. Despite the instrumental success of independent coping styles in the workplace, these competitive tendencies are likely to prove detrimental if applied in familial or social settings (Dunahoo, Geller, & Hobfoll, in press).

A broader vision would recognize the necessity for adults to participate as fully and as flexibly as possible in all aspects of life, including relationship and family maintenance as well as workplace productivity, and would endorse the utility of both individual and communal strategies for achieving goals. If psychology is able to expand its theoretical base by incorporating the experiences of both gendered styles, this synthesis will facilitate a transformation of our view of human nature and optimal functioning (Guisinger & Blatt, 1994; Hoffman, 1972). One way that psychology might be transformed would be to redefine the developmental tasks considered necessary for healthy adult functioning. For example, the same value would be given to the development of empathy and relatedness as is now given to the development of a distinct sense of self (Guisinger & Blatt, 1994; Jacklin, 1989). If both boys and girls were encouraged to develop skills useful for maintaining relationships as well as for achieving career objectives, their adult dyadic relationships could become truer, more egalitarian partnerships (Hall & Halberstadt, 1980).

Baruch et al. (1987) point out that men are as likely as women to benefit from new perspectives on workplace and family stress and coping, since they are increasingly permitted to acknowledge and attempt to resolve family concerns that previously they were expected to deny. These authors contend that well-being is achieved through a balance of agency and communion. They affirm that participation in multiple roles increases one's opportunities for expressing and fulfilling both of these functions. If both men and women developed roles in agentic *and* communal domains, couples would be better equipped to meet the demands of modern family life. Each partner's talents and resources would be more fully and flexibly utilized to meet goals that would be seen as mutual rather than as sources of conflict.

Inherent Biases of the Problem-Focused vs. the Emotion-Focused Distinction

The problem- vs. emotion-focused distinction has been the predominant theme of coping theory (Lazarus & Folkman, 1984). Whereas problem-focused copers direct attention toward changing the situation to fit their needs, emotion-focused copers direct their energies toward their emotional responses to the situation. Problem-focused coping emphasizes action and has been seen as most efficacious in promoting well-being. In contrast, emotion-focused coping has been found to be less effective and to be more frequently associated with psychological distress (e.g., Billings & Moos, 1984). In addition, some researchers have contended that men utilize problem-focused coping to a greater degree than women and that women are more likely than men to utilize emotion-focused coping (Billings & Moos, 1981, 1984; Pearlin & Schooler, 1978). These differences have been cited as one of the reasons women appear to be more susceptible than men to depression and other overcontrolled or internalizing disorders (Solomon & Rothblum, 1986). Thus, women's typical patterns of dysfunction and distress are self-punitive.

Because coping efficacy has been measured in terms of individual outcomes, the possibility that problem-focused coping may negatively affect individuals close to the coper has not been considered until recently (Hobfoll, Dunahoo, Ben-Porath, & Monnier, 1994). If it is the case that problem-focused coping often takes an antisocial form, its superiority as a general style may be called into question. The individualistic and at times emotionally impoverished nature of problem-focused coping may discourage cooperation by others and cause a decrease in social support resources (Eisler & Blalock, 1991). Various authors (e.g., Solomon & Rothblum, 1986; Strickland, 1992) note that men are overrepresented among those suffering from undercontrolled or externalizing disorders, and they characterize these disorders as disruptive and harmful to those *in proximity to* the disordered individual because of their antisocial approach.

The work of sustaining family life has traditionally been divided along gender lines, with men assigned responsibility for instrumental tasks and women delegated expressive and affective responsibilities (Eisler & Blalock, 1991). Feminist theorists have argued that this division of labor is hierarchical (e.g., Delphy, 1993). Psychology has mimicked society in valuing instrumental behavior over expressive behavior and in interpreting relationship-oriented behavior as reflective of inadequacy or dependency. In addition to paradoxically limiting individuality by encouraging stereotyped behavior, this viewpoint denies our mutual interdependence and degrades the status of those who maintain the conditions necessary for social functioning (Riger, 1993).

The current perceived crisis in American family life reflects in part our societal tendency to distance ourselves from responsibility for child welfare, to devalue the provision of child care, and to reward accomplishments in the workplace. Ironically, segregating tasks of family maintenance and economic well-being by gender has contributed to the devaluation of the family, yet those who most deplore the "breakdown of the family" are also generally the most eager to return to the traditional division of labor (Cohen & Katzenstein, 1988). To the extent that power is considered to be inconsistent with nurturance, empowered people will disown their ability to nurture. Riger (1993) discusses problems with the concept of empowerment. She suggests that empowerment and community are both necessary, despite their inherent conflict, and need to be valued equally. Until we do so, it will be difficult to envision a "successful family": one that both meets increasingly difficult economic challenges and provides for the emotional well-being of children in a turbulent, often violent society.

Do Coping Differences Reflect Differential Demands on Men and Women?

A contextual focus on social roles may illuminate the gender bias of traditional theories of coping. Demands traditionally faced by men have tended to involve a problem-solving component, whereas demands faced by women have tended to involve an emotional component. This distinction in role-related demands has most likely contributed to differences in the traditional coping styles of men and women (Aneshensel & Pearlin, 1987; Rosario et al., 1988; Roth & Cohen, 1986). Researchers on gender differences in stress and coping have found that women are more attuned to interpersonal sources of stress than are men (Groër, Thomas, & Shoffner, 1992; Kessler, McLeod, & Wethington, 1985). Flaherty and Richman (1989) question whether women in highly stressful professional settings may come to approximate the styles of their male counterparts, in response to role demands. If so, they may be acquiring the negative aspects of these coping styles (e.g., Type A personality) and their attendant risks as well (including increased risk of coronary artery disease) (Solomon & Rothblum, 1986).

Differences in coping styles may also reflect differences in power and control, and this differentiation may extend to family life. Women, still relatively disempowered and devalued in comparison to men, are more likely to face uncontrollable stressors (e.g., poverty, childrearing responsibilities, the "glass ceiling") (Belle, 1990; Dunahoo et al., in press; Strickland, 1992) that do not lend themselves to instrumental coping efforts. In fact, mothering has been characterized as an extremely high-risk activity due to its high-demand, low-control qualities. It is a role that assigns mothers full responsibility for the well-being of their children, even though no one can fully guarantee another person's well-being (Baruch et al., 1987). Thus, coping behavior labeled avoidant and stigmatized as inefficacious is highly likely to reflect environmental contingencies rather than an inherent biological inferiority (Solomon & Rothblum, 1986). Furthermore, simply occupying a deferent position in the social hierarchy may contribute to women's disproportionate share of psychological distress (Kaschak, 1992). Writers concerned with ethnic minorities have pointed out that discrimination results in a disparity in opportunities that may be linked to negative physical health consequences as well (David & Collins, 1991; Moritsugu & Sue, 1983). Similar processes may affect women.

One might argue that women have gained economic power in recent years as they have entered the workforce. In fact, women who attain high-status jobs experience greater satisfaction and fewer role conflicts than women in lower-status jobs (Baruch et al., 1987). However, women are still generally overrepresented in junior positions and are awarded lower levels of autonomy and salary even when they are in positions comparable to men's (LaCroix & Haynes, 1987). In addition, women's increased responsibility for the economic well-being of their families has not been matched by increased participation in household and childrearing duties on the part of men. Thus, women continue to fill their traditional service roles at home (Dunahoo et al., in press).

Rethinking the Bases of Coping Research

There are potential benefits to be derived from rethinking the evaluative and unidimensional posture that coping research has taken toward traditionally feminine coping. As an illustration of the advantages of a multidimensional perspective, we can return to women's communal style in the workplace. Women tend to be more team-oriented and less aggressive than men, indicating that they use prosocial, but also assertive (i.e., active), strategies (Powell, 1988). Thus, gender differences in coping may be better understood if active and social dimensions of coping are distinguished.

Increasing the contextual focus of coping models is important for another, very basic reason. Since women typically integrate contextual information (e.g., family functioning) into their understandings of self, goals, and behavioral options, any model that decontextualizes the process, tasks, or outcomes of coping will overlook information crucial to the understanding of women's coping (Gilligan, 1982; Riger, 1992, 1993). Numerous studies suggest that women are more influenced by and act more in reaction to social context than do men (Hobfoll & Stokes, 1988). Wertlieb, Weigel, and Feldstein (1987) have found evidence that gender differences in environment- vs. self-focused orientations begin in childhood. It is therefore important to consider contextual factors when studying women's coping.

At a fundamental level, problem-solving may be defined differently from a communal as opposed to an individualistic viewpoint. Communally oriented copers are more likely to utilize indirect social-network-based strategies. These copers may incorporate the needs of others in their attempts at problem solving. Unfortunately, current coping models may not recognize the positive problem-solving elements inherent in this approach. Expanding our understanding of coping to include dimensions other than problem-focused and emotion-focused may allow for more balanced gender comparisons. Including a prosocial–antisocial dimension allows for increased contextualization of coping as a social process with social effects. This aspect of the multidimensional view we are proposing is of special relevance for understanding the relationship of coping strategies to couples' conflicts. It may mitigate the misunderstandings that may arise when men and women place differing emphases on the relative importance of instrumental vs. relationship goals.

Social Support Utilization

Research on social support has increasingly characterized support seeking and support utilization as processes that differentially involve men and women. Men's and women's social behavior ultimately results in their cultivation of disparate social support resources. Differences in strategies for acquiring social coping resources (Ptacek, Smith, & Zanas, 1992) may lead to conflict. Men attain social support by linking to women and their established networks, yet women generally benefit more than men from social support (Flaherty & Richman, 1989;

Hobfoll & Stokes, 1988). Researchers have found that men utilize their wives as their primary confidantes, but women do not primarily rely on their husbands to fulfill this important function (Lowenthal & Haven, 1968). Women's friendships are more involving and emotionally supportive than men's (Belle, 1987; Solomon & Rothblum, 1986). In contrast, men's social support networks are typically larger but less intimate than women's (Hobfoll & Stokes, 1988; Reis, Senchak, & Solomon, 1985).

In addition, men and women may utilize their support systems differently, especially under stressful conditions. In the family context, this is like two trains trying to run in the same direction but on separate, nonconnecting tracks. Men may isolate under high stress conditions, whereas women may reach out to provide and receive more support under these circumstances, risking stress contagion in the process. The consequences of isolating or engaging support may be different for men and women, as well (Hobfoll, 1991). Not only do men utilize social support less than women do, but also social support may have negative rather than positive consequences for men. For example, Flaherty and Richman (1989) and Hobfoll (1991) found that men experienced more depressive symptoms as a function of increased intimate support. Therefore, women may find their husbands or partners emotionally unavailable and unable to provide support during stressful periods.

It may be that individualistic problem-solving approaches to coping are more likely to have an antisocial, aggressive, or even passive–aggressive aspect. If so, certain forms of problem-focused coping might lead to increased isolation and alienation (Lane & Hobfoll, 1992). Hostility engendered by this process may harm the coper's health or the health of those in proximity to him or her (Johnson, 1990). Social support in the form of intimacy with a spouse has been shown to be an important resource for both men and women, but as Rook (1984) and others have begun to explore, invalidating or conflictual exchanges exert a powerful negative impact that outweighs the beneficial impact of positive exchanges. Thus, aggressive coping not only may transfer the emotional consequences of a stressor from a husband to his wife, but also may require her to compensate with excessive efforts to regain emotional equilibrium by virtue of the potency of negative exchanges. Coping strategies that are active, but prosocial, may reflect and foster greater psychological health (Hobfoll & Lerman, 1989) for both men and women (Dunahoo, Monnier, Hobfoll, & Hulsizer, 1994).

THE MULTIAXIAL MODEL AND STRATEGIC APPROACH TO COPING SCALE

Hobfoll et al. (1994) initially developed the Dual-Axis Model of Coping, then expanded it to its current form as the Multiaxial Model of Coping, in order to address several of the limitations in the research literature on coping we have discussed. The Multiaxial Model of Coping was developed in an attempt to move away from culture- and gender-biased coping theory. As a dimensional model, it avoids the weaknesses of forced dichotomies: Coping strategies can fall toward the middle *or* on the end of a continuum. In order to test this model, Hobfoll and colleagues developed a measure, the Strategic Approach to Coping Scale (SACS), designed to tap the dimensions posited in the model. Research on this model has the potential to contribute to theory on family coping in a variety of ways.

First, the SACS measures behavioral strategies used in coping, rather than measuring emotional responses to stress that may confound outcomes of coping with coping style. Second, by incorporating multiple dimensions, and especially by distinguishing the prosocial–antisocial dimension from the active–passive dimension, the Multiaxial Model reflects a potentially more gender-fair theoretical orientation. Similarly, the indirect–direct dimension that was incorporated in response to early factor analytical findings with the initial Dual-Axis Model allows culturally specific styles to be incorporated into research, again, with less bias. Finally, the major theoretical contribution of the Multiaxial Model is its consideration of the interpersonal context of coping. Coping occurs in social contexts; therefore, measures of coping that focus solely on individual processes and outcomes miss a large portion of what is relevant and interesting about coping.

Description of the Model

The Multiaxial Model is a three-dimensional model that incorporates the axes described above: prosocial–antisocial, active–passive, and direct–indirect (see Figure 1). Coping behavior is seen as existing along each of the three continua simultaneously. For example, a strategy might be highly active, moderately antisocial, and more indirect than direct. Behavior that is active and prosocial is seen as potentially most psychologically healthy (Adler, 1929/1969; Erikson, 1963, 1968; Maslow, 1987). Directness, however, is more cultural and situational, as some situations call for more direct action than others. For example, support for an employee might be depicted to be active, prosocial, and indirect when a boss simply includes an employee in a dinner engagement with upper management, quietly designating the employee as a front-runner for promotion.

Initially, coping strategies were posited to fall anywhere within the three-dimensional space defined by the model. However, as Figure 1 depicts, empirical evidence has suggested that not all octants of the model correspond to existing behavioral strategies. Specifically, as coping becomes more passive, it is less readily characterized as antisocial or prosocial. Conversely, as coping becomes more active, its orientation toward the social environment becomes more relevant (Dunahoo et al., 1994). Passivity means inaction, and therefore cannot be directed pro- or antisocially. Instead, passive–aggressive strategies are conceptually and empirically better represented as indirect, antisocial, and active.

Subscales

Nine subscales, representing general coping strategies, have emerged from factor analytical studies of the original SACS and have been named to reflect the

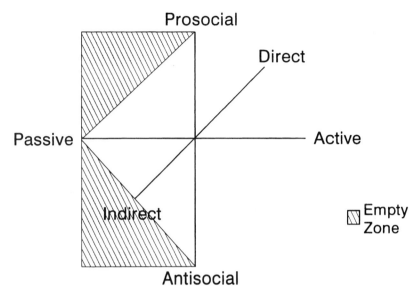

Figure 1. Multiaxial Model of Coping.

commonalities among the individual items that make up each subscale. These subscales can be located in the three-dimensional space of the model, as indicated in Table 1. The subscales can be characterized by the dimensions they reflect most clearly. They vary in their emphasis on active–passive or prosocial–antisocial distinctions, with only one reflecting the dimension of direct–indirect.

Several studies have been conducted to investigate the reliability and validity of the SACS (Dunahoo et al., 1994; Hobfoll et al., 1994). Both a Dispositional SACS-D) and a Situational (SACS-S) form have been developed, allowing for more precise application of the model and clearer evaluation of predictive validity. Psychometric properties reported below refer to the SACS-D, but are comparable to those for the SACS-S.

Two-week test–retest reliabilities for the subscales of an early version of the SACS-D were calculated for a group of 100 undergraduates at a Midwestern university. These coefficients ranged from .46 to .72, with most above .50. Internal reliabilities were calculated for these subscales utilizing a variety of samples; among a group of 205 undergraduates, Cronbach's alpha values ranged from .54 to .88, with only one alpha below .60. Internal reliability was also evaluated for the subscales among a group of inner-city residents. For this group, internal re-liabilities of the subscales ranged from .51 to .85, with only one subscale below .65. Three items were added to the subscale with the lowest internal reliability, and the subscales were retested with another group of 116 undergraduates. This modifica-tion resulted in subscale reliability ranging from .61 to .86. SACS-S internal reliabilities were even higher (.65–.90). These results compare favorably to those

Table 1. Strategic Approach to Coping Subscales and Sample Items

Active, prosocial
    Assertive action
        Be strong and forceful, but avoid harming others.
    Social joining
        Join together with others to deal with the situation.
Prosocial, active
    Seeking social support
        Ask friends or family for their opinions about your plan of action.
Passive, prosocial (moderately passive)
    Cautious action
        Go forward, but don't use all your resources until you know full well
            what you're up against.
Passive, asocial/antisocial
    Avoidance
        If it doesn't get worse, just avoid the whole thing.
Active, antisocial
    Antisocial action
        Move aggressively; often, if you get another person off guard, things
            will work to your advantage.
    Aggressive action
        Take the bull by the horns; adopt a take-charge attitude.
    Instinctive action
        Follow your first impulse; things usually work out best that way.
Indirect/direct
    Indirect action
        Others often need to feel they are the boss, so you have to work
            around them to get things done.

with other coping instruments. For example, the Carver (COPE) (Carver, Scheier, & Weintraub, 1989), one of the best available coping scales, reports subscale reliabilities as low as .40.

Explorations of the structure of the SACS measure indicated that subscales correlate with each other in predictable patterns. For example, antisocial strategies (instinctive, aggressive, and antisocial action) were positively correlated with each other. Similarly, action strategies (assertive, aggressive) were positively related to each other, but assertive action was negatively associated with antisocial action, indicating a distinction between prosocial and antisocial action. Social joining, support seeking, and cautious action were theoretically seen as active and prosocial, and were positively correlated. In contrast, social joining and support seeking were negatively related to instinctive and antisocial action, indicating the pro- vs. antisocial distinction. Avoidance was negatively related to assertive, aggressive, and cautious action strategies, indicating the passive–active continuum. Thus, the distinctions between the prosocial–antisocial dimension and the active–passive dimension were supported, and subscales that conceptually fall at one end of an axis tend to correlate positively with each other and negatively with the subscales that reflect the other end of the axis.

Relationship to Measures of Psychological Adjustment

Dunahoo et al. (1994) studied the relationships between SACS subscales and several measures of psychological adjustment. Exploring people's general coping patterns, they found that avoidant (passive) and instinctive action (antisocial) strategies were related prospectively to increased depression. As stress increased, failure to use social joining, support seeking, and cautious action (all active, prosocial strategies) was also associated with increased depression. Avoidance was related to increased anxiety, whereas cautious action and support-seeking strategies were protective against anxiety. Aggressive and antisocial actions were related to increased anger, although for antisocial action, this effect was found only under low-stress conditions.

An examination of the effects of situational coping (as opposed to general strategies) on concurrent emotional states revealed a few differences. Notably, aggressive action served a protective function against anger and anxiety under high-stress conditions. That is, individual, short-term outcomes may be enhanced by coping that directs stress-generated negative emotions toward others.

The general conclusion to be drawn from these results is that active, prosocial coping is related to lower levels of psychological distress, a relationship that is accentuated under high-stress conditions. Outright antisocial action was generally not beneficial for emotional outcomes, but the more moderately antisocial strategy, aggressive action, was found to be beneficial under certain circumstances. Antisocial action appears to be most detrimental under low-stress conditions, suggesting that antisocial action may have more repercussions for the coper in situations that do not provide clear justification for hostility. These findings highlight the possibility that problem-focused coping may take aggressive forms that do appear to enhance the well-being of the coper under certain circumstances. An important point, however, is that these strategies may simultaneously result in worse outcomes for those involved with the coper and may in the long run result in negative psychological and social outcomes for the coper.

Relationship of the SACS-D to the COPE: How Different Methods Lead to Different Conclusions

Dunahoo et al. (1994) investigated the relationship between the SACS-D and the COPE (Carver et al., 1989) in order to evaluate the potential presence of a hidden prosocial–antisocial dimension in the active–passive dimension measured by the COPE. The COPE was chosen because of its status as one of the best available coping scales. For this study, 5 of the 13 COPE subscales were used, all relating to the active–passive dimension: active coping, planning, suppression of competing activities, denial, and behavioral disengagement. Correlations between these 5 subscales of the COPE and the 6 SACS subscales that most clearly reflect active prosocial or active antisocial strategies (assertive and cautious action, social joining, support seeking, aggressive and antisocial action) were calculated.

Results revealed hidden social components of the COPE. Active coping, thought to be a healthy coping strategy, was found to be related to aggressive and antisocial coping as well as to more prosocial strategies. Suppression of competing activities is not simply a passive or neutral approach, but is also related to aggressive and antisocial coping. It involves focusing intently on the problem at hand and disregarding other, competing demands. Denial and behavioral disengagement were found to be related to antisocial action. This result suggests that these strategies do not simply reflect a passive or an avoidant response to stress, but may be associated with being intensely self-focused while directing negative affect toward others.

These results suggest that even the recent, more theoretically based and sophisticated coping research has overlooked the impact on loved ones of coping strategies thought to be psychologically healthy for the coper. Active coping as measured by the COPE can be individualistic or communal in orientation and therefore more or less costly for the partner or family. Along the same lines, it appears that some behaviors that are clearly functional for the coper, such as withdrawing from distractions, may involve implicitly delegating communal responsibilities to a partner, who may or may not be prepared to assume these added burdens. Less desirable coping strategies, such as behavioral disengagement and denial, that also imply regulating one's own level of involvement in a problem may involve disregarding the needs of family members and others. Therefore, these strategies have clear implications for couples' interactions and their sense of partnership. These tactics are inherently individualistic, although the COPE measure, as currently presented, does not acknowledge social dimensions of coping. It would be useful to compare the SACS with other coping measures in order to further explore these interpersonal facets of coping. The SACS offers a qualitatively distinct view of coping that can potentially enrich our understanding of the social context in which behavioral strategies are employed.

IMPLICATIONS FOR COUPLES

We have found differences in coping associated with gender and gender roles that clearly have implications for couples. Divergent interaction patterns may not be problematic under low-stress conditions. Under high stress, however, the differences in men's and women's response styles may be accentuated, potentially resulting in marital distress (Gottman & Levenson, 1988; Ptacek et al., 1992). Additionally, Gottman and Levenson (1988) assert that gender-stereotyped behaviors are more pronounced in highly distressed marriages than in less distressed marriages.

Early work with the Dual-Axis Model explored the relationship between interpersonal coping and gender as well as gender-role orientation (Hobfoll et al., 1994). Women were found to utilize prosocial strategies, including assertive action, support seeking, and cautious action, more often than men. In contrast, men used more antisocial action strategies than women. In addition, traditional men and women used more antisocial action and social joining strategies than did nontraditional men and women, respectively. Traditional women also used more cautious action than did nontraditional women. Thus, gender-role orientation also influences coping style.

Studies of the Multiaxial Model of Coping have provided evidence for gender distinctions consistent with those reported above for the Dual-Axis Model (Dunahoo et al., 1994). For example, women have been found to utilize more social joining and support seeking than men; men have been found to utilize more aggressive and antisocial action than women; and no differences have been found on active–passive distinctions. This reflects coping appropriate for family structures that exempt men from responsibility for the maintenance of connectedness and partnership while at the same time defining women by their success in these maintenance activities.

Coping and Social Support

Couples influence each other's perceptions of their social environment. These perceptions, in turn, are related to each partner's choice of coping strategies. For example, Hobfoll et al. (1994) found that assertive action and support seeking were positively related to perceptions of social support for both men and women. For men, social joining was also positively related to perceived social support. Although these findings are correlational, they potentially have implications for how couples' interactions evolve over time. Reciprocal causal relationships are likely, in which assertive, prosocial behaviors by one partner might lead to a response of increased social support from the other. This process results in increased mutually supportive socially oriented behavior by both partners.

The findings of Dunkel-Schetter, Folkman, and Lazarus (1987) similarly suggest that coping strategies can function to elicit or discourage social support from partners. Specifically, problem solving and support seeking were associated with receiving several forms of social support. Coping by confronting the problem was associated with receiving specifically informational support. These authors further suggest that coping by distancing may signal others that social support is not desired. They concur that the most accurate model of the relationship between coping and social support is probably recursive and dynamic. Therefore, gendered styles may be self-perpetuating. Traditional women's prosocial styles may elicit further social interaction and mutual obligation, and traditional men's antisocial styles may function to alienate support within the couple.

Consequences of Gendered Coping in Couples

The most important implication of these findings for couples' interactions is that men's strategies for coping tend to be oriented more antisocially than women's more prosocial, but also generally active, strategies. Among more traditional couples, even more stereotyped coping differences may be found. Women appear to be gearing their coping efforts toward the needs of their loved ones, whereas men are more likely to disregard the consequences their coping efforts may have for others. This disregard may potentially contribute to women's being at greater risk for dysphoria, powerlessness, and loneliness, and may be the root of conflict and poor communication between partners (Fitzpatrick, 1988). To the extent that couples are not meeting each other's needs, there may be consequences for children (Fruzzetti & Jacobson, 1991; Grych & Fincham, 1990). Marital conflict, perhaps more than divorce per se, has been linked to childhood emotional problems (Amato & Keith, 1991).

Although some have argued that the complementarity of roles that traditional men and women fulfill is ideal for family functioning, it seems clear that the costs of rigid role responsibilities are higher than the benefits on many levels: societal, familial, and individual. In contrast, nontraditional men and women are more likely to be characterized by a flexible coping style that is both active and prosocial (Hobfoll et al., 1994). This style has more to do with psychological health and maturity than with gender. Men and women who take an active, problem-solving approach to problems, but do so without losing sight of their connections to others, are likely to be well suited to the challenges of intimate relationships.

Future research on gendered coping among couples and families should incorporate measures of gender-role orientation in order to maximize statistical power and conceptual clarity. This distinction between gender and gender role is akin to the distinction made by various authors between race and culture as units for analysis (Betancourt & Lopez, 1993). Yoder and Kahn (1993) have also noted that gender differences are not simply biological distinctions, but are modified by cultural factors.

Men, Women, and Conflict

Gottman and Levenson (1988) review evidence for the negative consequences of differences in men's and women's coping. They argue that men's conflict-related behavior is greatly influenced by their poor tolerance for negative affect. As a result, men engage in more reconciling behaviors at low levels of conflict, but withdraw at higher levels of conflict, becoming either avoidant or actively antisocial. This tendency is especially problematic due to women's willingness to express negative feelings. Women may even find that their relationships with other women are enhanced by exchanges in which negative feelings are expressed and acknowledged. In relationships with men, this style may be met with avoidance, leading to decreased intimacy.

Jacobson (1989) offers an additional perspective on the consequences of gendered coping for couple functioning that aligns well with the Multiaxial Model. He asserts that affiliation–independence conflicts result in interaction patterns that are extremely difficult to circumvent. In his clinical work with distressed couples, he finds that positive communication skills readily learned and applied in the therapy room are quickly abandoned as arguments about these issues escalate at home. To address this dynamic, he proposes a three-stage intervention process: (1) Identify the thematic pattern of the conflict; (2) teach couples to self-monitor and then process their conflicts in terms of this theme; and

(3) utilize role-playing and homework assignments to interrupt and change the pattern. Usually the first two stages of intervention are adequate to improve the couple's functioning. Because Jacobson makes the connection between men's use of distancing and their greater power in relationships, he sees these therapeutic tasks as embedded in a political context that forces therapists to choose between facilitating oppressive (active, antisocial) relationships or fostering egalitarianism (active, prosocial).

CONCLUSIONS

Our research suggests that the active–prosocial coping style synthesizes problem-solving and relationship-enhancing aspects of coping that have traditionally been conceptualized as dichotomous and oppositional. As we incorporate contextual aspects of coping into research, we will likely conclude that the active, prosocial coper should replace the problem-focused coper as the epitome of mental health under stress. The active, prosocial coper has successfully integrated his or her potential for agency *and* community. Having done so, this person can serve as a model for theorists who view individuality and communality as complementary facets of human functioning. Changing our culturally sanctioned norms and ideals for human development goes hand in hand with changing our gendered role responsibilities and eliminating putative biologically destined social hierarchies.

Although we have focused on the obvious implications of the Multiaxial Model of Coping and highlighted the benefits of a more flexible and gender-fair evaluation of coping styles, there are those who would argue that the recommendations we have made bear more radical and potentially threatening implications. Delphy (1993) suggests that because gendered styles are the product of a hierarchical system, a more egalitarian society may not give rise to what we think of as traditionally feminine and masculine characteristics. Therefore, people of this egalitarian society may not *combine* masculine and feminine qualities, but actually cope in ways that we cannot currently anticipate. We do not believe it to be necessarily true, however, that nurturing is solely a function of being lower in the social hierarchy. Rather, there will always be a need for nurturance, and nurturance is likely to be a more highly valued function if we all participate in it. We would therefore suggest that increased male involvement in child care and other caretaking roles will foster the more mutual, well-rounded style initially given impetus by women's participation in the workplace.

Sampson (1977) provides yet another counterpoint to our worldview. He suggests that androgyny is a highly individualistic concept and that proposing an ideal of human functioning that combines and balances divergent tasks and styles within the same person is essentially countercommunal. He describes androgyny as an ideal that is uniquely a function of our current historical and social milieu. Although we agree with the spirit of much of his critique, it lacks recognition of two major points. First, the interdependent communities he proposes run the risk of imposing biologically defined hierarchics (by racc, castc, or gender) that promote inevitable conflict. Second, we would reiterate that our model of healthy coping does not require an impossible level of integration. Nontraditional men and women do typically achieve this style and its benefits. In addition, an essential feature of the androgynous style we advocate is connectedness. Sampson's concern that androgyny promotes isolation is directly contradicted by this provision.

Future directions for research should include attempts to elucidate the interpersonal, interactive nature of coping and social resource acquisition. Admittedly, processes are more difficult to operationalize than are individual states, but combining several approaches and viewpoints should allow for convergence. Our model offers one avenue toward this goal. First, it extends coping outcomes to families and relationships in addition to individuals. Second, the SACS, based on this model, permits more gender-fair and culture-fair investigations of coping processes. Research should examine each partner's coping styles and how they impact their own and their other partner's outcomes. Empirical work that directly examines couples' conflictual interactions is also of relevance (for several examples, see Noller & Fitzpatrick, 1988).

The study of coping as it relates to couples and families highlights the limitations of the problem- vs. emotion-focused distinction. Applying coping models that are based on male norms to family stress research consistently biases our perception of female family members' coping strategies. As a result, men's coping strengths are emphasized and women's coping efforts are portrayed as weaknesses. By incorporating a focus on both individual and communal aspects of coping, we are likely to paint a truer picture of family coping. Such a picture will facilitate increasingly contextualized and balanced coping research.

ACKNOWLEDGMENTS

Work on this chapter was supported, in part, by a grant from the NIH (1 R01 HD24901-01) and by the Kent State University Applied Psychology Center, which was established through the support of the Ohio Board of Regents.

REFERENCES

Adler, A. (1929/1969). *The science of living.* Garden City, NY: Doubleday.

Amato, P. R., & Keith, B. (1991). Parental divorce and the well-being of children: A meta-analysis. *Psychological Bulletin, 110,* 26–46.

Aneshensel, C. S., & Pearlin, L. I. (1987). Structural contexts of sex differences in stress. In R. C. Barnett, L. Biener, & G. K. Baruch (Eds.), *Gender and stress* (pp. 75–95). New York: Free Press.

Baber, K. M., & Allen, K. R. (1992). *Women and families.* New York: Guilford Press.

Barnett, R. C. (1993). Multiple roles, gender, and psychological distress. In L. Goldberger & S. Breznitz (Eds.), *Handbook of stress* (pp. 427–445). New York: Free Press.

Baruch, G. K., Biener, L., & Barnett, R. C. (1987). Women and gender in research on work and family stress. *American Psychologist, 42,* 130–136.

Belle, D. (1987). Gender differences in the social moderators of stress. In R. C. Barnett, L. Biener, & G. K. Baruch (Eds.), *Gender and stress* (pp. 257–277). New York: Free Press.

Belle, D. (1990). Poverty and women's mental health. *American Psychologist, 45*, 385–389.

Betancourt, H., & Lopez, S. R. (1993). The study of culture, ethnicity, and race in American psychology. *American Psychologist, 48*, 629–637.

Billings, A. G., & Moos, R. H. (1984). Coping, stress, and social resources among adults with unipolar depression. *Journal of Personality and Social Psychology, 46*, 877–891.

Block, J. H. (1983). Differential premises arising from differential socialization of the sexes: Some conjectures. *Child Development, 54*, 1335–1354.

Carver, C. S., Scheier, M. F., & Weintraub, J. K. (1989). Assessing coping strategies: A theoretically based approach. *Journal of Personality and Social Psychology, 56*, 267–283.

Chodorow, N. (1978). *The reproduction of mothering: Psychoanalysis and the sociology of gender.* Berkeley: University of California Press.

Chodorow, N. (1989). *Feminism and psychoanalytic theory.* New Haven, CT: Yale University Press.

Christensen, A. (1988). Dysfunctional interaction patterns in couples. In P. Noller & M. A. Fitzpatrick (Eds.), *Perspectives on marital interaction* (pp. 31–52). Clevedon, England: Multilingual Matters.

Cohen, S., & Katzenstein, M. F. (1988). The war over the family is not over the family. In S. M. Dornbusch & M. H. Strober (Eds.), *Feminism, children, and the new families* (pp. 25–46). New York: Guilford Press.

David, R. J., & Collins, J. W. (1991). Bad outcomes in black babies: Race or racism? *Ethnicity & Disease, 1*, 236–244.

Delphy, C. (1993). Rethinking sex and gender. *Women's Studies International Forum, 16(1)*, 1–9.

Denmark, F. L. (1994). Engendering psychology. *American Psychologist, 49*, 329–334.

Dunahoo, C., Geller, P., & Hobfoll, S. E. (in press). Women's coping: Communal versus individualistic orientation. In M. J. Schabracq, J. A. Winnubst, & C. L. Cooper (Eds.), *Handbook of work and health psychology.* Chichester, Great Britain: Wiley.

Dunahoo, C. L., Monnier, J., Hobfoll, S. E., & Hulsizer, M. R. (1994). *Even the Lone Ranger had Tonto: There's more than rugged individualism in coping* (submitted).

Dunkel-Schetter, C., Folkman, S., & Lazarus, R. S. (1987). Correlates of social support receipt. *Journal of Personality and Social Psychology, 53*, 71–80.

Eisler, R. M., & Blalock, J. A. (1991). Masculine gender role stress: Implications for the assessment of men. *Clinical Psychology Review, 11*, 45–60.

Erickson, E. H. (1963). *Childhood and society*, 2nd ed. New York: W. W. Norton.

Erickson, E. H. (1968). *Identity: Youth and crisis.* New York: W. W. Norton.

Fitzpatrick, M. A. (1988). Approaches to marital interaction. In P. Noller & M. A. Fitzpatrick (Eds.), *Perspectives on marital interaction* (pp. 1–28). Clevedon, England: Multilingual Matters.

Flaherty, J., & Richman, J. (1989). Gender differences in the perception and utilization of social support: Theoretical persepctives and an empirical test. *Social Science Medicine, 28*, 1221–1228.

Fondacaro, M. R., & Moos, R. H. (1987). Social support and coping: A longitudinal analysis. *American Journal of Community Psychology, 15*, 653–673.

Fruzzetti, A. E., & Jacobson, N. S. (1990). Toward a behavioral conceptualization of adult intimacy: Implications for marital therapy. In E. Blechman (Ed.), *Emotions and the Family* (pp. 117–135). Hillsdale, NJ: Lawrence Erlbaum.

Fruzzetti, A. E., & Jacobson, N. S. (1991). Marital and family therapy. In M. Hersen, A. E. Kazdin, & A. S. Bellack (Eds.), *The clinical psychology handbook* (pp. 643–666). New York: Pergamon Press.

Gilligan, C. (1982). *In a different voice.* Cambridge, MA: Harvard University Press.

Goldner, V. (1985). Feminism and family therapy. *Family Process, 24*, 31–47.

Gottman, J. M., & Levenson, R. W. (1988). The social psychophysiology of marriage. In P. Noller & M. A. Fitzpatrick (Eds.), *Perspectives on marital interaction* (pp. 182–200). Clevedon, England: Multilingual Matters.

Groër, M. W., Thomas, S. P., & Shoffner, D. (1992). Adolescent stress and coping: A longitudinal study. *Research in Nursing and Health, 15*, 209–217.

Grych, J. H., & Fincham, F. D. (1990). Marital conflict and children's adjustment: A cognitive–contextual framework. *Psychological Bulletin, 108*, 267–290.

Guisinger, S., & Blatt, S. J. (1994). Individuality and relatedness: Evolution of a fundamental dialectic. *American Psychologist, 49*, 104–111.

Hall, J. A., & Halberstadt, A. G. (1980). Masculinity and femininity in children: Development of the children's personal attributes questionnaire. *Developmental Psychology, 16*, 270–280.

Hobfoll, S. F. (1991). Gender differences in stress reactions: Women filling the gaps. *Psychology and Health, 5*, 95–109.

Hobfoll, S. E., Dunahoo, C. L., Ben-Porath, Y., & Monnier, J. (1994). Gender and coping: The Dual-Axis Model of Coping. *American Journal of Community Psychology, 22*, 49–82.

Hobfoll, S. E., & Lerman, M. (1989). Predicting receipt of social support: A longitudinal study of parents' reactions to their child's illness. *Health Psychology, 8*, 61–77.

Hobfoll, S. E., & Stokes, J. P. (1988). The process and mechanisms of social support. In S. W. Duck (Ed.), *Handbook of personal relationships* (pp. 497–517). New York: Wiley.

Hoffman, L. W. (1972). Early childhood experiences and women's achievement motives. *Journal of Social Issues, 28(2)*, 129–155.

Jacklin, C. N. (1989). Female and male: Issues of gender. *American Psychologist, 44*, 127–133.

Jacobson, N. S. (1989). The politics of intimacy. *Behavior Therapist, 12(2)*, 29–32.

Johnson, E. H. (1990). *The deadly emotions: The role of anger, hostility, and aggression in health and emotional well-being.* New York: Praeger.

Kaschak, E. (1992). *Engendered lives: A new psychology of women's experience.* New York: Basic Books.

Kessler, R. C., McLeod, J. D., & Wethington, E. (1985). The costs of caring: A perspective on the relationship between sex and psychological distress. In I. G. Sarason & B. R. Sarason (Eds.), *Social support: Theory, research, and applications* (pp. 491–506). Dordrecht: Martinus Nijhoff Publishers.

LaCroix, A. Z., & Haynes, S. G. (1987). Gender differences in the health effects of workplace roles. In R. C. Barnett, L. Biener, & G. K. Baruch (Eds.), *Gender and stress* (pp. 96–121). New York: Free Press.

Lane, C., & Hobfoll, S. E. (1992). How loss affects anger and alienates potential supporters. *Journal of Consulting and Clinical Psychology, 60*, 935–942.

Lazarus, R. S., & Folkman, S. (1984). *Stress, appraisal, and coping.* New York: Springer.

Lowenthal, M. F., & Haven, C. (1968). Interaction and adaptation: Intimacy as a critical variable. *American Sociological Review, 33*, 20–30.

Markus, H. R., & Kitayama, S. (1991). Culture and the self: Implications for cognition, emotion, and motivation. *Psychological Review, 98(2)*, 224–253.

Maslow, A. H. (1987). *Motivation and personality,* 3rd ed. New York: HarperCollins.

McGoldrick, M., Preto, N. G., Hines, P. M., & Lee, E. (1991). Ethnicity and family therapy. In A. S. Gurman & D. P. Kniskern (Eds.), *Handbook of family therapy,* Vol. II (pp. 546–582). New York: Brunner/Mazel.

Miller, J. B. (1976). *Toward a new psychology of women.* Boston: Beacon Press.

Moritsugu, J., & Sue, S. (1983). Minority status as a stressor. In R. D. Felner, L. A. Jason, J. N. Moritsugu, & S. S. Farber (Eds.), *Preventive psychology: Theory, research and practice* (pp. 162–174). New York: Pergamon Press.

Noller, P. (1988). Overview and implications. In P. Noller & M. A. Fitzpatrick (Eds.), *Perspectives on marital interaction* (pp. 323–344). Clevedon, England: Multilingual Matters.

Noller, P., & Fitzpatrick, M. A. (Eds.) (1988). *Perspectives on marital interaction.* Clevedon, England: Multilingual Matters.

Pearlin, L. I., & Schooler, C. (1978). The structure of coping. *Journal of Health and Social Behavior, 19*, 2–21.

Powell, G. N. (1988). *Women and men in management.* Newbury Park, CA: Sage Publications.

Ptacek, J. T., Smith, R. E., & Zanas, J. (1992). Gender, appraisal, and coping: A longitudinal analysis. *Journal of Personality, 60*, 747–770.

Reis, H. T., Senchak, M., & Solomon, B. (1985). Sex differences in the intimacy of social interaction: Further examination of potential explanations. *Journal of Personality and Social Psychology, 48*, 1204–1217.

Riger, S. (1992). Epistemological debates, feminist voices: Science, social values, and the study of women. *American Psychologist, 47*, 730–740.

Riger, S. (1993). What's wrong with empowerment. *American Journal of Psychology, 21(3)*, 279–292.

Robinson, B. E., & Barret, R. L. (1986). *The developing father: Emerging roles in contemporary society*. New York: Guilford Press.

Rook, K. S. (1984). The negative side of social interaction. *Journal of Personality and Social Psychology, 46*, 1097–1108.

Rosario, M., Shinn, M., Morch, H., & Huckabee, C. B. (1988). Gender differences in coping and social supports: Testing socialization and role constraint theories. *Journal of Community Psychology, 16*, 55–69.

Roth, S., & Cohen, L. J. (1986). Approach, avoidance, and coping with stress. *American Psychologist, 41*, 813–819.

Sampson, E. E. (1977). Psychology and the American ideal. *Journal of Personality and Social Psychology, 35*, 767–782.

Shumaker, S. A., & Hill, D. R. (1991). Gender differences in social support and physical health. *Health Psychology, 10*, 102–111.

Solomon, L. J., & Rothblum, E. D. (1986). Stress, coping and social support in women. *Behavior Therapist, 9(10)*, 199–204.

Strickland, B. R. (1992). Women and depression. *Current Directions in Psychological Science, 1(4)*, 132–135.

Strober, M. H. (1988). Two-earner families. In S. M. Dornbusch & M. H. Strober (Eds.), *Feminism, children, and the new families* (pp. 161–190). New York: Guilford Press.

Vetere, A. (1992). Working with families. In J. M. Ussher & P. Nicolson (Eds.), *Gender issues in clinical psychology* (pp. 129–152). London: Routledge.

Weisz, J. R., Rothbaum, F. M., & Blackburn, T. C. (1984). Standing out and standing in: The psychology of control in America and Japan. *American Psychologist, 39*, 955–969.

Wertlieb, D., Weigel, C., & Feldstein, M. (1987). Measuring children's coping. *American Journal of Orthopsychiatry, 57(4)*, 548–560.

Yoder, J. D., & Kahn, A. S. (1993). Working toward an inclusive psychology of women. *American Psychologist, 48*, 846–850.

18

Social Support and Preventive and Therapeutic Interventions

BRIAN LAKEY and CATHERINE J. LUTZ

Social support has been one of the most intensely studied psychosocial factors in health since research in this area began in the mid-1970s. From the very beginning, a major goal of social support research has been to guide novel preventive and treatment interventions (Heller, 1979). This hope has been sustained by the consistent finding that persons with low levels of perceived social support have more negative mental and physical health outcomes than their more fortunate counterparts (Barrera, 1986; Cohen & Wills, 1985; B. R. Sarason, I. G. Sarason, & Pierce, 1990a). In fact, the relation between perceived support and health appears to be one of the more replicable effects in psychology.

The purpose of this chapter is to review existing knowledge of how to change social support. We begin by reviewing intervention studies that have attempted to improve some aspect of social support. The majority of these studies have important methodological problems, and the few well-conducted studies have provided disappointing results. Although some interventions have had moderate health effects, they have rarely been able to change naturally occurring social support. Thus, support appears to be much more difficult to influence than scholars initially imagined. In our view, translating social support research into effective interventions has been difficult because the necessary basic research on the mechanisms by which social support has its effects have not been completed. In addition, the field prematurely adopted a theoretical model of social support that has important empirical problems.

In the second section of this chapter, we review the theoretical models of perceived support and their implications for intervention. Research indicates that

BRIAN LAKEY and CATHERINE J. LUTZ • Department of Psychology, Wayne State University, Detroit, Michigan 48202.

Handbook of Social Support and the Family, edited by Gregory R. Pierce, Barbara R. Sarason, and Irwin G. Sarason. Plenum Press, New York, 1996.

there are at least three important components of perceived support: an aspect of the perceiver's personality, objective characteristics of supporters, and the perceiver–supporter interaction.

In the final section, we draw from our clinical experience in working with low perceived support individuals to describe potential interventions for targeting each aspect of perceived support.

REVIEW OF SOCIAL SUPPORT INTERVENTIONS

Reviewing the intervention literature on social support presents the dilemma of what types of studies to include. The broadest perspective would be to include any intervention that involves one person providing interpersonal assistance to another under stress. However, this would include reviewing the entire body of research on psychological therapy. Although social support is probably an important ingredient in therapeutic effectiveness, the latter literature developed independently from social support research and deals primarily with professional helping, a process generally excluded from the social support literature. There is a similar literature on the effectiveness of paraprofessional helpers (Christensen & Jacobson, 1994; Durlak, 1979), and both literatures indicate that interpersonal assistance can substantially reduce psychological disorder (Christensen & Jacobson, 1994; Durlak, 1979; Robinson, Berman, & Robinson, 1990; Shapiro & Shapiro, 1982). The psychotherapy literature, however, is not generally considered to provide evidence for the role of social support.

The promise of social support research has been that individuals' naturally existing social relations can protect them from future psychological disorder, reducing the need for formal intervention (Heller, 1979). Thus, to go beyond the therapy outcome literature, social support research needs to show that we can produce enduring changes in naturally occurring social support and that such changes prevent future psychological problems. In our review, we focus on interventions that attempt to change social support levels in at-risk individuals. Unfortunately, there have been a number of studies in which a social support intervention was provided, but there was no assessment of whether the intervention changed naturally occurring social support. Such studies are more similar to investigations of paraprofessional therapy than to investigations of naturally occurring social support. Such studies will be reviewed if the authors conceptualized them as social support interventions, but in our opinion, they do not tell us much about how to improve social support because measures of the construct were not included.

We also place greater emphasis on findings that demonstrate changes in perceived social support rather than changes in social networks or changes in enacted support. Perceived social support reflects an individual's subjective appraisal that others would provide support if needed, as well as a general sense of being loved and valued. Enacted support refers to the provisions of specific supportive behaviors under stress, such as advice or reassurance. Social networks reflect structural aspects of relationships, such as the number of persons with whom one comes into contact on a regular basis or the percentage of these persons who are friends vs. family. Basic research has demonstrated that perceived, enacted, and network support are not closely related and reflect different constructs (Barrera, 1986; Dunkel-Schetter & Bennett, 1990; Heller & Lakey, 1985; Wethington & Kessler, 1986). We emphasize perceived support in this review because this same body of research has shown that only perceived support is related to psychological and physical health.

A wide range of intervention programs have been developed to increase the social support of at-risk populations. A popular approach has been to rely on trained volunteers or staff members to provide social support. Other interventions have consisted of support groups, social skills training, or restructuring social environments. Interventions that provide social support from volunteers, staff, or support groups have identical conceptual underpinnings and differ only in how and by whom social support is provided. The rationale is that enacted support provided by others (e.g., advice or reassurance) will strengthen an individual's coping resources and thereby lead to a generalized sense of being supported and a reduction of psychological symptoms. Social skills training has a different conceptual basis and targets skills deficits in low social support individuals (B. R. Sarason, I. G. Sarason, Hacker, & Basham, 1985). The rationale here is that people can directly influence their own naturally occurring social relations if they have the requisite skills.

In addition to utilizing a number of different interventions, these programs have targeted a wide range of participants as well. Participants have included the elderly, pregnant adolescents, women during labor, parents of children with conduct disorder, widows, college students, and high school students. The elderly have been the most frequently targeted single group because many scholars believe that they are more vulnerable to weak social ties (Heller, Thompson, Trueba, Hogg, & Vlachos-Weber, 1991). Unfortunately, although there are a number of studies reporting evaluations of social support interventions, many suffer from serious methodological flaws. Moreover, the outcome studies with the greatest methodological rigor frequently fail to demonstrate significant changes in naturally occurring social support.

Interventions That Provide Social Support from Volunteers or Staff

Several interventions have attempted to improve social support by providing it through trained volunteers or staff. For example, Scharlach (1988) attempted to increase the social adjustment of elderly patients newly admitted into a nursing home through the use of a structured program of peer counseling. Every second admission into a community nursing home was assigned to a peer counselor who greeted the patient upon admission, imparted information regarding institutional life, and attempted to initiate conversations about the challenges of institutional living. Peer counselors were residents of the nursing home who agreed to undergo training involving active listening skills. Control admissions did not receive any special attention. Measures of social competence and physical functioning were administered upon admission and 2 months later. Although the author reported that a higher percentage of intervention participants improved than did controls, no inferential statistics were reported, and no information was provided regarding how the classification of "improved" was determined. Furthermore, no measure of social support was administered, and so it was impossible to determine whether the intervention actually influenced the construct of interest.

Bogat and Jason (1983) compared two different visiting programs with no-contact controls among elderly participants. Although participants were randomly assigned to the two experimental groups, the control group was drawn from a slightly different elderly sample. In one visiting condition, college students were trained to provide an empathetic and caring atmosphere. In the second visiting condition, college students systematically encouraged and rewarded social participation and attempted to extinguish expressions of isolation and depression. After 3 months, the experimental groups did not differ from controls on life satisfaction, locus of control, health, depression, or current social networks. The only significant difference was that treated subjects reported greater increases in the social "networks in which they would like to participate, but were not currently involved." Thus, the intervention appears to have increased a desire for a larger social network, without increasing the size of the current network.

In one study, an extensive outreach program was organized within a government-subsidized housing project for the elderly (Baumgarten, Thomas, de Courval, & Infante-Rivard, 1988). Outreach services included two major components: (1) individual social support provided by resident volunteers and (2) leisure and cultural group activities, again coordinated by resident volunteers. Residents of another government-subsidized building in the neighborhood were used as the control group. Standardized measures of depression, social network size, and perceived social support were administered at pretest and 16 months later at posttest. Interviewers were blind to hypotheses. Despite a large sample size ($N = 93$), there were no significant differences between intervention and control subjects in the number of social ties or in perceived social support. Surprisingly, there was a trend for the intervention group to show greater increases in depressive symptoms.

Another study that attempted to provide supportive others for at-risk individuals is probably the most impressive intervention study in this literature. This study is impressive both because of its methodological rigor and because the intervention was carefully planned and implemented. Heller et al. (1991) attempted to increase perceived social support of elderly women through the use of telephone dyads. Low-income elderly women scoring below the median on a standardized measure of perceived social support were selected to participate in the study. Participants were randomly assigned to the control group or an experimental condition consisting of weekly telephone calls from a supportive staff member. Measures of depression, perceived social support, social networks, morale, health, and loneliness were administered at pretest and after 10 weeks. At the end of the 10 weeks, subjects in the experimental condition were randomly assigned to one of three groups: (1) continued staff contact, (2) conversation initiator, or (3) conversation recipient. Subjects in the latter two groups were randomly paired, and the conversation initiators were instructed to contact their assigned partners for an additional 10 weeks. Assigning participants to contact each other was an important component of the intervention because rather than being encouraged to depend on paraprofessional help, women were helped to develop new supportive relationships. Although peer dyads were not required to meet each other in person, they were not discouraged from doing so if they desired. Subjects who refused to participate in the peer-dyad portion of the experiment were reassigned to a "refuser" group and continued to receive phone calls from a staff member. At the end of this phase of the study, subjects completed the same measures administered at times 1 and 2.

Despite a well-conducted intervention, tight experimental design, and large sample ($N = 291$), intervention participants did not display significantly greater changes on any of the social support or mental health measures compared to controls. Similarly, there were no significant differences between the different experimental groups. All conditions demonstrated within-group improvements over time in morale and loneliness. One possible explanation for these puzzling results is that the peer-dyad component was ineffective in establishing close relationships between these women. However, the observation that 56% of these dyads were still in contact at the 10-week follow-up and described their partners in positive terms suggests that the intervention was implemented as planned.

The studies discussed above focused on providing social support for elderly populations. Such interventions have been applied to other at-risk populations as well. For example, Unger and Wandersman (1985 [Study 2]) randomly assigned teen mothers to a control group or to a group visited monthly by a "resource mother" who provided informational and emotional support. The authors reported a number of benefits associated with the program. There was a significant differences between the groups in the percentage of low birthweight babies, but the statistical tests that provided this information were not reported, and so it is difficult to examine their appropriateness. The authors also reported better outcomes on variables such as knowledge about their babies, satisfaction with mothering, and staying in school. However, they did not claim that these differences were significant and did not report any statistics. Although the authors emphasized that perceived social support was associated with better infant health and with greater satisfaction with mothering and maternal responsiveness, differences between treated and control subjects in perceived social support were not reported. We interpret this to mean that the intervention was not successful in increasing perceived social support.

Vachon and colleagues (Vachon, Lyall, Rogers, Freedman-Letofsky, & Freeman, 1980; Vachon et al., 1982) randomly assigned widows to a social support intervention group or a nontreatment control group. Widows in the intervention group received supportive telephone calls and visits from women who had successfully coped with the death of their husbands. Intervention subjects displayed greater improvement in psychological distress than did controls at the 2-year follow-up. The size of this effect was rather small, however, accounting for only 2% of the variance (Vachon et al., 1982). However, the two groups did not differ on an overall index of interpersonal functioning that included a wide range of heterogeneous factors including social support. At 12 months, the intervention group was more likely to have reported making new friends, but this effect was not obtained at 1 month or 24 months. Moreover, because of unhappy randomization, the intervention group had significantly larger social networks at pretest, which may have accounted for some of the effects. Thus, although this innovative program had a small effect on adjustment, it does not appear to have been successful in increasing levels of naturally occurring social support.

Bloom, Hodges, and Caldwell (1982) randomly assigned newly separated men and women to a no-intervention control group or to an intervention program that involved supportive contact from trained program staff and optional training programs in separation-related problems (e.g., parenting, legal issues). The intervention lasted 6 months and involved an average of 10 supportive contacts. Training sessions were much less frequently utilized than supportive contacts. At 6- and 18-month follow-up, intervention subjects displayed greater improvement in psychological symptoms than did controls (Bloom et al., 1982; Hodges & Bloom, 1986). At no point, however, did intervention subjects display greater changes than controls on any socialization measure, including perceived support from friends, number of friends lost, or family's acceptance of the separation. Thus, similar to the Vachon et al. (1980, 1982) studies, extensive support provided by project staff had significant effects on psychological symptomatology. However, these interventions did not change subjects' perceptions of naturally occurring social support.

Kennell, Klaus, McGrath, Robertson, and Hinkley (1991) randomly assigned women in labor to one of three conditions: (1) a control group, (2) an observer group, or (3) a supported group that received continuous emotional support throughout labor from a trained female assistant. As in the control group, subjects in the observer group received routine hospital care during labor, but with the presence of an unfamiliar observer who inconspicuously recorded the patients' progress. Women in the supported group were less likely to require a cesarean section than controls and less likely to require forceps delivery than controls and observer groups. Supported women were less likely than the other two groups to use epidural anesthesia, and the authors speculated that this may have been the reason fewer supported women developed maternal fever, thus necessitating a sepsis evaluation of the newborn infant. However, the groups did not differ in their use of two other types of anesthesia. This study is impressive in that it demonstrates how an interpersonal intervention can be effective in aiding labor and delivery. It is especially impressive because the study replicates prior trials conducted in Honduras (Klaus, Kennell, Robertson, & Sosa, 1986; Sosa, Kennell, Klaus, Robertson, & Urrutia, 1980).

The studies are limited, however, from the perspective of helping us understand how to increase naturally occurring social support. For example, it is not clear whether the active ingredient in this study was, in fact, social support, as no measure of the construct was obtained. An alternative explanation is that the presence of observers and supporters influenced the behavior of medical staff. For example, supporters may have acted as advocates for the women they were assisting. The mere presence of observers may have influenced staff behavior as well. Staff may have been more conservative in administering medication or in performing cesarean sections when it was salient that they too were being observed. For example, women in the observer-only condition were less likely to receive epidural anesthesia than controls, and supported women were not less likely to have cesarean sections than observed women.

Thus, although a number of studies have attempted to provide social support from trained staff and volunteers, they have not been very effective in producing changes in naturally occurring social support. This is an important limitation, because unless staff- or volunteer-provided social support produces changes in naturally occurring support, low support individuals will be protected from disorder only as long as they are in the program. No enduring strengthening of stress resistance will have been provided. Thus, such social support interventions would be limited to reducing symptoms among persons undergoing specific stressors (e.g., Bloom et al., 1982; Kennell et al., 1991; Vachon et al., 1980). This is useful knowledge, but it falls short of the original promise of social support research. Under these circumstances, the primary advantage of social support interventions would be that paraprofessionals are less expensive than professionals. However, producing semipermanent changes in naturally occurring social support would confer much more long-lasting and cost-effective benefits.

Support Groups as Vehicles for Providing Social Support

Another popular intervention has been to increase social support by providing support groups for at-risk individuals. These interventions are conceptually identical to those that provide support from volunteers or staff, but differ in who provides social support. Because support is not provided by volunteers or staff, there should be greater opportunities for support group members to become part of at-risk individuals' permanent social support resources. Consistent with research on project-provided support, however, there are a number of studies with important methodological limitations, and the overall results do not present an encouraging picture.

Unger and Wandersman (1985 [Study 1]) randomly assigned teenagers in their last trimester of pregnancy to an educational support group or a control group that received child development information in the mail. However, the effectiveness of the support intervention could not be evaluated because of the large number of dropouts in the support condition, resulting in a small sample size.

Andersson (1985) attempted to decrease loneliness among elderly women through small group meetings. A sample of elderly female applicants was randomly selected from a group of applicants for senior citizen housing. Participants were then randomly assigned to a control group or to the experimental condition, which consisted of 4 group meetings of 3–5 persons each. Two of the meetings were led by project staff, and topics for discussion included "the role of retiree" and "the residential area." Standardized measures of physical health, loneliness, and social contacts were employed. Compared to controls, subjects in the peer group condition demonstrated increases in their number of social contacts and decreases in blood pressure. However, they did not experience significantly greater improvements in self-esteem or loneliness (a strong correlate of perceived social support).

Haley, Brown, and Levine (1987) randomly assigned primary caregivers of demented relatives to (1) a support group, (2) a support group with stress management training, or (3) a waiting list control. The support group was highly structured and involved the provision of extensive information from professionals about dementia and coping with a demented relative. The stress management component involved instruction in progressive muscle relaxation and cognitive restructuring. Both intervention groups reported receiving social support from their group. For example, most participants reported deriving "belonging (i.e., being an involved member of the group; feeling close to others)." However, the groups did not differ from controls on perceived social support, depression, life satisfaction, or social activity.

Toseland, Rossiter, and Labrecque (1989a,b) report two separate studies in which caregivers of elderly parents were randomly assigned to (1) a professionally led support group, (2) a peer-led support group, or (3) a respite-only control group. The professionally led support group encompassed education, emotional support, and instruction on social problem solving. In the peer-led support group, participants were encouraged to share information and coping skills that they had found helpful. Toseland et al. (1989b) added a fourth group consisting of stress management training provided by professionals. This group focused on problem solving with additional training in progressive muscle relaxation. Although Toseland et al. (1989a) reported significantly greater reductions in psychological distress among treated vs. control participants, this difference was not observed in Toseland et al. (1989b). All intervention groups produced greater changes in social network size than did the control groups, and the stress management condition produced greater increases than the peer-led support group in Toseland et al. (1989b). However, there are limitations to these findings. Treated subjects did not display greater changes than controls in support satisfaction in either study, the network measure was a retrospective estimate of change at posttest, and the measures were administered by a nonblinded interviewer. A third experiment compared the problem-solving/stress-management group with a no-treatment control (Toseland, Labrecque, Goebel, & Whitney, 1992). Unlike the results of the earlier studies, this investigation kept participants blind to condition, but failed to find significant treatment effects for psychological distress, network size, or support satisfaction.

In summary, the results of support group interventions are similar to those that utilized project-provided social support. Like the outreach intervention of

Baumgarten et al. (1988) described above, the interventions of Andersson (1985) and Toseland et al. (1989a,b) were able to produce changes in social networks, but these changes did not result in improved perceived social support. This limitation is important, because only perceived social support appears to have a strong relation to health outcomes (Barerra, 1986; Wethington & Kessler, 1986). Like Bloom et al. (1982) and Vachon et al. (1980), Toseland et al. (1989a) found that success in reducing distress levels does not guarantee changes in perceived social support.

Skills Training to Increase Social Support

Another approach to increasing social support is to help at-risk persons develop the personal qualities needed to improve or develop their own naturally occurring relationships. These studies have focused on a wide range of constructs such as social skills, self-esteem, and requesting social support. Again, although there have been a number of intervention studies of this kind, there are a number of studies with methodological problems or weak results.

Lovell and Hawkins (1988) conducted a 26-week group, designed to increase the social networks of mothers currently in counseling for child abuse or neglect. The intervention consisted of a group didactic followed by an informal luncheon to encourage the development of friendships within the group. The didactic covered such topics as stress management, anger management, positive self-talk, problem solving, assertiveness, and child management. This study has several methodological limitations, including the lack of a control group and small sample size. But despite the generous nature of a pre–post design, no significant changes in social networks were observed, suggesting that the intervention was not successful.

Yahne and Long (1988) attempted to raise self-esteem by skills training including the development of social support. Participants in this study were graduate and undergraduate female volunteers. Subjects were randomly assigned to the treatment condition or a waiting list control. The treatment group met 2 hours a week for 6 weeks and was led by two cofacilitators trained by the researcher. Treatment consisted of skills training in problem solving and reframing, professional and peer counseling, and developing social support. In terms of the latter component, group participants were encouraged to form friendships with the other members and were taught skills in requesting social support, as well as ways to refuse or limit inappropriate support. The results indicated greater increases on the self-esteem measure among experimental subjects than among controls. Unfortunately, measures of social support were not administered.

Hawkins, Catalano, and Wells (1986) attempted to increase prosocial networks of substance abusers. Participants were randomly assigned to the program or to a treatment-as-usual control group. The program combined behavioral skills training, scheduled group activities, and network development components. Behavioral skills training, including assertiveness, social problem solving, and stress management, were taught during the first 10 weeks of the program. Modeling, role playing, and videotaped feedback were utilized to facilitate the learning of these skills. The remaining 6 months of the program consisted of planned activities between group participants and community volunteers. Although results showed an improvement in social problem solving and avoidance of alcohol and drugs as a function of treatment, no measures of social support or social relationships were administered.

Barth and Schinke (1984) attempted to enhance the social and cognitive skills of adolescent mothers in order to improve relationships with family and friends, thereby increasing perceived social support. The social skills component of this program focused on three common problem areas of adolescent parents: (1) making positive social contacts, (2) requesting help, and (3) resolving conflicts with parents. Cognitive skills included positive self-talk and thinking broadly about potential social resources. Barth and Schinke (1984) reported that participants in the program, compared to controls, demonstrated improvements in interpersonal and cognitive skills, as well as increases on some measures of social support. This study suffers from several methodological problems, however, making interpretations tenuous. Subjects were not randomly assigned to condition, the specific measures utilized were not stated, and assessment was not blind to condition.

Schinke, Schilling, Barth, Gilchrist, and Maxwell (1986) reported a much improved extension of Barth and Schinke (1984) that evaluated a 12-week stress management program for pregnant teenagers. The intervention consisted of training in problem solving, self-instruction, self-reinforcement, communication skill, relaxation, and social-network development. At posttest, intervention subjects displayed more favorable scores on measures of problem solving, perceived support, and behavioral assertion than did no-treatment controls. At 3-month follow-up, intervention subjects had higher scores on problem solving, support, self-esteem, and self-reinforcement. The behavioral assertion measure was not administered at follow-up. Although this is a promising investigation of how skills training may increase social support, subjects were not randomly assigned to condition, and the method of assignment was not reported. Thus, intervention subjects may have differed from controls in some important characteristics that may have led them to be more likely to improve during the study period regardless of the intervention.

Brand, Lakey, and Berman (1995) tested an intervention that incorporated both social skills training and cognitive restructuring. Cognitive techniques were designed to improve the perception both of self and of significant others. This approach was based on research and theory that suggested that self-esteem and perceived support are intimately connected (Lakey & Cassady, 1990). In addition, an important component was to reconceptualize important, troubled relationships with family members. Most participants had family relationships that were characterized by genuinely unsupportive or abusive interactions. Training encouraged subjects to develop more complex attributional theories of their family members' behaviors. Training encouraged participants not to attribute the unsupportive behaviors to subjects' deficient personal worth or lovableness, but to consider other factors as well (e.g., parental levels of stress, psychopathology, and skills in emotional expression). Subjects were widowed, divorced, and never-married community residents who scored below the mean on a standard measure of perceived social support. They were randomly assigned to a waiting list control or the interpersonal skills training condition. Compared to controls, intervention subjects demonstrated significant increases in perceived social support from family, self-esteem, and frequency of self-reinforcement. There were no differences between groups in perceived support from friends or in assertion skills. As predicted by the authors, mediational analyses suggested that changes in self-esteem and frequency of self-reinforcement could account for changes in perceived support. Nonetheless, although trained participants demonstrated significant changes in perceived social support, these changes were small and of little practical significance. Interestingly, changes in self-esteem and frequency of self-reinforcement were much larger, leading the authors to speculate that it may be easier to change cognition about the self than about supportiveness.

Wolchick et al. (1993) conducted a randomized investigation of a program for divorced mothers and their children that placed a strong emphasis on improving the quality of the parent–child relationship. Extensive training was provided for mothers in promoting positive family activities, quality time, positive attention for desirable behaviors, and listening skills. Compared to waiting-list controls, mother's reports of their interactions with their children improved on three relationship dimensions: communication, positive routines, and acceptance/rejection. Unfortunately, these results were not replicated in children's reports. Program children did not show significantly greater changes on most measures of adjustment than controls, although structural equation modeling indicated a significant indirect effect of the program in influencing behavior problems (mothers' reports) through improved relationship quality (mothers' reports). However, the relations between treatment and changes in family environment and between family environment and behavior problems were rather small (betas = 0.35 and −0.22, respectively), raising questions about the practical usefulness of this intervention. Last, although there was some evidence that family environment improved, it is not clear how these particular constructs (communication, acceptance/rejection, positive routines) relate to social support.

In summary, skills training appears to have some promise as a technique to increase social support. Although several of the studies suffer from important methodological problems, or failed to measure social support, the results of Brand et al. (1995) and Wolchik et al. (1993) are encouraging. Although these studies provide rare demonstrations that perceived social relations can be modified, both studies found small effects that may not be practically useful.

Other Social Support Interventions

In an innovative support program, Felner, Ginter, and Primavera (1982) attempted to prevent the onset of problems in academic and emotional adjustment that occurs during the transition from middle school to high school. In this

study, a randomly selected sample of students entering a large urban high school
were randomly assigned to either a control group or the transition project. The
transition project consisted of restructuring the role of the homeroom teachers
and partially modifying project students' social systems in order to enhance
feelings of stability and belongingness. The homeroom teachers' role was expanded to include counseling and administrative duties. In a sense, homeroom
teachers of project students were trained to serve as advocates for the students.
Project students were also assigned to all their core courses with other project
members in order to decrease the degree of flux in their social systems. The results
indicated that project students remained stable throughout the school year on a
variety of dimensions, while the control group evidenced a steady decline. This
effect was observed in grades, attendance, self-concepts, and several aspects of
perceived social climate. Most important for our purposes, control students saw
their teachers as less supportive as the year progressed, whereas project students
remained stable. Unfortunately, although one of the stated goals of this study was
to increase social integration among students, no measure of perceived social
support from peers was obtained. In addition, there were no significant changes
on students' sense of affiliation with teachers. This important and well-designed
study is another rare demonstration that perceived support can be modified.
Mediational analyses would have been helpful to determine the extent to which
changes in perceived support from teachers could account for changes in academic performance and what factors were most important in producing changes
in perceived support.

    One frequent criticism of social support interventions is the temporary,
artificial nature of the support provided. The research of Dadds and McHugh
(1992) is unique because it attempted to change the behavior of participants'
existing social network members. Single parents with conduct-disordered children were randomly assigned to either a behavioral family therapy condition or
behavioral family therapy with ally support training. In the latter condition,
participants chose a member of their social network to undergo support training
as the ally. Allies were given instructions on specific supportive tasks that they were
to perform, including responding to subjects' problems, engaging in casual
conversation with the participants on a weekly basis, and participating in problem-
solving sessions. Children of parents in both groups demonstrated improvements
in their behavior, but no group differences were found in perceived social support.

Summary of Social Support Interventions

    Studies designed to increase perceived social support have not provided
strong evidence that social support can be improved very easily. A number of
different interventions have been attempted, yet few have produced impressive
results. Interventions that have provided social support from trained volunteers or
staff have occasionally been able to reduce symptom levels, but they have not
translated into enduring changes in participants' social support. Support group
interventions have produced similar outcomes. There is some evidence that skills

training can improve social support, but the size of this effect has been relatively small. Felner et al. (1982) influenced perceptions of support by making organizational changes in a school environment, but this work needs to be replicated, and such interventions may be limited to school environments.

Our understanding of how to improve social support is limited by the large number of studies with important methodological limitations, including failure to use random assignment, blind assessors, standard measures, and appropriate statistics. Another problem is that although several investigations explicitly targeted improving social support, many did not include measures of this construct. Thus, it is impossible to determine whether the interventions actually influenced social support.

Conceptual Issues in Translating Social Support Research into Interventions

As we have seen, controlled trials of social support interventions have not been very successful in showing that perceived social support can be modified. These studies have been very successful, however, in raising hard questions about our understanding of this construct. Because several of these investigations were very competently conducted, their failure to produce changes in perceived support suggests that our assumptions about its nature may be flawed. This situation results from a lack of basic research on social support processes. We do not know how perceived support has its influence on symptoms, or even the extent to which it is a characteristic of the social environment, a personality characteristic of the perceiver, or some interaction between the two. In the absence of such fundamental knowledge, it is difficult to imagine how we could design interventions to influence perceived support. Thus, the next section of this chapter is designed to critically review some of the basic models of perceived social support that have guided and will continue to shape social support interventions.

The traditional models conceptualize perceived support as an aspect of the social environment (Cutrona & Russell, 1990; B. R. Sarason, I. G. Sarason, & Pierce, 1990b; Thoits, 1986). Persons under stress receive socially supportive behaviors such as advice or reassurance (i.e., enacted support), which enhance their ability to cope with the stressor. As a result of more effective coping, persons with high levels of support develop fewer stress-related psychological and physical symptoms (i.e., stress-buffering effects [Cohen & Wills, 1985]). According to this view, measures of perceived social support reflect the overall availability and quality of enacted social support in the social environment. These models have had tremendous influence on social support research, in part because of the strong intuitive appeal of social support. The mere term "social support" conjures up such processes, and most people believe that they routinely observe such processes in their daily lives. Virtually all the intervention studies reviewed previously were generated from such conceptions. However, there are important empirical problems with these models.

The most important empirical problem for the traditional models is that measures of perceived and enacted support do not appear to be strongly related.

This weak correlation is important because these models assume that perceived support is a reflection of the social support actually received and that enacted support is the mechanism that links perceived support with symptoms. As early as 1986, however, Barrera (1986) had observed that the correlation between self-report measures of perceived and of enacted support typically was about $r = 0.30$ or lower. Subsequent reviews and investigations have reached similar conclusions (e.g., Dunkel-Schetter & Bennett, 1990; B. R. Sarason, Shearin, Pierce, & I. G. Sarason, 1987). Although a correlation of this magnitude is not trivial in psychological research, it is too small to support the view that perceived support is rooted primarily in enacted support. In addition, other research has found that high perceived support subjects have better memory for supportive behaviors (Lakey & Cassady, 1990; Lakey, Moineau, & Drew, 1992). Thus, the weak correlation between self-report measures of perceived and enacted support may say more about memory for support-relevant behaviors than it does about the types of social support actually received.

Behavioral observation studies have also revealed limited evidence for an association between measures of perceived support and measures of enacted support. Heller and Lakey (1985) and Lakey and Heller (1988) observed high and low perceived support subjects interacting with their friends while facing laboratory stressors. The behaviors of subjects and their companions were coded to reflect a wide range of supportive behaviors. However, perceived support was unrelated to the actual supportive behaviors provided by friends. The results of Lakey and Heller (1988) are particularly noteworthy because they documented a relation between a behavioral measure of enacted support and a behavioral measure of subjects' subsequent problem-solving behavior. Thus, the absence of a relation between perceived and enacted support cannot be explained as a result of the poor measurement of enacted support. Similarly, Belcher and Costello (1991) observed the supportive interactions of clinically depressed individuals, normal controls, and their confidants in a laboratory situation. Although clinically depressed persons had much lower levels of perceived support than did normal controls, their confidants did not provide lower levels of enacted support. Cutrona, Suhr, and MacFarlane (1990) observed a supportive interaction between subjects and strangers in a laboratory setting. Subjects' ratings of the supportiveness of their interaction partners were unrelated to their partner's actual behavior.

In contrast, Gurung, Sarason, and Sarason (1994) recently reported significant relations between students' perceptions of their mothers' supportiveness and their mothers' actual behavior in a social-support interaction. However, this relation accounted for only 5% of the variance and was much smaller than the relation between students' perceptions of maternal conflict and mothers' critical behavior (21%). This study does suggest that stronger relations between measures of perceived support and behavioral measures of enacted support might be obtained if researchers used relationship-specific measures.

As a whole, these behavioral observation studies converge with the self-report studies in suggesting a less than strong relation between perceived and enacted support.

Other problems with the traditional model involve the relation between enacted support and symptoms. Although enacted support is hypothesized to be the mechanism by which perceived support is related to mental health, research has consistently shown that unlike perceived support, enacted support is unrelated to measures of psychological symptoms (Barrera, 1986; Dunkel-Schetter & Bennett, 1990). In addition, enacted support rarely demonstrates stress-buffering effects (Cohen & Wills, 1985), even though traditional models hypothesize that enacted support moderates reactions to stressful life events. In conclusion, we find little compelling evidence for traditional models of social support. Given this premise, it is not surprising that interventions based on this model have not been very effective.

Perceived Support as a Personality Characteristic

The main alternative to traditional views of social support has been models that conceptualize perceived support as a personality characteristic. Although other scholars had raised the possibility that social support could be confounded with personality processes (e.g., Heller, 1979), the Sarasons and their colleagues were the first to conceptualize perceived support as a personality characteristic in its own right (I. G. Sarason, B.R. Sarason, & Shearin, 1986). They hypothesized that perceived support was a generalized sense of acceptance that was rooted, in part, in early parent–child attachment (B. R. Sarason, Pierce, & I. G. Sarason, 1990). From attachment experiences, persons develop working models of self and others that represent the world as benign and supportive and the self as worthy of love and respect. This generalized sense of acceptance is hypothesized to enhance coping ability, social competence, and one's ability to form close interpersonal relations. Similarly, Lakey and his colleagues (e.g., Lakey & Cassady, 1990) have taken a social cognition perspective and hypothesized that perceived support operates according to schematic processes and thereby influences interpretation, attention, memory, and the efficiency of social information processing.

Over the past decade, there has been a gradual accumulation of evidence supporting the role of personality processes in perceived social support. I. G. Sarason et al. (1986) found that perceived support was as stable as other personality characteristics over 3 years. In addition, they found that perceived support was related to measures of parental bonding, leadership, social problem solving, and friendliness. Lakey and Cassady (1990) found that perceived support was more strongly related to measures of self-referent cognition (e.g., self-esteem, dysfunctional attitudes) than to enacted support and that the relation between perceived support and distress largely overlapped with the negative cognition–distress relation.

Several studies have found that low perceived support individuals interpret the same social information more negatively than do their counterparts. For example, Lakey and Cassady (1990) presented subjects with written descriptions of hypothetical stressful situations and supportive statements that might be made by friends or relatives. Low perceived support individuals rated the supportive behaviors as less helpful, and this result could not be explained by dysphoria or self-referent cognition. Lakey et al. (1992) replicated these effects with videotaped supportive behaviors. Again, the effect could not be explained in terms of dysphoria, social desirability, or self-esteem. To determine whether these laboratory findings generalized to naturally occurring relationships, Lakey and Dickinson (1994) studied the development of perceived support among freshmen who had moved away from home for the first time to attend college. Perceived support from family, assessed within the first week of college, predicted the perceived supportiveness of friendships developed at college by the end of the first semester. Thus, perceived support from the family of origin appeared to be generalized to new social relations. This effect held beyond the effects of prior social desirability, negative affectivity, extraversion, or agreeableness. Drew, Lakey, and Sirl (1995) compared low–socioeconomic status (SES), clinically depressed subjects and controls who viewed a series of videotapes in which one person described a problem to another. Clinically depressed subjects had lower levels of perceived support and rated female listeners as less supportive than did controls. Thus, the effects observed previously among college students were obtained in a clinical, low-SES sample as well. Lakey, Drew, Anan, Sirl, and Butler (1995) studied two samples of divorced individuals and asked them to interpret a wide range of divorce-related social situations. Although none of these situations involved social support per se, low perceived support subjects interpreted them more negatively. Thus, Lakey, Drew, et al. (1995) provide another replication of this effect in community samples and suggest that the interpretive biases associated with perceived support extend to social interactions in general, not merely to social support.

Other researchers have found interpretive biases associated with perceived support as well. B. R. Sarason et al. (1991) presented various slides of college students to subjects and then asked them to rate the typical level of social support enjoyed by the typical student. They found that low perceived support individuals rated anonymous peers as having lower levels of support than did high perceived support subjects. Pierce, Sarason, and Sarason (1992) studied subjects' interactions with their mothers. Mothers were instructed to copy a supportive message to their children in their own handwriting. Subjects with low perceived support from their mothers rated the message as less supportive, even though every mother provided the same message. Cutrona et al. (1990) studied strangers engaged in a laboratory social support interaction. Though the actual behaviors of these previously unknown companions did not influence subjects' perception of the stranger as supportive, low perceived support subject *interpreted* their companions as less supportive. Similarly, Mallinckrodt (1991) found that patients' perceptions of parental care and current social support appeared to be generalized to perceptions of their therapists.

Thus, there is some evidence that perceived support may act, in part, as a personality process. Perceived social support appears to be more highly correlated with personality variables than with aspects of the social environment (Lakey & Cassady, 1990), is as stable as traditional personality characteristics (I. G. Sarason et al., 1986), and is associated with biases in interpreting social information (e.g., Lakey & Cassady, 1990).

However, there are important conceptual and empirical problems with personality perspectives as well. Conceptually, these models need to explain how perceived support is linked to the social environment. It seems unlikely that any personality variable is completely divorced from the social world. Empirically, although the presence of interpretive biases associated with perceived support appears to be well-documented, the size of these effects is not large, indicating that perceived support is not merely a matter of interpretive bias. The most important empirical challenge to personality models, however, is the results of a recent study that suggest that perceptual biases account for less than 10% of the variance in supportiveness judgments.

Generalizability theory provides the conceptual and methodological tools to determine the extent to which various causes determine a group of scores or ratings (Cronbach, Gleser, Nanda, & Rajaratnam, 1972). These tools can be applied to the study of social support when a group of subjects rate the same individuals for supportiveness. Variance can be partitioned as effects due to supporters, perceivers, and their interaction. Effects due to supporters represent the extent to which all subjects see the same targets as supportive. This corresponds to the aspect of social support that resides in the actual qualities of supporters. Effects due to perceivers represent the extent to which different persons perceive supporters as more or less supportive, regardless of their actual characteristics. This corresponds to the interpretive biases of the perceivers. Effects due to the supporter–perceiver interaction reflect a process whereby different persons see different supporters as more or less supportive.

Lakey, McCabe, Fisicaro, and Drew (in press) conducted three such generalizability studies and found that each determinant of perceived support made a significant contribution. However, in contrast to what we have emphasized in our prior work, perceived social support as a personality process was the least important determinant, accounting for an average of 8% of the variance. Perceived support as a characteristic of supporters accounted for an average of 20%. However, the lion's share was contributed by the perceiver–supporter interaction, which accounted for an average of 41%. The magnitude of the perceiver–supporter interaction is important theoretically, because it suggests that there is little in the way of objective supportiveness. To a large extent, supportiveness is in the eye of the beholder. What is supportive for one person will be unsupportive for another.

What is the nature of the perceiver–supporter interaction? People may have a direct influence in shaping the supportive behaviors or qualities of the support providers. Thus, a given supporter may behave supportively to some persons and unsupportively to others. Of course, this leaves unanswered the question of what does "behaving supportively" means. Another possibility is that recipient and provider each have a preferred style of enacted support and the supportiveness of a relationship depends on the match between the recipients' and the providers' styles. A provider who prefers to give advice will be seen as very supportive by some and very unsupportive by others. These differing viewpoints would explain the lack of a strong relation between perceived and enacted support, because existing studies have not examined the match between the style of support received and the style desired. Alternatively, support judgments could be inferred from global liking judgments. Persons are seen as supportive insofar as they are liked. In this case, the perceiver–supporter interaction reflects the fact that people vary greatly in what they consider to be attractive. Another possibility is that people infer supportiveness on the basis of global person characteristics, but people differ in what qualities they use to drive supportiveness judgments. One person may weight a sense of humor highly, but another may emphasize warmth. Thus, a given humorous person would be judged as supportive by one person, but as unsupportive by another.

Further clues to the nature of the perceiver–supporter interaction come from recent research on how persons make perceived support judgments (Lakey, Ross, Butler, & Bentley, in press). Relying on both experimental and correlational methods in three studies, these researchers found that the most powerful determinant of supportiveness was the similarity of supporters to targets in terms of global attitudes and values. The only other factor to emerge consistently was supporter conscientiousness. Thus, support judgments are inferred, in large part, on the basis of similarity, and these inferences are further adjusted on the basis of target conscientiousness. Of course, similarity reflects a perceiver–supporter interaction because what is similar and supportive to one person will be dissimilar and unsupportive to another. Conscientiousness reflects a component of the main effects for supporters.

IMPLICATIONS OF BASIC RESEARCH FOR INTERVENTION

The basic research that we have reviewed has important implications for social support intervention. First, because perceived and enacted support are not strongly related, and because enacted support is not related to mental health, interventions designed to increase enacted support are not likely to be effective in improving perceived support or in reducing symptoms. Second, perceived support appears to have multiple determinants involving characteristics of the social environment, personality characteristics of the perceiver, and their interaction. Each source can serve as a useful focus for intervention, and intervention programs can increase their effectiveness by targeting each component. The remainder of this chapter will describe potential interventions targeting each component of perceived support. This section of the chapter draws primarily from our clinical experience with low perceived support individuals. Although we recognize that clinically derived knowledge is frequently not confirmed by research findings, we offer these insights as hypotheses to help guide clinicians and future research.

Perceived Support as a Personality Process: Perceptual Biases of the Perceiver

As described earlier in this review, there is substantial evidence that cognitive biases make significant contributions to perceived social support. Given the same relationships or the same enacted support, some individuals will see them as less supportive than will others. Fortunately, cognitive therapy of depression has provided a number of useful strategies for examining and correcting such interpretive biases (Beck, Rush, Shaw, & Emery, 1979). In the pages that follow, we will describe strategies and techniques derived from books such as *Cognitive Therapy of Depression* (Beck et al., 1979) as well as from our own clinical experience. Although many of these techniques were derived from individual therapy, they can be applied with minimal modification for use in group formats or in preventive interventions. Indeed, several programs have successfully applied such techniques to group or preventive interventions (Brand et al., 1995; Terri & Lewinsohn, 1986).

A basic premise of cognitive approaches is that distressed persons' negative view of their social relations frequently are unrealistically negative in that they represent inaccurate interpretations of social information. These interpretations can be corrected, however, by examining them systematically and objectively.

Because cognitive therapy places such an emphasis on correcting distorted thinking, it is extremely important to determine whether a low perceived support individual's thinking is, in fact, inaccurate. For example, low perceived support frequently presents itself clinically in statements such as "No one cares about me" or "No one understands." If these conclusions are distortions, then the client needs to learn the skills for evaluating the accuracy of negative thinking. But if these beliefs are accurate, it would be a great disservice to try to persuade the client that people really do care when, in fact, they don't. In the latter circumstance, low perceived support persons need to acquire the skills necessary to cultivate new supportive relationships.

Determining the accuracy of support cognitions is difficult because one does not usually have access to objective information about a person's social relations. Occasionally, one might have a copy of a letter written to the client, or observe his or her interactions with a romantic partner in session, but in most cases all the information must be gathered through the client's report. This is problematic because if the low perceived support person is engaging in cognitive distortions, how can we get unbiased information? In our view, obtaining descriptive information about actual transactions is less likely to yield a biased view than is simply accepting summary judgments of a relationship. For example, if a man believes that his wife no longer cares for him, it is important to find out exactly what has been said. Many times, low perceived support persons will report their global reaction to a conversation. He may report that "she basically said that our relationship was over" when she actually said she was angry and didn't feel close to him. Further inquiry may find that she actually made statements suggesting her commitment to the relationship, such as, "This relationship is more important to me than anything." Thus, descriptive information about what actually occurred frequently disagrees with the client's summary evaluation of a difficult transaction.

Given that one has identified low perceived support as involving distortions, there are a number of ways to try to correct them. The basic principle is to treat negative thoughts as hypotheses to be tested by gathering information. Rather than being allowed to rely on a therapist or group leader to guide all these efforts, it is important that low perceived support individuals acquire the skills themselves. Otherwise, they will not be able to use these techniques to solve future support-related distortions after the intervention has ended.

There are a number of cognitive strategies that we believe are useful in correcting support-related cognitive distortions. We will describe a few of them derived from our clinical experience to provide examples of how cognitive therapy techniques can be used to correct cognitive distortions involved in low perceived support. Low perceived support individuals sometimes experience genuinely unsupportive interpersonal transactions, but draw unnecessarily negative conclusions from them (overgeneralization). Intervention in these cases consists of scrutinizing the attributions that persons have made for these transactions. For example, a woman reported that she and her husband were no longer close, that this meant that he no longer cared for her, and that she simply could not function well in relationships. However, a detailed examination of the situation revealed that although her husband had been feeling distant, this feeling had nothing to do with her or her ability to function in relationships. He had reported to her that he hadn't felt close to anyone for a while and that, indeed, he hadn't been able to feel anything. Further inquiry revealed that he was displaying several symptoms of depression and that his mother had died within the last year. Unfortunately, this man was not especially psychologically minded, and so he had been unable to recognize or communicate to his wife that he was depressed. However, understanding the true origins of her husband's distance provided this woman with a completely different and more positive interpretation of her marital experience. Of course, the complete intervention also targeted means by which to improve her interactions with her husband and to help him address his depression. This example illustrates how a genuinely negative support-related event can be interpreted much more negatively than it really is. The requisite cognitive coping skill was to examine the accuracy of the attribution for the negative outcome.

A similar approach taken in the Brand et al. (1995) study was designed to address the problem frequently reported by low perceived support clients: that their parents didn't love or care for them sufficiently. Although this report was typically based on genuinely unsupportive acts, we attempted to modify clients' attributions for these events. Many of our clients had concluded that their parents' misbehavior was a result of a lack of caring or a deliberate attempt to be hurtful. We attempted to help clients see their parents as flawed human beings who misbehaved for a variety of reasons. Clients were helped to develop more elaborate theories about how various factors and limitations (e.g., their parents' own abuse as children, a lack of skill in expressing emotions, presence of an emotional disorder, high levels of life stress) conspired to lead to this behavior. When successful, clients were able to reconceptualize their parents' disappointing behaviors as resulting from multiple factors that said relatively little about the client, or even about the parents' true feelings for the client.

Occasionally, low perceived support individuals have concluded that nobody really cares about them, but this conclusion does not seem to be based on anyone's actual behaviors. In dealing with selective abstractions such as these, it is important to try to determine whether the judgment is accurate, and frequently one can find numerous indications that others genuinely care. When these indications are drawn to the client's attention, he frequently has some other explanation for the caring behaviors. He may have concluded that others merely feel sorry for him, or that his friends seek him out only because they have impoverished social lives as well. Here it is useful to consider the evidence for these attributions. Would friends really seek out a low perceived support person because of pity? Are people's social behaviors really generated by this kind of altruism? If not, what is a better explanation for their behavior?

Sometimes reviewing such evidence changes a low perceived support individual's conclusions that other don't really care. In other instances, the person will report that despite all this evidence, she still doesn't feel supported. In these circumstances, one must work harder to determine upon what this conclusion is based. Sometimes it isn't really based on anything at all, and the client hasn't considered her definition of what caring means. Here the client can benefit from considering the question of what it means for someone to really care about someone else. How does the client behave when she really cares about someone? Does this involve listening to the mundane details of daily life with interest? Listening attentively to the repetition of favorite stories? Calling on the phone? Asking for someone's company on an outing? How often does one do this? Once the defining behaviors of really caring are established, she can determine the extent to which her friends and family perform these behaviors and, by implication, are supportive of her.

Sometimes clients have unrealistic expectations and engage in dichotomous thinking. Caring becomes a discrete category, and the client has no conception of caring a moderate amount or caring a great deal. Anything short of complete devotion counts for nothing. Some low perceived support clients act as though they believe that people really care only if they always say the right things when you're down or they always want to be with you. The problem with this is that everyone is flawed in some way and no one can behave as you would like every single time. In addition, persons who care a moderate amount are placed into a category of not caring at all. This is problematic, because although one might not have friends who care about one as much as one would like, something is better than nothing.

How can clients learn to use a continuum of evaluation rather than a dichotomy? One approach is to simply practice using more of the scale. By being asked to make repeated judgments of others and by being required to use the midrange, clients can become more accustomed to thinking in this fashion. The mood benefits of concluding that someone cares about you a moderate amount, vs. concluding that the person doesn't care at all, provide powerful reinforcement for changing thinking. In addition, one can examine the client's own level of caring for others. The client probably has persons that he cares about a moderate amount, but for whom there are certain limits. He may be perfectly willing to have lunch with the person and listen to him describe his romantic frustrations during the work week, but not really want to spend a lot of time in the evenings or weekends listening to such concerns. But does this mean that the client's genuine caring about his friend is invalid? Put the other way, would it be fair for his friend to conclude that the client's attention and concern amounted to nothing?

Another approach to the problem of believing that no one cares, despite contradictory evidence, is to consider other sources for this conclusion. Essentially, we ask the client, given that these conclusions aren't based on other people's behavior, on what are they based? Sometimes conclusions about a lack of support are inferred from negative emotional states. Thus, when a client asks herself whether anyone really cares, she bases the answer on her emotional state. If she feels depressed, it must be because nobody cares. Basic research has shown that persons sometimes use their emotional states to guide their judgments when the source of their emotions is unclear (Clore, Schwarz, & Conway, 1994). When persons have a clear attribution for their emotion, they are less likely to base judgments on affect. Similarly, persons may overgeneralize conclusions from past relationships to new ones. A person who grew up feeling that his parents didn't love him may find himself believing this about a romantic partner. In both of these instances, interventions can focus on helping clients learn to be skeptical of their thinking and conclusions. Clients learn to catch themselves when drawing this conclusion and wonder, "Could this be an example of basing my thoughts on my depression? I frequently decide that someone doesn't care based on how I feel. I'm feeling depressed now, so this negative thought may say more about my mood than about the other person's feelings. So I'll take this with a grain of salt."

We have provided a number of examples of how cognitive therapy strategies can be used to attempt to influence low perceived support. One advantage of such approaches is that there is extensive empirical evidence supporting their effectiveness in the treatment of depression (Robinson et al., 1990), which involves low perceived support. Although the results of Brand et al. (1995) suggest that such approaches may be useful in modifying perceived support, more research of this kind is needed. In any event, because cognitive biases account for only part of the variance, cognitive approaches to treatment and prevention will need to be supplemented with other strategies.

Social Support in the Social Environment

An important portion of the variance in perceived support appears to result from the presence of genuinely supportive individuals (Lakey, McCabe, et al., in press). Although many interventions have attempted to increase perceived support by providing enacted support, these attempts have not been very effective. As discussed previously, basic research on social support suggests that manipulating enacted support would have little effect on symptoms or on perceived support. Although people are seen by others as supportive to differing extents, this difference does not seem to result from how much enacted support they provide.

Rather, their supportiveness appears to be inferred from other, more global personal characteristics (Lakey, Ross, et al., in press). But if the environmental component of perceived support cannot be manipulated by providing persons with enacted support, how can low perceived support persons have greater access to supportive others? One possibility is to recruit more persons with supportive qualities into their social networks.

Research on the development of perceived support in new social situations has found that persons with low levels of distress, high levels of social competence, and high levels of agreeableness develop higher levels of perceived support (Lakey, 1989; Lakey & Dickinson, 1994). Presumably, these individuals are engaging in behaviors that promote the development of supportive relationships. Thus, one potential way to increase the development of perceived support is to train individuals in the skills necessary to develop supportive relationships. Given the weak link between enacted support and perceived support, however, this training should not focus on learning to ask for assistance, although this skill may be important for some individuals. Rather, the focus should be on developing close relationships.

There is a large body of literature on training individuals in social skills, although the influence of such training on perceived support has rarely been investigated. Overall, the literature indicates that social skills training produces increases in social competence and is an effective treatment for depression and social phobia (Hersen, Bellack, Himmelhoch, & Thase, 1984; Öst, Jerremalm, & Johansson, 1981). In addition, the social skills training literature is unique in having established some of the factors that determine effective training. For example, research has documented the importance of rehearsal, coaching, elaboration, and covert rehearsal (McFall & Twentyman, 1976; Kazdin, 1980, 1982).

Although it has been established that social skills training is effective, it is not completely clear how to modify it for use in improving perceived support. A fundamental question is which social skills to target. The bulk of social skills training research has focused on assertion, frequently emphasizing techniques for refusing unreasonable requests. But it is not clear how this would enhance perceived support. Conflict resolution is also an important aspect of social skill, but is it important in improving perceived support? Although early reports seemed to suggest that social conflict was actually the driving force behind perceived support effects (Coyne & DeLongis, 1986; Pagel, Erdly, & Becker, 1987), other research appears to indicate that social support and social conflict are largely independent constructs with different mechanisms (Finch, Okun, Barrera, Zautra, & Reich, 1989; Lakey, Tardiff, & Drew, 1994; Rook, 1984).

Our basic research suggests to us that judgments of an individual's supportiveness may be developed in contexts that are not stress- or helping-related (Lakey, Ross, et al., in press). If this is so, then people may be able to improve their perceptions by developing friendships with persons who have supportive qualities. In fact, at least in the early stages, supportive relationships might best be developed by avoiding talking about personal problems, as this practice can alienate others.

Our clinical experience with low perceived support individuals suggests that many of them have difficulty with the early forms of friendship development and in deepening the level of intimacy in existing acquaintanceships. Thus, we have trained them in a variety of skills, including initiating conversation, initiating social interaction, self-disclosure, and expressing positive emotion.

Training in initiating conversation usually involves training persons in making small talk. Depending on the clients' skills, we usually try to teach them to draw others out. This is essentially a modified version of client-centered therapy techniques, stripped of what have become clinical clichés (e.g., "What I hear you saying is that you feel that I'm mimicking you"). Most people are gratified by the opportunity to talk at length about things that interest them, and active listening skills are relatively easy for most low perceived support individuals to learn. Such skills seem easier to learn in part because many of our low perceived support clients believe that they have little to say that would be interesting. Of course, for our clients to spend time drawing others out has the additional advantage of finding interests that other persons share with them.

Of course, sooner or later, clients need to say something themselves. Much of the time their inhibition results from a lack of confidence, rather than a lack of interesting things to talk about. They assume that their conversation partner wouldn't find their interests engaging and so they don't say anything, thus creating a self-fulfilling prophecy. To help clients develop this aspect of themselves, we like to ask them to talk about their interests in session. Low perceived support individuals can usually talk at some length about several topics. The therapist or group leader then summarizes what they had to say and comments on the extensiveness and appropriateness of the topic. Clients are usually surprised to find that they can speak so much on a topic.

Sometimes negative attitudes about small talk inhibit low perceived support individuals' ability to initiate social interaction. Some say that they are not interested in small talk because it is superficial. We see this as a misunderstanding of the function of small talk. The point is not to convey important information, but rather to provide a vehicle for a pleasant social exchange. The important thing is to convey affect and interest and to create opportunities for humor. Small talk is supposed to be superficial, because substantial conversation among acquaintances frequently makes people uncomfortable (e.g., "Is life really utterly meaningless, or does it just seem that way?").

Some low perceived support clients have the disadvantage of not having much to say about anything, or perhaps their interests are so esoteric that it is difficult for them to engage ordinary people in conversation (e.g., the medieval literature Ph.D. on the assembly line). Our tactic under these circumstances is to encourage them to learn about topics in which other people are interested. One of the advantages of living in Indiana or Carolina, say, is that you can have a perfectly delightful conversation with just about anyone about college basketball— no matter how different you are from them on most other variables. Of course, to do this, you have to know something about Hoosier or Tar Heel hoops. Besides sports, a lot of small talk is oriented toward movies or TV, and so learning about these media creates grist for the small-talk mill.

Beyond initiating conversation, low perceived support individuals frequently need assistance in initiating social activities. Such persons sometimes have a passive style. They have observed that some persons always seem to get invited to do things with others. Our view, however, is that the people who get many invitations extend many invitations as well. Thus, they help create a network of persons who initiate activities. Many times, low perceived support persons are worried that their overtures will be rejected. The therapist must help them to select persons who would be more likely to accept (e.g., persons with whom they have a lot in common, or go to lunch with at work) and to prepare the client to deal with potential rejection by thinking about how to interpret it. Even if a reasonable explanation is offered, a low perceived support person is likely to interpret someone's declining his invitation as meaning that the person dislikes him and that he is defective.

Other low perceived support individuals are able to interact smoothly on a superficial level, yet their relationships lack depth or intimacy. Sometimes this lack of depth seems to result from a lack of awareness of the role of self-disclosure in developing intimacy (Collins & Miller, 1994). A person may not feel supported because her friends don't really know who she is or what concerns her. Of course, because self-disclosure tends to be reciprocal, low levels of self-disclosure in a low perceived support person are likely to inhibit self-disclosure in others as well. Frequently, the barrier to self-disclosure is the expectation that if others really knew the client's thoughts and emotions, they would reject him. Responsibly encouraging self-disclosure involves helping the client judge what is appropriate. The statement "Sometimes I get discouraged" is probably not enough, but "I frequently think of killing myself" is too much, at least in the earlier stages of friendship development. The client is likely to find self-disclosure a bit risky at first, however, and one must be careful to target the right amount of disclosure and the right targets who are likely to be sympathetic. Small, low-risk experiments can help the low perceived support individual learn that people are not as rejecting as expected. This expectancy can be weakened beforehand by asking the client to judge how she would respond to a similar self-disclosure from someone else. For example, if someone told the client that she had marital problems, would the client be repulsed? The answer is usually no, which suggests that most reasonable others would respond similarly.

Another social skills problem that we have observed among low perceived support individuals is a deficit in expressing positive emotion to others. Some low perceived support persons express too many negative views about the world, other persons, or themselves. Frequently, social relations are improved if one more frequently refrains from making very negative statements. Other clients never give others compliments. One client with whom we worked initially had no concept of how to do this. When asked to generate a compliment that she might make to anyone that she knew, she could not think of anything. In this case, it seemed to reflect a more generalized difficulty in recognizing small positive qualities in others, although more typically, the problem is not understanding how sincere positive feedback can facilitate intimacy.

Perceiver–Supporter Interaction

Lakey, McCabe, et al. (in press) found that the largest single determinant of supportiveness judgments was the perceiver–supporter interaction. This finding suggests that certain individuals will be seen as supportive by some but not by others. Lakey, Ross, et al. (in press) found that much of this interaction is driven by the similarity between supporter and perceiver. That it is presents a formidable challenge to understanding how to increase perceived support, because it suggests that one can't simply provide the same supportive behaviors or supportive individuals to everyone. Perhaps the Heller et al. (1991) intervention would have been more effective if participants had not been randomly paired with one another. If participants had been matched on the basis of similarity, their relationships may have been seen as more supportive.

Although similarity appears to be a powerful determinant of perceived support judgments, much more needs to be understood about this effect before we can use it optimally in intervention. For example, although Lakey, Ross, et al. (in press) assessed similarity in terms of sociopolitical attitudes, other aspects may be more important. For example, how important is similarity in personality, gender, ethnicity, religion, or social class? Further, these dimensions might vary in importance for different persons. Ethnicity may be very important for one person, but be eclipsed by education for another. If social support interventions are going to match persons on the basis of similarity, it would be helpful to know what the most important dimensions are. In addition, it would be helpful to know why similarity leads to greater perceptions of support. Perhaps similar others are assumed to be able to understand your situation and not to be judgmental. They may be more likely to have similar scripts for supportive interactions. For example, it has been suggested that men and women differ in their idea of what is supportive behavior. Men may be more likely to give advice, whereas women may be more likely to provide emotional support. Thus, receiving advice may be more helpful if this also happens to be your idea of what persons are supposed to do when providing help. Finally, similarity may lead to supportiveness judgments because they lead to liking (Byrne, 1971). Many personality inferences of others appear to be driven by a general evaluative person concept (Srull & Wyer, 1989), and perceived support may act similarly. If it does, then perceived support may simply reflect whether persons like those in their social networks and whether they believe persons in their networks like them. If this is the case, then social support interventions do not need to focus on social support at all, but only on developing enjoyable relationships.

Social support interventions based on matching supporters to perceivers will be fairly complicated and different from existing interventions. Although support groups bring together similar others, their similarity is limited to having the same type of problem. Although this similarity is probably helpful to some extent, the efficacy of support groups may lie in the fact that they increase one's odds of finding attitudinally similar others, leading to friendship formation. We would predict that joining a group of persons without the same problems, but sharing the same attitudes and values, would actually be more effective than joining a support group composed of persons with dissimilar attitudes and values.

From a technical standpoint, the big difficulty is identifying highly similar subgroups and bringing them together. Doing so could be accomplished by borrowing techniques from dating services. These services attempt to measure people's characteristics and then match them with similar others. Unfortunately, such an approach requires getting a large group of persons to respond to questionnaire items for this purpose, and low perceived support persons might be unlikely to do so. Centering such an approach in existing institutions or targeting specific life transitions might be helpful. For example, members of large churches, retirement centers, and schools could complete attitude questionnaires and be brought into contact with similar others.

One problem with the dating service approach, however, is getting people to cooperate. High perceived support persons may not see the need for or have the time to bother with such an approach. Low perceived support individuals may want to avoid the stigma of needing this kind of assistance in forming relationships. Acceptability could be enhanced by applying the intervention to everyone. In a school setting, students could complete attitude information, and similar others could be brought together to work on a joint project. This approach could be presented as a school activity designed to bring students into contact with a wider range of peers than they would meet in classes.

In addition to interventions that attempt to match low perceived support individuals with similar others, individually oriented approaches are possible as well. For example, low perceived support individuals presumably see fewer persons in their social worlds as similar. In some cases, such persons may be underestimating the similarity that is actually there. For example, shy persons might not self-disclose enough to find out that people share many of their attitudes and values. Other persons might have particularly low tolerance for slightly dissimilar others. They may need to learn that dissimilarity in a few domains does not mean that the person is not highly similar in other important domains.

SUMMARY

In summary, the relationship between perceived social support and mental and physical health is among the most widely documented effects in applied psychology. From the very beginning, scholars have been interested in applying this knowledge to generate new interventions to increase social support. Unfortunately, although there have been a number of studies of social support interventions, they have produced disappointing results. A large number of the studies have important methodological flaws that leave their findings uninterpretable.

Another group of studies were extremely well conducted both experimentally and clinically, yet found no intervention effects. A few interventions produced statistically significant changes in perceived social support, but these effects were relatively small and probably lack practical usefulness.

Although these studies have had a low yield in terms of providing experimentally proven and clinically significant interventions, they have had a high theoretical payoff. In our view, the difficulties in this field suggest that some of the basic assumptions that have driven social support interventions are incorrect. In our view, the field prematurely adopted a particular theoretical model of social support that lacks strong empirical support. Moreover, we currently lack the underpinning of basic research to inform intervention. For example, although some knowledge is being developed, we still have a poor understanding of the extent to which social support is rooted in the social environment or in the personalities of the perceivers. In addition, we do not have enough knowledge of how persons make social support judgments. This deficiency of knowledge leaves us uncertain as to what participants are telling us when they complete social support measures.

Nonetheless, scientist practitioners will continue to develop social support interventions. The available research suggests that perceived social support is composed of characteristics of the perceivers, characteristics of supporters, and the perceiver–supporter interaction. Drawing from our own clinical experience, we have described a number of strategies and tactics that appear to be clinically useful and may actually be effective. Of course, more research is needed on how to improve perceived social support. But it is even more important to conduct the basic research on fundamental social support processes and to link interventions to this research.

REFERENCES

Andersson, L. (1985). Intervention against loneliness in a group of elderly women: An impact evaluation. *Journal of Social Science and Medicine, 20(4)*, 355–364.

Barrera, M., Jr. (1986). Distinctions between social support concepts, measures, and models. *American Journal of Community Psychology, 14*, 413–455.

Barth, R. P., & Schinke, S. P. (1984). Enhancing the social supports of teenage mothers. *Social Casework, 65(9)*, 523–531.

Baumgarten, M., Thomas, D., de Courval, L., & Infante-Rivard, C. (1988). Evaluation of a mutual help network for the elderly residents of planned housing. *Psychology and Aging, 3(4)*, 393–398.

Beck, A. T., Rush, A. J., Shaw, B. F., & Emery, G. (1979). *Cognitive therapy of depression.* New York: Guilford Press.

Belcher, G., & Costello, C. G. (1991). Do confidants of depressed women provide less social support than confidants of nondepressed women? *Journal of Abnormal Psychology, 100*, 516–525.

Bloom, B. L., Hodges, W. F., & Caldwell, R. A. (1982). A preventive program for the newly separated: Initial evaluation. *American Journal of Community Psychology, 10*, 251–264.

Bogat, G. A., & Jason, L. A. (1983). An evaluation of two visiting programs for elderly community residents. *International Journal of Aging and Human Development, 17*, 267–279.

Brand, E. F., Lakey, B., & Berman, S. (1995). A preventive, psychoeducational approach to increase perceived support. *American Journal of Community Psychology, 23*, 117–136.

Byrne, D. (1971). *The attraction paradigm.* New York: Academic Press.

Christensen, A., & Jacobson, N. S. (1994). Who (or what) can do psychotherapy: The status and challenge of nonprofessional therapies. *Psychological Science, 5,* 8–14.

Clore, G. L., Schwarz, N., & Conway, M. (1994). Affective causes and consequences of social information processing. In R. S. Wyer & T. K. Srull (Eds.), *Handbook of social cognition* (pp. 323–417). Hillsdale, NJ: Lawrence Erlbaum.

Cohen, S., & Wills, T. (1985). Stress, social support and the buffering hypotheses. *Psychological Bulletin, 98,* 310–357.

Collins, N. L., & Miller, L. C. (1994). Self-disclosure and liking: A meta-analytic review. *Psychological Bulletin, 116,* 457–475.

Coyne, J. S., & DeLongis, A. M. (1986). Going beyond social support: The role of social relationships in adaptation. *Journal of Consulting and Clinical Psychology, 54,* 454–560.

Cronbach, L. J., Gleser, G. C., Nanda, H., & Rajaratnam, N. (1972). *The dependability of behavioral measurements: Theory of generalizability of scores and profiles.* New York: Wiley.

Cutrona, C. E., & Russell, D. W. (1990). Type of social support and specific stress: Toward a theory of optimal matching. In B. R. Sarason, I. G. Sarason, & G. R. Pierce (Eds.), *Social support: An interactional view* (pp. 319–366). New York: Wiley.

Cutrona, C. E., Suhr, J. A., & MacFarlane, R. (1990). Interpersonal transactions and the psychological sense of support. In S. Duck with R. C. Silver (Eds.), *Personal relationships and social support* (pp. 30–45). London: Sage Publications.

Dadds, M. R., & McHugh, T. A. (1992). Social support and treatment outcome in behavioral family therapy for child conduct problems. *Journal of Consulting and Clinical Psychology, 60(2),* 252–259.

Drew, J. B., Lakey, B., & Sirl, K. (1995). *Clinical depression and cognitive processes in perceived social support.* Presented at the annual meeting of the Association for the Advancement of Behavior Therapy, Washington, DC.

Dunkel-Schetter, C., & Bennett, T. L. (1990). Differentiating the cognitive and behavioral aspects of social support. In B. R. Sarason, I. G. Sarason, & G. R. Pierce (Eds.), *Social support: An interactional view* (pp. 267–296). New York: Wiley.

Durlak, J. (1979). Comparative effectiveness of paraprofessional and professional helpers. *Psychological Bulletin, 86,* 80–92.

Felner, R. D., Ginter, M., & Primavera, J. (1982). Primary prevention during school transitions: Social support and environmental structure. *American Journal of Community Psychology, 10(3),* 277–290.

Finch, J. F., Okun, M. A., Barrera, M., Jr., Zautra, A. J., & Reich, J. W. (1989). Positive and negative social ties among older adults: Measurement models and the prediction of psychological distress and well-being. *American Journal of Community Psychology, 17,* 585–605.

Gurung, R. A. R., Sarason, B. R., & Sarason, I. G. (1994). Observing conflict and support: Global vs. behavioral-specific approaches. Paper presented at the American Psychological Association Annual Convention. Los Angeles.

Haley, W. E., Brown, S. L., & Levine, E. G. (1987). Experimental evaluation of the effectiveness of group intervention for dementia caregivers. *Gerontologist, 27(3),* 376–382.

Hawkins, J. D., Catalano, R. F., & Wells, E. A. (1986). Measuring effects of a skills training intervention for drug abusers. *Journal of Consulting and Clinical Psychology, 54(5),* 661–664.

Heller, K. (1979). The effects of social support: Prevention and treatment implications. In A. P. Goldstein & F. H. Kanfer (Eds.), *Maximizing treatment gains: Transfer enhancement in psychotherapy* (pp. 253–382). New York: Academic Press.

Heller, K., & Lakey, B. (1985) Perceived support and social interaction among friends and confidants. In I. G. Sarason & B. R. Sarason (Eds.), *Social support: Theory, research and applications* (pp. 287–300). The Hague: Martinus Nijhoff.

Heller, K., Thompson, M. G., Trueba, P. E., Hogg, J. R., & Vlachos-Weber, I. (1991). Peer support telephone dyads for elderly women: Was this the wrong intervention? *American Journal of Community Psychology, 19(1),* 53–74.

Hersen, M., Bellack, A. S., Himmelhoch, J. M., & Thase, M. E. (1984). Effects of social skills training, amitriptyline, and psychotherapy in unipolar depressed women. *Behavior Therapy, 15,* 21–40.

Hodges, W. F., & Bloom, B. L. (1986). A preventive intervention program for the newly separated: One year follow-up. *Journal of Preventive Psychiatry, 3,* 35–49.

Kazdin, A. F.. (1980). Covert and overt rehearsal and elaboration during treatment in the development of assertive behavior. *Behavior Research and Therapy, 18,* 191–201.

Kazdin, A. E. (1982) The separate and combined effects of covert and overt rehearsal in developing assertive behavior. *Behavior Research and Therapy, 20,* 17–25.

Kennell, J., Klaus, M., McGrath, S., Robertson, S., & Hinkley, C. (1991). Continuous emotional support during labor in a U.S. hospital. *Journal of the American Medical Association, 265,* 2197–2201.

Klaus, M. H., Kennell, J. H., Robertson, S. S., & Sosa, R. (1986). Effects of social support during parturition on maternal and infant morbidity. *British Medical Journal, 293,* 585–587.

Lakey, B. (1989). Personal and environmental antecedents of perceived social support. *American Journal of Community Psychology, 17,* 503–519.

Lakey, B., & Cassady, P. B. (1990). Cognitive processes in perceived social support. *Journal of Personality and Social Psychology, 59,* 337–348.

Lakey, B., & Dickinson, L. G. (1994). Antecedents of perceived support: Is perceived family environment generalized to new social relationships? *Cognitive Therapy and Research, 18,* 39–53.

Lakey, B., Drew, J. B., Anan, R. M., Sirl, K., & Butler, C. (1995). Dysfunctional attitudes and perceived social support in adult's adjustment to divorce. Presented at the annual meeting of the Association for the Advancement of Behavior Therapy, Washington, DC.

Lakey, B., & Heller, K. (1988). Social support from a friend, perceived support, and social problem solving. *American Journal of Community Psychology, 16,* 811–824.

Lakey, B., McCabe, K. M., Fisicaro, S. A., & Drew, J. B. (in press). Environmental and perceived determinants of support perceptions: Three generalizability studies. *Journal of Personality and Social Psychology.*

Lakey, B., Moineau, S., & Drew, J. B. (1992). Perceived social support and individual differences in the interpretation and recall of supportive behavior. *Journal of Social and Clinical Psychology, 11,* 336–348.

Lakey, B., Ross, L. T., Butler, C., & Bentley, K. (in press). Making social support judgments: The role of similarity and conscientiousness. *Journal of Social and Clinical Psychology.*

Lakey, B., Tardiff, T. A., & Drew, J. B. (1994). Negative social interactions: Assessment and relations to social support, cognition and psychological distress. *Journal of Social and Clinical Psychology, 13,* 42–62.

Lovell, M. L., & Hawkins, J. D. (1988). An evaluation of a group intervention to increase the personal social networks of abusive mothers. *Children and Youth Services Review, 10,* 174–188.

Mallinckrodt, B. (1991). Clients' representations of childhood emotional bonds with parents, social support and formation of the working alliance. *Journal of Counseling Psychology, 38,* 401–409.

McFall, R. M., & Twentyman, C. T. (1976). Four experiments on the relative contributions of rehearsal, modeling and coaching to assertion training. *Journal of Abnormal Psychology, 81,* 199–218.

Öst, L. G., Jerremalm, A., & Johansson, J. (1981). Individual response patterns and the effects of different behavioral methods in the treatment of social phobia. *Behavior Research and Therapy, 19,* 1–16.

Pagel, M. D., Erdly, W. W., & Becker, J. (1987). Social networks: We get by with (and in spite of) a little help from our friends. *Journal of Personality and Social Psychology, 53,* 793–804.

Pierce, G. R., Sarason, B. R., & Sarason, I. G. (1992). General and specific support expectations and stress as predictors of perceived supportiveness: An experimental study. *Journal of Personality and Social Psychology, 63,* 297–307.

Robinson, L. A., Berman, J. S., & Neimeyer, R. A. (1990). Psychotherapy for the treatment of depression: A comprehensive review of controlled outcome research. *Psychological Bulletin, 108,* 30–49.

Rook, K. (1984). The negative side of social interaction: Impact on psychological well-being. *Journal of Personality and Social Psychology, 46,* 1097–1108.

Sarason, B. R., Pierce, G. R., & Sarason, I. G. (1990). Social support: The sense of acceptance and the role of relationships. In B. R. Sarason, I. G. Sarason, & G. R. Pierce (Eds.), *Social support: An interactional view* (pp. 97–128). New York: Wiley.

Sarason, B. R., Pierce, G. R., Shearin, E. N., Sarason, I. G., Waltz, J. A., & Poppe, L. (1991). Perceived social support and working models of self and actual others. *Journal of Personality and Social Psychology, 60,* 273–287.

Sarason, B. R., Sarason, I. G., Hacker, T. A., & Basham, R. B. (1985). Concomitants of social support: Social skills, physical attractiveness, and gender. *Journal of Personality and Social Psychology, 49,* 469–480.

Sarason, B. R., Sarason, I. G., & Pierce, G. R. (Eds.). (1990a). *Social support: An interactional view.* New York: Wiley.

Sarason, B. R., Sarason, I. G., & Pierce, G. R. (1990b). Traditional views of social support and their impact on assessment. In B. R. Sarason, I. G. Sarason, & G. R. Pierce (Eds.), *Social support: An interactional view* (pp. 9–25). New York: Wiley.

Sarason, B. R., Shearin, E. N., Pierce, G. R., & Sarason, I. G. (1987). Interrelationships among social support measures: Theoretical and practical implications. *Journal of Personality and Social Psychology, 52,* 813–832.

Sarason, I. G., Sarason, B. R., & Shearin, E. N. (1986). Social support as an individual difference variable: Its stability, origins, and relational aspects. *Journal of Personality and Social Psychology, 50,* 845–855.

Scharlach, A. E. (1988). Peer counselor training for nursing home residents. *Gerontologist, 28(4),* 499–502.

Schinke, S. P., Schilling, R. F., Barth, R. P., Gilchrist, L. D., & Maxwell, J. S. (1986). Stress-management intervention to prevent family violence. *Journal of Family Violence, 1,* 13–26.

Shapiro, D. A., & Shapiro, D. (1982). Comparative therapy outcome studies. A replication and refinement. *Psychological Bulletin, 92,* 42–53.

Sosa, R., Kennell, J., Klaus, M., Robertson, S., & Urrutia, J. (1980). The effect of a supportive companion on perinatal problems, length of labor, and mother–infant interaction. *New England Journal of Medicine, 303,* 597–600.

Srull, T. K., & Wyer, R. S., Jr. (1989). Person memory and judgment. *Psychological Review, 96,* 58–83.

Terri, L., & Lewinsohn, P. M. (1986). Individual and group treatment of unipolar depression: Comparison of treatment outcome and identification of predictors of successful treatment outcome. *Behavior Therapy, 14,* 215–228.

Thoits, P. A. (1986). Social support as coping assistance. *Journal of Consulting and Clinical Psychology, 154,* 416–424.

Toseland, R. W., Labrecque, M. S., Goebel, S. T., & Whitney, M. H. (1992). An evaluation of a group program for spouses of frail elderly veterans. *Gerontologist, 32,* 382–390.

Toseland, R. W., Rossiter, C. M., & Labrecque, M. S. (1989a). The effectiveness of peer-led and professionally led groups to support family caregivers. *Gerontologist, 29,* 465–480.

Toseland, R. W., Rossiter, C. M., & Labrecque, M. S. (1989b). The effectiveness of three group intervention strategies to support family caregivers. *American Journal of Orthopsychiatry, 59,* 420–429.

Unger, D. G., & Wandersman, L. P. (1985). Social support and adolescent mothers: Action research contributions to theory and application. *Journal of Social Issues, 41(1),* 29–45.

Vachon, M. L. S., Lyall, W. A. L., Rogers, J., Freedman-Letofsky, K., & Freeman, S. J. J. (1980). A controlled study of self-help intervention for widows. *American Journal of Psychiatry, 137,* 1380–1384.

Vachon, M. L. S., Rogers, J., Lyall, W. A., Lancee, W. J., Sheldon, A. R., & Freeman, S. J. J. (1982). Predictors and correlates of adaptation to conjugal bereavement. *American Journal of Psychiatry, 139,* 998–1002.

Wethington, E., & Kessler, R. C. (1986). Perceived support, received support, and adjustment to life events. *Journal of Health and Social Behavior, 27,* 78–79.

Wolchik, S. A., West, S. G., Westover, S., Sandler, I. N., Martin, A., Lustig, J., Tein, J. Y., & Fisher, J. (1993). The children of divorce parenting intervention: Outcome evaluation of an empirically based program. *American Journal of Community Psychology, 21,* 293–331.

Yahne, C. E., & Long, V. O. (1988). The use of support groups to raise self-esteem for women clients. *College Health, 37,* 79–84.

19

Family Stress and Social Support among Caregivers to Persons with Alzheimer's Disease

KARL PILLEMER and JILL SUITOR

INTRODUCTION

Despite the current emphasis on "productive" and "successful" aging, the fact remains that many elderly people spend the last part of their lives suffering from chronic debilitating ailments. Moreover, contrary to deep-seated societal fears about the abandonment of the aged by their relatives, responsibility for caring for impaired elderly persons is usually assumed by kin. Although families have cared for the aged throughout recorded history, only in the past three decades has the topic become a vigorous and rapidly expanding area of research interest.

Part of the interest is due to a demographic imperative: The unprecedented growth in the elderly population is fundamentally changing the age structure of our society. The dramatic increase in the number of elderly citizens—and in particular in the number of persons 85 and older—will create tremendous demands on health and social service systems and on families who provide care. As life expectancy continues to increase, the prevalence of family caregiving is also likely to increase (Himes, 1994).

Beyond demographic trends, research interest has also been spurred by the well-documented negative effects on family members of providing care. In the most comprehensive reviews of the literature to date, Schulz and colleagues (Schulz & Williamson, 1994; Schulz, Williamson, Morcyz, & Biegel, 1990) found

KARL PILLEMER • Department of Human Development and Family Studies, Cornell University, Ithaca, New York 14583.   **JILL SUITOR** • Department of Sociology, Louisiana State University, Baton Rouge, Louisiana 70803.

Handbook of Social Support and the Family, edited by Gregory R. Pierce, Barbara R. Sarason, and Irwin G. Sarason. Plenum Press, New York, 1996.

overwhelming evidence for increased psychological distress among caregivers. Both self-report and clinical assessment studies have found caregivers more likely to experience elevated rates of depression and other forms of distress. Physical health may also be affected. For example, caregivers report themselves to be in poorer health than comparison groups, and there is evidence suggesting that the stress of caregiving has a negative impact on the functioning of the immune system, which may in turn lead to increased physical morbidity (Kiecolt-Glaser & Glaser, 1994).

One subset of caregivers has been a particular target of increased research attention: persons who care for family members with Alzheimer's disease (AD) or a related dementing illness. The prevalence of dementia merits such interest: Rates increase dramatically as people age, from a prevalence of 2–3% at age 65 to estimates of as high as 30% among persons 85 and over (Barker, 1992). The hallmark of dementia is irreversible memory loss, almost always accompanied over time by a decline in other cognitive functioning, including intellectual skills, judgment, and language (Cowan, Levitan, & Nelson, 1992).

The consequences of dementia are devastating not only for the patient, but also for members of the patient's family who provide care. As the disease progresses, demands for care increase, usually involving dependency for activities such as shopping, household maintenance, and financial management, as well as personal care. Often most distressing to family caregivers are the behaviors that frequently accompany the disease, such as failure to recognize family and friends, incontinence, sleeplessness, wandering, and verbal and physical aggression (D. Cohen & Eisdorfer, 1986). Further, the family experiences the loss of the loved one as a companion or confidant as their role becomes almost exclusively that of care provider (Fiore, Coppel, Becker, & Cox, 1986).

Because of these characteristics, families caring for dementia patients are highly appropriate for studies of the effects of social support on persons under chronic stress. The devastating nature of the disease and concomitant responsibilities of family members are likely to affect social relationships. In turn, the deterioration of potentially supportive relationships may have profound negative effects on caregivers' physical and psychological well-being.

It is therefore surprising that relatively little systematic research has focused on determinants and consequences of social support among Alzheimer's caregivers. A number of studies have included one or more measures of social contact and support as control variables, but few have made social relationships the major focus of inquiry. Nevertheless, there are some suggestive findings that can provide guidance for future research.

We have several goals in this chapter. First, we provide a critical review of the literature on this topic, focusing on two main areas: (1) the effects of social relationships on psychological well-being and on the decision to place the care recipient in a nursing home and (2) the patterns of support and interpersonal stress among caregivers and factors that account for those patterns. Next, we provide a conceptual framework and several empirical examples from our longitudinal study of AD caregivers that attempt to overcome selected gaps in the research literature. The chapter concludes with recommendations for future research.

REVIEW OF PREVIOUS RESEARCH

As noted earlier, there are only a few studies that have focused primarily on social relationships of AD caregivers. In most cases, one or a few social network or support measures have been included as control variables in studies that examined the more general impact of caregiving on distress. Further, we must repeat here the familiar lament of scholars who attempt to integrate findings from the caregiving literature: Differences in definitions of the study population, sample selection, and independent and dependent variables make it very difficult to compare results of various studies. Detailed critiques of this literature have been conducted by others (cf. Barer & Johnson, 1990) and do not need to be repeated here. It is important to note, however, that inconsistencies in the research limit the ability to make meaningful comparisons of some of the results.

The research on social relationships and AD caregiving can be broadly grouped into two major areas: studies that explore the impact of various aspects of social relationships on caregiver outcomes and studies that examine the effect of caregiving on social relationships.

Effects of Social Relationships on Caregiving Outcomes

Most of the available studies have focused on two potential effects of support: psychological well-being and the decision to place the care recipient in a nursing home. We will take these two outcomes in turn.

Social Support and Psychological Well-Being. The aforementioned problems of inconsistency in study samples, definitions, and independent and dependent variables are particularly apparent in this area. Any generalizations about the relationship between social support and psychological well-being among caregivers must therefore be made with caution. However, the more methodologically sound studies indicate, at least in a preliminary way, that perceptions about the adequacy of social support are predictive of well-being measures.

Fiore et al. (1986) studied 65 caregivers to spouses with AD. A Global Satisfaction Scale was used to measure perceived satisfaction with nine dimensions of social support. Other items measured the frequency of contact with network members, the frequency with which the respondent called on network members for support, and the extent to which the network members were perceived as available for support. Two measures of mental health were used: the Beck Depression Inventory and the Symptom Checklist-90 (SCL-90), which is an overall measure of psychological functioning and symptoms. Satisfaction with support was the best predictor of depression and SCL-90 scores. The other three support variables were not related to either measure of psychological well-being.

Similarly, George and Gwyther (1986) examined the impact of a measure of perceived need for more social support on several well-being measures. This item was strongly predictive of both self-rated physical health and several measures of psychological well-being. Zarit, Todd, and Zarit (1986) also found that only caregivers' subjective ratings of the adequacy of support received predicted caregiver burden. Creasey, Meyers, Epperson, and Taylor (1990) examined the impact of the spousal relationship on caregiver burden. Again, perception of support from the spouse was negatively associated with burden.

It does not appear, however, that mere contact or the *potential* provision of support results in either higher levels of actual provision of support or better psychological outcomes for caregivers. For example, Chiriboga, Weiler, and Nielsen (1990) examined the impact of social support on three indicators of psychological well-being: affect balance, anxiety, and depression. The social support measures generally were not related to any of these three indicators. However, the measures used in this study generally relate to the simple presence of *possible* supporters, as indicated by number of friends living nearby, number of siblings, marital status, involvement in self-help groups, and other factors, rather than to perceived adequacy of support. Similarly, Moritz, Kasl, and Berkman (1989) found no relationship between social isolation and depression. In their study, social isolation was defined as having no monthly "visual contacts" with friends or relatives other than children.

C. Cohen, Teresi, and Blum (1994) included measures of both network structure (e.g., size and density) and social support (e.g., frequency of contact and intimacy with network members). They also examined contact with social institutions, such as churches, senior centers, and support groups. In their study of 58 Alzheimer's caregivers, they found that the dimensions of social structure had very little impact on caregiver well-being, as measured by the Hopkins symptom checklist. None of the social network variables had a direct or a buffering effect, and only support from formal sources had an indirect effect.

It appears, then, that perceptions of social support have some potential for explaining caregiver well-being, while measures of contact, network structure, and instrumental support have a less clear effect. However, although most researchers have emphasized the positive effects of social support on psychological well-being, there are both theoretical and empirical bases upon which to suggest that *negative* interactions with network members may have particularly detrimental effects (Rook, 1984). In the past decade, investigators have begun to pay increasing attention to what has been variously described as "negative support," or "interpersonal stress" (we prefer the latter term, as it avoids the oxymoronic tone of the former).

Interestingly, one of the earliest studies of AD caregivers provided evidence that negative interactions were particularly predictive of distress. Fiore, Becker, and Coppel (1983) studied 44 spousal Alzheimer's caregivers, using an extensive battery of social support measures that provided detailed data on both supportive and upsetting aspects of the social network. Respondents rated up to 10 network members on the degree to which they were perceived as supportive or upsetting in five categories of social support: socializing, tangible assistance, cognitive guidance, emotional support, and self-disclosure.

Fiore and colleagues found that experiencing upset within the social network due to unmet support expectations or to negative interactions with others was by far the best predictor of depression. Upset in the area of cognitive guidance was most strongly predictive of depression; this area includes interactions that are designed to increase the caregiver's understanding of problems like the illness course and that help to put the situation into perspective. Social network helpfulness was not found to be related to depression in this study.

Considering the strength of this finding, it is curious that with only a few exceptions, subsequent research has virtually ignored the importance of interpersonal stress with network members in the experience of Alzheimer's caregivers. Indeed, this finding may help explain the overall lack of relationship among measures of support and outcomes noted above. As Fiore and colleagues suggest, it is possible that caregivers calculate an "average" of sorts between the support and the upset they experience from the network. When the negative interactions are examined separately, the upset component rises to prominence.

Some supporting evidence is available for the importance of interpersonal stress in predicting caregiving outcomes. For example, Creasey et al. (1990) found that for adult daughters caring for elderly parents with Alzheimer's, negative interactions with their spouses were very strongly positively associated with burden. Semple's (1992) study of family conflict in Alzheimer's caregiving families also provides support for the importance of interpersonal stress as a predictor of psychological distress. In a study of 555 caregivers, conflict over family members' attitudes and actions toward the caregiver were related to depression. The items included in this measure were: not telephoning enough, not giving the caregiver enough help, not showing enough appreciation for one's work as a caregiver, and giving the caregiver unwanted advice.

Franks and Stephens (1992) provide a relatively sophisticated analysis of the impact of interpersonal relationships on the well-being of family caregivers. Although their study is not directly comparable, in that they included caregivers to physically as well as mentally disabled relatives, the findings are nevertheless worth noting here. Their work is framed in the context of roles and role stress, rather than social support per se; however, the measures of role stress are very similar to those used in studies of "negative" social support.

Franks and Stephens interviewed 106 female primary caregivers to elderly family members who were living in the community. In addition to the caregiving role, they examined stress in two other roles: those of wife and mother. Most of the wife and mother role stress items measure various types of negative interactions (e.g., in the wife role: conflicts over children, insufficient emotional support, not enough appreciation).

Stress in both roles was negatively related to psychological well-being, with stress in the mother role being a particularly strong predictor. In a related study, Stephens, Franks, and Townsend (1994) examined not only the stressful aspects of roles, but also the rewards received from them. Again, stress in the mother role most strongly predicted the measures of distress. Thus, interpersonal stress with intimates appears to be a potentially powerful predictor of caregiver distress.

Social Support and Institutionalization. Considering the somewhat inconsistent findings related to well-being, studies of predictors of institutional placement are surprisingly consistent: Social support for the caregiver, regardless of how measured, does not appear to be related to the decision to place the relative in a nursing home.

This lack of relationship has been found in studies that have used a wide variety of measures, including frequency of instrumental support and participation in social and recreational activities (Colerick & George, 1986), number of family members and friends who provide hands-on assistance to the care recipient (Pruchno, Michaels, & Potashnik, 1990), weekly frequency of contact with formal and informal supporters and a subjective measure of quality of support (Zarit et al., 1986), number and closeness of friends and relatives and satisfaction provided by the network (Mittleman et al., 1993), an overall measure of lack of social support (Lieberman & Kramer, 1991), frequency of family interaction and the availability of backup help (Morycz, 1985), and scales measuring emotional, care-related, and task-related support (Aneshensel, Pearlin, & Schuler, 1993).

The lack of relationship between social support and institutionalization is somewhat counterintuitive. It might be expected that the presence of other helpers would lessen the strain of providing care. Further, a network of people who support the person's decision to provide care in the home would be expected to bolster positive feelings about the self and therefore reinforce the decision to continue in the role.

However, alternative explanations are possible. First, the studies of institutionalization have not systematically examined negative interactions with network members. Consistent with the research on psychological well-being noted above, perhaps interpersonal stress with network members will be more predictive of institutionalization. Second, it is possible that two countervailing forces are operating simultaneously. Although support may to some extent deter institutional placement, supportive network members may also *encourage* such placement. Qualitative data from our study of AD caregivers (described below) indicate that associates at times suggest that caregivers *should* be considering nursing home care, because they perceive that the stress is overwhelming the caregiver. Additional research is needed to better understand the role of social relationships in the decision to use nursing home care.

In sum, this literature shows that social support and particularly interpersonal stress have important effects on caregivers' psychological well-being, while the effects on the decision to institutionalize the relative are negligible. This brings us to our next question: To what extent are caregivers provided with adequate levels of support and shielded from interpersonal stress, and what factors account for these patterns?

Patterns of Support and Interpersonal Stress among Caregivers

A common finding of early studies and case reports was that individuals' involvement with friends and family often declined after they became primary caregivers (Archbold, 1982; Brody & Lang, 1982; Cantor, 1983; Chenoweth & Spencer, 1986; Fengler & Goodrich, 1979; Mace, 1984). More recent research has confirmed these findings. Moritz et al. (1989), in one of the few studies that allowed for systematic comparison, found that persons living with a cognitively impaired spouse engaged in less socializing outside the home than people whose spouses were not cognitively impaired.

George and Gwyther (1986) compared a sample of 510 dementia caregivers with data from several representative samples of the general elderly population. They examined the impact of caring for a dementia patient on various aspects of social participation, including frequency of phone contacts and visits with friends and family, church and club attendance, and satisfaction with social and recreational activities. Contact and visits with social network members were substantially lower in the caregiver group, as were other types of social participation.

Among married adult children, caregiving can have a serious impact on the relationship with the caregiver's spouse. Kleban, Brody, Schoonover, and Hoffman (1989) documented that a major effect of caregiving was interference with the couples' social lives. This effect was magnified when the care recipient shared a residence with the couple: Co-residential caregivers were most likely to have decreased social participation.

Thus, becoming a caregiver to a person with AD appears to have a major impact on social relationships. However, the question arises: Are the effects due simply to caregiving, or are there special characteristics of AD that cause greater disruptions in social relationships than occur in situations where the care recipient is not demented? Birkel and Jones (1989) contrasted aspects of the social networks of caregivers to demented and nondemented elders. They argue that the presence of dementia can actually *decrease* the amount of help others provide to the care recipient.

Birkel and Jones suggest that such a decrease can occur for several reasons. First, the mood swings and disruptive behaviors that often accompany dementia may discourage others from providing assistance. Second, the shame associated with mental illness may cause the caregivers to isolate themselves. Third, nondemented elders can help maintain relationships with persons outside the household, while demented persons generally cannot. They hypothesize that families caring for demented persons will rely on resources within the household and that the primary caregiver will be less likely to receive help from persons outside the household.

Birkel and Jones compared 20 elderly physically disabled persons without dementia with 20 elders who had both physical disability and dementia. The social network measures included the number of people who provided help when the caregiver was absent, as well as people who provided emotional support, advice, encouragement, and financial help. The hours of time provided by these network members were calculated.

As hypothesized, the dementia group had smaller overall networks and fewer helpers from outside the household. Household members provided a greater number of hours of care for dementia patients, while fewer hours were provided by non-household members. Overall, dementia caregivers identified fewer out-of-household supporters. Thus, this study indicates that responsibility for caring for nondemented individuals is shared to a greater extent than the care of demented persons. When the care recipient had dementia, responsibility fell on a smaller number of household members.

Other research supports these findings. Shaw, O'Bryant, and Meddaugh (1991) compared the support received by caregivers to Alzheimer's patients and caregivers to frail, nondemented elders. Alzheimer's caregivers were more likely to identify unmet needs for social support. They also reported having fewer nonkin supporters. Similarly, Clipp and George (1993) compared caregivers to dementia patients with persons caring for cancer patients. Overall satisfaction with social activities was substantially lower for dementia caregivers. They also were more likely to report feeling alone and to need more help from friends and family (for an exception, however, see Catternach & Tebes, 1991).

Thus, becoming an AD caregiver appears to reduce social interaction. Further, caregivers cannot assume that they will be provided with adequate support. Unfortunately, despite the important role of interpersonal stress for caregivers' well-being, no study has explored the prevalence of interpersonal stress in the networks of caregivers, nor has any study conducted comparisons with other groups regarding the amount of interpersonal stress.

Another critical question has been virtually unexplored: What factors explain patterns of social support to caregivers? For example, do patterns of support remain relatively stable throughout the course of the illness? What factors differentiate between caregivers who do and do not receive adequate levels of support?

In the only study to address either of these issues, Clipp and George (1990) used data on 376 caregivers to Alzheimer's patients to test whether six sets of caregiver characteristics and needs predicted levels of support over time. In general, patterns of support remained stable over the course of 1 year, with only about 15% of the respondents reporting decreases in either instrumental support or perceived support over that time period.

Persons who either had high instrumental support at both time points or received increasing support over the year were likely to be better educated and have higher incomes, to have frequent contact with friends and family, and to be caregivers to a person who was institutionalized. Those persons who either had low instrumental support at both times or decreased in support were disproportionately older and had lower incomes. They reported higher stress and were mostly caring for the relatives in their homes. Results were similar regarding perceived support. Thus, it appears that caregivers who are in greatest need of support are paradoxically those who are least likely to receive it.

Both of these findings, and the importance of support for well-being discussed above, suggest that it is critical to understand factors that affect patterns of support and interpersonal stress. Following a summary of the preceding review, the next section presents data that attempt to shed light on this issue.

Summary

The research review just presented indicates that the role of social relationships in AD caregiving is more complex than has generally been acknowledged.

Rather than straightforward direct or buffering relationships between social support and caregiving outcomes, effects seem to vary according to the way support is measured and the outcome under consideration. It will be useful to summarize the key points in the review, keeping in mind the limitations of existing studies:

1. Becoming an AD caregiver has serious and detrimental effects on social relationships. Caregivers experience constrictions in their social lives and disruptions in relations with friends and family.
2. Perceived adequacy of support appears to be related to measures of psychological well-being among caregivers.
3. Quantitative measures of contact and instrumental assistance are not consistently related to caregiver well-being.
4. Social support is not related to the decision to place the care recipient in a nursing home.

We believe that it is possible to move beyond such descriptive findings and to advance our knowledge of caregiving and social support in important new directions. On the basis of our review of the literature, four issues seem especially critical to address.

First, with notable exceptions (e.g., the work of Pearlin and colleagues), few studies have attempted to study the issue of social support and caregiving in the context of broader sociological theory regarding interpersonal relationships. We believe it is important to connect the study of caregiving to other bodies of theory and to develop conceptual frameworks for research that are theory-driven.

Second, much previous research on family caregiving has focused on the *content* of support, with only limited attention to the *social structural* factors that may affect support provision and receipt. In contrast, we concur with the call by House (1987) for greater attention to structural factors in the study of social support. We believe that a focus on the structure of social networks can substantially increase our understanding of factors that affect both the quality and the quantity of support received by family caregivers, as well as the outcomes of such support for the recipients.

A third direction for investigation was also offered by House (1981), who posed a classic question regarding social support: "*Who* gives *what* to *whom* regarding *which* problems? (p. 22). A great deal of work has been directed toward answering this question in the intervening years, with considerable attention focused on identifying associates who are most likely to be sources of support and on differences in the particular types of support provided (Suitor, Pillemer, & Keeton, 1995). This line of research, however, has not been extended to the study of AD caregivers.

Fourth, it is critical to examine more systematically the role of interpersonal stress in AD caregiving relationships. The preliminary evidence discussed above suggests that negative interactions with network members are more strongly related to caregiving outcomes than are emotional and instrumental support. It is therefore important to identify both the sources and the consequences of interpersonal stress.

Over the past several years, we have been involved in a program of research designed to begin to address these issues. In the remainder of this chapter, we summarize the conceptual framework we have developed to guide this research and provide three examples of empirical research we have conducted to test components of the theoretical framework.

ALZHEIMER'S DISEASE CAREGIVING AS A STATUS TRANSITION: A NEW FRAMEWORK FOR STUDYING SOCIAL SUPPORT AND WELL-BEING

As earlier sections of this chapter have indicated, although prior research shows some aspects of social support to be related to caregiver well-being, the findings are less consistent than might be expected, particularly given the salience of social support for well-being in other populations. We believe that future research on the effects of caregiving could provide more consistent findings by developing designs that draw upon the broader literature on status transitions, social support, and psychological well-being. Such a focus can substantially increase our understanding of factors that affect both the quality and the quantity of support received by family caregivers, as well as the outcomes of such support for the recipients.

Family Caregiver as a Social Status

The atheoretical nature of most research on family caregivers may be the result of the way in which caregiving has been conceptualized. In particular, family caregiving has generally been viewed as a specific activity, rather than as a social status (Suitor & Pillemer, 1990). We would argue, however, that "family caregiver" meets the sociological definition of a social status—particularly when individuals assume *primary* responsibility for the care of an elderly relative (see Brody, 1985; Pearlin, Mullan, Semple, & Skaff, 1990; Treas & Bengtson, 1988; Walker, Pratt, Shin, & Jones, 1990).

One ground for this argument is that "family caregiver" is a position in society that has specific behavioral and attitudinal expectations attached to it. Individuals who assume the care of an elderly relative are expected to provide both physical and emotional support for the care recipient and to do so with a minimum of resentment (Cicirelli, 1981; George, 1986; Gubrium, 1988).

Research on attitudes regarding filial responsibility illustrates the persistence of these norms. Friends and relatives expect adult children and spouses to provide elderly parents with assistance with activities of daily living and expenses, even when doing so requires that the caregiver alter family plans and work responsibilities (Brody, 1990; George, 1986; Gubrium, 1988; Jarrett, 1985). In most states, these informal prescriptions to provide assistance are reinforced by laws regarding elder neglect that provide formal standards for adequate performance of caregiving responsibilities (cf. Crystal, 1986; Wolf & Pillemer, 1989).

On the basis of this argument, we suggest that becoming a caregiver involves a status transition that is similar in many ways to that experienced when an individual assumes another new social status in adulthood, such as becoming a parent, becoming divorced, retiring, or entering the labor force or college. The event that brings on the status transition to family caregiver is usually the onset of the relative's illness or injury or the relative's discharge from the hospital following serious illness or injury. In the case of AD, the status transition is most likely to begin at the time a formal diagnosis is made (for a full discussion of the importance of diagnosis, see Suitor & Pillemer, 1990).

Status Transitions and the Benefits of Status-Similar Others

Viewing assumption of the role of family caregiver as a status transition allows us to draw on the broader literature on status transitions and social support in forming hypotheses about structural characteristics of networks that buffer against psychological distress. This literature shows that acquiring a new social status generally produces changes in an individuals' social networks that affect both the provision of social support and psychological well-being. When people acquire new statuses, they often reduce contact with associates to whom they have become less similar and intensify existing relationships (or develop new ones) with others to whom they have become more similar (see Bell, 1981; Belsky & Rovine, 1984; Gottlieb & Pancer, 1988; Gouldner & Strong, 1987; Hetherington, Cox, & Cox, 1976; Suitor, 1987a,b).

This pattern of increased status homophily appears to augment the positive effect of social support on psychological well-being. Lin and colleagues (Lin, 1986; Lin, Woelfel, & Light, 1985) found that support from individuals who were similar to the respondents (e.g., who were of similar age or occupational prestige) was associated with lower levels of depression following undesirable life events than was support from individuals with whom the respondents did not share those statuses.

Thoits (1986) has cogently argued that similarity of *situational experience* is particularly important. This assertion is based in part on experimental research demonstrating that individuals seek out and affiliate with others who have been through the same stressful experience. Thoits holds that empathic understanding, which is critical to the support process, is more likely to come from similar others.

Thoits proposes several reasons that coping assistance from similar others should be particularly efficacious. She notes that distressed persons frequently fear that something is seriously wrong with them. Others who have been through the same experience can help the stressed individual to view his or her feelings as expectable and within the range of normality. Further, similar others may be less likely to reject persons because of their distress or strong emotions. This greater sense of acceptance allows the stressed individual more freedom to discuss his or her feelings than occurs with nonsimilar associates.

Thus, Thoits argues that a distressed person must perceive empathic understanding from potential helpers in order to benefit from their assistance. Situationally similar persons will provide the most efficacious coping assistance because they can offer the stressed individual precisely this: understanding based on shared experience.

While we agree with this argument, we believe that the greater buffering effect also occurs because similarity decreases the likelihood that social interactions will have detrimental consequences for well-being. As suggested earlier, there are both theoretical and empirical bases on which to suggest that interactions with network members may have detrimental as well as beneficial effects.

For example, principles of exchange theory suggest that receiving support could have a detrimental effect on well-being if individuals are in a structural position that makes reciprocity difficult. When people are unable to return social support, they often feel in violation of the norm of reciprocity, a feeling that in turn leads to psychological distress (cf. Riley & Eckenrode, 1986). We suggest that the potentially negative consequences of social support are less likely when support is offered by network members to whom the individual is more similar.

The basis for this expectation is that individuals who share social statuses may be more accepting of one another's temporary inability to reciprocate support. This acceptance may occur in part because status similarity is associated with greater closeness, and there is more tolerance of short-term violation of the norm of reciprocity among intimates. But it is also likely that individuals who are status-similar have a greater understanding of one another's resources and ability to reciprocate and are therefore more tolerant of temporary periods of non-reciprocity (for a more complete discussion of this issue, see Suitor & Pillemer, 1990).

Another potential source of stress associated with network contact has been alluded to above: Unmet expectations of support and negative input from network members possibly have more significant consequences for psychological well-being than does perceived helpfulness. The greater similarity of values associated with status similarity is likely to reduce criticism (cf. Suitor, 1987a,b). Research on ineffective and miscarried support attempts further supports the importance of similar others. Advice and intervention from dissimilar others is more likely to be perceived as unwelcome and coercive (Thoits, 1986).

We hypothesize that experiential similarity will be particularly important in explaining which associates will be sources of support and stress and in predicting psychological well-being. It is likely, however, that other dimensions of structural similarity will also affect patterns and consequences of support. The structural similarities that will be most important following status transitions are those that (1) involve socialization processes or life events similar to those experienced by the respondent or (2) lead the associate to anticipate experiencing the same transition.

To provide an example, age similarity is likely to be an important structural factor explaining support for transitions that are specific to particular stages in the life course, as well as their outcomes. Associates who are in the middle years might be more supportive of similar-age individuals caring for their elderly parents than would those who are in earlier life stages and have not begun anticipating this transition.

Similarly, gender similarity may be important in predicting patterns of support and caregiving outcomes, and especially so for women. Women become caregivers primarily as the result of decision-making processes that are affected by gender-role socialization throughout the life course. Given the ubiquitous nature of such traditional socialization patterns among women in their middle years, even women who have not become caregivers themselves are likely to be able to identify with and understand the decision-making processes involved in such experiences.

ILLUSTRATIVE FINDINGS FROM THE ALZHEIMER'S DISEASE CAREGIVERS STUDY

Thus, there is ample theoretical justification for the assertion that the presence of individuals who share the status of an individual undergoing a status transition will be positively related to both the provision of support and psychological well-being. We now turn to three related analyses from our longitudinal study of AD caregivers hat explored issues of status similarity in the caregiving experience. Space limitations do not permit us to describe the analyses in full detail; rather, our goal is to provide illustrations of ways in which the conceptual framework just described can be empirically tested.

Data reported here come from the first wave of interviews from a panel study of AD caregivers. The methods used for the current study have been described in detail elsewhere (Pillemer & Suitor, 1992; Suitor & Pillemer, 1993) and will be reviewed only briefly here.

Data Collection

The first wave of data was collected between January 1989 and March 1992 during 2-hour interviews with individuals who were identified as the primary caregivers to elderly relatives with some form of irreversible dementia. The caregivers were interviewed a second time 1 year later and again a third time 1 year after that. The analyses reported here rely only on the first wave of data collection.

Of the participants, 91% were referred to the study by physicians at 13 major medical centers in the northeastern United States that have dementia screening programs. The remainder of the participants were referred by psychiatrists and neurologists who work extensively with dementia patients. One of the major considerations in the design was to interview the individuals shortly after they had acquired the formal status of caregiver. In order to accomplish this, we attempted to limit our sample to individuals whose parents had been given a diagnosis of dementia within the previous 6 months. (Due to errors in the referral process, a small number of the care recipients had been diagnosed more than 6 months prior to the interview.)

We completed interviews with 60% of the individuals who were eligible for participation, resulting in a sample of 256 caregivers. The sample included 118 daughters, 14 sons, 30 daughters-in-law, 53 wives, 25 husbands, 7 siblings, 6 other relatives, and 3 nonrelatives who were viewed by the respondents as equivalent to kin.

Measures of Social Network Structure and Function

We used the name-elicitation approaches developed by Fischer (1982) and Wellman (Wellman & Wortley, 1989) to collect information on the structure and function of the caregivers' social networks. We asked each respondent whether there was anyone on whom he or she relied for a variety of instrumental and emotional tasks, including tasks related to caregiving and those not directly related to caregiving. We also asked whether anyone had been critical of his or her caregiving or made his or her caregiving more difficult. For each item, we asked the first names of the people who had served as sources of these dimensions of support and interpersonal stress.

For each of the network members named, we collected data on the individual's demographic characteristics (e.g., age, educational attainment, gender, marital status, employment status) and whether the associate had experience caring for an elderly relative.

We measured support using the following items: (1) "In the past year, has anyone done anything to try to make it easier for you to care for your [relative]?" (2) "Does anyone else besides you help your [relative] with [any of the activities of daily living just listed]?" (3) "Whom do you talk to about your [relative]?" Each respondent who answered yes to either of the first two questions was asked both who had provided that support and specifically what that individual had done to make things easier.

A network member was categorized as a source of emotional support if the caregiver's response met at least one of two criteria: (1) The caregiver *directly stated* that a network member had provided emotional support (e.g., "She always supports me emotionally"; "He tries to cheer me up when I'm upset about my mother") or (2) the caregiver's response met the classic definition of emotional support given by Cobb (1976)—the caregivers' statements indicated that the caregiver viewed herself or himself as loved, cared for, and esteemed in terms of the caregiving context (e.g., "My friend Susan is just there for me in terms of my mother"). We considered any associate to be a source of emotional support who was coded positively on either of the first two items or who was someone the caregiver talked to about his or her relative.

Each network member was also categorized as having been or not having been a source of interpersonal stress depending on whether he or she was mentioned when the respondent was asked whether anyone had (1) criticized his or her caregiving; (2) made it harder for him or her to provide care to [the relative]; (3) made him or her feel neglected; (4) complained that the respondent had not spent enough time with him or her; or (5) provided less help in caring for the parent than the respondent thought was appropriate.

Independent Variables: Similarity

Experiential similarity was a dummy-coded variable: 0 = associate has not cared for an elderly relative; 1 = associate has cared for an elderly relative.

Although the focus of the study was on the effects of experiential similarity, we felt that it was important to include several structural dimensions of similarity in the multivariate analysis, since these factors are often found to predict patterns of support and stress in network studies that do not focus on recent transitions (e.g., Bell, 1981; Feld, 1982; Fischer, 1982; Gouldner & Strong, 1987; Wellman & Wortley, 1990). We selected dimensions of homophily that have been found most often to be predictors of patterns of support and stress for women—similarity of age, gender, marital status, and labor force status.

Age similarity and employment similarity were created using a combination of data on the respondent and each of his or her network members. Age similarity is the absolute difference between the respondent's age and that of his or her associate. Employment similarity is a dummy-coded variable: 0 = not same employment status; 1 = both employed or both not employed. Since all the caregivers in the subsample used in this analysis were married daughters, the associate's gender (0 = male; 1 = female) and marital status (0 = not married; 1 = married) were used to measure gender similarity and marital status similarity.

Analysis I: Extent of Support and Interpersonal Stress

For the examination of the extent and sources of support and stress, we restricted the analysis to the modal category of caregivers—married women caring for their parents ($N = 95$). We did this because preliminary analysis indicated that the structure and function of the caregivers' social networks varied substantially by gender, marital status, and relationship to the patient. Therefore, it was not appropriate to combine the various categories of caregivers for any of the analyses involving patterns of support and interpersonal stress (for a description of this subsample, see Suitor & Pillemer, 1993).

Almost all the caregivers reported that someone had provided some form of support. In all, 97% of the respondents reported that they had received instrumental support (i.e., concrete assistance), and 30% reported that they had received emotional support specific to caregiving. Further, 88% of the caregivers reported that someone had been a source of interpersonal stress. The most frequently reported form of interpersonal stress involved unmet expectations for support; 63% of the respondents stated that they felt that someone should have provided more help with caregiving.

We next examined which categories of associates served as sources of support and interpersonal stress. To accomplish this, we defined eight categories of associates: spouses, children, siblings, other kin, in-laws, friends, formal service providers, and a residual "other" category. We then examined the distribution of support and stress among these categories of associates. The distributions are shown in Table 1. To be sure, one could make many comparisons among the categories of associates and support and interpersonal stress. We have chosen to focus on only a few particularly striking comparisons.

One of the most interesting findings is the relative importance of friends and siblings as sources of support and interpersonal stress. Given the structural position of siblings, we might expect them to be by far the most important source of support. However, they provided only about the same amount of support, overall, as did friends. While siblings were a greater source of instrumental support than were friends, they played a far less important role than friends in providing emotional support. In fact, friends were clearly the greatest source of emotional support for these caregivers. Conversely, siblings were the greatest source of caregivers' interpersonal stress.

It should be noted that there were relatively few cases in which the same network member was identified as a source of both support and interpersonal stress. Of the total 614 associates who were mentioned as sources of either support or stress (349 support and 265 stress), only 49 (8%) were mentioned as a source of both. More than half of these cases involved siblings who provided some instrumental support, but were sources of stress because they did not adequately meet the caregivers' expectations for support.

Interesting differences occurred in sisters' and brothers' patterns of support and stress. Although we found that sisters were a greater source of emotional support than were brothers, they did not differ from brothers in terms of either instrumental support or interpersonal stress.

The findings regarding the roles played by siblings are particularly interesting in light of the gerontological literature on caregiving and support. This literature focuses on kin as a source of support for adult children caring for parents (cf. Biegel & Blum, 1990; Brody, 1990), with less recognition of the role of friends. Yet as these findings indicate, friends serve as an important source of support, while creating relatively little interpersonal stress. In contrast, siblings appear to be a substantially greater source of stress than of support.

These patterns greatly parallel the findings reported in other studies of siblings and friends, both within and outside the caregiving context. As cited earlier, Wellman and Wortley (1989, 1990) found that friends and siblings were almost equally likely to be sources of social support. Further, the findings of Brody, Hoffman, Kleban, and Schoonover (1989) suggest that conflict among siblings regarding care of their aging parents is common.

Other studies suggest that conflict among siblings may occur in the middle years, even when caregiving to elderly parents is not a focus of attention. Bedford (1989) recently found that siblings sometimes experience increases in conflict across the midadult years, while Ross and Milgram (1982) reported that almost half of the adults they interviewed admitted that they continued to harbor feelings of rivalry toward siblings. Bedford proposed that continued or increased conflict

Table 1. Percentages of Support and Interpersonal Stress by Category of Associate[a]

Associates	Support			Interpersonal stress					
	Total	Emotional	Instrumental	Total	Should have helped more	Neglected caregiver	Criticized caregiver regarding care	Complained caregiver spent less time with them	Made caregiving harder
Spouse	11.2%	14.7%	11.1%	5.3%	—	3.3%	12.3%	7.1%	8.9%
Children	13.5%	11.8%	14.0%	15.5%	17.3%	3.3%	3.5%	18.6%	8.9%
Sibling	20.9%	16.2%	23.9%	37.4%	66.1%	49.2%	52.6%	2.9%	62.2%
Other kin	10.9%	2.9%	11.8%	10.9%	10.2%	8.2%	14.0%	8.6%	13.3%
In-law	8.6%	13.2%	7.6%	5.7%	3.9%	8.2%	7.0%	4.3%	—
Friend	16.3%	35.3%	10.8%	23.8%	2.4%	26.2%	7.0%	58.6%	4.4%
Formal service provider	14.9%	2.9%	16.6%	1.1%	—	1.6%	1.8%	—	2.2%
Other	3.7%	2.9%	4.1%	0.4%	—	—	1.8%	—	—
Number mentioned	349	68	314	265	127	61	57	70	45

[a]The total number of associates identified was 1195. Some columns do not total exactly 100% due to rounding.

across the midadult years might occur because siblings have relatively little contact at this life stage and, as a result, continue to relate to one another as they did in the childhood and early adult years—years that tend to be characterized by more conflictual interpersonal relationships.

We agree with her interpretation and suggest that, furthermore, parent care may exacerbate any unresolved conflicts from the earlier stages of the sibling relationship in much the same way that Steinman (1979) suggested that conflicts between parents and adult children may become reactivated. The suggestion by Allan (1979) that past conflicts among siblings might become reactivated if they had to live together or work closely is consistent with our suggestion. Both living together and working closely involve involuntary contact and joint decision making among siblings—experiences that are also produced by a parent's need for care. Thus, while it appears that sibling relations become closer and less conflictual in the *later* years (cf. Cicirelli, 1985; Gold, 1989), the needs of aging parents may create relatively less comfortable relations among siblings during the middle years.

Analysis II: Explaining Support and Interpersonal Stress

Next we conducted a multivariate analysis of factors affecting support and stress. For this analysis, we combined emotional and instrumental support into one measure of support and combined all five measures of relational conflicts and unmet expectations into one measure of interpersonal stress. We omitted from this part of the analysis associates who were minors (children, grandchildren, nieces, and others under the age of 18 [$N = 73$]) and those who were formal service providers (e.g., social workers, physicians, paid helpers [$N = 85$]). (Additionally, 88 more associates were excluded from the analysis because the demographic data necessary to compute the similarity variables could not be provided by the caregivers.)

For this part of the analysis, we collapsed the categories of associates into nonkin and kin (0 = nonkin; 1 = kin) and entered this dichotomous variable into the regression analysis as a control.

To measure proximity, the caregivers were asked how far they lived from each of their associates. The distances ranged from less than 1 mile to more than 3000 miles; however, almost two thirds of the associates lived within 10 miles of the caregivers. Given the skewness of the data, the decision was made to use the natural log of the variable in the regression analysis.

Table 2 shows the findings of the logistic regression analysis. As shown in the left-hand columns, individuals who had themselves provided care to an elderly relative were more likely to have been sources of support, as were women and relatives (as opposed to friends); individuals who lived farther from the caregiver were less likely to have been sources of support than were those who lived closer.

The right-hand columns in Table 2 show the findings of the analysis for caregivers' interpersonal stress. All four of the factors that affected support also affected interpersonal stress; however, three of the four had positive rather than

Table 2. Logistic Regression Analysis of Support and Interpersonal Stress[a]

Independent variable	Support		Interpersonal stress	
	B	Standard error	B	Standard error
Associate's caregiving experience	0.800[d]	0.155	−0.854[d]	0.168
Associate's marital status	0.272	0.187	0.106	0.191
Associate's gender	0.360[c]	0.179	0.342[b]	0.182
Age similarity	−0.002	0.008	−0.020[c]	0.009
Similarity of labor force participation	0.012	0.162	0.099	0.169
Distance (miles)	−0.145[d]	0.039	0.090[c]	0.036
Relationship to caregiver	1.473[c]	0.203	1.333[d]	0.212
Model χ^2	94.35[d]		93.92[d]	
df	7		7	

[a]The analysis included a total of 949 adult associates.
[b-d]Significance: [b]$p < 0.10$; [c]$p < 0.05$; [d]$p < 0.01$.

negative effects. Network members with caregiving experience were less likely to have been sources of stress; however, both women and relatives were *more* likely to have been sources of stress, as were associates who lived farther away. Similarity of age, which was not important in explaining support, did distinguish between network members who were and were not sources of interpersonal stress. Specifically, network members who were more similar in age to the caregiver were less likely to have been sources of stress.

This analysis clearly demonstrates the importance of status similarity in explaining whether individual network members were sources of support or of interpersonal stress. The most consistently important dimension of similarity involved caregiving experience. Individuals who had themselves cared for an elderly relative were more likely to have been sources of support and less likely to have been sources of interpersonal stress, such as criticism, direct interference, or unmet expectations for support.

The respondents were often aware of the importance of caregiving similarity in explaining which associates were most likely to be sources of support or stress. In particular, many of the women indicated that relatives and friends who were sources of stress had little sense of the responsibilities and emotions involved in caring for a parent suffering from dementia, due to their inexperience as caregivers. The following statements from some of the respondents illustrate this point:

> Everyone will put their two cents in on how they think it should be ... if you don't live with an Alzheimer's patient, you have no idea. It's like you're in a world unto yourself because [my mother] will go out and do absolutely nothing in front of somebody else and be as normal as normal can be and [my relatives and friends] think that [I'm] exaggerating. Walk in my shoes kind of thing....
>
> ... [I told my brother that mother] is just really terrible. She wets all over the place, she couldn't remember anything or anyone. [He] just didn't want to believe me ... he

> thought I was just being ridiculous and crazy and all that.... I think that not being involved in giving care made it [hard] for him to [understand] what was going on.

> ... people don't really [understand].... [A friend] annoyed me because I always felt, you're not walking in my shoes and I said [to myself] you don't know what you're talking about. I never told her but it made me feel, you know, bad.

In sum, the finding that network members who had caregiving experience were more likely to have been sources of support and less likely to have been sources of stress contributes to a growing literature showing the benefits that caregivers receive from associating with others who share or have shared the status of family caregiver (Chiriboga et al., 1990; Maddox, 1984).

The findings also revealed that the associates' gender helped to explain patterns of both support and stress. As we anticipated, women were more likely to have been sources of support than were men. Contrary to our expectations, however, women were also greater sources of stress. The explanation for this may lie in differences in men's and women's patterns of interaction. Women generally appear to be more likely to become involved in their friends' and relatives' problems (cf. Allan, 1989; Bell, 1981; Wellman & Wortley, 1989). It would not be surprising if that increased involvement resulted in greater interpersonal conflict, as well as support, since contact increases the opportunities for stressful interactions.

Further, the analysis revealed that similarity of age was important in explaining which network members were more likely to be sources of interpersonal stress but, surprisingly, did not help to explain patterns of support. Given these inconsistent results, it is difficult to say with certainty whether any effects can be accounted for by age homophily. It is possible that the relationship between age similarity and stress can be explained by an entirely different set of factors. In particular, network members who were less age-similar to the caregiver were disproportionately younger, and age has been found consistently to be inversely related to interpersonal conflict among adult family members (Suitor & Pillemer, 1987, 1988).

Taken together, these findings suggest that some dimensions of status similarity are substantially more important than others in explaining patterns of support and interpersonal stress among family caregivers. For example, while similarity of caregiving experience consistently differentiated between network members who were and were not sources of support or stress, similarity of age did not do so consistently, and similarity of marital status and employment failed to differentiate at all.

One explanation for this pattern of findings may lie in the greater salience of some dimensions of status similarity. Given the importance of caregiving in the respondents' lives, this dimension of similarity may far outweigh others that might be important at other points in the life course.

Another explanation may lie in our selection of individuals in the early stages of caregiving. We expect that as caregiving responsibilities become more intense over time, the greater empathy that is likely to exist between individuals who are status-similar will increase the likelihood that these individuals will be important sources of support. If this is the case, similarity of age, as well as of marital status and employment, may begin to play a role in explaining patterns of support at later stages in the caregiving career.

Analysis III: Effects of Status-Similar Others on the Well-Being of Caregivers

The preceding analysis demonstrated that status similarity is a powerful predictor of the provision of support and interpersonal stress by network members. The theoretical framework outlined above also proposed that the presence of status-similar others in social networks would reduce psychological distress among caregivers. In this analysis, we will investigate this second question by examining the effect of experiential and structural similarity on caregivers' well-being. We anticipate that among persons who have recently assumed the status of family caregiver, the presence of a larger proportion of other caregivers in their social networks will be positively related to psychological well-being (for a complete discussion of this analysis, see Pillemer & Suitor, 1993).

In addition, we hypothesize that the benefits of status-similar network members will differ depending upon the degree of responsibility and stress imposed by the transition. Numerous studies have shown that the beneficial effects of social support are most likely to be found when a stronger stressor is present (cf. House, Umberson, & Landis, 1988). Perhaps the best indicator of demands on the caregiver is the degree to which the parent exhibits disruptive behaviors. Many studies have found that psychological distress results from the care recipient's wandering, embarrassing behavior, and verbal outbursts (cf. Deimling & Bass, 1986; Pillemer & Suitor, 1992).

We therefore hypothesize that in situations in which disruptive behaviors are low, the presence of other caregivers in the network would have little or no effect on distress. When disruptive behaviors are high, we anticipate that persons with networks consisting more predominantly of status-similar others will experience lower levels of distress. As before, we expect that caregiver status similarity will be more strongly related to depression than will the other network similarity variables.

Variables in the Analysis. To maximize comparability with the previous analysis, we used the subsample of 146 women who were caring for a parent or parent-in-law. In this case, we are interested in the relationship between network structure and well-being, rather than determinants of support by associates, so it was not necessary to restrict the sample according to marital status. Among the associates, professional helpers and minor children were excluded.

For the analyses here, four variables were created (all range from 0 to a maximum of 15). *Caregiving similarity* is the number of network associates who have had caregiving experience (mean = 5.2, SD = 3.4). *Age similarity* was calculated as the number of associates who were within 5 years of the respondent's age (mean = 4.7, SD = 2.7). *Employment similarity* is the number of associates who shared the same employment status, that is, both employed or both unemployed (mean = 6.4, SD = 3.3). *Gender similarity* is the number of associates who are women (mean = 7.2,

SD = 3.3). To avoid a confound with network size, each of these four variables was divided by the total number of associates named, to create proportional measures.

We included in the analysis as controls three variables that have been found in previous research to be related to caregiver distress. These are: living arrangement (coded as 0 = patient does not live with respondent; 1 = patient lives with respondent), amount of assistance provided (the number of activities the caregiver helps with, on a scale of 0–6), and self-reported health (1 = poor, 2 = fair, 3 = good, 4 = excellent).

The dependent variable was depression, measured by the Center for Epidemiological Studies Depression scale (Radloff, 1977). The items comprising the scale ask how many days in the preceding week the respondent felt a certain way (e.g., "You felt depressed"; "You felt hopeful about the future"). Response categories are: less than 1 day, 1–2 days, 3–4 days, 5–7 days. The items were combined in a scale in which a higher score indicates more severe depression (mean = 17.5, SD = 9.9; Cronbach's alpha = 0.89).

We tested the hypothesis that respondents whose social networks contain a higher proportion of experientially similar associates (i.e., those who have been caregivers) will experience lower levels of depression. Further, we anticipated that the presence of other caregivers in the network will be related to how demanding the caregiving situation is. To test this hypothesis, we subdivided the sample according to the amount of disruptive behavior exhibited by the respondent. We used a shortened version of George's index of disruptive behaviors (George & Gwyther, 1986). The scale consists of 8 items that ask how often problematic behaviors occur (1 = never, 2 = rarely, 3 = occasionally, 4 = frequently). The behaviors include the following: wanders or gets lost, is agitated or fidgety, does not recognize family or friends, has problems expressing thoughts, is depressed, does not like to be left alone with strangers, hears voices or sees things that aren't there, and cannot control bladder or bowels. The scale ranged from a score of 10 to 30 (mean = 21.5, SD = 4.3). For the purposes of the analysis, the scale was divided at the median (21) and dummy-coded as 0 = low disruptive behaviors and 1 = high disruptive behaviors.

The analysis presented in Table 3 confirms our hypotheses. In the subsample with low disruptive behaviors, only self-reported health was related to depression. However, in the regression with persons whose parents exhibited a high frequency of disruptive behaviors, the proportion of caregivers in the network was the *strongest* predictor of depression. In this case, caregiving-status similarity emerged as more strongly related to depression than self-reported health, amount of help provided, or living arrangement. Age similarity, gender similarity, and employment similarity of network members were not related to depression.

In our earlier discussion, we hypothesized a mechanism for the effect of similar others on depression: that similar other caregivers would be more likely to provide support and fewer hassles. Certainly, the findings of Analyses I and II support this assertion. In order to explore this issue further, we conducted regression analyses that included variables in Table 3, with three additional ones: the proportion of instrumental supporters in the network, the proportion of emotional supporters in the network, and the proportion of people who had

Table 3. Regression of Depression on Status Similarity and Control Variables Separated by Parent's Disruptive Behaviors

Variable	Low disruptive behaviors		High disruptive behaviors	
	B (Se B)	Beta	B (Se B)	Beta
Helping	0.281 (0.805)	0.052	1.650[a] (0.651)	0.280
Living arrangement	−1.93 (2.656)	−0.110	−1.259 (2.690)	−0.054
Health	−4.452[b] (1.335)	−0.385	−4.736[b] (1.624)	−0.329
Age similarity	0.183 (0.464)	0.059	0.426 (0.545)	0.098
Gender similarity	0.453 (0.436)	0.184	0.199 (0.538)	0.056
Employment similarity	−0.378 (0.417)	−0.136	−0.023 (0.429)	−0.007
Caregiving similarity	−0.272 (0.426)	−0.111	−1.477[b] (0.497)	−0.429
R^2	0.181		0.326[b]	
N	72		73	

[a,b]Significance: [a]$p < 0.05$; [b]$p < 0.01$.

caused interpersonal stress for the caregiver. The proportion of supporters in either category had no effect on the results. The inclusion of the proportion of stressful network members did reduce the impact of the proportion of caregiving network members, providing support for an indirect effect. It should be noted, however, that the proportion of caregivers in the network remained a strong and significant predictor of depression (table not shown).

In summary, these analyses examined the degree to which the presence of status-similar others in caregivers' social networks affects patterns of support and psychological distress. The results supported our conceptual framework, in which we argued that individuals undergoing a status transition—in this case to the status of AD caregiver—are benefited by networks with heavier concentrations of associates who have experienced the same transition. Similar associates were more likely to provide support and less likely to be sources of interpersonal stress. Further, respondents who named a larger proportion of other caregivers in their networks had lower depression scores, especially in situations in which the provision of care was more difficult.

Taking all three analyses together, one consideration for further research on the issue of status similarity is worthy of note. In the analyses described above, we selected those dimensions of status similarity that we believed would be especially salient to women who had recently begun caring for their elderly parents, such as age, gender, labor force participation, and marital status. However, the dimensions of structural similarity that are likely to be important may well vary across the life course, depending on the particular circumstances of an individual's life at any one point.

Further, the particular measure of similarity may affect the patterns of finding. For example, in this study, we operationalized similarity of employment simply by classifying individuals and their associates on the basis of whether they were or were not both in the labor force. However, a different pattern of findings might have been revealed if we had examined similarity of occupation. It is likely that individuals who share the same occupation are even more sensitive to one another's needs and constraints than are those who are both employed, but in different occupations. Thus, individuals who are occupationally similar may be especially likely to provide one another with support and unlikely to be a source of stress to one another. Future studies should attempt to use more refined measures of similarity to provide a more comprehensive picture of the ways in which similarity affects patterns of support and stress.

FUTURE DIRECTIONS

In this chapter, we have attempted to identify both consistent findings and major gaps in the literature on the social relationships of caregivers to Alzheimer's disease patients. In addition, we provided a conceptual framework and three empirical analyses to demonstrate a new, and we believe promising, approach to the study of caregiving and social support.

Where, then, do we go from here? We believe that it is important for researchers to avoid methodological problems that limit the utility of many of the research findings. As noted earlier, we do not wish to provide a full critique of this literature; rather, we limit ourselves to a few comments directly related to social support. First, and most obvious, many studies have been largely atheoretical, examining questions that seem to have emerged from social work practice rather than to have been developed from sociological and psychological theory. We believe that the research project described above, which used theory related to status transitions and status similarity, provides an example of the benefits of such theoretical grounding.

Another weakness of most studies of social support to AD caregivers is selection bias: Much research has used membership lists of advocacy organizations (such as the Alzheimer's Association). Recruiting subjects through caregiver support organizations selects for those caregivers who have already sought additional support in some way. Other studies use media advertisements; persons who take the initiative to respond to such solicitations may share special characteristics (e.g., greater social isolation or psychological distress). Promising alternative recruitment strategies include using population survey data (Moritz et al., 1989) or relying on referrals from medical centers after diagnosis.

Further, the use of meaningful comparison groups should be encouraged. We do not know whether the changes in network structure and function that appear to occur after becoming a caregiver parallel those experienced when individuals acquire other new statuses, nor do we know how these changes differ from those experienced over time in the general population.

Beyond these methodological problem, three more general issues are important. First, we would argue that the field lacks a dynamic life course focus on processes that over time affect both the need for and the availability of social support, as well as the nature and types of social relationships that promote well-being. Long-term assessment of social relationships is critically necessary. Researchers need to employ methodologies that permit examination of changes in the structure and function of individuals' social networks throughout the caregiving career. The paucity of such findings has made it particularly difficult to translate research on social integration into interventions. Some information is becoming available (cf. Suitor et al., 1995; Aneshensel et al., 1993), but most studies have involved cross-sectional designs.

Second, little is known about the *mechanisms* through which social support and social networks affect caregivers. For example, it is likely that social relationships can affect well-being directly, by reducing feelings of isolation, as well as indirectly, by promoting preventive health behavior, enhancing health-related resources and choices, and providing instrumental and emotional support. Research should focus on these mechanisms, in an attempt to understand not only *whether* social relationships provide benefits but also, if they do, *how* and under what circumstances they do.

Third, studies should devote more attention to issues of *gender*. Gender has a pervasive influence on both the structure and the function of social networks and on the role options of men and women. To some extent, both men and women face threats to social well-being when they become AD caregivers. However, the challenges of caregiving may affect men and women in different ways. Gender-role socialization, prior patterns of social integration and support, and levels of psychological well-being all differ systematically between men and women. It is therefore to be expected that the consequences of caregiving, and the social resources individuals possess as caregivers, will be affected by gender.

Ultimately, the beneficiaries of these refinements will be not only the scientific community, but also persons professionally and personally concerned with assisting family caregivers to AD patients. Ideally, the fruits of an improved research effort will be improvements in practice. Examining changes in social support, interpersonal stress, and psychological distress across the caregiving career will increase our ability to target interventions to persons who need them most, at the times when they will have the greatest benefit. Theoretically grounded and empirically sound research on this topic will enhance our ability to successfully provide support to caregivers, and in turn to ease the strain and distress they experience.

ACKNOWLEDGMENTS

This research was supported by grants from the National Institute of Mental Health (1 R01 MH42163) and from the National Institute on Aging (1 P50AG11711-01).

REFERENCES

Allan, G. (1979). *A sociology of friendship and kinship.* London: Allen & Unwin.
Allan, G. (1989). *Friendship: Developing a sociological perspective.* Boulder, CO: Westview Press.
Aneshensel, C. S., Pearlin, L. I., & Schuler, R. H. (1993). Stress, role captivity, and the cessation of caregiving. *Journal of Health and Social Behavior, 34,* 54–70.
Archbold, P. G. (1982). All-consuming activity: The family as caregiver. *Generations, 7,* 12–13, 40.
Barer, B. M., & Johnson, Colleen L. (1990). A critique of the caregiving literature. *Gerontologist, 30.*
Barker, W. H. (1992). Prevention of disability in older persons. In J. M. Last & R. B. Wallace (Eds.), *Public health and preventive medicine,* 13th ed. (pp. 973–981). Norwalk, CT: Appleton & Lange.

Bedford, V. H. (1989). Understanding the value of siblings in old age. *American Behavioral Scientist, 33*, 33–44.

Bell, R. R. (1981). *Worlds of friendship*. Beverly Hills: Sage Publications.

Belsky, J., & Rovine, M. (1984). Social-network contact, family support, and the transition to parenthood. *Journal of Marriage and the Family, 46*, 455–462.

Biegel, D. E., & Blum, A. (1990). *Aging and caregiving: Theory, research, and policy*. Newbury Park, CA: Sage Publications.

Birkel, R. C., & Jones, C. J. (1989). A comparison of the caregiving networks of dependent elderly individuals who are lucid and those who are demented. *Gerontologist, 29*, 114–119.

Brody, E. M. (1985). Parent care as a normative family stress. *Gerontologist, 25*, 19–29.

Brody, E. M. (1990). *Women in the middle: Their parent-care years*. New York: Springer.

Brody, E. M., Hoffman, C., Kleban, M., & Schoonover, C. B. (1989). Caregiving daughters and their local siblings: Perceptions, strains, and interactions. *Journal of Gerontology, 29*, 529–538.

Brody, E. M., & Lang, A. (1982). They can't do it all: Aging daughters with aged mothers. *Generations, 7*, 18–20, 37.

Cantor, M. (1983). Strain among caregivers: A study of experience in the United States. *Gerontologist, 23*, 597–604.

Catternach, L., & Tebes, J. K. (1991). The nature of elder impairment and its impact on family caregivers' health and psychosocial functioning. *Gerontologist, 31*, 246–255.

Chenoweth, B., & Spencer, R. (1986). Dementia: The experience of family caregivers. *Gerontologist, 26*, 267–272.

Chiriboga, D. A., Weiler, P. G., & Nielsen, K. (1990). The stress of caregivers. In D. E. Biegel & A. Blum (Eds.), *Aging and caregiving: Theory, research, and policy* (pp. 1221–1237). Newbury Park, CA: Sage Publications.

Cicirelli, V. G. (1981). *Helping elderly parents: Role of adult children*. Boston: Auburn House.

Cicirelli, V. G. (1985). Sibling relations through the life cycle. In L. L'Abate (Ed.), *Handbook of family psychology*. Homewood, IL: Dorsey.

Clipp, E. C., & George, L. K. (1990). Caregiver needs and patterns of social support. *Journal of Gerontology: Social Sciences, 45*, S102–S111.

Clipp, E. C., & George, L. K. (1993). Dementia and cancer: A comparison of spousal caregivers. *Gerontologist, 33*, 534–541.

Cobb, S., (1976). Social support as a moderator of life stress. *Psychosomatic Medicine, 38*, 300–314.

Cohen, C., Teresi, J., & Blum, C. (1994). The role of caregiver social networks in Alzheimer's disease. *Social Science and Medicine, 38*, 1483–1490.

Cohen, D., & Eisdorfer, C. (1986). *The loss of self*. New York: NAL Penguin.

Colerick, E. J., & George, L. K. (1986). Predictor of institutionalization among caregivers of patients with Alzheimer's disease. *Journal of the American Geriatrics Society, 34*, 493–498.

Cowan, L. D., Levitan, A., & Nelson, K. B. (1992). Neurological disorders. In J. M. Last & R. B. Wallace (Eds.), *Public health and preventive medicine*, 13th ed. (pp. 929–935). Norwalk, CT: Appleton & Lange.

Creasey, G. L., Myers, B. J., Epperson, M. J., & Taylor, J. (1990). Couples with an elderly parent with Alzheimer's disease: Perceptions of family relationships. *Psychiatry, 53*, 44–51.

Crystal, S. (1986). Social policy and elder abuse. In K. Pillemer & R. S. Wolf (Eds.), *Elder abuse: Conflict in the family* (pp. 331–340). Dover, MA: Auburn House.

Deimling, G. T., & Bass, D. M. (1986). Symptoms of mental impairment among elderly adults and their effects on family caregivers. *Journal of Gerontology, 41(6)*, 778–784.

Feld, S. L. (1982). Social structural determinants of similarity among associates. *American Sociological Review, 47*, 797–801.

Fengler, A. P., & Goodrich, N. (1979). Wives of elderly disabled men: The hidden patients. *Gerontologist, 19*, 175–183.

Fiore, J., Becker, J., & Coppel, D. B. (1983). Social network interactions: A buffer or a stress? *American Journal of Community Psychology, 11*, 423–439.

Fiore, J., Coppel, D. B., Becker, J., & Cox, G. B. (1986). Social support as a multifaceted concept: Examination of important dimensions for adjustment. *American Journal of Community Psychology, 14*, 93–111.

Fischer, C. S. (1982). *To dwell among friends: Personal networks in town and city.* Chicago: University of Chicago Press.

Franks, M. M., & Stephens, M. A. P. (1992). Multiple roles of middle-generation caregivers: Contextual effects and psychological mechanisms. *Journal of Gerontology: Psychological Sciences, 47*, S123–S129.

George, L. K. (1986). Caregiver burden: Conflict between norms of reciprocity and solidarity. In K. Pillemer & R. S. Wolf (Eds.), *Elder abuse: Conflict in the family* (pp. 67–92). Dover, MA: Auburn House.

George, L. K., & Gwyther, L. P. (1986). Caregiver well-being: A multidimensional examination of family caregivers of demented adults. *Gerontologist, 26*, 253–259.

Gold, D. T. (1989). Generational solidarity: Conceptual antecedents and consequences. *American Behavioral Scientist, 33*, 19–32.

Gottlieb, B. H., & Pancer, S. M. (1988). Social networks and the transition to parenthood. In G. Y. Michaels & W. A. Goldberg (Eds.), *The transition to parenthood: Current theory and research* (pp. 235–269). New York: Cambridge University Press.

Gouldner, H., & Strong, M. S. (1987). *Speaking of friendship: Middle-class women and their friends.* New York: Greenwood Press.

Gubrium, J. F. (1988). Family responsibility and caregiving in the qualitative analysis of the Alzheimer's disease experience. *Journal of Marriage and the Family, 50*, 197–207.

Hetherington, E. M., Cox, M., & Cox, R. (1976). Divorced fathers. *Family Coordinator, 25*, 417–428.

Himes, C. L. (1994). Parental caregiving by adult women. *Research on Aging, 16*, 191–211.

House, J. (1981). *Work stress and family support.* Reading, MA: Addison Wesley.

House, J. (1987). Social support and social structure. *Sociological Forum, 2*, 135–146.

House, J., Umberson, D., & Landis, K. (1988). Structures and processes of social support. *Annual Review of Sociology, 14*, 293–318.

Jarrett, W. H. (1985). Caregiving within kinship systems: Is affection really necessary? *Gerontologist, 25*, 5–10.

Kiecolt-Glaser, J. K., & Glaser, R. (1994). Caregivers, mental health, and immune function. In E. Light, G. Niederehe, & B. D. Lebowitz (Eds.), *Stress effects on family caregivers of Alzheimer's patients* (pp. 64–75). New York: Springer.

Kleban, M. H., Brody, E. M., Schoonover, C. B., & Hoffman, C. (1989). Family help to the elderly: Perceptions of sons-in-law regarding parent care. *Journal of Marriage and the Family, 51*, 303–312.

Lieberman, M. A., & Kramer, J. H. (1991). Factors affecting decisions to institutionalize demented elderly. *Gerontologist, 31*, 371–374.

Lin, N. (1986). Conceptualizing social support. In N. Lin, A. Dean, & W. Ensel (Eds.), *Social support, life events, and depression* (pp. 17–30). New York: Academic Press.

Lin, N., Woelfel, M. W., & Light, S. C. (1985). The buffering effect of social support subsequent to an important life event. *Journal of Health and Social Behavior, 26*, 247–263.

Mace, N. (1984). Self-help for the family. In W. E. Kelly (Ed.), *Alzheimer's disease and related disorders* (pp. 185–202). Springfield, IL: Charles C Thomas.

Maddox, G. L. (1984). Mutual help groups for caregivers in the management of senile dementia: A research agenda. In J. Wertheimer & M. Marois (Eds.), *Senile dementia: Outlook for the future.* New York: Alan R. Liss.

Mittelman, M. S., Ferris, S. H., Steinberg, G., Shulman, E., Mackell, J. A., Ambinder, A., & Cohen, J. (1993). An intervention that delays institutionalization of Alzheimer's disease patients: Treatment of spouse-caregivers. *Gerontologist, 33*, 730–741.

Moritz, D. J., Kasl, S. V., & Berkman, L. F. (1989). The health impact of living with a cognitively impaired elderly spouse: Depressive symptoms and social functioning. *Journal of Gerontology: Social Sciences, 44*, S17–S27.

Morycz, R. K. (1985). Caregiving strain and the desire to institutionalize family members with Alzheimer's disease. *Research on Aging, 7*, 329–361.

Pearlin, L. I., Mullan, J. T., Semple, S. J., & Skaff, M. M. (1990). Caregiving and the stress process: An overview of concepts and their measures. *Gerontologist, 30*, 383–394.

Pillemer, K., & Suitor, J. J. (1992). Violence and violent feelings: What causes them among family caregivers? *Journal of Gerontology: Social Sciences, 47*, S165–S172.

Pillemer, K., & Suitor, J. J. (1993). Status similarity and well-being of family caregivers to relatives with dementia. Working Paper No. 18. Ithaca, NY: Bronfenbrenner Life Course Institute.

Pruchno, R. A., Michaels, J. E., & Potashnik, S. L. (1990). Predictors of institutionalization among Alzheimer disease victims with caregiving spouses. *Journal of Gerontology: Social Sciences, 45,* S259–S266.

Radloff, L. S., (1977). The CES-D Scale: A self-report depression scale for research in the general population. *Journal of Applied Psychological Measurement, 1,* 385–401.

Riley, D., & Eckenrode, J. (1986). Social ties: Subgroup differences in costs and benefits. *Journal of Personality and Social Psychology, 51,* 770–778.

Rook, K. (1984). The negative side of social interactions: Impact on psychological well-being. *Journal of Personality and Social Psychology, 46,* 1097–1108.

Ross, H. G., & Milgram, J. I. (1982). Important variables in adult sibling relationships: A qualitative study. In M. E. Lamb & B. Sutton-Smith (Eds.), *Sibling relationships: Their nature and significance across the lifespan* (pp. 225–249). Hillsdale, NJ: Lawrence Erlbaum.

Schulz, R., & Williamson, G. (1994). Health effects of caregiving: Prevalence of mental and physical illness in Alzheimer's caregivers. In E. Light, G. Niederehe, & B. D. Lebowitz (Eds.), *Stress effects on family caregivers of Alzheimer's patients* (pp. 38–63). New York: Springer.

Schulz, R., Williamson, G., Morycz, R., & Biegel, D. E. (1990). Psychiatric and physical morbidity effects of caregiving. *Journal of Gerontology: Psychological Sciences, 45,* 181–191.

Semple, S. J. (1992) Conflict in Alzheimer's caregiving families: Its dimensions and consequences. *Gerontologist, 32,* 648–655.

Shaw, L. B., O'Bryant, S. L., & Meddaugh, D. L. (1991). Support system participation in spousal caregiving: Alzheimer's disease versus other illness. *Journal of Applied Gerontology, 10,* 359–371.

Steinman, L. A. (1979). Reactivated conflicts with aging parents. In P. Ragan (Ed.), *Aging parents.* Los Angeles: University of Southern California Press.

Stephens, M. A. P., Franks, M. M., & Townsend, A. L. (1994). Stress and rewards in women's multiple roles: The case of women in the middle. *Psychology and Aging, 9,* 43–52.

Suitor, J. J. (1987a). Mother–daughter relations when married daughters return to school: Effects of status similarity. *Journal of Marriage and the Family, 49 (May),* 435–444.

Suitor, J. J. (1987b). Social networks in transition: Married mothers return to school. *Journal of Social and Personal Relationships, 4,* 445–461.

Suitor, J. J., & Pillemer, K. (1987). The presence of adult children: A source of stress for elderly couples' marriages? *Journal of Marriage and the Family, 49,* 717–725.

Suitor, J. J., & Pillemer, K. (1988). Explaining intergenerational conflict when adult children and elderly parents live together. *Journal of Marriage and the Family, 50,* 1037–1047.

Suitor, J. J., & Pillemer, K. (1990). Family caregiver as a social status: A new conceptual framework for studying social support and well-being. In S. Stahl (Ed.), *The legacy of longevity: Health, illness, and long-term care in later life.* Newbury Park, CA: Sage Publications.

Suitor, J. J., & Pillemer, K. (1993). Support and interpersonal stress in the social networks of married daughters caring for parents with dementia. *Journal of Gerontology: Social Sciences, 48,* S1–S8.

Suitor, J. J., Pillemer, K., & Keeton, S. (1995). When experience counts: The effects of experiential and structural similarity on patterns of support and interpersonal stress. *Social Forces, 73,* 1573–1588.

Thoits, P. A. (1986). Social support as coping assistance. *Journal of Consulting and Clinical Psychology, 54,* 416–423.

Treas, J., & Bengtson, V. L. (1988). The family in later years. In M. B. Sussman & S. K. Steinmetz (Eds.), *Handbook of marriage and the family* (pp. 625–650). New York: Plenum Press.

Walker, A. J., Pratt, C. C., Shin, H.-Y., & Jones, L. L. (1990). Motives for parental caregiving and relationship quality. *Family Relations, 39,* 51–56.

Wellman, B., & Wortley, S. (1989). Brothers' keepers: Situating kinship relations in broader networks. *Sociological Perspectives, 32,* 273–306.

Wellman, B., & Wortley, S. (1990). Different strokes from different strokes: Community ties and social support. *American Journal of Sociology, 96,* 558–588.

Wolf, R. S., & Pillemer, K. (1989). *Helping elderly victims.* New York: Columbia University Press.

Zarit, S. H., Todd, P. A., & Zarit, J. M. (1986). Subjective burden of husbands and wives as caregivers: A longitudinal study. *Gerontologist, 26,* 260–266.

20

The Role of Attachment in Perceived Support and the Stress and Coping Process

J. T. PTACEK

INTRODUCTION

Sandy, a 43-year-old married mother of three, was recently diagnosed with and treated for breast cancer. Despite having had a radical mastectomy and 6 weeks of adjunctive radiation treatment, Sandy has maintained a positive mood. She attributes her good adjustment to her resolve to "beat the disease," her commitment to follow all her physician's recommendations, and a husband and friends who "have been there for her" when things were at their toughest.

Vicki is in a situation very similar to Sandy's: same family structure, same disease, same treatment regimen. Vicki, however, has been despondent throughout treatment, and her marital relationship has deteriorated markedly. Vicki has isolated herself from family and friends, has blamed herself for not discovering the disease sooner, and has attempted to escape her situation by watching old movies.

Why have Sandy and Vicki, despite great similarities in their situations, responded so differently? Two constructs, which perhaps share similar origins in early family relationships, are important contributors to these two women's different patterns of behavior—social support and coping. For the preceding 20 years, research concerned with the constructs of social support and that concerned with coping have traveled down parallel paths. Although this state of affairs was discussed at some length a decade ago (Gore, 1985), research aimed at drawing

J. T. PTACEK • Department of Psychology, Bucknell University, Lewisburg, Pennsylvania 17837.

Handbook of Social Support and the Family, edited by Gregory R. Pierce, Barbara R. Sarason, and Irwin G. Sarason. Plenum Press, New York, 1996.

the disciplines together remains relatively sparse. This lack of convergence between research domains is surprising given that at their inception, they shared a
common goal: explaining the inconsistent associations between stress and adjustment. Whether in the context of a given stressful transaction (as in dealing with
cancer) or with respect to general personality-like dispositions, both social support and coping are believed to reduce (or, at times, exacerbate) the deleterious
effects of stress on a host of cognitive, behavioral, emotional, and physiological
outcomes (Cohen & Syme, 1985). Although there remain nagging concerns about
the validity of research instruments used (House & Kahn, 1985; Stone, Greenberg,
Kennedy-Moore, & Newman, 1991) and methodologies employed (Ptacek, Smith,
Espi, & Raffety, 1994), most researchers maintain their conviction about the
important role played by each construct in the stress–outcome link.

The primary goal of this chapter is to examine the association between social
support and coping: to provide an intersection for the two lines of research. A
handbook on social support and the family may seem a curious place to engage in
such a task. After having taken a rather circuitous route, however, I will have
argued by the chapter's end not only that coping and social support are related in
the context of a specific stressful transaction, but also that the two constructs share
a common beginning: attachment relations with primary support providers.
Making such links is important for two reasons. First, because support and coping
processes each figure prominently in adjustment and well-being, understanding
their relations and joint functioning may well increase the predictive utility of
each concept. Second, though few would deny the importance of coping processes in adjustment, researchers know seemingly little about coping development. By understanding the links among attachment, support, and coping, researchers and clinicians should be in a better position to develop interventions
designed to enhance coping efficacy.

To the extent that attachment processes operate on both support and coping,
we might expect to observe several patterns of associations, depicted in Figure 1.
First, attachment should relate, at least theoretically, to both constructs. Second,
empirical evidence should reveal correlations between social support and coping
in children, adolescents, and adults. Because the effects of attachment processes
are observable by 6 months of age and are thought to have lasting and stable
effects across the life span, the pattern of associations observed in persons of
differing ages should be fairly constant, though the magnitude of associations may
be variable. Finally, to the extent that attachment operates on both social support
and coping through similar processes (working models and a secure base), these
two constructs may covary similarly with other constructs. For instance, we might
expect that persons who are avoidantly attached will, because of a fear of intimacy,
perceive less support available to them and be less likely to seek the support of
others. It would therefore be reasonable to find that a generalized fear of intimacy
(or a lack of trust) should correlate with both processes. One must recognize,
however, that because coping and support are themselves multiply determined,
the extent to which they intercorrelate or correlate with other constructs may not
always be large.

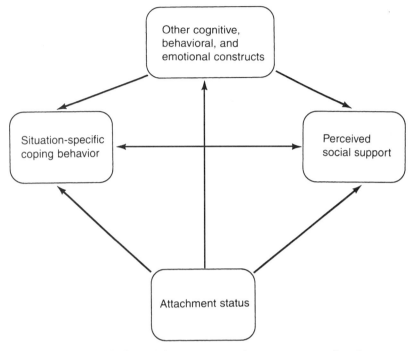

Figure 1. Model of associations among attachment, support, and coping.

ATTACHMENT: THE LINK BETWEEN SUPPORT AND COPING

The goal of this section is to provide a brief overview of the theoretical and empirical work being done by attachment researchers. In doing so, I will attempt to highlight the plausibility of attachment experiences as developmental antecedents for subsequent support and coping processes.

Although there are undoubtedly numerous physiological (temperament) and social (imitation) determinants of perceived support and coping, the attachment relationship with a primary caregiver is perhaps the critical component in the development of these two constructs and may well account for the observed links between support and coping. Attachment is thought to be a biologically based homeostatic system with the function of maintaining the proximity-promoting behaviors of children toward their caregivers (Bowlby, 1969, 1973, 1980, 1988). Although attachment is initially behavioral, and involves the social interplay among children, caregivers, and the environment, it eventually becomes internalized cognitively by the child. As attachment becomes increasingly a characteristic of the child himself or herself, it also begins operating at an unconscious level (Bowlby, 1988).

Working Models

Termed "working models," these internalized cognitive structures are based on the child's "expectations of regularities in what happens to him or her" (Ainsworth, 1989) and operate as lenses through which experiences are filtered. These expectations are one mechanism through which attachment influences the development of both perceived support and coping.

Support.   The role of working models in support perceptions has been well articulated by the Sarasons and their colleagues (e.g., B. R. Sarason, Pierce, & I. R. Sarason, 1990). According to these researchers, perceived support in adults is a manifestation of one attachment-based working model (B. R. Sarason et al., 1991). Early primary relationships are hypothesized to relate directly to a sense of being accepted and cared about in later life. Thus, persons who have had a positive attachment relationship are likely to believe that others can be trusted to help and that they themselves are worthy of help and of being cared for. These beliefs and feelings are then carried forward and form the basis of subsequent support perceptions. Patterns of relationships early in life also eventually relate to enacted support and perceptions of received support (B. R. Sarason et al., 1990). Once internalized, working models are relatively resistant to change, though constant updating based on ongoing transactions is thought to occur. Consistent with this theoretical perspective is evidence suggesting the stability of both attachment relationships and working models.

Coping.   It is important to recognize, however, that people have available to them many working models that can be applied to any given person, situation, or experience. Bowlby (1973) maintained that we simultaneously use multiple working models, only one of which is attachment-specific. Other working models, equally attributable to early parental relationships, may relate to coping via either personal resources or stylistic appraisals. Important among these are locus of control and generalized efficacy beliefs. Regardless of whether the working model is of other, self, or the environment, these models are thought to impact much of our functioning, including that related to coping behaviors. As Bowlby (1988, p. 132) notes:

> When a mother responds favourably only to certain of her child's emotional communi-
> cations and turns a blind eye or actively discourages others, a pattern is set for the child
> to identify with the favoured responses and to disown the others. It is along these lines
> that attachment theory explains the differential development of the resilient and
> mentally healthy personalities, and also of personalities prone to anxiety and depres-
> sion, or to developing a false self or some other form of vulnerability....

As cognitive processes, these working models are most likely to influence actual coping behavior through the primary and secondary appraisal processes (which will be discussed shortly). Important among such appraisals are one's beliefs about who is available to help and what they will or will not do to provide aid, one's perceptions of skills, talents, and weakness, and one's ideas regarding whether one controls the occurrence of stressful events and their outcomes. Because working models are thought to be resistant to change, they should relate to coping efforts consistently across time. On the point of temporal consistency in working models, Bowlby (1988) recognized the stability but allowed for constant updating of models through new experience. The consistency comes because "new information is assimilated to existing models" (Bretherton, 1985, p. 12).

Bowlby (1980) suggests not only that working models are stable components of individuals but also that they impose themselves on subsequent relationships, thus potentially influencing what stressful events are experienced and what resources are available for coping. Researchers have also demonstrated that one's relationship to a secure base (i.e., attachment classification) remains fairly stable (Rothbard & Shaver, 1994). Indeed, longitudinal studies of young children (Main & Cassidy, 1988) have found impressively high levels of stability in attachment classification, particularly with mother, from age 1 month to 6 years. Research indicates that the quality of and behaviors in romantic relationships can be predicted from attachment classification (Simpson, 1990), a finding that attests to their imposition on other relationships. Working models also manifest themselves through overt behavior, including support seeking when under stress. Simpson, Rholes, and Nelligan (1992) have demonstrated that the propensity for the securely attached person to seek support when experiencing anxiety carries over into early adulthood; they found that securely attached women were more likely than avoidant women to seek support in the face of increasing anxiety.

In summary, working models that develop from early relationships with the primary caregiver appear to be relatively stable across time. Stable perceptions about the extent to which we are cared for and loved, about our abilities and weaknesses, and about the availability of others under times of stress suggest that coping and support processes will indeed relate across time.

Secure Base

The second important component of attachment theory is the notion of a secure base, which Bowlby (1988) has eloquently described as "that from which a child or adolescent can make sorties into the outside world and to which he can return knowing for sure that he will be welcomed when he gets there, nourished physically and emotionally, comforted if distressed, reassured if frightened" (p. 11). According to Ainsworth (1967), knowing that her mother is available if needed allows the securely attached child to "explore other objects and interact with other people" (p. 345). By exploring and experimenting in the world, the child with a secure base should develop a broader coping repertoire. In addition, through making contacts with a variety of other people (including peers and strangers), the child with a secure base should have a larger network on which she can depend if need be (Ainsworth, 1989).

As with working models, the attachment-related concept of a secure base can account for the development of perceived support and coping and their relation. The nature of an infant's tie to this base has been described in detail by Ainsworth,

Blehar, Waters, and Wall (1978). Work on attachment classification, as defined by infants' reactions to a series of 3-minute reunions with a primary care provider in the Ainsworth Strange Situation, has consistently documented three patterns. Securely attached infants (B) are those who seek out the primary caregiver upon reunion, particularly if these infants have been highly distressed. Avoidant infants (A) fail to seek such contact and may ignore the primary caregiver altogether. Insecure–ambivalent infants (C) alternate between seeking attachment and displaying anger toward the caregiver or resisting contact. These researchers also identified, although inconsistently, a fourth pattern (D) in which infants appear disorganized or disoriented upon reunion with the caregiver.

Consistent with Ainsworth's notion of a secure base, as related to the development of coping skills, Gottlieb (1985) suggests that with the "knowledge that others are poised to assist them, they [people in general] gain confidence to cope independently" (p. 359). Thus, having a strong perception of support will both render situations less stressful perceptually and, because of increased coping efficacy and the use of adoptive coping methods, reduce the need to call upon network members.

Attachment in Adults

Interest in adult attachment has increased markedly in the past several years (e.g., Feeney & Noller, 1990; Hazen & Shaver, 1987; Kobak & Sceery, 1988; Simpson, 1990; Simpson et al., 1992; Sperling & Berman, 1994), and the emergence of similar attachment patterns in late adolescence and early adulthood is secondary evidence of the hypothesized temporal stability of attachment. Although the bulk of the work on adult attachment has focused on relationship-related variables (for a review see Bartholomew, 1993), there is mounting evidence that suggests associations between attachment and important constructs in the support–stress–coping process in adults. For instance, Kobak and Sceery (1988) reported that college students who were classified as securely attached were rated as being less hostile and anxious by their peers. In addition, this group reported having greater perceived social support from friends and family. Hazen and Shaver (1990) found a similar pattern of associations in a working community sample, with those classified as avoidant reporting higher levels of loneliness, anxiety, and hostility. The tendency of individuals classified as avoidant to report seeking less support has been noted by Bartholomew and Horowitz (1991). Simpson and his colleagues have uncovered some intriguing findings that are consistent with the attachment-coping links suggested by Ainsworth (1989) and argued for here. When faced with an anxiety-provoking situation, more securely attached women tended to use their partners as sources of comfort, while avoidant women tended to withdraw physically and emotionally (Simpson et al., 1992).

Simpson (1990), in discovering that within-dyad correlations between attachment classification did not vary as a function of length of relationship, has also demonstrated that attachment style is a relatively enduring characteristic of the individual, even into late adolescence. Rothbard and Shaver (1994) not only present an impressive review of data on the temporal stability of attachment patterns but also present evidence that their procedure for measuring adult attachment relates in theoretically meaningful ways to recollections of attachment relationships with mother and father.

In terms of support seeking as a method of coping with stress, Andrews and Brown (1988) found that women who recalled having a lack of care or experiencing antipathy from their mothers during childhood reported receiving less support during a crisis from core support providers. An important point is that this finding did not depend on marital status. What this study fails to tell us, however, is whether this lack of support could be attributed to an unwillingness or inability of these individuals to seek and gain support. In a related study, Simpson et al. (1992) found results suggesting that different types of support may be differentially effective depending on the attachment classification of the person seeking and receiving the support.

In summary, two important components of attachment theory, working models and a secure base, can theoretically play a role in the development of perceived support and coping. Perceived support is a direct extension of working models developed in reference to primary care givers. Working models likely influence coping through primary ("What's at stake in this situation?") and secondary ("What resources do I have available to deal with the situation?") appraisal processes. Having a secure base in early childhood should foster perceptions that others can be trusted to provide support under times of stress and should, through more extensive and efficacious encounters in the environment, result in a broader array of coping options.

ATTACHMENT AND SUPPORT AND A MODEL OF STRESS AND COPING

The foregoing review of attachment, though necessarily brief, suggests that early parental relations should set the stage for the development of both lasting support perceptions and the strategies people employ when dealing with stress. Although the links among support, coping, and attachment appear fairly compelling, the plausibility of these associations would be enhanced to the extent that they are consistent with the dominant theoretical model of stress and coping. To that end, I will next examine how these variables related in the context of a transactional model of the stress–coping process. After briefly summarizing the various components of the model, I will consider at some length the role perceived support plays at each step of the transaction. As I explicate the role of these perceptions, keep in mind that nearly all components of this process (including perceptions of support themselves) are potentially influenced by attachment relationships.

Coping and support are both components of a process that begins with an event or situation and ends with a behavioral, physiological, or psychological outcome. From a transactional perspective (Lazarus, 1966; Lazarus & Folkman, 1984), multiple situational, cognitive, and behavioral factors are involved and

unfold across time. Moreover, this perspective recognizes the mutual and reciprocal influences the components exert on each other. Thus, how an individual copes
in a given stressful situation will be a function of the nature of the situation (e.g.,
life area, duration, suddenness of onset), cognitive appraisals (e.g., threat, loss,
control), physiological processes, and individual differences (e.g., personal and
social resources). Coping efforts will, in turn, alter subsequent cognitive appraisals
and physiological processes.

It is important to note that from this perspective, perceived social support is a
higher-order construct that influences each step of the stress–outcome process.
As do other individual difference variables (e.g., neuroticism, optimism, self-
esteem), perceived social support influences coping both directly and through its
effects on the types of situations encountered and the internal processes that
occur. In addition to the effects on outcomes that perceived support has through
coping, support is believed to influence outcomes directly.

Components of the Model

Events.   The stressfulness of any given situation is due in part to the characteristics of the situation itself. Some situations, given the demands they place on
the individual and the physical and psychological toll they exact, are likely to be
perceived as stressful by nearly everyone. Many events, such as developing a major
physical illness or experiencing the death of a close significant other, tax the
resources of individuals unfortunate enough to experience them. There are,
however, characteristics of the events themselves that may contribute to the
stressfulness they engender. These include event severity (major life events vs.
daily hassles), event category (performance vs. relationship), frequency with
which the event has occurred, suddenness of onset, and duration.

Internal Processes.   Although the nature of the situation is important, there
are few situations so powerful that all people would report identical levels of stress.
The question thus becomes: What makes an event stressful to a given person? In
large part, individual differences in the stress experienced are due to differences
in cognitive appraisal (e.g., Lazarus, 1966; Lazarus & Folkman, 1984; Folkman,
Lazarus, Dunkel-Schetter, DeLongis, & Gruen, 1986). Consistent with the notion
that cognitive appraisal is important, stress is often defined in terms of the
appraisal that the demands of the situation exceeds one's resources.

The transactional perspective differentiates between two broad classes of
appraisal, which can be examined on two dimensions: the content of the appraisal
and the time during the stress process when the appraisal is made. Individuals first
make a primary appraisal in which they analyze what is at stake in the situation,
determining what they have to lose or gain (Folkman et al., 1986). Stress is
experienced and coping efforts are mounted only when people believe that there
is something at stake. Primary appraisal—assuming, of course, that the person
believes she or he has something important to lose or gain—is followed by a
secondary appraisal. The individual must determine what, if anything, can be

done in the situation and evaluate whether he or she possesses the skills, re-sources, and energy to do it. Lazarus and Folkman (1984) argue that secondary appraisals are the "crucial feature of every stressful encounter" (p. 35). The importance of the appraisal process is highlighted by I. G. Sarason, B. R. Sarason, and Pierce (1990), who state: "A useful starting point in analyzing anxiety begins with the objective properties of situations. However, regardless of the objective situation, it is the cognitive appraisal or personal interpretation of the situation that leads to behavior" (p. 5). Cognitive appraisals thus operate similar to working models; the view we have of ourselves, our resources, and the environment in part determine what we do.

The second important internal process is physiological arousal. A substantial body of research indicates that appraisal of an imbalance between the demands of the situation and personal resources available is accompanied by physiological changes (for detailed accounts of these changes, see Burchfield, 1985; Dobson, 1982; Everly & Sobelman, 1987; Selye, 1956). According to Cohen (1980), these changes involve the autonomic nervous system, the immune system, hormonal systems, and neurotransmitters. The effects of cognition on physiology have been demonstrated by Bandura and his colleagues (Bandura, Cioffi, Taylor, & Brouillard, 1988; Bandura, O'Leary, Taylor, Gauthier, & Gossard, 1987). Physiological changes, however, not only are a result of stress appraisals but also may contribute to such appraisals. Several researchers, including Bandura (1986) and Schachter (1978), have postulated that information from physiological processes in part determines cognitive activity.

The personal meaning attached to the physiological arousal experienced is a function of not only the current situation but also past successes and failures in similar situations. When giving his first speech in junior high school, a student probably experiences an increased heart rate, dry mouth, upset stomach, and sweaty palms. These physical symptoms may well "indicate" to the student that the situation poses a threat, perhaps resulting in interfering thoughts and decrements in performance. The seasoned college professor, alternatively, may experience similar bodily symptoms prior to her first lecture of the quarter. Unlike the student, however, she may well view her arousal as a sign that the situation faced is a challenging one and rise to the occasion by giving an inspiring lecture.

Coping

Coping has been examined in terms of both stylistic preferences for dealing with stressful situations (repression–sensitization [Krohne & Rogner, 1982]) and what individuals actually do in the context of a stressful encounter. Faced with evidence about the limited predictive utility of stylistic coping tendencies and persuasive arguments of positive evidence about the transactional nature of the stress–coping process (Lazarus & Folkman, 1984), most researchers have limited their inquires to situation-specific coping efforts. There is renewed interest, however, in examining how coping styles relate to situation-specific coping efforts (Carver & Scheier, 1994; Terry, 1994).

From a situation-specific (or transactional) perspective, coping can be defined as the behavioral and cognitive efforts to reduce, master, or tolerate stressful situations and the emotions that accompany them. Thus, on the basis of these internal cognitive and physiological processes, individuals then engage specific coping strategies to deal with the situation as construed. The three classes of coping that have received the greatest theoretical and empirical attention are problem-focused coping, emotion-focused coping, and seeking social support, although the actual number of strategies has ranged from 2 (Hamilton & Fagot, 1988) to 16 or more (Carver, Scheier, & Weintraub, 1989). Lazarus and his associates have focused primarily on the distinction between problem-focused and emotion-focused coping (Folkman & Lazarus, 1980; Folkman et al., 1986; Lazarus & Folkman, 1984). Problem-focused coping is usually defined as attempts to deal instrumentally with the perceived source of stress. Emotion-focused coping, alternatively, is most often defined as efforts aimed at reducing the emotional distress evoked by stressful situations. In addition to these two dimensions of coping, researchers have also assessed seeking instrumental and emotional support (Amirkhan, 1990; Ptacek, Smith, & Zanas, 1992; Stone & Neale, 1984). Although the goal of each of these classes of coping differs (dealing with the problem vs. dealing with the emotion), research has consistently demonstrated that people use strategies from each class during nearly every stressful encounter and that coping strategies tend to be intercorrelated (e.g., Folkman & Lazarus, 1980; Hobfoll, Dunahoo, Ben-Porath, & Monnier, 1994; Ptacek et al., 1992; Stone & Neale, 1984).

In addition to what people do to deal with stress, some researchers are beginning to consider how people employ the coping methods they use. The notion of relative coping, or the percentage of one's coping effort that can be accounted for by a particular coping method, has been forwarded by Vitaliano and his colleagues and has been demonstrated to be a better predictor of adjustment than simple sums (Vitaliano, Maiuro, Russo, & Becker, 1987). The order in which coping methods are employed has also been considered (Ptacek et al., 1992; Ptacek, Smith, & Dodge, 1994).

Resources

Individual differences also play a major role in the stress and coping process. Broadly speaking, these individual differences can be conceptualized as resources: personal or environmental characteristics that affect what stresses are experienced, how these stresses are appraised, and what individuals do to cope. Gore (1985) distinguishes resources from actual behaviors and cognitions undertaken in an attempt to manage stress. She suggests that resources "reflect a latent dimension of coping because they define a potential for action, but not action itself" (p. 266). The conceptualization proposed by Gore is similar to the distinction made here between resources and coping.

One can delineate further by making a distinction between resources residing within the individual (such as an optimistic outlook, hardiness, internal locus of control, and perceived support) and those residing outside the individual (including the number of people to whom a person can turn). With respect to social support as a resource, researchers disagree about how best to quantify the construct; consequently, as with coping, the use of different operational definitions results in different patterns of results. Social support has been considered as a characteristic of the environment (e.g., network size, density, and interrelatedness) and as a characteristic of the individual (perceptions of available support and satisfaction with the support). Research indicates that instruments designed to assess different aspects of support are only modestly correlated (Seeman & Berkman, 1988), suggesting the utility of using both operationalizations.

Even within the domain of the individual, researchers have focused on generalized perceptions of who is available (I. G. Sarason, Levine, Basham, & B. R. Sarason, 1983) as well as what is available (Cutrona & Russell, 1987). Interestingly, Cutrona and Suhr (1994), in discussing the perceptions of what types of support are available, distinguish between action-facilitating and nurturant. This distinction is similar to that made by many coping researchers between problem-focused and emotion-focused coping: Problem-focused coping is action-oriented and aimed at dealing with the situation; emotion-focused coping involves attempts to make oneself feel better without necessarily attempting to alter the source of stress. It is possible to believe that others are there for us instrumentally but not emotionally, a possibility consonant with Bowlby's notion that we can hold multiple working models of a single person (Bowlby, 1988).

I. G. Sarason, B. R. Sarason, and Pierce (1994) have argued that social support is "a product of the individual's history of social experiences ..." (p. 91). As such, social support represents perceptions of support that are carried with the individual as internal working models (Bowlby, 1988) that have their roots in the individual's developmental history, are consistent across time, and have clear behavioral referents. The consistency of perceptions has been demonstrated by I. G. Sarason, B. R. Sarason, and Shearin (1986), who found that support perceptions have stability coefficients exceeding 0.65 for available support over a 36-month period. With regard to behaviors, these authors reported that coders blind to subjects' support classifications provided differential ratings of subjects' characteristics after viewing a videotaped sample of behavior. Coders rated subjects high in support as appearing more trustworthy, being better problem-solvers (a form of problem-focused coping), and being better team members.

Research by B. R. Sarason et al. (1991) suggests that others' perceptions of us are similar to our self-perceptions and that both perceptions relate to perceived support. According to these authors the hypothesized source for these shared perceptions is the "... responsive, supportive experiences in childhood [that] are likely to contribute to a growing sense of (a) oneself as loved and cared for by important others, (b) oneself as an appropriate stimulus for the positive regard of others, and (c) others as available and willing to provide assistance should it be desired" (p. 285). In a later study using a similar methodology, B. R. Sarason, Pierce, Bannerman, and I. G. Sarason (1993) found that parents' views of their child's positive and negative characteristics correlated with the child's perception of father's support and to general perceptions of available support. Consistent with these views, these authors concluded that their findings are consistent with a developmental perspective of social support, with perceptions of having been "loved, valued, and accepted by others" (p. 1083) contributing to perceived support. It thus is clear that the empirical evidence supports the idea that social support has characteristics resembling those of personality.

Despite evidence about the dispositional qualities of support perceptions such as that presented above, some authors have urged researchers to focus more on support "processes" than on dispositional (perceptual) approaches (e.g., Hobfoll & Stokes, 1988). Such an emphasis encompasses not only support seeking as a coping strategy but also many other questions: What do we seek? What do we get? From whom do we get it? How satisfied are we with what we get? Although distinct from the dispositional approach advocated by the Sarasons, each approach is relevant to coping with stress. The building of ties, seeking of support, and development of internal working models relate to coping with stress and must, in part, have their foundations in early attachment relationships.

Resources and Other Components of the Model

Having briefly reviewed the important components of the stress and coping process, I will now examine in some detail how perceived support (as a personality-like resource) may relate to each of the other components.

Resources and Events. Regardless of conceptualization, either type of resource (internal or external) can exert an influence on the type of situations experienced. For example, Snyder (1983) and Emmons, Diener, and Larson (1986) have reported that individual differences in personality are predictive of the types of situations that people select. Stress and negative emotional reactions may be more likely in those situations into which the individual is forced or those that arise unexpectedly. If individuals select situations they believe are consistent with their competencies, then nonselected, yet experienced, situations may leave individuals wanting for effective strategies of coping.

Specific to social support, research suggests that it can be a source of stress. For instance, people with larger, more integrated social networks may experience more interpersonal stresses, particularly women (Solomon & Rothblum, 1986). Moreover, in the context of coping research, interpersonal stresses are often selected when subjects are free to choose the most stressful event recently experienced. In a sample of 9- to 14-year-olds, Spirito, Stark, Grace, and Stamoulis (1991) found that the percentage of children reporting a stress related to parent–child conflict or to sibling conflict ranged from 24.9% (for those age 12) to 36.6% (for those age 14). When friends and boyfriends or girlfriends were considered as well, these percentages rose to as high as 48.6%. A review by Honig (1986a,b) indicates that many stresses experienced by children are specific to the family and to disrupted family networks (e.g., birth of a sibling, divorce, loss of a parent). Network- or family-related stresses appear commonly in adolescent and adult samples as well (Folkman & Lazarus, 1980; Holahan & Moos, 1987; Ptacek et al., 1992). Thus, the family environment and having many people to whom one can turn may be beneficial, but may also be a source of conflict (Pierce, Sarason, & Sarason, 1991) and stress. An important finding is that when interpersonal stresses involve the disruption of networks, distressed individuals may be at added risk; they are not only experiencing stress, but also being denied one of their social resources (Ptacek, Dodge, & Ptacek, 1994).

Resources and Internal Processes. Appraisals about the stressfulness of a situation are based, in part, on beliefs that we have social resources at our disposal to aid us if needed. Demands of the situation and preferences and desires of the stressed individual as well as the relation between support provider and recipient help determine one's satisfaction with support received from a member of the support network. The notion of "fit" between what is wanted or needed in a stressful transaction and what is offered or provided is becoming increasingly important (Cutrona & Suhr, 1994). The notion of "fit" is central in the coping literature as well; one requisite of adaptive coping is that it fit the demands and parameters of the situation.

The support literature has repeatedly addressed the question of which aspects of support are important when support is sought and received. Hobfoll, Nadler, and Lieberman (1986) have concluded that satisfaction with the support received during a stressful encounter is the key ingredient to its effectiveness. This conclusion echoes arguments made by Gottlieb (1985) that the effects of social support on coping operate largely through primary and secondary appraisal processes. Heller, Swindle, and Dusenbury (1986), in presenting a model similar to the one presented here, distinguished between perceived support (which I am considering personal resource) and supportive transactions (which can be thought of as a form of coping). These authors have suggested that supportive acts are filtered through a person's cognitive and emotional biases and represent associations that are part of a complex appraisal process in which coping efforts are evaluated in terms of their effectiveness, which is itself determined by global support perceptions.

The relation between social support and physiological processes has also been established, particularly as support relates to immune functioning (Baron, Cutrona, Hicklin, Russell, & Lubaroff, 1990; Jemmott & Magloire, 1988). Baron and his colleagues found, in spouses of cancer patients, that a higher level of perceived social support was associated with greater immunocompetence.

Resources and Coping

Perceived support may impact the use of coping strategy either through its effects on the types of stressful events a person experiences or via appraisal and physiological processes. Regarding appraisal, those people with greater perceived support may simply appraise situations as being less stressful and thus have less need to engage in extended coping efforts. Moreover, recognizing that support is available if other coping efforts are ineffective frees individuals to engage in creative efforts to manage the stress without having to enlist support. Although such associations are feasible from a theoretical perspective, I have yet to examine their empirical validity. In the sections that follow, I examine the empirical evidence linking support perceptions to coping in adolescents and adults and in children.

Adolescents and Adults. The belief that our early childhood experiences with parents have lifelong implications for the strategies we use to deal with stress and anxiety has a rich theoretical history (Freud, Horney, Adler). The issues of whether and how perceived social support—which has been shown to be an extension of these early experiences—relates to coping, including the seeking of support, continues to be vigorously researched. To the extent that attachment relationships form the basis of lasting support perceptions and coping, research with adolescents and adults should reveal significant covariation between social support and the use of specific coping strategies in dealing with stress. The research literature is beginning to support this hypothesis, though longitudinal studies on the topic are still sorely needed.

Parkes (1986) found that work-related support, one aspect of what she considered environmental factors, correlated with the use of a General coping strategy (defined as "representing a wide variety of cognitive and behavioral strategies" [p. 1281] on the Ways of Coping Questionnaire). Nurses who reported having more support tended to report using less of this type of coping, though shared variance was small (3.61%). One possible reason for the modest effect of support was that nurses' perceptions were specific to the work environment and thus may not have been tapping what is most critical: support from intimate others. Another possibility addressed by Parkes is that perceptions of support interacted with other personality characteristics or other appraised aspects of the stressful situation encountered. Specifically Parkes uncovered an interaction between support and appraised importance of the event on the use of Direct coping. An examination of the nature of the interaction revealed that as the appraised importance of the event was increased, nurses high in support tended to use more Direct coping, while nurses low in support tended to use less.

Like Parkes, Terry (1991, 1994) has argued that a fuller account of the coping process will be achieved by considering both stable and situational factors. Using a prospective design and a classroom examination as a stressor, Terry (1991) found that social support (defined via a composite score constructed from the availability of friendship and attachment support) predicted the use of Seeking Emotional Support and Minimization. Students reporting higher levels of support tended to seek more emotional support ($r = 0.35$) and to rely less on minimization ($r = -0.18$). More important, the ability of support to predict these forms of coping remained significant even after controlling for a host of other resources (e.g., internal locus of control, self-esteem, neuroticism) and situational appraisal (e.g., control, efficacy, importance). Terry also discovered that the association between stress and the use of Minimization was moderated by level of support. As stress level increased, individuals with low support tended to engage in more Minimization, whereas those high in support engaged in less. Using self-selected stresses and prospective design, Terry (1994) found that support was an independent predictor of the reported use of Minimization 6 weeks later (having controlled for a host of resource and situation variables). Considering only the resource variables (social support, internal locus of control, self-esteem, neuroticism, denial, and type A behavior), social support was also an independent predictor of Seeking Support (the scale included both emotional and instrumental support items).

In their attempt to design a more socially oriented coping questionnaire, Hobfoll et al. (1994) have also examined the association between support perceptions and coping. In a cross-sectional study using the Social Support Questionnaire (I. G. Sarason et al., 1983), Hobfoll and his colleagues found associations between support and several of their subscales. Most notably, respondents with greater perceived support reported engaging in more assertive action, seeking more support, and using less antisocial action. No correlation between support and coping exceeded 0.29.

Greenglass (1993), in a study of support and coping with job-related stress, collected data from 114 male and female government supervisors. Data indicated that perceptions of support received from spouses, relatives, and friends correlated positively with the use of preventive coping and negatively with the use of palliative coping, self-blame, and wishful thinking. The observed associations between support and coping were particularly strong for women (that women demonstrated a stronger link between support and coping is consistent with the findings of Moos and colleagues). In discussing these findings, Greenglass noted that other researchers have obtained similar findings linking support to both adaptive and less adaptive coping (Coates, Wortman, & Abbey, 1979).

By far the most consistent work on the topic of coping and social support has been carried out by Moos and his colleagues. These authors (e.g., Holahan & Moos, 1987, 1990; Moos & Schaefer, 1986) as well as others (Heller et al., 1986) have proposed that personal resources should have both a direct and an indirect effect on functioning. The indirect effects of support are hypothesized to operate through its impact on coping. Cronkite and Moos (1984) argue that in attempting to deal with a stressful event, three elements come into play: (1) social resources, such as perceptions of family support; (2) coping resources, such as personality characteristics including optimism, self-esteem, and locus of control; and (3) coping responses, such as approaching or avoiding the stressor.

Consistent with predictions arising from their model, Holahan and Moos (1990) found that perception of family support assessed at the beginning of the study predicted the percentage of approach coping behaviors reported a year later. In addition, these authors found that "stable functioning under high stressors was predicted by personal and social resources at the beginning of the year that were linked to functioning through their influence on increased approach coping during the year" (p. 914). In other work, Holahan and Moos (1987) found that reports of family support correlated positively with Active–cognitive and Active–behavioral coping strategies and negatively with Avoidance for both a community and a patient sample. Family support assessed at the beginning of the study predicted reports of situation-specific avoidance coping a year later, even after controlling for coping reports provided at the study's inception.

Using structural equation modeling, Bennet (1993) tested a model similar to that espoused by Moos and his colleagues with data from a sample of postmyocardial infarction patients. She found that the paths from perceived support to both problem-focused and emotion-focused coping were significant, as was the path from support to coping effectiveness. These results are consistent with Moos's model, though, interestingly, neither form of coping predicted coping effectiveness.

Although the data support the idea that perceived support and coping are generally related, the links between these constructs appear to differ in their magnitude across sexes. For instance, Cronkite and Moos (1984) found that family support was significantly associated with the reported use of avoidance coping only for the women in their sample. In addition, even though the use of avoidance coping related to poorer adjustment in both sexes, only for women was the correlation between support and adjustment significant. Greenglass (1993) also reported sex differences in the support–coping correlation.

In summary, as would be expected if coping and perceived support shared a common developmental history, the two constructs are correlated in the context of a stressful transaction. Although the findings are fairly consistent across studies, the effect sizes are generally small. These generally low correlations are likely a function of (1) mixing levels of analysis and (2) using constructs that are multiply determined, as is particularly true in situation-specific coping. Regarding level of analysis, social support, as I have examined it, is a dispositional variable, whereas coping is a transactional variable that unfolds during the course of a stressful transaction. It has long been understood that predicting single acts from dispositional variables is often unsuccessful (Kendrick & Funder, 1988; Mischel, 1968). None of the studies examined here considered coping dispositionally or relied upon the beneficial effects of aggregating coping across multiple stressful events. In terms of behavior's being multiply determined, Ahadi and Diener (1989) have demonstrated that as the number of determinants of a behavior increase, the amount of variance for which any one predictor can account decreases. According to the model presented here, situational, cognitive, physiological, and a host of personal and social resources all influence what one does when confronted with a stressful situation.

Also important, as several writers have noted, is the complexity of the associations between support perceptions and coping, particularly the active seeking of support (Gore, 1985; I. G. Sarason, B. R. Sarason, & Pierce, 1988). The argument can be made that those with the highest levels of support should need to seek support less often because they have broader coping repertoires. It is equally plausible, however, and consistent with the work reviewed here, that high levels of perceived support will be associated with greater support-seeking behavior under stress. Perhaps people who differ in their attachment histories differ in the types of support they seek and whether their support-seeking efforts are successful in eliciting the desired response.

Children.   Despite the voluminous literatures on social support and coping, relatively little is known about the nature of these constructs in children. Research on coping has focused primarily on explicating what children of various ages report doing in response to stressful events. With respect to coping, what does seem clear is that the use of certain strategies is a function of age. For instance, Spirito, et al. (1991) found age-related differences in coping reports for both self-selected and common events. Subjects aged 9–11 years tended to report using more cognitive restructuring, problem solving, emotional regulation, and wishful thinking than did 14-year-olds. On the basis of their work, these authors concluded that by ages 9–11, children have a variety of coping options available. A pattern of increasing reliance on cognitive and emotional coping methods with increasing age has been uncovered by other researchers. Curry and Russ (1985) reported that older children (age 10 years) used more cognitively oriented responses than did younger children, and Wertlieb, Weigel, and Feldstein (1987) found that older children (age 9 years) used more emotional management than their younger counterparts.

Having conducted a thorough review of the literature, Compas, Banez, Malcarne, and Worsham (1991) concluded that the use of problem-oriented coping, once established, is relatively stable. Emotional-focused coping, alternatively, seems to display some increased use with age. These authors theorized that the different developmental patterns in coping use are a function of two factors. First, the early emergence and stable use of problem-oriented coping is due to modeling cues of parents. The overt nature of many problem-focused coping methods lends itself to observational learning. Emotion-focused coping has a longer period of development because many of the behaviors are covert and thus fail to lend themselves to modeling. Second, children may have to reach a certain level of cognitive sophistication before they are able to recognize their own internal states and their ability to control those states. Band and Weisz (1988) have suggested that children must reach a certain age before they can recognize that problem-focused strategies (which these authors term "primary control strategies") are unworkable in certain situations.

Stress and coping processes in children are thought to include several components, including perceptions (cognitive appraisals) of the stressor, coping resources, social support systems, and coping skills (Honig, 1986a,b). Moreover, research by Dubow and Tisak (1989) indicates that social support and social problem solving (which can be considered a form of problem-focused coping) are each a protective factor for children facing stress. The associations among stress, support, coping, and adjustment in children are by no means simple (Wolchik, Ruehlman, Braver, & Sandler, 1989).

Although attachment classification appears to be fairly stable from early in life, Cauce, Reid, Landesman, and Gonzales (1990) provide some intriguing information about the developmental nature of social support. Looking across the ages 5–12, these authors found uniformly high ratings of the availability of informational support and help and guidance from mother and father, though ratings of both types were somewhat higher for the older children. Perhaps the most striking age-related differences occurred with respect to friends, with ratings of emotional support and companionship being much higher in older children. This increasing pattern of emotional support, particularly from friends, has been documented by other researchers (e.g., Berndt & Perry, 1986) and is consistent with the changes that seem to occur in coping.

Very few studies have attempted to examine how parenting and parent–child relationships relate to coping. One exception, however, is the recent work of Hardy, Power, and Jaedicke (1993). Using the work of Ainsworth and Bandura to guide their predictions, Hardy and coworkers reasoned that parental support (behaviors that make children feel accepted and approved of as people) should result in children's feeling secure in times of stress. As I have argued, secure children should be more likely than insecurely attached children to develop a broad assortment of coping strategies that can be used flexibly. These researchers examined the association between parental support and coping in 60 children averaging 10 years of age and found that high support (a combination of cohesion, cohesiveness, nurturance, monitoring, and adaptability) reported by mothers was associated with a greater variety of coping strategies used in response to stress. Support also correlated significantly and positively with avoidance coping, a finding opposite that reported by Holahan and Moos (1987) in adults. This later finding, however, was restricted to situations rated as uncontrollable. Thus, children high in support appear better able to distinguish the circumstances (low control) under which emotion-focused coping will be a more adaptive response than problem-focused coping. As would be predicted, better, more secure attachment bonds should be associated with greater flexibility in coping.

Although less direct, research with resilient children also provides some evidence for the association between support and coping in children. By definition resilient children are those who have coped well and continued to cope well (evidenced by their ability to maintain adequate levels of adjustment) in the face of substantial life stress. Evidence suggests that having a positive relationship with at least one parent is a protective factor (Rutter, 1979), as are the coping methods of self-reliance and seeking social support when needed (Parker, Cowen, Work, & Wyman, 1990). These findings are consistent with the notion that people with a positive attachment relationship may need to rely less on their social networks (being self-reliant), but that they are able to recognize when support is needed and how to best obtain it (Felsman & Vaillant, 1987).

To summarize, perceived support and coping are related in the context of a given stressful event. Research with children seems to suggest that both support and coping change somewhat during ages 5–12, though perceptions of support may be relatively less changeable than coping at an earlier age.

SUPPORT AND COPING: THEIR RELATION TO OTHER CONSTRUCTS

If perceived support and coping are, developmentally, in part functions of early attachment relationships and both play roles in the stress process, then it seems reasonable that they might covary with other constructs in a similar manner.

Indirect evidence for similarity in patterning of associations can come from examining how social support and coping relate to other constructs in separate studies. Both the support and the coping literatures have examined whether and how the respective processes related to a host of other cognitive, behavioral, and emotional variables. With regard to coping, researchers have shown relations between the reported use of specific coping strategies and self-confidence (e.g., greater self-confidence, greater use of Active Behavioral methods [Holahan & Moos, 1987]), self-esteem (higher self-esteem, greater use of Positive Comparison and Direct Action with occupational stresses [Fleishman, 1984]), neuroticism (higher neuroticism, greater use of Distancing [Bolger, 1990]), optimism (more optimistic, more Seeking Support and Problem-focused coping and less Disengagement [Scheier, Weintraub, & Carver, 1986]). Still other have argued persuasively that locus of control, whether situational or dispositional in nature (Folkman, 1984; Solomon & Rothblum, 1986), exerts an influence on one's choice of coping strategies. Social support research indicates that this construct is associated with other aspects of personality, including higher levels of self-esteem (Brown, Andrews, Harris, Adler, & Bridge, 1986; Hobfoll et al., 1986) and lower levels of neuroticism (I. G. Sarason et al., 1983), among others.

More compelling evidence of similarities in patterning would come from studies that include both support and coping and these other variables. Unfortunately, patterning of associations in such studies has not been consistent. For instance, although Terry (1991) found that self-esteem was positively correlated with the use of problem-focused coping and perceived support, neuroticism related only to coping (negatively with Seeking Support). Cronkite and Moos (1984) also found that self-esteem correlated with coping (Approach and Avoidance) but not with perceived support. Parkes (1986) found that extraversion related with both Direct coping and perceived support; the direction of association, however, differed. Moreover, in this study, coping, but not support, related to neuroticism. Finally, Holahan and Moos (1987) reported significant relations between coping (but not support) and self-confidence and easygoing disposition.

Thus, there appears to be some evidence that perceived support and coping do relate to similar constructs. The strength and direction of the relations vary markedly across studies, however, and an examination of studies that have included coping, support, and at least one other individual difference variable reveals, somewhat surprisingly, little convergence in patterning.

COPING AND ATTACHMENT

As discussed earlier, the association between attachment and perceived support has been well established. In this final substantive section of the chapter, I will examine the evidence linking attachment directly to coping.

Despite clear hypotheses about the role that attachment should play in the development and use of specific styles of coping, relatively little work has explored the empirical validity of this assumption. The work done to date, however, has generally supported attachment-related hypotheses. For instance, in a study of fear of death and attachment, Mikulincer, Florian, and Tolmacz (1990) found that students classified as secure reported fearing death less than those classified as insecure. These authors speculated that this pattern of findings was "consistent with the view that attachment styles influence affective responses" (p. 278), which in turn should relate to the need to engage in coping efforts and the types of coping enacted. Thus, according to Mikulincer et al. (1990), the "differences among attachment groups ... may reflect differences in the cognitive schema guiding individuals in distressing situations" (p. 279). In subsequent work (Mikulincer, Florian, & Weller, 1993), this research team examined how attachment classification related to coping with missile attacks in a group of college-age Israeli students. Consistent with their previous findings and their hypotheses about attachment-related coping differences, these authors reported finding that subjects classified as ambivalent used more Emotion-focused methods than did either avoidant or secure subjects. Avoidant subjects used more Distancing than subjects from the other two groups, whereas secure subjects used more Support Seeking. Interestingly, however, the three groups used similar amounts of Problem-focused coping. Regarding this latter finding, these authors suggested that the intense nature of the situation dictated the extent to which problem-focused methods could vary. Exploring the association between attachment and coping in situations that pull less strongly for certain coping responses may allow hypothesized differences in problem-focused coping to emerge.

Grossmann and Grossmann (1991 [cited in Rothbard & Shaver, 1994]) also explored the association between coping and attachment and found that group differences in coping were limited to situations evoking certain types of emotional responses. As did Mikulincer et al. (1993), Grossmann and Grossmann found that secure children tended to cope by seeking instrumental and emotional support. Group differences did emerge with respect to the use of problem solving, with avoidant children more often attempting to use this strategy by themselves. This latter finding is consonant with the notion that avoidant individual may act in a compulsively self-reliant fashion (Main, Kaplan, & Cassidy, 1985).

Another recent study, using college-age participants, has examined the association between attachment to mother, father, and peers and coping resources (Brack, Gay, & Matheny, 1993). With respect to which coping resources were the best predictors of each attachment relationship, this study found that attachment to mother was predicted by Social Support, Self-disclosure, and Physical Fitness, whereas attachment to father was predicted by Social Support and Self-disclosure. Attachment to friends was predicted only by Self-directedness. These authors concluded that "strong bonding with parents appeared to be related to greater resourcefulness" (p. 214), which is consistent with the idea that securely attached individuals have more coping skills upon which they can draw.

In discussing several lines of research that attempt to explain the development of coping skills and coping resources, Compas (1987) highlighted the role of attachment. Compas argued that future research should study "the relation between various social contexts or ecologies and the coping behavior of children and adolescents.... Foremost among these is the role of the family" (p. 401). I concur with this suggestion and believe that the preceding brief review indicates that there is empirical support for the link between attachment and coping. Clearly, the results to date are sufficiently compelling to warrant continued investigation.

CONCLUDING REMARKS

The intent of this chapter was to provide a framework through which research on perceived support and coping can be drawn together. To accomplish this aim, I examined the possibility not only that these two constructs are linked in the context of a particular stressful transaction, but also that they share a developmental history. With regard to Sandy and Vicki, I have suggested that differences in their support, coping, and adjustment processes are linked to their attachment histories. I have reviewed evidence on (1) attachment and perceived support, (2) attachment and coping, (3) the association between perceived support and coping in the context of stressful encounters, and (4) the covariation between other psychological constructs and perceived support and coping. These four lines of research have been considered, in part, within a transactional model of stress and coping. From this perspective, perceived support is conceptualized as a personal resource that affects each component of the stress–coping process. Moreover, attachment relationships, I have argued, contribute to both one's sense of support and the coping behaviors in which one engages when under stress.

The evidence related to the four sets of relations reviewed here is not entirely convincing. There has been, for most of the possible relations, too little research. Most surprisingly, though there are sound theoretical reasons for examining support and coping in conjunction—both constructs are thought to influence adaptive outcomes—the research literature linking the constructs remains sparse (Gore, 1985). The associations between attachment relationships and perceived support have been thoughtfully explored, whereas research examining the associations between attachment and coping is in its infancy.

Longitudinal studies designed to assess the relations among these constructs across time and stresses are sorely needed. To my knowledge, no work has been conducted that examines whether coping strategy use and perceived support change in similar ways during early and middle childhood, though there is some secondary evidence to suggest that they may. Few would deny that a person's level of support and the coping skills the person has at his or her disposal are, at least in part, constructs that arise in early childhood and develop over time. The research domains of support and coping may be successfully drawn together by examining their development and by using attachment theory as a conceptual guide.

REFERENCES

Ahadi, A., & Diener, E. (1989). Multiple determinants of effect size. *Journal of Personality and Social Psychology, 56*, 398–406.

Ainsworth, M. D. S. (1967). *Infancy in Uganda: Infant care and the growth of love.* Baltimore: Johns Hopkins Press.

Ainsworth, M. D. S. (1989). Attachments beyond infancy. *American Psychologists, 44,* 709–716.

Ainsworth, M. D. S., Blehar, M. C., Waters, E., & Wall, S. (1978). *Patterns of attachment: A psychological study of the strange situation.* Hillsdale, NJ: Lawrence Erlbaum.

Amirkhan, J. M. (1990). A factor analytically derived measure of coping: The coping strategy indicator. *Journal of Personality and Social Psychology, 59,* 1066–1074.

Andrews, B., & Brown, G. W. (1988). Social support, onset of depression and personality: An exploratory analysis. *Social Psychiatry and Psychiatric Epidemiology,* 99–108.

Band, E., & Weisz, J. R. (1988). How to feel better when it feels bad: Children's perspectives on coping with everyday stress. *Developmental Psychology, 24,* 247–253.

Bandura, A. (1986). *Social foundations of thought and action: A social–cognitive theory.* Englewood Cliffs, NJ: Prentice-Hall.

Bandura, A., Cioffi, D., Taylor, C. B., & Brouillard, M. E. (1988). Perceived self-efficacy in coping with cognitive stressors and opioid activation. *Journal of Personality and Social Psychology, 55* 479–488.

Bandura, A., O'Leary, A., Taylor, C. B., Gauthier, J., & Gossard, D. (1987). Perceived self-efficacy and pain control: Opioid and nonopioid mechanisms. *Journal of Personality and Social Psychology, 55,* 479–488.

Baron, R. S., Cutrona, C. E., Hicklin, D., Russell, D. W., & Lubaroff, D. M. (1990). Social support and immune function among spouses of cancer patients. *Journal of Personality and Social Psychology, 59,* 344–352.

Bartholomew, K. (1993). From childhood to adult relationships: Attachment theory and research. In S. Duck (Ed.), *Learning about relationships* (pp. 30–62). Newbury Park, CA: Sage Publications.

Bartholomew, K., & Horowitz, L. M. (1991). Attachment styles among young adults: A test of a four-category model. *Journal of Personality and Social Psychology, 61,* 226–244.

Bennet, S. J. (1993). Relationships among selected antecedent variables and coping effectiveness in postmyocardial infarction patients. *Research in Nursing and Health, 16,* 131–139.

Berndt, T. J., & Perry, T. B. (1986). Children's perceptions of friendship as supportive relationships. *Developmental Psychology, 22,* 640–648.

Bolger, N. (1990). Coping as a personality process: A prospective study. *Journal of Personality and Social Psychology, 59,* 525–537.

Bowlby, J. (1969). *Attachment and loss,* Vol. 1, *Attachment.* New York: Basic Books.

Bowlby J. (1973). *Attachment and loss,* Vol. 2, *Separation: Anxiety and anger.* New York: Basic Books.

Bowlby J. (1980). *Attachment and loss,* Vol. 3, *Sadness and depression.* New York: Basic Books.

Bowlby J, (1988). *A secure base: Parent–child attachment and healthy human development.* New York: Basic Books.

Brack, G., Gay, M. F., & Matheny, K. B. (1993). Relationships between attachment and coping resources among late adolescents. *Journal of College Student Development, 34,* 212–215.

Bretherton, I. (1985). Attachment theory: Retrospect and prospect. In I. Bretherton & E. Waters (Eds.), *Growing points of attachment theory and research* (pp. 3–35). *Monographs of the Society for Research in Child Development, 50(1–2),* Serial No. 209.

Brown, G. W., Andrews, B., Harris, T., Adler, Z., & Bridge, L. (1986). Social support, self-esteem and depression. *Psychosomatic Medicine, 16,* 813–831.

Burchfield, S. R. (1985). *Stress: Psychological and physiological interactions.* New York: Hemisphere Publishing.

Carver, C. S., & Scheier, M. F. (1994). Situational coping dispositions in a stressful transaction. *Journal of Personality and Social Psychology, 66,* 184–195.

Carver, C. S., Scheier, M. F., & Weintraub, J. K. (1989). Assessing coping strategies: A theoretically based approach. *Journal of Personality and Social Psychology, 56,* 267–283.

Cauce, A. M., Reid, M., Landesman, S., & Gonzales, N. (1990). Social support in young children: Measurement, structure, and behavioral impact. In B. R. Sarason, I. G. Sarason, & G. R. Pierce (Eds.), *Social support: An interactional view* (pp. 64–94). New York: Wiley.

Coates, D., Wortman, C. B., & Abbey, A. (1979). Reactions to victims. In I. H. Frieze, D. Bartal, & J. S. Carrol (Eds.), *New approaches to social problems.* San Francisco: Jossey-Bass.

Cohen, S. (1980). Aftereffects of stress on human performance and social behavior: A review of research and theory. *Psychological Bulletin, 88,* 82–108.

Cohen, S., & Syme, S. L. (1985). Issues in the study and application of social support. In S. Cohen & S. L. Syme (Eds.), *Social support and health* (pp. 3–22). New York: Academic Press.

Compas, B. E. (1987). Coping with stress during childhood and adolescence. *Psychological Bulletin, 101*, 393–403.

Compas, B. E., Banez, G. A., Malcarne, V., & Worsham, N. (1991). Perceived control and coping with stress: A developmental perspective. *Journal of Social Issues, 47*, 23–34.

Cronkite, R. C., & Moos, R. H. (1984). The role of predisposing and moderating factors in the stress–illness relationship. *Journal of Health and Social Behavior, 25*, 372–393.

Curry, S. L., & Russ, S. W. (1985). Identifying coping strategies in children. *Journal of Clinical Child Psychology, 14*, 61–69.

Cutrona, C. E., & Russell, D. (1987). The provisions of social relationships and adaptation to stress. In W. H. Jones & D. Perlman (Eds.), *Advances in personal relationships* Vol. 1 (pp. 37–67). Greenwich, CT: JAI.

Cutrona, C. E., & Suhr, J. E. (1994). Social support communication in the context of marriage: An analysis of couple's supportive interactions. In B. R. Burleson, T. L. Albrecht, & I. G. Sarason (Eds.), *Communication of social support: Messages, interactions, relationships, and community* (pp. 29–49). Thousand Oaks, CA: Sage Publications.

Dobson, C. B. (1982). *Stress: The hidden adversary.* Langcaster, England: MTP Press.

Dubow, E. F., & Tisak, J. (1989). The relation between stressful life events and adjustment in elementary school children: The role of social support and social problem-solving skills. *Child Development, 60*, 1412–1423.

Emmons, R. A., Diener, E., & Larson, R. J. (1986). Choice and avoidance of everyday situations and affect congruence: Two models of reciprocal interactionism. *Journal of Personality and Social Psychology, 51*, 815–826.

Everly, G. S., & Sobelman, S. A. (1987). *The assessment of the human stress response: Neurological, biochemical, and psychological foundations.* New York: AMS Press.

Feeney, J. A., & Noller, P. (1990). Attachment style as a predictor of adult romantic relationships. *Journal of Personality and Social Psychology, 8*, 187–215.

Felsman, J. K., & Vaillant, G. E. (1987). Invulnerability among abused and neglected children. In E. J. Anthony & B. J. Cohler (Eds.), *The invulnerable child* (pp. 253–288). New York: Guilford Press.

Fleishman, J. A. (1984). Personality characteristics and coping patterns. *Journal of Health and Social Behavior, 25*, 229–244.

Folkman, S. (1984). Personal control and stress and coping processes: A theoretical analysis. *Journal of Personality and Social Psychology, 46*, 839–852.

Folkman, S., & Lazarus, R. S. (1980). An analysis of coping in a middle-aged community sample. *Journal of Health and Social Behavior, 21*, 219–239.

Folkman, S., Lazarus, R. S., Dunkel-Schetter, C., DeLongis, A., & Gruen, R. (1986). The dynamics of a stressful encounter: Cognitive appraisal, coping and encounter outcomes. *Journal of Personality and Social Psychology, 50*, 992–1003.

Gore, S. (1985). Social support and styles of coping with stress. In S. Cohen & S. L. Syme (Eds.), *Social support and health* (pp. 263–280). New York: Academic Press.

Gottlieb, B. H. (1985). The study of close relationships. *Journal of Social and Personal Relationships, 2*, 351–375.

Greenglass, E. R. (1993). Structural and social–psychological factors associated with job functioning by women managers. *Psychological Reports, 73*, 979–986.

Grossmann, K. E., & Grossmann, K. (1991). Attachment quality as an organizer of emotion and behavioral responses in a longitudinal perspective. In C. M. Parkes, J. Stevenson-Hinde, & P. Marris (Eds.), *Attachment across the life cycle* (pp. 93–114). London: Tavistock/Routledge.

Hamilton, S., & Fagot, B. I. (1988). Chronic stress and coping styles: A comparison of male and female undergraduates. *Journal of Personality and Social Psychology, 55*, 819–823.

Hardy, D. F., Power, T. G., & Jaedicke, S. (1993). Examining the relation of parenting to children's coping with everyday stress. *Child Development, 64*, 1829–1841.

Hazen, C., & Shaver, P. R. (1987). Romantic love conceptualized as an attachment process. *Journal of Personality and Social Psychology, 51*, 511–524.

Hazen, C., & Shaver, P. R. (1990). Love and work: An attachment-theoretical perspective. *Journal of Personality and Social Psychology, 59,* 270–280.

Heller, K., Swindle, R. W., & Dusenbury, L. (1986). Component social support processes: Comments and integration. *Journal of Consulting and Clinical Psychology, 54,* 466–470.

Hobfoll, S. E., Dunahoo, C. L., Ben-Porath, Y., & Monnier, J. (1994). Gender and coping: The dual-axis model of coping. *American Journal of Community Psychology, 22,* 49–82.

Hobfoll, S. E., Nadler, A., & Leiberman J. (1986). Satisfaction with social support during a crisis: Intimacy and self esteem as critical determinants. *Journal of Personality and Social Psychology, 51,* 296–304.

Hobfoll, S. E., & Stokes, J. P. (1988). The process and mechanics of social support. In S. Duck, D. F. Hay, S. E. Hobfoll, W. Ickes, & B. M. Montgomery (Eds.), *Handbook of personal relationships: Theory, research, and interventions* (pp. 497–515). London: Wiley.

Holahan, C. J., & Moos, R. H. (1987). Personal and contextual determinants of coping strategies. *Journal of Personality and Social Psychology, 52,* 946–955.

Holahan, C. J., & Moos, R. H. (1990). Life stressors, resistance factors, and improved psychological functioning: An extension of the stress resistance paradigm. *Journal of Personality and Social Psychology, 58,* 909–917.

Honig, A. S. (1986a). Stressing and coping in children (Part 1). *Young Children, 3,* 50–63.

Honig, A. S. (1986b). Stressing and coping in children (Part 2). *Young Children, 4,* 47–59.

House, J. S., & Kahn, R. L. (1985). Measuring concepts of social support. In S. Cohen & S. L. Syme (Eds.), *Social support and health* (pp. 83–108). New York: Academic Press.

Jemmott, J. B., III, & Magloire, K. (1988). Academic stress, social support, and secretory immunoglobulin A. *Journal of Personality and Social Psychology, 55,* 803–810.

Kendrick, D. T., & Funder, D. C. (1988). Profiting from controversy: Lessons from the person–situation debate. *American Psychologist, 43,* 23–34.

Kobak, R. R., & Sceery, A. (1988). Attachment in late adolescence: Working models, affect regulation, and perceptions of self and others. *Child Development, 88,* 135–146.

Krohne, H. W., & Rogner, J. (1982). Repression–sensitization as a central construct in coping research. In H. W. Krohne & L. Laux (Eds.), *Achievement, stress, and anxiety.* Washington, DC: Hemisphere.

Lazarus, R. S. (1966). *Psychological stress and the coping process.* New York: McGraw-Hill.

Lazarus, R. S., & Folkman, S. (1984). *Stress, appraisal, and coping.* New York: Springer.

Main, M., & Cassidy, J. (1988). Categories of response to reunion with the parent at age 6: Predictable from infant attachment classification and stable over a 1-month period. *Developmental Psychology, 24,* 415–426.

Main, M., Kaplan, N., & Cassidy, J. (1985). Security in infancy, childhood, and adulthood: A move to the level of representation. In I. Bretherton & E. Waters (Eds.), *Growing points of attachment theory and research* (pp. 66–106). *Monographs of the Society for Research in Child Development, 50(1 2),* Serial No. 209.

Mikulincer, M., Florian, V., & Tolmacz, R. (1990). Attachment styles and fear of personal death: A case study of affect regulation. *Journal of Personality and Social Psychology, 58,* 273–280.

Mikulincer, M., Florian, V., & Weller, A. (1993). Attachment styles, coping strategies, and post-traumatic psychological distress: The impact of the Gulf War in Israel. *Journal of Personality and Social Psychology, 64,* 817–826.

Mischel, W. (1968). *Personality assessment.* New York: Wiley.

Moos, R. H., & Schaefer, J. (1986). Life transitions and crises: A conceptual overview. In R. H. Moos (Ed.), *Coping with life crises: An integrated approach* (pp. 3–28). New York: Plenum Press.

Parker, G. R., Cowen, E. L., Work, W. C., & Wyman, P. A. (1990). Test correlates of stress resilience among urban school children. *Journal of Primary Prevention, 11,* 19–35.

Parkes, K. R. (1986). Coping in stressful episodes: The role of individual differences, environmental factors, and situational characteristics. *Journal of Personality and Social Psychology, 51,* 1277–1292.

Pierce, G. R., Sarason, I. G., & Sarason, B. R. (1991). General and relationship-based perceptions of social support: Are two constructs better than one? *Journal of Personality and Social Psychology, 61,* 1028–1039.

Ptacek, J. T., Dodge, K. E., & Ptacek, J. J. (1994). Social support in spouses of cancer patients: What do they get and to what end? Unpublished manuscript. Lewisburg, PA: Bucknell University.

Ptacek, J. T., Smith, R. E., & Dodge, K. E. (1994). Gender differences in coping with stress: When stressor and appraisal do not differ. *Personality and Social Psychology Bulletin, 20,* 421–430.

Ptacek, J. T., Smith, R. E., Espi, K., & Rafety, B. (1994). Limited correspondence between daily coping reports and retrospective coping recall. *Psychological Assessment, 6,* 41–48.

Ptacek, J. T., Smith, R. E., & Zanas, J. (1992). Gender, appraisal, and coping: A longitudinal analysis. *Journal of Personality, 60,* 747–770.

Rothbard, J. C., & Shaver, P. R. (1994). Continuity of attachment across the life span. In M. B. Spearling & W. H. Berman (Eds.), *Attachment in adults: Clinical and developmental perspectives* (pp. 31–71). New York: Guilford Press.

Rutter, M. (1979). Protective factors in children's responses to stress and disadvantage. In M. W. Kent & J. E. Rolf (Eds.), *Primary prevention of psychopathology: Social competence in children,* Vol. 3 (pp. 49–74). Hanover, NH: University Press of New England.

Sarason, B. R., Pierce, G. R., Bannerman, A., & Sarason, I. G. (1993). Investigating the antecedents of perceived social support: Parents' views of and behavior toward their children. *Journal of Personality and Social Psychology, 65,* 1071–1085.

Sarason, B. R., Pierce, G. R., & Sarason, I. G. (1990). Social support: The sense of acceptance and the role of relationships. In B. R. Sarason, I. G. Sarason, & G. R. Pierce (Eds.), *Social support: An interactional view* (pp. 97–128). New York: Wiley.

Sarason, B. R., Pierce, G. R., Shearin, G. R., Sarason, I. G., Waltz, J. A., & Poppe, L. (1991). Perceived support and working models of self and actual others. *Journal of Personality and Social Psychology, 60,* 273–287.

Sarason, I. G., Levine, H. M., Basham, R. B., & Sarason, B. R. (1983). Assessing social support: The Social Support Questionnaire. *Journal of Personality and Social Psychology, 44,* 127–139.

Sarason, I. G., Sarason, B. R., & Pierce, G. R. (1988). Social support, personality, and health. In S. Maes, C. D. Spielberger, P. B. Defares, & I. G. Sarason (Eds.), *Topics in health psychology* (pp. 245–256). New York: Wiley.

Sarason, I. G., Sarason B. R., & Pierce, G. R. (1990). Anxiety, cognitive interference, and performance. *Communication, Cognition, and Anxiety, 5,* 1–18.

Sarason, I. G., Sarason, B. R., & Pierce, G. R. (1994). Relationship-specific social support: Toward a model for the analysis of supportive interactions. In B. R. Burleson, T. L. Albrecht, & I. G. Sarason (Eds.), *Communication of social support* (pp. 91–112). London: Sage Publications.

Sarason, I. G., Sarason, B. R., & Shearin, E. N. (1986). Social support as an individual difference variable: Its stability, origins, and relational aspects. *Journal of Personality and Social Psychology, 50,* 845–855.

Schachter, S. (1978). The interaction of cognitive and physiological determinants of emotional state. In L. Berkowitz (Ed.), *Cognitive theories in social psychology* (pp. 401–452). New York: Academic Press.

Scheier, M. F., Weintraub, J. K., & Carver, C. S. (1986). Coping with stress: Divergent strategies of optimists and pessimists. *Journal of Personality and Social Psychology, 51,* 1257–1264.

Seeman, T. E., & Berkman, L. F. (1988). Structural characteristics of social networks and their relationship with social support in the elderly: Who provides support? *Social Science and Medicine, 26,* 737–749.

Selye, H. (1956). *The stress of life.* New York: McGraw-Hill.

Simpson, J. A. (1990). The influence of attachment styles on romantic relationships. *Journal of Personality and Social Psychology, 59,* 971–980.

Simpson, J. A., Rholes, W. S., & Nelligan, J. S. (1992). Support seeking and support-giving within couple members in an anxiety-provoking situation: The role of attachment styles. *Journal of Personality and Social Psychology, 62,* 434–446.

Snyder, M. (1983). The influence of individuals on situations: Implications for understanding the links between personality and social behavior. *Journal of Personality, 51,* 487–516.

Solomon, L. J., & Rothblum, E. D. (1986). Stress, coping, and social support in women. *Behavior Therapist, 9,* 199–204.

Sperling, M. B., & Berman, W. H. (Eds.). (1994). *Attachment in adults: Clinical and developmental perspectives.* New York: Guilford Press.

Spirito, A., Stark, L. J., Grace, N., & Stamoulis, D. (1991). Common problems and coping strategies reported in childhood and early adolescence. *Journal of Youth and Adolescence, 20,* 531–544.

Stone, A. A., Greenberg, M. A., Kennedy-Moore, E., & Newman, M. G. (1991). Self-report, situation-specific coping questionnaires: What are they measuring? *Journal of Personality and Social Psychology, 61,* 648–658.

Stone, A. A., & Neale, J. M. (1984). New measure of daily coping: Development and preliminary results. *Journal of Personality and Social Psychology, 46,* 892–906.

Terry, D. J. (1991). Coping resources and situational appraisals as predictors of coping behavior. *Personality and Individual Differences, 12,* 1031–1047.

Terry, D. J. (1994). Determinants of coping: The role of stable and situational factors. *Journal of Personality and Social Psychology, 66,* 895–910.

Vitaliano, P. P., Maiuro, R. D., Russo, J., & Becker, J. (1987). Raw versus relative scores in the assessment of coping strategies. *Journal of Behavioral Medicine, 10,* 1–18.

Wertlieb, D., Weigel, C., & Feldstein, M. (1987). Measuring children's coping. *American Journal of Orthopsychiatry, 57,* 548–560.

Wolchik, S. A., Ruehlman, L. S., Braver, S. L., & Sandler, I. N. (1989). Social support of children of divorce: Direct and stress buffering effects. *American Journal of Community Psychology, 17,* 485–501.

21

The Role of Family and Peer Relationships in Adolescent Substance Use

THOMAS A. WILLS, JOHN MARIANI, and MARNIE FILER

This chapter considers how family and peer relationships, respectively, act to decrease or increase adolescents' likelihood of involvement in substance use. The qualifying word "respectively" indicates that these two types of relationships may serve different roles for adolescents. Support from parents typically is indicated as a protective factor, inversely related to level of adolescent substance use. In contrast, support from peers under some conditions is positively related to substance use. The contrast between results for the parental and peer support systems indicates the theoretical complexity of considering how social networks operate for substance use in general and adolescent substance use in particular (Wills, 1990a) and has implications for the understanding of resilience effects (Haggerty, Sherrod, Garmezy, & Rutter, 1994; Wills, Blechman, & McNamara, 1996). In this chapter, we develop a framework for considering how parental and peer support operate in adolescence, report findings from our research program with adolescents, and discuss implications for the theory of social support. A specific emphasis derived from this research is that parental support has a powerful impact on adolescents' coping, competence, and self-control ability. We try in this chapter to elucidate the question of why parental support is so important. We also make the point that a problem behavior such as early substance use is best predicted from the interaction of parent and peer support systems and that

THOMAS A. WILLS, JOHN MARIANI, and MARNIE FILER • Ferkauf Graduate School of Psychology and Department of Epidemiology and Social Medicine, Albert Einstein College of Medicine, Bronx, New York 10461-1924.

Handbook of Social Support and the Family, edited by Gregory R. Pierce, Barbara R. Sarason, and Irwin G. Sarason. Plenum Press, New York, 1996.

adolescents seem to be particularly vulnerable when they have a low level of parental support but are strongly immersed in peer social activity.

Several definitions will introduce the general approach taken in our research program. The research uses the model of social epidemiology, studying factors associated with use or nonuse of substances in the general population of adolescents. Data are derived from questionnaires administered in school settings to reasonably large samples of adolescents in the age range from 12 to 15 years. Our approach to the measurement of social support is derived from a functional model (Wills, 1985; Cutrona & Russell, 1987) that posits that family support has impact because parents provide supportive functions that help adolescents deal with problems they may have. We have focused on emotional and instrumental support as the functions most likely to assist adolescents in adaptation (Wills, Vaccaro, & McNamara, 1992). Though we would not downplay the potential importance of functions such as informational support or social companionship, or the ability of parental relationships to help link adolescents with "diffuse support" from community networks (see Wills, 1991), we have posited that emotional and instrumental support are the functions of major importance, and we have used these functions to index "parental support."

"Peer support" has been defined as the ability of age peers to provide support when an adolescent has a problem, so the research includes parallel measures of parental and peer support (cf. Carver, Scheier, & Weintraub, 1989; Procidano & Heller, 1983; Wills & Vaughan, 1989). Note that we do not measure parental or peer support for substance use (which is a different construct), but rather the perceived emotional supportiveness of the parent or peer network. In some studies, we have also measured a somewhat different construct, termed "peer competence": the perception of being able to form good relationships with peers (Harter, 1985); this construct produces generally similar results, but we distinguish social competence constructs when they are discussed.

"Substance use" as studied in this research means the use of so-called "gateway substances": cigarette smoking, beer or wine drinking, and marijuana use. Substance use in adolescence typically begins with initiation of occasional smoking or drinking, and for a subgroup of adolescents, there is an increase in frequency and quantity of use during adolescence (Kandel, 1975; Kandel & Yamaguchi, 1985). While the majority of the general population of adolescents can be defined as nonusers or minimal experimenters, there is a detectable prevalence of regular (monthly, weekly, or daily) substance use in adolescent samples, which rises from low single-digit figures in early adolescence to rates of 15–30% in later adolescence (Johnston, O'Malley, & Bachman, 1989; Wills, McNamara, Vaccaro, & Hirky, in press). It is also typical in adolescent samples to find substantial correlations among tobacco, alcohol, and marijuana use, so the dependent variable is a total score for the combined frequency of use of these different substances (cf. Hays, Widaman, DiMatteo, & Stacy, 1987; Needle, Su, & Lavee, 1989).

Early substance use is of particular significance because follow-back studies of adults and follow-up studies of adolescents have shown that persons who began using substances early (before the age of 14 years) are at elevated risk for substance use problems in adulthood (Kandel & Davies, 1992; Robins & Przybeck, 1985). For this reason, our research has focused on substance use during the period from 12 to 15 years of age, both because of the prognostic significance of early-onset use and because this period represents the "time window" during which rapid escalation occurs for a vulnerable group of adolescents. The goal of the research, then, is to study a large population of adolescents, investigating the extent to which family and peer variables distinguish users from nonusers, early users from other types of users, or adolescents who show escalation in use from those who show a pattern of minimal experimentation.

The goal of this chapter is to present and discuss a program of epidemiological research testing a functional model of parental and peer support in relation to substance use in early adolescence. In the following sections, we first discuss some prior research on adolescent stress and support and then discuss findings from our research on adolescents. Finally, we consider what the findings may imply for the larger theory of social support.

PRIOR RESEARCH ON ADOLESCENT STRESS AND SUPPORT

Research on adolescent stress and support occurs against a background of research on stress, social support, and substance use among adults, which has shown some of the complexities that characterize the operation of social relationships. Life stress is a risk factor for substance use across the phases of substance use, from initiation to relapse, and the way in which persons respond to stressful situations is an important predictor of substance use (Wills, 1990c; Wills & Hirky, 1996). Social relationships may be protective against substance use, but much depends on the characteristics of the social network and on what aspect of social support is assessed (Wills, 1990a). For example, social integration is inversely related to substance abuse (Umberson, 1987), and measures of emotional support from close friends help to protect against relapse for several different types of substance use (Rhoads, 1983; Rosenberg, 1983). However, even though close relationships may provide emotional support for coping with stress, having a partner or confidant who is a substance user greatly increases the risk of relapse (Mermelstein, Cohen, Lichtenstein, Kamarck, & Baer, 1986; Tucker, 1985). Thus, social relationships cannot be classified a priori as either protective or risk-promoting with respect to substance use; social integration in the community, the availability of emotional support from a confidant, and the amount of substance use among network members are all relevant for predicting substance use, yet these variables may operate in opposite directions.

For adolescents, the general orientation in research on family and peer relationships has come from literature on adolescent sociology, which posits that the nature of adolescence is a move away from the family as a primary support source and into peer reference and membership groups (Glynn, 1981; Kandel & Lesser, 1972). Though it does not follow from this model that parents lack any influence on adolescents, a number of studies have indicated that peer groups have an important influence on adolescents, either through normative influences or through explicit social pressure (Chassin, Presson, Sherman, Montello, & McGrew, 1986; Kandel & Andrews, 1977; Wright & Keple, 1981). Research on adolescent substance use has been consistent with this proposition and has shown that initiation of substance use and other proscribed behavior tends to occur in groups of age peers, and having friends who are substance users is empirically a strong predictor of adolescents' substance use (Friedman, Lichtenstein, & Biglan, 1985; Mosbach & Leventhal, 1988). Whether this use occurs because of explicit social pressure or because of identification with peer users as desirable social image models has not really been clarified, though these processes are quite different theoretically (Barton, Chassin, Presson, & Sherman, 1982; Graham, Marks, & Hansen, 1991; Sussman et al., 1988).

Research on Family and Peer Relationships

Research on the role of family and peer relationships has tended to focus on family support as a protective factor (e.g., see Brook, Brook, Gordon, Whiteman, & Cohen, 1990; Bry, 1983; Dishion, Reid, & Patterson, 1988; Sandler, Miller, Short, & Wolchik, 1989), but several studies have examined the contributions of both parental and peer relationships to adolescents' adjustment. Burke and Weir (1978, 1979) conducted exploratory research with adolescents on the basis of perceived supportiveness from parents and peers, and correlated measures of parental and peer support with mental health indices. They found that parental and peer support had approximately equal effects on mental health. Greenberg, Siegel, and Leitch (1983) specifically tested stress-buffering effects of the two types of support in an adolescent sample, with indices of self-concept and life satisfaction as outcome measures. They found that although peer support was utilized more often in terms of frequency, the (beneficial) effect of parental emotional support on outcomes was much greater than the effect of peer support. Moreover, these investigators found that parental support produced stress-buffering effects, but peer support did not. These findings suggest that even though adolescents may perceive supportiveness from peer networks and utilize peer support with considerable frequency, the effect of parental support for helping adolescents to cope with problems may be greater in actuality. Steinberg, Dornbusch, and Brown (1992) found that an important predictor of academic success for an adolescent is having support for academics from both parents and peers; youngsters whose friends and parents both support academics have much higher achievement than those who receive support from only one source. Thus, the findings suggest that the interaction of parental and peer support systems is crucial for predicting competence.

With respect to substance use as an outcome, research with adolescents and young adults has shown a complex picture. In a longitudinal study with a high school sample, Kandel, Kessler, and Margulies (1978) found differing results for various indices of parent and peer relationships. An index of the quality of the parent–child relationship, termed "closeness to parents," was indicated as a protective factor, inversely related to substance use. For peer relationships, an index of the amount of time spent in peer activity was positively related to substance use, but an index of "intimacy of relationship with best friend" was inversely related to substance use. A study of adolescents' daily experiences by Larson (1983) found that adolescents experienced more positive affect in interactions with peers than in interactions with parents, but correlations of daily-experience indices with external criteria indicated that adolescents with a high level of peer activity had lower academic performance. It was suggested by Larson (1983) that while peer relationships may provide more positive hedonic experiences, they may not contribute to developing competence in instrumental tasks and problem-solving performance in the way that parental relationships do.

With a sample of college students, Fondacaro and Heller (1983) obtained measures of several indices of social network structure and functional support. Even in this somewhat older sample, the subjects perceived parents as a significant source of social support (aside from providing money). Analyses predicting level of heavy alcohol use showed that measures of functional support from network members (e.g., problem-solving support) were inversely related to heavy drinking, and inclusion of family members in the subject's nominated social network also was a protective factor. However, network indices such as amount of social contact and a measure of perceived dating competence were positively related to drinking. Similarly, Wills, Baker, and Botvin (1989) studied measures of assertiveness with a younger adolescent sample and found that assertiveness specifically against substance offers was inversely related to substance use, whereas social assertiveness was positively related to substance use. Thus, divergent effects for different types and sources of social support and social competence are suggested.

Several methodological issues are attendant on this research. The studies have been conducted with subjects of quite different ages, and there is relatively little evidence on the role of social support in early use. The measures used in the research generally have not been derived from functional models and tend to represent global indices that do not clearly distinguish emotional support, instrumental support, informational support, and companionship functions (see Wills, 1990b). Measures of peer activity often have not distinguished between constructs such as frequency of social activity and competence in social relationships, on one hand, and characteristics of peer support such as emotional support or intimacy, on the other. Also, the exact nature of the peer network has not always been characterized, so it is often not clear whether the peers who provide support tend to be mainstream (conventional) peers or, possibly, more deviant peers.

Research on Resilience

Theory and research on resilience are relevant for our work because family support is repeatedly suggested as a protective factor in developmental research with long-term follow-ups (e.g., see Luthar & Zigler, 1991; Masten, Morison, Pellegrini, & Tellegen, 1990; Rutter, 1985, 1990). The typical research paradigm in this area is to follow a sample of children who grew up in an environment characterized by chronic stress (e.g., economic hardship) and to obtain indices of their long-term outcomes. Children who are able to develop competent performance and satisfactory mental health are termed "resilient"; the goals of the research are to determine environmental, parental, and personality factors that differentiate resilient children from those who are adversely affected by their early environment.

For example, a study by Werner was conducted with a birth cohort of children on the Hawaiian island of Kauai (Werner & Smith, 1982). Assessments of the child and family were first conducted shortly after birth, and subsequent assessments, including records from archival sources (e.g., schools, courts, and community agencies), were obtained at ages 2, 10, and 18 years. From the larger sample, Werner (1986) identified a subgroup of 49 subjects who grew up in families characterized by parental substance abuse. In this subsample of children, all faced with early adversity from parental alcohol abuse and associated poverty, 41% developed adjustment problems by adolescence, but 59% did not (i.e., were resilient). Analyses of study data suggested that the resilient children were differentiated by a supportive caregiving environment (including more parental attention and less parental conflict) and by better intellectual development and academic competence.

Werner (1986) suggested that effects of risk factors on children can be buffered by the existence of protective factors such as social competencies, communication skills, and social support, which help to reduce the impact of parental alcoholism and poverty. Similar conclusions have emerged from other studies of resilient populations. It is consistently noted that resilience is attributable in part to a family environment that provides cohesion and warmth, encourages the child's coping efforts, and helps children to develop feelings of competence and self-efficacy (cf. Garmezy & Masten, 1991; Luthar & Zigler, 1991; Wills, 1994). Several studies suggest that a network of social relationships with other adults, such as coaches, teachers, or ministers, also contributes to resilience (Braithwaite & Gordon, 1992; Lewis & Looney, 1983). It has been suggested that essential elements in social networks that contribute to resilience are that they engender trust in people as supportive resources, provide information and access to knowledge about the community, and reinforce competent behavior while continually providing challenges (Blechman & Culhane, 1993; Cauce, 1986; Masten et al., 1990). This position is consistent with evidence we previously discussed on the operation of family support.

Research on resiliency has provided some intriguing findings, but also poses some methodological questions. The measures of parental support tend to be global ones and, particularly with longitudinal studies that were initiated some time ago, it can be difficult to determine exactly what aspect of the parent–child relationship was indexed. While it is often suggested in this research that parental support leads to better coping by children, the studies did not include direct measures of coping, so conclusions about how parental support contributes to resilience are inferential. The resilience literature has suggested that competence in relationships with both peers and adults is an important factor, but there is little direct evidence on social competence. Finally, because of the specialized nature of the samples, it remains unclear how parental support is related to other demographic characteristics of parents such as ethnicity. Thus, there is still much to be clarified about how resilience effects occur.

Explication of Our Functional Model

From previous research and theory, we derived a functional model of parental support. It is proposed that parents may provide supportive functions that help adolescents to cope with life strains and problems that they experience. As in the theory of functional support among adults (S. Cohen & Wills, 1985; Wills, 1991), it is proposed that support contributes to adjustment because children receive assistance for dealing with emotional distress; children receive assistance that helps them learn instrumental skills; and the perception of available support provides encouragement for pursuing more effortful types of coping (e.g., problem solving) rather than avoidant types of coping (e.g., getting angry at others or giving up on trying to solve a problem). In this way, emotional and instrumental support from parents may contribute to better adjustment among children. The buffering model of social support (S. Cohen & Wills, 1985) predicts that these kinds of supportive functions will be most relevant for persons who are experiencing a high level of life stress, and thus this model predicts that stress-buffering effects of parental support will be observed for adolescents.

In considering how parental support leads to better adjustment, previous research has tested specific predictions about coping mechanisms, derived from the transactional model of Lazarus and Folkman (1984). It is proposed that behavioral (or problem-solving) coping and cognitive (or emotion-focused) coping represent active coping mechanisms that will contribute to better adjustment, whereas avoidant ways of coping with problems (including anger and helplessness) will be detrimental to adjustment (Wills, 1990b; Wills & Filer, 1996; Wills & Shiffman, 1985). In recent work, we have drawn increasingly on models positing that lack of self-regulation ability is a basic pathway to development of behavior problems (Rothbart & Ahadi, 1994; Tarter, Moss, & Vanyukov, 1995) and have tested hypotheses about the effect of parental support on self-control ability.

In summary, we have proposed a functional model of parental support as a protective factor with respect to adolescent substance use, and we study this issue in the context of epidemiological research conducted over the age range from early to middle adolescence. In addition to testing the essential propositions of the functional model, we investigate the relative effects of parental and peer support, examine whether parental support serves as a buffering agent, and test models of how parental support works. The following section reports findings from this research.

EMPIRICAL STUDIES OF PARENTAL AND PEER SUPPORT

Methodological Approach

Our recent research has examined questions about family and peer support in five studies. Several methodological characteristics are common across studies. One is school-based data collection: Questionnaires are administered to students in classrooms by trained project staff who follow a standardized protocol in giving instructions to students and answering questions. The sampling frame is the entire population of students in a given grade level at the school, and we typically survey over 90% of the eligible population. Subjects participate under a consent procedure in which parents are informed of the nature of the research through a notice sent by direct mail and are informed that they can have their child excluded from the study if they wish. Students can decline participation at the time the questionnaire is administered. Under this procedure, rates of parental refusals and student refusals are usually around 1%, and the majority of case loss comes from student absenteeism. Sample size is mostly in the range of 1200–1800 cases, a characteristic conservatively figured to provide adequate power for detecting relatively small effect sizes that may occur because of the skewed distributions of predictors and substance use in younger populations. Some of the research has used cross-sectional designs; other studies have employed longitudinal designs, in which students are surveyed once per year between 7th grade and 10th grade.

The participants in this research are students in public school districts in the New York metropolitan area. The samples in our recent research have been about 30% African-American, 25% Hispanic, 35% white, and 10% other ethnicity. The communities the schools draw from are usually representative of the New York State population in terms of census statistics; the modal parental education level is around high school graduate, indicating a population that is working class on the average. Family structure also is typical for urban areas, with about 55% of the students living in intact two-parent families, 35% living with a single parent (usually single mothers, sometimes with relatives), and 10% living in blended families (one biological parent and one stepparent).

Adolescent substance use is indexed with a standard set of items. Three items ask about the typical frequency of use for cigarettes, alcohol, and marijuana. Responses for these items are on a scale with the numbers 1–6 corresponding to Never Used, Used Once–Twice, Used Four–Five Times, Use a Few Times a Month, Use a Few Times a Week, and Use Every Day. An item to specifically index heavy drinking asks whether there was a time in the past month when the respondent had three or more drinks on one occasion; response points for this item are No, Happened Once, and Happened Twice or More. The correlation between items is in the range from $r = 0.30$ to $r = 0.50$, reflecting the typical intercorrelation of different types of substance use in adolescent populations (Wills, Cleary, Filer, & Mariani, June, 1994). For multiple regression or structural modeling analysis, the four items are combined in a composite score representing total substance use (cf. Hays et al., 1987; Needle et al., 1989).

The prevalence of substance use in these samples is consistent with rates from national and regional studies (Johnston et al., 1989). For example, in a longitudinal panel surveyed between 1990 and 1992, the rates of monthly, weekly, and daily smoking were 2%, 1%, and 1%, respectively, for data from 7th-grade subjects (mean subject age: 12.4 years). These percentages increased to 6%, 3%, and 10% by the 9th-grade measurement, reflecting the typical increase in substance use from early to middle adolescence. The rate of heavy drinking (twice or more per month) in this sample was 3% in the 7th grade, 5% in the 8th grade, and 10% in the 9th grade, so it is evident that the levels of use are not trivial.

The methods of statistical analysis are generally similar across studies. In multiple regression, the composite substance use score is the criterion variable, and support measures are entered simultaneously, to test for their unique contributions to substance use (J. Cohen & P. Cohen, 1983). An analogous procedure is used in structuring modeling analyses with LISREL (Jöreskog & Sörbom, 1988), where the criterion construct of adolescent substance use is specified as a latent construct measured by indicators of smoking, alcohol, and marijuana use. These analyses are always replicated with demographic controls, entering indices for gender, ethnicity (African-American vs. Hispanic vs. white), family structure (single vs. blended vs. intact), and parental education (grade school to college graduate) together with the support variables. Thus, the analyses partial out any correlation of support variables with demographic characteristics.

Parental Support and Adolescent Substance Use in the Inner City

Our research on parental support has aimed to test a model that assumes that supportive functions from parents provide the "glue" that bonds children to mainstream institutions and builds self-control skills. The first study was conducted to test this conceptualization of support with an inner-city population. The subjects were 1289 middle school students (25% African-American, 51% Hispanic, 17% white, and 7% other ethnicity) from parochial schools in lower-income areas of Manhattan and the Bronx. The census statistics for these areas indicated very low income compared with either the city or the state average, and characterize this sample as a disadvantaged one.

Using as the base the extended version of the Interpersonal Support Evaluation List (ISEL) (S. Cohen, Mermelstein, Kamarck, & Hoberman, 1985), a 15-item inventory was developed to assess emotional and instrumental support functions in the context of adolescents' relationships with parents. The inventory was keyed to support seeking in the context of personal problems, and so was introduced with a setting statement about "a person that you talk to when you have a problem or when you need advice." Subjects were instructed to answer with respect to "the parent you talk to the most," to ensure that the support measures were not biased by the prevalence of single-parent families in the sample.[1] The instructions told subjects to circle a response (on a 1–4 Likert scale: "Not at All True for Me" to "Very True for Me") to show how they felt about talking to this parent; thus, the instructional set was oriented toward perceived support availability, the feeling that the parent would be available if there was a problem (not whether the subject had utilized support recently). The items for the emotional support scale indexed the constructs of availability ("When I feel bad about something, my parent will listen"), empathy ("If I talk to my parent I think they try to understand how I

---

[1]This caution is not meant to imply that the additive effects of support are unimportant. It is possible that support from father and support from mother each contribute unique effects to children's adjustment or that there are interactive effects (e.g., from father–son and mother–daughter relationships). In some kinds of samples, however, the prevalence of single parents will be substantial, and this fact must be recognized in measurement design.

feel"), and trustworthiness ("I can share my feelings with my parent"; "I feel that I can trust my parent as someone to talk to"). The items for the instrumental support scale indexed assistance with a variety of instrumental tasks including homework ("If I need help with my school work I can ask my parent about it"), transportation ("If I need help in getting somewhere I can ask my parent for a way to get there"), health ("If I have a problem with my health I think I can talk to my parent about it"), entertainment ("If I'm feeling bored, my parent has suggestions about things to do"), and social relationships ("If I'm having a problem with a friend, my parent would have advice about what to do"). A factor analysis indicated a two-factor solution with clear scales for emotional support (7 items, alpha = 0.81) and instrumental support (8 items, alpha = 0.74). The reliabilities are consistent with those found for other scales in epidemiological research with adolescents. The two scales were correlated ($r = 0.57$), so they are not exactly independent, but this is typical for functional measures (cf. Cutrona & Russell, 1987).

Multiple regression analyses with the two parental support scales entered simultaneously showed that the scales made independent contributions to substance use, with standardized regression coefficients of beta = -0.16 for emotional support and beta = -0.13 for instrumental support ($p < 0.0001$ for both). This finding provides evidence for the functional model, as direct measures of supportive functions from the parental relationship are shown to be related to adolescents' substance use. This evidence does not by itself prove that support for helping children deal with problems is the primary causal agent in protecting them against life strains, but it does suggest that supportive functions are relevant for this process. Two other points should be noted. One is that emotional and instrumental support make independent contributions in the multivariate analysis despite their substantial correlation (which works against demonstration of unique effects), so it is clear that they are not interchangeable or redundant— each has an independent role in the protective process. A second point is that the inverse correlation between parental support and adolescent substance use is not merely reflecting a confounded relationship with demographic characteristics. Though there are significant correlations of parental support with characteristics such as socioeconomic status or family structure, the observed effects of parental support cannot be attributed to confounding because the observed effects are obtained with control for demographic factors.

We also tested a corollary of the functional model, namely, the prediction of stress-buffering effects. It was noted in the S. Cohen and Wills (1985) paper that buffering effects of social support are observed consistently for functional measures that tap emotional, instrumental, and sometimes informational support: There is a substantial correlation between negative life events and depression among persons with a low level of social support, but this correlation is reduced (or eliminated) for persons with high support. Though it does not necessarily follow that buffering effects would be observed for adolescents with drug use as an outcome, we included a 23-item measure indexing negative life events that occurred during the previous year (to either the parents or the adolescent subject) and tested Life Events × Parental Support interactions with substance use as the criterion variable. Results showed that these interactions were significant for both emotional and instrumental support (see Wills, Vaccaro, & McNamara, 1992) and were consistent in form with stress-buffering: There was a strong relation between life events and substance use for adolescents with low family support, whereas this relationship was reduced among adolescents with high family support. Though a finding of buffering effects does not constitute unique proof for a theoretical model, it strengthens confidence that supportive functions from parents provide a generally protective effect and help adolescents to deal better with adverse events that otherwise could lead to problem behavior.

In this study, measures of several other variables were obtained, including positive and negative affect (from Zevon & Tellegen, 1982) and perceived competence (from Harter, 1985). Parental support was correlated with these other variables in a consistent manner: Support was related to greater academic competence, more positive affect, and less negative affect. Thus, we could begin to see some widespread effects—ripple effects if you wish—from parental support to variables that contribute to better adjustment. Some of these effects had been suggested in the resilience studies; for example, good parental relationships and better academic performance were observed retrospectively to be characteristic of children who showed resilience under adversity. Here, the effects were observed in a real-time mode, with parental support and adolescent competence measured in early adolescence. Because of the cross-sectional design, it was difficult to make firm inferences about causal direction, but the convergence with suggestions from the resilience literature was striking and suggested that resilience could be based in the ability of parents to help children cope with problems.

Parental Support and Adolescent Substance Use in a Metropolitan Sample

In subsequent research, we aimed to test the replicability of these findings in a longitudinal study with a larger sample. This study was initiated with a sample of 1702 students (29% African-American, 23% Hispanic, 37% white, and 11% other ethnicity) from public schools in the metropolitan area. The census statistics for the areas the schools draw from are close to those for the state as a whole, and study data on parental education indicated that the sample was working class on the average. We administered the inventory of parental emotional and instrumental support, and standard items on substance use, in a questionnaire that included measures of stress, coping, and competence (Wills et al., 1992). In this longitudinal study, students were surveyed four times over the interval from 7th grade to 10th grade.

The results for parental support and adolescent substance use over this 4-year period are summarized in Table 1. Descriptive statistics indicated that the scores for emotional and instrumental support were skewed toward the favorable end of the dimension, which is typical for functional measures, as most persons tend to perceive relatively high levels of support availability (see Wills, 1991); thus, in this respect, the measures for adolescents' support from parents produce findings

**Table 1. Analyses of Emotional and Instrumental Support
for the Seventh through Tenth Grades[a]**

Grade	Skewness	Zero-order r	Beta	Interaction (t)
Seventh				
PES scale	−1.07	−0.27[f]	−0.21[f]	−1.72[b]
PIS scale	−1.25	−0.24[f]	−0.10[e]	−1.20
(Intercorrelation r: 0.65)				
Eighth				
PES scale	−0.63	−0.29[f]	−0.26[f]	−3.71[f]
PIS scale	−1.02	−0.23[f]	−0.05	−2.39[c]
(Intercorrelation r: 0.70)				
Ninth				
PES scale	−0.60	−0.22[f]	−0.14[f]	−3.46[e]
PIS scale	−0.94	−0.22[f]	−0.12[e]	−3.71[e]
(Intercorrelation r: 0.73)				
Tenth				
PES scale	−0.54	−0.23[f]	−0.17[f]	−0.71
PIS scale	−0.76	−0.21[f]	−0.08[c]	−0.13
(Intercorrelation r: 0.74)				

[a](PES) Parental Emotional Support; (PIS) Parental Instrumental Support. A negative skewness value indicates a distribution shifted toward higher scores. The zero-order r is for correlation of support scale with substance use score; beta is a standardized regression coefficient in multiple regression with both support measures entered simultaneously, with substance use score as the criterion variable. Interaction t is for the Life Events × Parental Support interaction term, entered with main effect terms for events and support, with substance use score as the criterion variable.
[b-f]Significance: [b]$p < 0.10$; [c]$p < 0.05$; [d]$p < 0.01$; [e]$p < 0.001$; [f]$p < 0.0001$.

resembling those for measures of adults' functional support. The intercorrelations of the support scales were higher than in the previous study, at a level that was troublesome (though not impossible) for the multiple regressions.

Findings on the relation between parental support and adolescent substance use were replicated in this new sample. In the 7th-grade data, for example, independent contributions were noted for emotional support ($p < 0.0001$) and instrumental support ($p < 0.001$). The unique effects for instrumental support were smaller in this study, but this result should be considered cautiously in light of the higher correlation between the two scales. In fact, the zero-order correlations of the emotional and instrumental support scales with substance use were not very different, but in multiple regression with correlated predictors, the one having the slightly higher correlation with the criterion will "grab most of the shared variance from its neighbor" (J. Cohen & P. Cohen, 1983). It would be tempting to conclude that in this somewhat better off (though by no means affluent) population, instrumental support was less relevant than is the case for inner-city children, but the statistical characteristics of the data are not amenable to a definitive conclusion on this issue.

The relation between parental support and adolescent substance use was consistent across the age range studied. While it is suggested in these data that the effect of parental support was somewhat stronger at the first measurement (taken around 12 years of age), the really striking thing about the data is that effects of parental support are significant throughout the period from 7th grade through 10th grade. The notion that parental support becomes unimportant as teenagers move into the peer environment does not receive any confirmation in these data.

The buffering effects found in the inner-city sample were replicated in this study. Table 1 includes the t-test for the Life Events × Parent Support cross-product (i.e., buffering effect) when added to the main effects. The buffering effect was marginal in the 7th grade, but significant in the 8th grade (interaction for emotional support, $p < 0.0001$) and in the 9th grade ($p < 0.001$). The buffer interaction was nonsignificant in the 10th grade. We interpret this as evidence of a dynamic process, because the majority of initiation of substance use by the subjects occurred between 7th grade and 9th grade, and there was relatively little change between the 9th and 10th grades. Thus, a buffering effect of parental support was replicated in this sample, and the evidence suggests that the buffering process occurred during the crucial time window for onset.

To address questions about the temporal relationship between parental support and adolescent substance use, we performed prospective analyses, using parental support at one time point (e.g., 7th grade) to predict adolescent substance use score at a subsequent time point (e.g., 8th grade), with initial level of adolescent substance use included as a covariate. These analyses showed significant prospective effects for both emotional and instrumental support (Wills, Vaccaro, McNamara, & Hirky, August, 1993). Parental support was inversely related to change in substance use over time. This result suggests that parental support serves as a "brake," making it less likely that adolescents will initiate substance use or experience any substantial increase in frequency of use. Thus, parental support acts over time to deter onset of problem behavior.

How does parental support work to deter adolescents from becoming involved in substance use? It is possible that the protective effect of parental support occurs because it is related to other variables that are involved in onset of substance use. If so, this would produce a model of the mediational process like that portrayed in Figure 1; that is, support acts through increasing adolescents' level of self-control ability and decreasing the number of negative events that the teen experiences. To address this question, we performed mediation analyses (per Baron & Kenny, 1986), identifying variables that reduced the statistical relationship between support and substance use. Several variables were identified as mediators; these included two other protective factors (behavioral coping and behavioral competence) and four risk factors (deviant attitudes, anger coping, negative life events, and affiliation with substance-using peers). These variables were tested in a structural modeling analysis (Wills, McNamara, Riccobono, & Vaccaro, March, 1992). The results showed a process like that illustrated in Figure 1. The protective effect of parental support occurred because it was related to more adaptive coping, lower deviance proneness (e.g., less anger), and fewer negative life events. This circumstance in turn influenced the likelihood of associating with substance-using peers, which was indicated as the proximal vari-

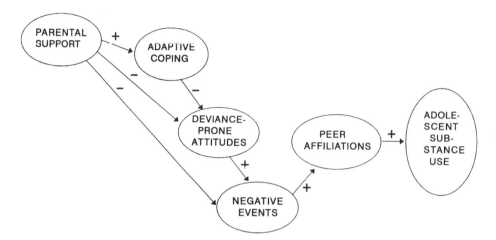

Figure 1. Theoretical model for mediation of effect of parental support. Symbols: (+) predicted positive coefficient; (−) predicted negative coefficient.

able (i.e., most immediate causal factor) for becoming involved in substance use (cf. Patterson, DeBaryshe, & Ramsey, 1989). Thus, the relation between parental support and adolescent substance use is not a direct one, but involves other variables. It should be noted that the analyses showed independent paths from parental support to coping, deviance proneness, and negative life events, indicating that functional support works through multiple pathways, not through just one factor.

Peer Support and Substance Use

The relation between peer support and adolescent substance use has been examined from several perspectives. An initial study was conducted with midsize samples (600–900 students) from public junior high schools in Manhattan (see Wills, 1985, 1986). In this study, the focus was more on stress-coping mechanisms (Lazarus & Folkman, 1984). The coping inventory introduced the items to the students with instructions about how they were to read some things that people might do when they had a problem; subjects were then asked to indicate the extent to which they used a particular response when they had a problem at school or at home. The coping inventory included items such as these: "Let out my feelings with someone I feel close to," "Find someone special to share my problem with," and "Talk with one of my friends," together with the item "Talk with my mother or father." These factored into two scales, with most of the items loading on a first factor (labeled Peer Support Coping) and the item about parents loading on a second factor (labeled Parental Support Coping). These scales tap support-seeking that is explicitly perceived as a means of coping. Our analyses of data from subsequent studies showed the Parental Support Coping measure to be substantially correlated with the measure of parental support availability, so they appear to index similar constructs.

Analyses testing the relation of parental and peer support to adolescents' substance use indicated that parental support was inversely related to substance use, but somewhat to the surprise of the investigators, peer support was positively related to substance use—the more peer support the higher the level of substance use (Wills & Vaughan, 1989). Additional analyses were performed that helped somewhat to understand this effect. For example, there was an interaction of peer support and peer substance use. When a person had few friends who had smoked or drunk alcohol, the relation between peer support and the subject's substance use was virtually zero; in contrast, when a person had several friends who were smokers or drinkers, there was a strong positive relationship between peer support and the subject's level of substance use. It appeared that peer support acted to strengthen the modeling effect of the peer network. Other analyses showed a significant interaction of parental support and peer support: Substance use was particularly elevated for adolescents with low parental support and high peer support. This finding suggested that adolescents were particularly vulnerable to substance use if they felt that they had little support from their parents but perceived their peer network as very supportive. Thus, this study indicated that parental support and peer support have different effects and suggested that the interaction of parental and peer systems is important for predicting substance use.

Our current research has followed up on these findings in several different ways. In the metropolitan-area sample, measures from the inventory of Harter (1985) were included to index subjects' perceptions of their competence in academic performance and in social relationships. Items in the Peer Competence scale ask the subject to indicate agreement/disagreement with statements such as "I find it easy to make friends with other kids," "I feel that I'm popular with other kids," and "I feel like I'm an important member of my class." To obtain parallel measures of peer and adult competence, we took the items from the Peer Competence scale and reworded them to index perceived competence in relationships with adults (e.g., "I find it easy to make friends with adults," "I feel that I'm well liked by adults," "I feel that adults treat me like I'm a real person").

Part of the thinking behind the design of this study was that measures of social competence might tap a different aspect of peer relationships than was indexed by measures of peer support as a coping mechanism.[2] Analyses predicting substance use from the set of competence scales entered together showed complex results. Academic competence and adult competence were related to lower levels of substance use, as predicted, but peer competence was positively related to substance use in the multivariate model (Wills, Vaccaro, McNamara, & Spellman, August, 1991). Moreover, this relation occurred as a suppression effect: The zero-order correlation of peer competence with substance use was nonsignificant, but

---

[2]It was not possible in this study to include measures both for social competence and for support-related coping. In field research of this type, there is usually a crunch of priorities, and it is typical that the investigator cannot include all the measures he or she would like (see S. Cohen, 1986).

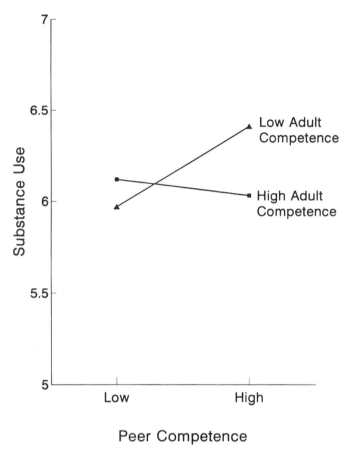

Figure 2. Interaction of adult and peer competence, substance use score as criterion variable. Predicted values are plotted at levels of mean ± 1 SD for each variable.

the coefficient for peer competence in the multiple regression was positive in sign and usually significant (similar to findings in Wills, Vaccaro, & McNamara, 1992). This suppression effect missed significance in the 7th-grade data ($r = -0.03$; beta = 0.04; both NS), but was significant in comparable models in the 8th grade ($r = 0.03$, NS; beta = 0.09, $p < 0.001$), the 9th grade ($r = 0.02$, NS; beta = 0.11, $p < 0.0001$), and the 10th grade ($r = -0.03$, NS; beta = 0.06, $p < 0.05$). The usual interpretation of such effects is that the other variables suppress irrelevant variance that produced the nonsignificant zero-order correlation, thereby making evident a relationship for peer competence that occurs in the context of other factors (Tzelgov & Henik, 1991).

We thought that the nonsignificant zero-order correlation for peer competence might occur in part because of an interaction with adult competence. We therefore tested the interaction of peer and adult competence, comparable to the interaction effects noted previously by Wills and Vaughan (1989) for measures of peer and adult support. This interaction was marginal in the 7th-grade data ($p = 0.07$) and significant in 8th grade ($p = 0.02$), but nonsignificant in 9th grade. Figure 2 provides a graphic representation of the interaction effect. The form of the interaction was similar to that found previously: Among adolescents with low adult competence, there was a positive relationship between peer competence and substance use; among adolescents with high adult competence, there was a slight inverse relationship for peer competence. Thus, this finding could help account for the nonsignificant zero-order correlation, as the relation between peer competence and substance use goes in opposite directions for different subgroups in the population.

We also tested whether peer competence interacted with substance use in the peer network, as Wills and Vaughan (1989) found for peer support. There was little evidence for such an interaction. Neither for peer competence nor for adult competence were there consistent interactions with friends' use across the four waves of the study. Thus, it is apparent that in this respect, competence measures work differently from support measures. Moreover, there was a consistent interaction for Stress × Peer Competence, significant at two measurement points (7th grade: interaction $t = 2.06$, $p < 0.05$; 8th grade: interaction $t = 3.65$, $p < 0.0001$), but this was a reverse interaction; that is, high peer competence *increased* the impact of life events on substance use. So, having looked at the issue in several different ways with competence measures, we find that most of the analyses show complex effects through which, in one way or another, peer competence is positively related to substance use.[3]

The reader should not think that peer support and parental support represent a zero-sum process and therefore must be inversely related. This is a general-population study, and it is possible in such research for constructs to vary with relative independence within the population. To be clear on this point, we checked the correlations between parental support and the competence measures for data from 7th grade through 9th grade. Results were quite consistent across waves, showing emotional and instrumental support positively related to all three types of competence. The magnitude of effect was similar for the three dimensions of competence. Correlations of parental support with academic competence were in the range of $r = 0.22–0.26$; correlations with peer competence were in the range of $r = 0.19–0.23$; correlations with adult competence were in the

---

[3]There is one exception, and perhaps a significant one. In a study testing the Cloninger (1987) theory of substance abuse (Wills, Vaccaro, & McNamara, 1994), we found a crossed interaction between a risk factor termed Novelty Seeking and a construct termed Social Reward Dependence (roughly analogous to social support). For low Novelty Seeking, adolescents with high Social Reward Dependence showed somewhat more substance use, but for high Novelty Seeking, Social Reward Dependence was related to less substance use (i.e., persons with low social dependence had more use). We have found similar interactions in 7th-grade data for peer competence in relation to friends' substance use: For low level of friends' use, peer competence is related to more substance use; for high level of friends' use, peer competence is related to less use. This finding was obtained in two replications, but only for 7th-grade data. We think this study illustrates the complexity of the construct of peer support.

range of $r = 0.24–0.28$. Thus, it is clear that the positive relationship of peer competence to substance use does not occur simply because less parental support means more peer support; this relationship occurs because of the complex relationships of peer competence with other variables.

Relative Contributions of Parental and Peer Support

The relative contributions of parental and peer support were examined in a second study with a sample of 1826 students, initially in 7th grade, from the metropolitan area. In this study, the measures of parent and peer support were taken directly from the COPE (Carver et al., 1989), which has parallel 4-item scales for seeking emotional support to help cope with problems. The items for peer support are: "I discuss my feelings with a friend I feel close to," "I try to get emotional support from one of my friends," "I get sympathy and understanding from a friend," and "I talk to a friend about how I feel." In the parallel scale for parental support, the word "friend" is replaced by "mother/father." We thought having exactly parallel scales that tap emotional support might help to better understand the effects of peer support.

In 7th-grade data, parental support was significantly correlated with lower levels of adolescent substance use ($p < 0.0001$), whereas the correlation for peer support was virtually zero ($r = 0.01$, NS). Multiple regression with both support measures entered simultaneously showed an inverse effect for parental support (beta $= -0.20$, $p < 0.0001$), whereas peer support was positively related to substance use (beta $= 0.07$, $p < 0.01$). So again, with a different measurement method, peer support was positively related to substance use, and this relation occurred as a suppression effect.

These data showed general replications of interactions between parental and peer support systems (as in Wills & Vaughan, 1989). A buffer-type interaction for Parental Support $\times$ Friends' use ($p < 0.01$) indicated that the inverse effect of parental support on adolescent substance use was strongest at a high level of friends' use. The interaction of Parental Support $\times$ Peer Support indicated that students with low parental support and high peer support had disproportionately high levels of substance use; the significance level was marginal ($p = 0.06$), but the form of the interaction was exactly the same as in the previous study. We followed up these subjects in the 9th grade and found that results for parental and peer support were replicated at a different age. Zero-order correlations for parental and peer support were both significant (though opposite in sign), and multiple regression showed a significant inverse effect for parental support (beta $= -0.22$, $p < 0.0001$) and a significant positive effect for peer support (beta $= 0.16$, $p < 0.001$). Thus, with a different measurement method, with exactly parallel measures for parent and support, and across the age range from 12 to 15 years, we find replicable results for the support measures. The effect of parental support is found to be greater than the effect of peer support, buffering effects are found for parental support, and peer support is positively related to substance use.

Parental Support and Self-Control

Our most recent work on early-onset substance use has been based on the proposition that difficulty in self-regulation is a central factor in risk for substance use and other behavior problems. It is not possible here to go into the rich theoretical background on this topic (e.g., for children, see Block, Block, & Keyes, 1988; Eisenberg & Fabes, 1992; Mischel, Shoda, & Rodriguez, 1989; for adults, see Derryberry & Rothbart, 1988; Khantzian, 1990; Miller & Brown, 1991; Rothbart & Posner, 1985; Tarter & Mezzich, 1992). We shall briefly note two implications for the present work. One is that generalized poor self-control ability is a basis for adjustment problems in childhood and adolescence. Following this reasoning, we have been using a measure of generalized self-control (Kendall & Wilcox, 1979; Kendall & Williams, 1982) and testing structural models in which a deficit in self-control ability is posited to contribute to adjustment and substance use problems. A second proposition is that development of self-regulation skills is shaped by the interaction of a child's temperament characteristics and the supportiveness of the family environment in which he or she grows up (Rothbart & Ahadi, 1994). Thus, we have been examining the relation of parental emotional support to self-control in samples of children and adolescents.

A first test of these propositions was conducted in the study of 1826 middle-school students discussed in the preceding section, which included a measure of parental support, the Revised Dimensions of Temperament Survey (Windle & Lerner, 1986), and several indices of self-control, including the Kendall and Wilcox (1979) Self-Control Schedule. We tested a mediational model of how temperament is related to adolescent substance use (Wills, DuHamel, & Vaccaro, 1995). The results showed that indices of "difficult" temperament were related to lower levels of parental support, as several have hypothesized (Lerner & Lerner, 1986; Rothbart & Ahadi, 1994). We found that parental support was related to more adaptive coping and better self-control ability, and these latter effects largely mediated the protective effect of parental support.[4] Thus, this study suggested that parental support is a protective factor because it is conducive to the development of self-control skills. The data also suggested that the level of parental supportiveness may be shaped to some extent by temperament characteristics of the child, as some children are more difficult to care for than others, and this difficulty can have an adverse effect on the development of the parental relationship.

A new study investigating very early substance use is being conducted with a sample of 1810 subjects, initially surveyed around the age of 11 years. In addition to an extensive temperament inventory, this study included a measure of parental

---

[4]This analysis also showed parental support as having a direct (inverse) effect on adolescent substance use, net of all the other mediators. This direct effect suggests that the protective effect of parental support also involves the operation of other variables. These variables could include other aspects of parenting behavior such as monitoring and supervision of the child, or it could involve parents' communication of attitudes and beliefs about substance use.

functional support as well as measures of parental conflict and parental substance use. Mediational analyses of factors related to early substance use by children again have indicated parental support to be an important factor. Parental support was positively related to a construct of good self-control and inversely related to a construct of undercontrol (Wills, Cleary, Filer, Mariani, & Spera, 1995). In contrast, parental conflict and parental substance use were indicated as significant risk factors, both related independently to early substance use (cf. Wills, Schreibman, Benson, & Vaccaro, 1994). This study therefore provides further evidence on how relationship with parents is important for children's adjustment. The contribution of parental support to the development of adaptive coping and self-regulation skills is emphasized as an important factor.

IMPLICATIONS FOR THE THEORY OF SOCIAL SUPPORT

This research was conducted to test predictions derived from a functional theory of family support. The findings were generally consistent with our model. We find that supportive functions of the parental relationship can be reliably measured, they produce replicable results, and parental support is consistently indicated as a protective factor with respect to adolescent substance use. The notion that parental support becomes irrelevant to adolescents once they move into peer networks receives little confirmation in these data; rather, the results indicate that parental support is an important factor throughout the period of adolescence. In addition to finding parental support inversely related to adolescent substance use, we have also observed stress-buffering effects in several samples. The replicability of the findings and their consistence with prediction gives confidence to a functional model of social support in parent–child relationships.

The findings on peer support were more complex. With regard to substance use as an outcome, it is typical to find no zero-order correlation between peer support and substance use, but to observe significant positive coefficients that occur through suppression effects when peer support is entered with other variables in multiple regression. Moreover, peer support interacts with other factors, such as parental support. Thus, when the correlations of peer support with other characteristics are partialed out, peer sociability is often indicated as being positively related to substance use. We think this result shows that the effects of peer support are complex ones, as others have also noted (e.g., see Chassin, Pillow, Curran, Molina, & Barrera, 1993). Thus, we think it is not meaningful to use an adolescent's level of peer support as a predictor, without considering his or her level of parental support; it is the interaction of parental and peer systems that is important.

Strengths and Limitations of the Research

The strengths of this research could be said to lie in external validity. The samples are large and representative, and the findings we discuss are replicated across samples. The criterion variable, early substance use, is related to health outcomes and has clinical importance, because adolescent problem behaviors tend to be intercorrelated. The findings for parental support are replicated across measurement methods, so we think the construct of parental emotional/instrumental support is tapping the right dimension. Last but not least, the findings are consistent with prediction and thereby lend confidence to a functional model of social support.

The limitations of the research, we think, lie in the global assessment of peer support. If there is one thing clearly indicated by our data, it is that the construct of peer support is complex. This complexity suggests a need for very detailed assessment of the structure and function of peer social networks, with particular attention to the deviance proneness of network members. Constructs of peer support and peer social competence need to be assessed with different measurement methods, including behavioral assessment and ratings by third-party observers, so as to get outside the self-report mode and test whether self-reports of support and competence produce the same findings as other methods (cf. Dubow & Tisak, 1989; Leadbeater, Hellner, Allen, & Aber, 1989; Pentz, 1985).[5] At the theoretical level, there is a need for detailed attention to the convergence between clinical models of peer relationships, which generally link adolescent depression and problem behavior to *lack* of social acceptance (e.g., Asher & Coie, 1990; Hymel, Rubin, Rowden, & LeMare, 1990; Parker & Asher, 1987), and the epidemiological evidence discussed here, which generally shows peer-group social activity to be *positively* related to substance use. There is a marked divergence between these two bodies of theory, and someone with a good grasp of clinical and social relationship theory could get to work on bringing them together.

Why Is Parental Support So Important?

Investigators immersed in research on family relationships may wonder why this kind of question is asked at all, when the issue seems self-evident. However, research on adolescent drug use has generally taken the view that teenage smoking and alcohol use occur because of "peer pressure," and whatever role parents might play is only that they sometimes contribute to the process through modeling of cigarette smoking or alcohol use.

As new measures of parental support have become available, the role of the family as a protective factor for various adolescent problem behaviors has become increasingly evident. Yet it is one thing to show that parental support is related to some criterion, another to show how this occurs. We think the data presented in this chapter show something about why parental support is important. One reason is that we see widespread effects of parental support on adolescents' coping and competence, as well as on deviance-prone attributes such as anger and tolerance

---

[5]Not discussed because of space limitation are two studies that have obtained teacher ratings of competence and temperament, in addition to self-reports from students. The patterns of findings noted in teacher ratings are identical to those found in self-report data, so we do not think that the substantive findings reported here are off base.

for deviant behavior. The latter two variables may act to encourage affiliation with deviant peers—itself a powerful predictor of deviant behavior—and in addition sometimes have direct effects on substance use. Several bodies of theory suggest that family support contributes to adaptation because it helps teach children to cope effectively (Blechman & Culhane, 1993; Rutter, 1985; Thoits, 1986; Werner & Smith, 1982). Our research, with measures taken during the time when onset of problem behavior is occurring, shows that the effect of parental support on adolescents' coping is an important pathway for protective effects. It is worth noting once again that this protective effect obtains independent of social class, ethnicity, and the number of parents in the family (Wills, Blechman, & McNamara, 1996).

Another reason for the importance of parental support is that it contributes to the development of self-control skills. More complete arguments concerning the reasons for this contribution have been presented elsewhere (see Rothbart & Ahadi, 1994; Wills, DuHamel, & Vaccaro, 1995). The data presented here suggest that self-regulation ability is a basic determinant of adolescent achievement and adaptation vs. problem behavior. The extent to which self-control develops from early temperamental characteristics, and how this development is influenced by the family environment, are questions for current research (Lerner & Lerner, 1986; Rothbart, Derryberry, & Posner, 1994).

Early Attachment and Models of Relationships

Though our research was not designed to provide a detailed investigation of children's perceptions of relationships, the results are consistent with the proposition that models of social relationships are developed in the context of early interactions with parents (Sarason, Pierce, & Sarason, 1990; Sarason et al., 1991). The positive correlations between parental support and other types of support and competence suggest that children who feel secure in their relationship with parents are better able to build support and competence in other domains (cf. Parke & Ladd, 1992). Though it is stretching a bit theoretically, our recent work on temperament makes us think it not implausible to link adolescents' perceptions of supportive relationships to early attachment relationships. The pioneer work by investigators such as Bowlby (1969) and Ainsworth, Blehar, Waters, and Wall (1978) has indicated that the development of a secure attachment with a primary caregiver is of great importance for a child. The expectations a child develops about whether the parent will be responsive to his or her needs may give rise to internal representations or "mental models" of relationships with others (Bowlby, 1973). Developmental research has suggested the continuity of these mental models over time, and their effects on the development of emotional regulation and problem-solving interactions with the environment, that is, the development of coping skills (e.g., Bowlby, 1980; Kobak & Sceery, 1988). Subsequent research has provided support for the proposition that attachment styles carry over into adult relationships (Hazan & Shaver, 1987; Simpson, Rholes, & Nelligan, 1992).

This work suggests another aspect of how parental support operates. If children form positive working models of relationships from an early age, they may be more likely to form secure and intimate friendships with other children and adults (cf. Reis, 1990). A positive working model makes it easier for a child to learn to self-disclose about emotions and problems and thereby more likely to be able to utilize the supportive functions potentially available from adults and peers. The ability to draw on the supportive functions of social networks seems likely to contribute to good adaptation.

The converse of secure attachment is often indicated as anger and hostility, distrust of others, and a cynical or manipulative approach to social relationships, qualities that are unlikely to help a person achieve successful adjustment in instrumental performance or social settings but instead are likely to contribute to the development of antisocial behavior. These considerations argue for detailed study of the working models of relationships that adolescents have, the relation of these models to early attachment and temperament characteristics, and their relation to subsequent outcomes.

Functional Support and Resistance to Stressors

The existence of stress-buffering effects of social support has been demonstrated with both adults and adolescents (Garmezy & Masten, 1991; Rutter, 1990; Wills, 1991; Wills, Vaccaro, & McNamara, 1992). However, there is still not a complete understanding of how buffering effects occur. There are several approaches to this question. With large-scale questionnaire research, it is possible to identify variables that are involved in the mediation of support effects and study how these variables are involved in reducing the impact of life stressors. With longitudinal data, it is possible to test the extent to which family support reduces the development of risk-related attributes, prevents the occurrence of negative events, or directly modifies the impact of acute or chronic stressors.

We suggest it would also be useful to conduct detailed studies of the daily lives of adolescents (cf. Larson, 1983; Larson, Csikszentmihalyi, & Freeman, 1984) or to study in detail how adolescents cope with a specific stressor such as parental substance abuse (Wills, Schreibman, et al., 1994). Such research may yield more information on the ramifications of a problem as they occur on a day-to-day basis, how people cope with these demands, and what eventually leads to a successful resolution.

Finally, it might be useful to study specific subgroups of adolescents. For example, those with low adult support and high peer support are a significant group from a risk standpoint, and they represent the reverse of buffering because their support characteristics put them at highest risk for substance use. It would be interesting to characterize this subgroup in terms of their profile of other variables (e.g., temperament, risk-taking orientation, coping mechanisms) and compare this profile with the profile for other selected groups, such as adolescents who are high on both adult support and peer support. In this way, research might provide a deeper understanding of the relation between the parent and peer systems.

ACKNOWLEDGMENTS

This research was supported by Grants 5-RO1-DA05950 and 1-RO1-DA08880 from the National Institute on Drug Abuse and S-184A-00035 from the U.S. Department of Education.

The authors thank the participating schools and students for their cooperation and Gregory Benson, Kate DuHamel, A. Elizabeth Hirky, Grace McNamara, Angela Riccobono, Daniel Schreibman, Donato Vaccaro, Jody Wallach, and Caroline Zeoli for their assistance with the research.

REFERENCES

Ainsworth, M. D., Blehar, M., Waters, E., & Wall, S. (1978). *Patterns of attachment.* Hillsdale, NJ: Lawrence Erlbaum.

Asher, S. R., & Cole, J. D. (1990) (Eds.). *Peer rejection in childhood.* New York: Cambridge University Press.

Baron, R. M., & Kenny, D. A. (1986). The moderator–mediator distinction in social-psychological research. *Journal of Personality and Social Psychology, 51,* 1173–1182.

Barton, J., Chassin, L., Presson, C. C., & Sherman, S. J. (1982). Social image factors as motivators of smoking initiation in early and middle adolescence. *Child Development, 53,* 1499–1511.

Blechman, E. A., & Culhane, S. E. (1993). Aggressive, depressive, and prosocial coping with affective challenges in adolescence. *Journal of Early Adolescence, 13,* 361–382.

Block, J., Block, J., & Keyes, S. (1988). Longitudinally foretelling drug use in adolescence: Early childhood personality and environmental precursors. *Child Development, 59,* 336–355.

Bowlby, J. (1969). *Attachment and loss,* Vol. 1, *Attachment.* New York: Basic Books.

Bowlby, J. (1973). *Attachment and loss,* Vol. 2, *Separation: Anxiety and anger.* New York: Basic Books.

Bowlby, J. (1980). *Attachment and loss,* Vol. 3, *Loss: Sadness and depression.* New York: Basic Books.

Braithwaite, R. L., & Gordon, E. W. (1992). *Success against the odds.* Washington, DC: Howard University Press.

Brook, J. S., Brook, D. W., Gordon, A. S., Whiteman, M., & Cohen, P. (1990). The psychosocial etiology of adolescent drug use: A family interactional approach. *Genetic, Social, and General Psychology Monographs, 116(2),* 111–267.

Bry, B. H. (1983). Family-based approaches to adolescent substance abuse prevention. In T. J. Glynn, C. G. Leukefeld, & J. P. Ludford (Eds.), *Preventing adolescent drug abuse* (pp. 154–171). Rockville, MD: National Institute on Drug Abuse.

Burke, R. J., & Weir, T. (1978). Benefits to adolescents of informal helping relationships with their parents and peers. *Psychological Reports, 42,* 1175–1184.

Burke, R. J., & Weir, T. (1979). Helping responses of parents and peers and adolescent well-being. *Journal of Psychology, 102,* 49–62.

Carver, C. S., Scheier, M. F., & Weintraub, J. K. (1989). Assessing coping strategies. *Journal of Personality and Social Psychology, 56,* 267–283.

Cauce, A. M. (1986). Social networks and social competence: Exploring the effects of early adolescent friendships. *American Journal of Community Psychology, 14,* 607–628.

Chassin, L. A., Pillow, D. R., Curran, P. J., Molina, B., & Barrera, M. (1993). Relation of parental alcoholism to adolescent substance use: A test of mediating mechanisms. *Journal of Abnormal Psychology, 102,* 3–19.

Chassin, L., Presson, C. C., Sherman, S. J., Montello, D., & McGrew, J. (1986). Changes in parent and peer influence during adolescence: Longitudinal versus cross-sectional perspectives on smoking initiation. *Developmental Psychology, 22,* 327–334.

Cloninger, C. R. (1987). Neurogenetic adaptive mechanisms in alcoholism. *Science, 236,* 410–416.

Cohen, S. (1986). Correlational field methodology in the study of stress. In S. Cohen, G. Evans, D.

Stokols, & D. Krantz (Eds.), *Behavior, health, and environmental stress* (pp. 25–45). New York: Plenum Press.

Cohen, J., & Cohen, P. (1983). *Applied multiple regression/correlation research for the behavioral sciences.* Hillsdale, NJ: Lawrence Erlbaum.

Cohen, S., Mermelstein, R., Kamarck, T., & Hoberman, H. N. (1985). Measuring the functional components of social support. In I. G. Sarason & B. R. Sarason (Eds.), *Social support: Theory, research, and applications* (pp. 73–94). Dordrecht, The Netherlands: Martinus Nijhoff.

Cohen, S., & Wills, T. A. (1985). Stress, social support, and the buffering hypothesis. *Psychological Bulletin, 98*, 310–357.

Cutrona, C. E., & Russell, D. W. (1987). The provisions of social relationships and adaptation to stress. In W. H. Jones & D. Perlman (Eds.), *Advances in personal relationships*, Vol. 1 (pp. 37–67). Greenwich, CT: JAI Press.

Derryberry, D., & Rothbart, M. K. (1988). Arousal, affect, and attention as components of temperament. *Journal of Personality and Social Psychology, 55*, 958–966.

Dishion, T. J., Reid, J. B., & Patterson, G. R. (1988). Empirical guidelines for a family intervention for adolescent drug use. In R. H. Coombs (Ed.), *The family context of adolescent drug use* (pp. 189–224). New York: Haworth Press.

Dubow, E. F., & Tisak, J. (1989). The relation between stressful life events and adjustment in elementary school children: The role of social support and problem-solving skills. *Child Development, 60*, 1412–1423.

Eisenberg, N., & Fabes, R. A. (1992). Emotion regulation and the development of social competence. In M. S. Clark (Ed.), *Review of personality and social psychology*, Vol. 14, *Emotion and social behavior* (pp. 119–150). Newbury Park, CA: Sage Publications.

Fondacaro, M. R., & Heller, K. (1983). Social support factors and drinking among college student males. *Journal of Youth and Adolescence, 12*, 285–299.

Friedman, L. S., Lichtenstein, E., & Biglan, A. (1985). Smoking onset among teens: An empirical analysis of initial situations. *Addictive Behaviors, 10*, 1–13.

Garmezy, N., & Masten, A. S. (1991). The protective role of competence indicators in children at risk. In E. M. Cummings, A. L. Greene, & K. H. Karraker (Eds.), *Life span developmental psychology: Perspectives on stress and coping* (pp. 151–174). Hillsdale, NJ: Lawrence Erlbaum.

Glynn, T. J. (1981). From family to peer: Transitions of influence among drug-using youth. *Journal of Youth and Adolescence, 10*, 363–383.

Graham, J. W., Marks, G., & Hansen, W. B. (1991). Social influence processes affecting adolescent substance use. *Journal of Applied Psychology, 76*, 291–298.

Greenberg, M. T., Siegel, J. M., & Leitch, C. J. (1983). The nature and importance of attachment relationships to parents and peers during adolescence. *Journal of Youth and Adolescence, 12*, 373–386.

Haggerty, R. J., Sherrod, L. R., Garmezy, N., & Rutter, M. (Eds.). (1994). *Stress, risk, and resilience in children and adolescents.* New York: Cambridge University Press.

Harter, S. (1985). *Manual for the self-perception profile for children and adolescents.* Denver: University of Denver.

Hays, R. D., Widaman, K. F., DiMatteo, M. R., & Stacy, A. W. (1987). Structural equation models of current drug use. *Journal of Personality and Social Psychology, 52*, 134–144.

Hazan, C., & Shaver, P. (1987). Romantic love conceptualized as an attachment process. *Journal of Personality and Social Psychology, 52*, 511–524.

Hymel, S., Rubin, K. H., Rowden, L., & LeMare, L. (1990). Children's peer relationships: Longitudinal prediction of internalizing and externalizing problems from middle to late childhood. *Child Development, 61*, 2004–2021.

Johnston, L. D., O'Malley, P. M., & Bachman, J. G. (1989). *Drug use, drinking, and smoking: National survey results from high school, college, and young adult populations 1975–1988.* Rockville, MD: National Institute on Drug Abuse.

Jöreskog, K. G., & Sörbom, D. (1988). *LISREL 7: A guide to the program and applications.* Chicago: SPSS.

Kandel, D. B. (1975). Stages of adolescent involvement in drug use. *Science, 190*, 912–914.

Kandel, D. B., & Andrews, K. (1987). Processes of adolescent socialization by parents and peers. *International Journal of the Addictions, 22,* 319–342.

Kandel, D., & Davies, M. (1992). Progression to regular marijuana involvement: Phenomenology and risk factors for near-daily use. In M. Glantz & R. Pickens (Eds.), *Vulnerability to drug abuse* (pp. 211–253). Washington, DC: American Psychological Association.

Kandel, D. B., & Lesser, G. S. (1972). *Youth in two worlds.* San Francisco: Jossey-Bass.

Kandel, D. B., Kessler, R. C., & Margulies, R. Z. (1978). Antecedents of adolescent initiation into stages of drug use. In D. B. Kandel (Ed.), *Longitudinal research on drug use* (pp. 73–100). New York: Wiley.

Kandel, D. B., & Yamaguchi, K. (1985). Developmental patterns of the use of legal, illegal, and prescribed drugs. In C. L. Jones & R. J. Battjes (Eds.), *Etiology of drug abuse* (pp. 193–235). Rockville, MD: National Institute on Drug Abuse.

Kendall, P. C., & Wilcox, L. E. (1979). Self-control in children: Development of a rating scale. *Journal of Consulting and Clinical Psychology, 47,* 1020–1029.

Kendall, P. C., & Williams, C. L. (1982). Assessing the cognitive and behavioral components of children self-management. In P. Karoly & F. Kanfer (Eds.), *Self-management and behavior change* (pp. 240–284). Elmsford, NY: Pergamon Press.

Khantzian, E. J. (1990). Self-regulation and self-medication factors in alcoholism and the addictions. In M. Galanter (Ed.), *Recent developments in alcoholism,* Vol. 8 (pp. 255–271). New York: Plenum Press.

Kobak, R. R., & Sceery, A. (1988). Attachment in late adolescence: Working models, affect regulation, and representation of self and others. *Child Development, 59,* 135–146.

Larson, R. W. (1983). Adolescents' daily experience with family and friends: Contrasting opportunity systems. *Journal of Marriage and the Family, 45,* 739–750.

Larson, R., Csikszentmihalyi, M., & Freeman, M. (1984). Alcohol and marijuana use in adolescents' daily lives: A random sample of experiences. *International Journal of the Addictions, 19,* 367–381.

Lazarus, R. S., & Folkman, S. (1984). *Stress, appraisal, and coping.* New York: Springer.

Leadbeater, B. J., Hellner, I., Allen, J. P., & Aber, J. L. (1989). Assessment of interpersonal negotiation strategies of youth engaged in problem behaviors. *Developmental Psychology, 25,* 465–472.

Lerner, R. M., & Lerner, J. V. (1986). Children and adolescents in their contexts: Tests of a goodness of fit model. In R. Plomin & J. Dunn (Eds.), *The study of temperament* (pp. 99–114). Hillsdale, NJ: Lawrence Erlbaum.

Lewis, J. M., & Looney, J. G. (1983). *The long struggle: Well-functioning working class black families.* New York: Brunner/Mazel.

Luthar, S. S., & Zigler, E. (1991). Vulnerability and competence: A review of research on resilience in childhood. *American Journal of Orthopsychiatry, 61,* 6–22.

Masten, A. S., Morison, P., Pellegrini, D., & Tellegen, A. (1990). Competence under stress: Risk and protective factors. In J. Rolf, A. S. Masten, D. Cicchetti, K. H. Nuechterlein, & S. Weintraub (Eds.), *Risk and protective factors in development of psychopathology* (pp. 236–256). New York: Cambridge University Press.

Mermelstein, R., Cohen, S., Lichtenstein, E., Baer, J. S., & Kamarck, T. (1986). Social support and smoking cessation and maintenance. *Journal of Consulting and Clinical Psychology, 54,* 447–453.

Miller, W. R., & Brown, J. M. (1991). Self-regulation as a conceptual basis for the prevention of addictive behaviours. In N. Heather, W. Miller, & J. Greeley (Eds.), *Self-control and the addictive behaviors* (pp. 3–79). Sydney: Maxwell Macmillan.

Mischel, W., Shoda, Y., & Rodriguez, M. L. (1989). Delay of gratification in children. *Science, 244,* 933–938.

Mosbach, P., & Leventhal, H. (1988). Peer group identification and smoking. *Journal of Abnormal Psychology, 97,* 238–245.

Needle, R., Su, S., & Lavee, Y. (1989). A comparison of the empirical utility of three composite measures of adolescent drug involvement. *Addictive Behaviors, 14,* 429–441.

Parke, R. D., & Ladd, G. W. (1992). *Family and peer relationships: Models of linkage.* Hillsdale, NJ: Lawrence Erlbaum.

Parker, J. G., & Asher, S. R. (1987). Peer relations and later personal adjustment: Are low-accepted children at risk? *Psychological Bulletin, 102,* 357–389.

Patterson, G. R., DeBaryshe, B. D., & Ramsey, E. (1989). A developmental perspective on antisocial behavior. *American Psychologist, 44,* 329–335.

Pentz, M. A. (1985). Social competence and self-efficacy as determinants of substance use in adolescence. In S. Shiffman & T. A. Wills (Eds.), *Coping and substance use* (pp. 117–142). Orlando, FL: Academic Press.

Procidano, M., & Heller, K. (1983). Measures of perceived social support from friends and from family. *American Journal of Community Psychology, 11*, 1–24.

Reis, H. T. (1990). The role of intimacy and interpersonal relations. *Journal of Social and Clinical Psychology, 9*, 15–30.

Rhoads, D. L. (1983). A longitudinal study of life stress and social support among drug abusers. *International Journal of the Addictions, 18*, 195–222.

Robins, L. N., & Przybeck, T. R. (1985). Age of onset of drug use as a factor in drug and other disorders. In C. L. Jones & R. J. Battjes (Eds.), *Etiology of drug abuse* (pp. 178–192). Rockville, MD: National Institute on Drug Abuse.

Rosenberg, H. (1983). Relapsed versus non-relapsed alcohol abusers: Coping skills, life events, and social support. *Addictive Behaviors, 8*, 183–186.

Rothbart, M. K., & Ahadi, S. A. (1994). Temperament and the development of personality. *Journal of Abnormal Psychology, 103*, 55–66.

Rothbart, M. K., Derryberry, D., & Posner, M. J. (1994). A psychobiological approach to the development of temperament. In J. E. Bates & T. D. Wachs (Eds.), *Temperament: Individual differences at the interface of biology and behavior* (pp. 83–116). Washington, DC: American Psychological Association.

Rothbart, M. K., & Posner, M. (1985). Temperament and the development of self-regulation. In L. C. Hartlage & C. F. Telzrow (Eds.), *The neuropsychology of individual differences* (pp. 93–123). New York: Plenum Press.

Rutter, M. (1985). Resilience in the face of adversity: Protective factors and resistance to psychiatric disorder. *British Journal of Psychiatry, 147*, 598–611.

Rutter, M. (1990). Psychosocial resilience and protective mechanisms. In J. Rolf, A. S. Masten, D. Cicchetti, K. H. Nuechterlein, & S. Weintraub (Eds.), *Risk and protective factors in the development of psychopathology* (pp. 181–214). New York: Cambridge University Press.

Sandler, I. N., Miller, P., Short, J., & Wolchik, S. A. (1989). Social support as a protective factor for children in stress. In D. Belle (Ed.), *Children's social networks and social supports* (pp. 277–307). New York: Wiley.

Sarason, B. R., Pierce, G. R., & Sarason, I. G. (1990). Social support: The sense of acceptance and the role of relationships. In B. R. Sarason, I. G. Sarason, & G. R. Pierce (Eds.), *Social support: An interactional view* (pp. 97–128). New York: Wiley.

Sarason, B. R., Pierce, G., Shearin, E. N., Sarason, I. G., Waltz, J. A., & Poppe, L. (1991). Perceived social support and working models of self and actual others. *Journal of Personality and Social Psychology, 60*, 273–287.

Simpson, J., Rholes, W., & Nelligan, J. (1992). Support seeking and giving within couples in an anxiety-provoking situation: The role of attachment style. *Journal of Personality and Social Psychology, 62*, 434–446.

Steinberg, L., Dornbusch, S. M., & Brown, B. B. (1992). Ethnic differences in adolescent achievement: An ecological perspective. *American Psychologist, 47*, 723–729.

Sussman, S., Dent, C. W., Mestel-Rauch, J., Johnson, C. A., Hansen, W. B., & Flay, B. R. (1988). Adolescent nonsmokers, triers, and regular smokers' estimates of cigarette smoking prevalence: When do overestimations occur and by whom? *Journal of Applied Social Psychology, 18*, 537–551.

Tarter, R. E., & Mezzich, A. C. (1992). Ontogeny of substance abuse: Perspectives and findings. In M. Glantz & R. Pickens (Eds.), *Vulnerability to drug abuse* (pp. 149–177). Washington, DC: American Psychological Association.

Tarter, R. E., Moss, H. B., & Vanyukov, M. M. (1995). Behavior genetic perspective of alcoholism etiology. In H. Begleiter & B. Kissin (Eds.), *Alcohol and alcoholism*, Vol. 1 (pp. 294–326). New York: Oxford University Press.

Thoits, P. A. (1986). Social support as coping assistance. *Journal of Consulting and Clinical Psychology, 54*, 416–423.

Tucker, M. B. (1985). Coping and drug use among heroin-addicted women and men. In S. Shiffman & T. A. Wills (Eds.), *Coping and substance use* (pp. 143–170). Orlando, FL: Academic Press.

Tzelgov, J., & Henik, A. (1991). Suppression situations in psychological research: Definitions, implications, and applications. *Psychological Bulletin, 109*, 524–536.

Umberson, D. (1987). Family status and health behaviors: Social control as a dimension of social integration. *Journal of Health and Social Behavior, 28*, 306–319.

Werner, E. E. (1986). Resilient offspring of alcoholics: A longitudinal study from birth to age 18. *Journal of Studies on Alcohol, 47*, 34–40.

Werner, E. E., & Smith, R. S. (1982). *Vulnerable but invincible: A longitudinal study of resilient children and youth.* New York: McGraw-Hill.

Wills, T. A. (1985). Supportive functions of interpersonal relationships. In S. Cohen & S. L. Syme (Eds.), *Social support and health* (pp. 61–82). Orlando, FL: Academic Press.

Wills, T. A. (1986). Stress and coping in early adolescence: Relationships to substance use in urban school samples. *Health Psychology, 5*, 503–529.

Wills, T. A. (1990a). Multiple networks and substance use. *Journal of Social and Clinical Psychology, 9*, 78–90.

Wills, T. A. (1990b). Social support and the family. In E. Blechman (Ed.), *Emotions and the family* (pp. 75–98). Hillsdale, NJ: Lawrence Erlbaum.

Wills, T. A. (1990c). Stress and coping factors in the epidemiology of substance use. In L. T. Kozlowski, H. M. Annis, H. D. Cappell, et al. (Eds.), *Research advances in alcohol and drug problems*, Vol. 10 (pp. 215–250). New York: Plenum Press.

Wills, T. A. (1991). Social support and interpersonal relationships. In M. S. Clark (Ed.), *Review of personality and social psychology*, Vol. 12 (pp. 265–289). Newbury Park, CA: Sage Publications.

Wills, T. A. (1994). Self-esteem and perceived control in adolescent substance use: Comparative tests in concurrent and prospective analyses. *Psychology of Addictive Behaviors, 8*, 223–234.

Wills, T. A., Baker, E., & Botvin, G. J. (1989). Dimensions of assertiveness: Differential relationships to substance use in adolescent populations. *Journal of Consulting and Clinical Psychology, 57*, 473–478.

Wills, T. A., Blechman, E. A., & McNamara, G. (1996). Family support, coping and competence. In E. M. Hetherington (Ed.), *Stress, coping, and resiliency in children and the family* (pp. 107–133). Hillsdale, NJ: Lawrence Erlbaum.

Wills, T. A., Cleary, S. D., Filer, M., Mariani, J., & Spera, K. (1995). Temperament and early-onset substance use: A test of two theoretical models (submitted).

Wills, T. A., Cleary, S. D., Filer, M., & Mariani, J. (June, 1994). Coping motives and substance use intensity in an adolescent sample. Paper presented at the meeting of the Society for Prevention Research. Palm Beach, Florida.

Wills, T. A., DuHamel, K., & Vaccaro, D. (1995). Activity and mood temperament as predictors of adolescent substance use: Test of a self-regulation mediational model. *Journal of Personality and Social Psychology, 68*, 901–916.

Wills, T. A., & Filer, M. (1996). Stress–coping model of adolescent behavior problems. In T. H. Ollendick & R. J. Prinz (Eds.), *Advances in clinical child psychology*, Vol. 18 (pp. 91–132). New York: Plenum Press.

Wills, T. A., & Hirky, A. E. (1996). Coping and substance abuse. In M. Zeidner & N. Endler (Eds.), *Handbook of coping: Theory, research, and applications* (pp. 279–302). New York: Wiley.

Wills, T. A., McNamara, G., Riccobono, A., & Vaccaro, D. (March, 1992). Family support and substance use in urban adolescents: A path model. Paper presented at the meeting of the Society for Research on Adolescence. Washington, DC.

Wills, T. A., McNamara, G., Vaccaro, D., & Hirky, A. E. (in press). Escalated substance use: A longitudinal grouping analysis in early adolescence. *Journal of Abnormal Psychology.*

Wills, T. A., Schreibman, D., Benson, G., & Vaccaro, D. (1994). The impact of parental substance use on adolescents: A test of a mediational model. *Journal of Pediatric Psychology, 19*, 537–555.

Wills, T. A., & Shiffman, S. (1985). Coping and substance use: A conceptual framework. In S. Shiffman & T. A. Wills (Eds.), *Coping and substance use* (pp. 3–24). Orlando, FL: Academic Press.

Wills, T. A., Vaccaro, D., & McNamara, G. (1992). The role of life events, family support, and competence in adolescent substance use: A test of vulnerability and protective factors. *American Journal of Community Psychology, 20*, 349–374.

Wills, T. A., Vaccaro, D., & McNamara, G. (1994). Novelty seeking, risk taking, and related constructs as predictors of adolescent substance use: An application of Cloninger's theory. *Journal of Substance Abuse, 6*, 1–20.

Wills, T. A., Vaccaro, D., McNamara, G., & Hirky, A. E. (August, 1993). Family support prospectively related to adolescents' competence and substance use. Paper presented at the meeting of the American Psychological Association. Toronto.

Wills, T. A., Vaccaro, D., McNamara, G., & Spellman, M. (August, 1991). Three competence domains relate to adolescent substance use. Paper presented at the meeting of the American Psychological Association. San Francisco.

Wills, T. A., & Vaughan, R. (1989). Social support and substance use in early adolescence. *Journal of Behavioral Medicine, 12*, 321–339.

Windle, M., & Lerner, R. M. (1986). Assessing the dimensions of temperament individuality across the life span: The Revised Dimensions of Temperament Survey. *Journal of Adolescent Research, 1*, 213–230.

Wright, P. H., & Keple, T. W. (1981). Friends and parents of a sample of high school juniors: An exploratory study of relationship intensity and interpersonal rewards. *Journal of Marriage and the Family, 43*, 559–570.

Zevon, M. A., & Tellegen, A. (1982). The structure of mood change. *Journal of Personality and Social Psychology, 43*, 111–122.

Author Index

Subject Index

ISBN 0-306-45232-4

90000